The
COOKING
ENTHUSIAST

The

COOKING
ENTHUSIAST

An Illustrated Culinary Encyclopedia

JOSCELINE DIMBLEBY

RUTLEDGE HILL PRESS®
Nashville, Tennessee

Copyright © 2000 Websters International Publishers
Text copyright © 2000 Josceline Dimbleby

Published by Rutledge Hill Press®, 211 Seventh Avenue North, Nashville, Tennessee 37219.

Distributed in Canada by H. B. Fenn & Company Ltd., 34 Nixon Road, Bolton, Ontario
L7E 1W2.

Created and designed by Websters International Publishers Limited, Axe and Bottle Court,
70 Newcomen Street, London SE1 1YT, U.K.

Library of Congress Cataloging-in-Publication Data

Dimbleby, Josceline.
    The cooking enthusiast / an illustrated culinary encyclopedia / Josceline Dimbleby.
        p.   cm.
    Includes index.
    ISBN 1-55853-797-x
    1. Cookery—Encyclopedias.   I. Title.
TX349.D55 2000
641.5'03—dc21   99-047735

Printed and bound in Hong Kong by Dai Nippon Printing
1 2 3 4 5 6 7 8 9—05 04 03 02 01 00 99

NOTES ON RECIPES

All spoon measures are level
1 tablespoon = 15ml
1 teaspoon = 5ml

Eggs are Medium unless otherwise stated.
Pepper is freshly ground black pepper unless otherwise states.

Ovens should be preheated to the specified temperature.
For all recipes, quantities are given in both imperial and metric measures.
Follow either imperial or metric measures but not a mixture of both.

CONTENTS

INTRODUCTION

Cooking is the great passion of my life. I have always enjoyed food but it is more than that; cooking, with its changing tastes, textures, smells and colors, and its infinite scope for variety, satisfies a deep creative urge. As a young child, moving from country to country with my diplomat parents, the kitchens of our temporary foreign homes became my haven. They were warm busy places full of exciting and unfamiliar foods; I watched, I smelled, I tasted, and my interest in food developed. Every three years as we moved to another part of the world the cuisine changed dramatically. Because of this I have always had an adventurous palate. But it was not until years later, in a tiny mildewed basement shared with a girlfriend, that I began to cook. I learned by experiment, and because I knew no rules I was able to cook in the way I still enjoy most: using straightforward methods to combine unusual tastes or to create real fantasies of my own. I soon realized that each basic cooking technique I mastered opened up a host of new possibilities. My hope in writing this book is that it will do the same for you.

I have always searched for methods which are the least time consuming, and do not require a great deal of practice or skill. The step-by-step recipes on these pages are those which I have found the most useful. Each chapter offers a framework for a different aspect of cooking designed to help you build up your repertoire. In the tinted boxes are ideas and suggestions which should give you the confidence to do this. If you are a reluctant cook I hope you will discover that by making small changes to your old standbys, what you think of as a chore can become something to enjoy and take pride in. If you are already an enthusiast I hope that I can lead you to new ways of cooking, to dishes or ideas you may not have tried before. In cooking and eating there are always more pleasures to discover. At the end of each chapter there are original recipes in which I have used variations of methods covered in that chapter and often unusual combinations of ingredients. These reinforce the techniques explained in the chapter and show how you can progress from them to produce something both personal and exciting.

When I started the book I thought that I would enjoy working on some of the chapters more than others. I knew that I would love the desserts chapter because I have always had a childish passion for them and have enjoyed the fun of making them. As I expected I could have written far more than there was space for about vegetables – their beauty and flavor and the increasing varieties available make them an inspiring subject. Fish is also something I like to write about because, although it is such delicious and healthy food, it is often ruined by careless cooking. It is important to learn quick and simple ways to bring out its delicate taste and succulence. However, in the end, there was not a single chapter which did not inspire me with renewed enthusiasm for the subject as I cooked and wrote. I worked on jams, jellies and pickles just before Christmas, so solving the problem of several presents. I have always made bread and cakes from time to time, but when I was working on these chapters I wondered why I did not make them every day. Even days of experiments with eggs, which might have become tedious, revealed what a magical ingredient they are.

I knew that this book should contain practical, comprehensive, reliable information. But I did not want it to be like a text book or manual. Instead I hope it becomes a friend. A friend you can trust, a friend you can turn to for advice and inspiration whenever you like. I would be happy if it made you feel that you are not alone in your kitchen, and that cooking is a more rewarding experience as a result.

Josceline Dimbleby

THE PANTRY

A well-stocked pantry should give you a satisfying sense of security. You will always be able to produce a last minute meal, impromptu guests will be impressed by your ingenuity, and you will be able to find something to vary or revive an ordinary dish. If you keep bottles of fruits in alcohol on your shelves, you can even be sure that you can produce a delicious dessert as well, when the occasion demands.

Your pantry can be anything from a standard, small cupboard in your kitchen to a cool, dry area in your basement. If you are lucky enough to have a root cellar, you can keep boxes of fruit such as apples and citrus fruits when in season, strings of fresh garlic and bunches of drying herbs – which look so attractive if you can hang them up on hooks. But most people have to make do with less space and warmer conditions, so we must rely on non-perishable items: cans, bottles, jars, vacuum-sealed packages and a variety of dried ingredients.

If you have enough shelves and keep your stores neatly arranged, you can fit a lot into a very small space. It is also necessary to be organized so that little containers do not get lost and totally forgotten. Put similar ingredients together and always keep certain spaces for particular items so that you get to know what is there and when it has run out. Always put a fresh container of something in back of an existing container of the same ingredient so that you use them up in order of age.

The skills required to stock a useful pantry come from learning which non-perishable ingredients work best to produce unplanned meals or quick dishes. All too often, cupboards contain packages and jars which are never used and become dusty with age at the back of the shelf. However, the possibilities available nowadays for long-lasting ingredients which will make impromptu meals easy and delicious are endless.

The following are things which I like to have in my cupboard, and a few ideas of what I use them for. I try to keep a similar supply in our vacation home so that if we arrive late with no time to shop, we can be sure of a good meal on the first night in next to no time.

Bottles and jars

• Jars of roasted peppers and marinated artichoke hearts can be used in salads or stirred into a tomato or cream sauce for rice or pasta.

• Any kind of tomato sauce is an excellent standby; it can be varied by adding some freshly chopped herbs.

• Capers are useful for sauces to go with fish, and for adding to salads.

• Mayonnaise is an invaluable standby; you can add ingredients such as fresh herbs, curry paste, crushed green peppercorns, chopped anchovies, tomato puree, crushed garlic, to suggest a few, to it, and then use it to dress cold chicken. Once opened keep in the refrigerator.

• Jars of pesto are excellent if you like pasta, but pesto is also delicious as a topping for baked potatoes. Caponata may be used in the same ways.

• Chutneys, relishes, salsas and pickles, can be added to an ordinary stew to make it into a kind of curry, as well as served with hot and cold meat and sandwiches.

• Jars (or cans) of olives are useful not only to nibble with drinks, but to add to stews, stuffings and sauces.

• With vine leaves in brine you can make a quick dish with alternate layers of ground beef and vine leaves baked in the oven and topped with cheese sauce.

• Fruit jellies are an excellent accompaniment to pork, game or lamb.

• I love really special honeys; it is worth using the most fragrant kind for making ice cream, but for baking and other cooking I keep a large jar of clover honey. Honey is also useful for sweetening dressings.

• Mustard has countless uses; it can be added to stews and casseroles, soups, sauces or bread doughs, or used as part of a marinade. I like mild whole grain and French Dijon mustard in sauces and salad dressings.

• Soy sauce is an invaluable flavor enhancer, and is by no means only for Chinese dishes. As well as using in stir-fried vegetables, soy sauce enormously enlivens a simple dish of green vegetables, and is very good on plain cold chicken, veal or pork.

• Various condiments, such as Worcestershire sauce, hot pepper sauce, steak sauce and anchovy paste are good flavor enhancers for casseroles, stews, sauces and gravies.

• Flower waters, either orange, rose or violet, give an authentic and romantic touch to ethnic desserts.

• Many different oils are available. Keep extra virgin olive oil for salad dressings and pasta sauces, and less expensive olive oil for sautéing. Walnut and hazelnut oils are lovely for leafy salads which include bitter leaves, but these oils must not be kept too long as they go rancid quickly once opened. Keep in the refrigerator after opening. Sunflower, grape seed and peanut oils are lighter alternatives to fruity olive oil in salad dressings and mayonnaise.

• The choice of vinegars is enormous. Sherry and balsamic vinegars are my favorites for adding to sauces and stews as well as salad dressings, but red and white wine and herb vinegars are excellent, too. Cider and white are the lightest vinegars and are useful for pickling. Raspberry and other fruit vinegars are lovely for more delicate salad dressings.

• Sun-dried tomato paste in a jar is good for enriching sauces, and really mouthwatering spread on hot toast with crushed garlic.

Cans

• I often use chopped canned tomatoes for quick pasta sauces and as an ingredient in casseroles, soups and countless other dishes.

• When you have no time, cans of beans, such as limas, white cannellini, kidney beans and chick peas, are a boon for salads and for making into a quick bean stew with added vegetables or bacon.

• Smoked oysters and mussels are delicious in salads, and also in stuffings for meat and chicken, because they add a smoky flavor.

• Canned beef, chicken and vegetable broths give a head start when making soups, stews and sauces.

• Tuna is universally popular and can be used in many dishes, including dips, quiches, pasta, stuffings, and, of course, salads and sandwiches.

• Sardines in olive oil are perfect for making sardine pâté or spread in seconds.

• Anchovies can be a wonderful flavor enhancer. They can be used on pizzas, with pasta, or chopped and added to stews, stuffings and sauces They can also be heated with their oil, traditional olive oil, and some sliced garlic to make Bagna Cauda for dipping fresh vegetables and bread.

Dried and dry ingredients

• The dried ingredient to keep on hand must be pasta. If you have pasta, olive oil and seasonings in the house, you will always have a complete meal ready to make in a hurry. Pasta comes, of course, in all shapes and sizes. Don't forget also oriental noodles which are useful for stir-fries.

• Rice is another invaluable standby, and wonderful varieties which have real flavor are now available. Arborio is the type of rice used for risotto, a useful dish if you have only leftovers or packaged ingredients in the house. Then there is my favorite – basmati, the delicate, long grain rice prized above all others in India. Brown basmati rice is to me the nicest of the whole grain rices, because it is lighter in texture and takes less time to cook.

• Flour becomes stale sooner than most people think, so always put the date on it when you buy it. I always keep a stock of bread flour, including whole wheat and

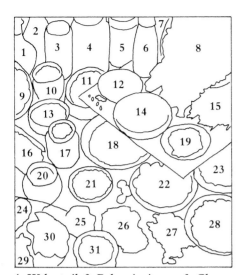

1. Walnut oil; 2. Balsamic vinegar; 3. Clams in shells; 4. Vine leaves in brine; 5. Sunflower oil; 6. Extra virgin olive oil; 7. Red wine vinegar; 8. Dried pasta twists and bows; 9. Dried apricots; 10. Clams; 11. Dried green lentils; 12. Pine kernels; 13. Whole wheat flour; 14. Dried beans; 15. Dried spaghetti; 16. White flour; 17. Whole grain mustard; 18. Arborio rice; 19. Sea salt; 20. Apricot jelly; 21. Light brown sugar; 22. Green and black olives; 23. Shelled walnut and pecan halves; 24. Dried black mushrooms; 25. Sun-dried tomatoes; 26. Basmati rice; 27. Dried chick peas; 28. Dried white beans; 29. Dried wild mushrooms; 30. Dried cèpes; 31. Tomato purée.

unbleached white, as well as all-purpose and cake flours. For variety, you can also keep a little rye flour to mix with wheat flour for homemade bread.

• I keep sunflower, pumpkin and sesame seeds as well as bulgar wheat to add to bread doughs and to use for toppings.

• I always keep a good store of dried fruits; these get eaten up very quickly as I used to try to make my children eat dried fruit instead of sweets, and they have become as addicted as I am. Dried fruit is useful to nibble after a meal when you have no dessert and have run out of fresh fruit.

• Dried mushrooms seem expensive, but the wonderfully pungent flavor of wild mushrooms which they give to dishes makes it worth the cost, and since their flavor is strong, you do not have to use a large quantity. Try adding a few dried mushrooms to the creamy sauce of a lasagne.

• Sun-dried tomatoes are a versatile ingredient to keep on hand. They have a rather addictive, intense flavor and you can buy them preserved in oil, or simply dried. The ones in oil are softer in texture and can be sliced and used in pasta and salads, while the dried ones are good in juicy casseroles.

• Nuts should not be stored for too long unless they are vacuum packed, but they are useful additions to cakes, puddings, salads,

stuffings and so on. You can buy shelled pistachio nuts which are marvelous for pâtés, stuffings and in ice cream – and I always keep ground almonds for baking.

• Pine nuts are a great favorite of mine; they are good toasted and added to salads, spicy ground meat dishes, stuffed vine leaves, eggplant and peppers, or simply on top of a dish of green vegetables.

• Green and red lentils, unlike most dried legumes, need no soaking before cooking; delicious green lentils can simply be boiled for 30–45 minutes until just soft, and used in salads, stews or as a vegetable on their own with plenty of butter and seasoning. Red lentils cook even more quickly and are useful for thickening stews, or can quickly transform stock into a sustaining soup.

• Spices of all kinds (page 12) are obvious candidates for the pantry shelf, but buy whole spices if possible and grind them yourself in a coffee grinder just before using.

• Most herbs are better fresh (page 10), but oregano is, in fact, best dried, so this is an extremely versatile herb which you can always keep. The other herbs which dry successfully are thyme, tarragon, dill (surprisingly) and bay leaves.

• Coconut milk powder comes in packages; it

is the quickest way of making coconut milk for spicy dishes or desserts.

• Aromatic tea, such as Earl Grey, makes an excellent poaching liquid for skinless chicken breasts or white fish.

Miscellaneous

• UHT cream and milk can be used for sauces and soups when you have run out of fresh; refrigerate after opening.

• Tubes of olive, garlic and tomato purees are perfect for flavoring ground meat mixtures, dips and pâtés, and for stirring into casseroles.

• I always keep plenty of the darkest cooking chocolate but I have a special hiding place or it gets eaten by members of my family. Stirred in before serving, a little dark chocolate enriches the juices of a game casserole and is also useful for quickly made sauces for ice cream or poached fruit.

• A few chicken, meat, fish and vegetable bouillon cubes should be kept for when you have no homemade stock, and they can also be used for intensifying the flavor of a sauce.

• Dehydrated egg whites and meringue powder are useful when you run out of fresh eggs. In addition, they are the best choice for recipes in which egg whites are not cooked enough to ensure safety.

HERBS

I realized what a miraculous effect the use of herbs can have in cookery when I first went to the Lubéron hills in the south of France. The dry hillsides are covered with wild thyme and rosemary, and these dusty little plants give off a wonderful smell as you walk through them. It was the exquisite combination of this aromatic thyme and pink, succulent baby lamb which fired my enthusiasm for using herbs in my own cooking.

Herbs really transform food, and some combinations seem to have been designed for each other: basil with tomato, tarragon with chicken, both thyme and rosemary with lamb and oregano with cheese and eggs. Yet there should be no compulsory combinations; what is exciting is that there is always more scope for experiment and the possibility of a new and successful mixture of tastes. I never tire of trying new fusions.

Herbs should be used fresh whenever possible, oregano being the one exception, as for some reason it has an even better aroma when dried. Most herbs are easy to grow, too. Thyme can be as good dried as fresh, but only if it has recently been dried. Now that it is so easy to obtain fresh herbs all year round,

it is strange to think that not so long ago you could only buy little cans of a limited selection of dried herbs. In any case, many of the tender herbs such as basil and parsley lose their character completely the moment they are dried; if you have a glut and want to preserve herbs you can either freeze small quantities in ice cubes (page 312) or, dry them in a dehydrator or the microwave. Once dried they keep best in an airtight container (though they will lose flavor over time).

Nothing matches the fragrance of fresh herbs in salads or sprinkled over cooked vegetables, and those with pretty shaped leaves make an effective garnish or stunning border to a dish. As long as you have some fresh herbs in the house you needn't worry if the dish you have made turns out to be colorless – if the basic taste of the food is good, you can easily improve the appearance with a scattering of herbs. Even perfectly executed casseroles, stews and soups almost always look more appetizing and attractive if you throw in a handful of coarsely chopped herbs at the last moment, and they make all the difference in gravies and sauces, too.

Angelica Dried or fresh, this is a useful herb for flavoring fish and salads. In candied form, the stalks can be chopped and used in fruit cakes or softened under warm water and then cut into decorations for the top of desserts, cakes and cookies. Angelica's flavor is often compared with juniper.

Aniseed Cultivated since the days of the Pharoahs, aniseed's most popular use today is in Mediterranean drinks like ouzo. You can also scatter a few seeds into fish soups, stews and cooked vegetables or into cookie doughs, cakes and even egg custards.

Arugula, originally from Italy, is a salad herb, used as whole, young leaves. It has a strong but delicious watercress-type taste which is enhanced by a good vinaigrette dressing (page 204). Arugula is also excellent stirred into cooked pasta with butter and crushed garlic or used in the place of lettuce on meat, cheese or roasted vegetable sandwiches.

Balm or lemon balm These fresh leaves have a flavor and scent resembling lemon. Use whole leaves in punches and fruit drinks and chopped leaves in soups and salads.

Basil One of the most versatile herbs to grow at home, basil is also one of my favorites. The green leaves have a tantalizingly heady aroma and pungent flavor. If you are cooking with it rather than using raw, add it at the end of cooking to preserve the flavor. Basil is used a great deal in Italian and French cooking to flavor tomatoes, with which it has an extraordinary affinity, and also in mixed salads and various sauces – the most popular being Italian pesto (page 207). Except when making pesto, basil leaves should not be chopped, which discolors them, but instead torn across with your fingers into pieces.

Bay Aromatic bay leaves are used fresh or dried for flavoring soups and stews and as an

essential part of bouquet garni. They go particularly well with fish and also with game and legumes. If you remove the ribs of the fresh leaves and chop them very finely they have a wonderful effect in cream and egg sauces. In sweet custards the whole leaves are infused in the hot milk before baking. Add to the water when boiling potatoes.

Borage This is a very easily grown herb with a pretty blue flower which is traditionally used in summer drinks. The flower is decorative but the leaves taste of cucumber and, when very young, can be added to salads. The flowers can also be crystallized (page 275) and used to decorate cakes or frozen in ice cubes for drinks (page 312).

Bouquet garni This is a bundle of fresh thyme, parsley stalks and bay leaves used to flavor soups, stews and sauces. Make up your own version of bouquet garni with any herbs and spices of your choice.

Chervil This is a pretty fine-leafed plant with the delicate aroma of aniseed. Use quickly because once picked the leaves wilt. Chervil is used a lot in French cooking for flavoring omelettes and fish dishes, but can also be used in salads.

Chives The bright green stems of this herb have an oniony taste, making them an ideal garnish for tomato salads, soups, baked potato fillings and egg dishes.

Cilantro The leaf, root, stem and seeds of this strongly aromatic herb all taste slightly different. The fresh leaves are pretty and add an instant exotic taste to any dish if added just before serving, but they are also excellent in salads and as a garnish. Cook the roots and stems in casseroles and soups but remove before serving.

Dill Available either fresh or dried, dill is mainly used for flavoring soups, sauces, pickles and cured salmon or gravlax (page

135). Fresh dill has a lovely flavor and enhances salads, fish stews, potatoes and other vegetables when added at the last moment. A mixture of shrimp, sour cream and fresh dill is a delicious, quick first course.

Elder Both the flowers and berries of this rampant weed can be used in the kitchen but, in the early summer, the flowers have a short, wonderful season as they won't freeze or dry. Their musky smell gives no hint of the fruity flavor (similar to muscatel grapes) they add to syrups, sorbets, jellies, jams and cordials and to stewed fresh or dried fruit. In the autumn the berries can be used in jams, jellies and chutneys.

Fennel The stalks and leaves of this aromatic herb have a delicate licorice flavor. Fennel's feathery leaves are an ideal garnish for vegetables and for fish dishes. The dried stalks are very effective as a bed to lay fish on when grilling.

Fenugreek leaves This is a soft green, clover-like herb, and the seed is often used in Indian cooking as its bitter aromatic flavor blends well with other spices. The leaves taste like a curry-flavored walnut.

Fines herbes A French term used to describe a blend of fresh herbs – usually parsley, tarragon, chives, chervil – which are finely chopped and often used to flavor omelettes.

Garlic Although really a member of the onion family, garlic is as much of a flavoring ingredient as any fresh herb. To me, the smell of garlic cooking is more appetizing than any other, and I would hate to live without it. It enhances all but the most delicate ingredients if used in the right way. When raw or briefly cooked, the taste is robust and strong, but cooked long and gently garlic becomes mild and sweet. Thus some dishes or sauces need the smallest addition of garlic while long-cooked dishes benefit from several cloves. Even people

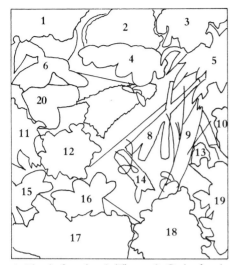

1. Flat-leaf parsley; 2. Thyme; 3. Coriander; 4. Arugula; 5. Sage; 6. Bay leaves; 7. Rosemary; 8. Lemon grass; 9. Chives; 10. Curly parsley; 11. Tarragon; 12. Marjoram; 13. Chopped chives; 14. Bouquet garni; 15. Mint; 16. Basil; 17. Dill; 18. Chervil; 19. Oregano; 20. Sorrel.

who claim not to like garlic are surprised at the flavor change.

Lemon grass Most frequently used in Thai and Vietnamese dishes, lemon grass is available both fresh and dried. It has a lemony flavor which goes well with fish. The dried variety should be soaked for a few hours before use.

Lovage The seeds, leaves and stems of this herb have a slight celery flavor but also a very definite pungent flavor of their own. The decorative leaves make a beautiful garnish around the side of a dish and they are also excellent coarsely chopped and thrown into soups and casseroles just before serving. Lovage is particularly good with tomato dishes. It is an attractive, easily grown herb which is extremely useful.

Marjoram This is a sweet herb similar to oregano, only far less assertive. The delicate flavor is destroyed by prolonged cooking, so it is best added shortly before serving. It is good stirred into chicken casseroles or vegetable soups.

Mint Among the most important of culinary herbs, mint has a wide range of flavors – such as spearmint or apple mint. As a change from mint sauce, mint is excellent chopped and inserted into slits in the surface of a lamb roast or cooked in a lamb casserole or meatballs. It is also an interesting flavor to add to chutneys and to stewed berries, plums and other summer fruits, and is excellent in fruit salads. Chopped mint is also good sprinkled on cooked vegetables.

Oregano Closely related to marjoram but stronger and more aromatic, oregano is very useful as it is the only herb which is arguably better dried than fresh. It goes well with meat and chicken and with cheese and eggs. It is much used in Italian and Greek cooking.

Parsley Although traditionally used as a garnish only, fresh parsley also adds a wonderful flavor to soups and sauces. Curly or flat-leaf varieties are available; the flat-leaf being more decorative, as well as having a stronger flavor. Lots of chopped flat-leaf parsley, a little crushed garlic and seasoned extra virgin olive oil is an excellent finishing touch to grilled meat and fish. Parsley can also be fried and added to fish, or pureed with butter to make a quick sauce to serve with chicken or veal. If you have an overabundance, it may be used as a salad green or finely chopped with garlic, olive oil and seasonings to make pesto (page 207).

Rosemary Often used with lamb, rosemary is also excellent with pork, game, chicken and sausages. It has a strong flavor, so is best used sparingly and finely chopped. Whole sprigs make a good bed on which to grill meat or poultry. Try it infused in sweet dishes, too, such as puddings, custards, syrups and vanilla ice cream.

Sage An excellent herb to combine with tomatoes, garlic and olive oil, sage is best used with meats such as pork or duck, or with liver. It also goes surprisingly well in beef casseroles which contain tomatoes as well and in hot cheese dishes. Sage has a powerful flavor, so use sparingly. It is a traditional herb to include in stuffings.

Savory The winter and summer varieties of this herb taste somewhat like thyme but are more bitter. Winter savory is slightly milder. Use (with discretion) in bean and pasta soups and in stews and meat casseroles.

Sorrel Especially popular in France, and with me, this sour, lemon-flavored herb makes the most delicious soups and sauces, stirred in at the end to cook only briefly. Sorrel leaves dissolve quickly and lose their bright green color when heated; often spinach is used with sorrel to add depth of color. A few raw leaves can also be added to salads.

Tarragon A pretty, fine-leaf herb with a strong but subtle flavor. If you grow any make sure you plant the French variety as the Russian type grows prolifically but has none of the flavor. Tarragon is famous for its use with chicken, eggs and fish and in butters and sauces. It can also be used with meat and game and in salad dressings.

Thyme Best suited to long, slow-cooking dishes and casseroles. Unlike most herbs, except oregano, thyme is as good dried or fresh. It is wonderful with young roast lamb but also good with pork, chicken, fish and eggs. Use sparingly, as it can easily overpower other flavorings.

SPICES

My passion for spices began at an age when most children scorn them. This was when my family went to live in Syria, and memories of the exciting smells and sights of the Street of Spices in the Damascus *souk*, or market, are still with me. In fact, spicy food does not mean food which burns the tongue; it means a complex variety of aromatics which can bring out unknown aspects of ingredients – only a few spices such as chilies, black pepper and ginger actually add heat.

In Damascus, I learned to love the typically Middle Eastern mixtures of cumin, coriander, cinnamon and so on; years later when I began traveling in India, I came across the same spices and many more, but combined and used in quite different ways. This was what led me to begin using spices in my own recipes, sometimes a mixture and sometimes just one spice sparingly added to a mild dish, which can often be extremely effective. A single spice can also be a miraculous last-minute seasoning to so many things, both savory and sweet; for example, grating nutmeg onto vegetables, puddings and cheese dishes, or adding caraway seeds to sweet potatoes and pumpkin.

Cardamom is one of the spices I feel almost addicted to; it is wonderful, not only with meat, poultry and fish – a crushed pod or two will transform a fish stew – but also to add a scented magic to puddings and ice creams. For savory dishes of all kinds, the mixture of cardamom with garlic and fresh ginger is – to me – one of the most mouthwatering combinations there can be.

Cinnamon is another spice which enhances both savory and sweet dishes; it is particularly good in chicken, using whole sticks to flavor a stew. Cinnamon toast, sticky cinnamon buns, cinnamon coffee cake and snickerdoodles are all irresistible.

Just as it is best to use fresh herbs, so the pungency of spices is far more pronounced if you buy them whole and grind them as you need them. When using either whole or ground spices you should heat them briefly in a dry frying pan first to bring out their full aromas. I keep an extra electric coffee grinder just to grind spices but if you use them only rarely you can wipe out your coffee grinder and use it, or pound them in a mortar and pestle, though this is more difficult with harder spices like cinnamon, cloves and star anise. In North Africa and the Middle East, coffee is often made with a pod of cardamom infused in it, and my husband often grinds the beans with a few cardamom seeds included.

You can experiment with different spices in the same way as you can with herbs but in my experience people are even more intrigued by the hard-to-define taste of a certain spice in a dish. You can also concoct your own mixture of spices to use in curries as housewives do in India. Careful spicing of food seems to excite people, and spiced food at a party always attracts more attention and is remembered. It is often difficult to know what drink to have with very spicy food; beer usually goes well and, when you want to celebrate, serve champagne or another sparkling wine.

Allspice This spice looks like large peppercorns but the taste resembles a mix of nutmeg, mace, cinnamon and especially cloves. Use it in fruit cakes, mince pies and spice cakes, and it is an important ingredient in mixed pickling spice. Ground allspice is a single spice, not a combination of spices as the name can imply.

Caraway A spice with brown, sickle-shaped seeds used for flavoring cakes, cookies, bread, cheese and pickles. Caraway seeds are also very effective scattered on cooked vegetables, particularly root vegetables, and are a classic with hot red cabbage.

Cardamom This spice tastes a bit like eucalyptus but, to me, sweeter and richer. I find it irresistible. The pods are naturally green but are sometimes bleached white; larger black cardamoms are much coarser and inferior in taste. Cardamom comes from an Indian plant and is much used in Indian dishes, both savory and sweet. It is wonderful in puddings (page 216). Use whole pods for a subtle flavor but break them open for a stronger one. Ground cardamom loses its best oils so use fresh seeds and grind them as required.

Cayenne pepper A very hot pungent spice, cayenne is derived from the dried pods of a red chili pepper native to Central America. Use this for adding heat to curries, and seasoning cheese and fish dishes.

Chili This member of the vast capsicum family comes in all shapes, sizes and colors. Chilies are the ingredient which gives heat and flavor to curries but individual ones vary in strength. Fresh green chilies are picked unripe, whereas red ones are ripe but not necessarily more pungent. On the whole, the fleshier, fatter chilies are milder than the small thin ones. The seeds are the hottest part of all and may be discarded. Always prepare chilies under water (page 49) and don't touch your eyes or mouth afterwards.

Chili powder This is a blend of ground chili pepper, cumin, garlic, onion and oregano. Essential for making Southwestern- and Mexican-style dishes in most parts of the country, this commercial blend is frowned upon in the Southwest where cooks mix their own.

Chinese five-spice powder This is a subtle blend of spices consisting of equal parts of finely ground Szechuan pepper, star anise, cinnamon, cloves and fennel seeds, widely used in oriental cooking.

Cinnamon Made from the bark of an evergreen native to Sri Lanka, cinnamon is sold either as sticks or as a ground spice, and has good keeping qualities. Cassia is similar to cinnamon but has a coarser texture and less delicate taste. Use cinnamon sticks for spicy chicken, lamb or vegetable casseroles, and ground cinnamon for baking and desserts. The flavor is especially good with apples, pears and chocolate.

Cloves A familiar spice, cloves are highly aromatic. They are traditionally married with apple dishes and also used with cinnamon in hot spiced wines and punches and in pickles. A few cloves are good in rich beef casseroles or stews and in curries.

Coriander The spicy dried seeds of this aromatic herb have a totally different taste than the fresh stems and leaves. Coriander seeds are good in pickles and curry and are excellent for flavoring pork, leafy green and root vegetables and any casserole.

Cumin Cumin seeds have a pungent, medium-hot and slightly bitter taste. They can be used whole or ground, and are useful for flavoring cheese, breads, sauces and curries. An excellent spice, particularly when combined with mint, for roast or stewed lamb, and also for ground beef dishes.

Dill Similar but milder in taste than caraway or fennel seeds, these seeds go well with mashed potatoes and boiled cabbage and with stewed or ground pork.

Fennel These delicate licorice-flavored seeds are used in curries, and are good with vegetable and dried bean casseroles.

Garam masala This name literally means 'hot mixture' and garam masala is a combination of roasted spices such as coriander seed, cumin, cardamom, cloves and cinnamon. Every Indian housewife makes up her own version and grinds the whole spices freshly for it.

Ginger Available fresh, ground, preserved in syrup and crystallized, ginger is a hot, spicy ingredient widely used in Indian and oriental dishes and baking. Fresh ginger is a revelation when you first try it as it has a clean flavor and wonderful lemony smell, quite different from dried or preserved ginger. It combines well with garlic and is excellent with shellfish, fish and chicken

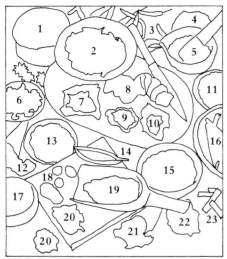

1. Star anise; 2. Dried red chilies; 3. Fresh red and green chilies; 4. Caraway seeds; 5. Juniper berries; 6. Green cardamom pods; 7. Cayenne pepper; 8. Whole and sliced fresh ginger; 9. Mace; 10. Saffron; 11. Ground turmeric; 12. Cumin seeds; 13. Tamarind; 14. Vanilla beans; 15. Pink, white and black dried peppercorns; 16. Cassia bark; 17. Black and white mustard seeds; 18. Whole and grated nutmeg; 19. Fennel seeds; 20. Cloves; 21. Dill seeds; 22. Green dried peppercorns; 23. Cinnamon sticks.

dishes. I like the flavor so much that I use it in an enormous range of dishes.

Juniper Famous as the flavor for gin, these small purply black, pine-scented berries are also useful in marinades, casseroles and terrines – in particular pork and game.

Mace A 'cage' surrounding the nutmeg seed, mace is bright red when fresh but changes to creamy brown when dried. It tastes only slightly like nutmeg, and whole blades can be used to improve the flavor of soups and stews. Ground mace is useful when baking cakes and cookies. I use it in creamy sauces for poultry, fish and game.

Mustard This is available in powdered and prepared forms. In addition to our mild yellow prepared mustard, English, French and German mustards are popular. Seeds may be white, black or brown – the last two are the hottest, and are often used in Indian dishes but can be effective in everyday dishes too. Whole grain prepared mustard is useful to stir into creamy sauces.

Nutmeg This is a versatile spice with a pungent nutty flavor. It is traditionally sprinkled on creamy desserts, such as rice pudding or custard, but is also a perfect accompaniment to pumpkin, spinach and pasta dishes, and is wonderful combined with cheese and in all root vegetable purees. Grate fresh nutmeg just before use as its essential oils and flavor are quickly lost.

Pepper As well as hot, spicy cayenne pepper made from chilies, this spice group also includes black, green and white peppercorns. These are the berries of vine peppers. You can buy ground pepper but it is far better to keep dried peppercorns in a pepper mill and grind it freshly as needed. Make up your own mixture for a grinder. Whole green peppercorns in brine are wonderful in sauces for chicken, beef and steaks. Although not a true pepper, pink peppercorns are milder, very aromatic and look pretty.

Saffron These dried stigmas of a special crocus are the most expensive spice in the world as they are harvested by hand. Saffron imparts a strong yellow color and has a unique, penetrating taste – only a pinch is needed to flavor and color any dish. To capture the most flavor, put a few filaments in boiling liquid to infuse for at least 15 minutes and then add the golden liquid with the saffron to the main ingredients. It is best used with rice and fish – for example, Spanish paella, Italian risottos and Indian pilafs. It is good with fish dishes which have creamy sauces, and saffron-flavored cream is excellent in mashed potatoes. It is used traditionally in European cakes and cookies.

Star anise A pretty star-shaped pod used in classic Chinese dishes, star anise has an overall flavor of licorice and aniseed but is spicier. Use in fish stews and root vegetable purees and with cabbage, leeks or pumpkin.

Tamarind Mainly used in curries, tamarind is a brown, slightly sticky substance which comes from the seed pods of the tamarind tree. It has a sour fruity taste which adds something more complex than just lemon juice to curries and other spicy stews and soups. Usually sold in a pressed or dried form, it is a vital ingredient in chutneys and many Indian and Far Eastern dishes.

Turmeric Usually sold as a ground orange/yellow powder, turmeric is often used instead of saffron to color food yellow but the taste – warm and spicy – is quite different. It is most often used in curries and pickles but is also good used sparingly in chicken and fish stews.

Vanilla This wonderful flavoring is derived from the pods of a Mexican orchid. The best vanilla is grown in Madagascar and it is the white crystals of vanillin which cling to the bean that provide the flavor and marvellous aroma. The beans are expensive but they can be used several times and can be stored in a jar of sugar which they will also flavor for use in desserts (page 235). Synthetic vanilla flavoring does not compare with the flavor you get from a real vanilla pod but you can buy real vanilla extract. Vanilla can also be used to flavor fish stews and sauces for fish.

BASIC KITCHEN EQUIPMENT

Cooking can be a pleasure, and it can be a chore. To prevent day-to-day meal preparation becoming a drudgery, it helps a great deal to have good, well-made kitchen equipment. That is not to say that you need indulge in expensive professional pans and tools, but you should buy the finest equipment you can afford, adding to your collection as your budget allows and when you have a better idea of what you will actually use.

Good equipment lasts for ever, so the investment is worth it,

paying you back time and time again with reliability and service. Poorly-made kitchen equipment that is flimsy and liable to break, buckle or burn, will cause you great frustration, and will make cooking an oppressive task that you will want to avoid.

Efficiency in the kitchen depends as much on the quality of the equipment being used as it does on your skills and organization, and together these can make cooking a very satisfying and pleasurable experience as well as making you less tired.

Bottle opener This works by prying off the cap of a bottle and sometimes forms the top of a corkscrew. It should be sturdy and comfortable to grip.

Can opener The most widely available is a butterfly-handled opener with a gear-driven cutting wheel, and it is easier to use than a simple ratchet opener or one with a blade and cog wheel. A wall-mounted version of the gear-driven opener is convenient although more expensive. Buy one that is easy to clean frequently. Electric can openers take up space on the work surface and are more difficult to clean but require no strength to use.

Colander This rigid bowl-shaped strainer can be metal, enamel, rigid plastic or earthenware and should have holes all over the bottom and partly up the sides to ensure speedy draining. For everyday washing and draining jobs a 2-handled colander with a broad pedestal base is best (on legs it is less sturdy). If you plan to use your colander as a steamer over a saucepan as well, choose one with a flat bottom, one long handle and, ideally, a hook on the side opposite the handle so it can rest securely on the pan's rim, as well as on bowls.

Corkscrew Many types are available so

choose one according to the strength of your hands. One of the easiest to use, a Screwpull, has a comfortable handle and large, open spiral screw for a better grip on the cork, and it works by pushing against the rim of the bottle for leverage to draw out the cork. A cork puller, with thin, flexible metal prongs that are eased down between cork and bottle, is good for fragile corks and can also be used to re-cork bottles.

Broad metal spatula or pancake turner These should have thin, flexible yet sturdy blades that will slide easily under food, and then be strong enough to lift or turn the food. Some are squarish or rectangular, and may have slots or holes to let excess fat or other liquid drain away; others are rounded or triangular, to fit against the walls of a saucepan.

Fork Sturdy forks with 2–4 straight or curved, sharply pointed metal (usually stainless steel) tines or prongs are used to lift food out of deep pans to taste it or test texture, to manipulate food that is being roasted or grilled, and to hold roasts or birds steady while they are being carved (pages 166 and 188). As with a good knife (page 16), a metal kitchen fork should be riveted at the handle, and the metal should extend through

to the end of the heat-resistant wooden or plastic handle for added strength.

Large strong, wooden forks, with 3–4 tines, have many uses, including swirling and separating spaghetti and vegetables, such as shredded cabbage, in their cooking water.

Metal spatula This spatula has a long, narrow blade that is thin and flexible yet sturdy; the tip is rounded, and one side of the blade may be serrated. Use this as a turner for thin flat items, such as small fish fillets or steak or pancakes, as well as for folding and mixing and lifting delicate cookies off a baking sheet. It can also be used to loosen a baked cake or cheesecake from its pan, spread soft mixtures such as icing or buttercream on a cake, or for making a decorative effect on a vegetable puree. A large spatula with a serrated edge is used to cut a cake into layers.

Metal spoon and ladle Large, long-handled metal spoons are used for stirring, folding, lifting and basting. They must be strongly made as the foods they stir and lift will often be stiff or heavy. The bowl of the spoon should also be shallow so that food is not caught in it. Ideally, choose spoons with heat-resistant handles.

Slotted or perforated metal spoons enable you to easily remove solid foods from liquid or fat, for tasting or serving. They may also be used for skimming fat or foam from the surface of a simmering liquid, although a circular perforated skimmer does this job more easily and thoroughly (the most thorough is a wire mesh skimmer). Wire skimmers, which are really shallow wire baskets, are best to use for removing items from deep hot fat.

Ladles used in the kitchen, for pouring a batter into a hot pan or for serving a soup or stew, should have a long handle, to keep your hand away from the hot food, and a deep bowl. Special basting ladles for skimming gravy have an oval bowl and should have a lip at one side to make pouring easy.

Nutcracker A cracker with a ratchet action is the easiest to use and is sturdy enough to crack the legs and claws of shellfish such as crabs and lobster, too. A wooden cracker with a screw is not as strong but is easy to use. The traditional nutcracker that employs a simple squeezing action requires the most effort and does not give as much control over pressure so the nut inside the shell may be crushed as well.

FOR A WELL-STOCKED BASIC KITCHEN

Anyone setting up home for the first time can use this as a guideline for stocking a kitchen. There will be very few cooking preparations that you won't be able to accomplish with these pieces of equipment. More expensive professional equipment (page 24) can be bought gradually as you become more experienced and accomplished.

- set of standard measuring spoons
- set of standard dry measuring cups
- glass measuring cup
- kitchen scales
- can opener
- bottle opener
- pair of strong kitchen scissors
- set of mixing bowls in varying sizes
- swivel-bladed vegetable peeler
- large, medium and small knives
- flat, sturdy chopping board
- grater
- medium-sized wire whisk
- wooden spoons of various sizes
- large plain metal spoon
- large 2-pronged metal fork
- slotted metal spatula

- rubber spatulas
- colander
- slotted spoon
- medium-sized sieve
- mortar and pestle
- rolling pin
- set of heavy saucepans in at least 4 sizes
- heavy frying pan
- omelette pan
- roasting pan with rack
- pie plate
- medium-sized Dutch ovens
- at least 2 baking sheets
- round and square cake pans in various sizes, from 8-10 in (20.5-25cm)
- 2–4 loaf pans, 7-9in (18-23cm)

1. *Tapered rolling pin*
2. *Rolling pin*
3. *Rolling pin with handles*
4. *Large deep ladle*
5. *Mini-ladle*
6. *Basting ladle*
7. *Shallow ladle*
8. *Nutcracker with ratchet action*
9. *Selection of wooden spoons*
10. *Scissors-style tongs*
11. *Two-handled colander with base*
12. *Wire skimmer*
13. *Flat perforated skimmer*
14. *Fine wire mesh skimmer*
15. *Wooden fork*
16. *Spaghetti tongs*
17. *Metal fork*
18. *Single-handled colander*
19. *Can opener*
20. *Metal spatula*
21. *Broad metal spatula*
22. *Long-handled metal spatula*
23. *Rubber spatula*
24. *Large metal spoon*
25. *Slotted spoon*
26. *Pastry brush*
27. *Pastry brush*
28. *Slotted wooden spatula*
29. *Bottle opener*
30. *Screwpull corkscrew*

Pastry brush These are handy for a multitude of uses, from greasing a pan or mold, to brushing an egg glaze over a pie before baking or moistening the edges of pastry to seal, to basting kebabs during grilling and so on. Choose brushes with natural bristles that will not melt like plastic ones. The brushes that look like paint brushes are the most versatile. It is best to have several, one for greasing, one for glazing and so on. Wash frequently in hot soapy water.

Rolling pin For general use, choose a long, heavy hardwood rolling pin without handles for closest contact with pastry. The smooth, silky finish will hold a dusting of flour, which ceramic and glass pins will not, and its weight and length will enable a smooth sheet of pastry to be rolled out almost effortlessly. Wooden rolling pins with handles that remain stationary as you roll are easy to use, but be sure the handles are not painted

because in time the paint will flake off into the pastry. An extra-long tapered rolling pin (at least 24in/60cm long) is worth having if you often make pasta dough by hand; it can be used for rolling out very thin, large pieces of pastry. Do not soak wooden ones in water or they may warp.

Spatula Pliable yet firm rubber spatulas are excellent for folding and blending light mixtures, such as whisked egg whites, and for scraping every bit of a mixture out of a bowl. Rubber spatulas should not be used in very hot mixtures or in hot pans, as the rubber will break down. Wooden spatulas, on the other hand, don't have this drawback and are suitable for mixing and folding all kinds of mixtures, as well as for doubling as a turner. Wooden spatulas come in a variety of shapes, both flat and curved, and may also be slotted.

Tongs Very hot or very cold food is best handled with metal or wooden tongs rather

than with your fingers. Tongs that use a scissor-action are more sturdy and flexible to use than simpler 2-sided tongs, unless you are proficient. Scissor-style tongs are also usually able to open wide enough for large items.

Wooden spoon Use these for beating, mixing and stirring, both during preparation and cooking. General-purpose spoons, in the traditional shape, are available in varying sizes. There are also a variety of flat spoons without bowls for creaming mixtures, and spoons that have an angled point or flat bottom to get into corners of pans or dishes. Wood does not conduct heat, so spoons stay cool while you are stirring a hot mixture; the long handle also helps to keep your hand and arm away from the source of the heat so you do not burn yourself. Do not keep wooden spoons in a pan during cooking – they can burn and even catch fire! Wooden spoons with holes need careful washing.

CUTTING *and* CHOPPING

Cooking is a matter of control – making your tools do exactly what you want. And nowhere is control more important than in the use of particular knives for specific jobs. I would rather have sharp knives in the kitchen than any other good equipment – an inefficient knife is very frustrating and a really sharp knife is much safer than a blunt one as it is less likely to slip.

Kitchen knives must be sturdy. The tang – the part of the blade that extends into the handle – should be 'full', that is it should extend all the way to the end of the handle and be visible all around. Ideally, the blade of the knife should be riveted to the handle, not glued, and the riveting should be flush to the handle. Finally, the handle should be heat-resistant and non-slip.

The metal of the blade may be carbon steel or high-carbon stainless steel alloy. Carbon steel will take a very sharp edge, sharper than the alloy will, but it will rust and stain unless meticulously cared for and dried after washing. High-carbon stainless steel resists discoloration, but is much more expensive than carbon steel. Most ordinary stainless steel knives cannot be sharpened as well as either of the carbon knives.

SHARPENING KNIVES

The difference between using a well-sharpened knife and a dull one is the difference between easy, accurate food preparation and hard labor. A sharpening steel, ideally with coarse rather than fine grooves, is the tool to use in the kitchen – any knife, whether carbon or steel alloy, needs a quick run over the steel from time to time, or even before every use. When you find a blade losing efficiency, wash it in soapy water, dry it thoroughly and then run it over the steel several times, holding it at a shallow angle (30–45°). This procedure will not really sharpen a knife; it just restores the edge on it temporarily. If you use your knives every day, they should be sharpened 3 or 4 times a year by a specialist. Only use your knives for cutting or chopping food and cut only on wooden or polyethylene boards.

Apple corer This hollow cylindrical blade has sharp edges to cut into fruit skin, and is long enough to go all the way through an apple or pear.

Boning knife Use this for removing bones from raw meat and poultry. The strong, rigid blade, 5–6in (12–15cm) long, has a fine, razor-sharp point to cut as close to the bone as possible. Choose a boning knife with a molded handle to prevent your hand from slipping onto the blade.

Bread knife Most of these are serrated to cut easily through the crust without mashing the crumb, but they may also be scalloped or fluted.

Butcher knife This is a large, fairly long knife with a broad, firm blade . Use to cut roasts, steaks and chops. The handle has a deep notch or 'shoulder' where it meets the blade to guard fingers and to give the hand maximum leverage when cutting.

Carving knife and fork Buy knives at least 10in (25cm) long of medium to thin width for carving hot meats. The blade does not need to be as sturdy as that of a chef's knife but should be quite firm with some flexibility towards the point. Poultry carvers have shorter blades (about 8in/20cm), and sometimes curve upwards towards the point; some have a gently fluted edge. Carving forks should have a guard to protect your hand if the knife accidentally slips.

Chef's knife Also called French knives, chef's knives have a rigid triangular blade with a sharp point and gently curved edge; the curve allows you to hold the point and rock the knife up and down, for fine chopping. The most versatile and frequently used one for chopping and slicing has a 6–8in (15–20cm) long blade. The smallest chef's knife, sometimes called paring knife, is a useful all-purpose knife. With a 3–4in (7–10cm) long blade, it is used for peeling, chopping and removing 'eyes' from potatoes and pineapple. The longer chef's knife, with a blade up to 14in (35cm) long, is used for cutting and slicing large foods.

Cleaver Available in several sizes and shapes, this versatile implement is used in as many ways as French knives: it can chop, slice, bone and flatten; the widest blade is an effective chopper, and is heavy enough to cut through chicken bones. For Chinese cooks it is their only knife and when very sharp it can do almost anything.

Cutting board The best wooden boards are heavy and thick, to act as good shock absorbers, and ideally made from one piece of densely grained wood (strips of wood glued together can eventually come apart); wooden surfaces are better for cutting and chopping because they will not blunt the knife. However, disadvantages of wood are many: it is porous and so absorbs moisture which can cause warping and cracking, and it can retain stains, odors and bacteria. It is important to wash wooden boards well, scrubbing in the direction of the grain. Rinse and dry well. Polyethylene cutting boards, available in many sizes, are usually considered more hygienic than wood because they can be thoroughly cleaned, even in a dishwasher, and are soft enough to avoid blunting a knife.

Personally, I much prefer the look and feel of wood and keep several boards of varying sizes for different ingredients. Using the same small board for crushing garlic only means other delicately flavored foods do not end up tasting of garlic.

Filleting knife Ideal for boning and skinning fresh fish without damaging the flesh, this knife has a slender and flexible blade, 7–9in (18–23cm) long. The sharp point is good for piercing fish skin and flesh, and the blade is ideal for skinning fish fillets. Because this knife is continuously wet during use, high-carbon stainless steel is best.

Grapefruit knife This has a curved, serrated flexible blade that cuts neatly around citrus fruit segments removing peel and membranes.

Grater Simple box graters, with 4 surfaces offering a choice of cutting holes, are more stable in use than flat graters. Metal ones are

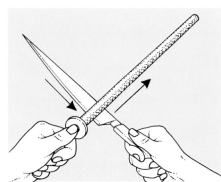

To sharpen a knife: **1** *Hold the steel level in front of you, pointing 45° away from your body. Place the wide end of the knife under the steel at the handle end of the steel. Pull the knife along the steel away from you in one swift movement, at the same time working from the knife heel to the point.*

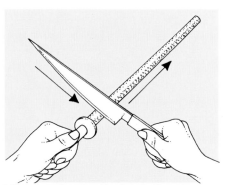

2 *Repeat on the other side of the knife on the top of the steel, again starting with the wide end of the knife at the handle end of the steel, and working along the steel in a single swift movement. Repeat both these steps several times until the blade is sharp, and again before using the knife next time.*

1. Slicer
2. Boning knife
3. Cleaver
4. Cleaver
5. Mezzaluna
6. Wooden chopping board
7. Box grater
8. Butcher knife
9. Coarse sharpening steel
10. Bread knife
11. Bread board
12. Rotary grater
13. Serrated knife
14. Paring knife
15. Grapefruit knife
16. Poultry shears
17. Small and large polyethylene chopping boards
18. Pine knife block
19. Kitchen scissors
20. Magnetic knife rack
21. Chef's knife
22. Chef's knife
23. Chef's knife
24. Oyster knife
25. Cheese knife
26. Filleting knife
27. Paring knife
28. Poultry carver
29. Carving knife
30. Carving fork
31. Serrated chef's knife
32. Nutmeg grater
33. Nutmeg grater
34. Swivel-bladed vegetable peeler
35. Apple corer

best and have sharper cutting holes. Safer is a rotary grater, with a selection of fine and coarse drums turned by a crank, although this can only be used for small food items. A nutmeg grater enables the cook to enjoy this spice at its freshest and most aromatic.

Japanese knife Similar in shape to a samurai sword, these traditional knives have flat backs and very sharp-angled edges so the cook can cut and slice very accurately. I find these beautiful knives are wonderfully satisfying to use; they make an excellent, if expensive, gift.

Knife rack If knives are stored in a drawer they bang together and the blades become dull, so protect your investment in knives with a wall-mounted magnetic rack or a slotted block. Don't hang heavy knives on a magnetic rack or they might fall.

Meat chopper This has a heavy, rectangular blade and will go through most bones. It is a useful general chopper and comes in varying sizes.

Mezzaluna This double-handled knife with a thick curving blade uses a rocking motion for fine chopping and mincing of herbs, vegetables and meat.

Oyster knife The short, pointed blade is used for prying open the oyster shells (page 123), and the horizontal guard protects your fingers from the shell's sharp edges.

Scissors and shears Kitchen scissors should be strong and sharp, and made from stainless steel so they can be thoroughly cleaned after use. One serrated blade gives a secure grip, especially when working with fish or other slippery items. Shears must be even stronger so they can cut through poultry bones; the best have a coiled spring between handles as well as a little notch in one blade to grasp chicken bones.

Slicer Use slicers to cut cold meats into even, thin slices. They are long and fairly narrow with a flexible blade and a straight, fluted or scalloped edge. A smoked salmon slicer is similar in shape but has a very narrow straight-edged blade.

Serrated knife This is used for cutting and slicing smooth-skinned fruits and vegetables and citrus fruits. The blade is long and narrow with a finely serrated edge that cuts cleanly through the skin without crushing the flesh. It is usually made of stainless steel as the acid in fruits and vegetables could cause carbon steel to corrode.

Vegetable peeler A swivel-action blade peels all vegetables and fruits easily and thinly, as the blade follows contours better than a stationary blade or knife; the pointed tip is used to dig out blemishes.

TOP OF THE STOVE

To cook efficiently and with pleasure, it is essential to supply your kitchen with the best equipment you can afford. Nowhere is this more important than in choosing pots and pans for cooking on top of the stove.

Saucepans, frying pans, Dutch ovens and so on receive heat only through their bases. For this reason, they should have thick or heavy bases; if they are too thin, the food being cooked in them is apt to burn and the pans themselves may buckle. In addition, the material used to make the pan must be able to conduct, or diffuse, the heat evenly from the base up the sides. Metal is the best conductor of direct heat which is why it is the material most frequently used. But, as you can see in the box below, a range of metals is used to make pots and pans. Pans should be well made so that they will last: lids should fit snugly and knobs and handles should be sturdy and securely fixed to the pan or lid. Also, be sure to lift up any stovetop equipment before buying. Many pieces, especially those made of cast iron, can be very heavy, and there isn't any point in spending the money on something you will find difficult to use.

It is also worth considering whether the chosen pans are easy to keep clean. Copper pans, for example, are beautiful, and they heat up and cool down rapidly, but they require regular maintenance because if stains are left on them too long the stains become almost impossible to remove. However, their incomparable way of diffusing the heat makes them a real joy to cook with, particularly for sautéing.

Crêpe pan Look for a pan made of good heat-conducting metal, such as cast iron, but lightweight enough and with a long handle so crêpes can be flipped easily. It has low, very sloping sides and comes in various sizes.
Deep-fat fryer Choose a deep pan with 2 short, sturdy handles and a long-handled basket; some have a charcoal filter in the lid, which prevents the unpleasant smell of fat escaping. Electric fryers are not worth the expense unless you intend to do a lot of deep-frying.
Double boiler The lower pan holds simmering water, while the upper pan sits securely on it so delicate mixtures, such as custards or sauces, can be cooked or kept warm over gentle, indirect heat. The lower pan may be made of tin-lined copper, enamelled steel or aluminum, and the upper pan is usually a thinner gauge metal or can be ceramic. A metal upper pan will cool more quickly than a ceramic one when removed from over simmering water. A double boiler can also serve as a bain-marie to make delicate sauces such as hollandaise without fear of curdling.

Dutch oven Sometimes made of cast iron but most often enamel-coated cast iron, these are heavy, fairly deep and straight-sided pots. They may be round or oval. After initial browning or other brisk cooking, food is left to cook more gently on top of the stove or in the oven. The lid should fit tightly to trap in moisture, and the handles should be strong. Dutch ovens are supremely practical for all-in-one dishes.
Fish kettle Long and narrow in shape to accommodate whole fish such as salmon, this has a perforated platform with handles so the fish can be lifted in and out of the poaching liquid without breaking up. Choose one made of tinned steel or tin-lined copper as other metals such as unlined copper could discolour acidulated poaching liquids. Squarer fish kettles are also available.
Frying pan These shallow, wide, flat-bottomed pans have gently sloping straight or curved sides so the food can be fried and turned easily. The base must be thick and the pan must be made of good heat-conducting metal. For prolonged frying over high heat, cast iron is best but very heavy. The handle should be long, strong and ideally of wood which is heat-resistant.
Griddle This wide flat pan has very low sides or none at all so as not to impede the turning of flat foods such as pancakes. Even, high heat is required for cooking, so choose one made of cast iron or enamelled cast iron.
Grill pan This is a very heavy, flat, cast iron pan that is rectangular- or frying pan- shaped, with parallel ridges over the base and a spout on the side for pouring off fat. The ridges keep steaks, chops and so on away from fat, which could make them soggy, and creates a seared exterior while retaining a moist interior, just like grilling and barbecuing.
Omelette pan The sloping sides should be slightly curved so omelettes can be rolled over and turned out; do not choose a big pan or the omelette will be difficult to turn; a 9in (23cm) pan is ideal to serve 2–3.
Saucepan For general cooking, choose straight-sided pans that are reasonably deep (to contain heat). For sauce-making, a pan

A GUIDE TO MATERIALS

Aluminum Good heavy-gauge aluminum pans are sturdy, conduct and hold heat well, will not dent easily or warp, are hard to scratch, and are relatively easy to clean. However, big pans are heavy, and the aluminum may affect the taste and color of some acidic or egg dishes cooked slowly in them, as well as being stained by the food. Some aluminum pans have non-stick linings, but this reduces heat conduction.
Cast iron This is an excellent material for frying pans in particular because it distributes the heat slowly, evenly, and with great intensity for good browning. It also cools slowly. Cast iron needs to be seasoned before first use, and carefully cleaned (without soap) and thoroughly dried after each use to prevent rusting. Wiping with an oiled paper towel helps.
Copper Beautiful – and expensive – copper pans conduct heat perfectly, heating and cooling more quickly than any other metal. Yet, unless they are lined with tin or stainless steel, copper pans can not be used to make chutneys or pickles because the high vinegar content of these preserves can cause a poisonous reaction with the metal; a tin lining cannot be scoured or it will deteriorate, but a stainless-steel lining can be cleaned easily and will last forever, so is the best buy. If, however, you do have a pan that needs re-lining, large kitchen equipment shops can usually arrange for this to be done. If you buy stainless steel-lined copper you will have the best pan possible as it will last forever. For copper pans to retain their beauty the outside must be polished regularly. Clean by rubbing with a cut lemon dipped in salt.
Enameled cast iron Pans made from this are sturdy and distribute heat well but they are heavy and slow to heat or cool, so they are not suitable for quick sautéing and preparing delicate sauces. The enamel may crack or chip if the pan is dropped, and the interior can be scratched if metal tools are used. Some enameled pans need treating before first use so follow the manufacturer's instructions. After use, if any food sticks to the lining, soak in warm water then use a plastic, not a metal scouring pad, to loosen.
Glass and porcelain These are suitable only for gentle cooking because they are used over a very low flame or heat-retarding mat. Glass 'pans' have average heat conduction but are easy to clean.
Stainless steel This excellent hard-wearing material is easy to clean, and does not scratch easily when scoured. On its own it is not a good heat conductor so most stainless steel pans have a layer of aluminum or copper, or both, in the base to retain and distribute heat better. Good stainless steel pans will last a lifetime.

1. **Stainless steel sauté pan with domed lid**
2. **Cast iron frying pan**
3. **Enamelled cast iron pan with pouring spouts**
4. **Expandable steaming basket**
5. **Two-handled stainless steel stockpot**
6. **Deep-frying wire basket**
7. **Stainless steel fish kettle**
8. **Small tin-lined copper saucepan**
9. **Stainless steel steamer and pan**
10. **Enamelled cast iron Dutch oven**
11. **Enamelled steel double boiler**
12. **Cast iron griddle**
13. **Cast iron omelette pan**
14. **Crêpe pan**
15. **Chinese bamboo steaming basket**
16. **Cast iron grill pan**
17. **Small stainless steel saucepan**

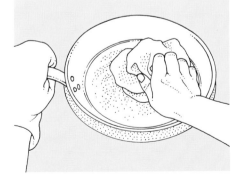

To season an omelette or crêpe pan before using the first time, thinly cover the inside with oil and a thick sprinkling of sea salt then heat until the oil is very hot. Wipe clean with a very thick wad of paper towel, taking care not to burn your fingers. After this, the pan shouldn't be washed without seasoning again, and it shouldn't need seasoning unless some food burns on and you have to soak and lightly scour it.

with sloped sides will allow more rapid reduction and easier stirring and whisking. Pans come in a range of sizes ; ideally a set of 4 pans, from 1 quart up to 5 quarts (1-4.75 liters) will meet most needs. Handles should be long enough to give a safe grip away from the heat, and if they are not heat-resistant, you will need to protect your hand with an oven glove when lifting the pan. Suitable materials are heavy-gauge aluminum, stainless steel with copper or aluminum in the base and steel-lined copper.

Sauce pot Larger than a saucepan, often 8-12 quarts (10-15 liters) in capacity, these are excellent for soup and large quantities of pasta and can double as a lobster pot.

Sauté pan Heavy and deep with a wide, flat base and straight sides, this pan is used for brisk sautéing. It needs to be made of a good heat-conductor such as tin or stainless steel-lined copper, or stainless steel with a copper bottom. Choose a sturdy pan with a handle that allows for a firm and relatively cool grip, so you can shake the pan to move food around quickly. This pan is more versatile than a frying pan, doubling as a chicken fryer when covered.

Steamer Steamers come in many shapes and sizes – round with a basket; tall and narrow with an inner perforated 'sleeve' for long vegetables such as asparagus; a double saucepan with holes in the base of the upper pan; and round stacking baskets made of bamboo. There are also expandable steaming baskets on legs that can be used in any size of pan, but these tend not to last very long. Any large stacking steamers with 2 or more layers, such as the decorative Chinese bamboo baskets, are extremely useful as you can steam different ingredients at the same time, removing a layer when cooked.

Stockpot This large, tall pot is relatively narrow to reduce evaporation of the liquid and to encourage flavors to be extracted from the ingredients. It is usually made of stainless steel. It needs 2 sturdy handles as the pot is heavy to lift when full.

IN THE OVEN

The heat conductor in baking and roasting is, primarily, the air of the oven. This means pans and molds used in the oven don't have to conduct heat especially well, and those made of aluminum, copper, steel, cast iron and glass are equally efficient. Yet, there are factors other than just heat conduction to consider in choosing equipment for baking and roasting.

The size of a pan for roasting can be crucial – if it is too large, the juices from the bird or roast could evaporate and even burn; too small and it is difficult to spoon the juices over the bird or roast to keep it moist. If a pan or mold is flimsy, it could buckle and warp, spilling its contents. Foods cooked in the oven are often large and heavy, and the pan or mold used will be very hot all over, so handles, a lip or a ridged side are needed to ensure a firm grip. Cooks who are not especially strong will prefer pans made from a lighter material, such as stainless steel or aluminum rather than cast iron.

Finally, bear in mind that many ovenproof dishes can be used for serving – copper, china, decorated oven-to-tableware, enamelled cast iron, glass and earthenware can all be very attractive – and this saves on washing up, too.

Au gratin dish This is an extremely versatile shallow, oval or round dish, with gently sloping sides and 2 flat handles or lips; it should be flameproof as the food cooked in it is often put under the grill for browning.

Baking dish Available in many shapes and sizes, baking dishes are relatively shallow and ideally have a handle or lipped rim to facilitate lifting. They should be ovenproof, and glass, earthenware and stoneware absorb heat best.

Baking sheets These should be flat, rigid, not too thin (or they can warp and buckle, causing uneven cooking) and fit into your oven leaving enough space all round for heat circulation. The sides, if any, should be no higher than ½in (1cm). Those made of dark-surfaced materials will quickly absorb heat and produce crisp, well-browned pastry, biscuits and so on; those made of shiny, light materials tend to deflect heat and so are preferable for delicate pastries and meringues.

Brioche mold Usually made from shiny tinned steel that deflects some of the oven heat from the rich yeast dough being baked, these molds are round with a distinctive flaring, fluted side. They are available in several sizes, including small ones for individual brioches. They can also do double duty as decorative molds for gelatin desserts or salads.

Casserole These are large, heavy pots with lids, made of good heat-absorbing and - retaining material, such as enamelled cast iron, earthenware (unglazed ones absorb heat more easily) and ovenproof porcelain (with unglazed base). The lids should fit snugly to keep in moisture, and the pots should have sturdy handles.

Cake pans These come in round, square, or rectangular shapes. Standard round and square pans are 8 or 9in (20.5 or 23cm); the most popular rectangular pan is 13 x 9in (33 x 23cm). Other sizes may be found in gourmet cookware and cake decorating supply stores. Usually made of aluminum, they may be found with nonstick finishes. Imported deep cake pans, some with removable bottoms, are available from specialty cookware catalogs and are good for fruit cakes and pound cakes

Cookie and biscuit cutter These are available in many shapes and sizes, either plastic or, preferably, metal. Buy ones that are sturdy with a sharp cutting edge.

Flan dish Also called a quiche dish, these are made of ovenproof porcelain, usually plain white, but many decorative ones are also available. The bottom of the dish is unglazed so the heat is efficiently absorbed to bake the bottom of the pastry shell; to intensify heat from the bottom and ensure a crisper baked crust underneath, place the dish on a preheated dark, heavy baking sheet. The classic shape is round with fluted, slightly sloping sides.

Flan ring Place this on a flat baking sheet to form a 'pan' for baking a pastry shell. After baking, the ring, usually made of tinned steel with a rolled edge, is just lifted off. Only buy ones which are rigid and sturdy. Available in imported cookware catalogs, these can be rectangular or round, with or without fluting inside.

Jelly-roll tin This is a large, rectangular pan with sides only ¾–1in (2–2.5cm) high. As the cake traditionally made in this pan is thin and the baking time is short, the pan should be made of good heat-conducting metal such as aluminum or black steel. Only buy pans that are sturdy so they do not warp or buckle. A 14 x 10½in (35 x 27cm) pan will make a jelly roll that will make approximately 10-12 servings. Lining the pan with waxed paper or parchment is usually recommended so the base of the cake remains soft enough to roll

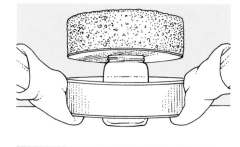

To remove a baked cake from a loose-bottomed cake pan, cool the cake in its pan on a wire rack according to the time specified in the recipe, until it comes away from the sides slightly. Place the pan on a can or jar and gently push down the outer ring. Remove the cake carefully from the base and transfer to a plate. Use this method also for a flan pan with a removable bottom.

without breaking (page 262).

Loaf pan Heavy, strong steel loaf pans keep their shape better than aluminum or non-stick ones. The standard sizes are 8 x 4½ x 2½ in(20.5cm) and 9 x 5 x 3 in(23cm), and those with a dark finish encourage a crisp crust all round.

Muffin pans These come with 6, 8, 12 or 24 cups and are usually deep and about 2½in (6.4cm) in diameter. Also available are pans with larger cups for making giant muffins, very shallow ones for making muffin tops and some fluted ones. Use for muffins, cupcakes, rolls and popovers. Most muffin pans are made of aluminum, and some have a nonstick finish for easy removal.

Pie pan This is a shallow round pan, usually made of heat-deflecting material such as stainless steel, with smooth, sloping sides and a wide rim.

Pie plate A traditional pie plate, made of earthenware or stoneware, is round. The best are at least 2in (5cm) deep, with a flat rim.

Roasting pan Look for a pan about 2in (5cm) deep (higher sides discourage browning and produce a moister result), and which will fit into your oven, with at least 2in (5cm) all round so that heat can circulate evenly. The pan must be strong, with rigid handles or a large lip for a good grip as a roast or bird can be heavy. They may be made of stainless steel, aluminum or enamelled cast iron. Some very deep pans have lids, in which food is more steamed or pot-roasted than roasted; for a crisp finish, the lid must be removed towards the end of cooking.

Skewers and needles Thin stainless steel skewers, 4–6in (10–15 cm) long, are used to hold boned roasts in shape and secure poultry cavities during cooking, while longer, flatter skewers are used for kebobs. Both kinds of skewers should have sharp points. Use a trussing needle, 8–10in (20–25cm) long for chicken and 14in (35cm) long for turkey, with kitchen string to truss birds.

Soufflé dish These round, deep dishes have straight, smooth insides so the soufflé mixture rises evenly. The outside of the dish usually has a traditional 'ridged' appearance, and the bottom should be unglazed to encourage oven heat to penetrate and cook the bottom of the soufflé. Available in many sizes, the 1, 2 and 3 quart (1-2.8 liter) dishes are the most

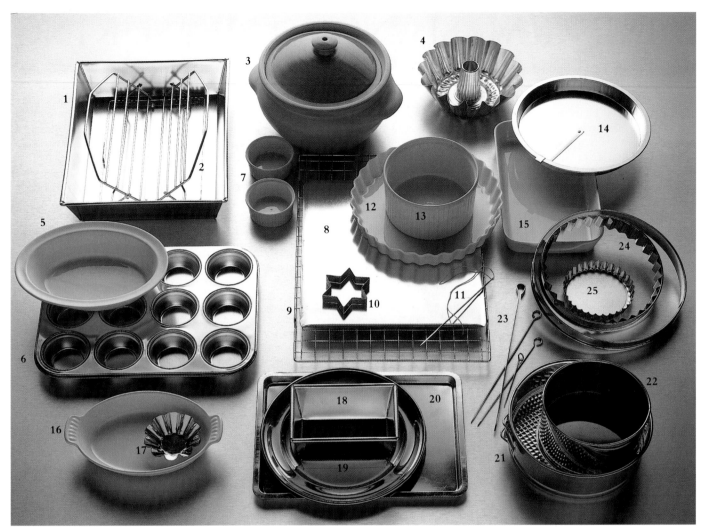

1. Roasting pan
2. V-shaped roasting rack
3. Earthenware bean pot
4. Fluted tube pan
5. Earthenware pie plate
6. Muffin pan
7. Ramekins

8. Baking sheet
9. Wire rack
10. Star cutter
11. Trussing needle and string
12. Fluted flan dish
13. Soufflé dish
14. Cake pan

15. Baking dish
16. Au gratin dish
17. Individual brioche pan
18. Loaf pan
19. Indented cake pan
20. Jelly-roll pan
21. Springform pan

22. Deep cake pan with
    removable bottom
23. Selection of metal skewers of
    various sizes
24. Flan rings
25. Individual tart pan with
    removable bottom

To remove a pound cake or cheesecake from a springform pan, let the cake cool if it has been baked according to the time specified in the recipe. Run a small spatula between the pan and the cake, then undo the spring-clip so that the ring gently pulls away from the side of the cake. Run the spatula between the base of the pan and the cake, remove the base and slide the cake carefully onto a serving plate.

common. Individual ones that look like large ramekins are available as well.

Springform pan Used for making delicate cakes, such as cheesecakes which can't be turned out, this pan has a loose, flat round bottom that fits into a deep, straight-sided ring; when the spring-clip is opened, the ring gently pulls away from the sides of the cake.

Tart pan A removable bottom sits in a fluted or plain rim, and after baking, the tart can be easily pushed up and out of the rim and then removed from the base (see left).

Tube pan This is a deep, round pan with a hollow tube in the centre to conduct heat to the middle of cakes for even baking; most often used for baking cakes such as angel food, chiffon, and sponge that are leavened by beaten egg whites. The best ones have little feet attached to the top rim to aid in cooling the cakes upside down, and a removable bottom to make it easier to loosen the cake from the pan. In Europe similar pans

are used for baking dry cakes that will subsequently be saturated with syrup or liqueur, or sweet, rich yeast-risen cakes. They may be shallow with a curved base (for baking savarins) or with a fluted base, or deep with a decoratively etched base and sides (for baking kugelhopfs).

Wire racks Wire cake racks are essential for cooling cakes, cookies and other baked goods, so buy the biggest rack you can accommodate, and check that it stands level and is sturdy enough to support a heavy cake. Wire racks for roasting meat are not essential but they hold the roast or bird above the fat in the pan. The most useful rack is V-shaped, and adjustable to hold different-sized roasts.

Grilling baskets consist of 2 layers of thin wire which hold food in between and usually have a handle. These enable delicate foods, such as whole fish, to be turned for even cooking without breaking up and are ideal for use on a barbecue.

MIXING, MASHING *and* MEASURING

Despite the advances of modern technology, many tasks in the kitchen are still done by traditional methods. This is particularly true in the way foods are mixed, minced and mashed. Electrical appliances such as blenders, food processors, mixers and beaters can take the hard work out of many everyday jobs, but they cannot entirely replace whisks, sieves, mashers and even the old-fashioned mortar and pestle. The traditional wire whisk, ideally in tandem with a copper bowl, incorporates more air into egg whites than an electric mixer.

All this is not to say that electrical appliances are unnecessary – the dough hook attachment on a heavy-duty electric mixer will knead dough perfectly, and with far less effort than doing it by hand; a blender purees cooked vegetables and stock into a cream soup in seconds; a food processor can mix cookies, cakes, pâtés, dips and sauces in no time at all and it can uniformly chop, shred, slice and grate vegetables even faster than a professional chef. However, with a food processor, people are apt to use the slicing blade too much; most salads look and taste better if the ingredients are prepared slightly unevenly by hand. For certain things such as finely slicing cucumber a food processor is invaluable. For accurately measuring ingredients use standard measuring cups and spoons and scales.

Citrus juicer and squeezer Many juicers and squeezers are available. The simple, cheap and efficient juicer, usually made of glass or plastic, has a ridged dome in the center of the dish onto which halved fruit is pressed and twisted. 'Teeth' around the dome will not always hold back seeds, so it is better to choose a juicer with a strainer that fits on the base dish.

Copper bowl Ideal for whisking egg whites because a chemical reaction between the egg and copper makes the volume of the egg white foam greater and more stable. Look for a rounded bottom and rolled edge.

Electric mixer Both small hand-held and large heavy-duty versions are available. A hand-held mixer is ideal for beating mixtures over the heat on top of the stove, as well as for light mixtures such as whipping cream. Choose a mixer with several speeds for maximum control. Heavy-duty mixers, although more bulky, efficiently cream large quantities of cake or cookie mixtures and knead bread dough if they have a bread hook. These mixers also have many attachments available for grinding, shredding, extracting juice, and so on.

Food mill This hand-cranked rotary food mill processes foods through holes with a metal blade, producing a puree. Seeds, fibers and other unwanted material are sieved out. Hooks on the rim hold it securely over a pan or bowl.

Food processor Most models come with a very sharp double-bladed knife for chopping, pureeing and mincing, with extra discs for slicing, grating and shredding. An optional plastic blade kneads dough, and there are optional juice extractors and coffee grinders. Ideally it should have rubber pads on the bottom to keep it in place while running.

Garlic press A sturdy press crushes garlic cloves and forces the flesh and juice of garlic through the holes. If the holes are too small the press can be difficult to clean.

Grinder An old-fashioned manually operated grinder with screw clamps to hold it securely on the counter is always useful, especially if it has a selection of discs – coarse, medium and fine. Be sure it can be dismantled for thorough cleaning.

Kitchen scales These may be the traditional balance scales, uncomplicated and precise but space-consuming; spring-balance scales, more suited to lighter loads but not good at weighing less than 1oz (25g); or beam scales, which are very accurate but again can be space-consuming. Be sure the scales show both U.S. and metric calibrations.

Masher The simplest and cheapest masher for potatoes and other root vegetables has a sturdy, meshed metal disc on the end of a long handle. For a smoother result, use a ricer that forces the vegetable through the mesh or cutting grid.

Measuring cups For measuring liquids, clear toughened glass such as Pyrex is best because the level of the ingredient being measured is easily seen, and the glass is not affected by boiling liquid. Use metal or plastic measuring cups for dry ingredients and fill level with the top.

Measuring spoons Standard measuring spoons give accurate measures of small quantities of dry and liquid ingredients; they are available in inexpensive sets made up of ¼tsp (1.25ml), ½tsp (2.5ml), 1tsp (5ml) and 1tbsp (15ml).

Meat mallet Usually made of wood, most meat mallets have both smooth and spiked sides; the smooth surface is used to flatten pieces of meat, such as scallops or chicken cutlets, for quick cooking; the spiked side breaks down fibers and thus tenderizes tough cuts of meat. It can also be used to crush whole spices such as cinnamon and star anise coarsely for use in marinades.

Mixing bowl Traditional bowls are heavy glazed porcelain, earthenware or stoneware, but more modern bowls are made of heatproof glass or stainless steel. Stainless steel is easy to clean, will not interact with any food like aluminium does, won't chip, shatter or melt, and cools and heats more quickly than ceramic, glass or plastic. Whatever kind of bowls you prefer, however, choose ones with rounded rather than straight sides so that a whisk or spoon will work efficiently, be sure they have flat bottoms so that they sit securely on the counter. Several bowls in graduated sizes will prove invaluable, and if they stack, they'll store easily.

Mortar and pestle A deep, curved bowl on a sturdy base and compatibly shaped pestle are used for grinding tiny, hard seeds, such as cumin and fennel, as well as garlic, anchovies and nuts. They can be made of white vitrified porcelain, heavyweight ceramic, tough unglazed porcelain, stone, wood, glass or marble. The end of the pestle and the inside bottom surface of the bowl should both be slightly rough for maximum friction.

Pastry scraper Shaped in a rectangle and sometimes with a handle along one side, this should be made of thin, stainless or carbon steel or plastic. Use for mixing and cutting pastry and bread doughs, for turning and lifting rolled-out pastry, for handling hot mixtures, for example when making candy, for scraping the counter clean, and for folding

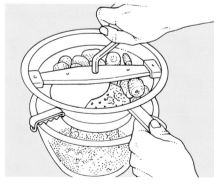

To use a food mill fit the appropriate disc for the desired texture and place the mill securely over a pan or bowl. A hand-operated crank forces food through the sieving disc into the bowl.

Use a sturdy mortar and pestle to grind whole spices, or for the traditional method of making pesto sauce. Work the pestle round and round against the sides and base of the mortar.

1. Nylon sieve
2. Kitchen scales
3. Glass mixing bowl
4. Citrus juicer
5. Wooden citrus juicer
6. Stainless steel mixing bowl
7. Food processor
8. Copper bowl
9. Mortar and pestle
10. Conical metal sieve
11. Hand-held electric mixer
12. Masher
13. Meat mallet
14. Wooden vegetable masher
15. Utensil container
16. Mixing bowl
17. Pudding mold
18. Pastry scraper
19. Tea strainer or mini-sieve
20. Fine conical strainer
21. Wire strainer
22. Grinder
23. Glass measuring cup
24. Food mill
25. Pudding mold
26. Measuring cups
27. Roasting thermometer
28. Oven thermometer
29. Small whisk for sauces
30. Flat whisk for batters
31. Wire whisk
32. Wire whisk
33. Garlic press

in any light cake or other mixtures.

Pudding mold Used primarily for cooking boiled and steamed puddings, these distinctive molds with sloping sides are made from earthenware or glazed porcelain. They must have a sturdy, flat bottom and a lip under the rim for securing a tied-on cover. Available mostly in antique stores or as reproductions these days, they can double as a mixing bowl and are indispensable if you do want to make a steamed pudding.

Sieve These can be bowl-shaped, conical or flat-bottomed, with a fine to coarse mesh or holes, according to use. Fine bowl-shaped and very pointed conical sieves (also called chinois) made from tinned wire, stainless steel or nylon (best for fruit and other foods that could be discolored by metal) are used for sifting, straining and gentle pureeing. For pureeing coarser mixtures, use a heavy conical stainless steel sieve with a less pointed bottom or strongly woven fine-mesh chinois and press food through with a narrow conical pestle. Chinois sieves are also used for straining fine sauces, custards, stocks and gravy. Wash all sieves by soaking in hot water first to dislodge particles of food and then scrub with a brush on both sides.

Thermometer These are essential for safe storage and preparation of food. Appliance thermometers for use in freezers, refrigerators and ovens check that correct temperatures are achieved and maintained; sugar and deep-frying thermometers measure the temperature of sugar syrup, a preserve or oil to be sure the required stage is reached and maintained; a meat thermometer, inserted into a large roast or bird, registers the internal temperature so you can tell when the food has been cooked through (page 159); an instant-read thermometer quickly gives the temperature of food cooked in a microwave oven or on the grill. It is a good investment if you do a lot of microwaving or grilling.

Whisk These come in many different sizes and shapes for different functions: a large, springy balloon-shaped whisk with 10–12 thin wires looping over each other, is used for whisking egg whites and is ideal for use with a copper bowl; a smaller, longer and relatively stiff whisk with only about 8 thicker wires is used for mixing and stirring sauces and gravies; a flat whisk with only a few wires is used for beating batters. Wires may be made of tinned steel or stainless steel, and the handles of metal or wood. Choose whisks that won't rust and ones with wires soldered into handles rather than removable wires because they will not pop out accidentally and are easier to clean.

SPECIALIZED EQUIPMENT

Once you have assembled the foundation of your kitchen equipment – good-quality pans, knives and so on – it may then be time to consider specialized tools that could make your style of cooking both more efficient and more artistic.

The utensils and appliances here are not essential in everyone's kitchen, but they may be useful in yours. It all depends on what you like to cook. If you make pasta often, for example, it may be worth investing in a pasta machine; if you like to serve molded desserts and savory terrines, you might want to have some pretty molds; pastry makers will value a marble board and lots of individual pans in different shapes; a Chinese wok is indispensable for anyone who likes the quick cooking style of stir-frying.

Many of the tools here do not involve spending a lot of money. A cheap salad spinner, for example, efficiently and quickly dries salad greens and other leafy vegetables. The cost of a zester or a melon baller is almost negligible, but they add a flair to food presentation.

Charlotte mold This plain, sloped-sided mold has 2 small handles to facilitate unmolding, and may be made of copper, aluminum or tin-lined steel. Desserts prepared in this mold are called charlottes (charlotte Russe, for example, consists of Bavarian cream surrounded by lady fingers and apple charlotte has an apple filling in a bread case) but the mold is also useful for savory mousses, terrines and so on.

Cheese slicer In my experience a simple cheese wire is useful for cutting close-textured cheeses like Gruyère or Emmental into really thin slices. The other option is a hand-held cheese slicer with either a rolling-action cutting wire or a slot in the blade.

Chinese wok Designed for stir-frying, woks are shallow, curved and often with a long handle. Long-handled woks are better to use, as you can then give the food a good toss without the fat splashing too much. The distribution of heat is important, so choose a wok made of rolled steel or iron rather than thin stainless steel or aluminum.

Citrus stripper This is a rounded stainless steel blade with a little V-shaped tooth in a horizontal hole on the side. Use it to peel single decorative strips about ¼in (5mm) wide from citrus fruits and to cut grooves in fruit and vegetables such as cucumbers . When the vegetables are then cut across, the slices have notched edges like flower petals.

Citrus zester This is a stainless steel blade with 5 little holes in a line along the downward-curving end. Use to peel fine strips of citrus skin or rind without taking off any of the bitter white pith.

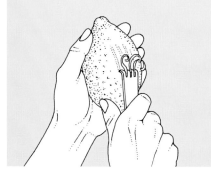

Use a citrus zester to remove thin, delicate strips of rind that are ideal for flavoring or garnishing foods. Draw the sharp side down the skin.

Couscoussière Used to cook couscous (page 110), the North African grain dish, this is a covered pot with perforations on the base that sits snugly on top of a round, deep pot. The semolina grains or couscous are steamed in the upper pot over an aromatic stock or a meat and vegetable stew in the lower pot. It may be made of earthenware, copper or aluminium, and is also useful for steaming rice, vegetables and fish.

Decorative molds These can transform even the most basic dessert or jellied dish into an ornamental centerpiece. Molds come in all shapes and designs and are made of many materials: expensive tin-lined copper (handsome enough to be displayed in the kitchen), porcelain, durable stainless steel (suitable for both hot and chilled preparations), earthenware, aluminum (may discolor), tin (may rust), glass (can be fragile), tinned steel and hard plastic. Molds for cooked dishes must be ovenproof; for chilled dishes, the molds are best made of thin metal which gets cold quickly and then warms again quickly to unmold easily. Be sure molds are seamless or they might leak, and that the design has shallow indentations or the food will be difficult to turn out without some sticking to the mold.

Ice cream scoop A sturdy cast aluminum scoop is best for solidly frozen ice cream because of a chemical sealed inside the handle that absorbs hand heat, softening the ice cream as you scrape.

Individual molds and pans Many molds for individual portions are available, such as the heart-shaped porcelain *coeur à la crème* mold with draining holes in the base to make a sweetened cheese dessert; ramekins, like very small soufflé dishes, sometimes oval, used for baked eggs, crème brûlée and so on; little porcelain or ceramic pots with lids for baked custard; metal timbale molds or glass custard cups with sloped sides for crème caramel, small bread puddings, vegetable purees and so on; shallow, oval metal molds for eggs in aspic; metal rings for rum babas; and small loaf pans. Pans for individual pastries may be round and shallow (for tartlets or flans), round or boat-shaped, plain or fluted (for pies) or conical (for cream horns). Small cake pans come in many shapes and sizes from tiny hearts, ovals and diamonds, to scallop-shaped madeleines.

Jelly bag A strongly made cloth bag with hanging loops or tapes will strain clear juice from the pulp of cooked or raw fruit, which is then used to make jelly (page 301) or wine; the finer the weave of the cloth, the clearer the juices will be. The loops or tapes are used to attach the bag to either a special plastic stand, a broom handle between two chairs or the legs of an upturned chair or stool, so the bag can be suspended over a bowl which catches the juice as it drips through the bag.

Melon baller Also called a ball cutter, this has small bowl-shaped cutters at each end, one larger than the other. Use to cut balls of fruit such as melons and vegetables such as carrots and potatoes, using a rotating movement.

Paella pan This large round pan is usually less than 2in (5cm) deep with sloping sides and a handle on each side. It may be made of steel, aluminum or, more traditionally, cast iron. Designed for cooking and serving the Spanish dish of the same name that consists of saffron rice with a variety of vegetables, meat and seafood. I also use mine for making large flat omelettes to feed crowds (page 73).

Pasta machine Adjustable rollers (ideally made of rust-resistant stainless steel) knead and roll dough, and cutters produce the desired width of noodles. Some are operated with a hand-turned crank, while others are electrically powered. Be sure hand-operated machines can be fixed securely to the worktop, for example with a clamp.

Pastry bag and metal tips Available in varying sizes, these cone-shaped bags should

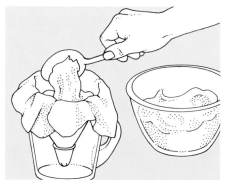

A clean and easy way to fill a pastry bag is by putting it, with a metal tip already inserted, point down in a measuring cup and rolling the end of the bag over the rim. Then spoon in the mixture. It can be messy filling the bag holding it in your hand.

1. Single-handled wok
2. Collapsible wire salad spinner
3. Pressure cooker
4. Couscoussière
5. Copper preserving pan
6. Jelly bag
7. Hand-operated pasta maker
8. Cast iron paella pan
9. Aluminum charlotte mold
10. Decorative copper mold
11. Individual bread pan
12. Timbale mold
13. Melon baller
14. Citrus stripper
15. Citrus zester
16. Boat-shaped pastry mold
17. Ice cream scoop
18. Cheese slicer
19. Individual tartlet pan
20. Earthenware terrine
21. Savory meat pie mold
22. Coeur à la crème mold
23. Metal decorating tips
24. Pastry bag

be made with double-stitched seams and hemmed ends. A flexible, tightly woven cotton or nylon bag will last longer than a plastic one. A set of tips, with openings in several sizes and shapes, gives variety for decorating cakes and desserts, piping fillings onto canapés and into pastries. An adapter enables you to change the tip without having to empty the bag first.

Preserving pan Buy a deep one so hot mixtures do not bubble over, and one wide enough to allow maximum evaporation. A heavy base prevents the mixture from burning and sticking, and 2 strong handles or a bucket-type handle are essential. They are usually made of heavy-gauge aluminum or lined copper.

Pressure cooker This is a heavy pan with a tightly fitting lid that has a pressure valve that works by trapping steam from boiling water, raising the pressure and temperature. Food cooks much faster than with conventional steaming, stewing or boiling while using up

relatively little energy. A pressure cooker is particularly useful for cooking dried legumes quickly without the need for presoaking, and for pot roasts.

Rice boiler This is a perforated aluminum ball that is suspended in boiling water, making boiled rice easy to drain. It can also be used for cooking and draining vegetables quickly and easily.

Salad spinner This may be a simple wire basket that is shaken (outdoors or over the sink) to remove excess water from salad greens, or a plastic basket inside a covered bowl that spins like a top, using centrifugal force to expel the water. Plastic spinners are bulky, whereas wire baskets can usually be collapsed flat for more convenient storage, but plastic spinners require much less effort to use.

Savory meat pie mold This is a large oval or rectangular tinned steel mold used for baking British-style meat pies and pâtés in pastry. The sides of the patterned or plain

mold are held together over the base by small clips; the clips and sides are removed after baking. This is expensive but pies baked in one of these molds do look attractive.

Terrine This is a heavy ovenproof dish, traditionally with a long rectangular shape but it may also be oval, round or square and is used for cooking pâtés, hence the name 'terrine' is sometimes used for baked pâtés. The lid should have a tiny steam hole to prevent the pâté from becoming soggy. As well as ovenproof porcelain or earthenware, this dish may also be made of enamelled cast iron. They are usually attractive dishes so you can serve directly from them.

Waffle iron The hand-held version with long handles can be used on either a gas or an electric heating unit, and may produce traditional heart-shaped waffles. Easier and more foolproof to use is the electric waffle iron, with non-stick grill plates. Some electric waffle irons have reversible plates so they can double as sandwich grills.

STOCKS and SOUPS

Stocks are the basis of much good cooking – thus the French word for stock, *fond*, which means foundation, is very apt. Soups, sauces, gravies and stews are all greatly enhanced if they are made with a good homemade stock. Still, I would never discourage someone from making a soup if they only had a bouillon cube as there are all sorts of additions such as lemon juice, wine and sherry which can transform the flavor. Nor do I feel, as we are told by chefs, that stocks must always be made with fresh ingredients not previously cooked ones – these stocks may be best but a stock is the obvious thing to make from carcasses and leftover trimmings, and a very good flavor can still be extracted from cooked bones and meat if they have not been overcooked.

Nevertheless, it is worth getting into the habit of making a stock from fresh ingredients. There is something very satisfying about it and it is a simple procedure. The best stocks are made from gelatinous parts of the animal such as marrow bones, oxtails, giblets and carcasses. Sweet root vegetables give flavor to a stock and onion is almost compulsory.

If you make a large amount of stock you can freeze it to use as needed. Stocks can also be reduced to an intensely flavored glaze which you can freeze in small containers, and then use in sauces or stews to give depth of flavor. If you plan to make a clear soup, it is nice to color the stock with ingredients such as beets, tomatoes, spinach or even carrots, which will give a warm glow. In fact, I find reduction the most useful way of keeping stocks, as they take up much less room in the freezer and so often it is the concentrated flavor, not a lot of extra liquid that you really need. If possible do not use an aluminum pan when making stock as the pan can affect the taste and color.

Soup has been a basic food almost all over the world for as long as what we eat has been recorded. Every culture has a long tradition of soups, and in some countries, such as Portugal, it is still unusual not to have soup every day. The homely French *potage* is a major part of everyday meals in rural France, and thin, aromatic soups are also part of everyday meals in China and the Far East. In this country, seafood soups such as clam chowder in New England, crab soup in Maryland and the Carolinas, and cioppino in San Francisco are traditions.

Soups range from the most delicate, clear variety to the thick main course soups which are almost like a stew. They can be smooth and creamy, thin and clear, thick with vegetable purees or full of chopped ingredients – the unifying factor is that soups are eaten with a spoon.

Homemade soup has no parallel and people tend to forget how simple it is to make, and how nutritious it is, too. A robust soup full of gently cooked vegetables and served with whole wheat bread can be a complete, healthy, balanced meal. I find this kind of soup invaluable for holiday lunches.

A good soup is always welcome; it is one of the ultimate comfort foods – when you are cold, hungry or simply depressed, or when you have eaten too much at the previous meal or are feeling tired or simply want a bowl of homey, soothing nourishment. Quite another thing is the first course soup; chilled or hot, with the purpose of being a tantalizing appetizer; this can be a fine vegetable puree with cream, or a crystal clear soup made from clarified stock with a few crisp ingredients or chopped fresh herbs.

Clockwise from top: Fish Bisque (page 39) a modern version of this traditional creamy soup, flavored with smoked fish fillets and spices, contains large prawns and red pepper rings; Shallot and Mustard Soup with Tarragon (page 38) is a pureed cream soup that makes an unusual start to any meal; Chicken Soup with Smoked Oysters (page 38) is a hearty mixture with mushrooms, red pepper and chopped chives for extra flavor; Clear Vegetable Soup with Eggs (page 39) has an aromatic stock with delicate eggs and fine lettuce shreds added at the last moment; Indian Summer Soup (page 38) combines eggplant and tomatoes in a spiced stock flavored with creamy coconut.

MEAT, POULTRY *and* GAME STOCKS

There are two basic kinds of meat stock – white and brown. Although raw meat and poultry make the best stock of all, you can, of course, use leftover carcasses and bones. In a white stock, like poultry stock, the ingredients are simply brought to a boil and then simmered slowly, but in a brown stock, like beef stock, the bones are first browned in a hot oven. It is important in all meat stocks to include bones for real depth of flavor, and a stock can be made very well with only raw meatless bones.

Boiling tends to make the stock cloudy so lower the heat to a very gentle simmer after it has come to a boil. Skimming the stock from time to time while it cooks will also help to reduce cloudiness. If you have little time you can make stock quickly, in about 20 minutes, in a pressure cooker but the result will be cloudy and it cannot be used for clear soups, though it is fine for thick soups.

Richly flavored homemade stocks are also the essential ingredient of clear bouillons or consommés (page 32). These soups are simply stocks that have been clarified with egg shells and whites, then strained through cheesecloth.

BONES FOR STOCK-MAKING

Bones contain collagen which dissolves during cooking to form gelatin. The best bones to use for stocks are the most gelatinous – beef shin, oxtail, veal and ham bones, knuckle bones and poultry and game carcasses. You should always break up carcasses or saw bones so all the collagen is extracted during cooking.

MAKING MEAT STOCK

White meat stocks are not really white but, in fact, paler in color and with a different character than brown stocks. Veal is the best meat to use for white stock, though it is possible to use pork as such lean pigs are bred today.

1 *Put cut-up bones and other flavoring ingredients into a large stockpot or saucepan with water to cover. Season lightly with salt, especially if using uncooked bones.*

2 *Bring to a boil. Skim off the foam that rises to the surface with a large spoon. Simmer, covered, adding a little water from time to time, if necessary.*

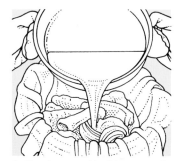

3 *Continue to add cold water and skim the stock until no more foam rises, then simmer gently for 2–3 hours. Strain through a colander lined with damp cheesecloth. Check the seasoning unless you are going to reduce the stock (opposite).*

To make brown stock, *brown the bones and onions in a pan in a hot oven, 425°F, 220°C, then boil to produce a rich, dark-colored stock. Unpeeled onions add extra color. Beef bones are particularly good.*

STOCK VARIATIONS

• Classic flavorings for meat, poultry and game stocks are onions (unskinned for brown stock), carrots and celery. I also use many other root vegetables such as parsnips, turnips and celeriac. Do not use potatoes if you want a clear stock. If making a very pale stock remember that carrots contribute quite a lot of color.
• Bulb fennel which is past cooking as a vegetable still adds an excellent flavor to stock.
• I add peeled and sliced garlic at the beginning of cooking for a mild sweet flavor, or just before the end for a strong garlicky taste.
• For a richly colored and flavored stock add slightly overripe tomatoes or some tomato puree. I sometimes add sweet red peppers, too, for extra flavor.
• Herbs should be as fresh as possible and tied into a bunch or added as a bouquet garni in a cheesecloth bag (page 10).
• Sage, which grows profusely and for which it can be difficult to find enough uses, is surprisingly good in beef stock if used sparingly.
• Spices are not a standard addition to stocks but peppercorns, whole cloves, blades of mace, cinnamon sticks, slices of fresh gingerroot, star anise and caraway, coriander and cumin seeds can be used to add extra character.

• Cinnamon sticks, tarragon leaves and sliced but unpeeled fresh gingerroot perk up a chicken stock.
• Sliced fresh gingerroot is also a good addition to beef stock.
• Try adding crushed juniper berries, whole allspice and bay leaves when you are making game stock.
• Salt should only be used sparingly at the beginning of cooking to draw out the flavors of the ingredients. Rather than salting stock at the end of cooking wait until you have incorporated it with the other ingredients in the final dish. Any stock that is going to be reduced as a sauce should not be salted until after reducing because reduction intensifies the flavors and the stock can end up tasting salty.
• Use whole peppercorns in stocks: ground pepper cooked for a long time can give an acrid taste.
• After you have carved all the meat from your holiday turkey, use the carcass to produce a wonderful stock with good flavor.
• It is also possible to make stocks in the microwave: put all the ingredients in a deep bowl, cover loosely and cook on High (100%) to boiling, then cook on Defrost (30%) for 45–60 minutes. (Check your user's manual for specific instructions.)

REDUCING STOCK

Stock that has been reduced by gentle boiling adds a rich flavor to soups and sauces. You can reduce the stock to varying intensities of flavor, and finally all the way down to a rich meat glaze which will set as a solid jelly. Keep reduced stock in the refrigerator for up to three days, after which it should be boiled again to prevent spoiling. Add a little meat glaze to sauces when they finish cooking for a really rich taste and shiny finish.

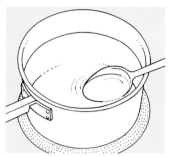 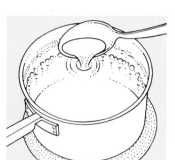

1 *Put the strained stock in a saucepan and boil gently, skimming the surface as necessary, until reduced by half.*

2 *To make a rich, glossy meat glaze continue reducing the stock until it is thick enough to coat a spoon. Chill until set.*

DEGREASING STOCK

Stock is degreased so it does not add fat to other ingredients, and to make the pure clear liquid essential for making consommé (page 32). For best results stock should be completely cold before degreasing but you can still remove excessive fat from warm stock.

 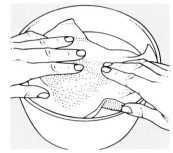

Allow the strained stock *to become completely cold, then chill it until the fat sets in a hard layer on the surface. Use a large metal spoon or spatula to lift off the solidified fat carefully and then discard it.*

If the stock is still warm *spoon off as much fat as possible from the surface using a shallow ladle or large tablespoon, then use several thicknesses of paper toweling to mop up the remaining fat from the surface.*

POULTRY OR GAME STOCK

Ideally use raw bones, with or without meat and giblets, excluding the liver. Or, use leftover carcasses. You can use bones from fattier types of poultry such as duck but avoid using the skin and any of the fat.

Break up the bones or carcasses and put them in a large pan with chopped onions – unpeeled for a richer-colored stock – carrots, celery and leeks. Game carcasses also make a dark stock. Add a bunch of fresh herbs – rosemary and tarragon are very good in poultry and game stocks – and some whole peppercorns. Pour on water to cover, then bring slowly to a boil, skimming until there is no more foam.

Reduce the heat and continue simmering, covered, for about 3 hours, skimming occasionally, if necessary. Strain and cool, then refrigerate the stock until the fat sets in a solid layer, then degrease (above).

Simmering poultry stock ingredients – bones, leeks, carrots, onions, onion skins, black peppercorns and fresh herbs in a bouquet garni. Adding salt at the start of cooking draws out the flavors.

FISH *and* VEGETABLE STOCKS

Fish and vegetable stocks are more delicate than meat, poultry and game stocks. Fish stock, in particular, should not be cooked for more than 25 minutes – simmering for even a little too long can make it unacceptably bitter, and if allowed to reduce too much the gelatinous fish bones will turn the stock into an inedible glue. If you want to reduce the cooked stock slightly you must strain the liquid before boiling it down further.

Gelatinous white fish, especially flat fish, make the best stock – plaice, sole, turbot, scrod, cod, whiting, hake and haddock are all suitable. Include as many thoroughly cleaned heads, tails and bones of filleted white fish as you can get from your fish market. For a smoky flavored stock use some smoked haddock. Salmon heads and tails are also good. Do not, however, use trimmings from oily fish such as mackerel, sardines or herring because you will just be adding excess oiliness and too strong a flavor. Prawn and lobster heads and shells and crab shells are wonderful as they contribute a delicious sweet flavor and a pretty color, too.

As fish stock tends to be rather grey looking you can add color by using onion skins as well as chopped onions and shallots to add flavor. Use carrots for color along with a little sweetness which I think is necessary in a good fish stock – you can even add a teaspoon or two of sugar. I often add tomatoes for flavor and color, and occasionally a dash of fresh orange juice. White wine or cider is something I also often include – as much of it as I can spare – and either a couple of tablespoons of lemon juice or a tablespoon of white wine vinegar. A little spice can be good, too: try coriander seed, one or two crushed cardamom pods or a blade of mace. Use whole black peppercorns, not ground pepper, and include a generous bundle of fresh herbs, with some dill and fennel, if you like. Do not use dried herbs.

COURT BOUILLON AND FUMET

A court bouillon is used for poaching delicate ingredients such as fish, shellfish and chicken. Usually prepared and cooled before using for poaching, court bouillon is made by boiling vegetables with water and wine or wine vinegar – normally white wine though red may be used – or lemon juice. A reduced fish stock is also known by its French name, *fumet*, and makes a richer poaching liquid.

VEGETABLE STOCKS

Now that more people are vegetarians vegetable stocks are gaining in popularity, and they can be useful for all sorts of vegetable soups and sauces. Almost any fresh vegetables can be used: cabbage, leeks and spinach produce a green-colored stock; parsnips, carrots and celeriac all add a rounded taste; tomatoes, red pepper, onions and garlic make a rosy Mediterranean-flavored stock, and chopped raw beets cooked with onions results in a beautiful scarlet stock which can be used as a clear broth or to make pink soups and sauces.

I nearly always add a little lemon juice or a tablespoon or two of sherry or cider vinegar to vegetable stocks, and caraway seed is an excellent spice for stocks made from root vegetables. The vegetables must be boiled until nearly mushy, then thrown away as all their goodness will have escaped into the water during the cooking.

VEGETABLE STOCK

Chop but don't peel about 1½lb (750g) mixed washed vegetables. Put the vegetables in a pan with 10 black peppercorns, 4 tablespoons lemon juice, 5 cups (1.2 liters) water and a little salt. Bring to a boil, skimming the surface with a large metal spoon, if necessary. Reduce the heat and simmer gently, covered, for 30–45 minutes. Strain through a fine sieve and discard the vegetables. Makes about 3¾ cups (900ml) stock. This can be stored for up to 2 days in the refrigerator.

A selection of vegetables and flavorings for vegetable stock.

FISH STOCK

For every 2lb (1kg) of fish trimmings use about 4⅓ cups (1 liter) water and 1¼ cups (300ml) white wine and include a carrot and an onion, both coarsely chopped, a generous bundle of fresh herbs (parsley and bay leaf, and fennel is particularly good, too), 2–3 tablespoons of lemon juice, 2 teaspoons sugar and 10–12 black peppercorns. Do not use any trimmings from oily fish. Makes about 5 cups (1.2 liters).

1 *Place all the fish trimmings in a large stockpot or saucepan with the chopped carrot, onion, bundle of herbs, lemon juice, sugar and black peppercorns.*

2 *Add the water and wine to the pan, bring to a boil, then simmer gently for 20–25 minutes, skimming the surface as necessary with a large spoon.*

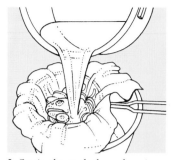

3 *Strain the stock through a sieve lined with cheesecloth. Use the stock at once or cool and then chill. Keep for up to 2 days in the refrigerator in a covered container.*

USING FISH AND VEGETABLE STOCKS

• Fish stock is used primarily as the base for fish soups. Use it either in the Mediterranean style as a thin liquid in which a variety of fish and shellfish are briefly cooked before serving, or thicken the stock with a little flour and plenty of cream to make a rich, smooth bisque.

• It is best to use clear, well-colored fish stock for clear soups. For a really clear broth I like to strain the stock a second time through a clean piece of fine cheesecloth.

• To turn fish stock into a soup, add breadcrumbs, rice or pureed cooked vegetables – try potatoes, sweet potatoes, peppers and zucchini.

• Add reduced fish stock to heavy cream and boil for a minute or two to make a delicious almost instant sauce to serve with poached or steamed fish (page 130).

• Strained fish stock can be made into aspic (page 33) in which to set prawns, other pieces of fish and fresh herbs. I serve this in the summer as a pretty first course.

• I make wonderful quick stews by briefly simmering slivers of vegetables and filleted fish or shellfish in well-flavored thickened fish stock. Cook lightly for 5–8 minutes before adding a handful of fresh herbs such as dill or cilantro leaves.

• Use thin or thick vegetable stock to make a variety of soups and sauces. It is also the perfect liquid in which to cook either vegetables, chicken or light meat for stews and casseroles.

• All sorts of pureed vegetables (page 53) and legumes (page 113) can be used to thicken vegetable stock – for example, pureed cauliflower is creamy and light, while a puree of cooked, dried white beans is a more substantial thickener. For extra smoothness I rub the puree through a sieve using a wooden spoon.

• Unthickened vegetable stock is ideal for minestrone-type soups with thickly sliced vegetables and pasta shapes lightly cooked in the liquid.

• Little pasta shapes and thin noodles can also transform a good vegetable stock into a hearty soup. Sprinkle over some freshly grated Parmesan cheese just before serving, if you like.

• To make simple and flavorful sauces, reduce the stock to intensify the flavor, then thicken with cream, a little cornstarch (page 199) or a fine vegetable puree (page 53).

• Arrowroot is the thickener which produces the most glossy, translucent effect (page 199).

• Strained vegetable stocks, especially ones with a good color, can be used to make an aspic (page 33) in which to set eggs, herbs and vegetables. Clear beet stock makes the most stunning aspic of all – a ruby-red mold in which you can set a feathery pattern of fresh green herbs.

Saffron, paprika and fresh herbs add colors and flavors to Mussel, Salmon and Scallop Soup (page 39), an elegant soup for occasions when you want to really impress.

CLEAR SOUPS *and* ASPICS

Clear soups are both beautiful and appetizing. They are also versatile as many different ingredients can be added to poach gently in the liquid– for example, thinly sliced vegetables, slivers of fish, shrimp or baby scallops .

Clear soups are made like stocks but with a lower proportion of water to other ingredients. They can be made from any kind of meat or vegetables except for starchy vegetables which cause cloudiness. Many Chinese soups, like the recipe opposite, are good examples of well-flavored clear soups made with a variety of ingredients. Straining the stock through a sieve lined with cheesecloth or a coffee filter usually clears it enough but if you want a really shiny clear soup you can clarify it as for consommé by using egg shells and whites (below).

CONSOMMÉ

Real consommé is a rich clear veal, beef or chicken stock made by cooking meat and vegetables in a thoroughly degreased stock. The consommé will sparkle even more served chilled and jellied: if the original stock has not been made with plenty of gelatinous bones you can add a little gelatin – about 1 envelope for each 2 cups (475ml) liquid – during the clarification process to make sure it will gel correctly. Chilled consommé is good either plain, sprinkled with herbs or with a swirl of sour cream.

ASPIC

Homemade aspic, made from concentrated, rich stock, is something of a labor of love but in terms of flavor it is well worth the effort for a special buffet or party dish. Coat cold cooked chicken, salmon or lamb chops by placing them on a wire rack and slowly spooning over a layer of aspic. Allow to set and arrange a garnish on top. Give it a second coat if required. Molded savory dishes look pretty if you arrange fresh herbs between two thin layers of aspic in the bottom of the mold.

BEEF CONSOMMÉ

To make crystal-clear consommé the stock should be clarified with egg whites and shells: these trap in a foam particles which might otherwise cloud the stock. Egg whites also remove flavor so more must be added in the form of fresh meat and vegetables – use 1 small onion, 1 carrot and 1 stick of celery, all chopped finely, plus 8oz (250g) very lean ground beef to every 7½ cups (1.8 liters) cold beef stock.

1 *Put the thoroughly degreased stock (page 28) in a very clean saucepan with the meat, vegetables and some salt and black peppercorns.*

2 *Add the lightly beaten whites and crushed shells of 2 eggs to the pan, then slowly bring to a boil, whisking constantly. A thick froth will form.*

3 *Stop whisking when the froth is quite firm and covers the top of the pan. Allow the soup to boil through the crust over medium heat for 20 minutes.*

QUICK ONION SOUP

When you have a clarified consommé on hand there are many ways in which you can use it as a shortcut to a delicious first course or light supper. Any sort of thinly sliced fresh vegetables can be cooked in simmering consommé until just tender for a delicious soup but onions are especially good.

For a very quick onion soup, heat 2 tablespoons butter until it bubbles in a medium-size Dutch oven or heavy saucepan. Add 4 large thinly sliced onions and cook, stirring occasionally, until the onions are soft and beautifully caramelized. Add 1 quart (.95 liter) of perfectly seasoned consommé or beef stock and cook 5 minutes. Divide into 6 flameproof soup bowls. Place a round of toasted bread on top of each and sprinkle with some shredded Gruyere and Parmesan cheeses. Place under a hot broiler just long enough to melt and lightly brown the cheese. Serve immediately.

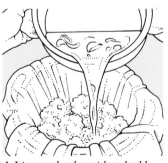

4 *Line a colander with a double layer of clean wet cheesecloth and set it over a large bowl. You can also use a jelly bag. Lift the crust into the center of the colander using a large perforated skimming spoon, then slowly pour the soup through it into the bowl.*

5 *If the consommé is not absolutely clear, you can pour it through the crust again into a clean bowl. Stir in 1 or 2 spoonfuls of sherry or Madeira and some finely chopped herbs. Serve hot or chilled. If chilled, lightly chop the consommé.*

CHINESE-STYLE CLEAR SOUP

The Chinese are great soup lovers. Their soups are light and clear but always full of flavor and visually very attractive. The variations are endless, as almost any fresh, good-quality vegetables can be used, along with meat, noodles or a combination of both. An essential start, however, is a good stock made with fresh chicken.

To make soup for 8 you will need a 3lb (1.5kg) chicken (if the giblets are provided do not use the liver) and 12oz (375g) pork sparerib bones.

Before cooking assemble 6 sliced green onions, 1 sliced carrot, 2 tablespoons chopped fresh gingerroot and 1 stick celery, chopped.

1 *Begin by making a simple flavorful chicken stock. Put the chicken and giblets, if using, into a large stockpot or saucepan with the pork sparerib bones, half the spring onions, the carrot, ginger, celery and a few crushed fresh parsley or coriander stalks. Stir in 2 tablespoons light soy sauce, ⅓ cup (150ml) white wine and 2½ quarts (2.4 liters) cold water. Season to taste.*

2 *Bring to a boil slowly, skimming the surface as necessary. Reduce the heat, cover and simmer for 1 hour. Strain the flavorings out of the stock, then chill and remove any fat from the surface (page 29). Using a knife or cleaver, shred the chicken breast meat finely and reserve; use the remaining chicken meat in salads or sandwiches. Return the stock to a clean pan.*

3 *Boil the stock, uncovered, for 10 minutes, add remaining green onions, shredded chicken, 4oz (125g) sliced oyster or shiitake mushrooms, 4oz (125g) broccoli florets and 2 tablespoons dry sherry. Simmer for 5 minutes, then add 1oz (25g) cooked or instant rice noodles, 1 teaspoon sesame oil, 1 teaspoon sugar and 2 tablespoons light soy sauce. Cook for 1 minute more.*

COLD SOUPS

Refreshing cold soups make an excellent first course for hot weather entertaining. To make the base for a clear soup use the instructions for consommé (opposite) and use either beef, chicken or fish stock. For a fresh-tasting vegetable soup, add julienned vegetables to the hot consommé, then chill until it is completely cold. The same may be done with thin slices of meat or fish. Top it with a sprinkling of fresh herbs for both flavor and color and serve it in a soup plate to accentuate its clarity. Prepared consommé may be gelled to make aspic for coating hors d'oeuvres or served as a main course topped with sour cream and some herbs. To gel the consommé, soften 1 package of unflavored gelatin in ½ cup (118ml) consommé for 5 minutes. Heat just until the gelatin dissolves, then stir it into 1½ cups (355ml) chilled consommé and spoon it over hors d'oeuvres or chill it until firm to serve as jellied consommé.

A flavorsome chicken stock is the basis of this Chinese-style clear soup with a selection of lightly cooked vegetables and noodles. Light soy sauce also adds an authentic oriental taste.

FLAVORING CLEAR SOUPS

• There are endless possibilities for additions to clear soup — try rice, eggs (either cooked in the soup or added hard-cooked and sliced), little pasta shapes, slivers of fresh vegetables, shellfish and pieces of fish, small slices of cooked meats, chicken and ham, chopped green onions and so on.
• One of my favorite fresh clear soups is made by cooking coarsely chopped ripe tomatoes in water with a squeeze of lemon juice and a teaspoon or two of sugar until tender. Then strain the mixture through clean, wet cheesecloth and reheat with little cubes of skinned fresh tomato and shredded strips of basil leaves added as a garnish.
• Drop small eggs into a hot clear soup and poach the eggs before serving.
• If you are serving consommé hot only add garnishes at the last moment so the consommé loses none of its clarity. You can add tiny slivers of ham or cold meats, fresh herbs or little bits of cooked vegetables or simply a hint of sherry.

THICKENED *and* PUREED SOUPS

Soups can be thickened in various ways. The most common way is with flour which you add to melted butter and the uncooked ingredients in the saucepan before stirring in the stock. You can also mix the flour with a little liquid until smooth, then stir it in at the end of cooking, stirring until the soup thickens. (Flour must always be cooked thoroughly or the soup will taste starchy.) Adding fresh breadcrumbs is another way I like to thicken more homey, filling soups.

Cream and/or egg yolks added at the last minute make a richer flavored and thicker soup. To thicken thin soups slightly, add cream and egg yolks, lightly whisked together, but only heat gently as boiling causes the eggs to scramble and light cream to curdle. I think a little flour

thickening at the beginning followed by a cream and egg addition at the end is the most successful method. Most cream soups, whether vegetable, chicken or fish, are thickened this way to achieve their smooth consistency.

Pureed cooked vegetables also make excellent thickeners for soups but will, of course, add distinctive flavors (page 53). Some people like the texture obtained by passing the vegetables through a food mill, but since I have had a food processor with which I can control the texture quite well, I have abandoned my food mill.

Using thoroughly cooked and pureed legumes as a thickener makes a more substantial soup (page 113). Red lentils, which cook more quickly than dried beans, are especially good for this, and add color as well.

THICKENING SOUPS WITH EGGS AND CREAM

Whisked egg yolks and cream thicken a soup slightly but mainly add a rich creamy finish. Do not let the soup boil after you have added eggs or light cream as the eggs will scramble and light cream will curdle. As the egg yolks cook they will thicken the soup. If the soup has been previously thickened with a little flour it will be less vulnerable to curdling but it should still not be boiled.

Allow ⅓ cup (75ml) heavy cream and 2 egg yolks for every 5 cups (1.2 liters) soup already thickened with flour; increase the number of yolks to 4 if the soup has not been previously thickened.

1 *Although soups can be made well in advance, only thicken them just before serving. To make the thickening mixture put the egg yolks and cream in a medium-sized mixing bowl. Using a fork or whisk, whisk them together lightly until well combined. It is best to use heavy cream because it will not curdle if the soup is boiled accidentally.*

CREAM OF VEGETABLE SOUP

This is a very versatile kind of soup as almost any vegetable can be used. For ultimate smoothness I find it best to puree the cooked vegetables and stock in a food processor first, then press the puree through a fine sieve. The amount of stock and exact cooking time depends on how thick or thin you like your soup and how much liquid there is in the vegetables used. Obviously, tomatoes will make a thinner soup than sweet peppers. These quantities serve 4.

1 *Melt about 1oz (25g) butter in a large saucepan, then stir in about 1½lb (750g) prepared chopped vegetables.*

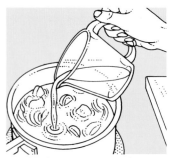

2 *Add about 5 cups (1.2 liters) stock or milk, or a mixture of both, then cover and simmer until the vegetables are tender.*

2 *Meanwhile, reheat but do not boil the soup. Add a ladleful of hot soup to the eggs and cream mixture. Use a wooden spoon to stir them together.*

3 *Stir the eggs, cream and soup mixture into the pan of hot soup. Continue to stir the soup over a low heat until it has thickened slightly but do not allow it to boil. Serve immediately.*

3 *Puree in a food processor or through a food mill. For a very smooth soup press the puree through a sieve with the back of a wooden spoon.*

4 *Add light or heavy cream or crème fraîche and reheat gently without boiling, stirring. Serve with your choice of garnishes (see box opposite for ideas).*

SIMPLE THICKENED SOUP

Whenever I want to make a soup quickly this is the method I choose. It is the easiest way of binding ingredients into a stock and, because the flour is added at the beginning, it cooks long enough so there is no danger of a raw, starchy taste.

You can, of course, use leftovers as well as freshly prepared ingredients. To add depth of color brown the ingredients in the butter before adding the flour and stock. If you want to enrich the soup stir in some cream just before serving.

All sorts of ingredients are suitable – just choose ones that all take about the same amount of time to cook; cut pieces to the same size for even cooking. Clam chowder is a delicious example; just add cooked bacon, cubes of potato, chopped onions, and fresh clams to a soup of fish stock and cream. These quantities serve 4–6.

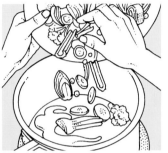

1 *Melt about 2oz (50g) butter in a saucepan and add about 1lb (500g) prepared chopped ingredients. Stir to coat the ingredients well with the butter.*

2 *Mix in about 4 tablespoons flour, then gradually stir in 5 cups (1.2 liters) stock. Bring to a boil, then simmer, covered, until the ingredients are tender. Season.*

MAKING CROUTONS

Croutons are a very traditional garnish for soups. To make your own, remove the crusts from slices of stale bread and cut the bread into even-sized cubes. Heat plenty of oil or fat – olive oil, chicken fat or garlic butter with some oil are especially good – in a large frying pan, then add the bread cubes in a single layer. Fry gently, tossing the cubes often, so they become crisp and evenly browned, then drain well on crumpled paper towels.

You can make fat-free croutons from slices of toast or day-old bread dried out in a warm oven.

Add flavor by rubbing the surfaces with a peeled garlic clove. For variety, cut into shapes using small cutters.

FINISHING TOUCHES

• I think garnishes of all kinds look most attractive if you add them after the soup has been ladled into individual bowls.

• I use fresh herbs more than anything else. Flat-leaf parsley, dill, fennel, strips of basil, sorrel and lovage, chives and summer savory all look extremely pretty as garnishes and add delicate flavors too.

• Cilantro is an especially suitable garnish for lightly spiced soups.

• Be cautious with tarragon as a garnish as it can be too strong for some soups. The same applies to rosemary, as well, which is too fibrous and intensely flavored.

• Swirl heavy cream, crème fraîche or plain yogurt into non-creamy soups or stir in an herb-flavored butter or soft cheese just before serving.

• Toasted sliced almonds are delicious sprinkled on top of cream soups.

• Finely grated Gruyère cheese sprinkled on top of hot soup melts in attractive, long strings.

• I add thin slivers of raw zucchini, red or green pepper, cucumber or carrot for a decorative crunchiness in smooth soups.

• Add a spoonful or two of pesto (page 307) to tomato soup.

• Crisp fried bacon crumbled over soup adds lots of flavor as well as texture.

Simple ways to add body

• Well-flavored, country-style vegetable soups can be thickened with bread. Use dry bread which dissolves and binds the broth, or stir in some fresh bread crumbs.

• Lay a slice of toasted or baked French bread in a soup bowl and ladle over the hot soup. The bread will swell up and thicken the soup most effectively.

• Top French onion soup with a slice of French bread sprinkled with some finely grated cheese, then brown it under a hot grill. Be sure to use a flameproof bowl.

• Small pieces of peeled starchy potatoes cooked in a good broth will eventually disintegrate and thicken the soup when stirred in.

Carrot and Cranberry Soup (page 38) has a refreshing taste as well as a vibrant color which makes a striking presentation. Ideal for Christmas, this can be made all year with frozen cranberries.

CHILLED SOUPS

With such a variety of vegetables now available to us, together with a wide range of yogurts and other milk products, there have never been so many possibilities for making chilled soups from both cooked and uncooked ingredients. Chilled soups are most welcome in the summer when you can make the most of tender young vegetables and flavor-packed soft fruit.

The variations of chilled soups are endless, and the techniques are simple. Easiest to make are uncooked blended soups, with pureed raw vegetables mixed with plain yogurt or sour cream. A bit more time consuming are soups like tomato and red pepper soup (below), made

from pureed cooked vegetables. Raspberry and mint soup (opposite) is made by a simple technique you can adapt for any fruit. Simply vary the amount of liquid in these soups depending on how much moisture or juice there is in the vegetable or fruit.

Many soups which are normally served hot can also be served chilled but flour-based soups tend to taste more starchy when cold, and, on the whole, starchy vegetables are not good in chilled soups. Creamy vichyssoise, made from potatoes and leeks, is a notable exception. I prefer to make chilled soups without butter or egg yolks as both of these ingredients make the soup too thick when chilled.

UNCOOKED BLENDED SOUPS

Quick delicious soups can be made in a food processor or blender using fresh vegetables such as cucumbers, tomatoes or avocados and creamy textured dairy products.

To make 6 servings you will need 1¼–2½ cups (300–600ml) fresh vegetable puree, depending on how watery the vegetable is, about 1 pint (600ml) yogurt and about 1¼ cups (300ml) sour cream.

Fresh herbs are a must for flavoring uncooked soups. Spiced oil garnish (right) is also a favorite of mine for garnishing chilled soups.

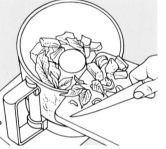

1 *Prepare the vegetable of your choice for the puree and put it in a food processor or electric blender with a generous handful of chopped fresh herbs and a little salt. (If you are using an avocado also add plenty of lemon juice to prevent discoloration.)*

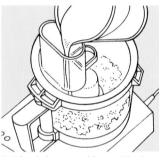

2 *Blend the vegetables and herbs to a puree. Gradually blend in the yogurt, then the sour cream. Pour into a bowl and chill thoroughly. Check the seasoning, then ladle the soup into individual bowls and garnish with fresh herbs or a swirl of the spiced oil.*

Spiced oil garnish *Toss 1–2 teaspoons cumin seeds in a small pan over medium heat for 30 seconds. Add 3 tablespoons olive oil and 2 teaspoons paprika, then stir for about 2 minutes without the oil bubbling. Pour into a small dish and set aside to cool.*

TOMATO AND RED PEPPER SOUP

This is an example of a chilled soup in which the vegetables are cooked first until tender, then pureed, flavored with herbs and seasonings. Chilled borsch and vichyssoise are two classic soups made by this simple method.

Cooking times depend on the vegetable used. Zucchini, for example, soften in about 5 minutes, while the red peppers in this recipe take about 20 minutes to become tender enough.

You will find it easy to adapt this recipe to use with all sorts of vegetables. The quantities suggested here will serve 4.

1 *Put l very large seeded and chopped red pepper in a pan with 1 large garlic clove, 2 tablespoons tomato puree and 2 cups (450ml) water. Season. Bring to a boil, then reduce the heat, cover and simmer gently for 15–20 minutes until the pepper and garlic are tender.*

2 *Puree the pepper, garlic and a little of the water. Stir back into the remaining liquid. Add 1½lb (750g) skinned, seeded and chopped tomatoes, juice of 1 lemon and 1 teaspoon sugar. Bring to a boil, cover and simmer for 8–10 minutes until cooked but not mushy.*

3 *Check the seasoning. Cool the soup, then chill it thoroughly. To serve, ladle the soup into individual bowls, drizzle a little olive oil over each bowl and sprinkle with chopped fresh herbs, if you like. I often add torn fresh basil leaves to this full-flavored soup just before serving.*

IDEAS FOR CHILLED SOUPS

- Small ice cubes added just before serving clink invitingly and look like crystals thrown into the soup.
- For a special effect freeze feathery herbs inside ice cubes to add to chilled soups at the last moment.
- The original seasonings must be added with care as the taste of the soup will change as it chills – adjust the seasoning just before serving.
- A jellied stock will result in a very pleasant slightly jellied soup when chilled.
- Uncooked chilled soups can be made from pureed blanched lettuce or watercress.
- Flavor chilled fruit soups with yogurt, light cream, thoroughly degreased chicken stock, fruit juices, cider or wine.
- Fruit can either be pureed completely in a food processor or through a sieve, or three-quarters of it pureed and the rest chopped into small pieces or left as small whole fruit which will be suspended in the puree.
- Chilled soups should be presented in individual bowls – glass bowls look very pretty.
- Fresh herbs, finely chopped raw vegetables, ribbons of lettuce, sprinklings of cayenne, paprika or grated nutmeg and swirls of cream, sour cream or yogurt are all ideal garnishes for light and refreshing chilled soups.

A selection of quick-and-easy chilled soups: tomato and red pepper soup (left), raspberry and mint soup (top right) and a quick uncooked blended soup of cucumber and yogurt topped with spiced oil.

RASPBERRY AND MINT SOUP

Especially in summer I think this style of chilled soup is very refreshing, and it makes an ideal first course.

The best fruits to choose are those which are full flavored and rather piquant – raspberries and cherries are excellent, as are tangy apples. Adjust the flavor with lemon juice and sugar to taste. Instead of wine or cider you can use stock, and, of course, a mixture of fruits. The quantities here serve 4.

1 *Put 1½lb (750g) (raspberries in a saucepan over a gentle heat with 4 tablespoons lemon juice and 1–2 tablespoons sugar and stir well with a wooden spoon.*

2 *When the sugar dissolves and the juices just begin to run, puree with about ⅔ cup (150ml) white wine or sweet cider. Press through a fine nylon sieve with a ladle.*

3 *Add another 1¼ cups (300ml) wine or cider and the strained juice of 1 orange and a handful of chopped fresh mint. Chill. Ladle into bowls and swirl with cream.*

CARROT AND CRANBERRY SOUP *(35)*

The vibrant combination of orange carrots and scarlet cranberries gives this soup a spectacular color. Because this is a smooth soup with a flavor which is slightly sweet and tangy, people find it hard to define the exact ingredients – but they always enjoy it. Use either fresh or frozen cranberries.   *SERVES 6*

1lb (500g) carrots, chopped coarsely
6 large cloves garlic
5 cups (1.2 liters) water
1¼ cups (300ml) freshly squeezed
  orange juice
2 teaspoons sugar
Sea salt and black pepper
6oz (175g) cranberries, thawed if frozen
Good handful of fresh dill or fennel leaves,
  chopped
1¼ cups (300ml) yogurt or sour cream

Put the carrots, garlic cloves, water, orange juice, sugar and a sprinkling of sea salt and black pepper in a large pan. Cover and bring to a boil, then reduce the heat and simmer gently for 30–40 minutes until the carrots are very soft.

Add the cranberries, cover and simmer for about 10 minutes. Pour into a food processor – you will probably have to do this in two or three batches depending on the size of your machine – and process until smooth. Strain the soup through a sieve into a clean saucepan. Taste and adjust the seasoning.

Reheat the soup and serve in individual bowls, sprinkled with some chopped dill or fennel. Spoon a dollop of yogurt or sour cream onto each serving bowl.

SHALLOT AND MUSTARD SOUP WITH TARRAGON *(26)*

Shallots are far sweeter than larger onions. My family loves this soup's mild mustardy flavor.   *SERVES 4*

1oz (25g) butter
4 cauliflower florets, chopped coarsely
1 large onion, sliced coarsely
3⅛ cups (750ml) chicken stock (page 29)
2 teaspoons Dijon mustard
1 tablespoon sugar
8oz (250g) shallots, halved lengthwise
2 tablespoons chopped fresh tarragon
⅔ cup (150ml) heavy or light cream
Salt and black pepper

Melt the butter in a large pan, add the cauliflower and onion and stir over a low heat for 10 minutes or until the onion is translucent and the cauliflower is tender. Puree in a food processor with 1¼ cups (300ml) stock, the mustard and sugar until smooth. Return to the pan and stir in the remaining stock. Season.

Bring to a rolling boil, then add the shallots. Cover and simmer 25–30 minutes. Stir in the tarragon and the cream; check the seasoning and serve.

CHICKEN SOUP WITH SMOKED OYSTERS *(26)*

An ideal soup to make ahead and reheat to serve. It also makes a good supper dish served with lots of French bread.   *SERVES 4*

3 tablespoons olive oil
1 large red pepper, cored, seeded and very
  thinly sliced (page 49)
2 teaspoons paprika
½ cup (125ml) lemon juice
2 large skinless boned chicken breasts,
  sliced into very thin strips
1¼ cups (300ml) heavy cream
4oz (125g) cremini mushrooms, stalks left
  on, very thinly sliced
1¼ cups (300ml) light cream
3½oz (105g) can smoked oysters, drained
Sea salt and black pepper
Generous bunch chives, chopped

Heat the olive oil in a large pan over a fairly low heat. Add the pepper and paprika, cover and cook gently for about 10 minutes until the pepper slices are soft. Stir in the lemon juice and chicken then cover the pan and cook for 5 minutes.

Remove from the heat and stir in the heavy cream and the mushrooms. Bring to a boil over medium heat, stirring. Still stirring, let the mixture boil for 2–3 minutes, then add the light cream and heat through but do not boil.

Stir in the oysters, remove from the heat and season to taste with sea salt and black pepper. Just before serving add the chopped chives.

INDIAN SUMMER SOUP *(26)*

This deliciously aromatic soup is Indian in character and can be served either hot or cold according to the weather.   *SERVES 6*

Salt
2 eggplants, cut into ½in (1cm) cubes
3 tablespoons peanut oil
1oz (25g) butter
2 teaspoons garam masala
1–2in (2.5–5cm) piece fresh gingerroot,
  peeled and finely chopped
3 large cloves garlic, peeled and
  finely chopped
2lb (1kg) tomatoes, chopped
2 tablespoons tomato puree
5 cups (1.2 liters) vegetable stock
  (page 30) or water
4 tablespoons lemon juice
2 teaspoons sugar
14oz (400ml) can coconut milk
2–5 pinches cayenne pepper
6 tablespoons plain yogurt

Rub the cubed eggplant all over with salt. Leave the cubes in a colander in the sink for about 30 minutes to drain off any bitter juices, then rinse off all the salt, drain and pat dry with paper towel.

Heat the oil in a large, heavy saucepan over fairly high heat. Add the eggplant cubes and brown them all over. Reduce the heat and stir in the butter, garam masala, chopped ginger and garlic. Stir for a minute or so, then add the tomatoes and tomato puree. Gradually stir in the stock or water, lemon juice and sugar. Bring to a boil, cover and simmer gently for about 45 minutes, stirring occasionally.

Reduce heat to low and add the coconut milk, stirring until smoothly mixed and hot through. Season with the cayenne pepper and salt to taste. Just before serving top each bowl of soup with a tablespoon of yogurt.

CLEAR VEGETABLE SOUP WITH EGGS (26)

The broth in this soup, which has a slightly Eastern flavor, can be made ahead and then reheated with the eggs and thin ribbons of lettuce dropped in to poach at the very last moment. *SERVES 4–6*

2 onions, unpeeled
8oz (250g) carrots, coarsely chopped
8 tomatoes, coarsely chopped
2 sticks celery, coarsely chopped
2in (5cm) piece fresh gingerroot, peeled and coarsely chopped
7½ cups (1.8 liters) water
Salt and black pepper
1 rounded teaspoon whole coriander seeds, crushed
4 cardamom pods, crushed
1 egg white, lightly beaten
4 tablespoons lemon juice
12 small eggs or quail eggs for special occasions
2 heads Bibb lettuce or 1 Boston lettuce, sliced very thinly crosswise
3 tablespoons coarsely chopped fresh cilantro leaves

Put the onions, carrots, tomatoes, celery, ginger and water in a saucepan with some salt and pepper. Add the crushed coriander seeds, cardamom pods and egg white and stir thoroughly. Bring to a boil, then reduce the heat, cover and simmer very gently for 1½ hours without stirring. Remove from the heat, skim off as much foam from the surface as you can with a large metal spoon, then stir in the lemon juice.

Put a double layer of clean, wet cheesecloth into a colander over a large bowl. Strain the liquid through the colander and discard the vegetables.

Put a clean piece of cheesecloth into the colander and strain the liquid back into the rinsed-out saucepan. Season to taste with salt and freshly ground black pepper.

Shortly before serving bring the soup to a rolling boil, then break in the eggs one by one, carefully but fairly quickly. Add the shredded lettuce and stir in very gently. The eggs will be poached after about 3–5 minutes.

Remove the saucepan from the heat, throw in the chopped fresh cilantro leaves and serve immediately in warmed soup plates, distributing the eggs evenly among the portions.

FISH BISQUE (26)

This is a delicate soup that is easy to make and has a wonderful flavor. The smoked fish cooked in the stock adds a faint smokiness, while fresh ginger contributes to the soup's sharp flavor. *SERVES 6*

1½–2lb (750g–1kg) fish bones
2lb (1kg) kippers or other smoked fish, coarsely chopped
1 small head celeriac, peeled and coarsely chopped
1 onion, halved
2 carrots, unpeeled and chopped
2in (5cm) piece fresh gingerroot, unpeeled and coarsely chopped
4 large cloves garlic, peeled and coarsely chopped
7½ cups (1.8 liters) water
Salt
3–4 pinches cayenne pepper
1 teaspoon turmeric
1 small red pepper, seeded and sliced into very thin rings (page 49)
4 tablespoons lemon juice
6 tablespoons heavy cream
8oz (250g) large peeled cooked prawns
Handful of lovage, cilantro or mint leaves, coarsely chopped

To make the stock, put the fish bones, smoked fish, celeriac, onion, carrots, ginger, garlic and water in a large saucepan or stockpot. Add a little salt, the cayenne pepper and turmeric, cover and bring to a boil, then reduce the heat and simmer very gently for 1 hour.

Strain the liquid through a fine sieve into a clean saucepan. If possible, refrigerate the soup overnight to make it easier to remove the fat before reheating the soup. Otherwise, remove the liquid fat with a large spoon or pieces of paper towel (page 29).

Return the soup to the heat. Add the pepper rings and bring slowly to a boil, then cover, reduce the heat and simmer for 10 minutes. Uncover and continue simmering another 5 minutes to reduce the soup and intensify the flavors. Stir in the lemon juice and remove the saucepan from the heat.

Just before serving stir the heavy cream into the soup and taste, adjusting the seasoning, if necessary. Return the soup to the heat and bring to just below boiling point, then remove from the heat, stir in the prawns and chopped fresh herbs and serve immediately.

MUSSEL, SALMON AND SCALLOP SOUP (31)

This is a rich but delicately flavored fish soup. If you like, keep a few of the cooked mussels in their shells to garnish the soup. *SERVES 4–6*

1¼ cups (300ml) white wine
2lb (1kg) fresh mussels, scrubbed and debearded (discard any open ones)
2½ cups (600ml) fish stock (page 31)
12–14 strands saffron
1 teaspoon paprika
1¼ cups (300ml) heavy cream
2oz (50g) butter
¼ cup (25g) all-purpose flour
Salt and black pepper
1¼lb (625g) salmon fillet, skinned and thinly sliced
4 scallops, sliced
Handful of fresh dill, coarsely chopped
Handful of fresh parsley, coarsely chopped
2 tablespoons lemon juice, strained

Boil the wine in a large pan. Add the mussels, cover and boil for about 2 minutes until the shells have opened. Transfer to a bowl, then remove them from their shells, discarding any that haven't opened. Pour the juices through a fine sieve into a clean pan and add the stock, saffron and paprika. Bring to a boil, remove from the heat, cover and leave for 30 minutes. Stir in the cream.

Melt the butter in a large heavy pan, then remove from the heat and stir in the flour. Add the stock and cream mixture, gradually at first, stirring until combined. Bring to a boil, then simmer gently, still stirring, for 4–5 minutes and remove from the heat. Season and cover.

To serve, bring to a rolling boil, stirring. Drop in the salmon and simmer for 2 minutes, then add the scallops and simmer for 2–3 minutes. Add the mussels, dill, parsley and lemon juice. Heat through for 30 seconds and serve.

VEGETABLES

Although I could never become a total vegetarian, vegetables are definitely the last food I would want to give up. They offer a vast scope of tastes, shapes, textures, colors and characters and, as a result they provide one of the most inspiring areas of cookery. Yet, vegetables are often not given much thought at all – carelessly prepared, overlooked and plunked on the table as if they were simply obligatory but unimportant accompaniments. These indifferent vegetables are nearly always boiled as if that was the only thing you could do with them. In fact, it is vegetables above all ingredients which adapt well to every kind of cooking method.

Vegetable cookery can change, chameleon-like, to suit the seasons and your moods. There are cold-weather, comforting dishes such as all kinds of vegetable gratins, stuffed and baked vegetables, root vegetable purees, fritters, toppings, vegetable stews and even vegetable pies. Then there is the thrill of summer vegetables eaten in season at their prime; delicately cooked, crisp and bright green, served with simple accompaniments such as butter, extra-virgin olive oil, fresh herbs, sour cream, hollandaise sauce, fresh tomato sauce, or a simple vinaigrette. There can also be ethereal results with vegetables in the form of featherlight soufflés, Japanese tempura, and vegetable mousses and terrines.

But with all their qualities, one exceptional bonus of vegetables is their beauty: their rhapsody of colors, their sculptural shapes, their tactile textures. I particularly like combining vegetables so that contrasting colors and textures will complement each other. I find shopping for vegetables, with all its variety, the most pleasurable kind of food shopping there is – as much a feast for the eye as the palate.

Knowing when a vegetable is cooked for the right amount of time is partly a matter of experience, and also, of course, of personal taste. However, it does seem to me a terrible waste if you overcook tender vegetables such as snow peas and sugar snap peas, young asparagus and spring greens. These, and other green vegetables, when they are young and fresh, should only be boiled or steamed briefly. Yet, some green vegetables, such as cabbage and leeks, can either be cooked briefly to retain crispness, or long and gently to a melting softness – both results are delicious, but very different.

My oldest daughter has been a vegetarian for several years, though luckily for me, she will eat fish. I don't believe in planning a meal entirely to suit one vegetarian in the family or party, and I don't really like the idea of one guest sitting eating something completely different which doesn't fit in with the rest of the meal. I do think, however, that a vegetarian in your midst inspires you to do more interesting things with the vegetable part of the meal, and as a result makes you appreciate vegetables as a main ingredient. Since my daughter stopped eating meat, I have grown to realize that combinations of vegetables can be made into really satisfying main courses which are welcomed by even the most voracious carnivores from time to time.

Vegetable main courses and side dishes, clockwise from top left: semolina gnocchi and Parmesan cheese top a Leek and Celeriac Pie (page 65); Carrot Salad with Oranges and Green Onions (page 64) adds a fresh taste to any meal; a golden puff pastry crust tops sliced vegetables and softly poached eggs in Egg, Fennel and Tomato Pie (page 64); Grilled Zucchini and Goat Cheese with Walnuts (page 62) makes an interesting first course; Sautéed Potatoes with Chopped Ginger and Spices (page 65) also contains cumin, caraway seeds and fresh parsley; Spinach and Pea Puree with Cabbage and Parmesan (page 64) can be made year round with frozen peas; Hot and Cold Salad (page 62) combines French green beans, mushrooms, pine nuts, radicchio and Bibb lettuce.

ROOTS *and* TUBERS

Root and tuberous vegetables, including potatoes, sweet potatoes, yams, carrots, parsnips, turnips, beets, salsify, radishes, rutabagas, celeriac and Jerusalem artichokes, are great favorites with me. They are extremely versatile and can form the base of marvelous soups, fritters, purees, soufflés and so on, while for vegetarians they can provide the sustaining body and sweetness which most green vegetables lack.

Celeriac, despite its unprepossessing, knobbly appearance, has a wonderful flavor, combining the freshness of celery and the sweet taste of a root. I also like the pepperiness of rutabaga, but it suffers from a rather watery consistency so it is best pureed and enriched with butter or cream, and sometimes combined with a finer, smoother root such as potatoes. The pleasurable qualities of carrots made into a puree or soup are by now well known, and their brilliant color and sweetness enhances many creations, both savory and sweet, cooked or raw. Parsnip is definitely one of the roots I eat most, perhaps because I so often use spices in my cooking, and all roots, but parsnips in particular, have a great affinity for spices.

But my favorite root of all must be the potato. Potatoes are so varied in type, taste and texture, making them suitable for quite different ways of serving, from a delicate dish of silky smooth new potatoes tossed in butter and fresh dill, to a crusty baked potato with its comfortingly soft and fluffy center. Potatoes must be the most versatile of all vegetables as they combine so well with all manner of flavorings and accompaniments, and can be cooked by every method, though unlike most other vegetables they are not good raw.

BUYING AND STORING

Ideally, store root and tuberous vegetables in a well-ventilated bag in a cool, dry and dark place, preferably not the refrigerator unless there really is nowhere else. In these conditions they should keep for a good two weeks. Exposure to daylight can cause potatoes to sprout and turn green in which case they should be discarded. Most potatoes are now sold already washed but still benefit from a light scrubbing if they are to be cooked in their skins. Very earthy potatoes can be soaked first in cold water to loosen the soil, then scrubbed in cold water or peeled before cooking, depending if you like the peel or not.

PREPARING ROOT VEGETABLES

For maximum vitamin retention, scrub or peel thinly and don't soak vegetables in cold water as the water-soluble vitamins B and C will leach out. Certain vegetables like celeriac, Jerusalem artichokes and salsify discolor when peeled so these must be prepared just before cooking or dropped into acidulated water, simply cold water with some added lemon juice or white vinegar. Beets are different – they need to be cooked first, then peeled to maintain their vibrant color.

To peel long, smooth vegetables, such as carrots and parsnips, with a swivel-bladed peeler, hold the vegetable root end pointing downwards in one hand. Use your other hand to run the blade away from you, scraping off the skin in thin strips. Hold rounder vegetables, such as potatoes and kohlrabi, in your hand and peel towards you.

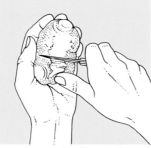

Use a paring knife to peel knobbly vegetables like Jerusalem artichokes and celeriac. Hold the knife in one hand and the vegetable in the other hand. For smaller vegetables place the thumb of your knife hand on the bottom of the vegetable to hold it still. Slice downwards to cut off the skin in thin strips or chop coarsely for soups or purees.

HOW TO CHOP VEGETABLES

A large chef's knife, about 8in (20cm) long, with a sharp blade is best for cutting vegetables. With practice you should be able to do this with the lightning quick precision of a chef. When chopping, it is vital to keep your fingers on the hand holding the vegetable firmly at right angles to the knife for safety's sake. This prevents you from cutting your fingertips. You can chop vegetables either into dice or slices. Use small dice for the classic mirepoix vegetable mixture for stuffings and larger cubes for chunky casseroles and stews. Make sure that chopped or sliced vegetables are cut evenly so they all cook within the same amount of time.

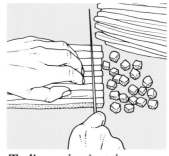

To dice, peel and cut the vegetable lengthwise into thick or thin slices depending on the size dice required. Pile slices on top of each other and cut downward into strips, then gather the strips together and cut across into square dice ready for cooking.

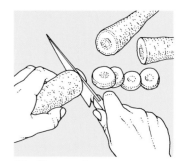

To slice parsnips, carrots or potatoes peel or scrub, then, holding the vegetable firmly, cut straight down crosswise or diagonally in thin or thick slices, depending on the end use. Paper-thin slices can be cut in a food processor using a slicing disc.

POTATO VARIETIES

Some potato varieties are more suitable than others for specific purposes. Until recently we simply had a choice between all-purpose and baking potatoes. Now farmers' markets and gourmet produce companies provide a few varieties by name. The guide below will help you choose the right potato for the cooking method you are planning to use.

Baking	Frontier, Russet or Idaho, White Cobbler, White Rose
Boiling	All Blue, Blue Caribe, German Fingerling, Kennebec, Peruvian Purple, Purple Chief, Red Norland, Red Pontiac, White Rose, Yellow Finn, Yellow Rose
French Frying	Russet or Idaho, White Cobbler, White Rose, Yukon Gold
Mashing	Irish Cobbler, Kennebec, Purple Chief, Russet or Idaho, Yukon Gold
Roasting	German Fingerling, Red Norland, Red Pontiac
Salads	Kennebec, Red Norland, Red Pontiac, White Cobbler
Steaming	Almost all varieties are suitable for steaming.

HANDLING VEGETABLES

• Only buy vegetables in peak condition – they should be hard and firm, crisp and brightly colored with no yellowing leaves or bruised, soft patches.
• All vegetables are best eaten as fresh as possible. From the moment vegetables are picked, the enzymes that cause decay start causing discoloration and destroying flavors. The vegetables then start to dehydrate and become limp. Two processes slow down this deterioration – cool temperatures and loosely covering food with plastic wrap to cut down on dehydration. This makes the refrigerator the ideal place to store most vegetables. But bags or containers should not be tightly closed or they will become too wet and the by-products of deterioration will cause mold.
• Remove packaged vegetables from any tight wrapping as soon as you get them home and store them loosely in food storage bags or plastic containers.
• Ideally, all vegetables should be prepared just before cooking to help maintain the maximum nutritive value and freshness. If you need to prepare them in advance, however, store them in a loosely closed plastic bag in the refrigerator.
• Root vegetables go limp when they begin to deteriorate and are difficult to peel, but they are fine for the stockpot.

PREPARING HOMEMADE FRENCH FRIES

For French fries it is important to choose a potato variety that holds its shape well and yet cooks to a light fluffiness inside (above). Fries can be made either with a sharp chef's knife for regular fries or in a food processor for pommes soufflées. After cutting, it is important to soak for about 30 minutes in water to remove excess starch. This prevents the potatoes from sticking together.

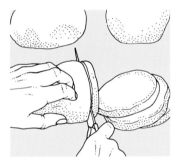

1 *Large potatoes are best for French fries. Peel them, then cut into ¼–½in (5mm–1cm) slices, depending on desired thickness.*

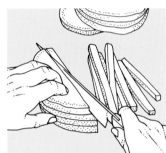

2 *Stack up several slices and cut down into ¼–½in (5mm–1cm) sticks. Soak the French fries in water for 30 minutes.*

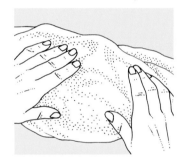

3 *Drain well, then place on a clean tea towel and pat dry. If not properly dried, the chips will spatter in the hot fat (page 54).*

If making your own French fries, you can cut them the thickness you like.

To make pommes soufflées, *fit a slicing disc into a food processor and twist on the lid. Cut the potatoes to fit the feed tube, then push them down with the plunger. The less you push the thinner the slices will be. Fry in 300 °F (150°C) oil until lightly browned. Drain and cool. Just before serving fry again in 375°F (190°C) and serve immediately.*

GREENS, PEAS *and* BEANS

This large group of vegetables provides great variety and pleasure. Peas and beans should be exceptionally fresh so that short and simple cooking will reveal their delicate flavor at its best. If you have ever picked peas and beans straight from the garden you will know that it is almost as difficult not to eat them immediately as it is when picking ripe fruit at the height of summer.

Ordinary cabbages are one of the most underrated vegetables; they are delicious if they are cooked briefly, remaining crisp and fresh, or equally good stewed long and gently in a little buttery stock until really soft and mellow flavored. Neither of these cooking methods will produce the terrible smell associated with cooking cabbage by old-fashioned methods; now I love a plate of vibrant green and tender kale leaves or sliced spring greens briefly cooked and sprinkled with dark soy sauce.

Cauliflower tastes good cooked fairly briefly, or for much longer with added flavorings, or raw in salads and for dips. I love it as a puree or as the base of a creamy soup. Look for ivory white, tightly clustered and unblemished florets surrounded by small leaves which are also good to eat. It is important to remember that broccoli, which is such an excellent and useful vegetable when still bright green and slightly crunchy, can become quite bitter when overcooked.

Spinach, to me as well as Popeye, is the wonder vegetable. It is tender, has a unique flavor, and retains its bright dark green color even when slightly overcooked. The small leaves of young spinach make a lovely raw salad.

BUYING AND STORING

It is best to use greens, peas and beans on the day of purchase but if buying ahead store loosely wrapped in the salad drawer. Do not buy any with yellow or limp leaves or tips. Fresh pods pop open easily, leafy vegetables should be firm and green and fresh beans snap easily if bent in half.

PREPARATION

Most vegetables today require only the minimum of preparation, either because they are harvested when young and tender, or because they are offered for sale already trimmed. Also, fashions have changed and over trimming is no longer thought necessary with some vegetables, like green beans. The tails of beans, for example, are quite edible, and look more natural left on. Also, many more people like crisp vegetables so it is not vital to prepare them for more thorough cooking. All these vegetables need only brief cooking in rapidly boiling water or by steaming (page 52) until bordering on what is now called tender-crisp – soft enough but still with a bite, and bright green.

When possible, prepare vegetables just before cooking, rather than hours in advance and leaving them to soak in a bowl of water. Soaking destroys the B-complex vitamins and vitamin C, which are water soluble and leach out into the water.

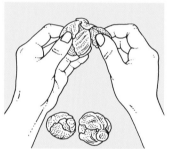

Brussels sprouts *Peel off the outer leaves, trim and discard the stems. If the sprouts are large and older, cut a cross on each stem base for even cooking.*

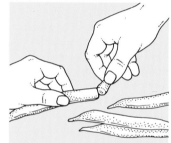

French beans *need their tops snapped or cut. Cut off the tails, too, if desired, bunching several beans together at a time so they are all the same size.*

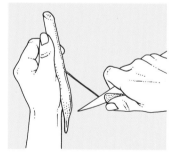

Older runner beans *need their tough string removed. Cut almost through the top, then pull it down on the inside curve, pulling away the string. Cut through the tail end and pull away the string on the outside. Cut into long diagonal slices.*

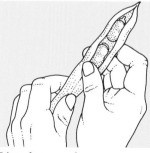

Lima beans and peas *pop open easily when the tail end is pressed firmly if they are fresh. Run your thumb along the curved side and scoop out the beans or peas. Purists will then pop lima beans out of their inner skins, too, after cooking – a treat if you have time.*

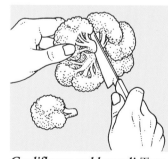

Cauliflower and broccoli *Turn the heads over and trim away the outside leaves, leaving on any thin light green ones. Cut off the florets, including a little of the thick stem. Large florets should be sliced in half. Slice off and discard the lower stalk.*

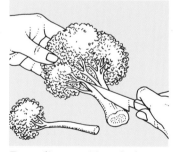

Broccoli spears *Trim the base stem from the head of florets down through the stalk to make spears. Or trim off the florets, then cut the thick stem into slices. Cook these first, adding the florets a few minutes later so they cook evenly.*

PREPARING SPINACH

Depending on the time of year, spinach leaves and stalks vary in size and tenderness. Only large thick and dark green leaves need to be trimmed of their stalks; younger stalks can be left on. Only buy leaves that are not damaged or yellow and without extra-hard stalks or any flowering shoots. Even prewashed spinach often contains some dirt, so a good rinsing in several changes of water really is necessary. Drain the leaves well, then cook with only the water left clinging to the leaves.

This colorful coleslaw is bursting with the flavors of shredded red and white cabbage, sliced green peppers, chopped green onions, raisins and caraway seeds.

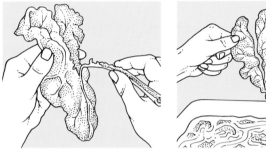 

1 *Carefully pick over and throw away any wilted and decayed leaves. Tear the stalks from large leaves and discard.*

2 *Tear the leaves into 2 or 3 pieces. Rinse in at least 2 changes of fresh clean water, then drain well, shaking off most of the water.*

PREPARING CABBAGE

COLESLAW

A really fresh cabbage, simply shredded and cooked in the smallest amount of water for the least possible time, must surely rate as one of the world's tastiest vegetables. It needs little adornment save adding a small lump of butter and no complicated preparation. Although it is a green leafy vegetable, cabbage retains its crispness for longer than lettuce or other greens. It is also a good source of vitamins B and C, but these deteriorate on long storage and leach out if soaked too long in water. There is no need to soak or cook cabbage with bicarbonate of soda as was done decades ago. Although this preserves color it destroys vitamins and gives a strange taste.

This is perhaps one of the world's most popular salads, but if badly made it can be the most dreary. Coleslaw, essentially a shredded raw cabbage salad, can be as simple or elaborate as you please, with the addition of grated carrot, chopped celery, thinly sliced green pepper, grated apple, raisins, finely chopped green onions and cucumber. Instead of dressing simply with homemade mayonnaise (page 202) and light or sour cream (below) coleslaw can also be dressed first with a little French mustard, wine vinegar, sea salt, sugar and caraway seeds and then left to stand for 30 minutes before tossing with a thick mayonnaise mixed with light or sour cream. For added interest use half white and half red cabbage. Leafy green vegetables, however, are not sufficiently firm to use in coleslaw.

Savoy cabbage *Cut the head in half vertically, then cut out the woody core in a 'V' shape. Pull off the large outer leaves and cut out the thick stalks. Roll the leaves together and shred finely. Halve the remaining cabbage and place each piece flat side down on a chopping board. Slice down into fine shreds.*

Regular cabbage *Cut the cabbage into quarters. Stand each quarter upright and cut out the hard core. Lay on its side and shred, finely for salads and coleslaw, thicker for cooking. For stuffing (page 60), peel whole leaves off the cabbage before quartering; cut out the stalks, then blanch and stuff.*

1 *Finely grate 3 carrots into a large bowl, then add any other crisp vegetable you like (above), either grated or very finely chopped. Mix together with 1¼ cups (300ml) homemade mayonnaise and a little light or sour cream.*

2 *Finely shred about 1lb (500g) cabbage in a food processor or by hand (left). Add to the grated carrot and mayonnaise mixture and stir until well coated. Season well with sea salt and freshly ground black pepper, then refrigerate for 30 minutes.*

ONIONS, STALKS *and* SHOOTS

My favorite of these vegetables is fennel; this has a totally different character and flavor when raw as opposed to cooked, but both are invaluable for producing interesting dishes. Cooking it produces a rounded, mellow flavor. Sliced thinly and eaten raw in salads, the anise flavor is much more pungent and refreshes the whole mouth.

Onions and shallots can hardly be overcooked; long and gentle frying or stewing brings out the best in them, a sweet and mild softness and the most enticing smell. If you cry when peeling and cutting onions the tears stop miraculously when you rinse your hands under running water.

Asparagus is a vegetable with a unique and fascinating flavor. It can be plump or thin, almost white, bright green or a dark purply green, which is the kind I prefer.

The globe artichoke is a member of the thistle family which belies its ferocious uncooked appearance. The base of the spiky leaves tastes divine, and last to be revealed, but best of all, is the artichoke heart.

Corn on the cob must be eaten as fresh as possible; immediately after picking, the corn is wonderfully sweet, tender and juicy, but as soon as corn is picked the sugar starts converting to starch so the longer the cob is stored before cooking, the more starchy it will become.

BUYING AND STORING

As with most vegetables, keep them cool and crisp in the bottom of the refrigerator, wrapped loosely in plastic wrap. Onions, however, need cool, dry and dark storage.

CHOPPING AN ONION

Chopping an onion correctly is deemed the art of a true professional cook! If you ever get the chance to watch a chef, you'll be amazed at the lightning speed. Once you have mastered the technique, regular practice will speed things up. The secrets are to make sure your chef's knife is good and sharp and to keep the onion root intact to act as an anchor. Chop just before using the onion so the juice will not dry up.

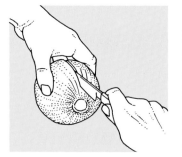

1 *Cut the onion in half leaving some of the root on each half. Peel each half and work with one at a time. Place the cut side down on a board.*

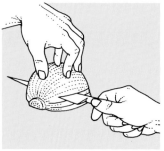

2 *With the knife held horizontally, make cuts almost right through to the root end at ¼in (5mm) intervals. Do not cut through the root.*

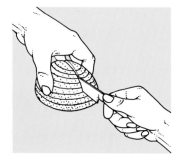

3 *Make vertical cuts down, at ¼in (5mm) intervals, again leaving the onion root attached and holding the onion firmly with your free hand.*

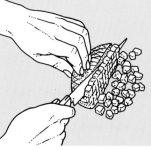

4 *Holding the onion with your fingers at a 90° angle, keep the knife tip on the board and rock the blade up and down, slicing as you go. Discard the root.*

PREPARING LEEKS

Even baby leeks need a little extra washing, but older loose ones sold with long dark green tops may well have a lot of dirt trapped inside. Wash off any obvious mud on the outside and cut off and discard the root and tough tops.

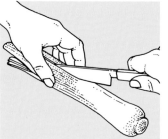

1 *Slash the leek twice lengthwise from the green tip down to the start of the white stalk. Wash well in at least 2 changes of cold water until all the dirt is removed.*

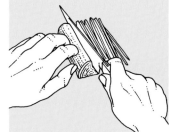

2 *Cut into 3 or 4 shorter lengths, then slice into thin strips. Alternatively, slice whole leeks across in rounds at ¼in (5mm) or ½in (1cm) intervals.*

PREPARING FENNEL

Fennel, often incorrectly labeled as anise, is sold in tight, flattish or round, oblong bulbs with small fronds which can be reserved and used as an attractive garnish. Look for pale green to white bulbs and do not buy any which are dark green or they will be too bitter tasting.

Fennel can be halved or quartered and cored and then braised, steamed or baked, or sliced thinly to use in salads, or in stir-fries and casseroles.

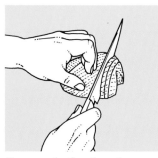

Remove the fronds *and reserve. Trim off the top stalks and halve the bulb. Cut out the root core in a 'V' shape, then lay cut side down and slice thinly crosswise.*

PREPARING GLOBE ARTICHOKES

Globe artichokes make one of the most attractive starters, and – once you've mastered the initial technique – are easy to prepare and cook. Look for ones with firm green leaves and avoid any with brown tips or a dried-up appearance. Once cooked, the artichoke can be served hot or cold. Pull off the leaves and dip the leaf base in dressing or melted butter. Then scrape off the soft flesh with your front teeth. Eat the heart separately with a knife and fork. Discard the hairy choke in the center.

1 *Score around the stem base with a sharp knife, then pull down sharply to remove. Use a sharp knife to cut off the top for presentation if you like.*

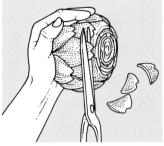

2 *Trim the tips of the leaves with scissors. Cook by simmering in water with some fresh lemon juice until the base leaves separate easily, about 40 minutes.*

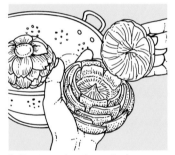

3 *Drain and cool upside down in a colander. Pull the top leaves apart to reveal the inner purple ones. Grasp these firmly and pull up hard, revealing the hairy choke.*

4 *Using a teaspoon, scrape out the choke in one piece as much as possible and discard, exposing the heart. Replace the purple leaves, reshape and serve.*

Tenderly cooked hot asparagus spears with melted butter, and Artichokes with Yellow Mystery Sauce (page 65).

PREPARING FRESH CORN

For the freshest flavor, sweetness and juiciness, fresh corn should be bought with the husks still intact, as the kernels become stale quickly when exposed to air. To capture the fresh flavor, eat corn on the day of purchase. Best of all is if you can pick your own and then go straight home to cook it immediately. Kernels also taste wonderful eaten raw as long as the corn is absolutely fresh.

PREPARING ASPARAGUS

Once only available for several weeks each spring, imports now mean we can enjoy asparagus all year round.

The stalks of thick asparagus, whether white or green, need peeling. After peeling, break off the woody base and discard. Young, thin, long asparagus stems, need little preparation, except trimming at the base. Prepare asparagus just before cooking (page 52) to prevent the stalks from drying out.

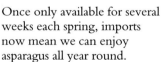

To peel thick asparagus, *use a swivel-bladed vegetable peeler or sharp paring knife and peel gently away from you from about half the way up the stalk to the base.*

1 *To prepare corn on the cob, hold the cob firmly in one hand, and pull off the green leafy husks. Trim the stalk, then peel away the brown corn silk. There is no need to wash before cooking.*

2 *To remove the kernels, hold the prepared cob upright, stalk end down on a board. Using a sharp chef's knife, cut straight down. The kernels may scatter a bit, so allow plenty of space.*

VEGETABLE FRUITS *and* SQUASHES

Vegetable fruits, which include tomatoes, peppers, eggplant, cucumbers and okra, are a delicious group which are botanically classified as fruits, but eaten as vegetables. In fact, they all contain an element of sweetness, as does the squash family. They combine well with each other in dishes such as ratatouille (page 59) or vegetable curries (page 58).

The joy of eggplant lies in its creamy consistency. So, whether they are baked, grilled, fried or stewed, eggplant must become completely soft before eating. Some people are wary of okra but if you buy them small and an unblemished green, they are excellent. The versatile squash family, including zucchini, winter squashes and pumpkin, all differ slightly in flavor and texture, but can be combined with all sorts of complementary ingredients.

BUYING AND STORING
Store most of these vegetables in the refrigerator, wrapped loosely in plastic wrap and use within a couple of days. Peppers and eggplant start to wrinkle with age but are still usable. Avocados are best kept at room temperature until ripened, then stored in the refrigerator to prevent over-ripening. Winter squash keep well in a cool, dry place.

PITTING AVOCADOS

Avocados are ripe if they feel slightly soft when pressed gently cupped in your hand. Although available all year round, there are different varieties and colors of avocado, but they are all prepared in the same way. Once you have cut one open, brush the flesh with lemon juice to prevent discoloration if you do not plan to eat it at once.

1 *Cut the avocado in half lengthwise right through to and around the stone. Holding in both hands, twist the halves in opposite directions and pull apart gently but still firmly.*

2 *Hold one half cupped in your hand and hit the stone firmly in the center with a chef's knife. Lift up the stone, which will stay on the knife. Serve in the skin or peel and slice for salads.*

DRAINING EGGPLANT

Look for firm full eggplant with smooth skins. Cooked whole, the flesh can then be scooped out for a smooth pâté (page 97), but normally eggplant are prepared in slices or dice. Classically, eggplant are drained by sprinkling them with salt so the bitter juices drain out and the flesh firms slightly. This is especially useful when frying slices so they don't absorb quite as much oil, and helps keep the texture soft. Draining is not necessary for chopped eggplant being put straight into a stew.

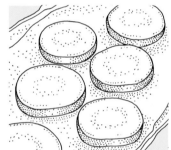

1 *Cut off the stalk and cut the flesh in slices ½in (1cm) thick, then layer in a colander, sprinkling each layer with salt.*

2 *Leave to drain for 30 minutes over a sink, then rinse well. Place the slices on several layers of paper towels and pat dry.*

PREPARING TOMATOES

It really is worth the small effort to skin fresh tomatoes for making stews, sauces, soups and coulis.

Choose firm, just ripe fruit. Single tomatoes can be skinned by spearing on a fork and holding over a gas flame until the skin blackens and pops, but for batches of tomatoes a brief dunk in boiling water to loosen the skins is easiest. For cooking, the plum variety, really ripe, are the best tomatoes to use.

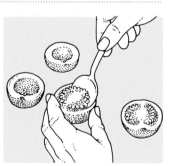

1 *Remove any stalks then cut a small cross on the opposite sides. Place the tomatoes in a deep heatproof bowl and pour over fresh boiling water.*

2 *Leave for 1 minute or until the skins split. Drain and pour over plenty of cold water so the tomatoes do not cook. Using a paring knife, remove the skins.*

To seed tomatoes, *remove the stalk core, then cut the tomato in half and scoop out the seeds. Chop if using in sauces or light casseroles, or slice.*

PREPARING PEPPERS

Versatile sweet peppers, members of the capsicum family, can be eaten either raw with a creamy dip, or even better, grilled (page 55) and sliced in salads, or cooked long and gently in stews and sauces. Hollowed out, they are an ideal container for stuffing and baking (page 61), or for holding a dip for other crudités. Peppers also make a wonderful puree.

Apart from the familiar red, green and yellow ones, look for orange or black-skinned peppers.

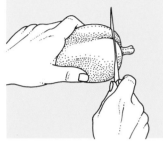

To hollow out, *cut off the top of the pepper with a sharp knife and reserve it as a lid if you plan to stuff the pepper. Use a spoon to scrape out the whole core and seeds. For rings, slice crosswise.*

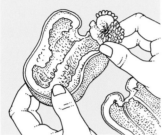

To slice or chop, *cut the peppers in half lengthwise, then remove the cores and seeds. Slice lengthwise or crosswise for half rings. For kebobs, quarter the peppers, then cut into square chunks.*

SEEDING CHILIES

These require care when handling if you are not to cause yourself great discomfort. The juice stings intensely so avoid rubbing your eyes or nose after cutting or handling a chili. I find preparing chilies under cold running water helps, but care is still the best course of action. If you have sensitive skin, wear a pair of rubber gloves.

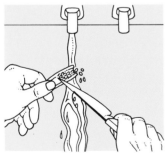

To seed a chili, *use a paring knife to slice it open, then use the tip of the knife to scrape out the seeds under running cold water. Chop or slice the chili as finely as required.*

TRIMMING OKRA

An important ingredient in all gumbos, okra is a favorite vegetable in African, Indian and Creole cuisines. Buy bright green firm pods without dark blemishes. Okra is often cooked whole because inside the pod is a sticky substance that acts as a thickening agent. Trim just before cooking to avoid the sticky juice oozing out, unless it is to be used as a thickener.

To prepare whole okra, *just before cooking, trim the very tip of the stem and then wash and drain thoroughly. Cut crosswise into chunks if desired.*

COOKING SQUASHES

Squashes are one of my favorite vegetables: they are delicious whether served as a side dish or stuffed and served as the main course.

They are divided into two categories by the time of year in which they mature. Although they are all of the same family, there is a great variety in flavor and texture. During the late spring and all summer we enjoy the quick-cooking zucchini, yellow and paty pan squashes and during the fall and early winter the markets are filled with the harder acorn, butternut, spaghetti, hubbard and buttercup squashes.

Both kinds may be cooked whole, cut into pieces, or split and stuffed with a flavorful filling. Summer squash have a thin, edible skin and may be cooked in 3 to 5 minutes on the grill or when cut into slices. When stuffed and baked they rarely take more than 20 minutes. Winter squashes are tough skinned and require a much longer cooking time to be tender and ready to eat. Peeled chunks of winter squashes cooked in water or as part of a stew will be tender in about 20 minutes while when roasted whole or stuffed they can take up to 1 hour. If you want to make winter squash puree and have the time, roasting the squash whole and then scooping it out of the shell is a lot easier than trying to peel and cut up the raw squash. Whipped cooked squash makes an excellent side dish with just the addition of a little butter and some herbs. Winter squash puree may also be used in place of pumpkin to make pies.

Warm, spicy Middle Eastern flavors permeate Eggplant and Okra Stew with Mint and Pine Nuts (page 62).

SALADS *and* RAW VEGETABLES

Lettuce, the most basic salad ingredient, varies greatly in type. By far the largest selling lettuce in America is Iceberg. Crisp and sweet, it was the first to make the long trip from California to east coast markets in the fall and winter. The other main choices in the market today are Boston which is sweet, pale green or red and elegant; Romaine, the star of Caesar salad; Bibb, with small, crisp, dark green heads, first bred in Kentucky; and the loose and fluffy heads of greenleaf or redleaf. Each may be used as the base for a salad of other ingredients or on its own with anything from a light vinaigrette to a creamy Blue cheese dressing. There are also very decorative lettuces which make salads so pretty. Watercress and arugula both have a peppery bite which is nice combined with creamy fla- vored, rich slices of avocado. Raw mushrooms are won- derful in salads, and absorb a flavorful vinaigrette made with extra-virgin olive oil.

BUYING AND STORING
Salad greens should be kept loosely wrapped in plastic bags in the bottom of the refrigerator and eaten as soon as pos- sible, particularly the more tender leaves.

THE PERFECT TOSSED SALAD

Aim to use at least 2 types of leaves, one sweet, like a Boston lettuce, and one frilly and bitter, such as frisée, or a different color, such as red radicchio. Optional extras include watercress or arugula, and lots of fresh chopped parsley, chives and other tender herbs. Crunchy vegetables like green onion, cucumber, and green peppers are best left for mixed salads. A well-flavored dressing (page 204) is essential but don't drench the salad. Use just enough to coat the leaves.

1 *Separate the lettuce leaves and tear into bite-size pieces, placing in a colander. Discard any damaged outer ones. Wash well with other smaller greens such as watercress and drain in a colander, shaking off any excess water.*

2 *Place the greens on a clean tea towel, top with another towel and pat lightly to dry, or dry by spinning in a salad spinner. (If preparing ahead, store in the refrigerator in a plastic bag to keep it crisp.)*

3 *Pour just enough vinaigrette to coat the greens into the bottom of a large mixing bowl. Add the greens and toss well with your hands or with salad servers. Transfer to a serving bowl immediately.*

IDEAS FOR SALADS

• Looseleaf lettuces are really best as a salad on their own, dressed with a good mustard vinaigrette, but the most decorative lettuces are good in mixed-green salads.
• All the chicories, with their slight bitterness, take well to a vinaigrette which has been sweetened with honey (page 204), or mixed with other sweet ingredients such as slices of orange, fresh apricots or watermelon. The colors also help make a pretty salad.
• Frisée tastes delicious with orange slices and a walnut-oil or hazelnut-oil vinaigrette.
• To make crudités to serve with taramasalata (page 137) cut carefully cleaned and prepared carrots, fennel, peppers and celery into neat, thin pieces.

• An excellent salad is finely sliced bulb fennel with thin slices of blood orange, simply dribbled with a little white wine vinegar and either olive or walnut oil, and sprinkled with crushed sea salt, pink peppercorns and a pinch or two of cayenne pepper.
• Another salad I really enjoy is watercress and arugula mixed with halved yellow cherry tomatoes and a hot bacon dressing, which also goes well with a spinach salad. Make the dressing by frying little pieces of bacon and then heating a vinaigrette mixture (page 204) in the skillet with the bacon and its fat before mixing it into the salad.
• Cucumber is best peeled and cubed, and mixed with seasoned yogurt and fresh mint.

MAKING A MIXED SALAD

I think a mixed salad is much more interesting if some of the ingredients are raw and some are lightly blanched vegetables such as snow peas, thin French beans or asparagus tips. Peeled and parboiled root vegetables can also enhance mixed salads; slices of parsnip, turnip, celeriac and rutabaga, steamed or boiled until just beginning to soften but still with a bite, are delicious. Strips of grilled peppers (page 55), with their mellow, smoky taste, are wonderful. Bulb fennel, sliced across, is excellent if grilled briefly before adding to salads. You can also pour boiling water onto fresh peas and then pop the peas out of their skins into the salad. A little finely shredded red cabbage adds crunch and color to a green salad.

I never use tomatoes, except whole or halved cherry tomatoes, in mixed salads as I think they are far better on their own with a generous sprinkling of fresh herbs and olive oil.

Prepare all the ingredients for a salad and assemble in a large bowl, adding chopped herbs if desired. Dress with a garlicky dressing, including whole grain mustard (page 204). Any root vegetables should be put into a separate bowl and tossed with some dressing while still hot so that they absorb the flavor of the dressing as they cool.

SALADE NIÇOISE

This classic Provençal salad is a glorious jumble of the ingredients that Mediterranean France excels in – tomatoes, black olives, crunchy green French beans and capers, topped with sliced anchovy fillets. Serve it as a starter or a light main course; to make it more of a main dish, add quartered hard-boiled egg and cold potato slices. A mustard-flavored vinaigrette (page 204) is particularly good with Salade Niçoise.

1 *Put 8oz (250g) each of cooked and still warm green beans and sliced all-purpose potatoes into a large bowl with 2 large coarsely chopped tomatoes.*

2 *Mix in 2 tablespoons capers, 7oz (200g) can tuna, drained and flaked, 1 handful small black olives, 1 tablespoon chopped flat-leaf parsley and 4–6 tablespoons vinaigrette.*

3 *Season well. Slice 2oz (50g) drained canned anchovy fillets, in half lengthwise. Quarter 1 or 2 hard-boiled eggs. Arrange the salad on a platter and garnish with the anchovies and eggs.*

The flavors of the south of France are captured in Salade Niçoise, ideal as a light meal just with chunks of French bread.

TOMATO SALAD

A simple tomato salad dressed with a drizzle of extra virgin olive oil, a sprinkle of crushed sea salt and garnished with chopped fresh basil is so good.

Slice the tomatoes and arrange on a serving dish. Vinaigrette dressing is often used on tomato salad but I prefer just oil as the tomato juices balance the oil; if they lack flavor add some lemon juice. After dressing, cover and leave for 1 hour.

Drizzle over *enough olive oil to lightly coat. Sprinkle with crushed sea salt, black pepper and chopped fresh basil.*

POTATO SALAD

The most important thing about a potato salad is that regardless of how the potatoes are ultimately going to be dressed, either with a garlicky mustard vinaigrette (page 204) with plenty of chopped dill, a yogurt dressing (page 205) or homemade mayonnaise flavored with dill (page 202), they should first be tossed in a bowl while still hot with extra virgin olive oil, a little vinegar and seasoning, then left to absorb the flavors. Serves 4.

1 *Scrub well or rub the skins off 1–1½lb (500–750g) new potatoes, and either leave whole or cut up, depending on size. Steam or boil (page 52) until just soft.*

2 *Put the hot potatoes in a bowl, toss with a vinaigrette (page 204) and leave until cold. Transfer to a serving bowl and then coat with your chosen dressing.*

PREPARING MUSHROOMS

Cultivated mushrooms, including oysters and shiitakes, are grown in sterilized compost so they don't need washing or peeling. A wipe with a clean damp cloth is more than sufficient. Baby-sized buttons can be used whole, while open caps can be sliced, quartered or skewered whole for kebobs. Portabella mushrooms, however, are best brushed with oil, stuffed and grilled (page 60).

Wipe mushrooms *with a clean, damp cloth. Trim the base of the stems, then slice thickly or thinly as required.*

STEAMING *and* BOILING

I nearly always steam vegetables rather than boil them, except for very quick-cooking vegetables like snow peas, which should be cooked for only a minute or two in a large pan of salted, rapidly boiling water, and leaves for blanching such as spinach and lettuce where boiling is more successful. I find that steaming keeps in more flavor, particularly with root vegetables, and produces less water-logged results. A wide range of steamers is available (page 19) and if you steam regularly and in large quantities buy a two-tiered steamer.

Traditionally, green vegetables were put directly into boiling water while roots and tubers went into cold water to be brought up to a boil. But if you start all vegetables off in a small amount of boiling water it helps preserve the vitamins. Boiled vegetables are usually cooked in salted water, while steamed vegetables are not salted. They need more seasoning before serving, but they do have more flavor in themselves. With both steaming and boiling, test frequently for doneness, because it is impossible to predict exactly when they will reach the right point.

BOILING CABBAGE

Cabbage is one of the most underrated vegetables; it can be supremely delicious if it is cooked carefully.

Either cook cabbage briefly, leaving it bright green and still slightly crunchy, or long and very gently so it becomes meltingly soft and almost sweet tasting. If you boil cabbage, it should be done in a minimum amount of water, really just enough to steam it – the more tender cabbages like green and savoy cabbages respond well to quick cooking, with crisper, fresh-tasting results.

Shred the cabbage finely (page 45) and rinse well. Bring about ½in (1cm) salted water to a vigorous boil in a heavy saucepan, then add the shredded cabbage, cover and boil for 5–8 minutes until softened, but still with a slight crunch to it.

STEAMING BROCCOLI

Broccoli should retain a bright-green color and a slight firmness, so it is very important not to cook it for too long. It can be too crunchy, however, so it is also vital to test it at least once or twice during the cooking. It is best to cut the broccoli into equal-sized florets (page 44), using only the green and tender part of the stem . The remainder of the stems may be peeled, cut crosswise into discs or lengthwise into julienne strips and cooked either with the florets or separately for use in salads.

Place the broccoli florets in the top half of a steamer over boiling water. Cover and steam for 5–10 minutes until just tender but still bright green. Season with salt and pepper and serve at once with plenty of melted butter or with hollandaise sauce (page 200).

COOKING ASPARAGUS

Because asparagus tips are more tender, care must be taken to ensure they do not overcook before the stems are ready. They are best cooked either upright in a tall pan so the tips steam while the stems simmer or flat in a shallow pan or frying pan.

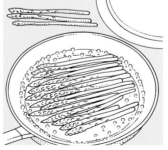 

1 Prepare the asparagus (page 47). Bring salted water to a boil in a shallow pan, then add the asparagus spears in a single layer without overcrowding. Reduce to a simmer and cover.

2 Cook for 5 minutes or until the stems are just tender. Remove with a spatula and drain well. Arrange on a hot serving dish and pour over melted butter or serve with hollandaise sauce (page 200).

USING BOILED AND STEAMED VEGETABLES
• Celeriac mashed with potato and lots of butter is a lovely topping for a shepherd's pie or may be served separately as a side dish with beef or game.
• Coarsely chopped sweet peppers, boiled with whole cloves of unpeeled garlic until soft, and then pureed together – first popping the soft garlic easily out of its skin – make an excellent puree. You can process in butter to serve as a hot puree, or olive oil for a cold one. Or sieve the puree with cream or vegetable stock to make it into a sauce.
• Peppers can also be boiled with other vegetables and pured together. Try carrots with red peppers, and zucchini or bulb fennel with green peppers.
• To enhance a dish of boiled or steamed vegetables, the easiest and most effective thing to do is to sprinkle them with soy sauce just before serving. This is also useful if you are on a low-fat diet and don't want to use butter.
• Fresh herbs such as mint, parsley and fennel leaves are good on all vegetables, with or without other flavorings.
• A sprinkling of hickory-flavored smoked salt is very good on green vegetables.
• Grated nutmeg seems to enhance all vegetables, and is marvellous included in a grated cheese topping.
• Freshly boiled, hot beets are nice with a white sauce (page 196) to which you have added sour cream or plain yogurt and chopped, fresh herbs at the end of cooking.

PUREEING VEGETABLES

Many vegetables make delicious purees to serve with roasts and comforting casseroles. The purees, however, should not be tasteless overcooked vegetable slurries but, instead, light creams retaining flavor and body. Suitable vegetables for pureeing include cauliflower, carrots, rutabagas, brussels sprouts, parsnips, celeriac, peas and spinach but root purees are best of all.

Often it is nice to combine two vegetables, one of which can be a vegetable that is too watery to puree on its own, but adds good flavor, such as leeks. The mixture of celeriac and potato is a well-known combination but celeriac is also delicious if combined with carrots, parsnips and rutabagas. Bulb fennel combines well with root vegetables in a puree, or is delicious as a puree on its own or blended with plain yogurt.

Enrich vegetable purees with butter, cream, crème fraîche, yogurt or olive oil. Serve topped with toasted nuts, spiced oil (page 36), fried breadcrumbs, chopped herbs or simply swirled attractively with a fork.

Spinach and Peppers in a Sweet Potato and Parsnip Bowl (page 63) uses two pureed root vegetables to make an unusual case for the spinach and red peppers.

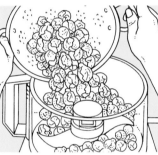

1 *Boil your chosen vegetable in a small amount of water until just tender but not overcooked. Drain, reserving the cooking liquid, and place in a food processor. Process until smooth, adding a little of the cooking liquid to moisten and make blending easier.*

2 *Add butter to taste or a couple tablespoons of crème fraîche or mascarpone. Freshly ground spices or chopped herbs such as nutmeg, cinnamon, thyme or cilantro can be added at this point. Taste again and season with salt and pepper.*

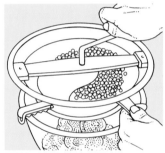

Purees can also be made *with a food mill (page 22), resulting in a thicker texture. Process the vegetable in batches. Return the pureed vegetable to the saucepan on low heat until any excess moisture is evaporated, stirring, and then beat in any flavorings.*

PERFECT MASHED POTATOES

There is something so comforting about good mashed potatoes – light, fluffy and creamy all at the same time. These are potatoes to go with fried chicken, chops, steaks or roasts, as well as homey stews, appealing to the young and old alike.

The secret to excellent mashed potatoes lies in choosing a variety of potato that boils to a soft texture without disintegrating (page 43). Luxury mashed potatoes can be made by mixing in saffron-infused milk or cream.

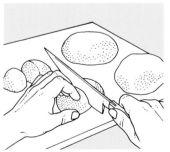

1 *Cut peeled potatoes into equal-sized pieces for even boiling. Cook in lightly salted boiling water until tender but not too soft. Drain well. Return the potatoes to the saucepan over a gentle heat to dry out slightly.*

2 *Using a hand masher, or small electric beater, mash the potatoes to a smooth puree. Do not mash potatoes in a food processor, as it turns the potatoes gluey. If you want saffron potatoes infuse several threads in hot milk or cream.*

3 *Beat in butter to taste and a little milk, hot for extra fluffy mashed potatoes. Season well, adding freshly grated nutmeg or ground mace. Mound up the potatoes on a hot serving dish and top with a chunk of butter.*

FRYING *and* GRILLING

Fried vegetables can be irresistible, but it is important to cook them carefully as they can burn easily. The oil or fat they are cooked in is important as it will become very much part of their flavor; a mixture of olive oil and butter can be brought to a higher temperature than just butter without burning, but for quickly fried vegetables, I think extra virgin olive oil is the best. For Chinese-style stir-fries the vegetables should be cut to the same size and, to add an authentic flavor, you can mix in some nutty-tasting toasted sesame oil with peanut or sunflower oil, but use it sparingly, as it is very overpowering.

Some people never think of grilling any vegetables other than tomatoes and mushrooms, but all the squash family, and other sliced vegetables which have a soft consistency, grill very well, and in the process lose much of their excess water. With grilling, it is best to keep the heat very high so the vegetables actually burn black in places, giving them a lovely smoky taste.

SAUTÉING

Sautéing vegetables adds a lovely flavor. As with all sautéing, vegetables are best cooked quickly in hot oil for a light crisp texture on the outside, leaving the inside just tender but still with a good bite. Sauté in a wide, heavy frying pan and use a little bit of good quality oil, such as olive, peanut or sunflower. Vegetables should be thinly sliced or grated. Mixing them with, or dipping them in, egg batters or breadcrumbs before frying helps protect the flesh from the heat. Grated potatoes can be pressed together and fried for traditional Jewish latkes or Swiss rösti.

To make zucchini fritters, mix 12oz (375g) grated zucchini and 1 small grated onion into a batter made with 1 cup (125g) flour, 1 egg, 1 teaspoon each salt and garam masala and ⅔ cup (50ml) milk. Drop tablespoons into hot shallow oil and fry for 5 minutes, turning once. Drain on paper towels.

To make potato latkes, grate 2lb (1kg) peeled potatoes and soak for 1 hour in cold water. Drain for 15 minutes. Beat 2 tablespoons self-rising flour with 2 eggs, 1 tablespoon grated onion, salt and pepper. Mix in the potatoes. Fry in tablespoonfuls in shallow hot oil for 3 minutes on each side until browned.

To make rösti, boil 1½lb (750g) unpeeled potatoes for 10 minutes. Drain, cool, peel and grate coarsely. Season. Heat 1 tablespoon oil and 2 tablespoons (25g) butter in a 9in (23cm) frying pan. Spoon in the potatoes, levelling the top. Fry 10 minutes, invert onto a plate, slide back to cook other side. Serve in wedges.

DEEP FRYING

Deep-fried potatoes and coated vegetables are crispest if eaten freshly cooked. For best results use peanut or sunflower oil as these can be heated to high temperatures. All vegetables, except roots, need protection in the form of batters or flour coatings, which add delicious flavors of their own.

Homemade French fries are one of the most popular deep-fried vegetables. These are cooked in two stages, the first to cook the potato and the second to crisp. After frying, keep the fries warm in a low oven, on several layers of crumpled paper towels.

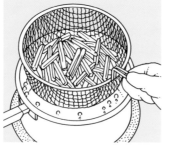

1 Prepare the French fries (page 43). Soak for 30 minutes, then drain and pat dry. Fill a deep, heavy saucepan one-third full with oil. Heat to 325°F, 160°C or until a cube of bread browns in 1 minute. Cover the base of the basket with raw French fries and fry for about 5 minutes until they are pale golden brown.

2 Remove the fries from the pan and drain well on paper towels. Cook the remaining fries. Raise the temperature to 375°F, 190°C or until a cube of bread browns in 30 seconds. Refry the fries for just 1 minute until crisp. Reheat the oil between batches. Drain the fries well on paper towels and sprinkle with salt.

For simple vegetable fritters, toss sliced onions, broccoli florets, parsnip sticks and button mushrooms in flour seasoned with mild curry spices. Heat oil to 360°F, 185°C, or until a cube of bread browns in 40 seconds. Fry the vegetables in batches for about 2 minutes. Drain well on paper towels

GRILLING PEPPERS

Grilled or broiled peppers are one of my favorite vegetables. The grilling transforms the slightly watery texture and taste to something smooth, mellow and sweet.

To remove pepper skins the peppers have to be grilled until charred and black. The slightly smoky taste grilling leaves once the peppers are skinned is an added bonus. Grilled and skinned peppers are excellent in salads, pasta and fish dishes.

To prepare peppers for grilling, cut in half lengthwise, and discard the core and seeds (page 49).

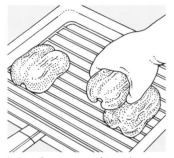 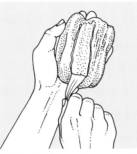

1 *Put the peppers, skin side toward the heat of an outdoor grill or indoor broiler. Leave until charred black nearly all over. Remove from the grill and wrap in a tea towel or place in a paper bag until cool enough to handle.*

2 *Using just your fingers, peel off the skin, bit by bit, and discard. Then slice the peppers as desired. Either add the peppers while still hot to cooked pasta or use later when cool in sandwiches or to add to a salad.*

IDEAS FOR GRILLING AND FRYING

• Oyster mushrooms are a most successful ingredient in a mixed vegetable grill (right).
• Sweetcorn can also be grilled as long as the cobs are very fresh and therefore juicy – they are best grilled still protected by their outside husk.
• A little beer added to a batter instead of some of the milk or water makes it lighter. You can also add herbs, grated lemon rind and ground or whole spices to batters for frying.
• Very thin slices of peeled root vegetables such as parsnip, celeriac or rutabaga are good fried briefly in olive oil with crushed garlic and chopped flat-leaf parsley added at the end of frying. They can be eaten as an appetizer or as a hot first course.
• For a real treat fry the thinnest slices of pumpkin swiftly in olive oil with a little crushed garlic over a fairly high heat so that the edges begin to blacken slightly, but the pumpkin is still fairly firm. Chopped fresh mint perfects

this dish, adding freshness to the sweet pumpkin.
• Zucchini flowers are a real delicacy served as the Italians do, sautéed in olive oil or stuffed with cheese, dipped in batter and deep-fried.
• The skin is arguably the best part of the potato; I love deep-fried pieces of skin. Choose long, narrow potatoes and cut them into fairly large slices which contain quite a lot of the flesh as well as the skin, parboil them very briefly in salted water just to soften a little and pat dry with paper towels before deep-frying in hot oil until crispy.
• Whole, medium-sized zucchini can be rubbed with olive oil and salt and grilled until blackened all over with the inside soft and white; cut into long strips, sprinkle with oregano and black pepper and drizzle with olive oil.
• Thinly shredded spring greens are irresistible deep fried and served in a crispy mound as the Chinese do.

A selection of charcoal-grilled vegetables – eggplant, yellow peppers, radicchio, tomatoes, zucchini and mushrooms.

MIXED VEGETABLE GRILL

Grilled or broiled vegetables can be absolutely wonderful. Zucchini, mushrooms, tomatoes, peppers, eggplant, slices of bulb fennel and clusters of radicchio leaves are particularly delicious grilled and can be served either on their own or as an accompaniment to roast meat or poultry. The grill should be very, very hot as the vegetables must become charred on the outside to give them their irresistible smoky flavor. If you are cooking indoors and lucky enough to have a ribbed grill pan or a grill on your stove, the vegetables can be attractively striped with black lines, but a broiler can also produce good results. In the summer, a charcoal or fruitwood barbecue, especially with a few rosemary, thyme or fennel sprigs on it, can be fantastic, but the cooking is harder to get right.

Prepare the vegetables as follows: Halve tomatoes and peppers or leave them whole; trim mushroom stalks so that they stay level on the grill; leave zucchini and eggplant unpeeled and slice thinly lengthwise, but score the cut surfaces of large eggplant in a criss-cross pattern so that the heat penetrates fully; radicchio simply needs halving lengthwise so the root end holds together the layers of leaves. Coat the vegetables all over with plenty of olive oil and a little salt, and also Mediterranean herbs such as oregano, rosemary or thyme.

 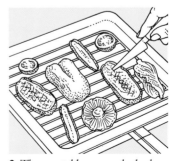

1 *Lay out the prepared vegetables on or under the hottest possible grill or broiler – when charred on one side, turn them over.*

2 *The vegetables are cooked when there is little resistance to a small pointed knife inserted in the center. Serve at once.*

ROASTING *and* BAKING

The most familiar roasted vegetables are, of course, potatoes, but other root vegetables can be roasted if you parboil them first. Vegetables which contain a lot of sugar such as sweet potatoes and parsnips burn quickly and should not be roasted too hot. Roasted vegetables should have a really crisp exterior and soft center, and are best roasted with a coating of butter or oil. One of the great treats are whole cloves of garlic, roasted in their skins with a slowly cooked beef or pork roast. They become brown and caramelized, with a sweet mellowness within the skin.

There are many possibilities for baking vegetables, again baked potatoes being the best known. Sweet potatoes also bake well and can be filled as ordinary potatoes. Vegetables can also be baked in shallow dishes in a béchamel or white sauce (page 196), or with crunchy toppings. Or you can arrange mixed layers of prepared vegetables with butter or olive oil and other flavorings in a covered terrine to be baked gently in the oven.

Baking is done at a moderate heat if you have not parboiled the vegetables first, whereas roasted vegetables, for the best crispness, should be parboiled and then roasted at a high heat which is then reduced to moderate after 20–30 minutes. For perfect roasting, vegetables need to be watched carefully as ovens often vary.

BAKED POTATOES

There are times when I feel I would like to eat a baked potato more than anything else; they are a most comforting food, either eaten simply (and to me best of all) with melted butter, or with a variety of fillings (below) to suit your mood.

Although it is extremely convenient to 'bake' potatoes quickly in a microwave, it is only by proper baking for at least an hour in a conventional oven, that you achieve a really crusty skin which contrasts irresistibly with the smooth, soft center. The chart on page 43 lists the varieties best for baking.

If you have any leftover drippings after roasting a chicken or turkey (page 178), you can use it to drizzle over the potatoes, otherwise use melted butter or olive oil – and sprinkle with crushed sea salt for its flavor, too. If you want the skin to be extra crunchy, cook the potatoes for a bit longer. Piercing the potatoes with metal skewers (right) conducts the heat and speeds up the cooking, but it is not essential.

Remember that you can bake sweet potatoes in the same way as white potatoes, and they will soften more quickly.

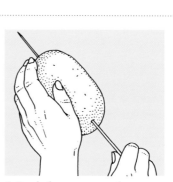

1 *Scrub the potatoes and cut out any blemishes. Either push a metal skewer through the center of each potato or cut a slit in the potato skin, so it has no chance of bursting while cooking. Rub the potatoes generously all over with butter or olive oil.*

2 *Sprinkle with crushed sea salt and lay on a baking sheet in the center of a preheated oven at 400°F, 200°C and bake for 1–1½ hours until soft. Remove the skewers. Cut a deep cross in each top and squeeze open for filling.*

IDEAS FOR ROASTING AND BAKING

• If you want to roast potatoes without parboiling, peel medium-sized potatoes and cut thinly almost right through so that they look a bit like a folded fan, then spread crushed garlic or pesto sauce (page 207) between the slices with a knife, sprinkle all over with sea salt, black pepper and olive oil and roast in a fairly hot oven.
• To make roast parsnips, peel them and cut into thick strips, then boil for 5 minutes. Drain well and roast as for potatoes (opposite) but at a slightly lower heat and for a shorter time.
• I love vegetables baked in the oven in a shallow gratin dish and topped with grated cheese or scattered with a mixture of

grated Parmesan, fresh breadcrumbs, crushed garlic and olive oil. The vegetables should be boiled until just tender first, then drained very well before spooning into the dish and adding the topping. A crunchy topping can also be achieved by mixing chopped nuts – hazelnuts or almonds especially – with the grated cheese.
• Pumpkin is spectacular baked whole with a filling (page 60) but large peeled pieces can also be tossed with oil and seasoning and roasted in an oven at 350°F, 180°C until brown outside and just tender in the center.
• You can also bake whole turnips with the stems cut off and skins rubbed with olive oil

and salt. Serve with a sauce made by beating honey with a little finely chopped garlic and balsamic vinegar, seasoned with salt and freshly ground black pepper.
• Baked dishes include vegetable soufflés and terrines – coarsely grated zucchini or pumpkin are excellent in a cheese soufflé mixture (page 76).
• Eggplant can be baked whole, or cut in half lengthwise while still raw then filled with a sautéed stuffing and baked.
• Good fillings for baked potatoes include crumbled crispy bacon on top of a little pureed spinach mixed with cream; sour cream topped with lumpfish or salmon roe (or real caviar if you

can afford it); chopped smoked salmon mixed with crème fraîche and lots of chopped fresh dill; chopped pickled herring mixed with sour cream, ground coriander and chopped chives – and the simplest but one of the best, a dollop of pesto sauce (page 207).
• A most wonderful vegetable to bake is beets. They need slow, long cooking and should be left unpeeled but wrapped in foil. Eat with sour cream or yogurt and plenty of black pepper.
• Sour cream or plain yogurt blended in the food processor with plenty of chives and/or mint make a marvellous green sauce for baked potatoes or baked beets.

BAKED SPAGHETTI SQUASH

Spaghetti squash, or vegetable spaghetti, has one of the best flavors of the squash family, a lovely yellow color, and an intriguing consistency after cooking. It looks like a tangled mass of spaghetti – hence its name.

This is most delicious served with a strong, cheesy sauce, flavored with grated nutmeg and put briefly under the broiler or in a hot oven before serving, so that the top browns a little. If you don't want to make a cheese sauce (page 196), simply mix the baked flesh with plenty of butter, salt and black pepper and sprinkle with grated Parmesan cheese on top.

Spaghetti squash seeds are usually tender and good to eat, so do not bother to remove.

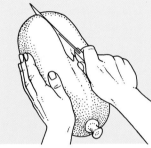 

1 Cut the spaghetti squash in half lengthwise and wrap the cut sides in foil. Put, foil sides down, on a baking sheet and bake at 350°F, 180°C for 40–50 minutes, until the flesh is soft when tested with the tip of a small knife.

2 Using a fork, scrape out the insides into a colander and transfer to a serving bowl. Top with a strong cheese sauce (page 196) flavored with grated nutmeg and plenty of pepper. Sprinkle with Parmesan and broil to brown slightly.

FENNEL GRATIN

Vegetables topped with cheese are very appetizing, but I think fennel is one of the best, especially when combined with Parmesan cheese, olive oil and garlic. The dish can be served hot or cold as an accompaniment or a first course. Serves 4.

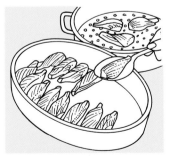 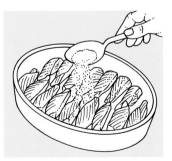

1 Cut the base and stalks off 4 large bulbs of fennel, then slice lengthwise into quarters, or sixths if very large. Steam or boil the fennel until soft, and drain, then arrange the pieces in a single layer in a shallow, lightly greased gratin dish, with their rounded sides facing up.

2 Drizzle 5–6 tablespoons olive oil over the fennel, sprinkle with 2 large finely chopped garlic cloves, ½ cup (50g) grated Parmesan cheese, crushed sea salt and plenty of black pepper. Bake at 400°F, 200°C for 20–30 minutes, until the surface is well browned.

ROAST POTATOES

It was my mother who made me realize how good roasted potatoes can be; richly golden and crunchy-crisp all over with a meltingly soft inside. She cuts her potatoes smaller than usual and boils them until just cooked, but not breaking up. A generous amount of very hot butter or oil is needed and it must have a good flavor, as this is absorbed by the potatoes. Butter is best but olive oil is also excellent. If you have other dishes in the oven, you can adjust the temperature but an initial high heat for at least 20 minutes is important.

1 Peel potatoes and cut up into 1-2in (2.5–5cm) pieces. Boil in salted water for about 15 minutes until just tender, then drain. Put enough butter or oil in a roasting pan to come at least ½in (1cm) up the side and place in the oven at 450°F, 230°C. When the fat is very hot, add the potatoes and turn them over.

2 Roast for about 20–30 minutes, turning them over once, then turn down the oven to 350°F, 180°C for 45–75 minutes until very crisp and golden brown. Check from time to time. Drain well on paper towels and sprinkle with crushed sea salt, then transfer to a serving dish. Serve hot.

Potatoes and Fennel Cooked with Cheese and Cream (page 63) makes a wonderful vegetarian main course or an ideal accompaniment to roasted meats.

BRAISING *and* STEWING

Gentle braising or stewing of vegetables gives very different results. Vegetables are usually braised by cooking slowly in a covered dish in the oven with the addition only of a little butter, olive oil or liquid, and seasonings such as herbs or spices, including garlic, fresh ginger or chilies. Use robust herbs such as bay leaves, rosemary, thyme and tarragon to braise with vegetables, but only stir in tender herbs such as leaf fennel, dill, basil, fresh cilantro and parsley at the end of cooking.

Vegetables can also be stewed in a saucepan or Dutch oven on top of the stove, or in the oven, with more liquid, like a normal stew – this can be done more quickly than braising, but doesn't achieve quite the same melting consistency and intensity of flavors which mingle together irresistibly. Apart from the delicious results, it is useful to have a braised vegetable cooking safely in the oven, and needing less attention before you serve the meal.

Certain vegetables are particularly suited to gentle braising or stewing, especially those which are slightly fibrous such as celery, bulb fennel, cabbage and leeks and also, above all, onions. It is only with slow cooking and absorption of seasoning and juices that the full and wonderful flavors of these vegetables really emerge. When you are braising or stewing several different vegetables together they should be added at different times, depending on the time they are going to take to cook, so none are overcooked. Garlic is almost always a welcome addition to braised or stewed vegetables; plenty can be used because with the long cooking it becomes beautifully sweet. Whole spices such as cinnamon also enhance a vegetable stew.

VEGETABLE CURRY

An easy vegetable curry can be made from all sorts of vegetables, according to what you have. This is a good way to use up vegetables which may be past their prime. All root vegetables are good with spices because of their sweetness, while the addition of legumes such as chick peas, will make the dish more substantial for a main course. Halved hard-boiled eggs are also a pleasing addition. This is a good lunch or supper dish, especially if you have a vegetarian in the family.

Remember that some vegetables take much longer to cook than others, and they should be added at different times. This is why I always make a vegetable curry in a Dutch oven on top of the stove. Serves 4.

2 tablespoons butter
3 tablespoons peanut oil
2 onions, peeled and sliced
1in (2.5cm) piece fresh gingerroot, finely chopped
3–4 cloves garlic, finely chopped

2 teaspoons ground coriander
1 teaspoon ground cumin
1 teaspoon ground cinnamon
½ teaspoon ground turmeric
½ teaspoon cayenne pepper
4 parsnips, peeled and diced
1 cauliflower, divided into florets
1 large red pepper, seeded and sliced (page 49)
1lb (500g) ripe tomatoes, skinned and chopped
2 tablespoons lemon juice
2 teaspoons sugar
8oz (250g) spinach, washed, drained and coarsely chopped
Salt

1 *Melt the butter and oil in a large Dutch oven. Add the onions and stir until they begin to soften. Add the ginger and garlic with the spices and cayenne pepper.*

IDEAS FOR BRAISING AND STEWING

• Chestnut mushrooms retain their body and are less watery even when cooked over a longish period than other mushrooms, so they are the best to use for braising and stewing. Mushrooms marry beautifully with Indian spices – try braising them in a covered dish with butter and a mixture of Indian spices or mild curry paste and some chopped fresh ginger or green chilli. Stir in chopped fresh coriander or mint leaves just before serving.
• Black onion seeds, available from Indian shops, are effective and look interesting in all braises and stews.
• Braised whole or halved chicory or fennel are mouthwatering if they are cooked gently in a covered dish with a little chicken stock, browned butter, brown sugar and seasoning – they are the most perfect accompaniment to pork, poultry and game.
• I also like to braise a little dish of whole peeled garlic cloves and shallots mixed with butter, olive oil, a dash of balsamic vinegar, 1–2 teaspoons of honey, salt and plenty of ground black pepper to be served as a side dish with roast or grilled poultry, meat or game.
• Coconut milk made up either from creamed or instant coconut powder is good stirred into spicy vegetable stews at the end of the cooking time.

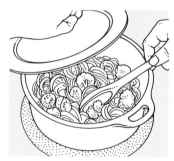

2 *Stir for 1 minute. Add the parsnips, cauliflower and red pepper and stir. Add the tomatoes, lemon juice and sugar. Cover the Dutch oven tightly and cook over the lowest possible heat, stirring once or twice with a wooden spoon, for 30–40 minutes until all the vegetables are very tender and the tomatoes have been reduced to a pulp.*

3 *Add the chopped spinach and stir in, cover and cook gently for another 8–10 minutes, or until the spinach is soft. Season with salt and more cayenne if you like a spicy taste. Boiled basmati rice (page 108) is an ideal accompaniment, or serve with Saffron and Chili Rice Cooked in Coconut Milk (page 115) or with Indian bread (page 293).*

SIMPLE VEGETABLE BRAISING

Certain vegetables which benefit from longer cooking like celery or roots are wonderful simply left in the oven to braise slowly, covered with stock or tomatoes and whatever herbs take your fancy. Braise at 350°F, 180°C for 40–50 minutes or until tender when pierced with a sharp knife.

To make braised celery, pull the tough outer ribs off a whole head of celery. Trim the leaves and slice crosswise.

Place the celery slices in a Dutch oven with 1 sliced red onion, 2 sliced carrots and 2½ cups (600ml) stock. Season and add herbs to taste. Cook as left.

RATATOUILLE

Ratatouille, a traditional Provençal vegetable stew, is a wonderfully versatile dish; it tastes as good hot or cold, and it can be eaten on its own or as an accompanying vegetable to meat, chicken and fish dishes. It is important to cook ratatouille gently so any wateriness evaporates and the vegetables become soft, sweet and mellow. Use only the best-quality ingredients, and really ripe tomatoes (the plum variety if available). Proportions and ingredients can be varied. It looks prettiest if you use different-colored peppers.

Prepare 1 large unpeeled eggplant by cutting across in thick slices and then in half, sprinkle with salt and leave in a colander for 30 minutes (page 48). Wash and drain thoroughly. You will also need 5–6 tablespoons extra virgin olive oil, 2–3 sliced onions, 2–3 peppers, cut into strips (page 49), 1lb (500g) skinned and chopped ripe tomatoes (page 48), 8oz (250g) sliced zucchini, 4 large cloves garlic, chopped, 2 tablespoons lemon juice, 2 teaspoons sugar, 1 handful coarsely chopped flat-leaf parsley and salt and black pepper. Serves 4.

Fennel or dill seeds add extra flavor to Braised Leeks with Tomatoes and Balsamic Vinegar (page 64). The slow, gentle braising brings out the leeks' sweet, mellow taste.

BRAISED RED CABBAGE

Delicious with roast pork and traditional with roast goose or duck, braised red cabbage improves if cooked ahead and then reheated just before serving. The sweet flavor of red cabbage marries well with tangy apple and rich comforting spices and it has a great affinity with beer, honey, chestnuts and caraway seeds. Braised red cabbage also looks very attractive.

If not serving at once, cool the cabbage, then refrigerate until ready to reheat for serving. This is an ideal supper dish for vegetarians. Serves 6.

1 Heat the olive oil in a large saucepan or Dutch oven over a medium heat. Add the onion slices and cook, stirring occasionally. When the onions have softened, after about 20 minutes, stir in the pieces of eggplant and pepper strips. Reduce the heat, cover the saucepan and cook gently for 15 minutes.

2 Add the tomatoes, zucchini, garlic, lemon juice and sugar. Cook, uncovered, over a low heat, stirring often, for 35–45 minutes until the tomatoes are thick and saucy and the vegetables very soft but still retaining their shape. Season with salt and plenty of black pepper and stir in the chopped parsley. Serve at once.

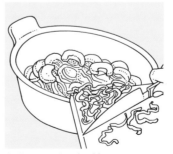

1 Quarter 1 red cabbage, weighing about 2lb (1kg). Cut out the core and shred (page 45). Place the cabbage in a Dutch oven with 1 sliced onion and 1 large cored and sliced cooking apple, such as a Jonathan, Winesap, Greening or Granny Smith.

2 Pour over 2½ cups (600ml) chicken or vegetable stock or water, or try half water and half light ale. Add 1 tablespoon honey, 1 teaspoon caraway seeds, 1 cinnamon stick, salt and freshly ground pepper. Cover and braise for 50 minutes at 325°F, 160°C, or until tender.

STUFFED VEGETABLE DISHES

It was my first visit to Turkey, where it seems as if almost every ingredient is stuffed, which fired my enthusiasm for stuffing vegetables. Stuffed vegetables always provide an element of surprise and ingenuity, and can be a wonderfully dense mingling of flavors. Served cold and drizzled with good olive oil, stuffed vegetables make a perfect first course. Several vegetables like sweet peppers, large onions, tomatoes, eggplant, every type and shape of the squash family and crisp, cup-like leaves of Iceberg lettuce and radicchio, are natural containers for stuffings, but round root vegetables can also be hollowed out and stuffed. Large leaves such as cabbage, spinach, spring greens and vine leaves can be softened and wrapped around stuffings.

Stuffings for juicy containers such as tomatoes should be absorbent enough, for instance containing breadcrumbs, to incorporate the juices which will escape during the cooking. Denser vegetables, however, should be given a more juicy or buttery stuffing to help enrich and moisten them. As well as butter, you can also include a little heavy cream or extra virgin olive oil.

SPICY STUFFED PUMPKIN

A pumpkin makes a good edible cooking container for a spicy meat or vegetable stuffing. A stuffed pumpkin looks extremely impressive but is easy to make and is less labor intensive than smaller, stuffed vegetables. A delectable dish for lunch or supper, it can be served by scooping out pieces of the soft, sweet pumpkin flesh and combining it with a spicy stuffing. This recipe includes a vegetable stuffing but as an alternative you can use a spicy ground meat stuffing.

To prepare a vegetable stuffing, mix thoroughly 1lb (500g) blanched and drained chopped spinach and 1 finely chopped small red pepper with 8oz (250g) soft, white cheese, such as grated part-skim mozzarella, 1-2in (2.5–5cm) piece fresh gingerroot, chopped, 1 large crushed clove of garlic, 2 teaspoons ground mace, 1 teaspoon ground cinnamon, ½ teaspoon cayenne pepper, 2 teaspoons sugar and a good sprinkling of sea salt. These quantities serve 4.

1 *Cut the top off a 3½–4lb (1.7–2kg) pumpkin using a large, sharp knife; reserve the top. Scrape out the seeds and pulp and spoon in the stuffing to fill pumpkin.*

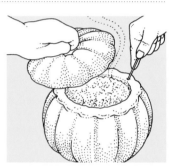

2 *Place the lid on top, rub with oil and put into a roasting pan. Roast at 350°F, 180°C for 45–60 minutes until the pumpkin feels tender when tested with a skewer.*

STUFFED MUSHROOMS

Large white or portabella mushrooms make lovely containers for stuffing. Trim the stalks from 4 large mushrooms and reserve. Fry a small chopped onion and a crushed garlic clove in 2 tablespoons olive oil with 2 chopped celery stalks, 2 chopped strips bacon, the chopped stalks and 1 skinned and chopped tomato until softened. Season well, add 1 tablespoon chopped fresh oregano or sage and 2 tablespoons heavy cream.

The spicy spinach and cheese stuffing inside this whole pumpkin contrasts nicely with its tender, sweet flesh.

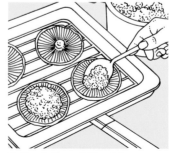

1 *Brush the outside of the mushrooms with more oil and broil on each side for about 5 minutes. Add the filling to the cups, spreading it out.*

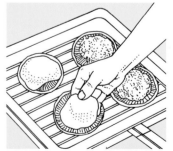

2 *Top with sliced mozzarella cheese. Return to the broiler until just melted, then serve sprinkled with chopped herbs on 4 rounds of hot buttered toast.*

BAKED STUFFED VEGETABLES

Baked stuffed vegetables are an exciting and mouthwatering fusion of taste and texture. You can serve small, stuffed vegetables as a first course, and larger ones such as eggplant and pumpkin as a more substantial main course. When baking stuffed vegetables in a roasting pan, you should put about ½in (1cm) water or olive oil in the bottom of the pan. For zucchini, cut in half lengthwise, scoop out the centers (which you can use in a salad or in the filling) and boil in salted water for 3–4 minutes before stuffing. Bake as for tomatoes (below). All stuffed vegetables are equally good hot or cold. Use the stuffing ideas below or try well-seasoned ricotta cheese mixed with chopped nuts, herbs, spices, sautéed onion slices and so on.

Rice and pine nut-filled dolmades (front) with a stuffed mushroom, a stuffed pepper and a stuffed tomato.

To stuff tomatoes, *slice the tops off very large ones. Carefully scoop out the inside flesh with a teaspoon, leaving the tomato shells as your containers. Fill with your chosen stuffing (see box below), including the tomato pulp. Place in a roasting pan and bake at 400°F, 200°C, for about 15 minutes.*

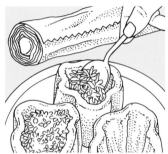

To stuff peppers, *cut the tops off the peppers and scoop out the core and seeds (page 49). Cook the scooped-out peppers and tops in boiling water for 5 minutes, then drain. Stuff the peppers, replace the tops, place in a roasting pan, loosely cover with foil and bake at 375°F, 190°C for 35–45 minutes.*

DOLMADES

An Eastern Mediterranean appetizer, dolmades are grapevine leaves enclosing a rice filling. Buy the leaves in brine in jars. One jar (227g) makes about 35 dolmades. Make a filling of 1 chopped onion fried in olive oil and mixed with ⅔ cup (125g) long grain rice, 3 tablespoons currants, 1 tablespoon each chopped fresh mint and fresh or dried dill, 2 tablespoons pine nuts, ⅔ cup (150ml) water, 1 teaspoon salt and pepper. Boil for 5 minutes.

1 *Drain and rinse the vine leaves in brine, then lay them out rib side up on a board. Put 1 teaspoon of filling at the stalk end of each leaf. Fold in the 2 sides to meet in the center.*

VEGETABLE STUFFINGS

• Spicy, ground meat stuffing is suitable for all kinds of vegetables and leaves. Fry ground beef, pork, veal, lamb or turkey, pressing with a wooden spoon to separate it. Add flavorings such as chopped garlic, sliced onions, chopped tomatoes, tomato puree, pesto sauce, curry paste, miso paste, chopped mushrooms, pine nuts, chopped walnuts, grated citrus rind, or herbs or spices.
• Ground meat mixtures or finely chopped and fried vegetables can be mixed with cooked rice – I always prefer basmati for its nutty flavor and texture (page 108).
• Fruit such as chopped fresh apricots, apples, pears and plums can also be mixed with well-seasoned rice, finely grated lemon rind and chopped green onions for a stuffing.

• Bread crumbs can be an alternative to rice when you want to make stuffings more solid and absorbing. Grated cheese – a combination of Gruyère and Parmesan is good – can be mixed with a stuffing, or sprinkled on top.
• Two vegetable purees of contrasting colors can be used for stuffing hollowed-out roast vegetables, especially if topped with grated cheese.
• One of the most homey but satisfying stuffed dishes, which can make a complete meal, is a whole cabbage. Hollow out the center and fill with a vegetable, rice or ground meat-based stuffing, putting stuffing between the remaining leaves as well as the center. Cook slowly in a covered saucepan with some butter and a little stock.

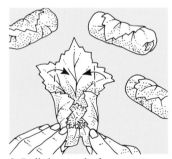

2 *Roll the vine leaf up, starting from the stalk end. Place seam side down in a large shallow pan with a lid. Repeat with the remaining leaves, fitting the rolls close together in a single layer.*

3 *Pour over water just to cover and the juice of ½ lemon and 4 tablespoons olive oil. Weigh down with a heatproof plate, cover and simmer 1 hour. Cool in the pan, then transfer to a plate.*

HOT AND COLD SALAD (40)

This special salad is wonderful for a summer lunch, and I like to serve it with smoked fish or cold poached chicken. The hot and cold effect, part raw and part cooked, brings out much more flavor than a salad would normally have. Shiitake mushrooms, when available, are ideal.   SERVES 4

½lb (250g) French green beans, trimmed
4oz (125g) cremini mushrooms, sliced not
   too thinly
1 small radicchio
2 Bibb lettuces
7 tablespoons extra-virgin olive oil
2 large cloves garlic, finely chopped
Sea salt
Black pepper
8–10 fresh basil leaves, sliced thinly or
   torn
3 tablespoons pine nuts
2 tablespoons sherry vinegar

Steam or boil the beans until just tender but still with a slight crunch to them. Drain and leave on one side. Add the sliced mushrooms to the beans. Separate the leaves of the radicchio and of the Bibb lettuce and arrange alternately around the outside of a fairly shallow large serving bowl or dish.

Very shortly before you want to eat, put 3 tablespoons olive oil in a large frying pan over a medium heat, add the finely chopped garlic and stir for 30 seconds or so.

Add the cooked beans and the mushrooms to the frying pan and cook, stirring, for 2–3 minutes until the mushrooms have softened. Season well with crushed sea salt and plenty of black pepper, then turn the mixture, including any oil and juices, into the serving bowl or dish surrounded by the lettuce leaves. Stir the sliced basil leaves into the hot green bean and mushroom mixture.

Put the empty frying pan back over a high heat and stir the pine nuts in it for a minute or so just to brown them, then scatter the pine nuts onto the salad. Drizzle the remaining 4 tablespoons olive oil all over the salad, including the lettuce leaves, followed by the sherry vinegar. Serve as soon as possible.

GRILLED ZUCCHINI AND GOAT CHEESE WITH WALNUTS (40)

Goat cheese is the best cheese for grilling there is. I also find grilled zucchini acquire a wonderful smoky flavor, so the two combined are unbelievably delicious. You can serve this simple quick recipe as a hot first course or side dish, or, with some crusty bread, as a light lunch or late supper. Small grilled zucchini can be served with drinks.   SERVES 4

1½lb (750g) medium zucchini, trimmed
   and halved lengthwise
Extra virgin olive oil
Salt
6oz (175g) round white goat cheese,
   sliced fairly thin
2 teaspoons dried oregano
¼ cup (25g) walnut pieces, finely
   chopped
Black pepper

Preheat the broiler to its highest heat. Steam or boil the zucchini (page 52) for only 3–4 minutes until bright green but still fairly firm. Drain the zucchini thoroughly and put them into a bowl, then sprinkle with olive oil and salt and toss around to coat well.

Arrange the zucchini on a grill pan, skin sides up, and put under the preheated broiler until the skins are blackened at places all over.

Lay the charred zucchini in a large, shallow flameproof earthenware dish, cut sides upwards, and arrange the slices of goat cheese on top. Sprinkle with the dried oregano and plenty of freshly ground black pepper, and scatter the chopped walnuts all over.

Put the dish back under the hot broiler for just a minute or two until the cheese is melted and browned; be sure to watch carefully while it browns.

Just before serving, drizzle a little olive oil over each zucchini half.

EGGPLANT AND OKRA STEW WITH MINT AND PINE NUTS (49)

This dish always reminds me of my childhood in the Middle East where I first grew to like the unique tastes and textures of both eggplant and the elegant pointed okra (known to me then by its British name of ladies' fingers). This is an easily made dish which can be eaten hot or cold, as an accompaniment to roast meat or chicken, or on its own, served with a green salad and crusty bread to help mop up the juices. There is no need to salt and drain the eggplant. Many people think they do not like okra because they may have had large ones which have been overcooked and become fibrous and slippery but I find they often change their minds when the okra is small, fresh and not overcooked as in this dish.   SERVES 4

1½–1¾lb (750–875g) small eggplant
White wine vinegar
1¼ cups (300ml) water
3 rounded tablespoons tomato puree
4 tablespoons lemon juice
4 tablespoons extra virgin olive oil
14½oz (411g) can chopped tomatoes
2 teaspoons ground coriander
1 rounded teaspoon paprika
1 rounded tablespoon honey
3 large cloves garlic, thinly sliced crosswise
   or lengthwise
1 large handful fresh mint leaves, finely
   chopped
3 tablespoons pine nuts
2–4 pinches cayenne pepper
Salt
8oz (250g) fresh small whole okra, tops
   trimmed (page 49)

Cut the eggplant across in ½in (1cm) slices, then cut the slices in half, sprinkling with wine vinegar as you do so and put to one side. Pour the water into a large, heavy saucepan and add the tomato puree, lemon juice, olive oil, chopped tomatoes, spices and honey. Bring to a boil, stirring well to dissolve the honey. Mix the ingredients thoroughly.

Rinse the eggplant, pat dry and stir into the boiling liquid with the sliced garlic and chopped mint. Cover the pan, reduce the heat and leave to simmer as gently as possible, stirring once or twice, for about 30 minutes until the eggplant are very soft.

Meanwhile, heat a dry frying pan over a medium heat. Toss the pine nuts around in it just until golden brown, then transfer to a plate and set aside until ready to serve.

When the eggplant are soft, remove the pan from the heat and season the juices to taste with cayenne pepper and salt. Return to the heat and bring to a boil again, then mix in the prepared okra, cover the saucepan and boil for 5–10 minutes or just until the okra feel soft when you insert a small, pointed knife, but are still bright green.

Transfer the mixture to a warm serving dish and scatter the toasted pine nuts on top, mixing some of them into the stew.

POTATOES AND FENNEL COOKED WITH CHEESE AND CREAM (57)

This is inspired by the classic *pommes dauphinoise*, where potatoes are cooked in a gratin dish with milk, cheese, cream and a hint of garlic. Cooked fennel is also wonderful with all these ingredients, and this recipe is quicker than most versions of *pommes dauphinoise* as you mix the ingredients together instead of layering them. The nutty taste of Gruyère cheese is an important element. All-purpose potatoes or new potatoes (page 43) are the best to use. For a real treat, use saffron-infused cream, which is made by putting a pinch of saffron threads into the cream, bringing it just up to boiling and then leaving it to cool while the saffron infuses before using.   *SERVES 6*

2lb (1kg) new potatoes, well scrubbed but
    not peeled and sliced about ⅛in
    (2.5mm) thick
1 large bulb fennel, trimmed, quartered
    and thinly sliced
3oz (75g) butter, cut into small pieces,
    plus a little extra
1 large clove garlic
4oz (125g) Gruyère cheese, cut into very
    small pieces
Sea salt and black pepper
1¼ cups (300ml) heavy cream
1 tablespoon grated Parmesan cheese

Steam or boil the potato and fennel slices together for about 10 minutes until they begin to soften. You may need to do this in two batches depending on the size of your steamer or saucepan. Drain and put into a mixing bowl. Stir the butter into the vegetables with a wooden spoon, then crush the garlic into the mixing bowl. Mix in the Gruyère cheese together with a seasoning of crushed sea salt and black pepper.

Spoon evenly into a large, shallow ovenproof dish. Pour over the cream slowly. Dot with a little more butter and sprinkle with the grated Parmesan cheese. Put the dish towards the top of a preheated oven, 350°F, 180°C for 40–50 minutes until the surface is browned in patches.

SPINACH AND PEPPERS IN A SWEET POTATO AND PARSNIP BOWL (53)

This dramatic-looking dish is an exciting way to serve your accompanying vegetables all in one – or, make it into a main course for a lunch or a light supper by arranging anchovy fillets alternately with the strips of red pepper.   *SERVES 4–6*

2–2½lb (1–1.2kg) sweet potatoes, peeled
    and coarsely chopped
1¼–1½lb (625–750g) parsnips, peeled
    and coarsely chopped
1 large red pepper, cored, halved
    lengthwise and seeded (page 49)
2oz (50g) butter
¼–½ whole nutmeg, grated
Sea salt
Black pepper
1lb (500g) spinach, well washed, thick
    stalks removed (page 45), chopped
Anchovy fillets (optional)
2–3 tablespoons extra virgin olive oil

Steam or boil the chopped sweet potatoes and parsnips together until very soft (page 52). Meanwhile, in order to skin the peppers later, put the pepper halves skin side upwards, under a very hot broiler until the skins are charred black (page 55). Remove the peppers from the grill and wrap in a tea towel or place in a paper bag until cool enough to handle.

Meanwhile, puree the sweet potatoes and parsnips with the butter in a food processor (you may have to do this in two or three batches, depending on the capacity of your food processor). Process in the freshly grated nutmeg with sea salt and black pepper to taste.

Spoon the sweet-potato mixture into a wide, shallow, ovenproof serving bowl, spreading it out and up the sides of the bowl with a rubber spatula so as to form a bowl shape within the bowl. Cover the bowl loosely with foil and put into the oven at the lowest possible temperature to keep warm while you skin the cooled peppers.

Remove the blackened skin from the pepper halves with your fingers, then cut the flesh lengthwise into thin strips with a sharp knife. Wrap these pepper strips in a piece of foil and keep warm in the oven with the bowl.

Shortly before you are ready to serve, steam or boil the spinach until soft (page 52), then drain in a colander and squeeze out the excess water.

Remove the bowl with the sweet-potato puree from the oven and spoon the cooked spinach into the center of the root puree. Sprinkle with sea salt and freshly ground black pepper. Remove the pepper strips from the oven and arrange them fanning out like a starburst on top of the spinach, adding the anchovy fillets if desired. Then drizzle the extra virgin olive oil all over the top and serve at once.

CARROT SALAD WITH ORANGES AND GREEN ONIONS *(40)*

This carrot salad was originally designed for my vegetarian daughter but meat-eaters also always enjoy it with roast duck or pork. *SERVES 4–6*

12oz–1lb (375–500g) carrots, coarsely grated
1 tablespoon orange flower water
1 tablespoon sugar
½ teaspoon salt
½ teaspoon cayenne pepper
4 tablespoons lemon juice
2 small oranges, peeled with white pith removed and thinly sliced
1 bunch green onions, trimmed and sliced (use as much of the green part as possible)
Handful flat-leaf parsley, coarsely chopped

Put the grated carrots in a salad bowl. Mix the orange flower water, sugar, salt, cayenne pepper and lemon juice together. Mix thoroughly with the carrots. Arrange the orange slices among the carrots and then sprinkle the whole salad with the green onions and chopped parsley.

EGG, FENNEL AND TOMATO PIE *(40)*

As the puff pastry lid cooks quickly the poached eggs underneath surrounded by fennel and tomatoes magically cook to perfection in this delicious vegetarian main course. Serve with a green vegetable such as spinach, brussels sprouts or crisply steamed cabbage.   *SERVES 6*

6 large eggs
2oz (50g) butter
2 tablespoons olive oil
4 large bulbs fennel, trimmed and thinly sliced
3 large cloves garlic, chopped
1 rounded teaspoon paprika
14½oz (411g) can chopped tomatoes
Salt
Black pepper
2–3 sprigs fresh tarragon or mint leaves, coarsely chopped
17.3oz (490g) package frozen puff pastry, thawed (use half)
1 egg yolk

Poach the eggs for about 2 minutes (page 69) until softly done. Carefully transfer them with a slotted spoon to a bowl of warm water so that they do not go on cooking but remain moist.

Melt 1oz (25g) of the butter and the olive oil together in a large, deep, heavy saucepan over a fairly low heat. Add the fennel pieces and cook, stirring often, for about 10 minutes until soft. Then add the chopped garlic cloves and the paprika and stir for another minute. Stir in the chopped tomatoes with their liquid and bring the mixture to boiling for a minute or two, stirring. Stir in the remaining 1oz (25g) butter.

Remove the saucepan from the heat and leave until the mixture is cool, then season well with salt and freshly ground black pepper and stir in the coarsely chopped tarragon or mint leaves.

Spoon half the fennel and tomato mixture into a pie plate or rectangular ovenproof dish. Lift the eggs from the bowl of water with a slotted spoon, one by one, and let any extra water drip off. Lay the drained, poached eggs on top of the mixture. Spoon the remaining fennel and tomato mixture on top, covering the eggs.

Roll out the puff pastry on a lightly floured surface to roughly the size of the top of the pie plate. Dampen the edges of the pie plate and lay the pastry on top. Trim the edges and use the scraps to roll out and make decorations for the top of the pie (page 245). Make 2 small slits in the pastry to allow steam to escape while baking. Refrigerate the pie for at least 30 minutes or until about 30 minutes before you want to eat.

To make the glaze, stir ½ teaspoon of salt into the egg yolk and then brush all over the decorated pastry crust. Bake the pie just above the center of a preheated oven, 425°F, 220°C, for 20–30 minutes until the puff pastry has risen and has become a dark golden brown. Serve the pie at once.

SPINACH AND PEA PUREE WITH CABBAGE AND PARMESAN *(40)*

The contrast of a smooth, rich vegetable puree topped with a crunchy green vegetable is always delicious, I find. Serve with new potatoes.   *SERVES 6–8*

1lb (500g) spinach, washed and stalks removed if coarse
8oz (250g) frozen peas
4oz (125g) butter, cut up roughly
Salt
Black pepper
1½lb (750g) green cabbage, shredded
½ cup (50g) Parmesan cheese, coarsely grated

Steam or boil the spinach until soft. Add the peas and cook for 4–5 minutes. Drain thoroughly in a colander, pressing the spinach to get rid of excess liquid. Put the spinach and peas into a food processor with the butter and process to a puree. Season with salt and black pepper. Put the mixture into a wide ovenproof serving bowl, cover loosely with foil and keep warm in a very low oven.

Just before serving, slice the cabbage fairly thinly (page 45) and steam or boil for 3–6 minutes just until bright green and still crisp. Drain the cabbage, pile on top of the green puree and sprinkle all over with grated Parmesan and freshly ground black pepper.

BRAISED LEEKS WITH TOMATOES AND BALSAMIC VINEGAR *(59)*

When leeks are cooked slowly in this way, a lovely sweet, mellow flavor emerges, which is enhanced in this recipe by the almost syrupy juices of tomatoes, balsamic vinegar and olive oil. Serve this with roast meats, chicken or game.   *SERVES 4*

1lb (500g) thin leeks, trimmed (retain as much of the green part as possible) and halved lengthwise
4 tablespoons olive oil
2 tablespoons balsamic vinegar
2 teaspoons fennel or dill seeds
Sea salt
Black pepper
2 large tomatoes, skinned (page 48)

Place the leek halves in a heavy Dutch oven or chicken fryer. Add the olive oil, balsamic vinegar, fennel or dill seeds and a sprinkling of sea salt and plenty of black pepper.

Chop the tomatoes thoroughly and spoon the tomatoes and their juice on top of the leeks, but don't mix in. Sprinkle with a little more salt and pepper. Cover the Dutch oven and cook over a very low heat for about 30 minutes, or until the leeks are very soft. Remove the lid of the Dutch oven, increase the heat and boil rapidly until the juices are thick and syrupy. Serve from the Dutch oven or transfer to a shallow baking dish.

SAUTÉED POTATOES WITH CHOPPED GINGER AND SPICES (40)

Potatoes with a firm texture such as waxy all-purpose potatoes are good for this recipe. If you want to sauté the potatoes in advance, you can keep them warm in the oven for up to half an hour, but remember to stir in the chopped parsley and salt just before serving.   *SERVES 4*

2lb (1kg) large potatoes, scrubbed but not
  peeled and cut into 1in (2.5cm) pieces
3 tablespoons olive oil or peanut oil
1oz (25g) butter
2–3 large cloves garlic, chopped finely
2in (5cm) piece fresh gingerroot, peeled
  and finely chopped
3 teaspoons ground cumin
4 teaspoons caraway seeds
Black pepper
Crushed sea salt
Generous bunch parsley, chopped

Steam or boil the potatoes until they are just cooked but not breaking up. Drain well and set aside.

Heat the oil and butter together in a large frying pan or wok over a medium heat. Add the garlic and ginger and stir for 1 minute, then add the ground cumin and caraway seeds and stir for another minute. Add the potatoes and sauté, stirring occasionally, over a medium heat for about 8 minutes until brown. Sprinkle with black pepper. Keep in a warm oven if you don't want to serve at once. Before serving, stir in a sprinkling of crushed sea salt and the chopped parsley. Turn into a warmed serving dish.

LEEK AND CELERIAC PIE (40)

As a main dish, accompanied by a tomato salad (page 51), this gnocchi topped pie is a delicious alternative to meat, fish or poultry, even for non-vegetarians.   *SERVES 4*

FOR THE TOPPING
  2½ cups (600ml) milk
  ¼ whole nutmeg, grated
  3–4 pinches cayenne pepper
  Salt
  4oz (125g) semolina
  3½oz (90g) mature Cheddar cheese,
    grated
  1oz (25g) butter, plus extra
  1 large egg, lightly beaten
  Grated Parmesan
FOR THE FILLING
  2oz (50g) butter
  2 tablespoons olive oil
  12oz (375g) celeriac, peeled and diced
  1½lb (750g) leeks, well washed and cut
    into 1in (2.5cm) slices
  2 teaspoons caraway seeds
  Sea salt
  Black pepper

Lightly grease a 9 x 12in (23 x 30cm) jelly roll pan. Make the gnocchi topping at least 2 hours in advance. Pour the milk into a saucepan with the nutmeg and season with the cayenne pepper and salt. Stir in the semolina. Bring the milk to the boil, then simmer for 3–4 minutes, stirring until thick. Remove from the heat and add the Cheddar cheese, butter and egg. Return to a low heat and stir for 1 minute more. Spread the semolina mixture evenly all over the bottom of the pan. Set aside to cool completely, then chill for at least 30 minutes.

Meanwhile, make the filling. Melt the butter with the olive oil in a large frying pan over a high heat. Add the celeriac and stir for 2–3 minutes, just to brown slightly. Add the leeks and caraway seeds, then cook gently, stirring often, until the leeks are soft. Season with sea salt and plenty of black pepper. Turn into a heated, shallow flameproof dish.

Preheat the broiler. Cut the gnocchi mixture into 2 x 1in (5 x 2.5cm) fingers or into circles.

Arrange in an overlapping pattern all over the leek and celeriac mixture, then dot with butter, sprinkle generously with Parmesan cheese and put under the broiler until golden brown.

ARTICHOKES WITH YELLOW MYSTERY SAUCE (47)

Artichokes always seem to be a treat – especially if they are prepared as cups in this way with the hairy choke and small leaves removed. In this simple recipe, they are eaten cold as a first course and can be prepared and refrigerated several hours in advance. See if anyone can guess what the subtle sauce is made of. If you drink water while eating artichokes, even tap water will taste as if it comes from a mountain spring.   *SERVES 8*

8 large artichokes
4 tablespoons lemon juice, plus extra for
  cooking artichokes
2–2½lb (1–1.2kg) pumpkin, seeds and
  skin removed and flesh coarsely chopped
1 tablespoon sugar
3fl oz (75ml) extra virgin olive oil
7oz (200g) crème fraîche
Salt
Cayenne pepper

Remove the artichoke stalks and for a neat presentation trim the leaves with scissors (page 47). Cook in simmering, lightly salted water with a little lemon juice for 40–45 minutes, until the base leaves separate easily. Drain and cool the artichokes upside down in a colander. Pull out the purple leaves revealing the hairy choke. Scoop out the choke with a teaspoon and discard, rinse the artichokes and drain upside down.

To make the sauce, steam or boil the pumpkin until soft. Then cool under cold water and drain. Put the flesh into a food processor with the 4 tablespoons lemon juice and the sugar and process until smooth, then gradually process in the olive oil. Finally process in the crème fraîche, season to taste with salt and cayenne pepper and chill.

To serve, put the artichokes on individual plates, spoon some yellow sauce into the center of each one and sprinkle a little cayenne pepper on top.

EGGS

When we talk about eggs we nearly always mean hens' eggs, but many other eggs are worth trying, too. Duck eggs, with their blue-tinted whites and distinctive taste, are much liked by some people; and are very popular in the Far East. I have never been offered a goose egg, perhaps because geese are not such prolific layers as hens and ducks, but their eggs are said to be excellent and milder in flavor than ducks' eggs. Both duck and goose eggs make deliciously rich sponge cakes.

One of the best eggs I have ever eaten was a pheasant's egg, which was delicate and creamy. And, I wish I could try pigeons' eggs, which, I am told, are absolutely delicious. After hens' eggs, quails' eggs now seem to be the most readily available commercially. Although quails' eggs are nearly always eaten hard-boiled, poached quails' eggs, either served plain in a salad or dropped into a clear soup, are truly magical. Fried quails' eggs make lovely canapé toppings.

We can now choose between mass produced eggs and free range. I think most people would rather pay more if they can for free range because, even if they can not distinguish any difference in taste and consistency, they prefer the idea of an egg which comes from a happier chicken. Real free-range eggs, which means the chickens have roamed over an open area where they pecked at grass and plants as well as corn, certainly do taste much better.

Very fresh eggs from home-kept chickens, as I knew so well until a fox visited mine one night, are superlative, with whites like whipped cream. My eggs were alluringly dark speckled brown, though the color of the eggshell has no relevance to the quality. Deep yellow yolks, however, are usually a sign that the chicken has been pecking at plenty of greenery.

Whatever theories come and go about eating eggs there can be no doubt that they are a highly nutritious food. Their pure nourishment is not surprising when you think that eggs are, after all, designed to feed the chick until it is strong enough to survive outside the egg. As well as protein eggs contain several important minerals including iron and calcium, and vitamins A, B and D.

Quite apart from the nutritional contribution of eggs to our diet they must also be about the most versatile food. Speedy breakfast-time favorites such as boiled, poached and scrambled eggs, spectacular dinner-party roulades and special occasion popovers and angel food cakes are just a few examples of the adaptability of eggs. Then there are the various types of omelettes and pancakes just waiting for exciting fillings to transform them into satisfying family meals or more extravagant special-occasion dishes. Hard-boiled eggs make wonderful picnic food.

Eggs are also the ultimate magic ingredient in cooking. It is helpful to remember that egg whites stiffen and lighten, whereas egg yolks thicken and enrich. Egg whites also have a wonderful ability to hold air. Whisked whole eggs bind together stuffings, meatballs and purees. Eggs are, of course, vital to many classic cakes, custards and sauces too, and these are described in separate chapters.

Without eggs the ever-popular soufflé would not exist. A soufflé has the same effect as fireworks – it causes amazement and excitement for a few intense moments. A good classic cheese soufflé (page 76) illustrates perfectly the supreme qualities of eggs; the golden appearance, the rich yolky flavor and the miraculously risen foam of the beaten whites which dissolves tantalizingly in your mouth.

Clockwise from top left: Hot Cheese, Egg and Anchovy Roulade, an adaptation of the basic soufflé mixture (page 78), served here with a mixed green salad; Very Special Toad-in-the-Hole (page 78) made with delicious homemade spicy sausages; Stuffed Rice Pancake (page 79) with a light oriental-flavor filling; Eggs and Vegetable Curry (page 79), a variation of poached eggs and garnished with fresh dill; and finally one of the most simple and versatile of all egg dishes, creamy scrambled eggs, here served with slices of smoked salmon and garnished with the feathery leaves of fresh dill. Dill is one of the most successful herbs for accompanying egg dishes.

BOILING *and* POACHING

'Can't even boil an egg' implies that someone can't cook at all. Yet many people can cook very well without managing to cook an egg successfully. Simmering and poaching are two ways of cooking eggs, that, although very simple, do require a bit of practice to get the exact result you want. Always use the freshest possible eggs.

Soft-cooked eggs, where the white is only just opaque and set and the yolk is still runny, are now considered chancy because of the possibility of salmonella poisoning. Intact eggs should be cooked to an internal temperature of 160°F (71°C). Medium-cooked eggs, or *oeufs mollets*, have a firm but not rubbery white, becoming softer towards the center with a semi-soft yolk. They are considered safer and are used in many more elaborate egg dishes. Hard-cooked eggs are set all through but are nicest when they have not been cooked so long that the whites become tough and the yolks powdery. Apart from being staples of packed lunches or picnics, hard-cooked eggs are often sliced for salads. Remember that an egg should not, in fact, be boiled but simmered. It is easier to achieve the consistency you like if you soft cook eggs using the hot-water method as they can be timed more exactly. But when cooking hard-cooked eggs start them off in cold water as this is less likely to result in rubbery whites. Never cook eggs straight from the refrigerator – at room temperature they cook more quickly and are less likely to crack.

HANDLING AND HYGIENE
Store eggs in a cool place. Buy them as fresh as possible and use within three weeks of the packing date. Make sure your hands, the work surfaces, utensils and containers are clean, and do not use any eggs that are cracked. Egg dishes should be eaten as soon as possible after preparation or cooled and then put in the refrigerator.

COOKING EGGS

The hot-water method *is best for soft-cooked eggs. Lower the eggs into a small saucepan of gently boiling water. Reduce the heat to a simmer and time from the moment the water returns to a simmer (see chart right).*

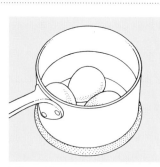

The cold-water method *is less likely to cause cracked shells if the eggs are cold. Put the eggs in a pan with cold water to cover and bring to a simmer. Start timing when the water boils (see chart right).*

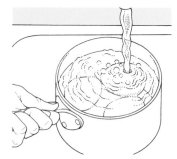

Use the cold-water method *for hard-cooked eggs. Time carefully (see chart right) and when cooked, cool immediately under cold running water to stop the cooking and to prevent black rings from forming around the yolks.*

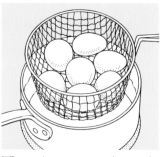

The easiest way *to cook several eggs at once is to use a wire basket. Lower the basket of eggs into a large pan of water, then lift out when the eggs are ready. The more eggs the longer the water will take to simmer.*

TIPS FOR HARD-COOKED EGGS
Although it takes a bit more time, the best way to avoid having a dark ring form around the yolks of your hard-cooked eggs is to cook the eggs in water that is no longer over the heat. Place the eggs in a single layer in a saucepan and add cold water to cover them by 1in (2.5cm). Set aside about 30 minutes until they come to room temperature. Then, heat the water to boiling over medium heat. Turn off the heat, cover the pan, and allow the eggs to stand in the water 15 minutes. Place in cool water immediately.

To make hard- or medium-cooked eggs easier to shell put them into cold water as soon as they are cooked (as you do anyway for hard-cooked eggs) and leave until cold. Tap the shells all over on a hard surface before peeling.

Shelling the eggs under cold running water also helps remove the membrane between the shell and the egg, and cools the egg if it's not quite cold.

Keep the shelled eggs in a bowl of cold water or in a plastic bag in the refrigerator until needed, as this prevents the whites from becoming tough. Pat dry with paper towels before using.

COOKING TIMES FOR BOILED EGGS (in minutes)
Use eggs at room temperature. Use soft-cooked eggs only in baked dishes where they will be heated for an additonal time.

Hot-water method (time from when water returns to boiling)

Egg size	Soft	Medium	Hard
Large	3½	5–6	12
Medium	3	4–5	10
Small	2	3	5

Cold-water method (time from when water first boils)

Egg size	Soft	Medium	Hard
Large	3	4	10
Medium	2	3	8

POACHING EGGS

Use a large frying pan as the more boiling water there is, the less the temperature drops when the eggs are added. Vinegar in the water also helps prevent the whites from spreading. Poached eggs should be cooked until the whites are set and turn opaque and the yolks are just set – test by pressing the yolk gently with your finger.

To keep poached eggs warm put them in a basin of warm water. If you are going to use the eggs cold put them in a basin of cold water so the whites stay supple.

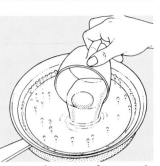

1 Bring a large pan of water and 2–3 tablespoons vinegar to a rolling boil in a deep frying pan. (I like to use a flavored vinegar such as dill which imparts a little of its taste to the eggs.) Break the egg into a cup, then slide it into the pan.

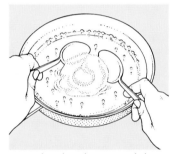

2 Gather the white around the yolk with two spoons if it is spreading too much. Reduce the heat to a simmer, cover and poach for 3–5 minutes.

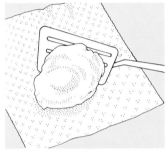

3 Lift out the egg using a slotted spatula or large spoon. Drain well on paper towels if eating at once, otherwise keep in warm or cold water until ready to serve.

USING A POACHER
Butter the cups, set them over simmering water and break in the eggs. Cover and cook gently until the whites are set and the yolks just set.

Or, put buttered metal cookie or biscuit cutters in a frying pan of simmering water. Break an egg into each one and cover the pan. When the eggs are cooked lift them out using a spatula.

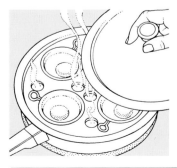

USING BOILED AND POACHED EGGS

• Eggs go extremely well with spinach, as in *oeufs à la Florentine*: poached eggs served on a bed of chopped cooked spinach and topped with a well-flavored cheese sauce (page 196).

• Medium-cooked eggs and poached eggs can be served hot or cold with a variety of sauces: with a good hollandaise sauce (page 200), a puree of grilled and skinned yellow peppers (page 49) mixed with a little sour cream or with a creamy white sauce (page 196) flavored with cheese and grated nutmeg, fresh chopped tarragon, chopped anchovy and a little crushed garlic or well-drained spinach puree and fennel seeds.

• Medium-cooked eggs, poached eggs or sliced hard-cooked eggs can be served cold with homemade mayonnaise (page 202) on a bed of salad greens. You can flavor the mayonnaise with, for example, spices or curry paste or with a little finely chopped spinach.

• For stuffed eggs scoop out the yolks of halved hard-cooked eggs and mix with chopped herbs and anchovies, or with spicy mayonnaise, or with finely chopped green onions and seasoning, then spoon the mixture back in the whites, mounding the mixture.

• As a first course I love cold poached eggs with fresh herbs set in aspic in little dishes – add a little wine or sherry to the aspic for flavor (page 33).

• Add well washed whole raw eggs in their shells to a slow-cooked spicy stew. During the long cooking the eggs absorb the flavors around them and become creamy textured. Before serving shell the eggs, halve them and return them to the dish.

• It is great fun to make tea eggs for salads. Cook the eggs in water with some aromatic tea leaves and whole spices for 3–4 minutes, then remove the eggs, reserving the liquid. Crack the shells all over and continue boiling the eggs in the liquid for another 10 minutes. When shelled the eggs will be beautifully marbled and taste faintly spicy.

• To make a quick egg curry, cover warm medium-boiled eggs with a creamy sauce; boil heavy cream with mild curry paste added to taste or ground turmeric and other Indian spices, then stir in 1 tablespoon plain yogurt and chopped fresh cilantro leaves or flat-leaf parsley.

Poached Egg on Spinach Sauce (page 78) makes an ideal cold first course or light meal. Both eggs and sauce can be made several hours ahead and assembled just before serving.

FRYING, SCRAMBLING *and* BAKING

These three methods of cooking eggs all involve oil or fat, and which oil or fat you use makes a great difference to the flavor of the eggs. Good olive oil such as extra virgin is hard to beat, but you can mix it with sunflower or peanut oil for greater economy. Olive oil and butter together not only taste marvelous but do not burn as quickly as just butter. Bacon fat adds a lot of flavor for frying, and the new flavored oils, if you have any, are also delicious. Butter should be used for scrambling and baking, and you can add a little good oil when baking, too – try hazelnut oil or olive oil that has had cheese and spices infused in it for adding flavor to the eggs.

Fried eggs can vary enormously. The whites can be gently set and white or they can be crisp, frilly and browned at the edges. If you add more oil and fat the eggs will bubble up in a way that I especially like. They can be cooked 'sunny side up'– the 'sunny' bit is the yolk which still shows because the egg hasn't been turned over – or 'easy over', which simply means turned over.

Frying and scrambling eggs must be the easiest and most convenient way of quickly producing a tasty meal. As the heat needs to be transmitted rapidly and evenly to fried foods, pans for frying eggs should be heavy bottomd and made of a heat-conducting metal such as iron or, best of all, stainless-steel lined copper. Non-stick pans are usually not heavy enough and the non-stick surface wears away quickly. The pan should be fairly shallow with sloping sides so that you can remove the cooked eggs easily. A new egg pan should be seasoned before use (page 19) and cleaned thoroughly after each time it is used.

FRYING EGGS

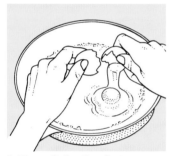

1 *Heat a little oil or fat in a heavy frying pan over a medium heat until hot but not smoking. Break the egg directly into the frying pan.*

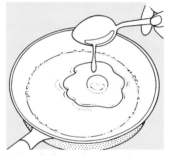

2 *Gently baste the egg with spoonfuls of fat, tipping the pan if necessary, until the top of the egg just begins to set.*

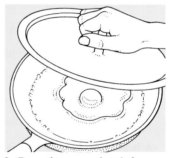

3 *Cover the pan and cook for about 1 minute until the white is set but the yolk is just set. Lift the egg out of the pan using a slotted spatula. Serve at once.*

For an 'easy-over' egg *turn it over carefully using a slotted spatula when the top is set and cook it until done on the other side. Serve at once.*

An egg frying in hot fat sunnyside up.

SERVING FRIED, SCRAMBLED AND BAKED EGGS

• **Fried eggs** are good served on top of full-flavored ingredients, for example a rich ratatouille (page 59) or a puree of root vegetables such as parsnip and celeriac with nutmeg (page 53). When you cut into the egg the flavor mingles with the food beneath and makes a nice combination. Another delicious pairing is sweet potatoes either mashed or sautéed with sliced onions.
• Enhance plain fried eggs by sprinkling them with a little soy sauce, freshly chopped herbs (try oregano) or spiced salt.
• **Tender scrambled eggs** become extra special with any smoked fish mixed in. Smoked salmon with fresh dill makes a delicious addition but add the salmon at the very end so it doesn't become tough.
• Sliced truffles or chopped sorrel sauteed in a little butter is excellent, too.
• For a Far Eastern touch stir a little canned coconut milk into an egg mixture before you scramble it. Season with a pinch or two of your favorite Thai or Indian spice mixture and stir in some chopped fresh cilantro leaves when you take the scrambled eggs off the heat.
• **Baked eggs** are very versatile. As a variation on plain baked eggs make depressions in a wide dish containing a baked spicy ground beef and onion mixture, drop in the eggs and top with cheese or cream. Return to the oven until the eggs are just set.
• For a different kind of baked egg with an Italian flavor, drop the yolk into a buttered ramekin dish, season and sprinkle with oregano, then cover with the stiffly beaten white and grated Parmesan cheese before putting into the oven to bake.
• Eggs can also be baked inside vegetables such as a baked potato (page 56), the inside mashed with cream and seasonings and put back, making an indentation to hold the eggs and a sprinkling of grated cheese on top.

SCRAMBLING EGGS

The tenderest scrambled eggs (page 66) are cooked over a very low heat for at least 5 minutes. The pan should be heavy bottomed for even heat distribution. For a really gentle heat cook the eggs in a bowl set over simmering water.

Before cooking whisk the eggs until they are frothy and season with salt and pepper, adding some fresh chopped herbs such as parsley, tarragon and chives, if you like. Allow 2–3 eggs per person.

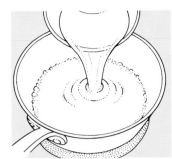

1 *Melt about 1 teaspoon unsalted butter per egg in a pan. When it stops foaming reduce the heat to low and add the whisked eggs. Stir with a wooden spoon.*

2 *Cook over a very gentle heat, stirring the cooked eggs from the sides of the pan into the liquid egg in the middle. (The eggs should reach 182°F, 83°C.)*

3 *Remove the pan from the heat when the eggs are just set (they will go on cooking in the hot pan) and continue to stir for 1 minute. Serve at once.*

BAKING EGGS

Eggs can be baked in several ways. *Oeufs en cocotte* are eggs baked in buttered little ramekins or cocotte dishes. The eggs are seasoned, topped with butter or a little cream and baked in a roasting pan half full of hot water.

Oeufs sur le plat are eggs baked in a shallow dish (right). You can cook ingredients such as bacon, mushrooms and tomatoes in the dish before adding the eggs, or cook others such as ratatouille beforehand and spoon them into the dish before breaking the eggs on top.

1 *To make oeufs en cocotte generously butter the inside of individual ramekin dishes or cocotte dishes using a small piece of waxed paper. It helps if the butter has been softened at room temperature. Preheat the oven to 350°F, 180°C.*

2 *Break 1 or 2 eggs into each ramekin. Season and top with butter and/or cream (season underneath the eggs if only adding butter so as not to speckle the tops). You can also add other flavorings such as finely chopped herbs or chopped anchovies.*

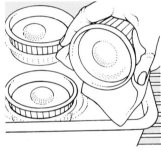

3 *Stand the ramekins in a roasting pan with enough boiling water to come half way up the sides. Bake for 8–10 minutes until the whites are firm and the yolks are just set. Test by tipping the ramekin a little; the white of egg should hold.*

BAKED EGGS IN A DISH

Melt about 1 tablespoon butter in a medium-sized gratin dish in a preheated oven, 400°F, 200°C. Add 2 eggs, spooning the butter over them. Season, cover with a little cream and return to the oven for 6–8 minutes until the whites are firm and the yolks are just set.

If you are combining the eggs with other ingredients that need cooking it is best to cook the other ingredients first, either in the same dish or separately. Then break the eggs on top of the cooked ingredients. Eggs cooked in this way will take slightly longer to cook.

Heavy cream and chives quickly and easily turn these baked eggs in a dish into a light meal.

OMELETTES

There are at least three very different kinds of omelette. A classic French omelette is light, soft and creamy. It is cooked very quickly and folded. It is served either folded over a filling such as cheese or mushrooms, or with added herbs, or completely plain. A fluffy soufflé omelette is much lighter than a classic omelette as the egg whites are beaten separately and folded into the beaten yolks before it is cooked. It is served sweet or savory, and can have a variety of fillings.

Both classic and soufflé omelettes must be eaten immediately after they are cooked so that they will remain fresh-tasting and very light in texture.

Flat omelettes are quite a different thing and even more versatile. With these the eggs do not provide the whole texture of the dish but hold a wide variety of fillings together. These omelettes are like a complete meal. Flat omelettes are best cooked slowly and can be served warm or lightly cooled. They are very useful to take on picnics, cut into wedges like a cake. There are several different types. The Italian *frittata* is about 1in (2.5cm) thick and can

either be plain or mixed with vegetables in the pan. The Spanish *tortilla* is a thicker, heartier dish – it is usually packed with cubes of cooked potato and fried onion, though it can also contain other ingredients. The Arabian *eggah* is even more like a cake with fillings of vegetables, noodles, meat and spices.

The pan used for French and soufflé omelettes should not be larger than 9in (23cm) in diameter as handling a bigger omelette is very difficult. This size pan is just right for a four to five egg omelette. Allow two or three eggs per person. The pan should be made of cast iron with sloping sides so you can slide the omelette out easily.

SEASONING AN OMELETTE PAN
A new omelette pan should be seasoned to prevent sticking before it is used: cover the base with a little oil and coarse salt and heat slowly until the oil is hot, then wipe the pan dry with crumpled paper towels (page 19). The pan should be simply wiped out, not washed, each time it is used and kept only for omelettes or plain fried eggs.

CLASSIC FRENCH OMELETTE

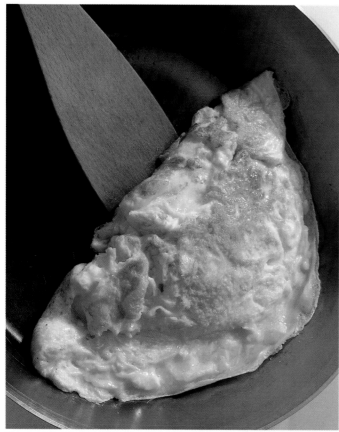

Serve a classic French omelette as soon as it is cooked. Gently *flip the omelette out of the pan onto a plate. Finely grated cheese can be spread over the cooked omelette just before it is folded over.*

1 *Heat 1 tablespoon butter per 2 eggs in a hot pan until foaming. Add the beaten, seasoned eggs and stir with a fork until they start to thicken.*

2 *Working quickly, pull back the egg that sets and tip the pan so that the uncooked egg pours to the sides of the pan. Continue until the mixture is completely set.*

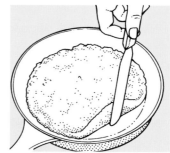

3 *Let the omelette cook for a minute or so until the bottom is slightly browned and the top completely set; test with a spatula. If using a filling, spoon it over half the omelette.*

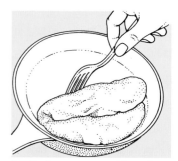

4 *Tilt the pan to one side and use a fork or spatula to roll up or fold the omelette. Slide the omelette carefully out of the pan onto a warm plate and serve immediately.*

SOUFFLÉ OMELETTE

Separated eggs can be whisked into a light, fluffy soufflé omelette. Allow 2 or 3 eggs per omelette.

Separate the eggs. Beat the yolks with some pepper until thick. In another bowl, whisk the egg whites with the salt until soft peaks form. Fold the whites carefully into the yolks, using a large spoon.

Heat an omelette pan, then add 1 tablespoon butter per 2 or 3 eggs. When it has stopped foaming, pour in the egg mixture. Cook gently over a low heat, without stirring, for 3–4 minutes until the underside of the omelette is pale golden and the top set. Check by lifting the edge

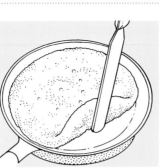

carefully with a spatula.

Tipping the pan, fold over the omelette and slide it out onto a warm plate. For a firmer set place the omelette under a hot broiler before folding. Serve at once. If you like, add a sweet or savory filling just before folding the omelette over. Have the filling warm and ready.

FRITTATA

This needs more filling than a classic French omelette. The following recipe is an example of what you can do but there are endless possible variations. Use fresh-cooked ingredients or leftover foods such as sliced potato, peas, cauliflower, spinach and ham.

To make the filling, fry the potatoes in half the oil in a heavy-bottomed frying pan, turning until well browned, then remove. Fry the onions and pepper in the remaining oil for 5–7 minutes until softened, then cool a little. Beat together the eggs,

grated Parmesan cheese, onions and pepper, herbs and seasoning. Serves 3.

12oz (375g) cooked potatoes, peeled and diced
4 tablespoons olive oil
2 red onions, sliced thinly
1 red or green pepper, cored, seeded and thinly sliced (page 49)
6 eggs, beaten
¼ cup (25g) Parmesan cheese, grated
1 tablespoon chopped fresh parsley or marjoram
1oz (25g) butter
Salt and ground black pepper

OMELETTE FLAVORINGS AND FILLINGS

• Classic fillings for French omelettes such as cheese and mushrooms can hardly be improved upon, but there is still plenty of room for improvisation. I like onions sautéed in good olive oil until soft, or thin slivers of Parma ham, or salami or ham.
• Add color to a French omelette with red onion rings and sautéed and buttered, lightly blanched tiny broccoli florets.
• Crème fraîche mixed with fresh chopped herbs, peeled and chopped tomatoes with fresh basil, or flakes of poached smoked cod all taste good in omelettes.
• Try cooked pumpkin mashed with butter, grated Parmesan cheese, caraway seed to taste and plenty of black pepper for an omelette filling.
• Ratatouille, finely chopped sautéed eggplant with cumin seed, grated zucchini seasoned and sautéed in butter for 30 seconds with 1 tablespoon of pine nuts, slivers of cooked chicken breast with fresh tarragon, chopped hard-cooked eggs with plenty of fresh dill or fresh cilantro and cooked, well-drained spinach mixed with a little olive oil all add a slight Mediterranean flavor to omelettes.
• Some chopped fresh sorrel or a little sprinkling of whole spices added to the uncooked egg mixture also makes a more unusual omelette – caraway, fennel and dill seeds all go well with eggs.
• The classic way to serve a light fluffy soufflé omelette is

with warm jam, but a delicious savory alternative is to surround it with a pool of fresh tomato sauce (page 206) flavored with parsley and basil or marjoram.
• For a Mediterranean flavor for a frittata, add fried eggplant cubes with Feta cheese cubes, black olive slivers and dried oregano.
• Cooked potatoes mixed with well-drained spinach, crushed garlic, mild curry paste and chopped fresh mint make an Indian-flavored frittata.
• To me, the nicest Spanish *tortillas* are filled to bursting with cooked potatoes and onions with perhaps a few slices of chorizo sausage included among them. They are wonderful for a beach picnic. These omelettes can also contain bacon, sweet peppers, tomatoes, spinach and peas and are a useful way to use up cooked chicken.
• Middle Eastern *eggahs* are cooked gently in a covered frying pan and are filled with either vegetables – often a single vegetable rather than a mixture in one omelette – such as eggplant, fava beans, leeks, zucchini and spinach, or spiced meats. Cook spice mixtures in the pan – minced or sliced chicken with potatoes or noodles – and mix the eggs into them or pour the eggs over them. Suitable spices to use are ground cumin, coriander, caraway, cardamom and paprika, with plenty of chopped fresh herbs – mainly mint, flat-leaf parsley or cilantro leaves.

1 *Melt the butter in the pan and when it stops foaming add the egg mixture, stirring lightly as you pour. Reduce the heat and scatter the fried potatoes over the egg.*

2 *Cook the egg mixture slowly for 10–15 minutes. When nearly set, cover the pan with a large heatproof plate and invert the frittata onto the plate.*

3 *Slide the frittata back into the pan and cook the other side. Or, if the omelette sticks to the bottom of the pan, place it under a hot broiler to brown the top.*

4 *Remove from the heat. Cut the frittata in wedges and serve it warm straight from the pan, or cool slightly and serve with a salad or take on a picnic.*

BATTERS

A batter is basically a mixture of flour and liquid with a pouring consistency. For most pancakes and crêpes eggs are vital to add richness, flavor and air for a light texture. Add melted butter for even more richness. Water makes the batter lighter and milk makes it smoother.

Mixing flour with water and a little oil and folding in a stiffly whisked egg white makes a very light, crisp coating batter for deep-frying vegetables. For a richer coating batter the egg yolk can be mixed into the flour and water or milk first. Using lager or beer instead of the water in a Yorkshire pudding batter not only makes the pudding rise more dramatically but also adds extra crispness and some subtle flavor, too.

A food processor makes batter far more swiftly than whisking by hand. However, a batter should never be over beaten – which can happen in the processor – as the gluten in the flour develops and makes the batter tough when cooked. Clarified butter or the high fat butter used by chefs is often recommended for cooking pancakes as it does not burn but if you do not have any, use a mixture of oil and butter, which won't burn as quickly as butter alone. Pancakes can be made ahead and frozen between sheets of waxed paper ready to thaw when needed.

USING THE RIGHT PAN
A crêpe pan should be shallow with sloping sides. Ideally, the pan should be made of cast iron but light enough to let you turn the pancake over by tossing it in the air if you like, though turning it with a wide spatula is perfectly satisfactory and much less risky. A new pan should be seasoned and then cared for in the same way as an omelette pan (page 72).

CRÊPES

The secret of making good wafer-thin crêpes is to heat the pan first and to use batter the consistency of light cream. All-purpose wheat flour produces the soft crêpes we are most used to and buckwheat flour the thin, lacy crêpes of Brittany. Makes 15 7-8in (18–20cm) crêpes.

1 cup (125g) all-purpose flour
Pinch of salt
1 egg
1¼ cups (300ml) milk or milk and water mixed
Butter or oil for greasing

1 Sift the flour and salt into a large bowl. Make a well in the center and break in the egg. Using a whisk or wooden spoon beat the egg, gradually drawing in flour from the sides and slowly adding the liquid.

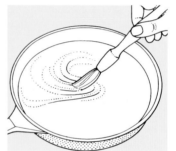

2 When the batter is smooth heat a crêpe pan or small- to medium-size flat frying pan steadily until hot but not smoking. Grease it lightly with butter or butter and oil mixed, using a pastry brush or paper towel.

3 Hold the pan in one hand and with the other ladle about 2 tablespoons batter into the hot pan, swirling to coat the pan with a thin layer of batter. Cook the crêpe until set and small holes appear on the surface.

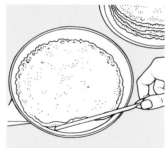

4 Loosen the crêpe with a spatula and flip over. Cook the second side until lightly browned. Remove from the pan and stack under a tea towel. Reheat the pan, regreasing as necessary and repeat with more of the mixture.

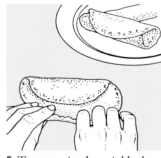

5 To serve, simply sprinkle the crêpes with sugar and lemon juice and roll up. Or, spoon a favorite filling in the center of each, then fold in half, quarters or thirds. If made in advance, the crêpes can be served at room temperature.

POPOVERS

Using bread flour gives a better rise, while a second egg makes it richer. This batter may also be used to make Yorkshire pudding
This recipe makes 18 popovers.

1 cup (125g) all-purpose flour
½ teaspoon salt
1 or 2 eggs
1¼ cups (300ml) milk and water mixed half and half
Oil, drippings or lard

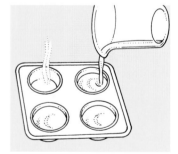

Mix the batter as for crêpes (left). Letting the batter stand for 30 minutes after making helps make lighter popovers. Put a little oil or fat in each pan and place in a preheated oven, 425°F, 220°C until just smoking. Fill each pan three-quarters full with batter. Bake for 20–25 minutes until risen and golden brown.

PANCAKES

These are made with a thicker batter than crêpes and traditionally are cooked on a griddle or you can use a heavy-bottomed frying pan. Flavorings such as honey, grated lemon rind, apple pie spice, grated apple or raisins can be added. This recipe makes about 20 pancakes.

2 cups (250g) all-purpose flour
Pinch of salt
½ teaspoon baking soda
1 teaspoon cream of tartar
1 egg
1 cup (300ml) milk
1 tablespoon sugar
Oil for greasing

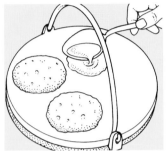 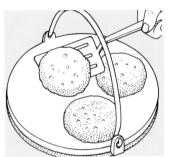

1 *Mix the batter as for crêpes (opposite). Heat a griddle or frying pan until hot but not smoking. Lightly grease with oil. Drop 2 or 3 tablespoons batter onto the griddle at a time.*

2 *Cook until holes appear on top and the batter has set. Flip the pancakes over and cook the other side for about 1 minute. Remove to a wire rack. Reheat the griddle and repeat with more batter.*

WAFFLES

To make about 10 waffles, mix the batter as for crêpes (opposite) using 2 cups (250g) self-rising flour, 2 egg yolks, 1¼ cups (300ml) milk, 1 tablespoon vanilla sugar (page 235) and 2oz (50g) melted butter. Quickly fold in 2 stiffly beaten egg whites with a large metal spoon to make a consistency like heavy cream.

Grease and heat the waffle iron over a gas flame or on an electric element, or use an electric waffle iron, following the manufacturer's instructions; turn the non-electric iron over so both sides are very hot. Hand-held irons made of aluminum will heat more quickly than those made of cast iron. Spoon in the batter without overfilling. Cook for 1½–2 minutes or until it stops steaming, turning once. If the iron does not open easily, cook for ½–1 minute longer.

CRÊPE FILLINGS AND FLAVORINGS

• For savory crêpe fillings I especially like cooked vegetables, such as spinach or broccoli, added to seasoned cream cheese or crème fraîche, or try chopped leeks sautéed slowly in butter with plenty of freshly ground black pepper and chopped chives stirred in at the last moment.
• Try peeled chopped tomatoes cooked in butter to a thick puree with cubes of crisp fried bacon stirred in at the end, or thinly sliced and softly sautéed bulb fennel mixed with fennel leaves and grated Parmesan cheese.
• Softly sautéed onions with 1 teaspoon of sugar added with the seasoning.
• Sliced cremini or shiitake mushrooms and chopped walnuts fried with chopped garlic and fresh ginger and a little ground coriander or cardamom.
• Fish and meat fillings include cooked and flaked smoked haddock or cod either mixed with chopped herbs or watercress or in a thick, creamy white sauce; pieces of smoked salmon or chopped anchovy stirred into crème fraîche with plenty of chopped dill.
• Try mixtures of seafood such as fresh mussels, prawns and scallops, or ham in a thick cheese sauce (page 196).
• Filled crêpes can be covered with a sauce. White sauce (page 196) is always adaptable with added cream, grated cheese, pureed sweet peppers, tomato puree and paprika, chopped spinach and herbs.
• A simple sauce of heavy cream, seasoned and boiled for 2–3 minutes to thicken slightly, with or without fresh herbs, can also be poured over filled crêpes.
• Seasoned crème fraîche, sour cream and plain yogurt all make quick sauces, but do not let them boil.
• A quick Italian-style filling is crumbled Gorgonzola cheese with slivers of Parma ham.

Feathery light crêpes can be folded or rolled to enclose a savory or sweet filling. Here, they are folded in quarters around a filling of sautéed mushrooms, bacon and tomatoes with fresh basil.

SOUFFLÉS

The dramatic rise of a soufflé and its brief moment of glory are unparalleled. The magic is caused by hot air expanding with stiffly beaten egg whites, which once beaten must be folded very carefully into the base sauce to produce maximum volume. Resist the temptation to open the oven door until five minutes before the end of the cooking time or your soufflé may collapse before your eyes!

Either savory or sweet flavorings can be used in soufflés. The flavoring ingredient must be intense as it will be diluted by the eggs, and it must be the right consistency – just soft enough to fall from the spoon, neither thicker nor thinner. The base sauce should be thin but not runny, and easily drop off a spoon. The volume of the strongly flavored base should never be more than half the volume

of the beaten egg whites and there should ideally be roughly one-third more egg whites than yolks. Beaten pasteurized egg whites can also be combined with gelatin to make chilled soufflés (page 229).

If you want to serve a soufflé at a dinner party you can prepare it up until after the egg yolks are stirred in well beforehand so that you only have to beat and fold in the egg whites and put it in the oven after your guests have arrived. You can even fold in the beaten egg whites an hour or two beforehand and keep the prepared, uncooked soufflé in the refrigerator until you are ready to cook it.

Roulades, which can be made with the same soufflé mixture, are baked in jelly-roll pans, then rolled around a filling. Roulades are even more adaptable than hot soufflés as they can also be served cold.

CLASSIC CHEESE SOUFFLÉ

Use a 1 quart (1.2 liter) classic soufflé dish. Serves 2 as a main course or 3–4 as an appetizer.

1oz (25g) butter
3 tablespoons all-purpose flour
½ teaspoon curry powder, dry mustard or ground nutmeg
Pinch of cayenne pepper
7fl oz (200ml) milk
½ cup (50g) sharp Cheddar cheese, grated
¼ cup (25g) Parmesan cheese, grated
4 eggs, separated
Salt and black pepper
1-2 extra egg whites (optional)
Bread crumbs

1 *To make the base sauce melt the butter in a medium-size saucepan, then stir in the flour and the curry powder, mustard or ground nutmeg and cayenne pepper. Cook for 1 minute, stirring constantly until the roux has a sandy texture.*

2 *Gradually add the milk, stirring until the sauce thickens, then simmer for 2 minutes. Remove from the heat, mix in all but a spoonful of the 2 cheeses until melted, then beat in the egg yolks. Season well with salt and black pepper.*

3 *Beat the egg whites until they form stiff, but not dry, peaks. (Include the extra egg whites if you want a very high soufflé.) Beat 1 tablespoon of egg white into the sauce to loosen it. This makes it easier to fold in the whites without losing any air.*

Few dishes make such an impressive start to a dinner party as a well-risen golden classic cheese soufflé. Adding extra egg whites helps to lift the soufflé further above the dish's rim.

4 *With a large metal spoon, gently fold in the rest of the beaten egg whites, turning the spoon in a figure eight movement. Butter the soufflé dish. You can coat the sides with dry bread crumbs to help the soufflé 'climb' up the side of the dish as it rises during cooking.*

5 *Spoon the soufflé into the prepared dish and sprinkle the top with the reserved cheese. Bake in a preheated oven, 375°F, 190°C for 20–25 minutes, until well risen and golden brown (see left) – the soufflé should wobble very slightly when shaken. Serve instantly.*

ROULADE

The classic cheese soufflé mixture (opposite) can also be used to make a savory roulade. Unlike a soufflé, a roulade can be made in advance and cooled to serve with a filling at room temperature. If you do this, roll up the roulade while still hot, incorporating the bottom piece of waxed paper inside. Before serving unroll the roulade, discard the paper, add the filling, then reroll.

Use a medium-sized jelly-roll pan (14 x 10½in/35 x 27cm). Serves 4–6.

1 *Cut a sheet of waxed paper about 2in (5cm) larger than the pan and snip the corners diagonally. Grease the pan and fit in the paper, folding in the corners. Grease the paper. Spread the soufflé mixture in the pan.*

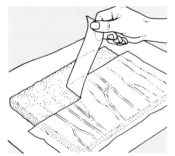

2 *Bake the roulade in a preheated oven, 375°F, 190°C for 15–17 minutes, until just firm to the touch. Turn out carefully onto a large sheet of waxed paper. Peel off the lining paper gently in strips and discard if it looks as if it is damaging the roulade.*

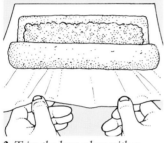

3 *Trim the long edges with a knife. Cover with a clean tea towel and allow to cool slightly. Spread with the chosen filling (see box). Fold over one edge of the roulade then roll up, holding the paper firmly underneath. Transfer to a serving plate and serve sliced.*

BEATING EGG WHITES

Soufflés rise to their impressive heights because of the air trapped in beaten egg whites. Using a food processor to beat egg white will not produce enough volume for a soufflé, though electric or rotary beaters give excellent results. The best-textured egg whites, however, are produced by whisking with a balloon whisk in a large copper bowl. Lift the whisk out of the whites each time, using large circular sweeps of your arm to incorporate as much air as possible. A small amount of salt helps to make the whites more stable and so able to trap the air longer.

FLAVORINGS AND FILLINGS

• Stir whole grain mustard, chopped fresh chives and cayenne pepper into a cheese soufflé base before you fold in the egg whites.

• Pureed root vegetables, especially parsnips, make a delicious soufflé base if mixed with Indian spices.

• Chopped smoked fish or shellfish such as crabmeat or fresh mussels added to the egg yolk base are excellent in a soufflé.

• Red peppers boiled until soft with several whole cloves of garlic and then pureed and added to the egg yolks and flour with a little paprika and cayenne pepper make a lovely colored soufflé.

• Sauces can often be very good finishing touches for soufflés – try heated cream with a soft white garlic cheese melted in it, a very smooth vegetable puree with added cream, a curried or cheese white sauce (page 196) with added cream, or a traditional rich hollandaise sauce (page 200).

• Put a little sauce such as homemade fresh tomato sauce (page 206) in the bottom of the prepared dish before adding the soufflé mixture.

• Easy and impressive roulades can be made by substituting a vegetable puree (page 53) for the butter, flour and egg mixture of the classic soufflé recipe. Fill with a hot mushroom béchamel sauce (page 196) or a garlic and herb cream cheese and serve with a fresh tomato sauce (page 206).

• Cream and cottage cheeses, fresh soft goat cheeses and seasoned crème fraîche make excellent fillings for roulades.

HINTS AND TIPS

Any trace of grease in the beating bowl will prevent the egg whites from rising properly, so wash it out before use with very hot water and a drop of detergent or wipe with a little vinegar. Dry the bowl thoroughly. Beaten egg whites should form slightly soft peaks. If the whites are beaten too much, they will be dry and will not fold well into the sauce.

The classic cheese soufflé recipe (opposite) can be cooked in individual ramekin dishes instead of one large dish: place the ramekins on a baking sheet and cook for about 12 minutes only. Individual unbaked soufflés can be frozen in freezerproof ramekin dishes but add an extra egg white when beating. Thaw at room temperature for 1 hour, then bake as usual.

Egg whites for soufflés should be stiffly beaten until the peak just slightly falls over when the beater or whisk is lifted. If they are not beaten enough the soufflé will not rise.

VERY SPECIAL TOAD-IN-THE-HOLE (66)

Instead of using commercial sausages, make your own spicy ones out of ground pork and red and yellow peppers.   SERVES 4

FOR THE SAUSAGES
  1lb (500g) ground pork
  1 each small–medium red and yellow
    peppers, cored, seeded and finely
    chopped (page 49)
  1 clove garlic, finely chopped
  2 teaspoons ground coriander
  1 teaspoon caraway seeds
  Sea salt and black pepper
  1 small egg
  Olive oil
FOR THE BATTER
  ⅔ cup (150ml) milk
  ⅔ cup(150ml) beer
  1 cup (125g) all-purpose flour
  ½ teaspoon salt
  2 large eggs
  Black pepper

Put the pork into a mixing bowl. Add the peppers, garlic, and coriander and caraway seeds and season generously with salt and pepper. Mix together thoroughly. Beat the egg lightly, then mix into the meat mixture.

Using wet hands form the mixture into sausage shapes. Rub them all over with a little olive oil. Spoon 2 tablespoons olive oil into a roasting pan and add the sausages in a single layer. Put the pan just above the center of a preheated oven, 425°F, 220°C for 10–15 minutes, turning the sausages once so they begin to brown on both sides.

Meanwhile, make the batter. Mix the milk and beer together. Sift the flour and salt into a food processor and add the eggs and half the liquid. Process until smooth, then gradually pour in the remaining liquid and process again thoroughly. Season with pepper. When the sausages are ready pour the batter around them. Bake for 40–45 minutes until the batter is well risen and golden brown.

HOT CHEESE, EGG AND ANCHOVY ROULADE (66)

Serve this light cheesy roulade either as a hot first course or as the main course of a light meal accompanied by a mixed salad. The roulade can be made, filled, then reheated just before serving so you can prepare it ahead, only having to put it briefly in the oven before serving. Use a 14 x 10½in (35 x 27cm) jelly-roll pan.   SERVES 6

FOR THE ROULADE
  Butter
  Grated Parmesan cheese
  1 cup (50g) fresh white breadcrumbs
  6oz (175g) sharp Cheddar cheese, finely
    grated
  4 large eggs, separated
  ⅔ cup (150ml) light cream
  3 pinches cayenne pepper
  Salt
  2 tablespoons warm water
FOR THE FILLING
  8oz (250g) cottage or cream cheese
  4 hard-cooked large eggs, chopped
  2 2oz (50g) cans anchovy fillets
  Large handful of chopped parsley
  2 tablespoons chopped fresh oregano
    or 2 teaspoons dried oregano
  Black pepper
  Olive oil

Butter the jelly-roll pan. Line with greased waxed paper or baking parchment (page 77) and sprinkle with grated Parmesan cheese.

Mix the bread crumbs and Cheddar cheese together, then add the egg yolks and cream. Mix lightly but thoroughly and season with the cayenne pepper and salt to taste. Stir in the warm water.

Put the egg whites in a large bowl. Add a pinch of salt and beat until they stand in soft peaks, then gradually fold into the cheese and yolk mixture using a metal spoon. Spoon into the prepared pan and bake in the center of a preheated oven, 400°F, 200°C for 10–15 minutes until risen and just firm to a light touch. Remove and cool slightly – it will shrink a little during cooling – then cover with a clean, damp tea towel and leave the roulade until cool.

Meanwhile, make the filling. Put the cottage or cream cheese in a bowl and soften slightly with a wooden spoon, then stir in the chopped eggs. Pour the oil from the anchovy cans into the mixture. Chop the anchovies finely, then mix

them in thoroughly with the herbs. Season with plenty of freshly ground black pepper – no salt, as the anchovies should make the mixture salty enough already.

When the roulade is cool loosen the edges with a knife. Sprinkle a large sheet of waxed paper or baking parchment evenly with Parmesan cheese and turn out the roulade onto the paper. Using a spatula spread the filling over the roulade to within ½in (1cm)) of the edges, then roll up from a short end by folding over one edge, then rolling, holding the paper underneath. Again with the help of the paper push the roll gently onto a large flat ovenproof dish. Brush the roll all over with olive oil and sprinkle with Parmesan cheese.

Shortly before you are ready to eat put the roulade in the center of a preheated oven, 375°F, 190°C, for 20 minutes. To serve cut across in thick slices using a sharp knife.

POACHED EGGS ON SPINACH SAUCE (69)

The element of surprise in this cold first course is a subtle puree of spinach and green pepper with just a bite of fresh green chilli.   SERVES 6

  5 tablespoons extra virgin olive oil
  1 large green pepper, cored,
    seeded and finely chopped (page 49)
  1 small fresh green chili, stemmed,
    seeded and coarsely chopped (page 49)
  1lb (500g) spinach, stemmed and washed
  1 clove garlic, crushed
  1 teaspoon sugar
  1 tablespoon white wine vinegar
  Salt
  6 large eggs
  1¼ cups (300ml) sour cream
  6 sprigs flat-leaf parsley, cilantro,
    fennel or dill leaves to garnish

Put 2 tablespoons of olive oil into a heavy frying pan over a medium heat. Add the green pepper and chili and fry gently, stirring often, until the pepper is completely soft but not browned. Move to one side of the pan.

Steam or boil the spinach leaves until soft, then drain and press out as much liquid as possible. Put into a food processor with the garlic, the fried peppers and their oil and the sugar and process to a smooth puree. Finally, process in the wine vinegar and the remaining olive oil. Season to taste with salt and leave until cold.

Meanwhile, poach the eggs for about 3–5 minutes until cooked (page 69) – the yolks should be opaque but feel just set to touch in the center. (I would poach the eggs one by one to get them right.) Put them straight into a bowl of cold water to stop further cooking, then refigerate.

Not more than an hour or so before you eat drain the eggs and gently pat dry with paper towels. Spoon the spinach and pepper puree onto individual plates, then swirl a little sour cream on top. Place a poached egg in the center and garnish with an herb sprig.

STUFFED RICE PANCAKES *(66)*

Using rice flour instead of wheat flour makes light, bubbly pancakes ideal for this stuffing with its delicate Far Eastern character. Serve the pancakes with a crisp green vegetable such as broccoli.   *SERVES 6*

FOR THE PANCAKES
  1¼ cups (150g) rice flour
  ¼ cup (25g) all-purpose flour
  1 level teaspoon salt
  3 pinches cayenne pepper
  1 large egg, beaten
  2 cups (450ml) milk
  Peanut oil
FOR THE FILLING
  2oz (50g) butter
  2 cloves garlic, chopped
  1in (2.5cm) piece fresh gingerroot,
    peeled and chopped
  ½ cup (150ml) canned coconut milk
  1 cup (250ml) milk
  Cayenne pepper
  Salt
  1 cup (125g) frozen baby peas
  6 hard-cooked large eggs, finely chopped
  Generous handful of fresh cilantro leaves,
    chopped
  3–4 tablespoons plain yogurt

To make the pancakes put the rice and wheat flours, salt and cayenne pepper in a bowl and mix thoroughly. Stir in the beaten egg and a little milk. Continue to add the rest of the milk, stirring, until you have a smooth, thin batter.

Pour just enough peanut oil into a heavy 8in (20cm) frying pan to coat the bottom. Put the pan over a high heat until the oil is smoking then reduce the heat a little. Stir the batter – it must be stirred before cooking each pancake otherwise the rice flour sinks to the bottom – and ladle about 2 tablespoons into the pan, swirling the pan immediately to coat the bottom. Cook until the batter is set and small holes start to appear, then loosen with a spatula and flip over. Cook the second side until lightly browned. Continue with the rest of the batter, placing the pancakes on a plate under a clean tea towel when they are ready. Add a little oil to the pan as necessary and adjust the heat if you find that the pancakes are browning too quickly.

To make the filling, put half the butter in a small pan over a low heat. Add the garlic and ginger and stir for a minute or so, then add the coconut milk and the milk. Stir over a low heat until heated through. Remove from the heat and season with cayenne pepper and salt. Boil the peas for 2–3 minutes. Put them in a bowl with the chopped eggs, add the coconut milk mixture and stir together. Taste and adjust the seasoning if necessary. Reserve a few whole cilantro leaves to garnish. Chop the rest coarsely and stir into the mixture.

Butter a large shallow ovenproof dish. Place the pancakes out on a flat surface and divide the filling evenly among them. Roll up the pancakes around the filling. Lay them close together in the dish and dot with the remaining butter. Cover with foil.

About 30 minutes before you want to eat put the dish in the center of a preheated oven, 375°F, 190°C for 25 minutes. Just before serving spoon the yogurt down the center of the pancakes and sprinkle with the reserved cilantro leaves.

EGGS AND VEGETABLE CURRY *(66)*

Eggs go well with spices, and the sweet flavor of parsnips, the main vegetable here, also lends itself specially well to spices. Dill is not a typically Indian herb but I find it goes well with this dish.   *SERVES 4*

  6–8 cardamom pods
  2 teaspoons coriander seeds
  1 teaspoon cumin seeds
  3oz (75g) butter
  2 red onions, finely chopped
  1lb (500g) parsnips, diced
  1 fresh green chili, stemmed, seeded and
    finely chopped (page 49)
  2 large cloves garlic, finely chopped
  1lb (500g) tomatoes, peeled and coarsely
    chopped (page 48)
  2 teaspoons sugar
  Salt
  Good handful of fresh dill, chopped
  4 large eggs

Grind the cardamom pods and coriander and cumin seeds finely in a coffee grinder or a mortar and pestle. Melt the butter over a medium heat in a large, heavy pan. Add the onions and stir for a few minutes until softened, then add the parsnips, ground spices, chili and garlic and stir for another minute or two.

Stir in the tomatoes and sugar, then cover and simmer over a fairly low heat for 15–20 minutes until the parsnips are soft. Remove the lid and increase the heat. Stirring all the time, let the mixture boil for a few minutes until it is very thick. Remove from the heat and season to taste with salt.

Just before you want to eat reheat the vegetable curry over a medium heat until just bubbling. Stir in half the dill. Quickly break in the eggs, spaced apart, then cover and cook for about 3 minutes until the egg whites are set and the yolks have just set. Sprinkle the remaining dill on top and serve immediately.

PASTA and PIZZA

Legend has it that pasta was invented in China and introduced to the West by Marco Polo but Chinese historians maintain that it came to them from the West. Whatever the truth, pasta has been eaten for centuries, and a form of pasta was even recorded at the time of the ancient Greeks. Now, above all, pasta is the gastronomic god of Italy, but noodles are just as popular in Asia, and there are the *udon* of Japan, the *pierogi* of Poland, the *spätzel* of Germany, the *nouilles* of France, even the *tel 'meni* of Siberia – and many, many more.

Pasta must surely be the world's most versatile food since it marries happily with almost any added ingredient and combination of flavors, seasonings and spices. Pasta can be – and has always been – eaten by paupers and princes: an excellent inexpensive food which can be elevated to luxurious sophistication according to what ingredients you combine with it.

Just as versatile are the small Italian dumplings called *gnocchi*. Often served simply with butter and Parmesan cheese, they are equally good with all pasta sauces.

I have never met anyone who didn't like pasta, but for the Italians it inspires real passion. This is shown by their unending fund of often affectionate names for different shapes of pasta – approximately 300 names for about 100 pasta shapes. The word *maccheroni* is thought to have evolved from *ma, che, carini!* which can be roughly translated as 'but what pretty little things!'. Then there are *amorini*, little loves; *tira baci*, kiss stealers; and *ziti*, bridegrooms, as well as all the familiar names such as tortellini, tagliatelle, fettucini, ravioli and so on.

Pasta is also the perfect convenience food. A package of dried pasta can always be kept in the cupboard, and even if you only have olive oil or butter and seasoning to add to it you will have a satisfying meal. Add a handful of fresh herbs, a few canned anchovies and a sprinkling of grated Parmesan cheese and it will be quite special. And any leftover pasta also tastes good cold. Throwing together a pasta dish at the last minute is ideal for informal occasions but if you are expecting several guests one of the baked, stuffed or layered pasta dishes is more practical. These dishes, such as the many varieties of lasagna and cannelloni, can be made in advance and then simply put in the oven just before you are ready to eat, allowing you to relax before your friends arrive. Usually only a salad and some bread is needed as an accompaniment, which makes preparing the meal even easier.

Although today there are countless pasta restaurants and pizzerias to choose from which provide an informal, inexpensive outing, it is still worthwhile making the dishes at home. Making your own pasta may be time-consuming but it is also very satisfying. The ingredients are basic and cheap yet the reward is rich and delicious. In your own home, too, there need be no rules about the combinations of ingredients you use for sauces or toppings – this is a chance to exercise your creative instincts and experiment to produce something really personal.

Tomatoes are often paired with pasta dishes and pizza although it is important to realize there are endless possibilities for pizza toppings and for pasta sauces which do not include them.

During this century pizza has followed pasta and broken through the Italian frontiers. Now pizzas seem to be an everyday food almost all over the world. I was amazed to see little pizza restaurants when I was traveling through a remote rural area of India recently. In fact, several of the Indian breads, topped with spiced meat, onions and herbs are like a form of pizza, and in Egypt and the Middle East there are delicious pizza-like breads topped with whole eggs and spices and sometimes meat. It is useful to remember that combinations of Indian and Middle Eastern spices go particularly well with pasta dishes and with pizzas.

Clockwise from top left: Salmon and Crab Cannelloni (page 92) is made with spinach lasagna wrapped around seafood; Pasta Bows with Spiced Meatballs (page 91); Spaghetti with Walnuts, Parsley and Gorgonzola (page 91) elevates spaghetti to dinner party status; a golden Cheddar cheese sauce tops spinach and tagliatelle in Noodle Pie (page 90); Tagliatelle Verdi with Squid and Green Cream Sauce (page 93); delicate pieces of poached salmon complement the smoked fish flavor in Sea Shell Pasta with Salmon, Smoked Haddock and Broccoli (page 90); Chick Pea, Mushroom and Leek Pizza (page 92) served with a mixed green salad. Center: Pasta with Parsnips and Pepperoni (page 93) with skinned yellow pepper strips.

PASTA

Pasta – the Italian word for dough – is simply flour and water, sometimes combined with an egg and other added flavoring. Italian dried pasta is made from hard durum wheat, and it can be bought made with egg or simply with water. Although fresh pasta is supremely light and delicate, you should not feel that dried pasta is inferior; it is simply different. Good-quality dried pasta has a mellow flavor and a strength of texture which homemade pasta cannot achieve. Where homemade pasta does triumph is in the colored and flavored pastas.

For homemade pasta white bread flour with its high gluten content is best and eggs are almost always added. Pasta can also be bought or made with whole wheat flour.

Personally, I think whole wheat flour is too heavy for pasta as lightness should be one of its most attractive features. The stronger flavor of the flour is also quite dominant. I prefer a mixture of buckwheat and bread flours.

It is very important to cook pasta *al dente*, which means that you still need to bite it slightly with your teeth. Prolonged cooking can make it soft and mushy. It is impossible to give an exact time for achieving the texture you want as pasta varies so much: always test it two or three times while it is cooking. Homemade pasta cooks extremely quickly – it is ready almost as soon as the water comes back to the boil in just two to three minutes – so watch it like a hawk!

MAKING FRESH PASTA

Making your own pasta may be time consuming, but it is very satisfying. The ingredients are basic and cheap, yet the result is so rich and delicious. Either make pasta dough by hand, as shown here, or process all the ingredients together in a food processor until the dough comes away from the sides of the bowl, adding extra flour if needed.

You can either cut the pasta by hand into the required shape or shapes or use a pasta rolling machine (opposite). Serves 6 as an appetizer or 4 as a main course.

1 *Sift 2½ cups (300g) white bread flour onto a clean work surface with 1 teaspoon salt. Make a well in the center. Break in 3 eggs and add 2 teaspoons olive oil (optional) to help keep the dough pliable while you work with it.*

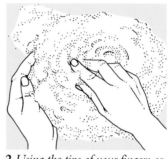

2 *Using the tips of your fingers or a fork mix the eggs and oil lightly together, then start to mix the flour into the eggs drawing in more and more flour until you have a thick dough. If the dough is moist and too sticky add a little more flour and mix in.*

3 *With a shaker filled with flour ready, knead the dough for 5–10 minutes until smooth, adding more flour as necessary. Cover the dough with plastic wrap or wrap in foil and leave it at room temperature for about 1 hour to rest before the next stage.*

4 *Divide the dough into 3 portions and work with 1 at a time, keeping the remaining pieces of dough covered with a clean tea towel. Lightly flour a work surface and roll out the dough to the thickness of a dime. Fold over four times, give a quarter turn and reroll. Repeat 4 times until the dough is smooth and no longer feels sticky.*

To cut into noodles, *lightly flour the rolled dough and fold it into a long, loose roll, slightly flattened. Cut across into thin slices with a sharp knife. Unfold and dry the noodles on a tea towel over the back of a chair; this will take 30 minutes to 2 hours, depending on room temperature. Dust, if necessary, with flour to prevent them from sticking together.*

To cook pasta, *bring a large saucepan of salted water to a boil. Add about 1 tablespoon oil, then add the pasta and stir so it does not stick together. Cook until al dente (above). Drain and rinse under cold running water. Return to the pan a little wet and reheat with your chosen sauce, or toss in oil and butter with seasoning to taste.*

COLORING PASTA
Homemade pasta can be colored in a number of ways which also give flavor and texture: finely chopped or pureed spinach for vibrant green pasta; tomato puree for orangy-red pasta; grated cooked beets for pink to crimson pasta (depending on how much you add); saffron and extra egg yolks for yellow pasta; and squid ink for black pasta. You can also add flavor by adding chopped herbs, ground spices or a little pesto sauce or olive paste from a jar. Add the extra ingredients at the same time as the eggs. You may need to use more flour as you knead.

USING A PASTA MACHINE

If you make pasta often it is well worth getting a pasta rolling machine. Hand-operated machines, as illustrated below, are reasonably priced, easily available and quite sturdy. There is a little technique involved – it is simply a matter of holding one end of the pasta dough while turning the handle.

Make the dough (steps 1–3 opposite). Have a clean tea towel spread out and feed the dough through the rollers in pieces the size of a large egg, keeping the remaining dough under a tea towel or wrapped in a plastic bag or foil to prevent it drying out.

The machine works like a clothes wringer – you feed the dough in at one end, turn a handle with your other hand and the dough comes out as a sheet of pasta. Repeat this a number of times with the same piece of pasta, progressively reducing the thickness each time. (Most pasta machines have six thickness settings.)

The dough will cut more cleanly and not stick if it is allowed to rest briefly after rolling and before cutting and again before cooking. To make lasagna or cannelloni, instead of noodles, simply cut the rolled-out dough (step 3 below) into the required lengths by hand and leave to rest before using.

Creamy Pasta with Chicken and Tarragon Cream Sauce (page 91) is made here with a mixture of spinach and egg noodles.

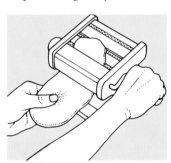

1 *Feed a small piece of dough through at the widest setting, holding the rolled-out end of the dough as it comes through. Fold in half and feed through again. Repeat this 4 more times. If the dough is at all sticky or breaks dust it with a little flour.*

2 *Set the rollers one setting thinner and feed the dough through again about 4 times. Reset the rollers to the next thinner setting and repeat. For pasta of normal thickness stop at this stage; for thinner pasta feed the dough through again.*

3 *Lay the sheets of rolled pasta out to rest on a clean dry tea towel, making sure they don't overlap otherwise they will stick together. Leave the pasta for about 1 hour at room temperature to dry it slightly so it will cut cleanly.*

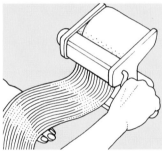

4 *To cut into noodles or spaghetti, fit the appropriate cutting rollers on the machine and refit the handle, if necessary. Feed the dough through as before, turning the handle with one hand and supporting the strands as they come out of the machine.*

SIMPLE SAUCES FOR PASTA

• Melted butter with plenty of freshly ground black pepper and chopped fresh herbs is one of the simplest pasta sauces you can make. I love it.
• Try slivers of sautéed fresh vegetables such as mushrooms, shallots and zucchini, or cooked ham or fish, tossed with single or double cream.
• Chopped walnuts or almonds or pine nuts sautéed in olive oil with garlic and plenty of chopped parsley adds a crunchy texture to pasta.
• Brightly colored sweet peppers fried until soft in oil and butter, then pureed, are a good topping

for noodles.
• For a lower-fat sauce, mix boiled and pureed sweet peppers with low-fat sour cream.
• Mix prawns into hot pasta with butter, seasoning and lots of chopped fresh dill.
• Canned tuna, cockles, mussels, crab meat or anchovies can be combined with olive oil or cream and fresh herbs.
• Fresh mussels, squid and scallops, cooked for just a minute or two and then mixed with cream and a small amount of the pasta cooking water, makes a delicious light sauce.
• Try cubed mozzarella or

crumbled blue cheese stirred into a cream, tomato or oil-and-butter sauce until the cheese just begins to melt.
• Cream with a little mild curry paste, lemon juice and chopped fresh cilantro or mint stirred in gives an Indian taste.
• And, of course, tomato sauce is always popular. Use canned chopped tomatoes for a quick tomato sauce (page 89) and add strips of fresh basil just before serving. Or, use the fresh tomato sauce recipe (page 206) without reducing it too much. Stir in some chopped fresh basil or dried oregano.

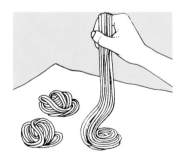

5 *Dry the noodles on the back of a chair and leave for 30 minutes to 2 hours. To make individual serving nests hold the noodles up, then curl them onto a tea towel; you should have about 3–4 nests per serving. Cook the noodles in a saucepan of boiling water until al dente (opposite).*

LAYERED *and* STUFFED PASTA

Baked layered and stuffed pasta dishes such as cannelloni and lasagna, and little filled parcels of pasta such as ravioli and tortellini, offer enormous scope for different ingredients and treatments.

The dough for filled pasta shapes should be fairly moist so it seals easily. Spinach pasta usually stays moist but if you are using egg pasta add a little oil to the dough. Roll out the dough thinly so the shapes will not be heavy, but not so thinly that they will tear when stuffed. You must not overfill them either or they may burst while cooking. After forming the little parcels arrange them spaced apart on a floured clean dry tea towel for an hour or so, turning them over once so they dry on both sides.

Dried cannelloni which do not need precooking are useful but still can be time-consuming to deal with. If you use the sort which have to be boiled before stuffing, take care not to overcook them or they may split when filled.

Cannelloni are, in fact, easiest to prepare if you use homemade fresh pasta sheets. Cut the pasta dough into rectangles like lasagna, and simply roll up round the filling, then lay the cannelloni cut side down in a shallow, rectangular ovenproof dish and cover with a sauce before baking. Always arrange them in the dish close together but in a single layer so they have the sauce both on and around them and don't dry out.

Stuffed pasta shapes are a boon for the home cook because they offer such variety with different colored and flavored pastas (page 82) and tasty fillings.

CLASSIC LASAGNA

Called *lasagne al forno*, this is a classic baked pasta dish layered with a ragù or ground beef sauce (page 213), pasta sheets, white sauce (page 196) and finely grated fresh Parmesan cheese. *Lasagne verdi* is made from spinach-flavored lasagna sheets. Homemade pasta sheets make the best lasagna of all but you can save yourself a great deal of time if you buy the dried 'no precooking' variety. These sheets will be even more successful if you soak them briefly in a large bowl of hot water before you assemble your lasagna, as this softens them slightly. It is also now possible to buy fresh lasagna sheets, making the whole process simpler still. When assembling lasagna, do not use more than 4 layers of pasta as too many layers with too little filling and sauce make a dry lasagna.

To serve 6–8 people, you will need 8–10 lasagna sheets, 3-4 cups (900ml–1.2 liters) white sauce and 3-4 cups (900ml–1.2 liters) ground beef sauce and grated Parmesan cheese. The exact quantities, of course, depend on the size of your ovenproof dish.

1 *Cook dried lasagna sheets that need precooking in a large pan of boiling salted water with a few drops of oil until al dente. Add the sheets a few at a time. Remove with a slotted spoon and drain on a clean tea towel, spacing well apart.*

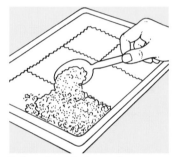

2 *Spread a thin layer of meat sauce in a greased ovenproof dish. Add a layer of pasta sheets, then a layer of meat sauce, a layer of white sauce and a sprinkling of Parmesan. Add a second layer of pasta and continue layering, finishing with pasta.*

3 *Top with a thick layer of white sauce sprinkled with more grated Parmesan cheese. Cook in a preheated oven, 350°F, 180°C for about 45 minutes until the top is just bubbling and golden brown.*

Bubbling Parmesan cheese tops classic lasagna.

STUFFED PASTA

As well as ravioli and tortellini there are numerous other small stuffed pasta shapes you can make just as easily. It's worth making your own because the pasta is more delicate in texture and the filling can be more varied and personal. *Lunette* are one of the easiest shapes to make. Just cut out circles of dough and place the stuffing along one side. Moisten the edges with water and press to seal, creating the distinctive half-moon shape.

Cook all fresh stuffed pasta in boiling salted water with a little oil for 5–7 minutes, or until *al dente*. Dried pasta shapes will take slightly longer to cook. Serve either with a sauce or simply with butter and grated Parmesan cheese.

MAKING RAVIOLI

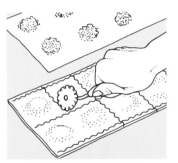

Spoon mounds *of filling (about ½ teaspoon each) onto a sheet of rolled pasta dough, about 2in (5cm) apart. Brush between the mounds with water. Lay a second sheet on top, then press with your fingers to seal between the mounds. Cut into squares with a fluted pastry wheel. Dry for about 1 hour before cooking*

If using a ravioli mold *place a sheet of rolled dough over the molds, pressing the dough into the hollows. Place a small amount of filling in each hollow, moisten and top with a second sheet of dough. Run a rolling pin over the top to cut. Cook in boiling salted water for 5–7 minutes, until al dente.*

SHAPING TORTELLINI

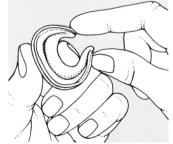

1 *Thinly roll out the pasta until it is about ⅛in (2.5mm) thick. Cut out circles of dough, about 2½in (6cm) in diameter, using a pastry cutter. Put about 1 teaspoon of filling on one half of each circle and moisten the edges of the dough with a little water.*

2 *Fold each dough circle in half over the filling and press the edges together firmly to seal. Carefully curve the half-moon shape round your forefinger, turning up the sealed edges like a hat brim. Pinch the pointed ends together. Repeat with the rest of the circles of dough. Cook the tortellini in the same way as ravioli (above).*

Creamy cheese-flavored white sauce tops Cannelloni Stuffed with Turkey and Fennel (page 90). Using fresh or 'no precooking' dried lasagna sheets makes this an easy dish.

PASTA FILLINGS AND FLAVORINGS

• A vegetable lasagna makes a complete and ideal meal for vegetarians. Use cooked vegetables and a suitable sauce such as yogurt stabilized with cornstarch so it doesn't curdle when heated instead of the usual white sauce.

• With a yogurt sauce you can crumble over ricotta or other white cheese.

• Sautéed sliced bulb fennel, eggplant, leeks, spinach or pumpkin and fresh tomatoes can all be layered with plain or cheesy white sauce for a lasagna with a difference.

• Toast pine nuts (see pesto page 207) or chopped walnuts and add to the lasagna layers. Scatter more untoasted ones on top before baking.

• Cremini mushrooms, which are more solid and keep their texture, are best for lasagna.

• Smoked fish goes well with a cheesy white sauce, as do mussels and other shellfish.

• For a light chicken lasagna filling, spread a creamy white sauce containing slivers of sautéed chicken breast and coarsely chopped tarragon between the pasta sheets.

• As a change from ground beef try ground veal, pork, chicken or turkey in stuffed pasta or for a meat sauce.

• Chopped ham or salami can be mixed with Parmesan cheese and ricotta or mascarpone.

• Smoked haddock or cod mixed with mascarpone and chopped dill or fennel is delicious in ravioli.

• A mixture of spinach and ricotta cheese – probably the best known pasta filling – is ideal for tortellini. Or, try ricotta mixed with cooked leeks, kale or broccoli.

• Spinach on its own can be an excellent filling for stuffed pasta, served with a cream or tomato sauce. Season with freshly grated nutmeg.

• Pumpkin mashed with butter and nutmeg is a popular Italian filling. Or, try mashed parsnip with ground coriander and fresh cilantro.

• Sauté some onions and bacon in butter until soft, then mix with ricotta and season with freshly grated nutmeg.

• Another favorite pasta filling of mine is goat cheese with chopped walnuts.

• Sprinkle crumbled crisply fried bacon over the stuffed pasta just before serving.

• Ricotta cheese with slivers of fresh basil or a little pesto sauce (page 207) makes a simple filling for pasta.

NOODLES *and* GNOCCHI

Noodles in various shapes and forms are eaten all over the world, and are particularly popular in Asia. Most noodles are made from some kind of wheat flour, with or without egg, but they can also be made from rice or buckwheat flour and from vegetable starches: mung bean, soy bean, chick pea, potato, yam and even seaweed.

Asian noodles range in shape from fairly thin egg noodles to wide flat rice noodles. Most can be boiled like European noodles but both rice and bean noodles must be soaked first to soften them before cooking. Very thin rice noodles can be deep-fried straight from the packet – they puff up into a crisp and delicious tangle that goes well with salads or stir-fried vegetables.

Gnocchi or 'little dumplings' vary greatly but are all irresistible. They can be made from potato and flour, from semolina and cheese (*gnocchi alla romana*) or even from spinach and ricotta or cottage cheese. Lightness should be one of the main characteristics of gnocchi, which is why potato gnocchi should be made with the driest potatoes, and not too much flour which would make the mixture heavy. Avoid adding eggs as this only means having to add more flour, and although eggs may bind the mixture they will also make it rubbery.

Chopped fresh herbs can be added to a potato gnocchi mixture to give it added flavor and pretty green specks, or you can make a beautifully colored version using orange-fleshed sweet potatoes. Serve gnocchi piping hot with plenty of grated Parmesan cheese and butter.

ORIENTAL-STYLE STIR-FRIED NOODLES

It is so easy to stir-fry precooked Chinese egg noodles with finely shredded vegetables and slivers of meat, fish or shellfish to make a variety of quick dishes.

As with all stir-fry recipes, the key to success is preparation. Have everything ready before you start cooking. Wash, peel and slice thinly the vegetables as appropriate. Cutting the vegetables into equal-sized pieces will help ensure even cooking. Cut any meat or fish into thin slivers.

Make sure the oil in your wok or pan is hot and constantly stir all the ingredients while they are cooking. It is best to use sunflower or peanut oil for stir-frying.

To prepare the noodles precook them in a large pan of boiling salted water for about 3 minutes until tender, then drain and rinse under cold water. If you want to cook the noodles in advance, keep them in plastic wrap in the refrigerator.

To serve 4, use about 1lb (500g) finely shredded vegetables and 8oz (250g) precooked noodles.

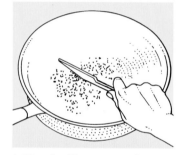

1 *Heat 3 tablespoons sunflower or peanut oil in a wok or frying pan over a medium-high heat. Add 2 finely chopped garlic cloves and fry until light brown, then stir in 2 teaspoons Chinese five-spice powder.*

2 *Add the prepared vegetables and stir-fry for 2–5 minutes, taking care not to overcook the vegetables, then add 3oz (75g) bean sprouts and the precooked noodles. Stir-fry for about 2 minutes more.*

Chinese Egg Noodles with Aromatic Vegetables (page 93) includes stir-fried garlic, gingerroot, sliced tomatoes and zucchini, fresh bean sprouts and chopped fresh cilantro leaves.

3 *When the vegetables are just tender but still slightly crisp, stir in 1 teaspoon light brown sugar, 3 tablespoons soy sauce and a small bunch of finely chopped green onions and just warm through. Season with salt and freshly ground black pepper and serve immediately. If you like you can sprinkle a little toasted sesame oil on top for extra flavor.*

POTATO GNOCCHI

These light 'dumplings' make a welcome alternative to pasta as a first course. Cooking the potatoes in a steamer before you mash them will make them extra dry, contributing to the desired lightness. Mash the potatoes by hand, because if you use a food processor it will turn them into unusable glue (page 53).

For every 2lb (1kg) mashed potatoes knead in about 1¾ cups (200g) all-purpose flour and salt and pepper to taste. Avoid adding eggs as they tend to make the gnocchi rubbery. These quantities serve 4–6.

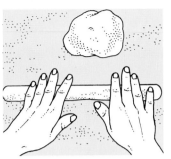

1 *Knead together the mashed potatoes, flour and seasoning to make a smooth, elastic dough on a work surface. Divide the dough into 3 pieces. Sprinkle each portion of dough with flour and roll into sausage shapes about ⅝in (1.5cm) wide.*

2 *Cut the 'sausages' across into 1in (2.5cm) lengths. Press each piece of dough against the back of a large, curved fork. At the same time pull it along the fork, then flick it off onto a floured surface. The gnocchi should look like ribbed shells.*

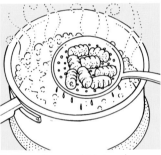

3 *Drop the gnocchi into a large pan of boiling, salted water. When cooked they will float to the surface. Lift out with a slotted spoon, drain well, then put into a warm, buttered serving dish. Add butter and grated Parmesan cheese or a sauce.*

SERVING NOODLES AND GNOCCHI

• Parsnip cubes browned in peanut oil with a little chopped garlic and ginger until almost soft with chopped fresh cilantro leaves added at the end are delicious with noodles.

• Noodles of any kind can be added to a broth or good chicken stock (page 29) or to a can of consommé. Include finely shredded vegetables to cook for a minute or so and slivers of cooked chicken, meat or fish for a quick soup. Soy sauce and finely chopped ginger can be added for a more Chinese flavor.

• Simply toss cooked noodles in a little oil with chopped garlic and ginger and some soy sauce for a really quick dish.

• Roughly chopped fresh cilantro and briefly fried chopped garlic add an instant oriental character to noodles.

• You can buy oriental sauces in jars – oyster sauce is one of my favourites – to add to stir-fried noodles, or you can make up a quick mixture of soy sauce, Chinese five-spice powder, tomato puree, some brown sugar and seasoning.

• Potato gnocchi are delicious served just with butter and grated cheese. Or, add a sprinkling of chopped fresh chives or dill for extra flavor.

• A rich fresh tomato sauce (page 206) combined with strips of basil is excellent to serve with gnocchi.

• You can make a variety of creamy sauces to serve with noodles and gnocchi by heating heavy cream and adding either crumbled Gorgonzola or a mixture of Parmesan and other cheeses, or finely chopped walnuts and parsley combined with chopped green onions.

• A green sauce for potato gnocchi can be made from chopped or pureed cooked spinach, crème fraîche and a little heated cream.

• Butter and cream warmed with tomato puree and seasoning make a pretty pink sauce for spinach gnocchi.

• As well as sea salt and freshly ground black pepper, grated nutmeg works well in all the above sauces. Try caraway seeds for a different flavor.

• Very light gnocchi can be made with ricotta mixed with spinach. Mix together 1lb (500g) cooked, drained and finely chopped spinach, which has been lightly sautéed in butter, with 6oz (175g) ricotta, 3oz (75g) plain flour, 2 egg yolks and 4oz (125g) grated Parmesan cheese. Season with salt, pepper and freshly grated nutmeg. Form the mixture into small ½in (1cm) balls and cook in boiling water in the same way as potato gnocchi (left) for 3–4 minutes.

BAKED SEMOLINA GNOCCHI

Semolina gnocchi are the easiest to make, and are served here baked with cheese. Make the mixture 2 hours in advance, so it cools before you cut it. Boil 2½ cups (600ml) milk with 1 cup (125g) semolina and grated nutmeg, salt and black pepper, stirring. Simmer gently, still stirring, until very thick. Remove from the heat and stir in ¾ cup (75g) grated Parmesan, 1oz (25g) butter and 1 egg plus 1 egg yolk beaten lightly together. Return to a low heat and stir for 1 minute. Serves 4–6.

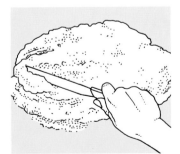

1 *Using a spatula spread the hot semolina mixture about ½in (1cm) thick over a cool work surface or in a buttered large shallow dish and leave until firm and cold. Take care not to burn your fingers on the hot mixture while you are spreading it.*

2 *Cut the cooled semolina mixture into 2in (5cm) rounds with a cookie cutter, then arrange in an overlapping pattern in a buttered shallow flameproof serving dish. Dot the tops with butter. Place any misshapen ones on the bottom underneath.*

3 *Bake towards the top of a preheated oven, 425°F, 220°C for 15 minutes or broil until the gnocchi are golden brown at the edges. Sprinkle with some finely grated fresh Parmesan cheese and serve at once, straight from the dish.*

PIZZA

Making a pizza must be one of the easiest ways to produce a complete and balanced meal. The variety of suitable toppings is endless, and you can invent toppings for all manner of occasions or to cater to the particular tastes of your family and friends.

A pizza crust is simply made with a bread dough using white bread flour. You can, of course, use brown or whole wheat flours but I find that these stronger-flavored flours compete too much with the toppings, and also they do not produce the thin, light and crisp Neapolitan-style crust which is ideal. Many commercially bought pizzas have a thick doughy base of bread, but, personally, I much prefer the original Neapolitan crust. Since part of the point of making a pizza is that it is quick and easy, I always use quick-rising dried yeast (page 282).

Part of the crunchiness of a truly authentic Neapolitan pizza base is the result of baking it on the floor of a traditional brick-lined bread oven at a very high temperature. You cannot do this at home but a similar effect can be achieved by putting a baking stone or unglazed terracotta tiles on the oven shelf to bake the pizza on without using a pizza pan.

Make sure you only use prime-quality ingredients for pizza toppings, and remember that seasoning is also important. Too much topping, however, can weigh down and dampen the crust. It is also important that the topping is not too wet or the crust will become soggy.

Eat your pizzas as soon as they come out of the oven because they lose much of their appeal as they become cold. If you do want to take a pizza on a picnic, I suggest wrapping it in foil and several layers of newspaper so it stays warm and delicious.

Classic pizza Napoletana with golden crusts and a bubbling topping made from fresh tomato sauce, mozzarella cheese, canned anchovies and a sprinkling of oregano.

CLASSIC PIZZA NAPOLETANA

This is the most famous of all pizzas, and you can use the basic recipe as a guide to making others with different toppings. The quick tomato sauce (opposite) should be made in advance and left to cool before using.

To make the dough, follow the white bread dough recipe, (page 282), but add 2 tablespoons extra virgin olive oil with the water. When the dough has risen divide it into 8 pieces to make 8 pizzas, each about 8in (20cm) wide, or make into 2 large pizzas. Use 2 baking sheets, if necessary.

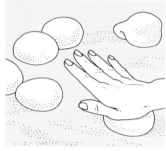

1 *Roll each piece of dough into a ball, then flatten into 8in (20cm) rounds about ⅛in (2.5mm) thick using the heel of your hand. Use your fingers to make the rounds a little thicker at the edges so the sauce does not run off the pizza during baking.*

2 *Place the pizzas on oiled baking sheets and leave to rise again, covered with lightly oiled plastic wrap. Brush each one with olive oil, then top with tomato sauce, sliced mozzarella cheese, a lattice of drained canned anchovies (optional) and dried oregano.*

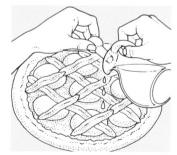

3 *Dribble over a little more olive oil, then bake the pizzas towards the top of a preheated oven, 450°F, 230°C for 10–15 minutes, rotating the baking sheets halfway through, until the edges are golden brown and the cheese bubbling.*

QUICK TOMATO SAUCE

A good, rich tomato sauce is essential for pizza toppings. My favorite sauce can quickly be made by mixing in a saucepan 2 tablespoons extra virgin olive oil, 1 finely chopped clove of garlic, 14½oz (411g) can chopped tomatoes, 2 tablespoons tomato puree, some black pepper and a little salt. Heat the mixture until it boils rapidly, stirring constantly until it is reduced to a thick sauce. Cool before using on pizzas. Or, you can make a fresh tomato sauce (page 206).

A calzone, here filled with gorgonzola cheese, sautéed thinly sliced onions and slivers of Parma ham, makes an excellent light lunch or supper dish served with a simple salad.

MAKING CALZONE

Calzones are the natural evolution of the pizza. The same white bread dough is used (opposite) but instead of being baked flat the dough is folded over a filling, like a turnover.

Calzones can be filled with any of the topping mixtures suggested for pizzas (see box right) but remember the filling must not be too wet initially. Be careful not to overfill the calzone or it may burst during cooking. Set the dough aside to rise before adding the filling.

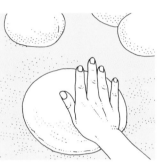

1 Divide the risen dough into 8 balls. Using the heel of your hand flatten each one on a lightly floured work surface to form a round as symmetrical as possible about 8in (20cm) in diameter and ⅛in (2.5mm) thick.

2 Brush the rounds with olive oil, then place about 3 rounded tablespoons filling on one half of each round. Brush the edges of the dough with beaten egg, then fold the rounds over the filling, making sure none of it seeps out. Press the edges to seal together firmly.

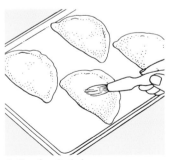

3 Brush a little beaten egg over each calzone for a shiny glaze. Place on an oiled baking sheet, or use 2 sheets if necessary, and bake in a preheated oven, 425°F, 220°C for 10–15 minutes until the dough is crisp and golden. Cool slightly before serving (the filling will be very hot).

IDEAS FOR PIZZAS AND CALZONES

• Use thinly sliced mozzarella cheese. If you do not have any mozzarella, use slices of Gruyère, Emmental or sharp Cheddar cheese.
• Goat cheese or Gorgonzola or other blue cheese mixed with ricotta makes a good pizza topping.
• My family likes pizza topped with very thinly sliced onions covered with grated cheese or with well-drained cooked spinach, greens or kale and slices of mozzarella cheese.
• Strips of grilled, peeled peppers (page 55), sliced tomatoes and thin slices of zucchini with cheese on top.
• Sautéed thinly sliced onions, especially the red-skinned variety, with crumbled Gorgonzola and a few slivers of thinly sliced Parma ham.
• Briefly sautéed thin slices of fennel with goat cheese on top. If the tomatoes are too juicy they can make a pizza too wet.
• Nuts are a good garnish for pizzas – frisée lettuce sautéed in olive oil with a few capers and chopped pitted black olives, topped with pine nuts or chopped walnuts and crumbled goat cheese, makes a delicious topping. Or, spread pesto sauce on the dough and top with pine nuts and grated Parmesan cheese.
• Thinly sliced cremini mushrooms, plenty of chopped garlic, ground coriander, cilantro, a little chopped chili and a generous drizzling of olive oil. I recommend this type of mushroom because they are more meaty than others.
• Thinly sliced dessert apples with ricotta cheese.
• Fresh pineapple with Gorgonzola cheese.
• Well-drained canned tuna with plenty of crushed garlic and freshly chopped herbs. Dill is specially good.
• Mussels, prawns, crab meat and briefly sautéed thinly sliced squid. (I always use plenty of chopped parsley and herbs with a seafood topping.)
• Thinly sliced dried sausages – salami, chorizo, pepperoni – with cheese.
• Miniature calzones made from 4in (10cm) circles of dough can be deep-fried in olive oil, making good snacks for picnics or parties. The quantity of white bread dough (opposite) makes 8–10.
• If you have time use fresh tomatoes when they are in season to make a tasty tomato sauce (page 206). Just remember to simmer the sauce until it reduces to the correct consistency.
• Sun-dried tomato paste enriches the flavor of the tomato sauce. It can also be spread onto pizza before adding other toppings.

SEA SHELL PASTA WITH SALMON, SMOKED HADDOCK AND BROCCOLI (80)

This pretty mixture of colors tastes every bit as good as it looks. It would not really be appropriate to add Parmesan cheese.　　*SERVES 6*

12oz (375g) broccoli florets,
*　trimmed and sliced thinly*
12-14oz (375–425g) small pasta shells
*　(depending on appetites)*
2 tablespoons extra virgin olive oil
1½oz (40g) butter
2 large cloves garlic, finely chopped
1in (2.5cm) piece fresh gingerroot,
*　peeled and finely chopped*
14oz (425g) salmon, filleted, skinned
*　and sliced into 1in (2.5cm) pieces*
10-12oz (300–375g) smoked haddock
*　or other smoked fish fillets, skinned and*
*　sliced into 1in (2.5cm) pieces*
3 tablespoons heavy cream
2 heaping tablespoons crème fraîche
Sea salt and black pepper

Cook the broccoli in boiling salted water for 3–4 minutes, then drain and set aside. Cook the pasta in plenty of boiling salted water until *al dente*.

Meanwhile, put the olive oil and butter in a deep frying pan over a medium heat. Add the chopped garlic and ginger and cook for 2 minutes, then add the sliced salmon and haddock and stir gently with a wooden spoon for 4–5 minutes until just cooked. Stir in the cooked broccoli, then the cream and crème fraîche and season to taste with plenty of black pepper and some sea salt. Remove the pan from the heat.

Drain the pasta and rinse under cold running water. Reheat in the rinsed-out saucepan, then turn it into a warm serving bowl. Add the sauce, mix it quickly into the pasta with a wooden spoon and serve at once.

CANNELLONI STUFFED WITH TURKEY AND FENNEL (85)

This recipe uses lasagna sheets which are not layered but instead wrapped round a filling of ground turkey, fennel and red pepper. The result is light, rather big cannelloni in a rich cheese sauce.　　*SERVES 4*

3 tablespoons olive oil
1 large red pepper, cored, seeded and finely
*　chopped (page 49)*
1 large bulb fennel, trimmed and finely
*　chopped (page 46)*
8 lasagna sheets (the 'no precooking' type)
2–3 large cloves garlic, chopped
1 heaping teaspoon ground mace
1lb (500g) ground turkey
Salt and black pepper
1oz (25g) butter
3 tablespoons all-purpose flour
2½ cups (600ml) milk
4oz (125g) sharp Cheddar cheese,
*　coarsely grated*
1 tablespoon grated Parmesan cheese

Lightly oil a rectangular ovenproof dish. Put the olive oil in a large, deep frying pan over a medium heat. Add the chopped pepper and fennel and stir, then cover and leave to cook, stirring occasionally, for 10–15 minutes.

Meanwhile, put the lasagna sheets into a bowl of hot water into which you have sprinkled a few drops of oil. Leave for 8–12 minutes until the pasta is just soft enough to bend but not so soft that it will tear easily. Drain the sheets separately on a flat surface.

When the vegetables are soft add the chopped garlic and stir for another 1–2 minutes, then increase the heat and stir in the mace, followed by the ground turkey. Stir with a wooden spoon over a high heat until the turkey meat has separated, then cook for about 5 minutes. Season to taste with salt and black pepper. Turn the mixture into a bowl and allow to cool slightly.

Spoon some of the cooked turkey and vegetable mixture onto the center of each lasagne sheet, then roll the pasta loosely round the filling and place the rolls carefully in the dish cut side down.

To make the sauce, gently melt the butter in a saucepan. Remove from the heat and using a wooden spoon stir in the flour until smooth. Gradually stir in the milk, return to the heat and bring to a

boil. Stir constantly until thickened. Remove the pan from the heat, add the grated Cheddar cheese and stir until melted, then season with plenty of black pepper and a little salt if necessary.

Gradually pour the sauce over the pasta rolls, letting it sink down to the bottom of the dish. Sprinkle the Parmesan cheese over the top. Bake just above the center of a preheated oven, 375°F, 190°C for 35–40 minutes until well browned.

NOODLE PIE (80)

I made this pasta pie during one of the school holidays and it has remained a family favorite ever since. It is a practical family dish as you can prepare it in advance and reheat when necessary.　　*SERVES 6*

4oz (125g) tagliatelle or other
*　wide flat egg noodles*
1lb (500g) spinach, stalks removed,
*　washed and drained*
1 tablespoon sunflower oil
1lb (500g) lean ground beef
1 tablespoon tomato puree
2 large cloves garlic, finely chopped
8–10 sage leaves, finely chopped
3–4 pinches cayenne pepper
Salt
1½oz (40g) butter
2 teaspoons ground mace
⅓ cup (40g) all-purpose flour
3¾ cups (900ml) milk
Black pepper
4oz (125g) grated Cheddar cheese

Cook the pasta in plenty of boiling salted water until *al dente*. Drain and rinse under cold running water, then keep on one side. Meanwhile, cook the spinach in a little boiling water in a covered pan for 1–2 minutes, just until limp. Drain thoroughly and set aside.

Heat the sunflower oil in a frying pan over a high heat. Add the ground beef and stir until browned, then add the tomato puree, chopped garlic and sage leaves. Boil the mixture, stirring, for another 3–4 minutes, then season generously with the cayenne pepper and salt. Transfer to a large, shallow ovenproof dish, spread the mixture out level and cover evenly with the cooked spinach leaves.

Melt the butter in a saucepan, stir in the mace and remove from the heat, then stir in the flour until smooth. Gradually add the milk. Return to the heat and bring to a boil, stirring all the time. Boil, still stirring, for about 3 minutes, then remove from the heat and season to taste with salt and black pepper. Pour half the sauce over the spinach leaves. Spread the cooked noodles over the sauce and pour the remaining sauce over the top. Finally sprinkle with the grated Cheddar cheese. Bake in a preheated oven, 400°F, 200°C for 25–35 minutes until the surface is rich golden brown.

PASTA WITH CHICKEN AND TARRAGON CREAM SAUCE (83)

The classic combination of chicken, cream and fresh tarragon is always a success. For extra interest, use half egg pasta and half a colored pasta, such as spinach or tomato. *SERVES 6*

12 oz (375g) noodles or pasta shapes
1 tablespoon olive oil
1½oz (40g) butter
1 red onion, halved and very thinly sliced
12oz (375g) skinless chicken breast fillets, very thinly sliced
4oz (125g) button mushrooms, halved if more than 1in (2.5cm)
1¼ cups (300ml) heavy cream
Small handful fresh tarragon leaves, coarsely chopped
2 teaspoons white wine vinegar
Salt and black pepper
Grated Parmesan cheese to serve

Cook the pasta in plenty of boiling salted water until *al dente*. Meanwhile, heat the olive oil and butter in a large, deep frying pan over a medium heat. Add the sliced onion and stir until softened, then add the chicken slices and cook for another 3 minutes. Add the mushrooms and stir for a further minute.

Add the cream and the chopped tarragon and bring just up to the boiling point, then remove from the heat. Gradually stir in the vinegar and season to taste with salt and black pepper.

When the pasta is ready drain it and rinse under cold running water. Reheat in the rinsed-out pan, then put it into a warm serving bowl. Pour the chicken sauce over the pasta, mix in lightly and serve immediately with a bowl of grated Parmesan cheese.

SPAGHETTI WITH WALNUTS, PARSLEY AND GORGONZOLA (80)

This is an example of how the most simple pasta dish, produced in minutes, can achieve a degree of excellence. The walnuts and Gorgonzola complement each other and plenty of chopped parsley adds a fresh element. *SERVES 4*

5 tablespoons extra virgin olive oil
2 cloves garlic, finely chopped
2oz (50g) walnuts, coarsely ground
2 handfuls fresh parsley, finely chopped
2 tablespoons very hot water
4oz (125g) Gorgonzola cheese, coarsely crumbled
Salt and black pepper
8-10oz (250–300g) spaghetti
Grated Parmesan cheese to serve

Gently heat 2 tablespoons of the olive oil in a pan. Add the garlic and stir for 30 seconds over a low heat, then add the ground walnuts and chopped parsley and stir for not more than 1 minute, or until heated through.

Add the remaining oil and the hot water followed by the Gorgonzola cheese. Stir for a moment until the cheese starts to melt. Season the sauce with a little salt and plenty of black pepper, then remove from the heat, cover and set aside until spaghetti has cooked.

Cook the spaghetti in plenty of boiling salted water until *al dente*, then drain and rinse under cold running water. Return to the rinsed-out pan, reheat, then add the sauce and mix together thoroughly. Transfer to a warm serving bowl and serve with grated Parmesan cheese.

PASTA BOWS WITH SPICED MEATBALLS (80)

This pasta dish is practical for a main course at a dinner party as you can make the meatball sauce in advance and all you need to do is reheat the sauce when you cook the pasta. For greatest ease you need only serve a green salad with the pasta, but green beans or French beans also go well with it. *SERVES 3–4*

12oz (375g) lean ground pork or veal
2 teaspoons ground coriander
1 teaspoon dill seeds
8–10 sage leaves, finely chopped
4 pinches cayenne pepper
3 cloves garlic, crushed
Salt
2 tablespoons olive oil
1oz (25g) butter
14½oz (411g) can chopped tomatoes
1 tablespoon tomato puree
Black pepper
Small handful fresh basil or lovage leaves, sliced into thin strips
12-14oz (375–425g) pasta bows
Grated Parmesan cheese to serve

Place the ground pork or veal in a medium-size bowl. Add the ground coriander, dill seeds, chopped sage leaves, cayenne pepper, about half the crushed garlic and a sprinkling of salt. Mix together thoroughly with a wooden spoon. Then, using wet hands, form the ground meat mixture into very small balls.

Heat the olive oil and butter in a large frying pan over a high heat. Add the meatballs and stir them around until browned all over. Reduce the heat to medium and add the remaining garlic, the chopped tomatoes and the tomato puree. Season with salt and freshly ground black pepper and let the sauce boil gently for 4–5 minutes. Remove the frying pan from the heat.

Shortly before you are ready to eat, cook the pasta bows in plenty of boiling salted water until *al dente*, then drain and rinse under cold running water. Return to the rinsed-out pan, reheat gently, then transfer to a warm serving dish.

Reheat the meatballs and sauce gently and add the sliced basil or lovage at the last moment. Spoon the sauce and meatballs on top of the pasta and serve at once with a bowl of grated Parmesan cheese.

CHICK PEA, MUSHROOM AND LEEK PIZZA *(80)*

The crust for this vegetarian pizza is made with quick-rising yeast which is mixed directly into the flour, needs only one rising and so is useful if you haven't much time. Bake the pizza on your largest baking sheet or shallow ovenproof dish. A rectangular-shaped pizza made in a shallow ovenproof dish is easier to cut and portion out than a round one. The chick pea and mint topping has a Middle Eastern flavor and has the advantage of tasting good when eaten cold, which is not the case with most pizzas.   *SERVES 4–5*

FOR THE DOUGH
3 cups (375g) bread flour
3 teaspoons crushed sea salt
1 package quick-rising dried yeast
1 cup (250ml) lukewarm water
About 2 tablespoons olive oil

FOR THE TOPPING
14oz (432g) can chick peas, drained
1 large handful fresh mint leaves, finely
*   chopped*
2 cloves garlic, finely chopped
2 tomatoes, chopped
4oz (125g) cremini mushrooms,
*   thinly sliced*
1 teaspoon cumin seeds
2 tablespoons tomato puree
About 2 tablespoons olive oil
Salt and black pepper
2 thin leeks, trimmed and very thinly
*   sliced*
2oz (50g) Feta cheese

Grease a very large baking sheet or shallow ovenproof dish. Put the flour into a bowl and add the sea salt and yeast. Stir in the water and olive oil with a wooden spoon, then gather the dough together and knead on a floured work surface with the palms of your hands for 5–10 minutes until the dough is smooth and elastic. Using a heavy rolling pin roll

out the dough firmly and thinly into a piece the same size as the baking sheet or dish. Place the dough on the baking sheet or in the dish. Cover loosely with oiled plastic wrap and set aside in a warm place for 45–60 minutes until the dough has risen moderately.

Meanwhile, prepare the topping. Using a fork coarsely crush the drained chick peas in a bowl, then add the chopped mint leaves, chopped garlic, chopped tomatoes, sliced mushrooms, cumin seeds, tomato puree and olive oil. Season with salt and black pepper. Mix together with a large spoon.

When the dough is ready brush it all over with olive oil. Spread the chick pea mixture evenly over the dough, leaving a ¾in (1.5cm) border around the edges, then sprinkle the sliced leeks over the chick pea mixture and crumble the Feta cheese on top. Bake at the top of a preheated oven, 450°F, 230°C for about 15 minutes until the edges of the dough are browned.

SALMON AND CRAB CANNELLONI *(80)*

For this luxurious dish of fish and crab wrapped in spinach pasta and enveloped in a creamy white sauce the cannelloni are formed using softened lasagna sheets. It is a perfect dinner party dish as it can be prepared in advance and needs only a crisp vegetable such as French beans or snow peas as an accompaniment. If you are serving it as a first course and your family or guests don't have gigantic appetites (unlike my family) this quantity will serve 6.   *SERVES 4*

8 strips (3 x 8in/7.5 x 20cm) fresh
*   spinach pasta or cooked dried lasagna*
*   noodles*
8oz (250g) crab meat (fresh or canned)
1½lb (750g) salmon, filleted, skinned
*   and cut into ½in (1cm) chunks*
3–4 teaspoons capers
3–4 pinches Cayenne pepper
Salt
1 egg, separated
1½oz (40g) butter
2 large cloves garlic, finely chopped
⅓ cup (40g) all-purpose flour
2 cups (450ml) milk
1¼ cups (300ml) heavy cream
Black pepper
Grated Parmesan cheese

Butter a fairly large, shallow ovenproof dish. Fill a bowl with hot water and sprinkle in a few drops of oil. Place the fresh pasta sheets in the water and soak for 1–2 minutes until the pasta is well moistened but not so soft that it will tear easily. Remove the pasta strips, drain well and lay separately on waxed paper while you prepare the filling. This is not necessary if using cooked lasagna.

Put the crab meat in a bowl with the salmon chunks and capers, season with the cayenne pepper and a little salt, then add the egg white and stir in thoroughly using a wooden spoon.

Pile the fish mixture evenly in lengthwise strips down the center of each pasta strip, then roll the pasta round the filling to make a tubular cannelloni shape. Arrange the tubes carefully, close together in a single layer in the buttered dish, cut side down.

To make the sauce melt the butter gently in a fairly large saucepan, add the garlic and cook for 1–2 minutes, stirring constantly, then remove from the heat. When the bubbles subside stir in the flour with a wooden spoon. Gradually add the milk, only a little at a time at first, stirring very thoroughly until smooth. Stir in the cream. Return the pan to a higher heat and bring to a boil, stirring vigorously all the time. Boil gently, still stirring, for 3–4 minutes. Remove from the heat, season the sauce generously with salt and freshly ground black pepper and stir in the egg yolk.

Spoon this thick sauce all over the cannelloni and sprinkle generously with grated Parmesan cheese. Bake just above the center of a preheated oven, 350°F, 180°C for 40 minutes until golden brown.

TAGLIATELLE VERDI WITH SQUID AND GREEN CREAM SAUCE *(80)*

Squid is a perfect ingredient for pasta sauces as it cooks so quickly – in fact, it must never be cooked for more than a few minutes or it will become rubbery. However, if cooked very briefly, it is tender and delicious. People are sometimes alarmed at the idea of preparing squid but once you have learned how it is not difficult and I even find it quite fun. *SERVES 6*

1–1¼lb (500–625g) small squid
14oz (425g) green tagliatelle
4oz (125g) fresh spinach, stalks removed, washed and drained
¾ cup (175ml) heavy cream
3 tablespoons olive oil
½ cup (125ml) dry white wine
2 cloves garlic, very thinly sliced
Salt and black pepper
Good handful fresh dill, coarsely chopped

Clean and prepare the squid as shown on page 126, reserving the tentacles and slicing the bodies across into very thin rings. Set aside.

Cook the tagliatelle in plenty of boiling, salted water until *al dente*.

Meanwhile, prepare the sauce. Put the spinach leaves into a food processor and process until chopped as finely as possible, then add the heavy cream and process again.

Heat the olive oil in a large, deep frying pan over a medium heat, then add the wine, sliced squid and tentacles and the sliced garlic and stir for 30 seconds only. Pour the spinach cream into the pan, bring to a boil and cook for 1 minute, then season to taste with salt and plenty of freshly ground black pepper and remove from the heat. Cover the pan with a lid or foil to keep the sauce warm.

When the tagliatelle is ready drain it and rinse well under cold running water, then return it to the rinsed-out pan with a spoonful of olive oil to keep it from sticking together and reheat. Stir in the squid and cream sauce and the chopped dill. Turn the mixture into a warm serving bowl and serve immediately.

CHINESE EGG NOODLES WITH AROMATIC VEGETABLES *(86)*

Serve this fresh-tasting stir-fry dish as an unusual vegetarian main course. You can cook the noodles and prepare all the vegetables beforehand so that it takes only minutes to prepare before your meal. *SERVES 4*

8oz (250g) Chinese egg noodles
2 tablespoons peanut oil, plus extra for coating the noodles
2 large cloves garlic, finely chopped
1in (2.5cm) piece fresh gingerroot, peeled and finely chopped
2 teaspoons Chinese five-spice powder
1lb (500g) small tomatoes, coarsely chopped
3–4 pinches cayenne pepper
12oz-1lb (375–500g) zucchini, cut into fairly thin 1in (2.5cm) strips
6oz (175g) fresh bean sprouts
2 teaspoons light brown sugar
2 tablespoons soy sauce
Handful fresh cilantro leaves, very coarsely chopped

Cook the Chinese egg noodles in plenty of boiling, salted water, for about 3 minutes until tender, then drain, rinse well in cold water, and turn into a bowl. Stir in a little peanut oil to stop the noodles from sticking together and set aside.

Put the peanut oil in a wok or large, deep frying pan over a medium heat and add the chopped garlic and ginger and the Chinese five-spice powder. Stir for 1 minute, then add the chopped tomatoes, cayenne pepper and zucchini. Stir over the heat for about 5 minutes or until the thin strips of zucchini are bright green

and not cooked through but still slightly crunchy.

Add the cooked egg noodles, the bean sprouts, light brown sugar and soy sauce. Cook, stirring, for 1 minute, just to heat through the noodles and bean sprouts. Finally stir in the chopped coriander leaves. Transfer to a warm serving dish and serve at once.

PASTA WITH PARSNIPS AND PEPPERONI *(80)*

Parsnips are far more versatile than you would imagine, as this easy recipe shows. With the smoky sweet additions of broiled peppers, garlicky and slightly spicy pepperoni slices and the light oniony taste of the leeks this is a wonderful combination. *SERVES 4*

2 large yellow peppers, halved lengthwise and seeded (page 49)
8-10oz (250–300g) pasta shapes, noodles or spaghetti
4 tablespoons olive oil
8oz (250g) pepperoni, very thinly sliced
12oz (375g) thin leeks, sliced into thin rings
12oz (375g) parsnips, very finely sliced
Salt and black pepper
Parmesan cheese to serve

Put the pepper halves under a hot broiler, skin side up, until blackened in patches all over. Wrap in a tea towel until cool enough to handle. Peel off the skin using your fingers, then cut the peppers lengthwise into thin strips. Cook the pasta in plenty of boiling, salted water until *al dente*.

Meanwhile, heat 2 tablespoons of the olive oil in a large, deep frying pan over a fairly high heat. Add the sliced pepperoni and cook for 1–2 minutes. Add the remaining olive oil and the sliced leeks and cook, stirring, for 1–2 minutes until they begin to soften, then add the sliced parsnips and stir for another minute. Then, stir in the sliced, broiled peppers and season to taste with salt and plenty of black pepper.

Drain and rinse the pasta well under cold running water. Return it to the rinsed-out pan and reheat very gently. Place the pasta in a warm serving bowl. Pour the sauce on top and mix thoroughly and serve with grated Parmesan cheese.

$\mathcal{P}$ÂTÉS

Nothing is more convenient for entertaining than an array of flavorful *pâtés*, spreads and loaves. These traditional meat, vegetable and fish mixtures have been a part of American hospitality since colonial days. In French the word *pâté* means pastry; and originally all pâtés were pork mixtures wrapped in pastry. Nowadays, all sorts of savory spreadable or sliceable combinations go by that name. Whether you choose to make the smoothly pureed versions or a loaf made by layering coarsely chopped meats, the fact that pâtés are even better if prepared a day ahead makes them a perfect choice for the busy cook.

Long ago, loaves baked in an earthenware dish were a way of preserving pork, and although pork fat and liver are still the most usual ingredients, all sorts of other things are now added to make the loaf more interesting, and more decorative, too. A variety of birds, including chicken, turkey, duck, pheasant and squab, lend their different colors and flavors. Venison and rabbit add their assertive character to game loaves, but pork and beef liver should be presoaked in milk to lessen their strong taste. Cooking the loaf in a water bath (page 216) helps keep in the moisture, and a certain amount of fat is necessary for both succulence and flavor. When onions or other vegetables are added to a loaf, they must be gently fried in butter first to soften them. Loaves are best pressed with weights after cooking to make them easier to slice, and can be arranged beautifully on a large plate for a buffet party. Appetizer loaves may also be served for a light lunch or supper, accompanied by good crusty bread and a salad.

Rather different from meat and poultry concoctions are fish and vegetable pâtés. These are ideal as a first course, or as part of a cold lunch, and they can also be far less rich than meat and liver pâtés since you can add ingredients, such as low-fat sour cream and yogurt. Some softer, smooth fish and vegetable spreads seem more like dips than pâtés.

Smoked fish pâtés, such as mackerel, trout, kipper, and salmon, are very easy to make, and always popular; they can also be used as a stuffing for hard-cooked eggs and tomatoes, or other vegetables. Fresh fish can be made into loaves and cooked in a water bath as you do meat loaves, but the fish is usually pureed and mixed with egg white, and often cream, (when it is called a mousseline) so the finished result is much lighter and more suitable for a first course.

Vegetable pâtés have also become extremely fashionable; they can be very pretty indeed, but they can also be laborious to assemble as the vegetables have to be carefully prepared. I would rather have a jumbled mixture of vegetables that tasted really appetizing than a perfect work of art. Seasoning really is crucial, as vegetable pâtés which are not seasoned well can be far from a pleasure to eat.

Pâtés, whether spreads, loaves or the lighter pureed mousselines and mousses produce a wide range of different effects, depending on the ingredients used, and how they are cooked. It is quite possible to deviate from the basic methods to produce different, exciting tastes and textures, which is what can make this an especially interesting and personal area of cookery.

Appetizer spreads and loaves in a variety of textures and flavors, clockwise from top: Glazed Pâté in Herbed Pastry (page 105) encases veal, pork, turkey and chicken livers in a crisp rosemary-flavored pastry; Smoky Fish Loaf with Mace and Pink Peppercorns (page 105) is made with smoked haddock, flounder and salmon and here served with a light saffron-flavored cheese sauce and fresh tarragon; Parsnip and Garlic Mousse with Cilantro Sauce (page 104) is a hot, baked mousse flavored with honey and mace, served with a simple sauce made from yogurt and fresh cilantro; a medley of lightly blanched fresh vegetables set in a wine-flavored aspic in Glossy Vegetable Pâté (page 104), with a lettuce garnish; Duck, Chicken and Pork Loaf with Prunes and Pistachios (page 104), flavored with orange liqueur, orange juice and ground mace and coriander, is served here with a garnish of lettuce and cucumber.

SPREADS or SMOOTH PÂTÉS

Spreads or smooth pâtés can be made from livers, chicken, game, marinated meats, fish or vegetables. They can either be cooked in a mold in a water bath (page 216) or by lightly cooking the ingredients in a frying pan, then pureeing and spooning into a dish to seal with clarified butter. Instead of clarifying your own butter (below) you can buy at gourmet stores the high-fat concentrated butter used by chefs which has been refined and had much of the liquid removed. Simply melt some and cook it for a minute before pouring it through a fine sieve on top of the pâté.

In cooked mixtures, herbs, cream or cream cheese, which will enrich and lighten the pâté, can be added to the pureed mixture before it goes in the oven, and as always with all pâtés, careful seasoning is vital.

But I prefer making the pan-prepared smooth pâtés, as they are so quick; flavor contributors such as mushrooms and bacon can be softened in the pan before adding the main quick-cooking ingredients, such as chopped chicken livers and slivers of chicken breast, tossing them around to cook lightly in the butter. To lighten the consistency after pureeing, add cream, or for a less rich effect, plain yogurt, crème fraîche or other milk products. With this method it is easier to get the seasoning right as you can taste the mixture in the final stage and adjust it if needed.

QUICK CHICKEN LIVER PÂTÉ

A smooth, rich chicken liver pâté is one of the quickest pâtés to make, but tastes even better if you take time to soak the livers in milk for at least an hour beforehand to give them a milder flavor. Other ingredients can be added which will also enhance the pâté. I like to add mushrooms, onions, bacon, or even slightly sweet ingredients like finely chopped parsnips – but they must be precooked in the skillet before adding the livers, which must be cooked only briefly.

A delicate mildness should be one of the characteristics of chicken liver pâté, so garlic should only be added if it has been cooked long and gently beforehand, to remove strength and induce sweetness, either by frying or by boiling the cloves in their skins. Blending the livers after cooking with unsalted butter and/or cream will make the mixture taste even milder. For flavoring, 1–2 tablespoons brandy, sherry or Marsala can be used according to taste.

To serve 4 use 8oz (250g) chicken livers, soaked in milk. Serve the pâté with some delicious crusty bread.

1 *Melt 2oz (50g) unsalted butter in a pan over a gentle heat, then add 1 teaspoon ground coriander and 1 finely chopped small onion. Stir until softened, then add the drained and coarsely chopped chicken livers and 1–2 tablespoons brandy.*

2 *Stir for about 5 minutes until the livers are completely cooked. Turn the mixture into a food processor and add another 1oz (25g) soft unsalted butter and 2 tablespoons heavy cream. Process to a smooth puree. Season to taste with sea salt and black pepper.*

3 *Spoon the chicken liver pâté into an earthenware dish, about 3¾ cups (900ml) capacity, or 6 small ramekin dishes and spread level. Melt 1-2oz (25–50g) clarified butter (right) and pour carefully over the top of the pâté to seal it. Chill the pâté overnight before serving to give the flavors time to mature.*

CLARIFYING BUTTER
Clarifying butter not only raises the temperature at which it can be cooked without burning, it also helps the butter last longer (up to 1 month) and so is useful for sealing. It is worth clarifying reasonable amounts of butter at a time, remelting as required. First melt the butter slowly in a heavy-bottomed saucepan. Pour the melted butter carefully through a sieve lined with cheesecloth into a bowl, leaving as much of the milk sediment behind as possible. Allow to settle then pour gently again into another bowl or cup or pour on top of your pâtés as required.

A homemade chicken liver pâté is always popular; it is one of the quickest and easiest pâtés to make, and inexpensive too.

EGGPLANT PÂTÉ

I learned to make this delectable puree years ago in a little Turkish restaurant above the covered market in Istanbul. The eggplant skin is burned black to impart a subtle smoky taste to the soft flesh within. This eggplant pâté is far softer than most pâtés, and makes a good first course piled onto thin toast. As the flavor is so delicate, it is better to use sunflower rather than olive oil which can be overpowering. This quantity serves 4.

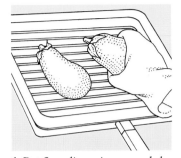

1 *Put 2 medium-size, unpeeled eggplants under the hottest possible broiler for 15–25 minutes, turning them once or twice until the skin is charred then plunge them into cold water.*

Eggplant pâté (left) and smoked salmon pâté are both easy to prepare and ideal for informal meals.

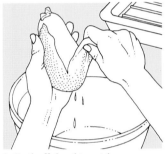

2 *Peel off the skin with your fingers and discard. Put the flesh into a fine sieve and press with a wooden spoon to push out as much of the liquid in it as possible. Put the drained flesh into a food processor and add 1 tablespoon lemon juice.*

3 *Process together, adding 3–5 tablespoons sunflower oil, a little at a time until smooth. The more oil you add, the lighter the texture. Season with salt and black pepper. Spoon into a dish and chill until ready to serve. Sprinkle with chopped herbs.*

SMOKED FISH PÂTÉ

If you use a food processor or blender, smooth pâtés made from smoked fish are very easy to make.

To make the pâté more impressive for a dinner party, serve it in hollowed-out lemon or orange shells instead of a terrine. It also looks pretty simply spooned into cups of crisp lettuce leaves with a scattering of fresh herbs on top. You can use any skinned and filleted smoked fish, including mackerel, kipper, trout, and salmon. Instead of crème fraîche you can use cottage or cream cheese. Serves 6.

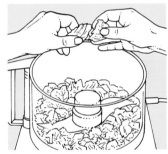

1 *Put 12oz (375g) coarsely flaked smoked fish into a food processor with 3oz (75g) soft unsalted butter, 4oz (125g) crème fraîche, 4 tablespoons heavy cream, 1 teaspoon sugar and 1 small clove crushed garlic (optional). Process to a smooth puree.*

MAKING THE MOST OF SMOOTH PÂTÉS

• Adding some finely chopped and sautéed red onions, fennel or wild mushrooms, or a smattering of finely chopped sour cherries, apples, dried apricots, prunes or pistachio nuts to chicken liver pâtés makes them more interesting and adds extra flavor too.
• When topping pâtés with melted clarified butter, it looks pretty if you lay a few whole leaves, such as flat-leaf parsley or bay leaves on top so they set in the butter.
• Ground spices such as coriander, mace, allspice and cinnamon go particularly well with meat mixtures.
• Finely grated lemon or orange rind is another good flavoring for most pâtés.
• Make chicken liver pâté even

milder and lighter by sautéing a few slivers of boneless chicken breast with, or in place of, some of the livers.
• I think smoked fish pâtés and pureed vegetable or dried bean pâtés look more impressive if you stuff them into containers such as halved red peppers or hollowed-out tomatoes, or into avocado shells, incorporating the avocado flesh mixed with lemon juice into the pâté.
• A quick smoked salmon pâté can be made by finely chopping scraps of smoked salmon and mixing them into softened cream cheese or mascarpone with plenty of finely chopped fresh dill, 1–2 teaspoons of whole grain mustard and a dash of lemon juice.

2 *Gradually process in 1 tablespoon lemon juice and then season to taste with salt and cayenne pepper. Stir in 1 tablespoon chopped fresh dill or fennel, reserving a few unchopped sprigs for garnishing.*

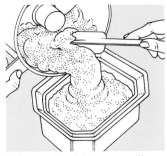

3 *Spoon the pâté into a small terrine or else use hollowed-out lemon or orange shells. Cover the pâté loosely with foil and chill until ready to serve. Before serving, garnish the top with fresh sprigs of dill or fennel.*

COUNTRY PÂTÉS

I love making this kind of baked appetizer loaf because, without the need for any skill, you can make it look so beautiful. You really can't go wrong – simply by arranging different-colored meats and livers, and sometimes other ingredients, such as nuts, dried fruits or olives, within the mixture, an intriguing mosaic of varying shapes and shades will be revealed when the loaf is sliced.

The meat for a baked pâté is usually cut up by hand into small pieces or long strips (though you can process some of it to vary the textures) and is best marinated overnight in a wine, oil and seasoning mixture to make it more tender, succulent and full of flavor. After cooking, weigh down the pâté while cooling, so the meats become pressed together and easier to slice.

The compactness of baked pâtés makes them a supremely portable food, ideal for picnics or to take friends as a present when you go to stay. Baked pâtés are also perfect for occasions like Christmas when you have a houseful of people who may become hungry at any time. They can be made ahead as their taste is at its best the day after cooking. You must keep the baked pâté in the refrigerator, but it should be eaten at room temperature.

MAKING COUNTRY PÂTÉS

Any shape of container or dish can be used to make this baked appetizer loaf – in fact, it looks very attractive made in a pie plate and turned out. Lining the container with strips of bacon is not essential but it helps to add moistness to the strips of lean meat .

Or, instead of turning out the loaf make it in a special earthenware dish (page 25) and garnish the top attractively with bay leaves, juniper berries and maybe at Christmas time with a few cranberries. For an appetizing gloss, brush the top with some cooled chicken aspic (page 33). Serves 8–10.

1 *Mix together in a large bowl 1lb (500g) ground or chopped pork shoulder, 8oz (250g) chopped pork liver, 1 chopped onion, 2 crushed cloves of garlic, 3 tablespoons brandy or sherry, ½ teaspoon ground allspice, 1 teaspoon dried sage, salt and black pepper. Marinate for 4–8 hours or overnight.*

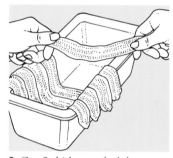

2 *Cut 2 chicken or duck breasts into strips and season. Mix in a bowl and cover. Stretch 8oz (250g) bacon strips with the back of a knife so they are easy to manipulate and lay flat (page 149); use them to line a greased 6¼ cup (1.5 liter) loaf pan or terrine, leaving a little on each side as an overlap.*

3 *Check the seasoning by frying a small amount of the marinated meats first, tasting, then adding more salt, pepper or spice if necessary. Spoon into the bacon-lined tin, alternating layers of marinated meats and the strips of poultry or game. Fold back the overlapping strips of bacon. Cover with greased foil.*

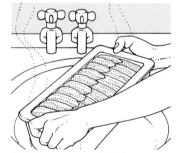

4 *Place in a water bath (page 216) and cook at 350°F, 180°C for 1½ hours. Remove from the water bath and cool, then chill, placing a board and some weights on top; leave to 'mature' in the refrigerator overnight. To serve remove the foil and unmold by dipping the pan very briefly in hot water. To serve, cut carefully into thin slices.*

A country pâté (left) and pâté en croûte can be made with your favorite flavorings and ingredients.

PÂTÉ EN CROÛTE

Wrapping a delicious and colorful mixture of meats (especially game, such as venison, pheasant or rabbit), herbs, nuts and dried fruits in a rich pastry case makes for a very special pâté, ideal for parties. Make sure, though, there are no cracks in the pastry for any juices to escape, and although the pastry case may sag a bit at the bottom this adds to the homemade appearance of the pâté. When cool, pour well-flavored aspic (page 33) mixed with extra gelatin through one or two small holes in the pastry to fill in any little gaps and hold the pâté and pastry together better.

For this recipe, to serve about 8, you will need pastry made with 3 cups (375g) all-purpose flour, ½ teaspoon salt, 6oz (175g) butter and 3–4 tablespoons water (page 246).

First of all prepare the ingredients for marinating: mix together 1lb (500g) ground game meat or pork or veal, 8oz (250g) diced fully cooked ham or Canadian bacon, 8oz (250g) pork fat cut into thin strips, 1 chopped onion, 2 cloves crushed garlic, salt and freshly ground black pepper and 1–2 tablespoons chopped fresh herbs, and a splash or two of brandy or sherry.

1 *Place the well-mixed meats and other flavoring ingredients in a large glass bowl and marinate overnight, stirring when possible. Check the seasoning by frying a small amount of the marinated mixture first, tasting, then adding more salt, or freshly ground black pepper if necessary.*

2 *Add flavorings such as green peppercorns, pistachio nuts, pitted olives or chopped ready-to-eat dried apricots to the marinated ingredients. Make the pastry and roll out slightly less than half to a large rectangle about ¼in (5mm) thick and place on a greased flat baking sheet.*

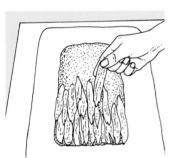

3 *Cut into strips an additional 6oz (175g) lean game or meat such as duck, goose, venison or pork tenderloin to provide an interesting contrast in the filling. Spoon the marinated ingredients into a long tall mound in the center of the rolled-out pastry, layering as you go with the strips of additional lean meat.*

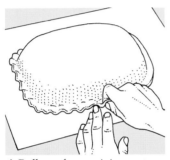

4 *Roll out the remaining pastry to a rectangle large enough to cover the pâté easily. Lay it on top, glaze the edges with beaten egg, trim and press the edges to seal. Make 2 steam holes in the top. Reroll any trimmings for decorations such as leaves or cut out letters spelling PÂTÉ or seasonal messages (page 245).*

5 *Glaze the top with beaten egg yolk, attach the decorations and glaze again. Chill for 20 minutes. Cook the pâté at 400°F, 200°C for 15 minutes, then reduce the temperature to 350°F, 180°C and cook for another hour. Remove from the oven and cool the pâté on the baking sheet.*

6 *Make up 1¼ cups (300ml) of aspic by dissolving 2 teaspoons softened gelatin in 1¼ cups (300ml) hot pork or chicken stock (page 28). Allow to cool before pouring carefully through the holes in the top of the pâté. Chill overnight before serving. Transfer to a serving dish and cut into slices with a serrated knife.*

ADDING COLORS AND FLAVORS TO COUNTRY PÂTÉS

• Coarse-textured country pâtés are a joy for the imaginative or artistically inclined cook. You can use different colored meats such as a combination of duck, turkey and Cornish hen breasts, pork, ham and pork fat, either arranged in simple layers or in more complicated patterns. Long strips of meat can be wrapped in blanched spinach leaves which will give a very pretty effect of green circles when the pâté is sliced.

• You can also stud the meat with pistachio nuts, walnuts or almonds, and with dried apricots, peaches, prunes, pitted black or stuffed olives, water chestnuts, cranberries, strips of colored peppers or pieces of blanched orange or lemon rind.

• Try pieces of lychee in a pork and chicken pâté, marinating the meat first in sherry with plenty of fresh ginger slivers.

• Green or pink peppercorns add aroma to pâtés, and juniper berries are good with game.

• I like to use bacon to wrap around pâté mixtures because of its attractive appearance.

• Marinades can be made up with some kind of alcohol – red or white wine, sherry, vermouth, brandy or port – or with fresh fruit juices. Mix the alcohol or juice with olive oil and seasonings which can include herbs, onions, garlic, ginger and spices such as ground cloves, allspice, mace, coriander and cinnamon.

• If you like, you can marinate the meats in different mixtures; for example, the dark meats such as venison in a wine mixture and the paler ones, such as turkey or chicken, in a yogurt marinade.

• Chopped chicken livers mixed among coarsely chopped meats in a pâté will add softness to the overall texture.

• A certain amount of ground or finely chopped pork fat should be included in all meat and game pâtés to keep them from becoming too dry and solid and to improve the consistency.

• I think it is nice to serve a thin slice of an attractively patterned pâté on individual plates as a first course. Place it on a layer of smoothly pureed sauce; try fresh tomatoes stewed and pureed with orange juice, or a savory fruit like red or golden stewed plums mixed with sherry vinegar.

SAVORY MOUSSES

Cold and hot savory mousses and mousselines are variations on a theme whose main characteristic is a delicate lightness. As long as the flavor is right, they can be a wonderful, sensual pleasure to eat. They are each made with a base of smooth puree which can be made from cooked or raw meats or poultry, fish or vegetables. In hot mousses, these purees are often enriched by egg yolks and lightened with beaten egg white or sometimes cream, too. Hot mousses are usually cooked, but they can also be steamed, or, in the case of quenelles, poached. Cold mousses are purees mixed with mayonnaise (page 202), or with a white sauce (page 196), lightened with whipped cream and set with either a small amount of gelatin dissolved in stock or prepared aspic – they should never be rubbery. Beaten egg whites are

sometimes added to lighten the mixture further. As in fish and vegetable terrines (page 102), the smoothly pureed mixtures of both hot and cold mousses can be dotted with pieces of vegetables, nuts, seafood, fish or simply with chopped fresh herbs.

A mousseline mixture is a puree of raw fish (either smoked or unsmoked), poultry or pale meat into which unbeaten egg whites and cream are gradually beaten. All the ingredients must be chilled to make a stiff mixture. It is often used as the basis of baked terrines, either layered or covered with whole ingredients, or just the mousseline can be spooned into ramekins and cooked like a terrine in a water bath (page 216) in the oven before serving hot with a sauce. Use a mousseline mixture also for making quenelles.

COLD SAVORY MOUSSE

Cucumber mousse is an attractive make-ahead cold buffet dish. To make other mousses, use this technique and substitute about 1¼ cups (300ml) of mashed fish, grated carrot or chopped tomatoes for the cucumber. Always season cold mousses well as chilling weakens flavors. The decorated shimmering aspic top is purely optional, but is a good way of showing off.

The mousse can be set in a 5 cup (1.2 liter) pretty glass dish or divided between 8 individual ramekin dishes or molds. Serve with a pretty salad garnish for a spectacular effect. Serves 8.

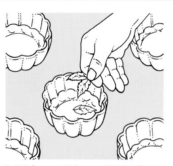

1 *Make up 1¼ cups (300ml) aspic (page 33) and use half to line eight ⅔ cup (150ml) individual molds, or a 5 cup (1.2 liter) mold. Chill until set, then place a few mint leaves on top of the aspic. Pour over the rest of the aspic and chill again until set. Or, use feathery dill, chervil or parsley instead of mint.*

2 *Meanwhile, peel, halve and seed 2 cucumbers. Coarsely grate into a bowl, then mix in 2 tablespoons each chopped green onion tops and chopped fresh mint. Mix in 5oz (150g) of softened low-fat soft cream cheese or 5oz (150g) crème fraîche, 2 tablespoons lemon juice and season well.*

3 *Soften 1 package unflavored gelatin in 3 tablespoons water, heat then mix in. Add to the cheese and cucumber mixture. Whip ¾ cup plus 2 tablespoons heavy cream and fold in, then pour the mixture into the molds. Chill until set. Loosen the sides with a knife, dip the molds very briefly in hot water and turn out.*

A cucumber savory mousse served with carrot matchsticks tossed with shredded fresh mint, sesame seeds and a light vinaigrette.

FLAVORING SAVORY MOUSSES

• Add tomato puree or sun-dried tomato paste, or olive, garlic, anchovy or curry pastes or coarsely crushed green or pink peppercorns to the basic mousse mixture to strengthen or enhance taste.
• Instead of a classic, creamy velouté sauce, such as sauce Nantua (page 197) to serve with quenelles, use a smooth cheese or curry-flavored white sauce (page 196).
• If you grow sorrel in your garden, a sauce made by wilting sorrel leaves in a little unsalted butter in a pan and

then pureeing and heating again with a little cream, is delicious to serve with savory mousses. Improve the sauce's color by including a leaf or two of spinach with the sorrel.
• Quick cold sauces can be made using sour cream or plain yogurt with thin vegetable purees (page 53) stirred into them.
• Make a garlic and saffron sauce by boiling 1¼ cups (300ml) heavy cream with 2 halved garlic cloves and a pinch of saffron. Cool and remove the garlic before serving.

MAKING MOUSSELINE

Food processors have made it possible to produce lovely, light fish mousselines, as well as smooth terrines without long arduous pounding and beating by hand with a wooden spoon. But if you want your puree to be extra smooth, you can press it through a sieve or pass it through a food mill.

Most firm fish, such as sole, haddock and salmon, is suitable, although oily fish like herring and mackerel are too rich and some shellfish, such as scallops, too watery. The other ingredients are simply heavy cream, egg white and lots of seasoning, ideally with sea salt and white pepper and maybe a good pinch of paprika. As it is difficult to season the mousseline after cooking, check by cooking a small spoonful of the mixture first, by poaching in a little stock or water.

The secret of a light mousseline is to keep the mixture well chilled while you beat in the cream. This helps the mixture maintain a firm texture and yet cook to a delicate lightness. Be sure to have crushed ice ready to use in step 2. Mousselines can be cooked simply in buttered molds or ramekins, with a delicious surprise base of chopped, lightly cooked asparagus, tomatoes, peppers or mushrooms, if you like. Serves 6.

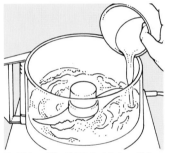

1 *Trim 1lb (500g) skinless fish fillet of membranes and stray bones. Cut into cubes, then puree in a food processor until smooth. Add 2 egg whites and season more generously than you would think. Process until well mixed and spoon into a bowl.*

2 *Place the bowl in a larger one containing crushed ice cubes, then gradually beat in 1¼-1½ cups (300-375ml) chilled heavy cream, depending on the fish; firmer fish need more cream. The mixture should be thick and smooth and hold its shape.*

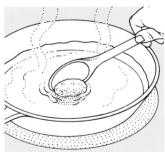

3 *Check the seasoning by poaching a spoonful in simmering water for 3 minutes and tasting. Spoon the mixture into a 3¾ cup (900ml) ovenproof dish or into 6 individual ⅔ cup (150ml) ramekins, on top of a base of lightly cooked vegetables if desired; cover with greased foil.*

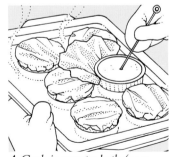

4 *Cook in a water bath (page 216) at 350°F, 180°C for 25–30 minutes until just firm in the center. Run a knife around the outside and unmold onto small serving plates. Serve warm with hollandaise or other hot buttery sauce (page 200) and an herb garnish if desired.*

QUENELLES

A delicate light mousseline mixture can be shaped into small 'dumplings' called quenelles and then poached for a few minutes until firm. Make up the mousseline mixture at left, then shape the individual quenelles using 2 soup spoons.

As quenelles only take a few minutes to cook and are nicest served freshly cooked, the mixture can be kept chilled in the refrigerator until nearly ready to serve. Prepare a wide, shallow pan of simmering fish stock (page 31) before you start shaping the quenelles. Cook the quenelles in batches of about 6 at a time. Serve with a hot, buttery sauce (page 200). Makes about 18 quenelles.

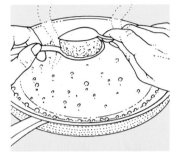

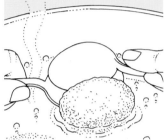

1 *Using 2 soup spoons, scoop up a spoonful of mousseline with 1 spoon and smooth over the top with the other spoon. Work over the pan of simmering stock while you continue shaping the quenelle. Scrape the other spoon down, scooping off the mixture towards you in one quick movement.*

2 *Then repeat the same movement with the first spoon. Repeat this twice more and finally drop the shaped quenelle straight into the stock. Poach for about 5 minutes until firm, shaking the pan gently to roll the quenelles. Lift out with a slotted spoon and keep warm.*

Attractive fish quenelles (left), here served with a creamy sauce Nantua (page 197), can be made from any fresh white fish. The hot salmon mousselines are served with a creamy, rich hollandaise sauce (page 200) and fresh dill.

FISH *and* VEGETABLE PÂTÉS

Fish and vegetable pâtés or loaves are lovely for first courses and summer lunches. Unlike meat, game and poultry pâtés which improve with a day of maturing, these should be eaten very fresh. If the ingredients are not perfect and the seasoning not well thought out and adjusted, vegetable pâtés can taste very dull.

Spinach is often used to line the mold for a vegetable pâté and make a pretty green edge on each slice – in this case, I oil the dish instead of buttering it, so that the leaves look glossy when the pâté is turned out.

A light and delicate fish pâté is one of my favorite preludes to a rich, meaty meal. I like hot fish pâtés best of all, and these can also be served as the main course of a light meal. Fish pâtés are made in the same way as meat pâtés,

using uncooked ingredients, but the time taken to cook the fish, with the dish usually set in a water bath, is far less, so as not to overcook and lose the succulence of the fish. Most fish pâtés, as below, are assembled in the dish using a mixture of fish mousseline (page 101) and pieces of fish or seafood added either in neat layers or at random which I think looks just as good.

Something not made in this way are potted shrimp, which can be served like a pâté when they are turned out of the pot. They are one of my great favorites. Despite the laborious peeling, it tastes far better if you use shrimp instead of the much larger prawns. With a combination of clarified unsalted butter (page 96) and a little mace and cayenne pepper, it is an irresistible dish.

FISH PÂTÉ

An attractive mousseline pâté to be served warm or lightly chilled can be made with one or two colored mousseline mixtures. Pâtés also look very pretty layered with strips of lightly cooked vegetables or long strips of a contrasting firm fish. The variations of color and flavor are endless.

For a special mousse or pâté, line a buttered mold with thin fillets of sole, skinned side facing inwards, and make a smoked fish mousseline speckled with chopped herbs or even pistachios or colored with a spice such as turmeric or paprika. Or, line the mold with blanched spinach leaves and stir into the mousseline some finely chopped herbs or 1–2 tablespoons sherry. Serve warm fish pâtés with a hot fresh tomato sauce (page 206).

For cold pâtés, line the container with blanched spinach leaves, cool, fill with your chosen mixture and then chill until ready to serve.

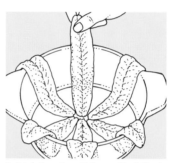

1 *Lightly oil a 6¼ cup (1.5 liter) round ovenproof dish and line the base with a greased disc of waxed paper. Arrange about 6 long thin fillets of sole or flounder in a pattern, extending from the center to the top edges. Let the fillets overlap a little to allow for shrinkage.*

2 *Make a double quantity of mousseline mixture (page 101) from smoked fish, such as haddock. Stir in 2 teaspoons turmeric to give the mousseline a yellow color, then add some coarsely chopped pistachio nuts and finely chopped fresh cilantro leaves to taste.*

Chopped pistachio nuts and chopped cilantro are mixed with a turmeric-flavored smoked fish mousseline and whitefish fillets.

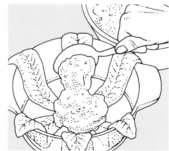

3 *Spoon the golden mousseline into the fish-lined dish, making sure it fills the gaps between the sole 'spokes'. Tap gently on the work surface to make sure the mousseline works its way down to the bottom. Use a wet spatula to smooth the top. Fold over the overhanging fillets.*

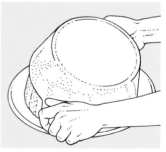

4 *Cover with greased foil, then place in a water bath (page 216) and cook at 350°F, 180°C for about 50 minutes until the center of the pâté feels firm when tested with a skewer. Allow to stand for a few minutes before inverting onto a warm serving plate. To serve, cut in wedges.*

VEGETABLE PÂTÉ

A pretty layered vegetable pâté can be served lightly chilled and cut into elegant slices. The 'binding base' is a delicate cheesy savory custard holding colorful cooked vegetables together. Choose vegetables of contrasting colors such as carrots, leeks, red pepper, green beans, asparagus spears and button mushrooms, and arrange them either randomly or symmetrically in layers. For best effect, line the base and sides of the pan with blanched spinach leaves.

Distinctive vegetable flavors and freshly grated nutmeg make this spinach-wrapped pâté with an egg custard base a popular first course or light main course.

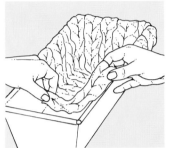

1 *Blanch 8oz (250g) large spinach leaves until just wilted. Place in ice water. Carefully line the base and sides of an oiled 9in (1kg) loaf pan, slightly overlapping to avoid gaps.*

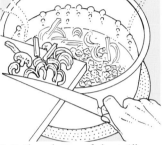

2 *Boil a selection of about 1lb (500g) mixed vegetables until tender. Add in stages, the harder ones first, to cook the vegetables to the same degree of tenderness. Drain the vegetables together.*

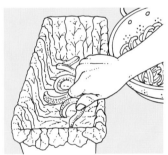

3 *Place the vegetables in ice water. Arrange the vegetables in the loaf pan in a random mixture lengthwise along the pan; mixing the colors and shapes and seasoning well in between the layers of vegetables.*

4 *Beat together 1 whole egg, 2 egg yolks and 1¼ cups (300ml) light cream with salt, pepper and freshly grated nutmeg. Add 2oz (50g) grated Cheddar cheese. Pour over the vegetables. Fold back the spinach leaves.*

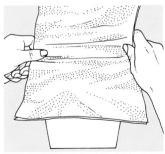

5 *Cover with a double thickness of greased foil and bake in a water bath (page 216) at 350°F, 180°C for 1–1¼ hours until the center is just set.*

6 *Remove the pan and cool, then chill before turning out onto a serving plate. If the custard has leaked out a little, scrape it off. Cut carefully into slices.*

IDEAS FOR FISH AND VEGETABLE PÂTÉS

• One of the most beautiful dishes is a vegetable pâté set in clear aspic; a simple and successful aspic can be made by dissolving softened gelatin in warmed dry wine diluted with a little mineral water, and seasoned well. Sometimes I add a little sherry vinegar. Different colors of steamed vegetables should be arranged in layers in a loaf pan, covering each layer with aspic and allowing it to set in the refrigerator before adding another layer. If you are in a hurry, you can simply pack the layers of vegetables closely together and spoon the aspic gradually into the filled dish until it has reached the top. Fresh herbs can be put on the bottom of the tin so that it looks pretty when it is turned out (see Glossy Vegetable Pâté page 104).

• Pumpkin puree with a small amount of lima bean puree, seasoned with nutmeg and a little mustard, bound with eggs, makes a nice autumn pâté.

• Use different colors of fish when making fish pâtés – the yellow of smoked fish looks very pretty with the pink of salmon, and, of course, shellfish add a lot of color. Whiting, cod or flounder can be used for the white fish, and I particularly like haddock.

• Pieces of seafood such as mussels, scallops, shrimp and lobster, add both color and texture to delicate fish mixtures.

• Both vegetable and fish pâtés are nicest served with a sauce such as a puree of peppers, tomatoes or zucchini, with a little oil and vinegar added. Or try something simple like plain yogurt, or sour cream with seasoning and chopped fresh herbs.

• For an excellent simple sauce for fish pâté season heavy cream with a trace of crushed garlic and a few threads of saffron, bring to a boil and then leave to cool and infuse, before stirring in 1–2 teaspoons sherry vinegar at the end.

• Individual molds or timbales made from a well-seasoned vegetable puree, such as parsnip, zucchini or spinach bound with whole eggs or egg whites, are lovely hot with a sauce as a first course.

GLOSSY VEGETABLE PÂTÉ (94)

This is my favorite kind of vegetable pâté. The key to a good pâté is that both the aspic and the vegetables should have real flavor – it is worth using organic vegetables if you can get them.   SERVES 6–8

2½ cups (600ml) white wine
2 bay leaves
½ teaspoon caraway seeds
1 large clove garlic, chopped
1in (2.5cm) piece fresh gingerroot, peeled and coarsely chopped
8oz (250g) broccoli florets, halved lengthwise
10oz (300g) small zucchini, trimmed and thinly sliced lengthwise
12oz (375g) small carrots, thinly sliced lengthwise
8oz (250g) cauliflower florets, thinly sliced lengthwise
1 cup (150g) frozen Fordhook lima beans
Salt
Cayenne pepper
1½ packages unflavored gelatin
½ cup (125ml) cold water
Sprigs flat-leaf parsley
1 large yellow pepper, cored, seeded and chopped as finely as possible (page 49)

Boil the wine with the bay leaves, caraway seeds, garlic and ginger, then cover and simmer for about 25 minutes.

Meanwhile, blanch the broccoli, zucchini, carrots and cauliflower separately in boiling salted water. Immediately drain and place in cold running water. Put the lima beans in a bowl, pour boiling water over them and immediately drain well in a colander. Transfer to a bowl and set aside.

When the wine mixture is ready strain it through a fine sieve into a bowl. Season to taste with salt and cayenne pepper. To make the aspic soften the gelatin in the water and stir into hot wine mixture until it has fully dissolved, then cool. Don't start to assemble the pâté until the aspic has cooled.

Pour a thin layer of the cooled aspic over the bottom of a 9in (1kg) loaf pan. Arrange sprigs of flat-leaf parsley in the bottom of the pan and chill until the aspic has set. Arrange the vegetables in alternating layers, interspersed with lima beans and yellow pepper. Pour in the remaining aspic, letting it flow through the vegetables and cover them. Chill the

pâté for several hours until well set. To serve, dip the pan briefly in a bowl of hot water, then turn out onto a serving plate, giving the pan a shake against the serving plate. Use a very sharp serrated knife to cut into slices.

PARSNIP AND GARLIC MOUSSE WITH CILANTRO SAUCE (94)

Here is a delicious example of how well-cooked garlic becomes mild and sweet.   SERVES 6

1lb (500g) parsnips, coarsely chopped
1 large head garlic cloves, separated but unpeeled
1 teaspoon paprika
1 large egg
1 large egg white
1¼ cups (300ml) heavy cream
1 teaspoon honey
1 teaspoon ground mace
Salt and black pepper
FOR THE SAUCE
1¼ cups (300ml) sour cream or plain yogurt
3 teaspoons white wine vinegar
1 good handful chopped fresh cilantro
Salt
Cayenne pepper

Cook the parsnips in salted water with the unpeeled garlic cloves until soft, then drain.

Generously oil a 5 cup (1.2 liter) mold or loaf pan. Sprinkle the paprika on the bottom, mainly in the center. Put a roasting pan of hot water in the oven and heat to 325°F, 160°C. Pop the garlic cloves out of their skins into a food processor with the parsnips, egg and egg white, cream, honey and mace. Process until very smooth, then season to taste with salt and black pepper. Pour slowly into the prepared mold and put into the roasting pan of water in the oven. Cook for 30–40 minutes until firm to a light touch in the center. Remove and leave until almost cold, then loosen the sides carefully, using a knife if necessary, and turn out onto a serving plate.

To make the sauce, simply mix the sour cream or yogurt, vinegar and chopped cilantro together and season to taste with salt and a little cayenne pepper. Put in a bowl and serve with the mousse, which should be served at room temperature, not chilled.

DUCK, CHICKEN AND PORK LOAF WITH PRUNES AND PISTACHIOS (94)

Make this at least a day before you plan to eat it as it will keep for several days in the refrigerator. It is an ideal standby accompanied by crusty bread. The duck skin adds the good flavor of duck fat and so keeps the loaf moist – just as you often add pork fat to a loaf, only duck has a richer taste.   SERVES 8–10

2 duck breast filets, about 10oz (300g)
2 skinless chicken breast filets, about 10oz (300g)
1lb (500g) salt pork, derind and diced
2 cloves garlic, crushed
1 teaspoon ground mace
1 teaspoon ground coriander
Finely grated rind and juice of 1 orange
⅔ cup (150ml) Cointreau or brandy
Black pepper
4oz (125g) soft pitted prunes, quartered
2oz (50g) shelled pistachio nuts
Salt
12oz (375g) thinly sliced bacon
Whole peppercorns

Skin the duck breast filets. Cut up the skin into very small pieces, then cut the duck and chicken meat into ½in (1cm) cubes. Mix together the meat and duck skin, and the pork in a small bowl with the garlic, mace and coriander, orange rind and juice, Cointreau and a generous sprinkling of black pepper. Cover and chill for at least 8 hours.

Put a roasting pan of water in the center of the oven and heat to 300°F, 150°C. Stir the prunes, pistachio nuts and a sprinkling of salt into the meat mixture. Line the bottom and sides of a medium-sized earthenware bowl or soufflé dish with about half the bacon, then spoon in the mixture with any juices and pack level. Lay the remaining bacon neatly all over the top and scatter 1 teaspoon of peppercorns in the center of the bacon for garnish. Cover with foil, place in the roasting pan and cook for about 2 hours until the loaf comes away from the sides of the dish.

When the juices and fat have started to cool, put a heavy weight on top of the foil and put the dish in the refrigerator. Remove the dish at least 30 minutes before you plan to serve the loaf and turn it out carefully.

GLAZED PÂTÉ IN HERBED PASTRY (94)

A wonderful fusion of flavors combined with a spectacular appearance makes this a perfect pâté for a lunch party, accompanied by a green salad and crusty bread in summer, or during colder weather, a bowl of hot new potatoes. Including herbs in the pastry is an easy way of adding extra flavor.   *SERVES 6–8*

FOR THE PÂTÉ
    8oz (250g) boneless stewing veal, finely diced
    6oz (175g) boneless pork, such as leg, finely diced
    6oz (175g) skinless turkey breast filets, finely diced
    1 cup (250ml) dry white wine
    ½ cup (125ml) dry sherry
    Black pepper
    4oz (125g) chicken livers, finely chopped
    Milk
    125g (4oz) pork fat, finely chopped
    2 teaspoons drained capers
    1 teaspoon juniper berries, crushed, plus extra for garnishing
    2 teaspoons green peppercorns
    3–4 large cloves garlic, finely chopped
    2oz (50g) can anchovy fillets
    Sea salt
    Several bay leaves
    Olive oil
    1 package unflavored gelatin
FOR THE PASTRY
    2 cups (250g) bread flour
    1 teaspoon salt
    1–2 sprigs fresh rosemary, finely chopped
    2 teaspoons dried oregano
    1 teaspoon dried thyme
    5oz (150g) butter
    5 tablespoons water

Place the veal, pork, turkey, white wine, sherry and a generous sprinkling of freshly ground black pepper in a large bowl and mix together thoroughly. Cover the bowl and place in the refrigerator for 12–24 hours. About halfway through the marinating time put the chopped chicken livers in a second bowl, cover with milk and chill.

While the meat is marinating, butter a 7in (18cm) springform pan with a loose base. To make the pastry, sift the flour and salt into a bowl and mix in the rosemary, oregano and thyme. Heat the butter and water in a small saucepan over low heat until the butter melts, then pour

into the flour and herbs and stir until you have a smooth, thick dough. Put the ball of dough into the pan and press the dough evenly over the bottom and up the sides of the pan to just beyond the rim. Refrigerate until needed.

Drain the meat and marinade mixture in a sieve over a bowl, then pour the liquid through a fine sieve into a small saucepan. Drain the chicken livers and discard the milk. Put the meat and chicken livers in a bowl and mix in the pork fat, capers, juniper berries, green peppercorns and garlic. Drain the oil from the anchovies and add it to the bowl. Season with sea salt and a little black pepper.

Spoon the mixture into the pan and spread evenly. Arrange a star pattern of alternate anchovy fillets and bay leaves on top, pressing them into the meat mixture. Brush with olive oil. Lay a piece of foil loosely on top and bake at 325°F, 160°C for 1¾–2 hours.

Towards the end of the cooking time, combine the gelatin and ¼ cup (60ml) cold water in a bowl. Boil the sieved marinade mixture for 1 minute, then pour into the bowl through a fine sieve lined with cheesecloth. Stir until the gelatin has fully dissolved. When the terrine is baked, you can replace the bay leaves with fresh ones for a more colorful effect if you wish. Spoon the slightly cooled gelatin liquid over the top of the meat so that it sinks into any gaps where the cooked meat has shrunk away from the pastry. Set aside until cold.

To serve, remove side of springform pan. Carefully remove the bottom before putting the pâté onto a serving plate. Serve cool, but not straight from the refrigerator.

SMOKY FISH LOAF WITH MACE AND PINK PEPPERCORNS (94)

I serve this loaf as a main course with a cheese sauce which I make slightly thinner than usual, adding threads of saffron and a clove of crushed garlic right at the beginning so that they infuse into the sauce as it cooks. New potatoes and either a green vegetable or salad are good accompaniments.   *SERVES 4*

    14oz (425g) smoked haddock fillet, skinned and coarsely chopped
    1 teaspoon ground mace
    2 eggs
    2 egg whites
    ⅔ cup (150ml) heavy cream
    1 teaspoon chopped fresh tarragon leaves
    1 teaspoon pink peppercorns
    3–4 pinches cayenne pepper
    1 flounder fillet, 6–8oz (175–250g), skinned and cut into thin strips lengthwise
    1¼–1½lb (625–750g) salmon, filleted, skinned and cut into ¾–1in (1.5–2.5cm) pieces
    Salt

Puree the smoked haddock in a food processor. Add the mace, then one at a time, the eggs and egg whites, processing very thoroughly after each addition. Gradually process in the cream. Turn the mixture into a bowl, stir in the tarragon and peppercorns and season with the cayenne pepper and salt. Cover and refrigerate for at least 30 minutes. Put a roasting pan of hot water in the oven and heat to 325°F, 160°C.

Butter a 5 cup (1.2 liter) earthenware dish generously and lay a piece of buttered parchment on the bottom, then layer the strips of flounder fillet across the terrine and up the sides, leaving a space between each strip. Stir the pieces of salmon fillet into the chilled haddock mixture and spoon into the dish. Top with a piece of buttered foil, pressing the edges to seal. Pierce 2 holes in the top of the foil to let the steam escape.

Set the earthenware dish in the roasting pan and cook for 60–70 minutes until the edges have slightly shrunk from the sides and a small knife inserted in the center comes out clean. Remove the foil and pour off any liquid around the loaf. (You can use this in your cheese sauce.) Set aside for 5 minutes before turning out onto a warm serving dish.

RICE, GRAINS and LEGUMES

Rice, grains and legumes have kept man alive and healthy for thousands of years, and still form the staple diet of more than half the world's population. Now, as a result of the high cost of meat and a growing number of vegetarians, the Western world is returning to a diet which previous generations might have scorned as peasant food. If you are a real vegetarian, a variety of legumes and grains, which are full of protein, vitamins and minerals, with the bonus of fiber too, can provide all the nutrients you need. Non-vegetarians can also benefit from the healthy properties of grains and legumes, and once you have realized their versatility in the kitchen, it is very possible you will not need to eat as much meat as you did before.

In any case, grains and legumes provide a huge and important area of cookery, and can be made into a wide variety of dishes, ranging from hearty stews to delicate purees trickled with the best olive oil. They should be eaten for their taste, texture and adaptability, as much as for their low cost and nutritious qualities.

If you have never had rice cooked well, it is easy to be bored by it. I still find that rice served as an accompaniment to meat or fish in restaurants is frequently dull, bland and unappealing. But basmati rice, with its aromatic grains, or a real risotto made with Italian arborio rice, can be ambrosial. The Egyptian way of cooking rice by the absorption method and then raising the heat and letting the grains on the bottom of the pan toast golden to dark brown before stirring them up into the rest of the rice is my favorite rice dish. Dark, spicy

wild rice although not a true rice but the seed of an aquatic grass grown in North America, can also be used cold in salads, or in stuffings.

Most dried legumes should be soaked in cold water for several hours – I usually leave them overnight, which makes the cooking time shorter. If you have a pressure cooker, it is the quickest way to cook them, and it also preserves the valuable B vitamins.

Among the countless possibilities for using legumes, you can make wonderful soups, subtle purees, or delectable cassoulet-type stews with a variety of the beans. When I am feeding large crowds during the holidays some kind of bean stew is one of the most useful and popular dishes to make. It can be simply beans: kidney, haricot, cannellini or chick peas in particular, slowly cooked with vegetables added at different stages, or more luxuriously, like a real cassoulet with pieces of goose or duck, smoked sausages and chunks of bacon – in either case the beans have to cook long and gently to become meltingly soft, absorbing the flavors of ingredients cooked with them, and forming creamy, self-thickened juices around them.

Grains and legumes, the first foods to be discovered by man, were also the first foods to be stored for later use. They offer enormous scope for nutritious and unusual meals. One great advantage is their keeping properties; rice can be kept in a dry atmosphere more or less indefinitely, and legumes and grains will last well for at least a year, after which they are still usable, but take longer to cook as they become harder.

Clockwise from top: My Cassoulet (page 114), a hearty stew of beans, pork, duck, sausages under a golden oregano-flavored bread crumb topping; Basmati Rice with Crisped Grains (page 114) is flavored with cinnamon sticks; Kidney Bean and Grilled Pepper Salad (page 115) combines red kidney beans with yellow peppers, green onions and flat-leaf parsley; Saffron and Chili Rice Cooked in Coconut Milk (page 115) makes a flavorful, golden accompaniment to curries and grilled meats; Golden Lentil Rolls Wrapped in Bacon (page 114) are baked with finely grated Parmesan cheese and served here with frisée lettuce.

RICE

There are literally thousands of varieties of this vital grain, all with different characteristics that lead to many ways of cooking. Yet in our cuisine rice remains a much underrated food, relegated to the side of the plate as a boring accompaniment, which it can be if not cooked properly. This is a great pity as rice's ability to absorb and enhance flavorings and textures makes it ideal to produce some unusual and even glorious dishes.

Rice comes in two main grain types – long (*indica*) and round (*japonica*). Round grains cook to either a creaminess or a light glutinous stickiness (ideal for chopsticks), depending on the variety. Light, long grains that stay separate and have real flavor are essential for spicy pilafs or for simply elegant fluffy rice as a side dish. Short round grains cooked long and slowly become a comforting pudding; medium round grains also with the same creamy quality make the memorable Italian classic risottos or colorful Spanish paellas. Brown rice with the outer bran layer intact has a deliciously nutty taste but does take longer to cook. Readily available converted rice has been refined by parboiling, which slightly hardens the outside layer and reduces the risk of overcooking. This rice is ideal for cooking in one-pot meals and casseroles as occasional stirring will not break up the grains.

PREPARING AND COOKING RICE

All U.S. grown rice has been cleaned so it is not necessary to rinse or soak. The cooking times given here are for unsoaked rice. There is no need to rinse or soak converted rices. Rinsing and soaking, though, is necessary for imported rices such as jasmine and basmati rice. To rinse, add the rice to a large bowl of cold water, stirring the grains round with your hand. Let it settle, then pour off the water. Repeat 2–3 times more until the water becomes clearer, then drain and cook. There are a variety of rice mixtures now on the market that make interesting accompaniments to meats.

Do not cook more than 1lb (500g) raw rice at a time (that's 8–10 portions). Allow 2oz (50g) raw rice per person for a side dish and 3oz (75g) for a main dish. Most rice absorbs at least 3 times its weight in liquid making this a generous serving. To test if rice is cooked scoop out some grains and press 1 or 2 between your thumb and forefinger. If a small hard core remains allow a few minutes extra. After cooking, rice continues to absorb moisture and it will fluff up even more if you allow it to stand for a few minutes before stirring and serving.

OPEN PAN METHOD

Many cooks have their own favorite ways of cooking rice. One method is the open pan or excess water method, boiling it in a lot of water like pasta. Allow 6¼ cups (1.5 liters) water to 8oz (250g) rice. Season with 1 teaspoon of salt either during cooking or afterwards, remembering that rice absorbs salt very easily. Long grain rice takes 12–15 minutes; brown rice 30–35 minutes; basmati rice 8–10 minutes. Converted rice needs a few minutes extra cooking time and because of its slightly harder outside layer doesn't spoil if overcooked.

Bring a large pan of *water to a good rolling boil. Add the measured rice, stir and return to a medium boil. Cook, uncovered, stirring once or twice with a large wooden spoon, according to the times (see left), then drain in a sieve and rinse with boiling water if desired. Toss with a little oil or melted butter.*

ABSORPTION METHOD

In this method the rice simmers slowly in a measured amount of water or stock in a covered pan and the rice should be cooked when the liquid has been absorbed and there are small holes between the grains.

Use the same measuring cup for the rice and water or stock. For long grain rice use double the amount of water or stock, 1¼–1½ times the amount of liquid for basmati and 2¼ times the amount of liquid for brown rice. Add any seasoning before cooking although basmati or Thai rices taste delicious unseasoned.

Place the water or stock *and rice in the pan, season and bring to a boil. Lower the heat to simmer, then cover tightly and cook for 15–20 minutes for long grain rice, 10 minutes for basmati and 30–35 minutes for brown rice. Remove from the heat without uncovering and leave for 5 minutes. Toss with oil or butter.*

MICROWAVE METHOD

Rice cooks beautifully in a microwave. Do not cook more than about 12oz (375g) rice at a time and you need a deep bowl for the water as it boils up. Use the same proportions of long grain and brown rice to water as in the absorption method (left), and 1½ times the amount of water for basmati rice. Use these times: for long grain rice cook 7 minutes on High, then 8 minutes on Defrost; for basmati cook 6 minutes on High, then 4–6 minutes on Defrost; for brown rice cook 7 minutes on High, then 25 minutes on Defrost.

Cover the bowl *with microwavable plastic wrap. Pierce. Cook on High (100%) for the specified time (left), then stir, recover and cook on Defrost (30%) for the remaining time. Remove from the microwave and leave for 5 minutes before removing the wrap and stirring with a fork. Toss with a little oil or butter.*

MAKING A PILAF

A pilaf is oil- or butter-enriched rice, cooked until the liquid, usually stock, has been absorbed, and then a few other cooked or sautéed ingredients such as shrimp, mushrooms or peas, are added. The rice is never stirred during the main cooking period.

Pilaf can either be cooked on top of the stove, as shown here, or cooked, covered, in the oven at 350°F, 180°C. Rinse and soak the rice in water for at least 1 hour before cooking. These quantities serve 4.

1 *Melt 1oz (25g) butter in a heavy pan and fry 1 finely chopped onion until golden. Add 8oz (250g) basmati rice and spices to taste and stir to coat with butter. Cook for 1–2 minutes until the grains are opaque.*

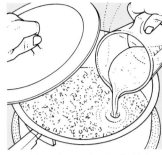

2 *Add 1¼ cups (300ml) chicken stock and bring to a boil, stir, then cover the pan and simmer as gently as possible for about 12–15 minutes until tender but still with a slight bite to it. Test for doneness (opposite).*

3 *If the rice is still too firm, and all the liquid is already absorbed, add a little more liquid, stir in the prepared ingredients and continue cooking until the rice is done. Fluff the rice with a fork and season. Mound on a serving dish.*

MAKING A RISOTTO

A real risotto is luxuriously creamy; this is achieved by stirring in small amounts of hot stock during the cooking process, and only adding more after the previous amount has been absorbed. The best risottos are made freshly to order so they retain their delicious creaminess. Use short grain Italian arborio rice. The method here is for a basic risotto; other prepared ingredients such as sautéed vegetables or fresh herbs can be added 5 minutes before the end of cooking. Serves 4.

1 *Melt 1½oz (40g) butter and 2 tablespoons olive oil in a large saucepan over medium heat. Add 1 finely chopped onion and fry until golden. Add 12oz (375g) arborio rice and stir for 1–2 minutes until a pale opaque color.*

2 *Heat 5-6¼ cups (1.2–1.8 liters) of chicken stock and add a ladleful to the rice, stirring until absorbed. Continue adding stock, a ladleful at a time, and stirring for 20–25 minutes until the rice is cooked but still firm.*

3 *After adding the stock stir in any prepared ingredients and warm through. Stir in 1oz (25g) butter and season to taste. Spoon onto individual plates and serve at once, topped with coarsely grated Parmesan cheese.*

SERVING RICE

• Paella, ideally using a medium round grain rice, is cooked with chopped tomatoes, onions, garlic, meat and fish in a stock, but the pan is shaken during cooking rather than stirred so the grains separate more.
• Good ingredients to add to both pilafs and risottos are sautéed slices of bulb fennel, parsnips, eggplant, mushrooms, zucchini or broccoli, as well as broiled, skinned and finely sliced peppers, pieces of smoked fish, shrimp, crab meat, crispy fried cubes of smoked bacon, smoked or fresh ham, and chicken. There is lots of opportunity for adding plenty of chopped fresh herbs. Squid ink can be added to risotto to make it a shimmering black color, which looks wonderful with chopped flat-leaf parsley, and beet juice will turn the rice pink.
• Rice mixtures are excellent for stuffing vegetables (page 61), or sometimes fish, wrapping in pastry or packing into molds to serve either hot or cold.
• Rice for salads should be dressed with vinaigrette (page 204) after draining and rinsing while still hot. Leave to cool before serving.

A risotto flavored with shrimp, asparagus and dill.

GRAINS

Grains can be the basis of much innovative cooking. Wheat in many forms, buckwheat, corn, rye, barley and millet are all dried grains which offer nourishment, taste and variety once they have absorbed liquid and softened. They are an invaluable way of stretching more expensive ingredients such as pieces of meat or fish and still producing an exciting and delicious dish.

Wheat could be called the king of grains, as it is the essential ingredient for most of our daily bread. There are also several forms of cracked wheat, including bulgar, which have been cracked by preboiling so only need soaking for use in salads, croquettes, stuffings and so on. Semolina and couscous are also forms of wheat.

Cooked whole grains are ideal cold and can be used in salads to provide a chewy element. Like rice, other grains are perfect vehicles for all kinds of sauces, and for added herbs, spices, garlic and other seasonings. Buckwheat, which you can buy either roasted or not, cooks more quickly than most grains: roasted buckwheat is particularly good and buckwheat flour makes the laciest, crispest pancakes possible (page 74). Millet is another quick-cooking grain which can be used for making rissoles, or in stews. Polenta, an Italian dish made from cornmeal, is cooked until thick and eaten immediately or cooled and cut into wedges, then fried and served with a sauce.

One of the things I look forward to when the weather gets colder is eating cooked cereal again. As well as for cereal, oatmeal can be used in cookies or as an addition to bread dough as it has a wonderful flavor and texture. Cookies made with oatmeal are another of my favorites.

PREPARING COUSCOUS

The staple grain of North Africa and becoming better known elsewhere, couscous is a form of semolina made from durum wheat and rolled into little pellets. Traditionally, it is cooked in a couscoussière (page 24), which looks like a steamer, and is put over a pot of a simmering spicy meat, vegetable or fish stew. If you don't have a couscoussière, you can just use an ordinary steamer with a tight-fitting lid. Allow 8oz (250g) couscous to serve 4.

Traditional couscous requires a time consuming process of repeated soaking, draining, rubbing and drying to allow it to swell and lighten somewhat before being placed in the couscoussière.

These days most people are looking for convenience and use the precooked type of couscous which is available in supermarkets either plain or as a mix with the spices included. Precooked couscous can be ready in a minute. Just reconstitute it with boiling water or stir it into the broth of a dish at the end of its cooking time.

It is particularly good in salads (see right) and as an easy accompaniment to stews and casseroles.

SUMMER COUSCOUS SALAD

Couscous is very good for salads as it absorbs some of whatever dressing you use and blends well with whatever flavors you choose to combine it with.

For a summer vegetable salad to serve 4, pour 1¼ cups (350ml) boiling water over 1 cup (250g) precooked couscous in a large bowl. Stir in 6 tablespoons (75ml) extra virgin olive oil, ¼ cup (50ml) white wine vinegar, 1 teaspoon sugar, and salt and black pepper to taste. Set aside about 20 minutes or until all the liquid has been absorbed and the couscous has cooled enough not to melt the cheese when you add it.

Stir 3oz (80g) coarsely shredded Swiss cheese, 2 firm tomatoes and 1 yellow pepper, cubed, 4 green onions, sliced crosswise, 12 oil-cured ripe olives, halved and pitted, 2 large handfuls flat-leaf parsely, finely chopped, and 2 large handfuls basil, also finely chopped, into the couscous mixture. Cover and refrigerate until ready to serve.

Just before serving, remove from the refrigerator, stir again and spoon out onto a serving platter lined with red and green leaf lettuce. This salad is good with grilled chicken, steak or hamburgers, or as a vegetarian main dish.

MAKING TABBOULEH

Tabbouleh is one of the most famous of the Middle Eastern *mezze*, meaning appetizers, which cover the whole table with countless little dishes. Serve it as a salad, or make it part of a cold summer meal.

The grain used is bulgar, which is preboiled, cracked wheat. The only preparation it needs is soaking. Traditionally, tabbouleh is made with chopped tomatoes, onion, parsley and mint leaves. Serves 6.

4oz (125g) bulgar soaked for 15–20 minutes and drained
6 tablespoons lemon juice
Salt
Black pepper
6-8 tablespoons extra virgin olive oil
3 large handfuls flat-leaf parsley, finely chopped
2 large handfuls mint leaves, finely chopped
1 red onion, finely chopped
4–5 firm tomatoes, cubed

1 *Use your hands to transfer the soaked and drained bulgar to a bowl, squeezing out all the water. Marinate with the lemon juice and salt and pepper for 30 minutes.*

2 *Stir in the remaining ingredients and mix together well with a wooden spoon. Spoon into a shallow serving dish. Stir again just before serving.*

POLENTA

Made from yellow cornmeal, polenta is a classic of Italian cooking. Freshly cooked polenta looks like cooked cereal. In Italy it is eaten in many different ways from a simple first course with butter and Parmesan cheese to an accompaniment for game casseroles. Or serve with fresh tomato sauce (page 206) or grilled meat.

You need 2 cups (300g) polenta to serve 4–6. In Italy, polenta is lovingly and continually stirred for up to an hour, but I find frequent stirring for 20 minutes is quite sufficient. If allowed to set in a shallow layer, polenta can be cut up and grilled.

1 Bring 7½ cups (1.8 liters) milk and water mixed to a boil in a large, heavy saucepan. Season with salt. Measure 2 cups (300g) cornmeal. With a long-handled spoon in one hand for stirring, drizzle the grains into the saucepan. Stir briskly, but not too vigorously, always in only one direction to avoid lumps, as you add the cornmeal.

Grains make a hearty start to the day – try homemade muesli or hot, creamy oatmeal with yogurt and brown sugar.

2 Continue to stir rapidly until smooth and thick, then turn down the heat to simmer and cook for 20 minutes. Ideally you should stir all the time, but as long as you stir frequently to keep the polenta from burning on the bottom of the saucepan it should be fine. Check the seasoning and stir in a good chunk of butter and grated Parmesan cheese.

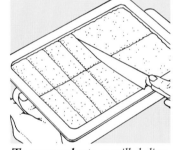

To serve polenta *as grilled slices pour the cooked polenta into a large, shallow ovenproof dish and spread out evenly. Cool and refrigerate until solid, then cut into narrow rectangles. Preheat a broiler until very hot and broil the slices until browned and crispy on both sides. Spread with butter to serve with stews or grilled meats or simply buttered on its own.*

OATMEAL

Traditional Irish oatmeal is made with cut oats and often cooked overnight in a very low oven. The method below uses rolled oats and takes only a few minutes to cook on top of the stove.

I like using old-fashioned rolled oats, which only take a little longer to cook than quick or instant oats, and have much more texture. To serve 4 allow 1¾cups (125g).

Place the rolled oats *and 2½ cups (600ml) water in a small saucepan and bring to a boil, stirring. Simmer gently, stirring constantly, for 3–5 minutes until it is the thickness you like. Season to taste with salt. Spoon the oatmeal into bowls and serve with milk, cream or yogurt, and brown sugar, honey or molasses.*

MUESLI

This mixture of uncooked grain flakes and dried fruit was introduced by a Dr Bircher at his clinic in Switzerland at the end of the nineteenth century. Today it is almost as familiar as granola on the breakfast table and just as easy to make.

Making muesli at home means you can put in more of your favorite ingredients and vary them each time. The following mixture is my personal choice: 1 cup dried apricots, ½ cup each dried apples and prunes, ½ cup dried bananas, ¼ cup hazelnuts, ¼ cup almonds in their skins, 2 cups old-fashioned rolled oats, 2 cups barley flakes, 3 teaspoons ground cinnamon, 1 tablespoon sesame seeds and ½ cup golden raisins.

Chop the dried fruit and nuts fairly small. Put into a bowl with the grains, cinnamon, sesame seeds and raisins, mixing well with a wooden spoon. Transfer to an airtight container for storage, and serve with milk, fruit juice or yogurt, and add pieces of fresh fruit and some brown sugar if you like.

USING GRAINS

• Boiled whole wheat, barley or rye grains are enhanced by stirring in some butter-sautéed onions or mushrooms to serve with roasted game birds, duck and chicken. You can also sprinkle the grains with soy sauce just before serving.
• Bulgar, so quick to prepare, can be made into various stuffings for vegetables, vine leaves or poultry. Mix it with spiced ground lamb, nuts or chopped sautéed vegetables.
• Cooked grains are also good served with vegetable sauces, such as pumpkin cooked with plenty of garlic, butter and spices until it becomes a mushy sauce, or a fresh tomato sauce (page 206) with strips of basil added at the end.
• Grains can be added to vegetable soups and stews to add body to the juices as well as texture and flavor.

LEGUMES

Legumes are the dried seeds of an enormous variety of bean and pea pods, many possessing very different flavors and characters. Whenever I travel abroad and discover legumes I haven't seen before I cannot resist bringing them home to try. The flavoring of legumes is very important; although they do not have a definite taste of their own, the long, slow cooking they need allows them to take on the flavors of the ingredients they are cooked with. Some legumes, such as white beans and lentils, break up more easily than others, making them more suitable for soups, purees or very mushy, comforting stews. Chick peas, however, never break up, however long they are cooked, although they can also be puréed to make hummus, the classic Middle Eastern appetizer.

Although legumes can make irresistible stews and casseroles, they can also be used for lighter dishes. Carefully seasoned and butter-enriched pureed legumes are excellent alternatives to potatoes or rice as a side dish, and cold purees make delicate dips or appetizers. Legumes can be added to salads. As well as being convenient, canned legumes hold their shape and color well which makes them ideal for salads (you may prefer to rinse them first).

SOAKING LEGUMES

Almost all dried legumes require presoaking to speed up the cooking process, and soaking is also supposed to help to reduce any tendency to flatulence. Although not essential, legumes intended for the pressure cooker are best presoaked as this cuts down on foaming. Legumes can be soaked in cold water for up to 8–12 hours. Smaller legumes, such as lentils, can be cooked without soaking, particularly red lentils which can be poured straight from the package into the cooking pot and only take 20 minutes or less to cook. Thicker green and brown lentils, however, cook far quicker if soaked for a couple of hours beforehand. If you forget to start soaking larger legumes well in advance, then you can cut the soaking time to 1–2 hours by covering in boiling water and then cooking them a little longer.

Remember, legumes yield about double their weight when cooked, so take that into account when calculating quantities. For 4 servings, use 4oz (125g) dried legumes. As cooked legumes can be stored in the refrigerator for up to 3 days, it is sensible to cook more than you need, to use for another meal.

Cover legumes with at least 4 times the amount of cold water. Swish around with your hands and leave to soak (see chart below). Drain and rinse under cold water. Cook legumes with added flavorings (but not salt) in more fresh cold water (right).

COOKING LEGUMES

It is important to boil some legumes for the first 10 minutes to destroy any potential toxins that may be present, but after that reduce the heat to a gentle simmer so they soften without breaking up. Simmering times in the chart are approximate because older legumes take longer to cook. Adzuki, kidney, lima and soy beans specifically require vigorous preboiling for 10 minutes to destroy toxins but it does no harm to preboil all legumes.

SOAKING AND COOKING CHART

Use these times as guidelines; how long the legumes have been soaked and stored will affect the cooking times. Older legumes and those that have not been soaked long, take longer to cook. First preboil the legumes for 10 minutes, then reduce the heat to a simmer.

Variety of legume	Soaking time	Approximate simmering time after 10 minutes' preboiling
Adzuki bean	At least 8 hours	40 minutes
Black-eyed peas	At least 8 hours	50 minutes
Chick peas (garbanzos)	At least 8 hours	1 hour
Cranberry bean	At least 8 hours	50 minutes
Fava bean	At least 8 hours	50 minutes
Haricot bean (navy bean, cannellini and flageolet)	At least 8 hours	50 minutes
Kidney bean, black	At least 8 hours	50 minutes
Kidney bean, red	At least 8 hours	1 hour
Lentils, green	Not necessary	45 minutes
Lentils, red	Not necessary	20 minutes
Lima bean	At least 8 hours	1 hour
Mung bean	At least 8 hours	25 minutes
Peas, split	Not necessary	30 minutes
Peas, whole	At least 8 hours	1–1¼ hours
Pinto bean	At least 8 hours	1 hour
Soy bean	12 hours	1¾ hours

Put the soaked legumes into a saucepan and cover with at least 4 times the volume of cold water. Add herbs, onion slices or diced carrots. Bring to a boil. Boil hard for 10 minutes and skim off any foam. Reduce to a simmer, cover and cook until tender (left). Add some boiling water, if necessary. Drain, discard the flavorings and season. Toss with olive oil or vinaigrette (page 204) if serving cold in salads.

SPROUTING BEANS AND SEEDS

Watching beans, peas and seeds sprout over a few days is quite magical. Fresh homegrown sprouts are also very nutritious, and an excellent inexpensive way of taking in fresh vitamins. The sprouting and germination process renders the beans digestible and all they need is time and water. Most legumes will sprout, but not split beans and split lentils, and it is a good idea to have 2 or 3 types growing at once. Sprouts can be used in pasta sauces, pilafs, homemade burgers, stir-fries, stews and even sandwich fillings as well as in salads.

1 *Soak about 3 tablespoons of legumes in at least 4 times the amount of fresh water for 12 hours. Drain, rinse in cold water and place the legumes in a clean glass jar. Cover with a piece of cheesecloth, secured with an elastic band. Pierce the top a few times with a skewer. Lay the jar on its side on a light, but not sunny, windowsill away from drafts.*

2 *Rinse well with warm running water each morning and night to wet the seeds and remove waste gases. It should not be necessary to remove the top. When sprouted (usually within 3 days), rinse and drain again, then store in a plastic bag in the refrigerator and eat within 2 days. If the legumes do not sprout this means they are too old so discard.*

MAKING PUREES AND DIPS

Legume purees can be either hot or cold, mushy or thick enough to form a solid cake. Hot purees should be made with legumes that break up easily, such as lentils, lima beans and cannellini beans. After draining the cooked legumes, you can simply mash them with a fork, adding butter and flavors as you mash, or use a food processor. Serve hot purees as a side dish instead of potatoes, or serve cold ones as a dip.

For extra-smooth purees *use a food processor. Put the drained, cooked legumes in the machine with spices or extra flavorings as you like. Process until the puree is smooth and creamy.*

For a thinner puree *add a little olive oil, nut oil or plain yogurt to the drained cooked legumes. Either add through the top of a food processor or beat in by hand with a fork after pureeing.*

IDEAS FOR LEGUMES

• Spices such as turmeric, cumin, coriander, caraway, nutmeg, cinnamon and mace all go well with legumes, as do herbs such as oregano, thyme, rosemary, cilantro, basil, mint, garlic, fresh ginger and chili.

• White beans are especially good for pureeing to form the basis of soups or pâtés. A puree of white beans and carrots in a well-seasoned chicken stock makes a wonderful soup. Top with a swirl of cream and fresh dill or basil.

• Thick lentil, chick pea, cannellini or kidney bean purees can be formed into rissoles or balls and shallow-fried until crisp all over. Mix with finely chopped fried onions or mushrooms, chopped green onions or simply with lots of chopped parsley and chopped garlic, adding spices if you like, or a spoonful of curry paste. The balls can be rolled in fresh bread crumbs, and deep fried for an extra crispy exterior.

• I think long and gently simmered stews and casseroles are perhaps the most satisfying way of cooking legumes. I always boil beans for a stew separately in unsalted water, until they are soft but not breaking up, and then cook them again with the other ingredients, long and gently. Seasoning should be adjusted at the end.

• Try navy and cannellini beans in stews, particularly with chunks of smoked bacon, tomatoes, onions and plenty of garlic. They are delicious but they do tend to break up more than kidney beans.

• Nutty-flavored chick peas are lovely in a chicken casserole with turmeric or saffron, garlic and bulb fennel with chopped fresh herbs such as cilantro or tarragon thrown in at the end.

• Imported flageolet beans or green lentils are excellent as a salad on their own mixed with finely chopped, raw red onion, plenty of chopped parsley and a vinaigrette dressing (page 204).

• Crunchy ingredients such as bulb fennel, celery, parboiled thin slices of parsnip, radishes and blanched slivers of broccoli, as well as plenty of fresh herbs, combine well with beans in a salad.

Clockwise from top: Butter Bean Puree with Onions and Garlic (page 115), chick pea puree with turmeric and cilantro and a hot green lentil puree topped with melting butter.

MY CASSOULET (106)

There is a lot of argument about what a true cassoulet consists of, but it seems to me that as long as it is a richly satisfying fusion of beans and meats, it is really up to personal taste, what ingredients you can get, and how much time you have. There is no point in thinking you can't make a cassoulet if you haven't got any preserved goose or Toulouse sausages. The crust of breadcrumbs on top of the cassoulet is an authentic touch worth doing. Serve with a green salad. *SERVES 8*

1lb (500g) dried white beans, soaked overnight in cold water
1oz (25g) butter
4 tablespoons olive oil
3 large onions, cut into ¼in (5mm) slices
6–8 large cloves garlic, chopped
2 large red peppers, halved, seeded and cut into ½in (1cm) slices (page 49)
2 large bulbs fennel, trimmed, halved and cut into ½in (1cm) slices (page 46)
2lb (1kg) pork shoulder, cut into chunks
4 boned duck breasts, halved
1lb (500g) garlic sausages, cut into 1in (2.5cm) pieces
1lb (500g) tomatoes, coarsely chopped
2½ cups (600ml) hard cider
2 tablespoons tomato puree
1 tablespoon chopped fresh rosemary
2 rounded teaspoons green peppercorns
Salt and black pepper
6 slices 2-day-old bread, made into crumbs
3 teaspoons dried oregano
Extra olive oil

Drain the soaked beans and put them in a saucepan. Cover generously with cold water. Bring to a boil for 10 minutes, then cover and simmer gently for 20–35 minutes until just soft and not losing their form. Drain and set aside.

Melt the butter with 2 tablespoons olive oil in a large, deep frying pan over a medium heat. Add the onions and cook, stirring, until soft and browned, then add the garlic and stir for 1 minute.

Transfer the onions and garlic to a large bowl. Add another tablespoon of oil and the sliced peppers and fennel to the pan and fry until they begin to soften, then add to the bowl of onions. Add the final tablespoon of oil and fry the pork until just browned all over. Remove it and add it to the mixture in the bowl, then fry the duck pieces just to brown them.

Put the beans in a large casserole and add all the ingredients from the bowl, the duck and any fat from the pan, the sausages, tomatoes, cider, tomato puree, rosemary and green peppercorns. Mix together and season with salt and black pepper. Cover the casserole and cook at 450°F, 230°C for 20–25 minutes, then reduce the heat to 275°F, 140°C, and cook for a further 2½–3 hours.

Mix the bread crumbs and oregano together. Stir the cassoulet to mix well, then sprinkle the bread crumb and herb mixture over the top. Drizzle olive oil over the top and return the cassoulet to the oven, uncovered, for another 30 minutes.

BASMATI RICE WITH CRISPED GRAINS (106)

Basmati rice has a unique elegant, fragrant flavor. This method of cooking is based on the Egyptian way of almost burning the rice on the bottom of the pan and then scraping up the toasted grains to mix them with the rest. *SERVES 6*

8oz (250g) basmati rice, rinsed and soaked in salted water for 1 hour
2oz (50g) butter
3 cinnamon sticks, each about 1-2in (2.5–5cm) long
1¼–2 cups (300–450ml) water
1 teaspoon salt

Drain the soaked rice. Melt the butter in a heavy saucepan, add the cinnamon sticks and rice and stir. Stir in the water and salt, then bring to a boil. Cover the saucepan tightly, reduce the heat to as low as possible and cook for 10–14 minutes until the rice has absorbed the liquid and is tender but still has a slight bite to it. Put a tea towel between the lid and the top of the rice, tying the corners together on top of the lid so that they don't burn.

Increase the heat to as high as possible and continue cooking rice – this is to toast the bottom layer of rice and takes about 8–12 minutes, occasionally more depending on individual stoves. Don't try to stir the rice to see if the bottom is browning. Instead look at the top rim of the rice – when you see that the sides are beginning to brown, it will be ready. In my experience it hardly ever burns too much.

Remove the pan from the heat and set aside for 10 minutes. With a fork, remove the rice to a serving plate, scraping out all the toasted bottom and stirring the crisp, brown grains into the rest of the rice.

GOLDEN LENTIL ROLLS WRAPPED IN BACON (106)

Serve this lovely supper or lunch dish with a crisply cooked green vegetable like broccoli, or just a salad. It can be made well ahead so that you can simply put it in the oven to bake shortly before the meal. *SERVES 6*

6oz (175g) split red lentils
2 cups (450ml) milk
1 onion, finely chopped
3oz (75g) sharp cheese, grated
1oz (25g) butter
2 teaspoons dried oregano
Salt and black pepper
1 egg, beaten
About 6oz (175g) thinly sliced Irish bacon
Grated Parmesan cheese

Place the lentils, milk and finely chopped onion in a saucepan and bring to a boil, then simmer very gently, stirring now and then, for 20 minutes or until thick and mushy. Remove from the heat and add the cheese, butter, oregano and salt and black pepper to taste. Stir in the egg, then set aside to cool.

Butter a fairly large, shallow, oven-proof dish. Using floured hands, roll small handfuls of the lentil mixture into 2½in (6cm) long sausage shapes. Wrap a piece of bacon around each one, leaving gaps of lentil still exposed.

Lay the rolls close together in the dish and sprinkle all over with grated Parmesan cheese. Bake at 450°F, 230°C for 20–30 minutes until the rolls are golden brown and crispy.

BUTTER BEAN PUREE WITH ONIONS AND GARLIC *(113)*

In the South, dried lima beans are called butter beans. They really do have a rich buttery flavor, and as they tend to break up when they cook, a puree or a soup is the best thing you can do with them. This simple puree is wonderful, and goes perfectly instead of potatoes or rice with any roast or grilled meats or birds, or as part of a vegetarian meal. Butter beans combine especially well with the flavour of bay so for extra flavoring add a bay leaf or two to the cooking water.   *SERVES 6*

> *10oz (300g) dried butter or lima beans,*
>   *soaked for 8 hours or overnight in cold*
>   *water*
> *3oz (75g) butter*
> *2 tablespoons olive oil*
> *1 onion, sliced thinly*
> *2 teaspoons sugar*
> *2 cloves garlic, crushed*
> *Salt and black pepper*
> *2 tablespoons fresh white bread crumbs*
> *1 tablespoon grated Parmesan cheese*
> *Extra butter*

Drain the soaked butter beans. Put them in a saucepan and cover generously with cold water. Bring to a boil, boil for 10 minutes, then cover and simmer for 1–1½ hours until very soft, skimming the surface as necessary to remove any foam.

Meanwhile, melt 1oz (25g) of the butter with 2 tablespoons olive oil in a frying pan over a medium heat. Add the sliced onion and fry, stirring until it is soft and dark golden brown. Stir in the sugar, remove from the heat and set aside.

Drain the cooked butter beans and place in a food processor with the crushed garlic and remaining butter. Process thoroughly to a smooth puree. Season to taste with salt and black pepper, then stir in the fried onion with its butter and oil. Spoon the mixture into a shallow earthenware or gratin dish.

Mix the breadcrumbs with the grated Parmesan cheese, sprinkle over the top and dot with little bits of butter. Bake at 400°F, 200°C for 20–30 minutes until golden brown on top – if you already have meat or poultry roasting in the oven at a different temperature, just put in the dish and leave it for either more or less time until the surface has browned.

SAFFRON AND CHILI RICE COOKED IN COCONUT MILK *(106)*

Rice cooked in this way has such a lovely discreet exotic flavor that I like serving it with grilled chicken or fish instead of a dish with a lot of sauce, so that the rice can be tasted separately.   *SERVES 6*

> *8–10 strands saffron*
> *1 rounded teaspoon salt*
> *1¼ cups (300ml) boiling water*
> *½ cup (118ml) canned coconut milk*
> *1⅓ cups (250g) basmati rice, rinsed and*
>   *soaked in salted water for at least 1 hour*
> *1½oz (40g) butter*
> *1–2 fresh red chilies, stemmed, seeded*
>   *and finely chopped (page 49)*

Put the saffron and the salt in a cup with the boiling water and stir. Add the coconut milk and stir until combined. Cover and set aside to infuse.

Drain the soaked rice. Melt the butter in a large, heavy saucepan over a low heat, add the rice and finely chopped chilies and stir. Then pour in the saffron-coconut milk, including every strand of saffron. Bring to a boil, cover the saucepan tightly and reduce the heat to as low as possible for 10–14 minutes until the rice is tender but still has a slight bite to it when tested. Remove the saucepan from the heat.

If you aren't ready to eat immediately, put a cloth between the rice and the lid and leave on top of the stove, with the heat turned off, for up to 20 minutes. To serve turn out the rice onto a warmed serving dish.

KIDNEY BEAN AND GRILLED PEPPER SALAD *(106)*

With its combination of smoky, grilled peppers, this is a salad which can be prepared well ahead. When you can find them, black kidney beans look particularly effective. Cooking dried beans with a selection of herbs and a coarsely chopped onion will add to their flavor when you want to use them for a salad, as here. It is much better to put on the dressing while the beans are still hot so that they will absorb it.   *SERVES 6*

> *8oz (250g) red or black kidney beans,*
>   *soaked overnight in cold water*
> *2 bay leaves*
> *2–3 sprigs rosemary*
> *1 onion, coarsely chopped*
> *3 yellow peppers, halved, cored and*
>   *seeded (page 49)*
> *1 bunch green onions, finely chopped*
> *2 good handfuls flat-leaf parsley, coarsely*
>   *chopped*
> *FOR THE VINAIGRETTE*
> *1 tablespoon sherry vinegar*
> *2 tablespoons lemon juice*
> *1 teaspoon caraway seeds*
> *1 small clove garlic, crushed*
> *2 teaspoons honey*
> *6 tablespoons extra virgin olive oil*
> *Salt and black pepper*

Drain the soaked beans and put in a saucepan with the bay leaves, rosemary sprigs and chopped onion. Cover generously with water and bring to a boil. Boil for 10 minutes, then lower the heat, cover and simmer very gently for 40–60 minutes, skimming as necessary, until the beans are soft but still holding their shape.

Meanwhile, broil the pepper halves until the skins have blackened (page 55). Wrap them in a tea towel and set aside to cool. Put all the vinaigrette ingredients into a jar, cover and shake to mix thoroughly.

When the beans are cooked, drain them, discarding the herbs and onion, and put them in a large bowl. Shake the vinaigrette again and pour over the beans, mixing gently. Set aside to cool.

Meanwhile, peel the grilled peppers and thinly slice. When the beans are cool, mix in the peppers, chopped green onions and coarsely chopped parsley. Serve the salad warm or at room temperature, not chilled.

FISH and SHELLFISH

Only a short time ago many fish markets used to say it was not worth their while stocking a wide variety of fish. Customers, they said, would not try anything except the old faithfuls such as cod and sole. Now, happily, more and more kinds of fish are available, including tropical, Mediterranean and freshwater fish, different varieties of smoked fish and fresh shellfish of all kinds. Perhaps because we are more aware of healthy eating, and perhaps because there is an increased interest in cooking, we are beginning to be more imaginative and daring with what fish we buy, and what we do with it. Many people are discovering for the first time in their lives how delicious fish can be.

Fish is exciting to buy because it is so beautiful to look at. I find it almost impossible to pass the fish counter without buying something, even if I have not planned to eat fish that day. Fish is quick and interesting to cook, adapting itself to all sorts of wonderful sauces. The character of fish can become decidedly sophisticated when it is lightly poached with a delicate sauce, or comfortingly homey in something like really good fish cakes or a fish chowder. For anyone who insists they hate fish and cannot bear that 'fishy' taste, the more meaty fish now available, like tuna, monkfish, shark and swordfish, are a good way to start converting them.

When shopping for fish the characteristics of freshness are easy to spot. The fish should look as much as possible as if it is still swimming in the sea; shining bright, the gills deep pink to red and the eyes protruding and glossy, never sunken and cloudy. The flesh should be slippery and firm – if you can press it with your finger and it leaves no indentation you can be sure of freshness. Fish should smell of the sea but the smell should never be 'fishy' and strong. The exception to this is skate, which can smell very faintly of ammonia; this fish will be at its sweetest and is more tender about two days after it is caught.

When you are buying fish fillets the flesh should look translucent and succulent with no sign of discoloration. If possible ask the fish store clerk to fillet the fish when you buy it, or do it for yourself at home, as fish deteriorates more quickly once it has been filleted.

Different methods of cooking fish produce very different results. Many people are put off trying to cook fish at all because they have chosen a tricky method for their first attempt, with disastrous results. I think the best way to gain the feeling of confidence that is needed to bring out the best in fish is by simply wrapping either a whole fish or steaks in foil with butter, lemon juice and seasoning and baking the package in the oven (page 132). In this way the fish can cook gently and never dries out, while producing a delicious sauce of its own. I still like this way of cooking fish more than any other. When you are much more confident you can try poaching which, as long as the heat is kept low enough, is a wonderfully delicate way of producing supreme texture and taste. Frying fish takes more practice but there are times when everyone longs for a piece of fried fish – juicy inside and with a golden crust – so it is worth learning how.

To overcook fish is to ruin it; moisture and flavor will be lost and texture destroyed. With such different kinds and shapes of fish, cooking times and methods vary, but the golden rule remains: do not overcook. To tell if a fish is cooked, gently pull back the flesh with a knife: it should be just opaque all the way through and flake easily. With filleted fish the appearance of soft white drippings is a sign that it is cooked.

Clockwise from top right: with its golden orange top of mashed sweet and white potatoes Golden Fish Pie (page 141) is a variation of the traditional British fish pie; Marinated Scallops with Avocado and Tomatoes (page 138) is a simple summer salad; The Emperor's Fan (page 141) is poached skate wing with a delicate sauce of citrus juices, fresh ginger and cilantro leaves; the pretty colors of Stuffed Salmon Fillets with Yellow Pepper and Saffron Sauce (page 140) make it a perfect treat for a dinner party; a fine mixed seafood platter with fresh oysters, mussels, shrimp and prawns set on crushed ice. Center: red mullet with their distinctive color grilled simply with olive oil and fresh herbs.

PREPARING ROUND FISH

Round fish include some of the most familiar fish such as cod, haddock, mackerel and herring, as well as Mediterranean fish like red mullet and tropical fish, such as the beautiful parrot fish with its brilliant colors. As well as an enormous variety of species, there is a wide range of flavors and textures.

Oily round fish, such as mackerel, with pale brown flesh, in particular, are as different from white fish as beef is from chicken. The flesh is richer with a more pronounced flavor which responds well to stronger seasonings and spices, and to full-bodied sauces. All fish are rich in protein, minerals and vitamins, but oily fish have the added bonus of healthy fish oil.

Many round fish are large and often sold cut into steaks or filleted. When possible buy a whole fish and ask for it to be scaled, trimmed, gutted and cut or filleted on the spot, or prepare it yourself at home. With smaller fish that I want to cook whole I always ask the fish store clerk to prepare and gut the fish, but to leave the head on as I think the appearance is better for serving. Even if you have an obliging fish market it is useful to learn the following techniques for times when you are given fresh fish.

SCALING, TRIMMING AND GUTTING

Most fish need scaling, otherwise the scales loosen during cooking and spoil the flesh. But, be warned, scaling is messy and it's best to work at the sink with cold running water and a drain basket fitted over the drain.

Some fish may need additional trimming of fins, tails and heads, although it is quite acceptable to present scaled fish looking more natural. All fish, except for very small fish like whitebait, need gutting. You can do this by slitting the belly or pulling the guts out through the gills.

1 *Cut off all fins. Hold the fish by the tail, gripping with hands dipped in coarse salt, and scrape towards the head using the back of a large knife or a special fish scaler. Rinse frequently under cold running water. Some scales can cut, so take care.*

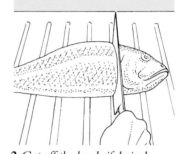

2 *Cut off the head, if desired, just behind the gills. The head can be saved for use in the stockpot (page 31); if you do not want to make stock at the moment, just freeze the head and any other bones until you have more time or need the stock.*

3 *To gut through the belly, slit from the head end to the vent just before the tail, then scrape out the innards. Wash thoroughly and using your finger or a teaspoon, scrape out any dark blood, especially along the backbone, which could make the fish bitter.*

• Fish is a highly perishable food so needs to be kept in peak condition if you are to get the best from it. An attractive, well laid out fish counter indicates a certain amount of care and attention on the part of the fish marketer – someone who cares about what he or she sells and prepares for you.
• Fresh fish have shiny, moist skin and firm flesh. Heads, where left on, will have bright eyes that do not appear sunken, and bright red or pink gills. A really fresh fish will remain stiff when you pick it up.
• White fillets should be a good translucent color, while smoked fish should look glossy, bright and have a healthy, subtle smoky aroma.

HANDLING SEAFOOD

• After buying fish, simply rinse, pat dry, cover loosely in plastic wrap and refrigerate.
• Cook fresh fish within 24 hours of purchase.
• The supply of fresh fish is dependent on a number of variables, not least the weather. If good fresh fish is not available or does not look appetizing, try frozen. Often, as it is frozen at sea within hours of catching, it can be even 'fresher' than some fresh fish.
• Frozen fish should be sold frozen hard in well-sealed, untorn packaging without any ice crystals.
• Thin fillets of frozen fish can be cooked from frozen, but thicker fillets and steaks and also whole fish are best thawed

before cooking (page 313).
• Thaw fish either quickly at room temperature and cook immediately, or thaw overnight in the refrigerator. Do not thaw fish in cold water.
• When thawing fish in the refrigerator place it on a large plate with a rim so none of the juices drip on other foods.
• For fast thawing use a microwave on the Defrost (30%) setting, then cook the fish as soon as possible. Watch fish thawing in the microwave so the thin parts do not cook before the other parts thaw.
• While you can freeze freshly caught fish, do not refreeze frozen fish unless it has been thoroughly cooked first, such as in fried fish.

GUTTING THROUGH THE GILLS

A fish with its head left on and stuffed whole makes an attractive presentation, and for the fish to keep its shape it is gutted through the gills. This technique is also useful if you want the fish to keep its round shape when you cut it into steaks.

To gut through the gills push your finger down inside the fish, through the gills. 'Hook' your finger around the innards, then pull them out and snap off the gills. Rinse the fish out thoroughly with cold running water. Pat dry inside and out with paper towels, stuffing them down inside the body cavity and then pulling them out.

FILLETING ROUND FISH

It is easier to fillet round fish before skinning, giving 1 meaty fillet on each side of the backbone. These can then be skinned (right) and coated and fried or cut into strips and breaded to make small pieces of fried fish.

Check that all the small 'pin' bones around the back fins are removed, as these can be annoying to come across when you are eating the fish. Begin by cutting off the head.

1 *A filleting knife is not necessary but its flexible blade makes neater fillets. Place the fish with its head end away from you and its back towards you. Cut through the backbone down to the tail, keeping the blade as close as possible to the bone.*

2 *Using a gentle sawing motion, starting from the head end, cut the flesh from the fine rib bones. Hold back the freed flesh with one hand and use your other hand to keep the knife's blade scraping back and forth in a gentle sawing motion against the bones, working as quickly as possible. This filleting technique gets easier the more you practice.*

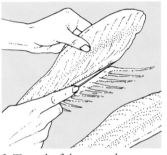

3 *Turn the fish over and remove the fillet from the other side in the same way. Check both fillets for any stray bones and pull them out with your fingers or tweezers. Skin the fillet (right) if you like. Save the bones for making stock (page 31). They can be put in a plastic food bag together with the head and frozen until you wish to make the stock.*

SKINNING FISH FILLETS

Round and flat fish fillets (page 120) are skinned in the same way. Like filleting (left), perfecting this technique really is just a matter of practice.

Lay the fillets skin side down on a board. Dip your fingers in coarse salt for a better grip or hold the tail with a cloth to prevent it from slipping.

Use a large-bladed knife and make a small cut through to the skin at the tail end and loosen the flesh just a little.

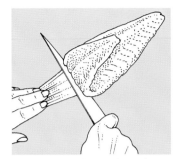

Pull the tail skin tight *and, holding the knife at a right angle to the flesh, use a gentle sawing motion to work the knife towards the other end.*

Jock's Grilled Stuffed Mackerel (page 140) has a simple bread crumb stuffing with chopped almonds and fresh tarragon.

BONING ROUND FISH FOR STUFFING

Stuffing a whole boned round fish makes an interesting and attractive meal. This can either be done by boning from the back (keeping the fish attached at the belly), or, as is more usual, by boning from the belly, shown here. You can either leave the head on or remove, as you like.

Use this technique for herring, mackerel, haddock, whiting and trout. Rinse the fish well with cold running water after boning, taking care to remove all the dark blood along the backbone, which causes a bitter taste.

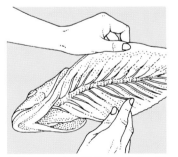

1 *Remove the gill flap and fins if you have not cut off the head. If the fish has not been gutted, cut it along the belly to the tail and open it up. Rinse well with cold running water. Use your fingers or a small sharp knife to free each of the long rib bones.*

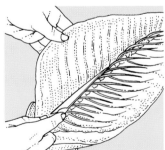

2 *When the rib bones are free on each side, run a sharp knife down either side of the backbone, scraping it free of flesh and not cutting through the skin. Make sure all small bones are removed. Along the backbone it is easier to free the flesh with your fingers.*

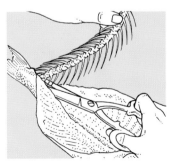

3 *Cut the backbone at each end with a sharp pair of scissors. Lift out the bone and save it for use in the stockpot (page 31), if you like; do not use bones from oily fish, such as mackerel, for making fish stock as the flavor is too strong and the stock could be oily.*

PREPARING FLAT FISH

Flat fish, which include flounder, sole, halibut, turbot and brill, all swim on their side – in fact, rather than swim they mostly lie on the seabed with both eyes on one side of their twisted faces looking for prey. Skates and rays also lie on the seabed and look like flat fish but they are actually cartilaginous fish, related to sharks.

Most flat fish are sold whole or in fillets, but large halibut and turbot can also be cut into steaks.

Flat fish fillets are versatile. They can be fried gently in butter, cut into strips and sautéed with fresh herbs, ginger or mild spices, covered in a sauce and baked or covered in a light batter and deep fried. Fillets are also ideal for stuffing and rolling, then poaching gently before finally covering with a sauce made with the thickened poaching liquid

(page 130). Whole flat fish, because of their characteristic thinness, can also be fried, grilled, broiled or baked.

Sole and turbot are the kings of flat fish; they are expensive but you are paying for real quality and a flavor which should never be disguised. Although there are countless recipes for sole, many with elaborate sauces and accompaniments, it is a fish of such delicate, sweet taste and fine, firm texture that it seems a pity to mask it with anything more than lightly seasoned butter or a light creamy sauce. I like sole grilled on the bone best of all and it is the easiest fish there is to separate from its skeleton on your plate. Because of turbot's large size it is less practical to grill, but its flesh is sweet, firm, moist and beautifully white. You can buy fillets or steaks and simply grill or poach them.

FILLETING FLAT FISH INTO FOUR FILLETS

A flat fish on the fish counter, complete with skin and head, can be a somewhat daunting sight if you are unsure of how to prepare it for the table. The price by weight is less than already prepared fillets, so it can be worth doing the preparation yourself. You can either cut the fish into 4 fillets, 2 from the top and 2 from the underside, as shown here, or 2 large fillets, one each from the top and the underside, as shown opposite.

Flat fish have a light side and a dark side that provides good camouflage against inquisitive predators. When filleting flat fish, it is easiest to cut the fillets from the skeleton first and then skin them if you want. Use the same technique for skinning flat fish fillets as for round fish fillets (page 119).

A filleting knife is not absolutely necessary, but its flexible thin, blade makes the job easier than if you use a chef's knife with its firm blade.

A fillet of flounder can be coated in batter and deep fried quickly in oil so it becomes golden and crisp on the outside and the flesh remains moist and juicy on the inside.

1 *Place the fish head toward you. Remove the head, cutting in a half circle just behind the gills, which removes all the insides from a flat fish. Discard the innards which are much smaller in a flat fish than a round one but save the head for the stockpot (page 31).*

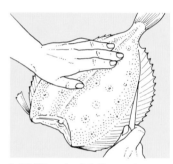

2 *Holding the fish firm so it doesn't slide, slice around the edge of the flesh where it meets the fins to cut an outline for the fillets. It is not necessary to cut off the fins. Slice along the backbone from the head end to the tail, cutting down to the bone.*

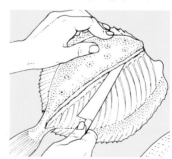

3 *Slide the knife under the flesh, almost flat along the rib bones. Use a gentle sawing motion to cut away the first fillet, keeping the knife as flat as possible and scraping firmly against the bones. Repeat this action on the other side of the backbone, to remove the second fillet.*

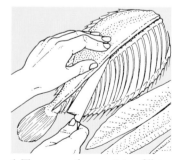

4 *To remove the remaining fillets, turn the fish over and repeat steps 2 and 3, making 4 fillets in total. If you want, remove both the dark and light skins from the fillets or just the dark upper skin if you are pressed for time (page 119). Save the skeleton for use in the stockpot (page 31).*

FILLETING INTO TWO FILLETS

For more generous-looking helpings keep the top and bottom fillets whole. This technique requires more practice than the technique for making 4 fillets (opposite).

Cut the head behind the gills and remove. Make a slit across the tail end and slice around the edge of the flesh where it meets the fins. Insert the knife flat along the backbone between the rib bones and flesh. Use a sawing motion to cut to one side, keeping the knife flat .

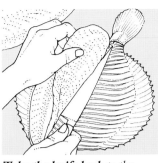

Take the knife back *to the backbone and repeat on the other side, making 1 large fillet. To make the second fillet, turn the fish over and use the same procedure on the other side.*

SKINNING A WHOLE FLAT FISH

This technique requires a great deal of strength, but it does yield a skinned whole fish suitable for boning and stuffing, as shown below. Or, remove only the top dark skin and then shallow fry the fish (page 128) so the unskinned side has a delicious crispy finish.

It is easiest to skin the smaller flat fish, such as plaice and sole, by this method. Turbot and halibut will be more difficult because of their large size.

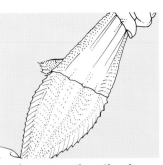

Make a cut at the tail end*. Hold the tail firmly with fingers wrapped in a cloth or dipped in salt. With your other hand, hold the skin and pull it back toward the head end in one swift tear.*

POCKET-BONING A FLAT FISH FOR STUFFING

Medium to large flat fish, such as sole and flounder, can be partially skinned, boned and left whole for stuffing, and then either baked as here, or breaded and fried (page 128).

Remove the head and gills (opposite). Trim the fins, if you like, and remove the dark skin (above).

To make the stuffing for 4 sole, cut 2 carrots, 2 well-washed leeks and 1 small bulb fennel into matchsticks, then stir-fry in 3oz (75g) butter with 2 teaspoons grated fresh ginger for 2 minutes. Add 3 tablespoons dry sherry and cook for 2 more minutes. Season well.

Any variety of ingredients can be used to make a stuffing for pocketed fish. Here, stir-fried ginger-flavored vegetables are used, and the fish is served with boiled new potatoes with thyme.

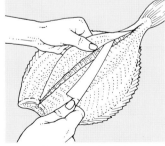

1 *Cut down one side of the backbone on the skinned side, starting ½in (1cm) from head end. Cut the flesh away in a sawing motion, keeping the knife flat to the rib bones. Do not remove the fillets. Repeat along the other side of the backbone.*

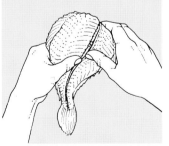

2 *To remove the backbone slide the knife in from the head end between the flesh and the backbone, to loosen the flesh on the other side of the bones. Fold the fish over and crack the bone in 2 or 3 places to make it easier to remove.*

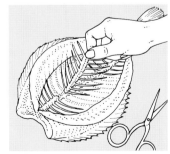

3 *Snip all the way around the edges of the bones and across the tail and head ends of the backbone with small scissors. Using your fingers, pull the backbone and rib bones out and discard. Double check that no small stray bones are still in the flesh.*

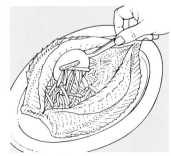

4 *Divide the stuffing between the boned sole. Place in a roasting pan, cover with foil and bake at 350°F, 180°C for 20 minutes. Serve with the cooking juices blended with a little cream and spooned on top, if you prefer a richer sauce.*

PREPARING MOLLUSKS

It is extremely important that all seafood is fresh when you buy it and particularly so with mollusks, the group of shellfish which includes mussels, scallops, oysters, and clams. To ensure freshness the shells should be tightly closed before eating raw or cooking, or, if the shells are open, they should close quickly when tapped. Discard any that remain open or have cracked shells.

Scallops are often sold shelled, but if you can get them in the shell, use the shells as serving containers. In Washington State it is possible to get scallops with their orange 'coral' which is just as delicious as the white part, with its contrasting rich taste and smooth texture.

Some people are passionate about oysters – if they want a real treat, oysters will probably be at the top of their list.

Local oysters are the most readily available and are cheaper than the many varieties imported from all over the world. Nowadays, the high price of oysters makes people think it a shame to cook them as when they are cooked their flavor and texture cannnot be fully appreciated. To eat them raw, just hold your head back and slip the oyster and juices down your throat, with or without chewing. The choice is yours.

Clams are becoming more available and are a delightful surprise and very easy to prepare. Clams make an excellent sauce for pasta and a delicious and unusual topping for pizza. Mussels are a traditional addition to soups, stews and sauces. Add them still in their beautiful black shells for an attractive presentation.

MOULES MARINIÈRE

Mussels are richly flavored, succulent and not expensive. The golden rule is to discard any not tightly closed or that do not close when tapped before cooking, and any that remain closed after cooking. Simply steam mussels until their shells open up.

This is my version of *moules marinière*, the classic dish of steamed mussels with flavored cooking juices. Allow 1lb (500g) of mussels per person; the shells take up bulk and there will probably be some to discard.

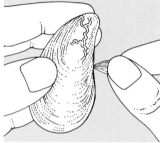

1 *Discard any mussels that are cracked or open and stay open when tapped. Wash the mussels in plenty of cold running water to remove any trapped sand. Scrape off any barnacles, pull off the beards and scrub well.*

2 *Put 2 chopped shallots and some parsley stprigs in a large pan with 1¼ cups (300ml) dry white wine, black pepper and the mussels. Cover and shake over a high heat until the shells open; it will take less than 2 minutes.*

3 *With a large spoon, transfer the mussels to a colander set over a bowl. Discard any mussels that remain closed. Put the remaining ones into a large warm serving bowl. Cover with foil and keep warm and moist.*

SERVING MOLLUSKS

• A richer version of *moules marinière* (above) can be made by reducing the juices as in step 4, then adding heavy cream and a little lemon juice, which will also thicken the sauce.
• Or, for extra flavor add chopped garlic to the white wine at the initial stage of steaming open the mussels.
• A peeled and finely chopped tomato added to the wine will give the resulting sauce a pretty pink tinge.
• Shelled mussels can be added to pasta and the juices reduced with cream to make the sauce.
• 'Stuffed' mussels on the half shell are, in fact, not really stuffed but covered with a variety of toppings. These can include garlic and parsley butter, cheese and breadcrumbs, or chopped spinach and Parmesan.
• Scallops with their delicate taste are best served simply: they need hardly any cooking and are also excellent served raw, either with a vinaigrette-type dressing, or briefly marinated.
• Scallops are wonderful lightly poached in a little seasoned cream with fresh dill.
• Stir-fry slices of scallop quickly with thin slivers of fresh gingerroot and a crunchy green vegetable, shredded lettuce, thin slices of mushrooms or simply a generous handful of fresh herbs.
• Crispy fried oysters are delicious on their own, in sandwiches such as the New Orleans "po' boy" or served as a garnish on meat dishes.
• Clams and cockles are excellent with pasta or any seafood mixtures.
• Add clams or mussels at the last moment to any kind of fish stew or soup so they do not overcook.
• All kinds of fresh, tender herbs can be used with seafood. Feathery fennel is a good additional or alternative herb to parsley. Mild seasoning with spices such as coriander or fennel seed can also be delicious.

4 *Strain the cooking liquid into a saucepan and reduce over high heat by about one third. Whisk in 2oz (50g) unsalted butter, a large handful of chopped parsley and some black pepper and adjust the seasoning if necessary. Pour over the mussels and serve. Chunks of good crusty bread are the only accompaniment necessary.*

PREPARING SCALLOPS

Scallops, particularly the smaller bay scallops, are available fresh or frozen throughout the year. They can be poached, baked, fried or steamed, and are excellent broiled if you wrap them in strips of bacon before broiling. Take care not to overcook scallops or they will toughen. Scallops are cooked when they turn opaque but are still translucent in the center.

Although we usually find scallops removed from the shell, it is a special treat to find them in the shell with their coral. Here's how to prepare them when you can get them.

Served on the half shell on a bed of crushed ice with plenty of lemon wedges, raw oysters make an impressive and wonderful first course for a dinner party.

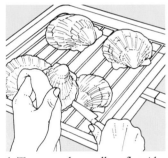

1 *To open, place scallops flat side down under a broiler or in a warm oven. As soon as the shells open remove the pan from the heat. Insert a sharp knife and cut the muscle which holds the top and bottom shells together. Carefully separate the 2 shells.*

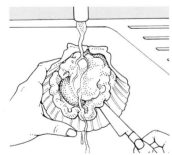

2 *Hold the lower shell under cold running water and scrape away the yellow-brown membrane. Discard this and the black intestine, then loosen the flesh and coral; the scallops are ready for cooking. Wash the shells to use as serving containers.*

SHUCKING OYSTERS

Live oysters are traditionally available in any month containing the letter 'r'. However, because of refrigerated transportation and aquaculture, you can now find some in the market all year. Only buy ones with tightly closed shells and keep in a bowl covered with a damp cloth in the refrigerator for up to 2 days. Always open just before serving or cooking.

When eaten raw, oysters are usually served on a bed of crushed ice with lemon wedges, and either hot pepper sauce to sprinkle on top, or horseradish or Worcestershire sauce. Allow 6–8 oysters per person.

Cooked oysters are usually served on their bottom shell with a sauce or breadcrumb topping. Broil or cook in the oven at 425°F, 220°C for 2–3 minutes until the edges curl back but the center is still soft.

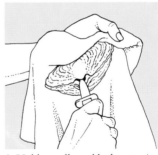

1 *Hold a well-scrubbed oyster in a thick cloth, flat side up. Stick an oyster knife, or short-bladed knife, into the hinged edge of the shell, and twist to pry open.*

2 *Still holding the shell firmly, cut through the muscle and lift off the top shell, taking care not to spill any of the liquid inside.*

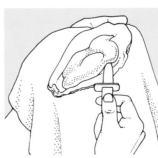

3 *Slip the knife under the oyster to separate it from the lower shell, and flip it over still in the shell, if desired, to show the smooth side.*

PREPARING CLAMS

Clams vary greatly in size and variety, and, depending on their size, should be dealt with like mussels or oysters.

Smaller clams can be steamed open like mussels and then cooked in a light tomato sauce to make *vongole*, a classic Italian pasta sauce. Larger clams should be treated like oysters and can be eaten raw, although they are also delicious cooked on an outdoor grill. You can also add them to soups and seafood salads.

To steam small clams, *place them in the top of a steamer over boiling water. Cover and steam until the shells open This should not take more than 2 minutes. Discard any that do not open. For extra flavor replace the water with wine or add herbs and lemon slices to the water.*

PREPARING CRUSTACEANS

Lobsters, crabs, prawns, shrimp and crawfish, known collectively as crustaceans, have the sweetest flavor of all shellfish. Some of these are relatively expensive, but if you choose, prepare and present shellfish well the quality of their delicate flesh make them worth their cost. These shellfish always seem like a real treat.

It is vitally important that shellfish are very fresh as they deteriorate quickly. Shellfish should really smell of the sea and still feel springy within the shell – not limp, which is an indication of staleness. If you buy cooked shrimp it is best to buy them in their shell – the shells are, in any case, valuable for making excellent stock (page 31) or for sauce Nantua (page 197). When you are able to buy large prawns and cook them yourself, it is worth the expense because the taste and texture are wonderful. Uncooked prawns and the smaller shrimp look grey when you buy them raw but they become pink when cooked. Tiny, delectable Arctic shrimp are available precooked frozen.

When choosing lobster or crab go by weight rather than size; the size of the shell can be far bigger than the flesh within it which may have shrunk. There should not be any sound of water when you shake a crab. Male crabs and lobsters are larger than the females but females often contain eggs or a coral which tastes wonderful and can also be used for garnishing.

Crab is my favorite shellfish, especially hard shell crabs. Picking at a whole freshly cooked crab, simply accompanied by good fresh bread and lemon juice or, perhaps, homemade mayonnaise, creates an intimate, friendly atmosphere at a relaxed meal. Crab meat, either lump, backfin, or the less expensive flake, can also be bought either fresh or pasteurized.

PREPARING A CRAB

You can buy whole cooked crabs to serve at home. Choose ones that feel heavy for their size, because they will be full of meat. A dressed crab makes a very special cold dish, with the meat attractively presented in the shell. Each of the meats has a very different texture and flavor; the lump is sweet and pure, and the claw is rich and creamy. The claw meat is also excellent added to pâtés or sauces. Plan a 1lb (500g) crab to serve 1 person as a main course, or 2 as a first course.

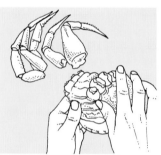

1 *To prepare a cooked crab, turn it on its back and pull off its claws and legs. Discard the legs unless they are big and contain lots of meat. Hold the crab bottom side up and twist off the tail, which you can discard.*

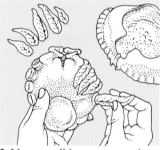

2 *Use a small hammer to crack the shell on the bottom around the body. Pull the central body part out of the shell. Discard the grey lungs which look like fingers, and pull away the spongy stomach. Discard.*

3 *Cut the central body in half with a heavy knife. With a metal skewer scoop out the lump meat into a bowl. Using a spoon, scoop out the meat from the main shell, under the area where the body was, keeping the backfin and lump meats separate.*

4 *Crack the claws with the hammer and extract any meat with the skewer. Mix claw and backfin meat with a little mayonnaise and seasoning and lump meat with fresh lemon juice. Arrange separately and serve with bread and butter.*

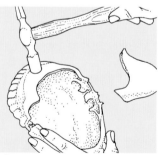

If you want to use *the crab shell as a serving container, lightly tap the line around the opening of the shell with a small hammer or rolling pin and pull away the shell to enlarge the opening. Wash well with soap and hot water, then dry.*

PREPARING SHRIMP

Half the joy of eating really fresh cooked shrimp is in peeling them yourself.

On the fish counter you will find shrimp of varying sizes, ranging from small to jumbo, and the largest European prawns. Cooked shrimp with their rosy orange shells are ready to eat or add to dishes such as Italian risotto or Spanish paella.

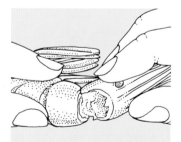

To peel whole shrimp *pull the heads from the bodies and discard. Pull off the legs first, then remove the body shell, leaving on the tail if you like. With larger shrimp you have to remove the thin black intestinal vein that runs along the back with the tip of a small knife. Sometimes the vein is clearly visible and at other times you have to slice along the whole back to find it and pull it out.*

PREPARING LOBSTER

In season all year long, a fresh lobster is a real treat and it can usually be bought already cooked. Be sure to check that both the claws are attached and that the lobster feels heavy for its size. If it is too light it means it is not fresh and the meat has had time to dry up a little. A 2½lb (1.2kg) lobster is ample for 2 servings with homemade mayonnaise (page 202) and a salad of mixed greens.

You will need a heavy sharp kitchen knife to cut through the shell or you can use a heavy Chinese-style cleaver.

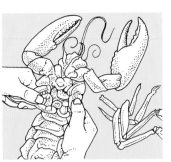

1 *Lay the cooked lobster on its back and pull off the legs and claws. For presentation purposes keep the attractive long wispy antennae. Small legs can be discarded because they do not contain much meat but keep the larger claws.*

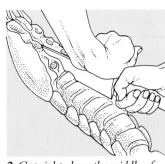

2 *Cut right along the middle of the lobster, stretching out the tail and pressing down firmly on the back of the knife blade. If pressing on the knife back is uncomfortable then press down on a clean, folded cloth.*

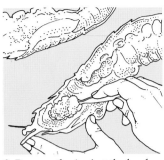

3 *Remove the 'sac' at the head end, and the long thin black intestine which runs down to the tail. Discard any feathery gills and bits of shell, too. The greenish liver, called tomalley, and the pink coral in the female can be eaten.*

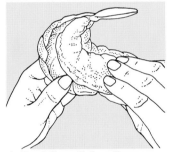

4 *Carefully pull the tail meat out of each lobster half. Clean out and wash the shells with plenty of hot soapy water if you plan to use them for serving. Rinse and dry the shells and arrange them on a bed of pretty salad greens, ready for filling.*

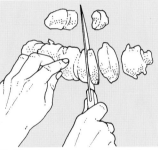

5 *Cut the tail meat neatly into chunks. Any pink coral, which is delicious, can be served on its own or used as a garnish. The tomalley or liver can be mixed with sauce for serving with the lobster meat.*

6 *Crack open the claws and pull out the firm pinky white meat. Cut this into chunks and mix with the tail meat. Pile the mixed meat into the shells, adding the antennae, if you like. Garnish with lemon quarters.*

SERVING CRUSTACEANS

• The most obvious way to serve shrimp, crab and lobster is to include them in a salad. Arranged among pretty greens and dressed simply with a good vinaigrette, they look beautiful, and their sweet, delicate flavor can be appreciated for what it is.
• Fresh herbs which go well with shellfish are dill, fennel and cilantro.
• Crab meat, both lump and backfin, makes wonderful sandwiches, particularly if you mix in fresh cilantro leaves.
• I like to add crab meat to fish cakes and sauces.
• When adding shrimp to fish stew, a sauce or a soup, do so only at the last moment or they will shrink and be tough.
• Prawns, especially the larger ones, are delicious grilled in their shells and served with really garlicky butter, or shelled and coated first with garlic and fresh herbs, then quickly fried in butter and served with lemon.
• There are many elaborate recipes for lobster but I think that if it is really fresh and meaty it is a pity to mask the flavor with any sauce other than homemade mayonnaise or melted butter, depending on whether you are serving the lobster cold or hot. Add dill to the mayonnaise.

A tempting individual Scallop, Crab and Prawn Tart (page 139) served with a simple green salad makes a delicious seafood first course or light lunch.

PREPARING SQUID *and* OCTOPUS

Squid are widely available and extremely good, as well as inexpensive. They are also far easier to prepare and cook than is often imagined. When my children were very young their favorite meal used to be 'squid and French fries'. This was after eating it every day in Spain, where they also watched with great fascination the octopus being beaten on the rocks to make them tender.

Smaller squid are perfectly tender as long as you don't cook them either too long or on too high a heat. Slices of squid literally need no more than a minute or two of fairly gentle cooking, just until they turn an opaque white.

I needed no encouragement from my children to cook squid frequently because I love that sweet, clean taste and texture, and their adaptability to so many flavorings and preparation methods. They are actually far easier to deal with and cook than most other fish and shellfish. If the squid you buy still contains its ink sac intact (this is what holds the ink which the creature squirts out in a thick black cloud if it wants to deter attack), save the rich and flavorful liquid to make a sauce for the squid.

Octopus are tough and need tenderizing before cooking; this is usually done by the fish market. Stewed gently and slowly with root vegetables, bulb fennel, tomatoes and lots of garlic, octopus produces an excellent, rich flavor and wonderful juices. I like to sprinkle chopped flat-leaf parsley over the mixture just before serving.

PREPARING SQUID

Don't be alarmed either by the appearance of uncooked squid or by the prospect of preparing them. The removal of the bone and internal organs is intriguing and, once you know what to do, easy. It is certainly easier than preparing ordinary fish, and much cleaner and more pleasurable, too.

The most important thing to remember once you have prepared your squid is not to ruin its tender texture by cooking it too long or with too high a heat. If deep-frying, the cooking time must be even shorter.

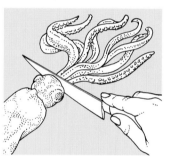

1 *Rinse the squid well. Cut the tentacles away from the head, discarding the beak-like mouth found in the center of the tentacles, just below the eyes. Reserve the tentacles which can be cooked with the main body meat or finely chopped and mixed with stuffing ingredients.*

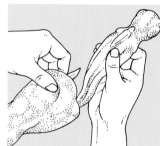

2 *Hold the body of the squid in one hand and pull the head gently with the other hand, which brings out the internal organs. Discard both head and internal organs but carefully retain the ink sac if needed in the recipe — it is pearly colored with a blue tinge. It is often used in pasta sauces.*

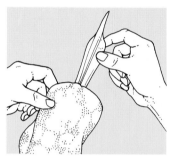

3 *Pull the transparent quill-like bone from the body pocket and discard. Use your fingers to check for any remaining internal organs and pull out and discard.*

USING SQUID AND OCTOPUS

• I like to stir-fry squid because of the short cooking time. Try squid slices stir-fried with red pepper, broccoli, snow peas and sliced spring greens with ground coriander.
• Squid always makes a fish stew seem more exotic. Add the slices only at the very last minute, just long enough for the heat to turn the pearly flesh an opaque white.
• Pasta with squid is wonderful. While the pasta is cooking toss slices of squid and chopped garlic briefly in a generous mixture of extra virgin olive oil and unsalted butter and stir in lots of chopped parsley before mixing into the drained pasta.
• If you want to barbecue larger pieces of squid, marinate the pieces in olive oil, lemon juice and herbs or spices for an hour or so beforehand. Grill very briefly over a high heat.
• As well as making an excellent stew, thin slices of octopus can be simmered gently in a little stock or water until very tender — they will turn pink and can be drained, cooled and then dressed with olive oil, lemon juice, garlic, lots of flat-leaf parsley and served as a first course.

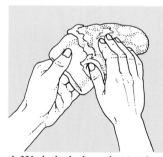

4 *Wash the body pocket inside and out thoroughly under cold running water, getting rid of any traces of internal organs that may remain. Peel and rub off the purple mottled skin from the outside. Pat dry with paper towels.*

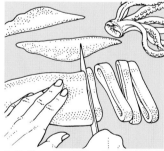

5 *Pull or cut off the fins and slice into strips for cooking with the main body meat. Slice the body across into fairly thin rings or leave whole if stuffing the squid (opposite). Divide the reserved tentacles into 2 or 3 pieces if the squid are fairly large and you are using them for stuffing.*

STUFFING AND COOKING SQUID

You can stuff squid of all sizes; with larger squid slice the stuffed body across in thick slices after cooking, then arrange them on a serving plate surrounded by the sauce. With smaller squid serve a whole one to each person. You can even stuff very small squid and then poach them in a sauce so each serving contains several squid. If you like add the ink sac to the sauce you cook the squid in, to make it rich and black.

Clean and prepare the squid (opposite), leaving the bodies whole. Chop up the fins and tentacles to use in the stuffing.

To make the stuffing for 4 small to medium-sized squid, put 3 tablespoons olive oil in a frying pan over a medium heat. Add 2 large finely chopped cloves of garlic, a finely chopped 1in (2.5cm) piece of fresh gingerroot and the chopped squid fins and tentacles, then stir for 1 minute only. Stir in 2oz (50g) can finely chopped anchovies, 8oz (250g) blanched and finely chopped spinach, 2 tablespoons fresh whole wheat bread crumbs and remove from the heat. Season with salt and freshly ground black pepper to taste.

Squid Rings with Leeks and Spinach (page 139) on a dramatic bed of red sauce.

1 *To stuff squid, spoon an equal amount of stuffing into each one, taking care not to fill them so full that they burst during cooking. For smaller squid you may find it easier to press the stuffing into the body cavity through a plastic funnel, or use a pastry bag without the tip attached.*

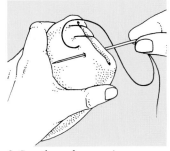

2 *Sew the ends up, using a trussing needle and kitchen string, or secure with wooden toothpicks. Put 2 tablespoons olive oil and 1oz (25g) butter in a Dutch oven over a medium heat. Add 2 finely chopped large cloves of garlic and 1 small seeded and chopped red pepper. Stir for 1 minute.*

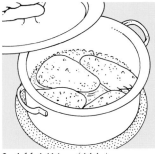

3 *Add 14½oz (411g) can chopped tomatoes, 1 tablespoon tomato puree, 4 tablespoons fresh orange juice, salt and pepper. Add the stuffed squid, cover and simmer very gently for 35–45 minutes until tender. Place the squid in a serving dish. Stir plenty of chopped parsley into the sauce and serve with the squid.*

PREPARING OCTOPUS

Most of the octopuses sold today have already been cleaned and tenderized. They can become tough when cooked, so try to find the variety with small heads and long tentacles as these are generally the most tender. If the octopus is not already cleaned you will have to gut it, remove the eyes, beak and skin and tenderize it before cooking, as shown here.

Octopuses can be fried, stuffed and stewed or grilled on an outdoor grill. Little ones are best fried in olive oil.

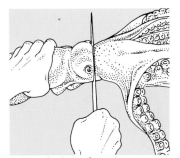

1 *Cut the body from the tentacles, and discard the contents of the body sac, including the internal organs and ink bag, if you are not using it for a sauce.*

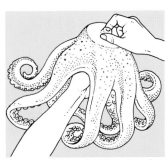

2 *Push the body inside out and cut away the eyes and beak and discard. Wash the head and tentacles under cold water, then blanch them in boiling water for 5–10 minutes.*

3 *Drain and rinse well under cold water, then peel off the skin and the thin membrane underneath. Tenderize the octopus by beating it against the sink or on a large chopping board about 40 times. It is now ready for cooking.*

FRYING

Frying fish can produce delicious results when done carefully and attentively. For small fish and fillets, shallow frying (also called pan frying), sautéing or stir-frying are the quickest and simplest methods to do at home. Deep-frying in breadcrumbs, seasoned flour or batter, however, produces irresistible results; a crisp crunchy coating on the outside, succulent fish on the inside.

Batters are useful for protecting deep-fried food during cooking. The correct temperature of oil is important in frying, especially deep-frying. If the temperature is too low the coating will not seal and will break up, and if it is too high the outside will burn before the inside is cooked. It is important to reheat oil between batches.

For sautéing and stir-frying, which involves constant stirring, use even-size pieces of close-textured firm fish. Monkfish, tuna, shark and shrimp are among the best.

As with all frying remember to watch the stove constantly and adjust the temperature when necessary.

SHALLOW FRYING

For shallow frying use vegetable oil or the high-fat butter used by chefs or make your own clarified butter (page 96). Both butters are good to use because they have no sediment to burn, while ordinary butter is unsuitable unless it is mixed with oil.

Use any thin fillet of fish, preferably skinned, or cut across into strips. A crisp homemade breadcrumb coating, ideal for shallow frying, is delicious and quite simple. Prepare three plates – one with seasoned flour, another with beaten egg and the third with dried breadcrumbs.

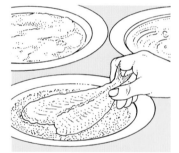 

1 Dip the fish pieces in the flour, then in the egg and finally in the crumbs, making sure the fish is well coated. Shake off the excess. Chill for 10–20 minutes.

2 Heat enough oil in a frying pan to cover the bottom by ¼in (5mm). Fry the fish in a single layer until golden, then turn and repeat. Drain on paper towels.

DEEP-FRYING

Fish coated in batter and fried quickly in hot deep oil is light and the flavor of the fish is preserved. The choice of oil is important not only for the flavor but also because the higher the temperature an oil can reach without developing a burned taste, the better. Vegetable oils are best to use, particularly sunflower and peanut.

For deep-frying fish, the temperature of the cooking oil should be between 350°F and 375°F (180°C and 190°C) or until a cube of white bread browns in about 30 seconds.

To make a simple batter for 4 cutlets or fillets, mix 1 egg and 1¼ cups (300ml) milk or water with 1 cup (125g) seasoned flour until smooth. Milk makes a thicker batter than water.

1 Prepare the batter and place in a relatively deep bowl. Dip each piece of fish into the batter, then allow the excess batter to drip off. It is best to cook the fish as soon as it is coated, so prepare and dip in batches, depending on how many pieces of fish fit in your frying basket at one time.

2 Use a deep heavy saucepan only one-third full of oil. Heat the oil steadily to the correct temperature, testing with a deep-frying thermometer or bread cube (above). Place the fish in a frying basket that fits the pan comfortably, then lower it gently. Cook until golden brown and crisp. Drain the fish well on absorbent paper towels and keep it warm in a low oven, until all the pieces have been fried and you are ready to serve.

*For special occasions these **Salmon Balls** (page 138) make the lightest fish cakes, with no mashed potatoes, just plenty of fish bound together in a rich white sauce.*

SHRIMP TEMPURA

Tempura must be one of the most universally popular of all the Japanese dishes – tender morsels of fresh fish and seafood, or vegetables, coated with the lightest batter and deep-fried for only a few minutes.

The secret of a good tempura is to make up the batter just before you use it and not to beat the mixture – it should be made with either a fork or chopsticks and left lumpy. To make the batter, use 1 beaten egg, ⅔ cup (75g) all-purpose flour, ¼ cup (25g) sifted cornstarch and ½ cup (100ml) water.

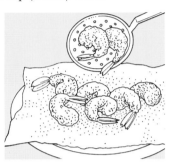

1 *Prepare raw shrimp (page 124). Score the undersides so they do not curl during frying. Rinse well and pat dry. Just before frying, dip each shrimp in the batter, holding it by its tail and shaking off the excess. Prepare in batches, if necessary.*

2 *Heat the oil to 350°F, 180°C or until a cube of white bread browns in about 30 seconds. Fry the shrimp in batches until the batter is pale golden and crisp and bubbling. Drain well on paper towels and keep warm until ready to serve.*

Shrimp tempura served with an oriental dipping sauce (page

FISH CAKES

I adore fish cakes as long as they are made with plenty of fish, never less than the amount of potato, and seasoned well. Use any filleted white fish, mackerel, smoked haddock or cod. A mixture of smoked and unsmoked fish is excellent.

To serve 6, mash 1lb (500g) boiled potatoes, adding 1oz (25g) butter and set aside. Simmer 1lb (500g) skinned fillets in ⅔ cup (150ml) milk in a covered saucepan for about 5 minutes until the fish flakes. Strain the milk into the potatoes and mix. Flake in the fish with 2 tablespoons chopped fresh chives, 1 beaten egg and salt and pepper. Mix and chill.

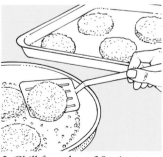

1 *Using floured hands form the mixture into balls about the size of a small orange. Flatten slightly, then brush with a little beaten egg and coat with 1 cup (50g) fresh breadcrumbs.*

2 *Chill for at least 30 minutes. Shallow fry in vegetable oil (opposite), turning once until golden brown on each side. Drain on paper towels and serve with fresh tomato sauce (page 206).*

FLAVORING FRIED FISH

- Flour for a coating can be seasoned with herbs and spices.
- Make red devilled fish by adding paprika and cayenne pepper to the coating flour.
- Nutty flavored Irish oatmeal is a good coating for fried herring and mackerel, but you can also use ground nuts, cornmeal, rice flour and semolina, all of which give a nice crunchy crust.
- A basic batter can be varied in many ways, including folding in beaten egg whites for lightness.
- Beer in a batter in place of the water or milk, and sometimes in place of the eggs, produces a lightness with a slightly bitter tang. I find it enhances the taste of the fish.
- Whole spices such as fennel, dill and caraway seeds are effective in various batters for deep-fried fish, as are herbs.
- Add color and spice to a batter by adding paprika or turmeric with other ground spices.
- Fish cakes are nicest coated with coarsely crumbled fresh white breadcrumbs.
- The mixture for the fish cakes themselves can vary as far as your imagination takes you. Mashed salt cod (page 137) makes very good fish cakes.
- Flavor fish cakes with either saffron, capers, crushed garlic, grated lemon rind, spices such as cardamom, coriander, cumin and turmeric, fresh herbs or chopped green onions.
- Fish cakes made in a saffron-flavored white sauce (page 196) are light and sophisticated enough to serve as a first course.
- Finely chopped hard-cooked eggs, anchovies or firm tomatoes can also add interest to a fish cake mixture.
- I sometimes add some nut-flavored oils to vegetable oil when frying for extra flavor. Try hazelnut or walnut oil.
- Bacon or duck fat both add a delicious flavor to fried fish.

POACHING *and* STEAMING

The important thing about poaching as a cooking method is its gentleness. It produces the most succulent, tender, evenly cooked fish. Poaching means cooking in a liquid, but it must never mean boiling; if fish is agitated in boiling liquid the flesh begins to fall apart, succulence escapes, tenderness is lost and the appearance is destroyed. The very most that the liquid should do is just to tremble on the surface. There shouldn't be any bubbles.

When poaching whole large fish you will need a container big enough, ideally a fish kettle (page 18). If you are going to eat fish cold you should start it in cold liquid and bring it slowly up to just boiling; then, after about 1 minute, remove it from the heat and leave it to become completely cold in the liquid. For eating hot, poach the fish, let it sit in the hot water for 15–20 minutes, then test to see if it is done by inserting a thin skewer or trussing needle; if it meets no resistance in the flesh it will be ready. The fish will feel firm if you press it lightly with your finger.

Steaming, as well as poaching, is a healthy, virtually fat-free way of cooking. Many types of inexpensive steamers are sold, including the excellent tiered Chinese baskets and a steaming rack to fit inside a wok.

Lightly steamed green vegetables and poached Fillets of Cod with Creamy Shrimp and Dill Sauce (page 141) make a luxurious main course for a dinner party.

POACHING FISH

Cutlets or fillets should be poached in a court bouillon (page 30), then after poaching, use the liquid to make a delicate sauce; strain and reduce the liquid, then whisk in small pieces of unsalted butter for extra richness.

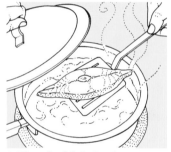

1 *Place the fish in barely simmering, just trembling, liquid to cover in a shallow pan that holds the fish in a single layer. Cover and poach for 5–10 minutes, depending on the thickness of the fish.*

2 *When cooked, the fish will be opaque and the flesh will flake if tested with the tip of a knife. Drain well on paper towels. Keep covered and warm in a low oven while you make a sauce out of the poaching liquid.*

SHAPING FISH FILLETS

Skinned fillets (page 119) can be rolled or folded into various shapes before poaching or steaming. Put the skinned side on the inside for a neater appearance when serving.

Enclosing a contrasting stuffing adds flavor and color. Although the fillets can be cooked plain, a stuffing, which can be as simple as chopped herbs and melted butter, helps compensate for the loss of flavor when the flesh is removed from the bones.

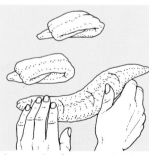

A very simple *presentation is to fold a fillet in half, tucking in the thin end. Lightly slash the skinned inside before folding, so the flesh does not contract during cooking and lose its shape.*

A 'turban' is *half a flat fish fillet rolled from the wide end to the thin end. Secure with wooden toothpicks or poach the 'turbans' close enough together so they do not uncurl during cooking.*

Two long thin *fillets of contrasting colored fish, such as salmon and lemon sole, look striking twisted together like a candy cane. Secure with toothpicks for poaching.*

STEAMING FISH

Steaming is a delicate way of cooking, ideal for cooking fish, but steamed fish can taste bland. To avoid this, lay flavorings such as herbs and vegetables underneath the fish and sprinkle other herbs or spices over the top. The fish can also be lightly marinated before steaming to add extra flavor.

If you want, after steaming reduce the liquid slightly to thicken and make a sauce for the fish. Or, you can serve the fish simply sprinkled with flavorings, such as fresh herbs, lemon juice or soy sauce. Pieces of steamed fish are also excellent cooled and then used in salads.

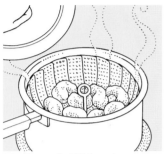

Delicate shellfish *such as scallops are ideal for steaming. Less gentle methods can make scallops tough, while steaming leaves them tender. Place the scallops in a steamer over boiling water, cover and steam for 2–3 minutes until opaque but still translucent in the centers and just lightly firm to the touch.*

Use 2 heatproof plates *to make an impromptu steamer for cooking thin fillets. Place a fillet over some herbs, if you like, on a lightly buttered heatproof plate. Cover with the second plate, turned upside down. Place over a saucepan of boiling water and steam for 5–10 minutes until the flesh flakes lightly.*

PERKING UP POACHED AND STEAMED FISH

• For someone on a diet, pieces of fish steamed with fresh ginger and served with soy sauce and crisp bean sprouts should not provoke complaints of deprivation.
• Flavorful quick sauces for poached or steamed fish can by made by reducing the poaching or steaming liquid and then whisking in butter or adding flour and egg yolks to thicken.
• You can also add cream to reduced cooking juices, or, if you want a low-fat sauce, use plain yogurt, but make sure you don't boil the sauce or the yogurt will curdle.
• A mixture of plain yogurt and crème fraîche makes a thicker sauce.
• Bland fish which has been given added flavor by being poached in a court bouillon (page 30) is excellent to use for fish cakes – then you can keep the court bouillon for soup or

reduce it and freeze it in ice cube trays in order to have a concentrated stock for sauces and soups at any time.
• Cold poached fish is most often served with mayonnaise, and you can vary this by adding fresh herbs such as dill, fennel and tarragon, a little cooked and well-drained spinach puree to make it green, sun-dried tomato paste and tomato puree, or spicy Indian condiments, such as lime pickle and mango chutney.
• If time is short use a good commercial brand of mayonnaise mixed with whipped cream and well seasoned.
• For both poached and steamed fish fresh tomato sauces are excellent, or sauces made with pureed peppers and other vegetables. Steamed fish pieces can be mixed into these thick sauces, then spooned into a dish and sprinkled with herbs.

HEARTY FISH STEW

In this stew, all the ingredients except the fish and tarragon are cooked first, then these are added so the fish is gently poached only for the last few minutes of the cooking time.

To serve 4 people, you will need 1lb (500g) peeled and chopped potatoes, 3 sliced garlic cloves, 2 bay leaves, 5 skinned and chopped tomatoes, 1 sliced yellow pepper, 4 tablespoons lemon juice, ⅔ cup (150ml) cider, 4 tablespoons olive oil, 1–1¼lb (500–625g) skinned and filleted white fish, cut into large chunks, 1 tablespoon chopped fresh tarragon, salt and pepper.

1 *Mix together the potatoes, garlic, bay leaves, tomatoes and yellow pepper in a large saucepan or Dutch oven. Season and pour over the lemon juice, cider and olive oil. Cover and cook gently for about 30 minutes until the potatoes are tender.*

2 *Carefully add the fish to the pan with the tarragon, cover again and gently poach over a low heat for 5–10 minutes until the fish is just opaque and flakes when tested with the tip of a knife. Serve at once, ladling into individual bowls.*

To make this simple hearty fish stew, fillets of monkfish are set on a bed of vegetables and poached in cider with chopped fresh tarragon and bay leaves.

BAKING *and* GRILLING

If you are nervous about cooking fish the most uncomplicated and foolproof method is baking. Baking is a loose term generally meaning to cook in the oven; it can mean that the fish is wrapped in parchment paper or foil or that you bake it in a dish, basting with the juices. Bake large fish at a lower temperature and small fish at a higher one because then the cooking time is so short that they will not have time to dry out.

Steaks or pieces of meaty fish such as tuna, shark and swordfish can be cooked gently and comparatively slowly in a covered casserole with vegetables all around them to make a complete and full-flavored dish. Whole fish can be stuffed with all sorts of good things or simply a bunch of fresh herbs which flavor the flesh during baking.

Broiling or grilling brings out the real flavor of fish in a unique way, and can be done either under or over a fierce heat. The flavor imparted to fish grilled over charcoal or some aromatic wood is best of all. Oily fish such as mackerel or herring, and larger fish like salmon and bass which have full, rich flavors, are especially good for grilling. Large uncooked shrimp cooked in their shells and basted with garlicky oil are wonderful.

All fish, whether whole, steaks or fillets should be basted several times during broiling to keep them moist. Use either the fish juices which collect beneath the fish, or spoon or brush over a sauce when you are barbecuing.

PAN-BAKED FISH

This style of baked fish can be a complete meal if it is cooked with vegetables, or you can just cook the fish in a little wine with olive oil, which effectively bastes the fish.

Cook stuffed whole fish (pages 119 and 121) or steaks in this way, but medium-sized steaks should be covered with foil to keep the moisture in. Large fish won't dry out so they don't need covering.

Place sliced, skinned tomatoes, mushrooms and thinly sliced onions in a buttered ovenproof dish, and season well. Rub the fish with butter and seasoning and place on top of the vegetables.

Add ¾ cup (175ml) *white wine and 3–4 tablespoons of olive oil and season with salt and pepper. Cover the dish loosely with foil and bake at 350°F, 180°C for 30–40 minutes for a medium-sized fish. The fish is cooked when the flesh looks opaque and flakes easily when tested with the tip of a knife.*

FOIL-BAKED FISH

After preparing the fish (right), lay the foil package on a large baking sheet and bake steaks at 300°F, 150°C for about 15 minutes or until firm to the touch. Bake whole fish at the same oven temperature for 12 minutes per 1lb (500g) for fish between 2–5lb (1–2.5kg) in weight and 8 minutes per 1lb (500g) for fish over 5lb (2.5kg) in weight. After cooking leave the fish in the foil for a few minutes before serving with the cooking juices.

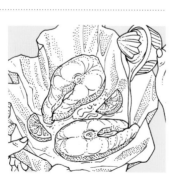

Generously butter *a piece of foil. Dot the fish with butter and seasonings such as herbs and lemon slices. Bring the foil up around the fish, add the juice of 1 lemon and wrap up securely.*

BAKING FISH IN PAPER CASES

Chunky fillets or steaks of fish are delicious baked in parchment paper or foil with chunks of butter, sprigs of fresh herbs, wafer-thin strips of vegetables or toasted split almonds and splashes of wine, sherry or vermouth.

The fish makes its own delicious juices while it cooks, then the packages are unwrapped at the table by each diner. As each package is opened it releases the most wonderful aroma.

Either simply wrap up in rectangles of parchment paper with a double fold on top, tucking the sides under, or try this more striking presentation.

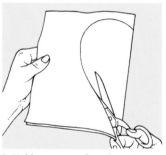

1 Fold a square of parchment paper in half and cut out a half heart, which when opened out forms a heart shape large enough to comfortably enclose the fish and any flavorings. Lightly brush the paper with melted butter or olive oil. (To cut out a number of hearts at once, fold several pieces of paper together.)

2 Place the fish steak or fillet on one side of the paper heart, with any finely chopped vegetables, almonds and/or fresh herbs as desired. Season to taste with salt and freshly ground black pepper. For extra flavoring, 1 tablespoon of dry white wine or vermouth can be added as well, if desired.

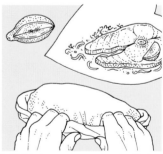

3 Fold the paper over and roll the sides in on themselves to seal in the juices. Place on a baking sheet and bake at 375°F, 190°C for about 20 minutes until the fish is cooked. Check by pressing the fish through the paper with your finger; it should be just firm.

FLAVORING BAKED AND GRILLED FISH

- You can transform the character of baked fish very easily by varying the flavors you add. The combination of tomatoes for their sweetness and lemon juice for its sharpness is always good, especially if it mingles with some well-flavored olive oil.
- A sprinkling of finely chopped garlic and fresh ginger is a favorite combination for baked fish in my family.
- Ground spices or Indian curry pastes can be smeared all over the outside of the fish, and into gashes in the skin before baking. If you do this it is a good idea to wrap the fish and leave it to absorb the seasoning for a few hours before cooking.
- I like spiced grilled fish with fresh cilantro butter.
- Robust whole fish can also be stuffed before baking. Chopped vegetables such as onions, leeks, peppers, eggplant and mushrooms should be softened first in butter or oil and cooled before spooning inside the fish and then baking.
- Chopped nuts, particularly hazelnuts, and chopped black olives and anchovies are a good addition to a stuffing for broiled or barbecued fish.
- Add chopped dried apricots to the stuffing for mackerel and herring for a sweet-and-sharp taste.
- Fresh apricots and green grapes contribute their lovely juices to the sauce surrounding a foil-baked fish.

BUTTERFLYING PRAWNS

Butterflying large uncooked European prawns or jumbo shrimp is an attractive way to prepare them for grilling or broiling. The prawn is opened flat to expose the translucent and pale grey flesh which turns white during cooking.

To keep the prawns flat while cooking, skewer several prawns side by side on soaked long wooden skewers with 1 skewer just above the tail ends and another near the head ends. Or, coat the butterflied prawns in breadcrumbs or cornmeal and then shallow fry in a skillet (page 128) so they curl slightly.

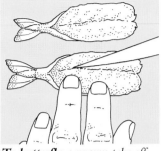

To butterfly a prawn take off the head and remove the shell (page 124). Cut along the outer curve from the head end to the tail, leaving the tail intact and without cutting all the way through. Flatten and use the tip of the knife to remove the black intestine that runs along the length of the prawn's back.

BROILING FISH

To preserve succulence and fresh flavor fish should never be broiled for too long: the broiler must be preheated and very hot so as to cook the fish swiftly, producing tender flesh and a crisp outside.

To broil fillets, the flesh side should always be broiled first, and thick fillets or steaks are the most successful. With a large whole fish it is best to make deep, slanting cuts in the skin at 1–2in (2.5–5cm) intervals so the heat penetrates all the way through the flesh, cooking it evenly.

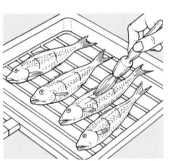

To broil fish brush the rack with oil, then brush the fish before cooking so the flesh remains moist and the skin crisps. Carefully turn the fish over halfway through the estimated cooking time and brush again.

BARBECUING FISH

For successful barbecuing choose rich-flavored or meaty fish such as mackerel, sardines, shark, tuna, salmon, monkfish or bass.

With large fish you can leave the scales on so the skin is protected, then lift off the skin in one piece after cooking. Another trick is to wrap the fish in unbuttered foil; then when the foil is peeled off after cooking the skin comes with it. White fish cubes can be wrapped in bacon if being made into kebobs so they don't fall apart.

Use a fish rack for easy turning of whole fish during barbecuing. Oil the rack thoroughly before use, then place the fish in it, with some herbs at either side, if desired. Put the rack on the grill, turning once halfway through cooking.

To make kebobs cut the fish into 1½–2in (3–5cm) pieces, then marinate in a mixture of lemon juice, oil and seasonings for at least 30 minutes. Skewer and cook on an oiled rack, turning 2 or 3 times until the flesh flakes.

Grilled Mullet in a Spicy Coating (page 140) looks attractive and is easy to prepare.

SALMON *and* SALMON TROUT

It seems only a few years ago that salmon ranked with lobster as one of the fish 'treats' for special occasions. Now, as a result of being farmed very successfully on a large scale, it is becoming cheaper than many other fish and is available, of consistently good quality, all year round.

Between February and August wild salmon is sometimes available; its flesh is delicate and succulent, and should be cooked very simply to make the most of its flavor and texture.

Salmon trout is a family of several species of brown trout which, like salmon, leave their rivers for the open sea and develop pink flesh – though not as orangy pink as

salmon – as a result of the crustaceans they eat. Although it is not as easily available, salmon trout is one of my favorite fish, even more smooth fleshed and moist than salmon, and less oily. Salmon trout is smaller than salmon with a more rounded stomach and stubbier tail.

Both salmon and salmon trout can be cooked in the same way; whole or cut into steaks or fillets, and served hot or cold. They are delicious baked or poached whole, but large steaks or fillets are also excellent grilled. The one thing to guard against, as with all fish, is overcooking. When perfectly cooked the pale pink flesh will still be slightly dark toward the center, but will come away from the bone easily.

POACHING AND SERVING A WHOLE SALMON

Especially if you are going to eat salmon cold I think this is the best way to produce cooked but still extremely moist flesh, particularly next to the bone. The poaching liquid can either be a flavored court bouillon (page 30), or simply salted water as salmon has such a unique flavor of its own.

Because salmon is a rich fish, 4–6oz (125–175g) per person is an adequate portion. When calculating what size fish to buy don't forget the head, tail, bones and viscera amount to about 1lb (500g) loss during cleaning.

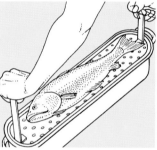

1 *Place the salmon in a fish kettle and cover with cold poaching liquid. Cover and bring to a boil on top of the stove. Poach for 1 minute for fish up to 5lb (2.5kg) and 2 minutes for larger fish. To serve hot, leave it for 15–20 minutes. To serve cold, leave the fish overnight in the liquid.*

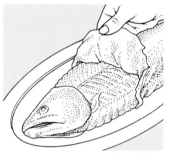

2 *Remove the fish from the kettle. To skin, score around the head and gills, then around the tail with a sharp knife. Carefully peel back the skin in long strips and discard. Scrape off any brown spots with the back of a knife, without disturbing the pink flesh underneath.*

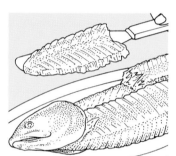

3 *To serve hot or cold salmon, cut along the backbone, then carefully slide a thin-bladed knife under the flesh to separate it from the rib bones. Use a spatula to lift off individual portions. After the top half of the fish has been served, lift off the bones and discard. Continue with remaining fish.*

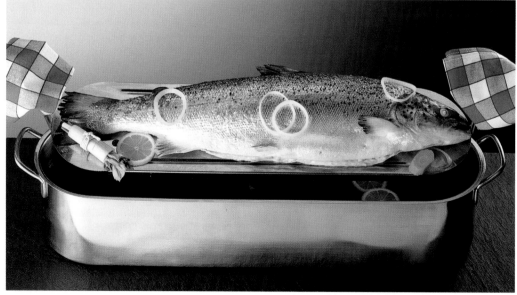

A whole poached salmon with flavorings ready to serve after cooling in a fish kettle.

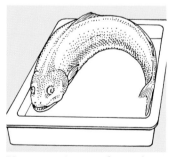

Use a roasting pan *for poaching a whole salmon if you do not have a fish kettle (page 18). Place the fish in a half-moon position and pour in the poaching liquid. Cover with foil and cook as in step 1 (above). After cooking, skin the fish. Serve hot salmon simply garnished with lemon and cold salmon on a bed of shredded lettuce leaves.*

BAKING SALMON

Whole gutted salmon and salmon trout can also be baked in the oven, wrapped in a well-buttered sheet of foil like other fish (page 132). If serving hot, rub generously with butter which will mingle with the fish juices and a little lemon juice to produce a good sauce. If you want to serve the fish cold, however, rub the foil with olive oil instead of butter before baking because butter solidifies when cold.

Leave the fish in the foil for 10 minutes after cooking and before serving. If you plan to eat the fish cold, it will be easiest to remove the skin while it is still warm.

MARINATING RAW SALMON

Now that gravlax (below) is beginning to rival smoked salmon and there are more Japanese restaurants serving sashimi (thinly sliced raw fish), people are getting used to the idea of eating raw fish. Lightly marinated raw salmon can be delicious, as it has such a smooth, dense texture. To marinate salmon begin a few hours before serving and use olive or hazelnut oil and lemon juice, a wine or spirit, such as brandy, plus seasoning.

Salmon to be eaten raw should be the freshest fish possible. Serve it filleted, skinned and thinly sliced on a plate with salad greens. Or, serve with soy sauce and Japanese horseradish (wasabi) powder mixed to a paste for dipping the salmon. For something a bit adventurous serve marinated raw fish as a main course with warm new potatoes and spinach.

GRAVLAX

Gravlax is a wonderful Scandinavian way of mildly pickling raw salmon, and is extremely easy to prepare. A salmon tail piece (approximately 2lb/1kg), cut into two pieces, will produce a considerable amount. Serve with plenty of pumpernickel and a sweetened mustard and dill-flavored mayonnaise (page 202). The salmon should be filleted but left unskinned.

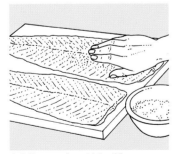

1 *Mix together 1½ tablespoons each crushed sea salt and sugar and 1 teaspoon crushed peppercorns. Rub the mixture into the flesh of both salmon pieces and place 1 piece skin side down in a shallow glass or china dish. Cover with plenty of finely chopped fresh dill. Place the second fillet on top, skin side up, and surround with more chopped dill.*

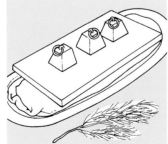

2 *Cover the salmon pieces with waxed paper and wrap tightly, then place a weighted board on top and chill for 2–3 days. Turn the fish and baste with the juices twice a day. Scrape off the pickling mixture before serving. Slice very thinly as for smoked salmon (right) or slightly thicker, in the Scandinavian style, which I prefer.*

SERVING SALMON

- A rich homemade mayonnaise (page 202) is the classic sauce for cold salmon, but you can vary it in many ways by adding herbs, crushed garlic, spices and other flavorings. The most effective fresh herbs for fish are dill, fennel, tarragon, basil, lovage and chervil, and chopped blanched watercress. A puree of cooked and well-drained spinach and sorrel produces a really green mayonnaise.
- Thick plain yogurt with whipped cream and any of the above flavorings also makes a good sauce for cold salmon.
- Of course, you can serve non-mayonnaise type sauces with cold salmon, too; skinned chopped tomatoes cooked until soft in olive oil with the addition of garlic and a little sherry or balsamic vinegar, and served cold, is excellent.
- For an oil-based green sauce you can use blanched and chopped spinach and sorrel with extra virgin olive oil.
- An easy sauce to make to serve with poached salmon is pureed avocado with lemon juice, a little oil and seasoning.
- Make salmon tartare the same way as steak tartare, mixing finely chopped raw salmon with olive oil, capers and herbs. Add some finely chopped onion as well, if you like.
- Flavored butters melt delectably onto hot salmon. Try butter softened with fresh parsley or other herbs, pounded anchovies, lemon rind and juice, crushed garlic or mustard.
- Peeled whole garlic can be sautéed gently until soft, golden and sweet and then pureed and stirred into cream to be heated and seasoned for an easy sauce to serve with salmon.
- Hollandaise sauce (page 200) is a favorite with me and can have many of the flavorings suggested for mayonnaise (left) added to it.
- Smoked salmon is also effective as a wrapping for fish pâtés or terrines or for stuffings of shellfish, or vegetables such as spinach or broccoli.
- Make scrambled eggs for a special occasion with slivers of smoked salmon stirred in at the last moment. Dill or chives are good flavorings for the eggs.
- Pasta with cream and slivers of smoked salmon tossed in at the last moment is a dreamy dish.

SLICING SMOKED SALMON

Although smoked salmon is expensive, a little goes a long way. Good-quality smoked salmon should be quite oily, slightly sweet and have a peachy pink color. Sliced smoked salmon is readily available but if you are serving it for large numbers it is more economical to buy a whole side and slice it yourself. Serve with lemon wedges and rye bread and butter.

1 *To slice your own smoked salmon lay the side of smoked salmon skin side down on a board or other flat surface. Check for any stray small bones, removing them with your fingers or a pair of clean tweezers.*

2 *With a long, thin serrated knife, cut wafer-thin slices starting at the tail end. Use your free hand to hold the uncut salmon firm. Lay the slices on waxed paper, placing some paper between each layer.*

SMOKED, DRIED *and* SALTED FISH

Smoking, drying and salting are early methods of preserving fish that we still use. Each has survived because of the particular flavor it gives to food. Smoking only preserves for a limited period but it must have been realized early on what wonderful results it can have on fish. Fish is either hot smoked, which lightly cooks the fish as well as flavoring it, or cold smoked, which leaves the fish raw as with smoked salmon (which is salted before smoking). Hot smoked fish include mackerel, trout and eel. As a rule look for plump, pale-colored fish. Kippers and Finnan haddie are both soaked in brine before smoking, then dried and lightly cold smoked.

Although smoked, dried and salted fish were important in the Colonial diet their use had declined until they were rediscovered by today's chefs..

The kind of wood used for cold smoking and the length of time (anything from two to twenty days) both affect the final flavor of the fish. Cod and haddock are normally cold smoked and it is sometimes possible to buy cold smoked mackerel as well. Other smoked delicacies to look for are smoked halibut, tuna, mussels and monkfish. Once found only in ethnic neighbourhood fish markets, smoked fish are now offered by all gourmet producers on both coasts. Available in gourmet markets locally, they may also be purchased by mail nationwide.

There are different kinds of salted fish; some of them salted and dried, others packed in a salt brine or simply closely packed in salt, which produces its own brine around them. Anchovies, for example, can be salted or brined. There are also fish which are simply dried in the sun or in drying sheds. The Spanish and Portuguese have what seems to me an almost obsessive passion for salt cod although they live in countries which abound with many types of wonderful fresh fish.

PREPARING KIPPERS

Although traditionally associated with a good British breakfast, kippers make excellent suppers or light lunches, too. They are cured herring, preserved further by cold smoking so they still need cooking before eating. You can buy kippers in gourmet markets. Fillets have been boned, although fine bones may still be present. Look for plump, firm flesh with a good sheen.

There are three ways of cooking kippers. Whole or filleted kippers can be broiled 5 minutes, immersed in boiling water 5–10 minutes or microwaved. To cook kippers in a microwave, place them on a lightly greased microwave-safe plate. Cover loosely, then cook on High (100%) for 3–5 minutes. Set aside 3 minutes, then serve.

Regardless which method you use, they are cooked when the flesh flakes easily. Serve with a squeeze of lemon juice, freshly black ground pepper and plenty of brown bread and butter.

WHITEFISH SALAD

Smoked fish of all kinds can be good in salads and sandwich fillings. Smoked whitefish salad is a New York deli specialty used to stuff bagels and generous rye bread sandwiches. On weekend mornings, people stand in line for this tradition, but in truth it is so easy to make that you can keep some on hand to avoid the line. This recipe serves 4 in most of the country, but a deli would put this amount on 2 bagels.

In a medium-size bowl, with a fork, mix together 8oz (250g) skinned, boned and flaked smoked whitefish (this will be about 12oz/375g when purchased) and 3oz (75g) cream cheese until uniformly combined. Add 3oz (75g) sour cream, 2 tablespoons finely chopped onion and some black pepper; stir to combine.

Turn the salad into a serving bowl, cover and refrigerate until ready to serve. Garnish with lots of dill and sprinkle with paprika. Serve with pumpernickel bread or bagels.

USING PRESERVED FISH

• Thinly sliced or flaked smoked fish mixed with salad vegetables or greens make wonderful salads. Toss with an herb, garlic or mustard vinaigrette (page 204) just before serving.
• Any filleted smoked fish can be made into a pâté (page 97) but smoked mackerel and kipper are the most usual; they can be made with added butter, cream, cottage cheese or crème fraîche – if you have a blender or food processor this takes only minutes to make, and not much longer by hand. Season to taste with herbs, spices or even a drop of alcohol such as Pernod.

• Stuff taramasalata into edible containers such as hollowed-out tomatoes and hard-boiled eggs or little pastry cases. Small cream puffs stuffed with taramasalata are delicious, too.
• For a first course, wrap taramasalata in smoked salmon packages.
• Smoked haddock can be very delicious when cooked in milk and then made into a soup or served with poached eggs and spinach. It can also be used for fish cakes.
• I love anchovies, fresh or salted. The anchovies which are most easily available are salted fillets in cans: these are a good

addition to pasta dishes, to pizzas, to stuffings for lamb or chicken, for flavoring butter and for all manner of sauces.
• I make my favorite potato salad by mixing hot, boiled potatoes with a mixture of finely chopped anchovies with their oil and extra olive oil, crushed garlic, a little balsamic vinegar and lots of black pepper, then leaving the potatoes to cool and absorb the flavors.
• Cooked gently, soaked dried cod can be treated like its fresh counterpart. It goes well with the strong Mediterranean flavors of garlic, olives and tomatoes.

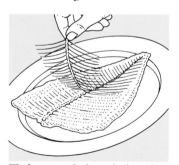

To bone a whole cooked smoked fish, place the fish flesh side up, and loosen the main bone. Slowly pull it up and discard. Even if the fish is skinned and already filleted there may still be fine bones on the skinned side so use clean tweezers to loosen them and pull away.

NEW ENGLAND CODFISH CAKES

The first colonists to North America were delighted to discover the waters full of the biggest codfish they had ever seen. Codfish became an important part of their diet and salt cod became an early New England commodity and one of this country's first exports to Europe. As Portugese communities developed along the shores of New England, they contributed to the culinary culture many new ways of preparing this mainstay of their diet. But this simple preparation has remained a regional tradition.

This recipe is pan fried for convenience, but may be deep fried if you wish. Codfish cakes are often deep fat fried which gives them an easy crispy surface with golden wisps of cod at the edges. All you need to add is a green vegetable, bread and salad for a delicious, traditional New England supper. This recipe serves 6 people.

Peel and quarter 2 medium-size potatoes, cover with water, and bring to a boil over high heat. Cook until very tender, about 20 minutes. Drain them very well and set aside.

Meanwhile, heat 1oz (25g) butter and sauté 1 small onion, finely chopped, until it is softened and just beginning to turn golden. Add the onion and butter mixture to the potatoes, along with 1 cup (125g) soaked, cooked and flaked salt cod (see below). Stir the mixture with a fork until it is evenly combined. It should still be a little lumpy.

With floured hands, divide the codfish mixture into 6 balls. Flatten the balls into 3in (7.5cm) round cakes. Dip the cakes in flour to coat them lightly on all sides. Place the cakes on a plate; cover and refrigerate for 1 hour to make them firmer and easier to fry.

In a large heavy skillet, shallow fry the codfish cakes in a mixture of butter and oil, turning once until golden brown on each side. Drain on paper towels and serve immediately.

The traditional accompaniment for codfish cakes is ketchup, but tartar sauce or just lemon wedges will do as well.

Pasta Spirals with Smoked Haddock (page 138) is an easy-to-prepare family dish that makes the most of the fish's smoky flavor. Fresh basil is used as the garnish here but you can, of course, use any fresh herb in season.

PREPARING SALT COD

Except for the traditional codfish cakes of New England, salt cod is mostly used in ethnic dishes. In order to prepare a dish with salt cod, you must prepare ahead as it should be soaked for at least 24 hours before cooking.

Look for fish with a beige-grey color with a dusting of salt, and ideally choose from the thicker middle of the fish.

One simple way to serve cooked salt cod is in pieces with plain boiled potatoes and a good garlicky mayonnaise.

My favorite way of serving it is in a brandade – a creamy puree of salt cod, garlic, olive oil and even cream – popular along the Mediterranean.

1 *With a very strong pair of scissors or a heavy kitchen knife, cut the salt cod into pieces to fit in a single layer in a large flat bowl. Cover the salt cod pieces with cold water and leave to soak for 24–48 hours, changing the water every 8 hours or so. This preparation is necessary so the cod loses its salty taste yet still retains a unique, firm texture.*

2 *Drain the salt cod pieces and place in a large saucepan with fresh cold water to cover. Add a bouquet garni and whole black peppercorns. Bring slowly to a boil. Cover the pan and simmer gently for 10–20 minutes, depending on thickness of the fish, until the salt cod is tender and flakes easily when tested with the tip of a knife.*

3 *Remove the salt cod from the cooking liquid with a slotted spoon and set aside until cool. Remove the skin and flake the flesh into meaty chunks. Serve with a sauce or mash and use for codfish cakes or a brandade mixed with garlic and olive oil (left). You can also use it like ordinary flaked fish in stews or in casseroles mixed with chunks of potatoes.*

MARINATED SCALLOPS WITH AVOCADO AND TOMATOES *(116)*

The small scallops are the best to use for this delectable first course. They are meltingly tender, and it is really pointless to cook them. They are much nicer either marinated and eaten cold as here, or simply warmed in a sauce or soup.

In this simple summer dish the scallops are marinated with lemon juice and then served with chopped fresh dill and basil and a lemon vinaigrette, accompanied by sliced avocados and tomatoes. If you can't find small scallops, use larger scallops, but slice them into thirds before adding the marinade. *SERVES 4*

1lb (500g) small scallops, thawed if
* frozen*
½ cup (125ml) lemon juice, preferably
* freshly squeezed*
Black pepper
Extra virgin olive oil
Salt
Small bunch of fresh dill, fairly finely
* chopped*
2 large avocados
Lemon juice for sprinkling
¾ lb (375g) tomatoes, skinned and cut
* across into thin slices*
8–10 fresh basil leaves, cut crosswise into
* thin strips*
Fresh dill sprigs to garnish (optional)

Put the scallops in a bowl and pour the lemon juice over them – it should be enough to cover the scallops. Sprinkle with black pepper. Cover the bowl and leave in the refrigerator for 30 minutes, or a little longer if convenient.

Pour the marinade off the scallops into a jar and add olive oil and seasoning.

Shake to make a vinaigrette dressing. Mix the chopped dill with the scallops.

Shortly before you want to eat cut the avocados in half, remove the stones and peel off the skins carefully. Slice across thinly in half-moon slices. Sprinkle with lemon juice as you slice them to prevent the flesh from browning.

Arrange the avocado slices alternately with the tomato slices on a serving dish, overlapping slightly. Spoon the scallops alongside. Sprinkle the basil strips over the avocado and tomato slices and finally spoon the vinaigrette dressing over the whole dish. Garnish with fresh dill, if desired, and serve at once.

PASTA SPIRALS WITH SMOKED HADDOCK *(137)*

You can use any of the pasta shapes which hold sauces well for this mouthwatering and quickly made supper dish. Any smoky-flavoured, fish blends well with this creamy sauce. *SERVES 4*

12oz (375g) pasta spirals
2oz (50g) butter
¾ lb (375g) smoked haddock fillet,
* skinned and cut into chunks*
2 teaspoons paprika
1 tablespoon tomato puree
2 cups (450ml) heavy cream
2 bunches green onions, trimmed and
* finely chopped (including the green parts)*
3–4 tablespoons lemon juice
Cayenne pepper
Salt
Fresh basil to garnish
Grated Parmesan cheese to serve (optional)

Cook the pasta in plenty of boiling salted water until *al dente* (page 82).

Meanwhile, melt the butter in a large frying pan over medium heat. Add the fish and stir gently for about 3 minutes until the fish is opaque, then stir in the paprika followed by the tomato puree. Add the cream and bring to a boil. Stir in the chopped green onions and boil gently for 1 minute, then remove from the heat and gradually stir in the lemon juice. Season with cayenne pepper and salt to taste.

When the pasta is ready drain it, put it into a warmed serving dish and mix in the haddock and cream sauce. Garnish with fresh basil and serve at once, with or without grated Parmesan cheese.

SALMON FISH BALLS *(128)*

These fish balls are very light and creamy as they contain no potato and instead have a base of white sauce. They are sophisticated enough to serve at a dinner party either as a hot first course or as a main course, accompanied by a mixed green salad. Prepare the mixture well in advance as it must chill thoroughly so you can form the fish balls easily. A mixture of salmon and smoked haddock is also delicious. *SERVES 4–6*

3oz (75g) butter
2 cloves garlic, chopped finely
⅔ cup (75g) all-purpose flour, sifted
1¼ cups (300ml) milk
1lb (500g) lightly poached salmon
* (page 130)*
Salt
3–4 pinches cayenne pepper
Bunch of fresh watercress leaves, finely
* chopped*
About 5 tablespoons fresh white
* breadcrumbs*
Peanut oil for frying

Melt the butter in a saucepan and add the chopped garlic. Remove from the heat and stir in the sifted flour. Gradually stir in the milk. Put the pan back on the heat and bring to a boil, stirring all the time with a wooden spoon. Boil gently, still stirring, for about 4 minutes until very thick. This also cooks the flour so it does not taste raw in the fish balls.

Remove the pan from the heat and flake in the poached salmon flesh. Season well with salt and the cayenne pepper and stir in the chopped watercress. Turn the mixture into a shallow dish or roasting pan and leave until cold. Cover with plastic wrap and chill thoroughly in the refrigerator for at least 1 hour.

Put the breadcrumbs in a bowl, and flour your hands. Take up small amounts of the chilled salmon mixture and lightly roll into round shapes, a little bigger than ping-pong balls. Dip the balls in the bread crumbs, one by one, and set aside until all are coated.

Heat peanut oil in a deep frying pan until very hot and fry the balls, a few at a time, over a high heat for a short time, until golden brown all over. Take out using a slotted spatula and drain well on paper towels. Arrange the cooked fish balls on a serving dish and keep warm in a low oven, until ready to serve.

SQUID RINGS WITH LEEKS AND SPINACH (127)

This is a wonderful way of serving larger stuffed squid; when cooked the squid is sliced and laid on a rich red sauce. When preparing the squid save the fins and tentacles and chop to include in the stuffing.   *SERVES 4*

1 tablespoon olive oil
½oz (15g) butter
12oz (375g) leeks, trimmed and cut into
  ½in (1cm) rings
2in (5cm) piece fresh gingerroot, peeled
  and chopped
1 large clove garlic, chopped
1½lb (750g) large squid, washed and
  prepared for stuffing (page 126)
4oz (125g) fresh spinach, stalks removed,
  washed, well drained and chopped
2oz (50g) pecans, chopped
Salt and black pepper
1 small egg, beaten lightly
FOR THE SAUCE
1 large red pepper, halved, seeded and
  cored (page 49)
1oz (25g) butter
1 clove garlic, finely chopped
12oz (375g) tomatoes, skinned and
  coarsely chopped (page 48)
2 teaspoons sugar
Salt and black pepper

Heat the olive oil and the butter in a large, deep frying pan over medium heat. Add the leeks and stir occasionally until softened – don't let them brown. Add the ginger and garlic, the chopped squid fins and tentacles and the spinach with only the water that clings to the leaves after draining. Stir over the heat, just until the spinach is limp – if there is a lot of liquid increase the heat and boil for a minute to reduce it slightly. Remove from the heat and add the pecans, with a good sprinkling of salt and black pepper. Turn into a bowl and leave the stuffing mixture until cool, then stir in the beaten egg.

Hold the squid firmly and spoon the stuffing mixture in, working it down to the bottom. Still holding the squid, stitch or skewer to enclose the stuffing (page 127).

Rub the stuffed squid with a little oil, place in a roasting pan and cover tightly with foil. Bake at 325°F, 160°C for 1–1¼ hours.

Meanwhile, make the sauce. Process the red pepper in a food processor until very finely chopped. Heat the butter in a large saucepan over medium heat, then add the chopped garlic, the red pepper and its juices, the chopped tomatoes and the sugar. Cover the pan and cook, stirring now and then, over a very low heat for 20–25 minutes until you have a fairly thick sauce. Remove from the heat and leave on one side.

When the squid is cooked transfer carefully to a chopping board and pour any pan juices into the tomato and pepper sauce. Bring the sauce to a boil, cook for a minute or two and season to taste with salt and black pepper. Pour into a fairly shallow, warm serving dish. Using a very sharp knife cut the squid across into ½–¾in (1–1.5cm) rings. Using a spatula, carefully arrange the squid rings, slightly overlapping, on top of the tomato sauce. If necessary, cover with foil and keep warm in a low oven.

SCALLOP, CRAB AND PRAWN TART (125)

If you can get the little scallops, they are the sweetest of all, and cheaper, too. To make 8 individual tarts, instead of 1 large one as below, use 4in (10cm) tartlet pans and increase the quantities of scallops, crab meat and prawns slightly. Bake the pastry blind (page 245) for only 15–20 minutes.   *SERVES 6–8*

FOR THE PASTRY
2 cups (250g) bread flour
½ teaspoon salt
3 tablespoons semolina
6oz (175g) chilled butter, cut into small
  pieces
1 egg
1 tablespoon cold water
FOR THE FILLING
8oz (250g) scallops, fairly thinly sliced
8oz (250g) mixed crab meat
3oz (75g) peeled prawns or shrimp
1 fresh red chili, seeded and finely chopped
  (page 49)
1 clove garlic, crushed
1 tablespoon coarsely chopped fresh
  tarragon
1 teaspoon ground mace
1¼ cups (300ml) heavy cream
1 egg, lightly beaten
2 tablespoons lemon juice
Salt and black pepper
1 teaspoon paprika
Lemon slices and extra tarragon to garnish
  (optional)

To make the pastry, sift the flour and salt into a bowl. Stir in the semolina, then rub in the butter lightly with your fingertips until the mixture resembles coarse breadcrumbs. Lightly beat the egg with the water and mix it into the flour and semolina with a fork until the mixture starts to stick together.

Gather the pastry mixture into a ball and roll it out on a lightly floured surface into a piece large enough to line a 10–11in (25–28cm) loose-bottomed flan pan. Line the pan with the pastry, pressing a rolling pin around the edges to cut off the excess neatly.

Refrigerate the pastry shell for at least 30 minutes. Take the pastry-lined pan out of the refrigerator, and line it with parchment paper and dried beans (page 245). Bake the pastry blind at 400°F, 200°C for 20–25 minutes until lightly golden. Remove the parchment paper and beans and leave the tart to cool in the pan on a wire rack.

To prepare the filling, place the thinly sliced scallops in a bowl with the crab meat and peeled prawns. Mix in the chopped chili, the crushed garlic, the chopped tarragon and the ground mace. In another bowl whip the cream until it begins to thicken, then add the lightly beaten egg, the lemon juice, salt and freshly ground black pepper. Continue beating until thick, then stir lightly into the fish mixture.

Pour the fish and cream mixture into the cooled pastry shell and sprinkle a dash of paprika across the center.

Bake the tart in the center of a preheated oven, 375°F, 190°C for 15–20 minutes, until the filling is set and lightly browned. Remove the tart from the oven and leave to cool a little, then carefully remove from the tart pan and place on a serving plate.

Garnish the tart with lemon slices and extra sprigs of fresh tarragon if you like, then serve. Serve lukewarm or at room temperature but never straight from the refrigerator.

JOCK'S GRILLED STUFFED MACKEREL (119)

I dream of landing a plump sea bass but the only fish I catch is the humble mackerel. However, very fresh mackerel tastes like a prince of fish. It has a beautiful soft yet dense texture and a characteristic flavor which is at its best when broiled so that the blackened skin adds a hint of smokiness. The inspiration for this recipe comes from a family friend who visits every summer.   *SERVES 4*

½ cup (75g) blanched almonds, chopped
A few sprigs of fresh tarragon
2 cloves garlic, finely chopped
2 tablespoons fresh brown breadcrumbs
1 small egg, lightly beaten
Salt and black pepper
4 small–medium mackerel, gutted through
* the gills and heads removed (page 118)*
Lime or lemon wedges and tarragon to
* garnish*

Toast the almonds in a dry frying pan over high heat. Put in a bowl. Pull the leaves off the tarragon, chop coarsely and add to the almonds with the garlic. Stir in the breadcrumbs and egg and season.

Preheat the broiler to the highest possible heat. Using a sharp knife, make 3 or 4 diagonal cuts on the side of each mackerel. Spoon the stuffing mixture into the body cavities of the fish and lay the fish on a broiler rack. Cook under the preheated broiler for about 5 minutes on each side until the flesh of the fish is opaque. Garnish and serve at once.

STUFFED SALMON FILLETS WITH YELLOW PEPPER AND SAFFRON SAUCE (116)

These are a perfect treat for a small dinner party and the mixture of pink, yellow and green is tempting. The filleted tail pieces of salmon are stuffed with shrimp (for a very special occasion you could use pieces of lobster) and plenty of fresh dill and cilantro. They are then cooked in a creamy yellow sauce which goes especially well with new potatoes and snow peas.   *SERVES 4*

2 tail pieces of salmon, about 1¼–1½lb
* (625–750g) each before filleting and*
* skinning*
Black pepper
Bunch of fresh dill, chopped
Generous handful of fresh cilantro leaves,
* chopped*
6oz (175g) peeled cooked shrimp
FOR THE SAUCE
¾ cup plus 2 tablespoons (200ml)
* white wine*
2 good pinches saffron strands
2 small–medium yellow peppers, halved,
* seeded and cored (page 49)*
½ pint (300ml) heavy cream
4 tablespoons balsamic or sherry vinegar
Salt and black pepper

Lay out the fillets of salmon and sprinkle generously with black pepper. Press the chopped dill and cilantro all over one side of the pieces of salmon. Place the shrimp in the center of each piece. Roll over the salmon lengthwise to enclose the shrimp and hold the rolls together with wooden skewers or toothpicks. Leave on one side while you prepare the sauce.

In a small saucepan, heat 6 tablespoons of the white wine with the saffron strands until boiling, then remove from the heat and leave on one side to infuse. Preheat a hot broiler. Put the pepper halves, skin side up, under a hot broiler until the skin has burned black nearly all over (page 55). Place in a tea towel until cool enough to handle, then peel off the skins using your fingers. Put the flesh in a food processor with the remaining white wine and process until as smooth as possible (press the puree through a fine sieve if not absolutely smooth).

Put the pepper puree into a Dutch oven which is wide enough to hold the rolled fillets of fish side by side. Stir the cream into the pepper puree with the

saffron infused and remaining wine. Place the rolled fish fillets on top of the sauce and cover with a lid.

Very shortly before eating put the Dutch oven over a high heat on top of the stove. Bring the sauce just up to boiling, then lower the heat and poach the fish very gently for 6–8 minutes – the salmon should not be allowed to overcook and should still be a slightly darker pink in the center if you gently test by sticking in the tip of a knife. Lift out the salmon fillets with a spatula and put carefully on to a heated serving plate.

Add the balsamic vinegar or sherry to the sauce, season to taste with salt and freshly ground black pepper, then bring up to boiling again. Stir for 1 minute, then strain before pouring it over the fish. Serve at once.

GRILLED MULLET IN A SPICY COATING (133)

Mullet is an inexpensive fish which grills and bakes well; if not available, substitute 2 catfish. I always find this way of cooking very useful when time is short but if possible start early in the day so that the spices permeate the flesh. Ask the fish counter clerk to gut the fish through the belly, leaving the head on, and to remove the scales, or do it yourself (page 118).   *SERVES 4*

1 mullet, about 3½lb (1.75kg)
2 rounded tablespoons plain yogurt
2 teaspoons paprika
1 teaspoon ground cinnamon
½ teaspoon cayenne pepper
1 large clove garlic, crushed
Sea salt
Flat-leaf parsley, bay leaves and lemon
* wedges to garnish*
1 tablespoon olive oil

Put the yogurt in a bowl and stir in the paprika, cinnamon, cayenne pepper, garlic, olive oil and a little sea salt. Cut diagonal deep slashes at 1in (2.5cm) intervals on each side of the fish. Rub the yogurt and spice mixture onto the fish outside and in, pressing it into the slashes. If time refrigerate for 30 minutes or more..

Preheat a very hot outdoor grill or indoor broiler. Cook the fish under the preheated grill or broiler for about 6–8 minutes on each side until blackened in patches. Garnish and serve.

FILLETS OF COD WITH CREAMY SHRIMP AND DILL SAUCE (130)

Cod is an often underrated fish, not associated with more sophisticated dishes. Cooked carefully, however, its large flakes should be moist and smooth with a delicate flavor. These fillets are poached lightly in a white wine and shrimp stock, which then becomes part of the creamy shrimp sauce, making it a luxurious dish. Serve with new potatoes and a green vegetable.   *SERVES 4*

12oz (375g) shrimp in their shells
3 large cloves garlic, sliced
2 rounded teaspoons paprika
1¼ cups (300ml) dry white wine
1¼ cups (300ml) water
4 thick pieces cod fillet, about
  8oz (250g) each
1 cup (250ml) heavy cream
2 teaspoons white wine vinegar
Salt and black pepper
1 rounded tablespoon coarsely chopped
  fresh dill

Peel the shrimp, putting the shells and heads into a saucepan and the shrimp into a bowl. Add the sliced garlic and paprika to the shrimp shells and pour in the white wine and water. Cover the saucepan and bring to a boil, then lower the heat and simmer very gently for 20 minutes. Strain the liquid through a sieve into a wide saucepan into which all the pieces of cod fillet will fit close together in a single layer.

Lay the fillets skin side up in the shrimp stock. Cover the saucepan, put over a medium to low heat and keep only just simmering for 8–10 minutes until the fish is opaque white all through. Using a wide slotted spatula carefully lift out the fillets and place on a warmed serving dish. Again carefully, peel off the skin and discard. Keep the fish loosely covered in a low oven or warm place while you make the sauce.

Boil the poaching liquid rapidly over a high heat for about 3 minutes until slightly reduced. Stir in the cream and boil rapidly for 1 minute until the sauce has thickened. Remove from the heat. Stir in the vinegar and season to taste with salt and freshly gound black pepper if necessary, then add the shrimp and the chopped dill. Spoon the sauce over the cod fillets and serve at once.

THE EMPEROR'S FAN (116)

My husband named this dish at first glance. You wouldn't think there was anything very imperial about skate, but the fan-shaped wings, glazed with a clear sauce flavored with orange and lemon juices, fresh ginger and coriander is certainly evocative of the Far East.   *SERVES 4*

1 orange
2½ cups (600ml) fish or chicken stock
  (pages 28–31)
4 tablespoons lemon juice
1in (2.5cm)piece fresh gingerroot, peeled
  and sliced
4 skate wings
2 rounded teaspoons arrowroot
1 tablespoon water
Salt and cayenne pepper (optional)
4oz (125g) button mushrooms, sliced
A good handful of fresh cilantro leaves,
  chopped
Orange wedges and extra rind and cilantro
  sprigs to garnish (optional)

Remove a few strips of peel from the orange and squeeze the juice. Pour the stock and orange and lemon juices into a large frying pan which has a lid with the ginger and orange peel. Warm the stock, then add 2 skate wings. Cover, bring the liquid up to barely simmering and poach for 5–6 minutes until the skate is just opaque. Remove the skate and arrange on a shallow serving dish, like overlapping fans. Cover with foil and put into a low oven while you poach the rest.

Then bring the liquid to a boil for 5 minutes. Strain through a fine sieve into a saucepan. Mix the arrowroot with the water until smooth, then stir into the strained liquid. Bring to a boil, stirring all the time, then boil, still stirring, for 3 minutes. Season if necessary with a little salt and cayenne pepper. Add the mushrooms and cook for another minute. Stir in the cilantro. Pour over the skate wings, garnish if desired and serve.

GOLDEN FISH PIE (116)

We often have variations of fish pie for a family supper, and this one is popular with its golden orange top of mashed sweet and white potato. For an extra treat, you can add a few shelled mussels to the fish. Serve with a simple green salad.   *SERVES 4–5*

1lb (500g) sweet potatoes (the large,
  orange-fleshed kind), peeled
12oz (375g) potatoes, peeled
3oz (75g) butter
2–3 pinches cayenne pepper
1½–1¾lb (750g–875g) haddock or cod
  fillets, skinned
2 heaping tablespoons cornstarch
2–3 tablespoons water
2½ cups (600ml) milk
⅔ cup (150ml) heavy cream
12oz (375g) small tomatoes, skinned and
  quartered (page 48)
1 rounded teaspoon of Dijon mustard
Salt and black pepper
2 tablespoons chopped fresh dill

Steam or boil the sweet potatoes and the white potatoes until very soft. This takes approximately 20 minutes. Mash the potatoes together with 2oz (50g) of the butter and season to taste with salt and the cayenne pepper.

While the potatoes are cooking steam the fish fillets until just cooked (page 131) – this should not take more than 5 minutes so keep checking so as not to overcook. Leave the fish and potatoes on one side.

Preheat the broiler to high and put a shallow ovenproof serving dish in a low oven to keep warm. Put the cornstarch and water in a cup and stir until smooth. Pour into a saucepan and gradually stir in the milk and the cream. Bring to a boil, stirring all the time, then boil, still stirring, for about 3 minutes.

Add the tomatoes and boil for another minute. Stir in the mustard with salt and black pepper to taste. Add the steamed fish and chopped fresh dill (and mussels if using). Remove immediately from the heat and pour into the warm serving dish.

Using a spatula carefully spoon the mashed potatoes all over the fish mixture and spread gently to form a topping. Dot with the remaining 1oz (25g) of butter and put under the broiler for 5–10 minutes until the surface is darkly speckled all over – the speckles should look black against the orange of the potato.

MEAT and GAME

Although I can very well go without meat for days I cannot imagine I will ever become a vegetarian. Meat adds enormous scope to both cooking and eating – a family Sunday dinner is epitomized by a large juicy roast, the appetizing smell of which fills the house during the cooking. In winter a slowly cooked meat stew with its rich juices and meltingly soft vegetables is a great comfort, while a rare, tender filet of beef wrapped in pastry is a luxurious treat. Another experience I would hate to miss out on in life is the pleasure of eating meat cooked outdoors. Given a beautiful garden or picnic spot, lamb grilled outside, ideally over a bundle of rosemary twigs whose aromatic smoke infuses into the meat and scents the air, can induce a sense of ecstasy, and should taste as good as anything the most exclusive restaurant could produce. As it is the juices of meat which are so wonderful it is important not to overcook and dry out grilled or roasted meat – in slow-cooked casseroles and stews it is these juices which literally make the dish.

The cheaper cuts of meat often have the most flavor, and if cooked with thought and time they produce a supremely satisfying meal. Ground meat is sometimes scorned, probably because it can be so badly cooked, resulting in a grey and tasteless mess. But seasoned well, with added herbs or spices, and cooked carefully, it can be transformed into an enormous variety of dishes. Even shepherd's pie can be made into a dish fit for a dinner party, not to mention lasagna, moussaka, stuffed peppers and zucchini and countless different meatballs.

The meats most widely eaten are beef from the steer, lamb from the sheep and pork from the pig. In our household, lamb is the meat we eat most although the occasional treat of a large rib roast of beef, on the bone

and properly hung in the traditional way, is well worth paying for. Both fresh and frozen lamb can be excellent, but fresh, really young spring lamb is sweet, mild and succulent and needs no added flavorings. As pork is bred so much leaner nowadays, which gives it a tendency to dryness, it must be cooked in a way which will add moisture; I find it a perfect meat for stews. Goat is often served in Mediterranean countries and baby kid is wonderfully tender and succulent. Venison, hare and rabbit are classed as game even though they are not always wild. Farmed venison can be so tender that you can treat it exactly like the best cuts of beef and cook it rare. Many people like the fact that it is low in fat and even prefer its milder flavor.

A light marbling of fat gives tenderness and flavor to pieces of meat which are to be grilled, roasted rare or lightly cooked, while leaner cuts of meat develop tenderness and flavor with long, slow cooking. But the texture and taste of the meat also vitally depends on the hanging of the animal – all meat except veal should have been hung, for varying amounts of time. Luckily, meat is now beginning to be hung for longer in the traditional way. Often this is indicated on the roast but if in doubt always check before buying.

All meat is muscle, and the harder the muscle works the tougher the meat is likely to be, yet the flavor will tend to be better, especially on an older animal. Many wonderful slowly cooked stews and casseroles can be made with the tougher parts of the animal. And then there are the variety meats, which some love and some hate; personally, I love variety meats for their wonderful and varied flavors. But, once again, careful cooking is essential.

Clockwise from top right: The flavorings used in Roast Veal with Prunes, Ginger and Pistachio Nuts (page 168) keep the meat moist and tender; Pork Chops Stuffed with Roquefort and Baked with Pears (page 170) are served with lightly steamed savoy cabbage; Grilled Lamb Filets with Mint and Yogurt Sauce (page 170) are quick and easy to make using boned lamb rib or loin, and served here with creamy purees of carrot, and spinach and potato; buttered Chinese noodles give an oriental touch to the more traditional combination of pork and apple in Stir-fried Pork Filet with Fruit and Lettuce (page 169); and the rich, strong flavor of rabbit is complemented by a smooth red pepper and tomato sauce in Stewed Rabbit with Quinces (page 171), accompanied by steamed potatoes.

BEEF *and* VEAL

Beef is the meat of a steer, and veal is the meat of the young calf, yet the characters of these meats are so different it is as if they come from two different animals. Beef is eaten fresher than it used to be, as the traditional longer hanging takes up space and raises the price of the meat. But now once again butchers are beginning to realize the virtues of hanging, which are increased flavor and tenderness. Look for darker red beef which indicates that it has been well hung, or look out for information to indicate that the meat has been matured in the traditional way.

Beef is, above all, an extremely versatile meat which suits either the most lavish or the most economical meal. Although cuts such as filet and sirloin are expensive they are never wasteful, and they are usually very simply cooked. Beef that is marbled with thin strands of creamy colored fat has more flavor. Some inexpensive beef roasts, such as brisket, have a marvelous flavor, but are very fatty; look for the least fatty piece you can find, then cook it long and gently, skimming off as much fat as you can from the surface. Richly delicious stews can be made with the cheapest cuts of beef, providing the meat is cooked gently for a long time – at least three hours.

Veal comes from calves up to five months old, but the best veal is from really young animals which have been fed entirely on milk. The flesh should be a very pale pink, soft and moist. Veal is nearly always tender but it has little fat so it is not ideal for grilling or roasting at a high heat. Gently roasted veal produces the most intensely flavored juices of all meat and the gelatinous bones make the best stock, thus pot-roasted and slowly stewed veal is delicious.

TYING MEAT WITH A BUTCHER'S KNOT

Meat is tied not only for a neater appearance, but also because it enables more even cooking and easier carving. Boned roasts, with or without a stuffing, obviously need tying, but it also helps to tie roasts with one large muscle, such as silvertip, so they retain their shape.

Professionals use this knot because of the control it gives over tightness. If you've boned a roast, or have unrolled one for stuffing this knot at regular intervals gives a neat shape for even cooking.

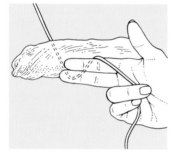

1 *Pass a piece of string under the roast, with the short end toward you. Make the shape of a pair of scissors with your right hand and pass the short end of string over the palm and hold it firm with your third and little finger.*

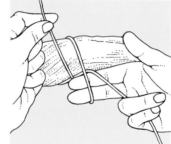

2 *Take the long end of string with your left hand and pass it over and behind the first two fingers of your right hand, parallel to the first piece of string. Pull with the left hand to keep the required tension.*

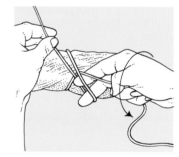

3 *Keeping your right hand in the scissor shape twist from the wrist in a counterclockwise direction towards you and out so that the back of the hand is uppermost. Keep the left hand holding onto the long end.*

HANDLING MEAT AND GAME

• Refrigeration prevents the growth of and cooking destroys bacteria which can cause food poisoning. You must take great care, however, that bacteria in raw meat do not cross-contaminate other foods.
• Your refrigerator should not be any warmer than 40°F (4°C) for safe storage of meat.
• Refrigerate meat as soon as you get it home. Meat sold on plastic trays can be left as it is; other meat should be put on a dish with a rim to catch any juices.
• Do not let juices from raw meat drip on any other foods.

• Never prepare raw and cooked meat on the same chopping board, unless it is thoroughly washed and dried in between. This cuts down on bacterial cross-contamination.
• Always wash your hands and utensils thoroughly after handling raw meat.
• All frozen meats are best thawed slowly and thoroughly before cooking. Unwrap, put on a plate with a rim or in a shallow container, cover loosely with foil or a plastic bag and always thaw in the refrigerator slowly to cut down on moisture loss.

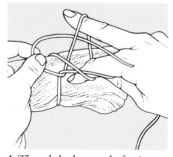

4 *Thread the long end of string through the loop made by the 'open scissors'. Remove these fingers from the loop carefully and draw the knot slightly closer, pulling the left hand end up tightly to close the loop and pull the string closer around the roast.*

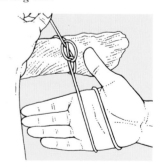

5 *Wrap the end of the string in the right hand around your palm, then yank the knot tight pulling the right hand toward you and down. This locks the knot. Finish with a right over left, left over right knot and cut off excess string with a pair of scissors or a sharp knife.*

STUFFED BONED VEAL BREAST

BEEF ROLLS

A boned and stuffed breast of veal makes a delicious and economical mid-week roast.

The stuffing flavor variations are endless, using fresh bread crumbs or rice, herbs, spices, chopped dried fruit, nuts and lemon. For a 2½lb (1.2kg) piece of meat before boning you will need about 8oz (250g) stuffing. Bind the stuffing with an egg if necessary.

Trim the roast well and remove the thick skin first. Lay skinned side down on a chopping board.

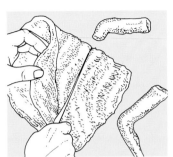

1 *Pull back the half flap of meat which covers the bones. Cut out the L-shaped rib bones singly, cutting back the meat flap until all bones are removed. Do not cut through to the other side. Open up the meat and press flat.*

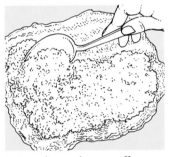

2 *Spread your chosen stuffing on the boned side of the breast. Be careful not to add too much stuffing or the roast will be difficult to roll up neatly.*

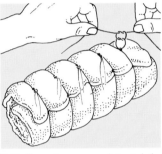

3 *Roll up the roast and tie tightly with 4–6 butchers' knots (opposite). Weigh and roast cut side down according to the chart on page 157.*

For this popular dish the meat must be cut into slices like thin steaks so it can be rolled up around a stuffing. To serve 6 you will need 1¾–2lb (875g–1kg) stewing beef, such as top round, sliced into 12 large, thin slices, tomato puree to taste, a handful finely chopped fresh sage leaves, 3 chopped cloves garlic, 2oz (50g) can anchovies, drained and sliced, black pepper, 6 tablespoons dry red wine, 1 rounded tablespoon cornstarch, salt and ⅔ cup (150ml) sour cream.

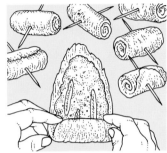

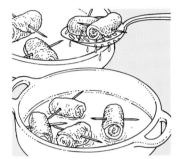

1 *Lay the beef slices between 2 sheets of wet parchment paper and pound the slices with a rolling pin or meat mallet until very thin. Rub each slice generously with tomato puree, then pat on some chopped sage leaves, garlic and anchovies. Season well with black pepper. Roll up and secure each slice with a wooden toothpick. Lay in a Dutch oven, add the wine and enough water to almost cover the beef.*

2 *Bring to a boil, then cover and cook in a preheated oven, 300°F, 150°C for 1¾–2½ hours until tender. Remove beef rolls with a slotted spoon and keep warm in a low oven. Pour the cooking juices into a saucepan. Mix the cornstarch with a little water until smooth, then stir into the juices. Bring to a boil for 3 minutes, stirring constantly until thickened. Season, pour the sauce over the beef and top with sour cream.*

BEEF CUTS

Allow 8–12oz (250–375g) meat on the bone and 4–6oz (125–175g) meat off the bone per person.

Cooking method	Cuts
Roast	Standing rib roast, rolled rib roast, rib eye, sirloin, tenderloin or filet, sirloin tip, standing rump, rolled rump, top round, eye round
Stew/Pot roast	Chuck, blade, arm, rolled shoulder, bottom round, heel of round skirt, brisket, flank
Grill/Fry/Broil	Steaks (T-bone, filet, sirloin, tri-tip, minute, porterhouse), hamburger

VEAL CUTS

Allow 250g (8oz) on the bone and 175g (6oz) off the bone per person.

Cooking method	Cuts
Roast	Rib roast, crown roast, loin, sirloin, tenderloin, round, rump, blade
Stew	Flank, neck, shin, rib, breast, middle neck cutlets, shoulder
Grill/Fry/Broil	Rib chop, loin chop, sirloin, medallions, scallops (not grill)

These gently stewed beef rolls are filled with a piquant anchovy and garlic mixture and topped with sour cream.

LAMB

Lamb is my favorite meat. Living in the Middle East as a young child, it was the only meat I knew, and I still love cooking it with coriander, cumin, yogurt, mint and even dried fruit – all accompaniments to lamb which I became used to at the time.

Lamb is sold when it is under one year old; pale pink flesh indicates young lamb, and the flesh darkens to light red as its age increases. As a general rule, the younger the lamb, the more tender it is. The best lamb easily available is usually spring lamb of under six months old; preferably its flesh should still be pale and its fat creamy white, never yellow. A blue tinge in the rib bones also indicates a young animal. Flavor, however, develops with age; mutton (sheep over two years old) can have a wonderful gamey flavor, but needs slow cooking to make it tender. It is difficult to obtain nowadays but if you ever come across any mutton, try it. To me, young lamb is most delicious when it is cooked slightly rare, pink rather than actually bloody. I think an expensive leg of lamb is wasted if it is overcooked but a larger shoulder can have great appeal when it is spiced, garlicked and roasted very gently. Shoulders have, in fact, a sweeter flesh than the leg. If you can't face the more difficult task of carving a shoulder you can have it boned and rolled. Boning takes away a little of the flavor but you can make up for this by stuffing the roast.

The most impressive roast of lamb for entertaining is the crown roast – literally a beautiful spiked crown of succulent cutlets which should always be roasted slightly rare, and the center filled with an interesting stuffing of vegetables, nuts, herbs and so on. The cheapest cuts can be made into a wide variety of stews and casseroles with all sorts of seasonings and other ingredients, including fruit.

PREPARING LAMB SHOULDER

Shoulder is one of the most economical cuts of lamb on the market. It is less tender than most other lamb cuts, although, since lamb is technically only a year old at most, the shoulder area is not as well developed as is beef shoulder and so is not as tough as it would be when mature. The most common lamb shoulder cuts in the meat counter are the blade or shoulder chop and the arm or round bone chop. In areas where lamb sales are high enough to have more variety, bone-in shoulder roasts, boned, rolled shoulder roasts, presliced shoulder roasts, and lamb neck slices are also available.

If lamb shoulder cuts, particularly the blade and arm chops, are marinated and cooked quickly, they can be grilleld, broiled, fried or roasted. However, all shoulder cuts do well when braised. Long, slow cooking in a liquid of some sort will tenderize and develop the flavor of the meat. This Lamb and Vegetable Stew (right) will serve 4-6 people.

Stuffed Shoulder of Lamb wrapped in Puff Pastry (page 168) with its spinach stuffing makes the most of a fully boned roast.

LAMB AND VEGETABLE STEW

1 tablespoon extra virgin olive oil
1oz (25g) butter
2lb (1kg) boned lamb shoulder, cut into large chunks or lamb stew cubes
2 large red onions, coarsely chopped
2 large cloves garlic, coarsely chopped
14½ oz (411g) can chopped tomatoes
1 cup (250ml) white wine
1½ teaspoons fresh or ½ teaspoon dried thyme leaves
1½ teaspoons fresh or ½ teaspoon dried marjoram leaves
1½ teaspoon fresh or ½ teaspoon dried rosemary leaves
Salt
Black pepper
½ cup (125ml) water
¼ cup (32g) all-purpose flour
1lb (500g) baby carrots, peeled
1lb (500g) small new potatoes, scrubbed or peeled and halved
½ lb (250g) small turnips, peeled and quartered
½ lb (250g) green beans, trimmed and halved
Good handful chopped fresh parsley

Heat the butter and oil in a large Dutch oven over a fairly high heat. Add the lamb and cook, turning occasionally, until well browned on all sides. Remove the meat to a bowl as it is browned, and set aside.

Add the chopped onions and garlic to the Dutch oven. Cook, stirring constantly, until softened and slightly browned, then add the tomatoes, wine, thyme, marjoram, rosemary, and salt and pepper to taste. Return the meat to the Dutch oven along with any juices. Bring to a boil over high heat. Cover and cook in the oven at 350°F, 180°C for 45 to 50 minutes or until almost tender.

Combine the water and flour and whisk into the liquid of the stew. Bring to a boil stirring constantly until thickened; add the carrots, potatoes, turnips and green beans. Return to the oven and cook for 15 or 20 minutes or until the meat and vegetables are just tender.

Sprinkle with parsley and serve straight from the Dutch oven.   *SERVES 4-6*

PREPARING A RACK OF LAMB

This cut is popular with cooks because it is sweet, tender and easy to carve between the chops. It is also very versatile to present, from impressive-looking crown roasts and European-style guards of honor to simple plain roasted racks.

Rack of lamb comes from the rib which is between the loin and the shoulder, with tender pieces of meat attached to elegant rib bones. The ribs are often left attached but scraped clean down to the succulent eye of meat to give the finished dish a more elegant presentation. Each rack of lamb contains six or seven ribs.

The backbone needs to be sawed where the vertebrae meet the ribs. For traditional roasting, leave the bone attached and carve the meat from it for serving. For crown roasts, guards of honor and racks of lamb it is removed before roasting.

For a crown roast, if the fat layer is thick, trim it slightly before curving inside. Both guards of honor and crown roasts can be roasted with a stuffing – put it between the racks for a guard of honor and in the center for a crown roast.

You can also roast a crown roast hollow and then fill the center afterwards with a pretty medley of crisp buttery vegetables or a spicy pilaf (page 109).

You can let your imagination go when making a guard of honor by varying the stuffing each time. Here, red peppers, celery and onions have been softened in butter with turmeric and then mixed with bread crumbs and a lightly beaten egg.

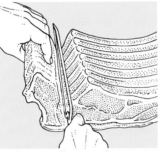

1 *Use a small saw or cleaver to cut just through the bone, leaving the meat underneath uncut, and just loosening but not cutting off the bone. For guards of honor and crown roasts remove completely. Cut off the skin, leaving the fat.*

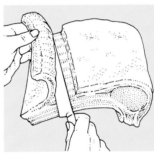

2 *For attractive presentation cut the fat and flesh off the end of the rib bones, leaving about 3in (7cm) of bones.*

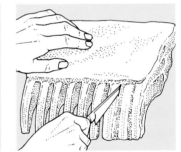

3 *Use a small sharp knife to scrape the rib bones clean, cutting and scraping between each one. Scrape as clean as possible.*

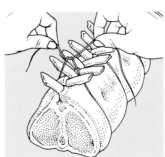

For a guard of honor*, choose 2 matching racks. Remove the bottom bone and prepare as in steps 1–3. Stand the racks upright and interlink, then tie. Score the fat in a criss-cross and stuff if you like. Roast according to the chart on page 159.*

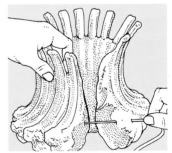

For a crown roast*, choose 2 matching racks. Remove the bottom bones and prepare as in steps 1–3. Curve around with the bones facing outwards and place end to end. Stitch together with kitchen string. Roast according to the chart on page 159.*

LAMB CUTS

Allow 8–12oz (250–375g) meat on the bone and 6–8oz (175–250g) meat off the bone per person.

Cooking method	Cuts
Roast	Leg , rolled shoulder, loin, saddle, rack, rolled breast, guard of honor, crown roast, rib
Stew	Shank, spareribs, rolled breast, shoulder chops, arm chops, neck
Grill/Fry/Broil	Shoulder chops, arm chops, cutlets, loin chops, rib chops

PORK, HAM *and* BACON

More food products are derived from the pig than from any other animal; they include pork, ham, bacon and an endless variety of fresh and cured sausages, and smoked or cured pieces of meat and fat. Almost every bit of the pig is edible, and it is the only animal whose skin we eat.

Pigs have been bred leaner and leaner over the years, and, although the meat is generally quite tender, it is very important to cook it in a way that doesn't lose moisture, such as in stews, casseroles, pies or pot roasts. When you roast or grill it you should cook it gently and rather slowly, basting often – slightly sweet liquids such as cider are good for basting, and beer is also excellent.

Real ham is the salted and aged back leg of the pig; cured and pressed shoulder is known as smoked pork shoulder or smoked pork butt and is often used as ham.

Only a country or aged ham keeps for long periods and some are eaten raw, such as the delicious Italian Parma or Spanish Serrano hams.

The smell of sizzling bacon is one of the most mouth-watering smells of all cooking. Bacon comes from the sides of the pig which have been soaked in brine and then may be smoked. My favorite bacon is the reduced-salt variety which is sweeter and milder because it is cured with less salt.

Sausages are another of my favorites – best of all I love spicy, meaty ones, and whenever I travel I search for the best local sausage. Pork is at its most succulent when it is used in a sausage, and a simple meal of good sausages, carefully cooked cabbage and buttery mashed potatoes never seems ordinary to me.

BONING AND ROLLING A LOIN OF PORK

Loin is an excellent special-occasion roast, either boned or whole. It is often difficult to roast the sides and bottom of a rolled pork roast successfully so that the rind becomes crisp, therefore it is usually removed before cooking. The advantage of a boned roast is that it is so much easier to carve, making it ideal for a tableful of hungry guests.

For a thicker rolled roast, buy a loin with rib bones still attached so you have a long belly flap after boning to roll round the loin and stuffing.

To stuff a 2lb (1kg) roast after boning you will need about 8oz (250g) stuffing, or spread with 4oz (125g) of a savory butter such as herb and garlic.

FRESH PORK CUTS

Allow 12oz (375g) meat on the bone and 6oz (175g) meat off the bone per person.

Cooking method	Cuts
Roast	Center loin, crown roast, sirloin roast, tenderloin, back ribs, spareribs, fresh ham
Stew/Braise	Shoulder, blade, spareribs, arm steak, fresh hock, fresh picnic
Grill/Fry/Broil	Spareribs, tenderloin, medallions, rib chops, blade chops, sirloin chops, fresh ham steak

CURED AND SMOKED PORK CUTS

Allow 12oz (375g) meat on the bone and 6oz (175g) meat off the bone per person.

Cooking method	Cuts
Boil	Smoked picnic, hock, butt
Bake	Ham (whole, half, bone-in, semi boneless, boneless, fully-cooked, uncooked, presliced, canned)
Grill/Fry/Broil	Ham steak; bacon

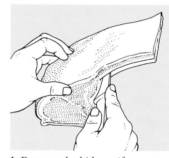
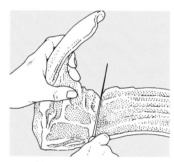

1 *Remove the kidney, if present, if you want, or leave it to be cooked with the roast. Remove the rind if you do not want it. Place the roast rib side up. Insert a boning knife between the meat and the bones at the tip of the rib bones.*

2 *Holding firmly with your free hand, cut downwards against the rib bones until you reach the bone on the bottom, releasing the meat as you go. Scrape as much meat away from the bones as possible, holding the knife very close to the bones.*

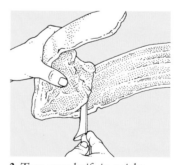

3 *Turn your knife in a right angle to the left and cut off the bottom bone. The bottom bone and rib bones will come away in one piece. It is not worth scraping meat from between the rib bones. Discard all the bones or save to make stock (page 28).*

4 *Flatten out the belly flap where the ribs were and spread with a stuffing or flavored butter and roll up. Tie at regular intervals (page 144). Score the fat and insert garlic slivers or herbs, if you like. Weigh and roast according to the chart on page 159.*

PREPARING BACON

Bacon is the name for the side of pork that has been cured and smoked. It is usually at least half fat because that is what gives it flavor. In addition to the regular sliced bacon, it is available thin sliced and thick sliced. Slab bacon still has the rind and has not been sliced. Specialty bacons that are available include Country-style which is usually saltier and smokier, Irish bacon which is a wider, meatier slice, Canadian bacon which is really a cured smoked loin, and Pancetta, an Italian-style spiced bacon which is often cooked and aded to salads.

This country-style Boneless Smoked Pork Loin with Spiced Garlic Potatoes (page 169) uses a flavorful and easy-to-cook cut of pork to make a filling dish for colder weather.

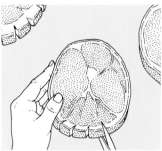 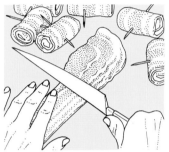

Because of the shape of boneless ham steaks and Canadian bacon, they curl up when cooked. To prevent this, snip or cut the rind at 1in (2.5cm) intervals before cooking. Smoked pork chops may need snipping, too, if they have the rind still attached. Extra large ham steaks can be cut into half-moon shapes for cooking.

To make Irish bacon rolls or to stretch Irish bacon for lining terrines (page 98), remove any rind from the strips, then lay flat on a board. Run the back of a knife along the strip holding one end firm. This stretches it and makes rolling up neater. Use a wooden toothpick to fasten each bacon roll before cooking.

TENDERLOIN

Turn a piece of lean pork tenderloin into a quick rolled roast by slicing lengthwise and pounding until thin. Spread with a stuffing of chopped herbs, nuts, spinach and herbs or simply a spicy, garlic paste, then roll up, tie, weigh and roast, according to the chart on page 159, basting well with oil or butter. For a 10–12oz (300–375g) tenderloin you will need about 4 tablespoons stuffing or 2 tablespoons garlic paste.

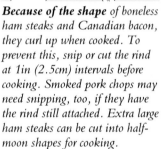 

1 Place the piece of tenderloin on a sheet of wet parchment paper. Slit down the center from one end to the other without cutting all the way through the meat. Open out and place another sheet of wet parchment paper on top.

2 Using a rolling pin or meat mallet, pound and flatten the meat. Uncover, spread the roast with stuffing or garlic paste and roll up. Tie at regular intervals, then weigh and roast according to the chart on page 159.

SAUSAGES

Type	Ingredients	Cooking method
Andouille (Cajun)	Chitterlings and tripe, spices (smoked)	Fry, add to gumbo
Beef	Beef, beef fat, salt, seasoning	Fry, grill
Frankfurter (hot dog)	Pork, beef or poultry, salt, seasoning, filler (precooked)	Boil, fry, grill, broil
Gourmet	Poultry or game with cheese, dried vegetables, mushrooms, or fruit, salt and seasonings	Fry, grill, broil, braise
Haggis (Scottish)	Sheep variety meats, oatmeal, parsley, onions, salt, seasonings	Boil, fry, bake
Hot Italian	Pork, pork fat, salt, fennel seeds, crushed red pepper	Fry, grill, braise
Kielbasa (Polish)	Pork, beef or poultry, salt, fat, garlic, seasonings	Fry, grill, broil, braise
Pepperoni	Pork or beef, garlic, salt, seasonings (cured and dried)	Slice; add to sauce or pizza
Pork	Pork, pork fat, sage, salt, pepper	Boil, then fry or grill
Pork and beef	Pork, beef, fat, sage, salt, pepper	Boil, then fry or grill
Poultry	Chicken or turkey, poultry fat, salt, seasonings	Boil, then fry or grill
Smoked	Pork, and/or beef, fat, sage, salt, pepper (smoked)	Boil then fry or grill
Sweet Italian	Pork, pork fat, salt, fennel seeds	Fry, grill, braise
Vienna	Pork, beef, or poultry, salt, seasoning, filler (precooked)	Boil, fry, grill

VARIETY MEATS

Variety meats, the organ meats of beef, pork, veal and lamb, are much appreciated in other parts of the world, but tend to be overlooked here in favor of the carcass meats of the same animals. Variety meats are high in vitamins and minerals, low in fat, and, with the exception of liver and sweetbreads, economically priced. Don't be put off by their anatomical sounding names - brains, chitterlings or chitlins (small intestines), heart, kidneys, liver, sweetbreads (thymus gland), tongue and tripe (stomach lining) - they offer a great selection of flavors and textures to experience in a wide range of dishes. Except for liver and kidneys, most are mild in taste and profit from the addition of a flavorful sauce. Lemon or cream sauces are good with brains or sweetbreads, wine or tomato sauces enhance chitterlings, heart, tongue and tripe, and just add sautéed onions to liver and kidneys.

PREPARING VARIETY MEATS

Organ meats are somewhat slippery so one of the most important pieces of equipment is a good sharp knife to remove any exterior fat. Brains and sweetbreads are the most fragile and should be soaked in lemon water (and, many people say, poached) before a quick sautéing. Liver and kidneys simply need tubes and vessels removed before cooking, while chitterlings, heart, tongue, and tripe require longer cooking to make them tender.

KIDNEYS

When you buy kidneys they should have just a mild smell and no discolored patches. They are sometimes sold with a layer of hard fat, called suet, around them that acts as a protective cushion while the animal is alive. It can be easily peeled off with your fingers. Either discard the fat or grate it to mix with seeds as a treat for the wild birds.

Lamb kidneys are fairly small while veal and pork kidneys are large.

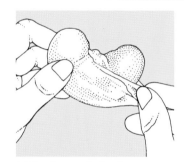

1 *Use the tip of a knife to cut any fine membrane surrounding the kidney, being careful not to cut the flesh. Then peel off and discard the membrane.*

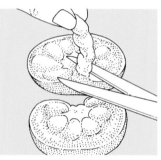

2 *Cut the kidney in half lengthwise through the core, then snip out the tubes and discard. Or, keep the kidney whole and cut crosswise in slices.*

USING VARIETY MEATS

• One of my favorite quick supper dishes is a sauté of kidneys with a slightly spicy sauce — with the addition of a little liquid kidneys make an instant, rich sauce of their own. I often add a little wine or brandy with ground spices (cinnamon is good) or some cream or sour cream and fresh herbs.

• Once prepared for cooking (see right), sweetbreads may be split and sautéed in butter until golden on each side. Remove them to a platter; in the same skillet, sauté mushrooms in more butter, then add white wine and thicken it to make a sauce to top the sweetbreads

• Soak sliced pork or beef liver and kidneys in milk and then cook in the oven at a gentle heat with tomatoes, garlic and a little sherry for at least 2 hours until tender.

• Make quick sauces for grilled or fried lamb or calf's liver by adding dry sherry, marsala, orange juice or Worcestershire sauce to the pan just as the liver finishes cooking. Remove the liver and let the liquid boil, then pour over the liver.

• Another sauce to try with liver is made by stewing a few fresh cranberries or apricots with sugar to taste and a little sherry vinegar.

Kidneys complement the flavor of ground beef in Steak and Kidney Meatballs with Fresh Tomato Sauce (page 168), served here with fresh noodles and broccoli.

LIVER

The best liver is calf's liver, sweet and meltingly tender. Lamb liver is also sweet but firmer when cooked.

Liver is generally sold ready to cook. If not, run your fingers over the surface to check for any tubes and remove. When buying lamb and calf's liver I look for the palest color as experience has taught me it is milder and more tender. As well as being pan fried, calf's and lamb livers are excellent stir-fried.

Pork liver is ideal for braising gently or for use in pâtés and terrines. Beef liver is best for long, slow cooking. Both pork and beef livers have strong flavors which can be mellowed by presoaking in milk for about 30 minutes.

Calf's and lamb liver are best sliced very thinly for quick sautéing or stir-frying. If the liver is sold as one piece, use a sharp knife and cut thin slices across the grain at a slight diagonal, firmly holding the piece of liver steady with one hand while cutting. As you will be cooking the liver so briefly, it is important to cut the liver into even-sized slices so no part of it remains raw or becomes overcooked.

Grilled calf's liver is served here with a delicious sauce made from the pan juices and a little sherry, fresh orange juice and parsley.

SWEETBREADS

Sweetbreads are the thymus glands from near the throat and heart of a calf. Sold as a pair, they have a delicate flavor and creamy soft texture that is a rich reward in itself. After preparing the sweetbreads (below) they can be either shallow fried in butter and oil, or coated with beaten egg and breadcrumbs and deep fried. You can also braise them in stock with chopped onion, carrot and celery, sherry and fresh herbs. Cook at 400°F, 200°C for about 45 minutes until tender.

For a delicious sweetbread curry, fry sweetbreads and sliced onions with butter and Indian spices over a low heat, stirring frequently until both are very soft. Then add some heavy cream and fresh cilantro leaves and boil for a minute.

1 *Sweetbreads are easier to peel if soaked and blanched first. Soak sweetbreads in cold salted water for 30 minutes to 4 hours to remove any blood, changing the water whenever it becomes pink. Place in a saucepan of fresh cold water, bring to a boil and simmer for 2 minutes.*

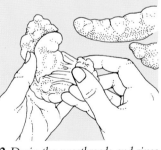

2 *Drain the sweetbreads and rinse well. Use your fingers to peel off the thin membrane and any small amount of fat and the tubes. If you want sweetbreads with a firmer texture, place a weight on top of the sweetbreads for 30 minutes, then cut thinly or chop before cooking.*

HEART

The heart is a muscle that works hard all the animal's lifetime so will be quite tough. Therefore, before cooking, all tubes and vessels need to be removed. Because heart is so lean, it needs a sauce to keep it moist during cooking.

Small lamb hearts are the best and most tender but still need long gentle cooking. Chopped root vegetables are good in stuffing for a lamb heart, together with fresh breadcrumbs and a little chopped spinach. A lamb heart stuffed with sage and onions is also very good. Veal heart is also very tender. As well as being good roasted, it is also good braised or stewed. Beef hearts are good cut up and slowly stewed with rich ingredients such as red wine, garlic and onions, with a parsnip puree to thicken the sauce. They are also delicious stuffed and braised with vegetables and stock.

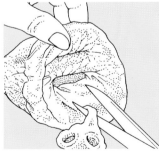

1 *Using scissors, carefully snip out all tubes and vessels. Rinse the heart well inside and out and pat dry with paper towels. Soak in lightly salted water for up to 1 hour before cooking, then drain very well.*

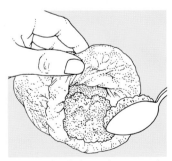

2 *To cook whole, make up a rich, moist and tasty stuffing (above). Spoon it into the heart taking care not to pack too much in and stitch with kitchen string. Brown well on all sides in hot fat before braising slowly.*

GROUND MEAT

The most important thing to realize about ground meat is that it does not have to become grey, granular and tasteless from overcooking; on the contrary, it is extraordinarily versatile, and when cooked properly ground beef can be both as safe and as succulent as the best steak. Ground meats, in fact, can be said to be one of the most useful ingredients for creative cookery. It is possible to buy very lean ground meat but a small proportion of fat adds flavor and tenderness. Adding extra flavor to ground meat is crucial and must not be forgotten – spices, herbs and many other additions make all the difference in the final cooked ground meat dishes.

Ground meat can be served in many ways from the simple hamburger to the sophisticated country pâté. The Greek moussaka is a layered casserole made from ground lamb with tender eggplant and a cheese custard on top. I love meatballs and make them in many different ways, not only from ground beef but also using pork, lamb and veal, with different seasonings and flavorings to suit the character of the meat and sometimes surprise stuffings too.

I use ground meat mixtures to stuff vegetables, pancakes and boned roasts, fill little pies and to make sauces for spaghetti, including Bolognese sauce or ragù (page 213). I also love making meat loaves, sometimes striped with two varieties of ground meat. The possibilities are endless and most of them don't take much time.

GRINDING MEAT

Grinding meat yourself is well worth the effort for inexpensive special occasion dishes, for memorable homemade burgers or if you want to use a different meat such as pork or lamb that is not available commercially ground. You also know exactly what meat has been used and can choose lovely, lean juicy cuts. For best results only grind meat just before cooking, because once ground it deteriorates rapidly.

Grinding can be done in a home grinder (hand or electric as an attachment to a mixer), in a food processor or by chopping finely using two very sharp, large, heavy knives. Each method gives a different texture. When done in a grinder, ground meat is ground and slightly twisted, processor ground meat is more pulverized and some say more tender, while chopped ground meat is firmer.

After grinding, season and add additional flavours such as fresh herbs, garlic or onion. If you don't have time to grind the beef for the Tacos (right), use commercial ground beef.

BEEF TACOS

1lb (500g) beef chuck, cut into
   chunks or preground
4 green onions, finely chopped
4 cloves garlic, finely chopped
2 teaspoons chili powder
1 teaspoon ground cumin
8 corn tortillas
1 cup salsa (page 206)
1 small avocado chopped
¼ cup (50g) chopped cilantro
1 tablespoon lemon juice
Salt
1 tablespoon peanut oil
8oz (250g) can tomatoes
1 tablespoon cornmeal
1½ cups shredded lettuce
8 tablespoons sour cream

Grind or chop the meat, along with the onions, garlic, chili powder, and cumin.

Wrap the tortillas in foil and keep warm in a low oven. Prepare the salsa. Combine the avocado, cilantro, lemon juice and a pinch salt.

Heat the oil in a large frying pan. Sauté the meat mixture until browned. Add tomatoes, cornmeal and a pinch salt; cook, stirring, until thickened.

Fill the tortillas with the beef mixture, top each with salsa, avocado, shredded lettuce and sour cream.   *SERVES 4*

MAKING THE MOST OF GROUND MEAT

• Try cumin, coriander, cardamom, cinnamon, paprika, allspice, nutmeg and caraway seeds to flavor ground meat.
• Fresh chopped herbs in ground meat both taste and look good, as does finely chopped red pepper.
• Tomato puree or sun-dried tomato paste adds a lot of flavor to all ground meats, and spoonfuls of mild curry pastes, pickles or even pesto sauce (page 207) can be very effective.
• Chopped raw nuts and grated Parmesan cheese are delicious with lots of garlic in a ground pork mixture.
• A meat loaf can be delicious; I like to use a combination of pork and veal flavored with plenty of garlic, tomato puree, chopped capers, chopped fresh rosemary and some grated cheese.
• The taste of shepherd's pie can also be varied by adding spices and herbs and the mashed potato top substituted with other root vegetables; golden sweet potato is delicious and so is celeriac or parsnip. All these vegetable toppings can be sprinkled with grated cheese.
• Fill meatballs with surprise fillings which can include a cube of cheese. This melts within as the meatball cooks. Whole nuts, dried fruits, whole dill seeds, lots of chopped fresh dill and wholegrain mustard are good inside pork meatballs.

Never dismiss hamburgers as mere junk food. When homemade with fresh accompaniments, such as blue cheese, capers and tomatoes, crispy lettuce and green peppers, burgers become a delicious meal especially if you have ground the meat yourself.

MAKING MEATBALLS

Meatballs are one of the easiest things to make with ground meat, and, not surprisingly, they are popular around the world. In the Middle East, koftas are highly spiced meatballs shaped around skewers, and in India meatballs are often the only tender meat available. Although the spicy, exotic meatballs are usually made with lamb or mutton, you can also use beef and pork, or a combination. The meat should be top quality and, if possible, more finely ground than for hamburgers. Meatballs can be round, oval-shaped or slightly flattened, but never very big.

For about 8–14 meatballs, use 1¼–1½lb (625–750g) finely ground lamb, 2 teaspoons ground cumin, 3 teaspoons ground coriander, 2 peeled and finely chopped cloves garlic, 1 handful finely chopped fresh mint and salt and black pepper. Serve with plain yogurt mixed with chopped cucumber and mint.

1 Put the finely ground lamb into a bowl, add the ground spices, the chopped garlic and chopped mint leaves and season generously with salt and freshly ground black pepper. Mix together thoroughly either with your hands or with a wooden spoon until all the ingredients are well combined.

2 Using wet hands, take about 2 tablespoons of the mixture and shape around skewers for koftas or form into walnut-size meatballs. Either grill (brushing with oil first) or fry in a little oil in a pan, over a medium heat for 8–12 minutes, turning the meatballs often until browned.

An ideal dish for an informal meal is small cumin-flavored lamb meatballs as in Aromatic Meatballs with Spinach and Mushrooms (page 170). Just before serving, the meatballs are topped with sour cream and dusted with paprika.

THE BEST HAMBURGERS

All hamburgers are extremely simple; they should taste of unadulterated meat so must not be bound with egg or coated with flour. Unlike meatball mixtures which can benefit from the addition of spices and chopped vegetables, hamburgers should be seasoned only with black pepper and sea salt, and possibly a little finely chopped onion and capers. I add some fresh green peppercorns and a little ground coriander seed, or a spoonful of tomato puree if I am not sure of the beef's quality. Ideally it should be top quality and fairly lean, and it must be coarsely ground.

Hamburger condiments and accompaniments which are added after cooking between meat and bun, or simply as a topping instead of a bun, provide scope for experiment. Classic combinations include: tomato slices and lettuce, pickles and sauces of various kinds, cheese which melts onto the hot meat, crisp strips of broiled bacon, avocado slices, and mayonnaise.

If you have a charcoal grill, hamburgers become especially delicious, but in any case the grill or skillet should always be at its hottest so that the meat becomes black in patches on the outside and remains succulent inside – there is nothing good about a dry, gray hamburger.

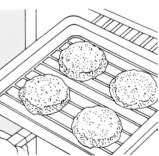

1 To make 4 burgers, put 1½lb (750g) coarsely ground lean beef into a bowl and mix in coarsely ground black pepper, a little sea salt and finely chopped onion and/or capers, if desired. Using wet hands form the meat into 4 balls, then flatten each slightly to form hamburgers about 1in (2.5cm) thick. If time, refrigerate them for 30 minutes.

2 Rub the hamburgers with a little oil. Place on a pan and broil under the highest heat or on a charcoal grill for about 5 minutes each side. For safety, burgers should be cooked until no longer pink inside (160°F, 71°C). Lightly toast the buns, then put the cooked hamburger between the bun halves with any additions or relishes.

GAME

Even if you don't have access to wild game, venison and rabbit are now readily available and make a special and often impressive meal. Because rabbit is bred domestically and most venison is farmed they are beautifully tender, even if they lack the intensity of flavor of the wild animals. Venison is also the leanest of all red meats, which is a healthy bonus.

All game should have been hung for a certain amount of time to develop its flavor and tenderness; after a few days hanging, enzymes in the flesh cause a chemical change which tenderizes the meat while strengthening the taste. Very young venison needs hanging most of all as it has the least flavor but older animals with more flavor can be very tough; they should be marinated for at least 24 hours and it is not unusual to marinate large roasts for up to four days. The best venison comes from animals aged between 18 and 24 months. When roasting, grilling or frying the meat should never be cooked too long as it is so lean and will become dull and dry – ideally it should be cooked fairly swiftly so it remains pink and juicy inside.

Domestic rabbit is not hung and is very mild in flavor, but has a lovely smooth-textured tenderness. It can be cooked exactly like chicken, using the same recipes, but it should be marinated first for added flavor, or it can be used as a vehicle for absorbing the character of strong ingredients which are cooked with it. As it is so lean it needs to be cooked with other moist ingredients.

All the cooking methods and seasonings you would use for a venison roast will be delicious with elk, moose, caribou or antelope, however the cooking time will be dependent upon age. Although not much bear is available, it is delicious in the ways that you would cook pork.

PREPARING GAME

Venison is the game most likely to be roasted. Most venison now is farmed and when cooked becomes deliciously tender, but that also means it lacks a strong gamy flavor which may disappoint some people. I, in fact, prefer it milder. The choicest cuts are leg, loin and saddle, and they are best served slightly pink and juicy. Because venison is so lean, it is advisable to bard roasts (page 156) and baste frequently during roasting, or rub with vegetable oil before roasting. the fuller flavor of venison means it takes beautifully to exciting marinades which also help to keep the meat moist and tender during roasting. The directions at right for roasting venison could be used with other large game as well.

After nearing extinction, buffalo are once again a part of the American heritage and food supply. Today, because of the success of breeding and farming programs, there is enough farm-raised buffalo to find its way to the retail as well as the food service market. No longer just a curiosity, buffalo steaks, burgers, roasts and even hot dogs are enjoyed because of their beef-like flavor and the fact that they are very lean. Although thought of as game, buffalo can really be used in any recipe that would be good with beef. However, because it is low in fat, those cuts that are going to be grilled, fried or broiled will be especially good if you take the time to marinate them before cooking. The following recipe for Buffalo Chili could also be made with other ground meats. It will serve 4 people.

Heat 1 tablespoon peanut oil in a large frying pan. Add 1lb (500g) ground buffalo. 1 large coarsely chopped onion, 1 large, coarsely chopped green pepper, 1 large, coarsely chopped red pepper, 6 finely chopped cloves garlic and 1 finely chopped jalapeño pepper, if desired. Sauté the ground buffalo and vegetable mixture, stirring occasionally, until lightly browned. Add a 14½oz (411g) can chunky tomatoes, a 15½oz (440g) can drained red kidney beans, 1-2 tablespoons chili powder, 1 tablespoon ground cumin, 1 tablespoon paprika, and salt to taste. Bring to a boil over high heat; reduce the heat and cook gently, stirring occasionally, 15 to 20 minutes.

1 *Prepare the marinade in a large pitcher by mixing together 1¼ cups (300ml) wine vinegar, ⅔ cup (150ml) olive oil, 2–3 crushed garlic cloves, 2 tablespoons crushed juniper berries and fresh herb sprigs. This makes enough for a 3lb (1.5kg) roast.*

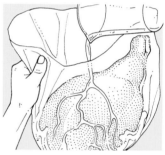

2 *Trim the venison roast, here a haunch, of any fat, membranes or gristle. Place the roast in a large plastic roasting or food storage bag. Pour in the marinade, then securely close the bag with a tie or tie in a knot if the bag is long enough.*

3 *Rub the roast all over in the bag, so it is well covered with the marinade. Place on a large platter and refrigerate for 2 days, turning every 8 hours or so. This allows the marinade flavors to permeate the meat.*

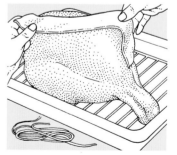

4 *To prepare for roasting, remove the roast from the marinade and weigh it. Place it on a rack in a roasting pan. Bard the roast (page 156) or rub it with vegetable oil and roast it according to the chart (opposite).*

VENISON CUTS

Allow 8oz (250g) meat on the bone and 6oz (175g) meat off the bone per person. Begin roasting in a preheated oven, 450°F, 230° C for 10 minutes, then at the temperature below:

Cooking method	Temperature	Time
Bone-in roasts		
Leg, saddle	350°F, 180°C	Rare: 12 minutes per 1lb (500g) plus 12 minutes if necessary Medium: 15 minutes per 1lb (500g) plus 15 minutes if necessary Well done: 20 minutes per 1lb (500g) plus 20 minutes if necessary
Boned rolled roasts		
Leg, shoulder	350°F, 180°C	Medium: 20 minutes per 1lb (500g) plus 20 minutes if necessary Well done: 25 minutes per 1lb (500g) plus 25 minutes if necessary
Stew		
Shoulder, boned and diced	350°F, 180°C	1½–2 hours
Broil/Grill/Fry		
Tenderloin chops or steaks	Medium heat	20–30 minutes

RABBIT CUTS

A cleaned and skinned rabbit weighing 3½lb (1.7kg) will serve 4 people; a 4½lb (2kg) wild rabbit will serve 6 people.

Cooking method	Temperature	Time
Roast		
Saddle	350°F, 180°C	35–40 minutes for up to 2lb (1kg) 40–50 minutes up to 4½lb (2kg)
Stew		
All parts including saddle	325°F, 160°C	1–1½ hours, depending on age

FLAVORING GAME

• Olive oil mixed with lemon juice, black pepper, garlic and a few herbs (but never salt which draws the juices out) is an easy and excellent marinade for game. A little sherry vinegar is also an effective addition.

• Marinades can be liquid or more like a thick paste of seasonings – this can be a generous mixture of spices and herbs moistened with a little lemon juice, red wine or fruit vinegar and oil, which is rubbed onto a roast and left for the flavors to be absorbed before roasting.

• Game roasts can be immersed for several hours or up to two days in liquid marinades containing not only oil, lemon juice and seasoning but wine as well and will become substantially tenderized and fuller flavored.

• More complicated liquid marinades can be made like a stock by cooking vegetables such as carrots, onions and celery with herbs and seasonings in an oil and wine mixture, then allowing it to cool before using.

• The strong taste of wild rabbit benefits from a rather sweet but garlicky marinade and then by stewing gently with both sweet and sharp ingredients – dried apricots, onions, yellow peppers and crushed juniper berries are a good combination, with ground cinnamon and a teaspoon of whole caraway seeds, and a little orange juice as the liquid.

• Rabbit is often cooked with mustard and cream – I stew rabbit pieces with whole shallots or pickling onions, whole grain mustard, green peppercorns and a glass of sweet cider. When the rabbit is cooked I add heavy cream and boil the sauce for a minute.

CUTTING UP RABBIT

Rabbits are best served cut into pieces, if only because they don't look too appetizing roasted whole, although they can be roasted with a stuffing in the cavity. The saddle or loin is the most tender cut and can be roasted, but the remainder is best cooked slowly as in a flavorful stew such as Rabbit and Pumpkin with Mustard (page 171), pictured below.

Cutting up a skinned and gutted rabbit by this method will give 7 pieces.

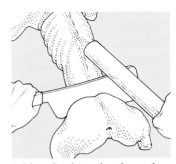

1 *Place the skinned and gutted rabbit belly side down. Using a rolling pin and meat cleaver cut crosswise to remove the hindlegs, and again to remove the forelegs, leaving the back whole.*

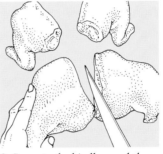

2 *Separate the hindlegs and the forelegs into 2 pieces each. On large rabbits the massive hindlegs can be cut into several more pieces.*

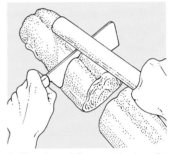

3 *Cut the saddle crosswise into 3 equal pieces depending on the size of the saddle, using a rolling pin to help push the meat cleaver through the bones.*

The classic combination of rabbit and mustard is enhanced with caraway in stewed Rabbit and Pumpkin with Mustard (page 171).

ROASTING BEEF *and* VEAL

Roasting is a wonderful cooking process for larger pieces of meat, producing a tempting smell as the roast sizzles in the oven. The most important thing to remember if you want to produce a perfect roast is that it needs care and attention. All too often a roast is treated as a convenience food: brought straight out of the refrigerator and put, unseasoned, into the oven for an allotted time during which it is forgotten – this will do nothing for the meat except to cook it.

Meat should always sit at room temperature for 30 to 45 minutes before roasting. Because both ovens and the meat itself are unpredictable you must never rely entirely on timing charts and suggested temperatures – you must check constantly during the cooking and adapt timing and heat, if necessary. I invariably like to start the meat off at a high temperature for 10 minutes and then lower the heat for the remainder of the cooking, somtimes lowering it even twice.

Basting the meat is also vital for succulence and to create a beautiful gloss. Vital, too, is allowing the roast to rest before carving. All roasts should be left in a warm place, or in the turned-off oven with the door open for 15–20 minutes after cooking – this will tenderize the meat and give it a better texture making it be easier to carve.

RIB ROAST

A beef roast, to my mind, should always be cooked so the flesh remains pale to dark pink within a glossy browned crust – those who insist on eating only grey meat can have the outside slices but they will miss out on the succulence. Flavor roasts off the bone with garlic cloves or herb sprigs inserted into small slices in the flesh. I don't usually add extra flavoring to prime cuts of beef, particularly when they are on the bone, except some olive oil and freshly ground black pepper and a bit of crushed sea salt for those who enjoy the fat (as I confess I do).

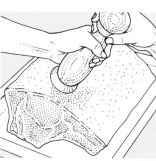

1 *About 30 to 45 minutes before roasting rub the skin side of the beef roast generously all over with olive oil or softened butter, then sprinkle with freshly ground black pepper to taste. Set the roast aside in the roasting pan, covered loosely in a cool place, until you are ready to put it in the oven to roast.*

2 *Weigh, calculate the cooking time and preheat the oven (see chart opposite). Keep in mind when calculating time that long, thin roasts tend to take less time than a compact roast, regardless of weight. Season the meat with herbs if desired and rub coarse sea salt into the fat. Place the pan in the oven.*

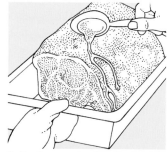

3 *During roasting baste occasionally with a large metal spoon, spooning the pan juices over the roast. Remove from the oven, transfer to a warm serving plate and keep warm for 15–20 minutes while you make the gravy. After 10 minutes pour any cooking juices from the serving plate into the gravy.*

BARDING LEAN ROASTS

Barding is the simple technique of covering a lean roast with thin sheets of pork fat or strips of bacon. (This is different from larding where strips of fat are actually threaded through the roast with a larding needle.) The fat bastes the meat as it roasts so it does not dry out. This technique can be used for venison and game birds as well as for beef and veal roasts. Pork fat is used because of its blander flavor and more pliable texture.

Season or flavor the roast *as desired, then wrap the fat over the top. Tie at intervals with kitchen string. Weigh the meat, roast and baste as normal. Discard the fat before serving.*

IDEAS FOR ROASTING BEEF AND VEAL

• The flavor and succulence of a good beef roast on the bone is so good that it needs little extra seasoning or complicated accompaniments. Leaner, boneless roasts such as round, can be enhanced by making deep slits in the meat with a knife, inserting well-crushed garlic and green peppercorns, capers or whole grain mustard and then pot-roasting (page 160). Whole grain mustard can be rubbed with olive oil onto any beef cut before roasting.

• Roast beef can be served with horseradish sauce (page 212), horseradish sauce stirred into whipped cream to give it a milder flavor, béarnaise sauce, or simply plain yogurt seasoned with finely chopped capers and black pepper.

• As an alternative to gravy for beef, heat heavy cream with the defatted pan juices, adding sea salt and crushed green peppercorns.

• Veal roasts are invariably boned and stuffings can play an important part. Fresh herbs such as marjoram, sage, thyme or rosemary added to bread crumbs with softened butter, sautéed mushrooms, onions, peppers, eggplant or even dried apricots go well with veal. Bind the stuffing ingredients with egg, or with cottage cheese.

• Veal roasts produce intensely flavored juices; add a little vermouth, sherry or cider to the pan and boil on top of the stove, stirring in all of the veal juices and drippings, then add heavy cream and boil again for a delicious sauce.

BEEF IN PASTRY

In the classic Beef Wellington the beef filet is surrounded by a mixture of chopped and sautéed onion and mushroom and a good liver pâté, but you can simplify this, as I often do by using only pâté with extra flavorings. You can make your own flaky pastry (page 250) or use ready-made puff pastry. Serve with béarnaise sauce (page 200) or horseradish and sour cream.

For a 2lb (1kg) filet of beef to serve 6–8 people you will need a mixture made from 2 teaspoons crushed green peppercorns, 1 tablespoon finely chopped fresh parsley and 6oz (175g) liver pâté.

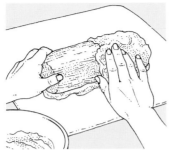

1 *On a lightly floured surface roll out both sheets from 17.3oz (490g) pastry to a rectangle large enough to enclose the beef. Spread one-third of the pâté mixture down the center of the pastry making sure it is as wide and as long as the filet. Place the beef on top, then cover the top and sides with the remaining mixture.*

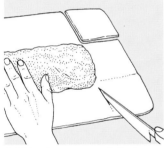

2 *Trim the corners and the long edges of the pastry so that the long edges meet on top of the filet and fold up to enclose. Moisten the edges with water and press to seal. Fold up the end pastry, moisten with water and seal to make a neat parcel. Cut out decorations from the pastry trimmings (page 245).*

3 *Place the roast cut side down on a baking sheet. Attach the decorations to the pastry with water, using a pastry brush. Pierce 2 holes for the steam to escape and chill for at least 30 minutes. Brush with beaten egg yolk. Cook at 425°F, 220°C for 45 minutes for rare; let stand for 10 minutes before carving.*

QUICK GRAVY

I never make a thickened gravy (page 199), which I know some people like. Instead, about 30 minutes before the end of cooking I add a glass of liquid to the roasting pan. While the roast is resting on its serving plate I boil the juices in the roasting pan, reducing or adding a little water or stock as necessary. To make an instant sauce, stir in heavy cream and boil until reduced.

Place the roasting pan on the stove and boil the juices, scraping the bottom. Add extra liquid or reduce and then season.

A tender, juicy filet of beef wrapped in an egg yolk-glazed crust of puff pastry is an impressive sight.

ROASTING CHART

Beef

All timings are guidelines only. Longer, thinner roasts may need less time, so it is best to check about three-quarters of the way through the calculated cooking time; it may not need the extra time. Internal temperature on a meat thermometer (page 159) should be: rare, 140°F, 60°C ; medium, 160°F, 70°C ; well done, 175°F, 80°C . Stuffed roasts need an extra 5–10 minutes per 1lb (500g). Begin roasting in a preheated oven, 450°F, 230°C for 10 minutes, then at the temperature below:

Cut	Temperature	Time per 500g (1lb)
Bone-in roast		
Standing-rib, sirloin,	350°F, 180°C	Rare: 10 minutes plus 10 minutes if necessary Medium: 12 minutes plus 12 minutes if necessary Well done: 20 minutes plus 20 minutes if necessary
Boneless or boned rolled roast		
Filet, rolled rib, top round, rib eye, sirloin tip	350°F, 180°C	Rare: 12 minutes plus 10 minutes if necessary Medium: 15 minutes plus 15 minutes if necessary Well done: 20 minutes plus 20 minutes if necessary

Veal

Internal temperature on a meat thermometer (page 159) should be: medium, 160°F, 70°C; well done,175°F, 80°C. Stuffed roasts need an extra 5–10 minutes per 1lb (500g). Begin roasting in a preheated oven, 450°F, 230°C for 10 minutes, then at the temperature below:

Cut	Temperature	Time per 1lb (500g)
Boned rolled roast		
Filet, loin, sirloin	350°F,180°C	Medium: 20 minutes plus 20 minutes if necessary Well done: 25 minutes plus 25 minutes if necessary

ROASTING LAMB *and* PORK

Lamb can be roasted in two equally delicious ways; either gently and long so it begins to fall apart and becomes meltingly tender but dark and crisp on the outside, or for a shorter time at a higher heat so the flesh is pale pink to a darker pink in the center and very juicy, as the French like it. The second method is best for a leg, saddle or crown roast, but a shoulder, which has the sweetest flavor, can be cooked either way. As it is a difficult cut to carve, lamb shoulder is usually sold cut into shoulder or round-bone chops. All lamb is delicious flavored with garlic.

Pork provides lots of dense meat and therefore is relatively inexpensive for a roast. As pigs are now bred so lean it is most important to keep the flesh moist, especially as it has to be thoroughly cooked. Stuffings are a good idea for pork roasts and can be flavored similar to those suggested for roast veal (page 156).

Roasts should never be wrapped in foil as it simply steams rather than roasts the meat, and there will be none of the glossy crispness on the outside which comes from frequent basting in an open roasting pan.

ROASTING A LEG OF LAMB

A leg of lamb is a lean cut with a delicate flavor and should always be cooked so it is still pink inside to retain its succulence. Prepare the leg at least 30 to 45 minutes before roasting so the flesh absorbs the flavors of this light coating: mix 2 cloves of crushed garlic with fresh thyme or oregano, black pepper and a little lemon juice. Make small, deep slits in the meat and push the mixture in. Rub the whole roast with a little lemon juice mixed with olive oil and set aside at room temperature.

1 *Just before roasting rub a little more olive oil all over the prepared roast, then rub the outside skin with crushed sea salt, if you like, and put into a roasting pan. Weigh and roast according to the chart (opposite), basting frequently.*

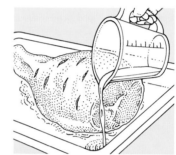

2 *About 20 minutes before the end of cooking add about ⅓ cup (75ml) dry vermouth to the roasting pan. After roasting, leave the lamb to rest on a warm serving plate in a warm place for 15–25 minutes. Use the pan juices to make gravy (page 157).*

BONED LEG OF LAMB

A completely boned leg of lamb is ideal for stuffing and is easy to carve. Bone it yourself (page 146) or ask the butcher to do it for you.

A 2½lb (1.2kg) boned and stuffed roast is enough to serve 6 people.

1 *Prepare a stuffing (see box). Open up the meat, skin side down, and evenly pat in the stuffing, making sure you press it into any pockets.*

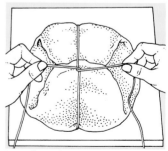

2 *Roll up the meat and tie with kitchen string. Rub the skin with olive oil and crushed sea salt and place in a roasting pan, cut side down. Roast the rolled leg of lamb according to the chart (opposite).*

FLAVORINGS AND STUFFINGS FOR LAMB AND PORK

- To stuff a 2½lb (1.2kg) boned leg of lamb mix together a good handful of finely chopped blanched spinach, 2 chopped garlic cloves, 2oz (50g) can anchovies, 2 teaspoons dried oregano, 2oz (50g) chopped walnuts and 1 beaten egg with black pepper to taste.
- An old-fashioned stuffing for lamb is a mixture of crab meat and bread crumbs.
- Vary basic olive oil and wine marinades for lamb by adding some soy sauce, mustard or mild curry paste.
- Yogurt is a good marinade in itself as it tenderizes the meat. You can mix it with chopped mint and cumin or with tomato paste, crushed garlic and ground coriander.
- Lamb does not need a substantial stuffing; insertions of

herbs, garlic and spices are usually enough.
- Lamb has a particular affinity for thyme and rosemary, and also for dried oregano.
- A mixture of mint and cumin adds a Middle Eastern touch to a lamb stuffing.
- Roast a boned piece of lamb rolled around a filling made from broiled or roasted peppers, onions and carrots. The wonderful juices of the vegetables add to the flavor of the lamb and to the pan juices.
- For pork roasts I rub plain yogurt marinades on the flesh but not on the skin of the roast. I often add a sweeter element such as orange juice. Beer is a good liquid to add to the pan to baste the roast with as it cooks.
- Sage and juniper berries are classic flavorings for pork.

- Finely chopped spinach spread onto a boned piece of pork, then seasoned and rolled before roasting, will add moisture to the flesh.
- For an easy, creamy sauce to serve with roast pork or lamb reduce the juices until they are almost sticky, then add heavy cream and boil in the pan, seasoning to taste. A little sherry or balsamic vinegar, stirred into the cream sauce gradually at the end is often a good idea, and tomato puree is another.
- Fresh chopped herbs added to a gravy or sauce at the last moment always improves the appearance.
- Red currant or red raspberry jelly stirred into lamb or pork gravy with a splash or two of port and a few shakes of soy sauce is wonderful.

ROASTING A LOIN OF PORK

It is advisable to cook pork thoroughly – that is until just done with no pinkness but still tender and juicy. A meat thermometer (below) helps you determine more accurately if the meat is cooked all the way through.

Leg and loin roasts are the prime cuts for roasting, and they can be roasted on or off the bone. If not boned ask the butcher to cut the bottom bone from loin roasts for easier carving.

Be sure the oven is preheated according to the chart (below) before you put the roast in if you want a really crisp surface.

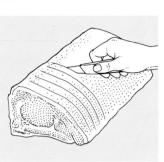

1 *To make a perfectly crisp surface, deeply score the rind (if not removed) and fat without cutting into the meat. The scores should be about ¼in (5mm) apart. You will need a very sharp knife. If the surface is not evenly scored, you will find it difficult to cut when carving the finished roast.*

2 *Wipe the surface with a clean, damp cloth, then sprinkle liberally with crushed sea salt and rub it into the rind or fat.*

3 *Place the roast on a rack in a roasting pan. Remove from the oven 3 or 4 times during roasting and splash with water.*

USING A MEAT THERMOMETER

One way of ensuring thoroughly cooked meat is to use a meat thermometer. Using one certainly takes all the guesswork out of calculating the roasting times.

Different meats are cooked to different internal temperatures. Stick the thermometer's point into the thickest part of the roast. While the meat is roasting watch the dial move up until it reaches the required internal temperature (see charts right and page 157). Or, use an instant-read thermometer toward the end of the estimated cooking time to check the temperature until the roast is done.

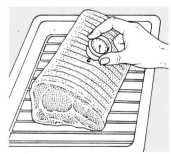

When putting *a meat thermometer in a large cut of meat avoid hitting the bone as this can give a false high reading. Once the thermometer is in position, do not move it or too many juices will escape. Try to buy a thermometer with a thin spike so it does not create a large hole in the roast.*

Apple rings quickly sautéed in butter and fresh sage are the traditional accompaniments for a golden roasted loin of pork.

ROASTING CHART

Lamb

All timings are guidelines only. Longer, thinner roasts may need less time, so it is best to check about three-quarters of the way through the calculated cooking time. Internal temperature on a meat thermometer should be: rare, 140°F, 60°C; medium,160°F, 70°C ; well done, 175°F, 80°C. Stuffed roasts need an extra 5–10 minutes per 1lb (500g). Begin roasting in a preheated oven, 450°F, 230°C for 10 minutes, then at the temperature below:

Cut	Temperature	Time per 500g (1lb)
Bone-in roast		
Rib roast, crown roast, guard of honor, loin, saddle, shoulder	350°F, 180°C	Medium: 15 minutes plus 15 minutes if necessary Well done: 20 minutes plus 20 minutes if necessary
Boned rolled roast		
Leg, loin, shoulder	350°F, 180°C	Medium: 25 minutes plus 25 minutes if necessary Well done: 30 minutes plus 30 minutes if necessary

Pork

Internal temperature on a meat thermometer should be 175°F, 80°C . Stuffed roasts need an extra 5–10 minutes per 1lb (500g). Begin roasting in a preheated oven, 450°F, 230°C for 10 minutes, then at the temperature below:

Cut	Temperature	Time per 1lb (500g)
Bone-in roast		
Fresh ham, loin, shoulder	350°F, 180°C	25 minutes plus 25 minutes if necessary
Boned rolled roast		
Leg, loin, shoulder	350°F, 180°C	30 minutes plus 30 minutes if necessary

STEWING *and* POT-ROASTING

The toughest cuts of meat often have the richest flavor; braising, pot-roasting and stewing are long, gentle methods of cooking in a pot which not only bring out the flavor to its fullest but also transform the meat to a melting tenderness. Vegetables and other ingredients cooked in the same pot add their goodness to the wonderful juices.

Braising and pot-roasting are similar in that they both involve cooking with small amounts of liquid with chopped vegetables. As a rule, however, pieces of meat are braised but whole roasts can be pot-roasted or braised. Likewise there is little difference between braising and stewing, except that in stewing the pieces are usually smaller and more liquid is used. In both the meat cooks in

gently simmering liquid for a long period of time. None of the terms are very exact, which is partly why these methods of cooking are so versatile and pleasing.

It is useful to know that it is not really necessary to seal the meat before cooking; browning the meat does not improve the dish but it will deepen the color of the sauce if that is what you want. Vegetables, however, do seem to take on a sweeter flavor if they are sautéed in a little fat in the pot first. Although marinating adds moisture to dry, lean meats, it is also not essential unless you feel you have a really tough piece of meat; if you add liquid such as wine, and also herbs or spices to the pot the meat will absorb their goodness during the long, slow cooking.

BEEF STEW

Beef needs longer and gentler cooking than other stewing meats to become tender, but it can produce a most satisfying, rich flavor. I like to use plenty of garlic which becomes sweet and mild during the extended cooking. Onions are also necessary, I feel, for their sweet softness. You can experiment with different vegetables such as celery and root vegetables, adding them when you add the onions. This quantity serves 4–5.

¼ cup (32g) all-purpose flour
Salt and pepper
2lb (1kg) stewing beef, such as chuck, cut into large chunks
3 rounded tablespoons butter or olive oil
2 large onions, coarsely chopped
4 large cloves garlic, coarsely chopped
1¼ cups (300ml) beef stock or red wine
14½ oz (411g) can chopped tomatoes
3 teaspoons whole grain mustard
1 teaspoon sugar
Chopped fresh parsley

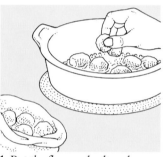

1 *Put the flour and salt and pepper into a plastic bag, add the beef and shake to coat evenly in the flour. Melt the butter in a Dutch oven over a fairly high heat. Add the beef.*

2 *Cook the beef until browned on all sides. Remove and set aside. Add the chopped onions to the Dutch oven, with more fat, if necessary. Stir until softened and slightly browned, then add the garlic. Stir in any surplus flour from the bag and cook for 3 minutes, then return the meat and any juices to the Dutch oven.*

3 *Gradually stir in the stock or wine, tomatoes and mustard. Continue stirring until bubbling and thickened, then season with salt, black pepper and sugar. Cover and cook at 300°F, 150°C for 3–3½ hours until tender. Before serving add a handful of chopped parsley.*

Few things can be more welcoming on a cold day than a hearty beef stew with tender chunks of meat and tasty root vegetables such as baby parsnips.

POT-ROASTING PORK

Blades, shoulders, picnics and hocks are ideal pork cuts for long, slow, delicious pot-roasting where the result is meltingly tender meat with a tasty sauce at the same time. If desired, bone the meat first. Have a selection of chopped vegetables ready as a base to cook the meat on.

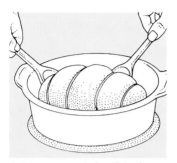 

1 *Remove any rind and tie the roast into a neat shape (page 144). Stud with slivers of garlic at intervals, if desired. In a large Dutch oven, brown the meat in hot oil, turning frequently. Remove the meat and set aside, then brown a selection of coarsely chopped vegetables. Return the roast to the pan on top of the browned vegetables, together with any juices.*

2 *Add enough hot stock or water to a depth of about 1½in (4cm), and bring to a boil. Season, cover and cook gently over a low heat, or in the oven at 325°F, 160°C for 45–50 minutes per 1lb (500g). After cooking, discard the vegetables and flavorings, strain the juices into a small pan and thicken them with a little cornstarch or flour to make a sauce (page 199).*

FLAVORING POT ROASTS AND STEWS

• All pot-roasted and stewed meat and game is improved by a certain sweetness in the ingredients: peeled and chopped parsnips lend a delicious flavor and at the same time often disintegrate and thicken the liquid; dried fruit such as prunes and apricots are often cooked with lamb and spices in Middle Eastern or North African dishes, and they also go particularly well with pork and veal.

• Slivers of orange peel and orange juice for the cooking liquid go particularly well in a beef stew, combined with a pinch or two of ground cloves and some crushed juniper berries.

• Lamb, veal and pork are enhanced by cumin, coriander, cardamom and paprika, while beef can take on cloves and allspice. Cinnamon goes well with all meat.

• If you don't want to thicken your dish with flour but would rather the sauce has some body,

include either very finely chopped onion, root vegetables or even sweet red pepper (for a beautiful scarlet effect). These will cook to such softness over the long cooking time that they blend into the thin liquid and so thicken it.

• Liquids added to stews and pot-roasts can be mixtures of stock and wine, beer and stout, marsala, sherry, citrus juices or even flamed brandy, in varying quantities depending on the style of the finished dish.

• Vegetables which do not suit long cooking, such as most green vegetables, can be added 20–30 minutes before the end of the cooking so that they don't lose their freshness. Apart from vegetables and fresh or dried fruits there are other things which add flavor and character to slow-cooked dishes; for example, black olives, walnuts, canned chestnuts, dried mushrooms, pickled lemons or simply a little grated orange zest.

SIMPLE LAMB CURRY

Ideally the spices for a curry, a simple braised dish, will be at their most aromatic when bought whole and freshly ground but when you are in a hurry a good curry, like this one, can be made by using a commercial curry paste or even powder. Fresh ginger and garlic, however, cannot be replaced, and fresh cilantro makes all the difference. This quantity serves 4–5 people.

2 tablespoons peanut oil
1oz (25g) butter
1 large onion, pureed
2–3 teaspoons mild curry paste
3 large cloves garlic, chopped
2in (5cm) piece fresh ginger, peeled and finely chopped
2lb (1kg) lamb neck, cubed
1 tablespoon tomato puree dissolved in 1¼ cups (300 ml) water
Juice of 1 lemon
Handful fresh cilantro leaves
Salt

1 *Heat the peanut oil and butter in a Dutch oven over a fairly high heat. Add the pureed onion and cook, stirring occasionally, until slightly brown. Stir in the curry paste, chopped garlic and ginger and pieces of lamb filet. Cook for about 2 minutes, stirring until the cubes of meat are browned all over.*

2 *Add the tomato puree and water and lemon juice, season with salt and bring up to boiling. Cover and cook in the oven at 325°F, 160°C for 1½–2 hours until the lamb is very tender but not breaking up, stirring once or twice. Stir in coarsely chopped cilantro leaves and serve with basmati rice.*

Fresh cilantro leaves add color and flavor to this simple lamb curry, served here with pappadams and spiced basmati rice.

BROILING, GRILLING *and* FRYING

Only the more expensive cuts of meat should be used for broiling and grilling, as the heat is fierce, which combined with the short cooking time, makes tough meat tougher. Lean meat such as veal and pork should ideally be marinated before broiling or grilling, and basting while grilling or barbecuing also helps meat remain moist.

Good quality, carefully grilled meat can be delicious – charred on the outside and succulent inside. Grilling on a barbecue over charcoal or wood, with its added aromatics, is best of all. Meat for grilling, or for roasting, should be at room temperature before beginning.

Frying is a more versatile method of cooking as it can be done in several ways with or without other ingredients. For tender meat, frying should either be done quickly over a high heat so that the meat remains pink inside, or over a low heat for much longer – anything in between will be inclined to produce tough meat, as meat toughens after the first minutes of fierce cooking and then becomes tender again with time and gentle cooking.

Sautéing or stir-frying in a little oil or melted butter are the quickest methods, but are only successful with small, even-sized, thin slices of boneless meat – marinating the meat before cooking is best, and thinly sliced vegetables can be added.

Shallow frying in oil, butter or fat in a heavy pan is better for larger pieces of meat such as chops and steaks. It is also possible to dry fry chops and steaks, starting in a cold non-stick pan with no added fat, so that those on a low-fat diet can pour away almost every scrap of fat which comes out of the meat during cooking.

BROILING OR GRILLING CHOPS

Use only prime quality chops, such as loin or rib, for broiling or grilling as the meat can toughen and dry out quickly with the high heat. Brush liberally with butter or oil before cooking or for low-fat cooking baste frequently with a marinade while grilling. The other essential hint is to preheat the grill well so the meat seals quickly. Use tongs or two wooden spoons to turn the meat rather than a fork so the flesh isn't punctured, allowing the juices to run out.

You can tell when a chop is cooked by pressing it with the flat edge of a knife. If the chop is slightly springy and soft it is still pink inside; a firmer texture indicates the chop is just done. Be careful not to overcook.

Broiled chops are delicious spread with a little honey or currant or mint jelly and popped back under the broiler quickly, or topped with pats of herb and garlic or mustard butter.

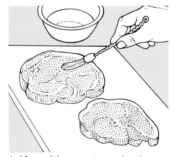

1 *If you like, marinate the chops before broiling for extra flavor and bring the excess marinade to a boil for brushing on the chops during broiling. Preheat the broiler to high. Brush the chops with oil or melted butter. Season with black pepper only and spices. Pork chops may need to have the skin and fat snipped at 1in (2.5cm) intervals to keep the chops flat during broiling.*

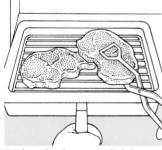

2 *Place the chops on a lightly greased broiler pan and quickly brown to seal on both sides. Turn down the heat to medium and continue cooking the chops until done as desired, turning the chops once more. Brush any remaining boiled marinade on the chops while broiling. Check for doneness by pressing with the flat edge of a knife. Season with salt and extra pepper, and serve.*

FRYING VEAL SCALLOPS

Veal scallops are thin slices cut across the grain from the larger end of the leg. The usual way to treat scallops is to coat them in egg and seasoned breadcrumbs (preferably made from 2-day-old bread) before frying. I also like to sauté the uncoated meat gently in butter, adding lemon juice and fresh herbs, and often some cream at the end of basting to form a delectable sauce.

Take care never to cook scallops too long or the lean meat will dry out and become tough. Scallops can also be cut in slivers for stir-frying.

1 *Place the scallops well spaced apart on a wet sheet of parchment paper and cover with a second wet sheet of parchment paper. Use a rolling pin or meat mallet to pound out the meat evenly until the scallops are very thin. Peel off and throw away the pieces of paper.*

2 *The scallops can either be fried with or without a breadcrumb coating. If desired, dip the scallops first in a bowl of beaten egg, then in one of breadcrumbs. If coated, chill the scallops for at least 15 minutes before frying to let the coating set.*

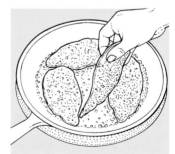

3 *Melt a small amount of olive oil and butter together in a large heavy frying pan. Add the scallops in a single layer and fry for 2–4 minutes on each side, turning only once. Serve at once, sprinkled with lemon juice and salt and pepper.*

COOKING STEAKS

Beef and lamb are the best steaks as they are good served slightly pink. Beef filet, sirloin, T-bone, shell, strip, club and Porterhouse steaks are the most tender, and rump, a less tender cut from the top of the leg, has the most flavor. Lamb steaks are from the leg and are not as tender as lamb chops; don't overcook as they may become tough. Cube steaks are tougher cuts that have been tenderized. Charcoal grilling adds an especially delicious flavor to all steaks.

With practice you can tell how well a steak is cooked by pressing it with your finger, rather than cutting it open and letting juices escape. Use this guide: rare – meat feels springy when pressed and drops of blood and juices appear on the outside; medium rare – meat feels quite firm but a little springy and pink juices are visible; well done – meat feels quite firm.

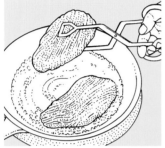 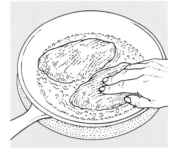

1 *Preheat a heavy frying pan or broiler until very hot. Add a small amount of olive oil and butter to the pan, or use a brush if broiling. Add the steaks and cook for 1–4 minutes on each side, turning once with tongs.*

2 *Test for doneness (above) and remove the steaks from the pan or broiler. If frying, add wine or stock to the pan juices, swirl, season and add a little cream or chunk of butter. Pour over the steaks and serve at once.*

FLAVORING GRILLED AND FRIED MEAT

• Marinades give grilled and fried meats many different flavors. The marinades can be a simple mixture of olive oil with lemon juice and coarsely ground pepper. Or, add flavorings such as herbs, spices, crushed garlic, juniper berries, capers, green peppercorns or fresh ginger.
• Liquids I like to use for marinades include lemon, orange, lime or pineapple juices, soy sauce, wine and sherry and other alcohols, including whiskey.
• Thicker marinades, ideal for grilled meats, can be made from seasoned plain yogurt. These are more like a paste, which softens the meat's texture if rubbed in and left for several hours or overnight. Stir spices such as cumin, coriander and cinnamon into the yogurt with lemon juice and chopped

garlic. I add a great deal of chopped mint, thyme or rosemary for lamb or pork.
• Make a thick sauce from grilled, skinned and pureed sweet peppers to serve with grilled meat – after pureeing reheat with a generous amount of butter, a little lemon juice and plenty of chopped fresh herbs, seasoned well.
• Grilled kebobs are popular in my family. Ideally, use prime quality cuts of beef, lamb, pork or veal, but less tender cuts can be used if marinated first. For lamb kebobs cut a boned rib into small medallions. Marinate in a mixture of yogurt or olive oil flavored with crushed garlic, grated ginger, lemon juice, ground cumin and seasoning, turning occasionally for at least 2 hours.
• Add chopped fresh herbs to bottled Chinese marinades.

A perfectly fried filet with its well-browned exterior and a still pink interior is served here with some homemade French fries (page 43) and a simple salad with grilled tomatoes.

BARBECUING SPARERIBS

Spare ribs are, as the name suggests, the leftover lower portion of the pork ribs. Normally pork ribs are used for barbecuing but lamb riblets are equally delicious and can be treated in the same way as the pork.

The secret of successful spareribs that are deliciously flavorful and tender enough to almost fall from the bones is to marinate them overnight in an intensely flavored mixture, then cook them long and slowly and finish them under high heat to caramelize the outside.

The Chinese have a saying 'the nearer the bone, the sweeter the meat' and nowhere is this better demonstrated than by their style of cooking very bony ribs. The sauce, a lovely blend of sweet and savory flavors, is almost as important as the meat itself.

Marinate the spareribs *overnight in a barbecue sauce made from a mixture of soy sauce, sherry, vinegar, sugar or honey, chopped garlic, ginger and Chinese five-spice powder. Transfer the ribs and the marinade to a roasting pan, cover and cook at 325°F, 160°C for about 1 hour. Either increase the oven to 400°F, 200°C and roast, uncovered, for 30 minutes, skimming off excess fat, or transfer the ribs to a barbecue grill or preheated broiler, spooning over excess marinade, and cook on high heat to brown and caramelize the outside.*

BOILING *and* POACHING

Boiling and poaching meat are methods which cannot really be distinguished; the most accurate term would be poaching, which implies gentleness, as meat should never be boiled. Instead, merely bring it slowly to a boil in cold water and then simmer as gently as possible to prevent the flesh from becoming tough. It is often a refreshingly pure experience to have a dish of tender, boiled meat with a green sauce such as they serve in Italy.

Cuts of meat which poach most successfully are brisket and corned beef, neck and shank of veal, breast and stewing cuts of lamb, the leg, belly or shank of pork, and, of course, country ham and smoked pork butt. A certain amount of fat is nicer, particularly with salted and cured meats as the curing gives it a unique texture and taste.

I love salted and cured meats, either to eat hot or cold. If we are going to have a boneless roast cold I wrap it in foil after poaching while it is still hot and refrigerate it overnight under some weights. This presses the meat together which gives it a finer consistency and makes it much easier to carve when you serve it cold. These days, only the old-fashioned country hams still need to be soaked before cooking.

BOILED DINNER WITH DUMPLINGS

This is a variation of a great classic recipe and a marvelous winter warmer. Smoked pork shoulder butts come in a variety of sizes, anywhere from 1-4lb (500g-1.8kg), so you can choose one that is right for your family. They are boneless and are pressed into a neat compact shape that will fit well into a large saucepan or Dutch oven. This also makes them easy to slice and serve when they have finished cooking.

Check the wrapper for cooking instructions. If the smoked shoulder butt you have purchased has been precooked, as many are these days, you will be able to prepare this recipe in much less time. This version of Boiled Dinner is prepared with just the addition of carrots, onion and celery. However, potatoes, turnips, or cabbage wedges could be added as well.

If serving with dumplings, prepare the dumpling mixture just before cooking and then cook on the lowest simmer so they don't break up.

For each serving, plan about 4-6oz (125-170g) meat, 1 large carrot, peeled and cut crosswise into 2in (5cm) pieces, 1 stalk celery cut crosswise into 2in (5cm) pieces, and 1 medium onion, cut into wedges.

Place the unwrapped smoked shoulder butt in a large saucepan or Dutch oven with a few bay leaves, whole black peppercorns, and juniper berries or whole cloves. Cover with cold water and bring slowly to a boil.

Skim as necessary, *then lower to a gentle simmer, cover and cook for 25 minutes per 1lb (500g) plus 30 minutes, or 1½ hours for butts less than 1½lb (750g). Add vegetable pieces 20 minutes before meat is done. Remove meat and vegetables before you cook the dumplings*

Mustard is the only accompaniment necessary to serve with boiled pork butt and herb dumplings.

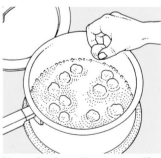

To make dumplings, *mix self-rising flour with a little softened butter, salt and pepper, herbs and just enough water to bind to a firm dough. Shape the dough into small balls. Carefully drop the balls into the pan, cover and cook on a very gentle simmer for 15–20 minutes until cooked and fluffy. If the dumplings start to break up the simmer is not gentle enough.*

BOILING AND TRIMMING A BEEF TONGUE

The best-flavored tongue is beef. It is usually cooked and trimmed to serve cold; it looks impressive and carves easily. Beef tongues are sold fresh, smoked or corned. Smoked or corned tongues need soaking before cooking. Any kind of boiled tongue is delicious served hot too. Serve with Cumberland sauce (page 206).

A 4lb (2kg) beef tongue is enough to serve 8 people if served hot and more if thinly sliced and served cold.

Soak a smoked or corned tongue for 2–3 hours in cold water, changing the water once.

1 After soaking simmer the tongue in a large saucepan of water for about 3 hours until tender, adding a little more boiling water if necessary to keep the tongue covered. Check for doneness with a fine skewer. Drain, reserving the cooking liquid, and plunge the tongue into a bowl of cold water.

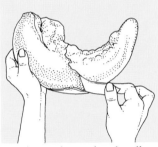

2 When cool enough to handle, remove the tongue from the bowl and discard the water. With a small sharp knife loosen the skin on the underneath and then peel away the remaining skin using your fingers.

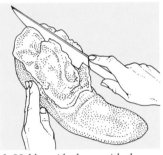

3 Hold upside down with the tongue pointing towards you. Cut lengthwise along the middle. Cut away any gristle and tiny bones from the thick end. If serving hot, slice and drizzle with a little of the cooking liquid.

COOKING CORNED BEEF

Corned beef may be purchased in either whole or half brisket pieces. Even though it is boneless, plan 6-8oz (170-250g) uncooked meat per person because it tends to shrink while boiling. Cooked corned beef is also good chilled and sliced for sandwiches. This recipe for Corned Beef Dinner is for 4.

2lb (1kg) corned beef brisket, rinsed
2 bay leaves
12 whole black peppercorns
6 whole cloves
4 medium potatoes, peeled and quartered
1 medium cabbage quartered
2 tablespoons apricot preserves mixed with 1 tablespoon prepared brown mustard

Place beef in a saucepan with bay leaves, peppercorns and cloves. Cover with water and bring slowly to a boil; cover and cook for 2 hours or until tender. Remove to a broiler rack; top with apricot mixture and broil. Keep warm.

Bring broth to a boil, add vegetables and cook 20 minutes or until tender.

MAKING THE MOST OF BOILED MEATS

• Corned brisket of beef is a great favorite of mine, as the flavor of both the meat and the fat is excellent. I often press green peppercorns and sometimes finely chopped yellow pepper deep into any cracks or cavities in the meat before cooking as this both looks and tastes interesting when the meat is sliced.

• An economical piece of boiled ham can be transformed for eating cold by rubbing the entire surface of the ham with a mixture of dark brown sugar and spices. Wrap the ham well in foil and cook at 350°F, 180°C for about 35 minutes per 1lb (500g) plus 30 minutes.

• The poaching liquid for cured meats can be plain water or an unsalted stock. Add whole spices such as blades of mace, cloves, allspice berries, bay leaves and sticks of cinnamon for extra flavor. Juniper berries and slivers of fresh ginger or chili are also good.

• Other sauces for boiled or poached meats are a delicious green sauce of chopped spinach, sorrel and parsley and a little wine vinegar, with or without chopped anchovies or a simple mixture of heavy cream boiled with chopped capers or green peppercorns.

• Or, I sometimes make a white sauce (page 196) and add chopped anchovies and parsley.

• Another quick sauce can be made by pureeing sweet peppers that have been cooked with the meat.

• Sweet and sour sauces for smoked meats and ham – such as apricots and slivered orange rind stewed in orange juice and sugar, with a little wine vinegar added at the end – can make a lively difference.

• When making pickled tongue stir chopped fresh parsley or other herbs into the vinegar mixture before pouring it over the sliced tongue in a non-metal bowl.

BOILING A HAM

Uncooked hams, smoked shoulder cuts, and hocks can all be cooked until tender by gentle poaching. Leaner, more prime cuts can be almost cooked, then removed from the saucepan, the rind peeled off and the ham roasted with breadcrumbs or a sugary glaze. If the meat is not wrapped with cooking instructions on the label weigh and cook it for 20 minutes per 1lb (500g).

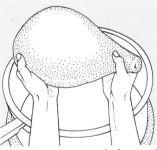

If soaking, remove the ham and discard the soaking water. Place the ham in a large saucepan and add fresh cold water to cover and any flavorings (above). Bring the water to a boil, then cover the pan and turn down the heat to a gentle simmer. When the ham has simmered for the calculated cooking time, allow it to cool in the water until tepid.

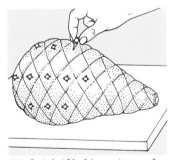

To finish if baking, simmer for two thirds the calculated cooking time, and cut off the skin. Score the fat in a neat criss-cross pattern and stud the centers of alternate diamonds with cloves. Sprinkle with soft brown sugar, pressing in well. Bake at 350°F, 180°C for the remaining time until a tempting golden brown glaze is formed.

CUTTING *and* CARVING

A truly sharp knife is vital to the carver, and one which is the right shape for the type of roast you are carving. Knives for carving should be slightly flexible, and should have a pointed end for roasts with a bone to cut the meat away from the bone (page 16).

The other crucial point to remember for successful carving of roasted meat is that you must always leave it to rest in a warm place, such as the turned-off oven with the door open, for 15–20 minutes after cooking. During this time, the juices, which move to the center of the meat while it is cooking, will filter back evenly through the roast so it won't be dry at the edges. The meat's texture will also become relaxed, softer and, therefore, far easier to carve and more tender to chew.

Meat should always be carved across the grain to shorten the fibers and make them more tender. The direction of the blade should never be altered in mid-slice as this will produce ragged pieces, and tougher cuts of meat should be sliced as thinly as possible.

Bad carving can destroy all the virtues of good meat – the texture, taste and the luscious appearance. It is probably better to carve away from the table so that you are not inhibited by the scrutiny of others hungrily waiting for their helping, and it is easier to carve on a surface slightly higher than a dining table like the kitchen counter.

Don't forget to save all the juices that run out during carving for adding extra flavor to the gravy or any accompanying sauce. If you have cooked an expensive cut of meat to perfection but are not entirely confident of your carving don't hesitate to ask if someone else will do it for you – some people are proud of their carving skills and will enjoy performing for you and your guests.

CARVING LARGE BEEF ROASTS

Beef roasts with large rib bones are each basically carved in the same way. The idea is to loosen the meat in a piece from one end of the bones and cut across the grain in neat slices. Traditionally, beef is carved thinly.

As with all carving an extra-sharp knife is essential so the meat is cut, not torn. Once you are experienced with sharpening knives with a steel (page 16) keep the steel handy so you sharpen after every several slices or so.

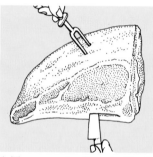

1 *To carve a standing rib of beef, place the roast fat side up and the side with the long bones down on a board. Slide the carving knife between the flesh and rib bones and loosen.*

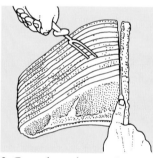

2 *Carve down the roast in neat slices, then loosen all the slices at the bottom bone. To keep the meat juicy only carve as much as you need at a time and serve the carving juices over the slices.*

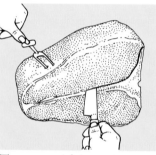

To carve a sirloin *roast run a carving knife between the bone and meat and then carve down to the bone in thin slices. Turn the roast over and repeat on the other side.*

CARVING ROLLED ROASTS

Small, round, rolled roasts are best laid meat side down on the board and carved horizontally. You will have to cut off the pieces of string as you come to them. If the roast has been barded (page 156), it is best to remove the fat before carving.

Larger rolled roasts which would be too tall to carve horizontally, are best laid fat side down on the board. Cut thin vertical slices down across the roast, holding the roast still with a carving fork.

Lay the roast *meat side down on a flat surface. Hold securely in position with a carving fork and cut horizontally across the grain into thin slices with a sharp carving knife.*

ACCOMPANIMENTS FOR CARVED MEATS

• Mix grated horseradish with whipped cream or a mixture of whipped cream and yogurt with chopped cucumbers and capers for a quick accompaniment to roast beef.
• Add a can of peeled chopped tomatoes to the pan juices of roasted veal with heavy cream and boil to a quick sauce.
• Very few things taste better with roast lamb than a simple homemade mint sauce (page 207). For a creamed mint sauce (page 207) stir in a little cream.
• A small bowl of red currant or red raspberry jam is one of the easiest accompaniments for a tender, pink leg of lamb.
• My family likes freshly made mustard or whole grain mustard with rare roast beef or ham slices. Mustards with many different flavorings are widely available, so it is easy to provide without any effort.
• For a lovely sauce intensify the flavor of the cooking juices by reducing them until almost sticky while the meat is resting, then add heavy cream and boil. Season to taste and add a little sherry or balsamic vinegar. Some freshly chopped herbs added at the end improves the appearance and taste.

CARVING A LEG OF LAMB

For successful carving, it helps to remember how the bones lie in a roast. In legs the bones will be down the center with one side of the leg more fleshy than the other, so start carving on the fleshy side, turning the roast over after all the meat is removed from the top. Hold the bony shank with a clean napkin to keep the roast steady as you carve. If the shank has been cut off by the butcher use a carving fork instead to steady the roast while you carve.

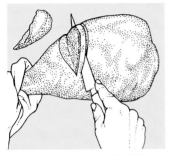 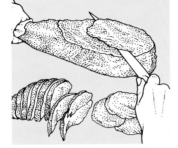

1 *With the rounded side of the leg up, make a wedge-shaped cut in the middle of the leg, cutting through to the bone. Lift out a slice. Continue cutting slices on each side of this first cut.*

2 *Turn the roast over and hold the shank end as in step 1. Cut down the roast in long angular slices to free and remove the rest of the meat.*

Here is a selection of simple accompaniments suggested in the box (opposite) to serve with carved roasted meats. Experiment with flavored mustards and jellies to find your favorite.

CARVING TIPS

There is nothing as spectacular as a crown roast of lamb or pork, but for your guests to enjoy its presentation, you must bring it to the table uncarved and either return to the kitchen to carve it or do so in front of everyone. In order to shape the roast, the bottom bone was either removed or sawed through between the rib bone. This will make carving easier. Insert the carving fork on one side of the roast, then slice down beside 2 adjacent rib bones on the other side of the roast, separating and serving one rib bone, its accompanying meat and a wedge of stuffing at a time.

Correctly carving a flat boneless beef roast such as a flank or a brisket can make all the difference between a tender slice of meat and a chewy one. Slice across the grain of the meat with a knife on the diagonal to produce very thin slices. The more nearly parallel the knife is to the meat, the larger the slices.

A lamb shoulder roast is one of the most difficult cuts of meat to carve. As they are rarely available in the supermarket, you will have gotten the roast from a butcher who will be able to remove or at least loosen the blade bone for you. Once cooked, if the blade was just loosened, remove it. Now carve the meat from the top down, across the grain, removing slices as you go. Then turn the roast over and cut diagonal slices from the sides until as much meat has been removed as is possible. Be sure to save the bone for soup as there will still be small pieces of meat attached to the bone.

A pork loin roast will be much easier to carve if the bottom bone has been removed. If your butcher or the supermarket did not remove or saw through the bone to separate the ribs, be sure to remove it in the kitchen before bringing the roast to the table for carving. Place the fork into the meat at one end of the roast and, starting at the other end, carve down between the ribs to separate the meat into chops.

Always have a warmed platter ready to hold the meat as you carve it. Be sure to arrange the slices attractively and have any garnish on hand so the carved meat can be passed at once.

Once carved, return the roast to the kitchen to add any juices that may have collected on the platter to the gravy. If seconds are required, carve them in the kitchen.

CARVING A WHOLE HAM

On a buffet table or at a large family get together, a whole ham looks impressive. One of the advantages of ham for a party is that it is delicious served hot or cold, which means you can prepare it in advance.

Ham is usually served in thin slices. If you don't buy it spiral-cut, it is best to carve a whole ham with a long thin knife with a slightly serrated edge. Although not essential, it does make for easier carving.

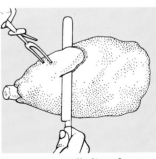

Remove a small slice *of meat from the shank end of the ham and then carve with the knife at an angle in long thin slices down as far as the bone. Loosen from bone.*

ROAST VEAL WITH PRUNES, GINGER AND PISTACHIO NUTS (142)

Although veal produces the best juices of all meat when roasted, the lean flesh can be slightly lacking in flavor. If you press flavorings deep into the cracks of a rolled, boned roast, it becomes something far more sophisticated. The juices combine with apple juice and cream to make a wonderful sauce.   *SERVES 8*

> *3 large cloves garlic, very finely chopped*
> *2in (5cm) piece fresh gingerroot, peeled and very finely chopped*
> *½ cup (75g) pitted prunes, sliced into 3 or 4 pieces*
> *⅓ cup (50g) shelled pistachio nuts*
> *1 rolled, boned veal roast, about 4lb (2kg), such as loin or leg*
> *Olive oil*
> *Black pepper*
> *8oz (250g) tomatoes, skinned and chopped finely (page 48)*
> *1¼ cups (300ml) unsweetened apple juice*
> *⅔ cup (150ml) heavy cream*
> *Sea salt*

In a small bowl, mix together the garlic, ginger, prunes and pistachio nuts. Untie the veal and lay out flat, flesh side up. Spread the filling over it, re-roll and tie again (page 144). If you don't want to untie the roast, press the garlic and ginger into the cracks in the meat from both ends and from the sides, as deep as you can with your fingers, then poke in the slices of prune and the pistachio nuts. Rub the roast generously all over with olive oil and sprinkle with plenty of pepper.

Spoon the chopped tomatoes into the center of a roasting pan and place the veal on top. Cook the meat in the center of a preheated oven, 325°F, 160°C for 2½–3 hours, basting with the juices now and then. About 15 minutes before the end of the cooking time add the apple juice. When the meat is done, turn off the oven, transfer the roast to a carving board and allow to rest in the oven with the door ajar for about 20 minutes.

Meanwhile, add the cream to the juices and tomato bits in the roasting pan and bring to a boil, stirring, on top of the stove. Still stirring, boil the sauce for about 2 minutes. Season to taste with sea salt and black pepper and pour into a sauceboat to serve with the veal.

STEAK AND KIDNEY MEATBALLS WITH FRESH TOMATO SAUCE (150)

Use veal kidneys if possible but lamb's kidneys will still give these meatballs a lovely softness and rich flavor. I like the meatballs best when they are served with spinach and egg noodles and sprigs of bright green and still very slightly crisp steamed broccoli.   *SERVES 4*

> *FOR THE SAUCE*
> *3 tablespoons extra virgin olive oil*
> *2oz (50g) butter*
> *1lb (500g) tomatoes (the plum variety if available), skinned and coarsely chopped (page 48)*
> *2 large cloves garlic, finely chopped*
> *Salt*
> *Black pepper*
> *1 tablespoon tomato puree*
> *FOR THE MEATBALLS*
> *1½lb (750g) ground sirloin*
> *2 veal or 4 lamb's kidneys, skinned and very finely chopped (page 150)*
> *Good handful chopped fresh dill, or 1 level tablespoon dried*
> *2 teaspoons ground coriander*
> *Salt*
> *Black pepper*
> *All-purpose flour*
> *Peanut oil for frying*
> *Fresh dill for garnishing (optional)*

Prepare the sauce first. Heat the olive oil and butter in a saucepan over a medium heat, add the chopped tomatoes and garlic and season with salt and black pepper. Cover the pan, reduce the heat and cook very gently for about 20 minutes until the tomatoes are completely soft. Stir in the tomato puree and adjust the seasoning if necessary. Remove the pan from the heat and set aside while you prepare the meatballs.

Put the ground sirloin in a bowl with the chopped kidneys and dill, the ground coriander and a generous seasoning of salt and black pepper. Mix together thoroughly with a wooden spoon. Put some flour into a separate bowl.

Shape the meat mixture with your hands into slightly flattened balls slightly bigger than a ping-pong ball. As you shape them dip the balls into the bowl of flour so that they are generously covered – this helps them hold together during cooking. To cook, heat a little oil in a large, heavy frying pan over a fairly high heat. Add the meatballs carefully and cook for 4–5 minutes on each side, turning once with a spatula.

Meanwhile, gently reheat the tomato sauce. Carefully transfer the meatballs to a shallow serving dish, pour over the reheated sauce and serve, garnished with fresh dill, if you like.

STUFFED LAMB SHOULDER WRAPPED IN PUFF PASTRY (146)

This is an impressive piece for a large dinner party. It can be prepared well ahead, even the day before, and simply put in the oven shortly before the meal to cook the pastry. As the meat is boned, the serving is simple, providing you use a large, well-sharpened knife.   *SERVES 8–10*

> *1 boned lamb shoulder, weighing about 2½–3lb (1.2–1.5kg)*
> *4 tablespoons lemon juice*
> *8oz (250g) spinach or kale, thick stalks removed, washed and drained*
> *4oz (125g) mushrooms (any kind), finely chopped*
> *2 large cloves garlic, finely chopped*
> *2oz (50g) shelled walnuts, finely chopped*
> *3oz (75g) sharp Cheddar cheese, coarsely grated*
> *Salt and black pepper*
> *17.3oz (490g) package frozen puff pastry, thawed*
> *1 egg, beaten*
> *FOR THE SAUCE*
> *3 tablespoons brandy*
> *1¼ cups (300ml) heavy cream*
> *Salt and black pepper*

If the lamb has been tied up, untie it and lay the meat out flat. Rub the flesh with the lemon juice. To make the stuffing, put the spinach leaves into a food processor and process until very finely chopped. Turn into a mixing bowl and add the finely chopped mushrooms, garlic, walnuts and the grated cheese. Season with a little salt and freshly ground black pepper, then mix together thoroughly with a wooden spoon.

Press the stuffing mixture onto the lamb and into any pockets in the meat. Roll up the lamb loosely to enclose the stuffing as much as possible, pressing it back in with your fingers if it falls out. Secure in as neat a shape as possible with string and/or skewers and put into a roasting pan. Rub the roast all over with sea salt.

Cook the meat in a preheated oven, 350°F, 180°C for 1½–2 hours according to the size of the roast and how well done you like your lamb, basting occasionally with the pan juices. Remove the meat from the oven and let cool in the pan no longer than 30 minutes.

When the meat is cold, remove and discard any solidified fat. Press any of the stuffing which may have come out of the roast back into the meat and carefully remove the string and/or skewers. Pour the pan juices into a small bowl and reserve in the refrigerator.

On a lightly floured surface place the pastry sheets one on top of the other and roll out into a piece big enough to completely enclose the meat. Wrap the meat in the pastry, moistening the pastry edges to seal and cutting off any excess pastry at the corners to make decorations.

Place the roast with the seam of pastry underneath in a greased roasting pan. Roll out the pastry trimmings and cut out decorations for the roast (page 245). Attach them with water. Cut 3–4 small slits in the pastry for the steam to escape. Refrigerate the pastry-covered meat for at least 30 minutes before cooking.

Brush the pastry all over with the beaten egg and cook in the center of a preheated oven, 400°F, 200°C for 30–40 minutes until a glossy, rich brown. Leave the roast in the oven with the heat turned off while you make the sauce.

Bring the reserved meat juices to a boil in a saucepan with the brandy and cream and boil them for a minute or two, or longer if you want to reduce them. Season to taste with salt and black pepper and pour into a sauceboat to serve with the meat. Cut the roast into slices to serve.

SMOKED BONELESS PORK LOIN WITH SPICED GARLIC POTATOES (149)

This is a simple but delicious dish. The smoky taste and succulence of the smoked pork permeates the potatoes which cook underneath it in a mixture of olive oil, garlic, cumin and mace, with onion and tomato to make a rich juice. Only a simple green vegetable, such as steamed broccoli, is needed as an accompaniment. *SERVES 6*

1½–2lb (750g–1kg) potatoes, scrubbed
  but unpeeled
4 large cloves garlic, finely chopped
3 teaspoons cumin seeds
About 6 blades mace
1 large onion, coarsely chopped
8–12oz (250–375g) tomatoes, finely
  chopped
2 bay leaves
3 tablespoons extra virgin olive oil
1 tablespoon wine vinegar
Salt
Black pepper
2–2½lb (1–1.2kg) boneless smoked pork
  loin

Cut the potatoes into ½in (1cm) thick slices and lay them in the bottom of a large, deep Dutch oven. Add three-quarters of the chopped garlic, 2 teaspoons of the cumin seeds, the mace, chopped onion and tomatoes, bay leaves, olive oil and the wine vinegar and mix together. Season with a little salt and plenty of black pepper.

Put the rest of the chopped garlic in a small bowl with the remaining teaspoon of cumin seeds and season with plenty of freshly ground black pepper. Rub this mixture all over the pork, then place the pork on top of the potatoes. Cover the Dutch oven and cook in the center of a preheated oven, 350°F, 180°C for 1¾–2 hours.

To serve, lift the pork onto a carving board and cut into thin slices with a sharp knife. Serve the potatoes and their juices straight from the Dutch oven.

STIR-FRIED PORK FILET WITH FRUIT AND LETTUCE (142)

This is ideal for an informal supper after a busy day, as it takes very little time to prepare. It has the familiar combination of pork and apple but with a Chinese character. Serve it with buttered Chinese noodles or with rice. *SERVES 3–4*

12oz–1lb (375–500g) pork tenderloin,
  cut crosswise into ½in (1cm) slices
3 tablespoons sunflower or peanut oil
3 Granny Smith apples, washed but
  unpeeled
1in (2.5cm) piece fresh gingerroot, peeled
  and cut into thin slivers
2 large cloves garlic, thinly sliced
½ cup (75g) dried apricots, halved
  lengthwise
1 small–medium Romaine lettuce, thinly
  sliced crosswise
4–5 pinches cayenne pepper
Salt
Soy sauce

Place the slices of pork, spaced apart, between two large sheets of wet parchment paper. Pound with a rolling pin until thin. Heat 1 tablespoon of sunflower oil in a wok or large frying pan. Fry the pork pieces over a high heat until lightly browned on both sides then, using a slotted spoon, transfer to a dish and keep warm in a low oven.

Core the apples, then cut in half and slice thinly in half-moon pieces. Put a second tablespoonful of oil into the wok or frying pan over a high heat. Add the ginger and garlic and stir for a minute, then add the apple slices and stir for another minute or so until the apples are tinged with brown. Stir in the halved apricots and add the mixture to the pork in the oven.

Put the remaining tablespoon of oil in the wok or pan, add the lettuce and stir over a high heat for about 30 seconds or so until the lettuce is limp. Add to the pork mixture. Season with cayenne pepper and salt and turn into a warmed serving dish. Sprinkle with soy sauce and serve immediately.

GRILLED LAMB WITH MINT AND YOGURT SAUCE *(142)*

Lamb loin is a marvelous choice when you want boned lamb; it is especially good when marinated and grilled, as this produces aromatic meat which remains pink and juicy inside. Pureed vegetables (page 53) are an ideal accompaniment to this dish.   *SERVES 4*

2 tablespoons olive oil
4 tablespoons lemon juice
3 cloves garlic, crushed
3 rounded teaspoons ground cumin
1 tablespoon tomato puree
Black pepper
1½–1¾lb (750–875g) boned lamb loin
Mint leaves to garnish
FOR THE YOGURT SAUCE
1 rounded teaspoon coriander seeds
2 teaspoons sesame seeds
Generous handful of fresh mint leaves, very finely chopped
8 tablespoons plain yogurt
Salt and black pepper

At least 4 hours in advance make the marinade mixture. Put the olive oil, lemon juice, crushed garlic, ground cumin and tomato puree in a bowl and mix together. Season generously with black pepper. Place the lamb in a shallow dish and brush all over with the marinade. Cover the dish and leave in the refrigerator, for 4 hours or overnight if possible.

Before cooking the lamb prepare the yogurt sauce. Put a dry frying pan over a high heat and toss the coriander and sesame seeds in it for a minute or two just to toast. Turn the seeds into a small mixing bowl. Add the chopped mint and the yogurt. Mix well, season with salt and black pepper and spoon into a serving bowl.

To cook the meat preheat the grill to its highest. Grill the lamb for about 10 minutes until dark brown all over, turning once or twice and spooning over any excess marinade during first half of cooking time. When cooked remove from the heat but leave the lamb on the grill pan for a few minutes before putting them on a board and slicing across into ½in (1cm) slices. To serve, arrange the lamb slices on a warm serving plate, garnish with a few fresh mint leaves and serve with the spicy yogurt sauce.

AROMATIC MEATBALLS WITH SPINACH AND MUSHROOMS *(153)*

This is a popular family dish in my house, full of goodness and lovely aromas. Serve with new potatoes or buttered noodles.   *SERVES 4*

1lb (500g) lean ground lamb or beef
Sea salt
Black pepper
1–2in (2.5–5cm) piece fresh gingerroot, peeled and finely chopped
2 teaspoons cumin seeds
1 tablespoon tomato puree
1–2 tablespoons peanut oil
2oz (50g) butter
1 onion, coarsely chopped
1lb (500g) spinach, stalks removed, washed and chopped roughly
6oz (175g) mushrooms, thinly sliced
4 large cloves garlic, sliced lengthwise
4 tablespoons sour cream
Cayenne pepper to garnish

Put the meat into a mixing bowl and season well with sea salt and black pepper. Add the chopped ginger, cumin seeds and tomato puree and mix thoroughly with a wooden spoon. Using damp hands, form the mixture into small balls the size of a large marble or walnut.

Put the peanut oil in a large frying pan over a high heat. When the oil is hot, add the meatballs and turn around carefully with a wooden spoon just to brown all over. Remove the pan from the heat and set aside.

Melt the butter in a large Dutch oven over a medium heat. Add the chopped onion and cook until soft and translucent. Add the coarsely chopped spinach, cover the Dutch oven and cook for a few minutes, opening the dish and stirring once or twice. Stir in the sliced mushrooms and garlic and season with salt and black pepper.

Using a slotted spatula, take the meatballs from the frying pan and arrange them on top of the spinach and mushroom mixture. Cover the Dutch oven again and continue to cook over a gentle heat for 15 minutes. Remove the lid of the Dutch oven, increase the heat and boil vigorously for 5–8 minutes until the juices have reduced by about half. Just before serving, spoon the sour cream over the top of the meatballs and vegetables then dust with a little cayenne pepper. Serve directly from the Dutch oven

PORK CHOPS STUFFED WITH ROQUEFORT AND BAKED WITH PEARS *(142)*

Both pork and onions call for a little sweetness, and this is a delicious way of combining them. The onions are given extra zip with fresh ginger, while the salty flavor of Roquefort mingles into the juices.   *SERVES 4*

4 thick boned loin or spare rib pork chops
4oz (125g) Roquefort cheese
Black pepper
Olive oil for frying
3 onions, coarsely chopped
2 cloves garlic, finely chopped
2in (5cm) piece fresh gingerroot, peeled and finely chopped
1 rounded tablespoon orange marmalade
Salt
2 large firm large pears
Sugar
Finely chopped fresh parsley to garnish

Using a sharp knife, slice a wide, deep pocket in each pork chop. Crumble the Roquefort into a bowl and season well with black pepper. Press the Roquefort into the chops, then press to enclose the cheese. Rub with olive oil and set aside.

Heat about 1 tablespoon olive oil in a cast-iron skillet over a medium heat, then add the onions and stir constantly until softened. Add the garlic and ginger and stir for another minute. Finally stir in the marmalade and season with salt. Lay the stuffed chops on top.

Cook in the open skillet in the center of a preheated oven, 325°F, 160°C for 1–1¼ hours. Meanwhile, peel the pears, then halve them and carefully cut out the cores. About 30 minutes before the end of cooking lay a pear half on each chop, rub with olive oil and sprinkle with a little sugar, salt and black pepper. Sprinkle with parsley to serve.

STEWED RABBIT WITH QUINCES (142)

This stew of spiced rabbit in a smooth red pepper and tomato sauce is perfect accompanied by boiled potatoes, rice or buttered noodles, and a crisp green salad or vegetable. Quinces contribute a unique flavor which is excellent with meat but if they are difficult to find use firm pears instead.   *SERVES 6*

2 red peppers, cored, seeded and coarsely chopped(page 49)
1lb (500g) tomatoes (the plum variety if available), coarsely chopped
1 very large onion, coarsely chopped
1 rounded tablespoon sugar
2½ cups (600ml) medium or dry cider
2 tablespoons sherry vinegar
Salt and black pepper
2 tablespoons peanut oil
3–3½lb (1.5–1.7kg) rabbit, cut into pieces (page 155)
3 large cloves garlic, peeled and finely chopped
½ teaspoon ground cloves
1 teaspoon ground mace
1 whole nutmeg, grated
1lb (500g) quinces, washed but unpeeled
Handful of chopped fresh parsley

Put the coarsely chopped peppers, tomatoes and onion in a large saucepan with the sugar, cider and sherry vinegar and season to taste with salt and black pepper. Place the pan over a high heat and bring to a boil, then cover the saucepan and simmer gently over a medium heat for about 30 minutes. Remove the saucepan from the heat and set aside.

Heat the peanut oil in a large frying pan over a high heat, and fry the rabbit pieces on both sides just to brown them. Remove the pieces from the frying pan with a slotted spoon and transfer them to a large Dutch oven. Sprinkle the rabbit with the chopped garlic and the other spices.

Pour the contents of the saucepan into a food processor and process until smooth. Work the puree through a fine sieve, taste and adjust the seasoning with more salt and black pepper if necessary. Pour the puree over the rabbit. Cover the Dutch oven and cook in the center of a preheated oven,475°F, 240°C, for 15 minutes, then reduce the oven temperature to 325°F, 160°C and cook for another 1½ hours or until the rabbit is

completely tender.

Finally, cut the washed quinces into quarters, cut out the cores and add the quince pieces to the casserole dish, mixing them in. Cover the dish and continue cooking for another 30 minutes or until the quinces are just soft. Sprinkle with the chopped fresh parsley just before serving.

RABBIT AND PUMPKIN WITH MUSTARD (155)

The mild tenderness of domestic rabbit is perfect for this lovely autumn dish. The pumpkin softens to form a delicious pale orange sauce, rich yet mild, and the mustard and green peppercorns add zest. *SERVES 4*

1 tablespoon olive oil
2 teaspoons caraway seeds
2–2¼lb (1–1.1kg) rabbit, cut into pieces (page 155)
4 cloves garlic, coarsely chopped
4oz (125g) butter, cut into pieces
2lb (1kg) piece pumpkin, peeled, seeded and chopped into small pieces
2 teaspoons bottled green peppercorns, drained and crushed
4 teaspoons Dijon mustard
⅔ cup (150ml) white wine or cider
Salt
⅔ cup (150ml) heavy cream
Flat-leaf parsley sprigs to garnish

Heat the olive oil in a large Dutch oven over a medium heat. Add the caraway seeds and stir for a minute, then add the rabbit pieces and sauté to seal them on both sides. Next add the chopped garlic and stir for 30 seconds. Remove from the heat and add the butter, then, when the butter has melted in the Dutch oven, add the chopped pumpkin, the crushed green peppercorns, the mustard, the white wine or cider and a sprinkling of salt. Stir with a wooden spoon to mix the ingredients thoroughly.

Cover the Dutch oven with a tight-fitting lid and cook in the center of a preheated oven, 350°F, 180°C for 1¼ hours. Stir with a wooden spoon to break up the pumpkin until it combines with the other ingredients to become a puree, then replace the lid and continue cooking for another 20–30 minutes.

Just before serving, pour the heavy cream over the top and garnish with parsley sprigs.

SADDLE OF BONED AND ROLLED VENISON WITH SPINACH

A boned and rolled saddle of venison looks splendid and the moist and piquant spinach filling is an added bonus.   *SERVES 6–8*

3½–4lb (1.7–2kg) piece of saddle of venison, boned
4 tablespoons lemon juice
Olive oil
Black pepper
1lb (500g) spinach, stalks removed and washed
2 rounded teaspoons bottled green peppercorns, drained and crushed
2 rounded teaspoons whole grain mustard
Sea salt
Pork fat for barding (optional)
1 tablespoon sherry or balsamic vinegar
2 teaspoons Dijon mustard
1¼ cups (300ml) heavy cream

Lay the venison skin side down in a roasting pan. Rub the flesh with the lemon juice and olive oil and sprinkle liberally with pepper. Cover and refrigerate for several hours or overnight.

Steam or boil the spinach leaves until very soft. Rinse with cold water and drain thoroughly, pressing out as much liquid as possible. Leave to cool for a few minutes.

Put the crushed green peppercorns in a bowl with the whole grain mustard. Mix in the spinach and press onto the inside of the venison roast and loosely roll the venison with the spinach inside. If any spinach comes out as you do this press it back in. Carefully turn the roast over, and either rub the top with olive oil and sprinkle with sea salt or if using, wrap the top half of the roast in the pork fat. Tie the roast at regular intervals (page 144). Put the roast in a preheated oven, 425°F, 220°C and cook for 45–60 minutes.

Meanwhile, put the vinegar and mustard in a bowl and stir in the cream. Season with salt and black pepper. When the venison is cooked, transfer it to a warm serving dish. Pour off any fat from the pan, then add the cream and mustard mixture into the roasting pan with the meat juices. Put over a high heat and bring the sauce to boiling, stirring all the time. Boil for a minute and then pour into a sauceboat to serve with the venison.

POULTRY and GAME BIRDS

Poultry – which includes chickens, turkeys, ducklings, ducks and geese – offers enormous possibilites in the kitchen and is becoming increasingly popular. Chicken and turkey are also the most economical of meats, and are ideal for entertaining because you can transform them into almost any type of dish. Chicken is a wonderful vehicle for herbs and spices, sauces and enhancing ingredients; this applies particularly to frozen birds as they often need added taste and texture. Fresh free-range birds have enough flavor, as a result of their more varied diet and roaming lifestyle, to be cooked simply. This applies to free-range turkeys just as much as to chickens.

The wide variety of poultry available is relatively inexpensive and is low in fat (except ducks and geese). Chicken and turkey, almost universally popular with both young and old, are therefore supremely practical for family meals. But there is no need to bore your household with the same old chicken dishes as the basic bird can be transformed by different ways of cooking and seasoning and by different sauces. Boned chicken breasts, for example, may be cooked in many ways. They can be grilled, roasted or steamed whole but I think they are far more exciting when sliced across thinly for quick stir-fry style dishes or put between sheets of parchment paper, pounded thin and rolled around a stuffing. Small Cornish hens are perfect for a single serving and fun to serve.

Chickens which are yellow skinned have been fed a special diet to add the color. Although they are factory raised, they usually have a moist, tender texture because they have a little more fat under the skin than free range chickens which have a better flavor.

Ducklings, ducks, and geese do not offer value for money in the same way as chickens and turkeys because they have shallow breasts with not much meat on them, and altogether a lot of bone in proportion to meat. They do, however, offer real character, and few foods seem more festive than a roast goose with a good fruit and nut stuffing. Commercially raised ducklings have a thick layer of fat under the skin which stops the meat from drying out or becoming tough. Since most are marketed quite young they are naturally tender and juicy. I particularly love the little mallard, or wild duck, which has an even stronger taste and the darkest flesh.

Duck breast is best and most succulent when eaten pink but as the legs should be more thoroughly cooked it is difficult to roast a bird like this. Individual breast filets, however, are now available and they can be cooked briefly under a hot broiler producing tender slivers of pink and juicy meat. Bone-in duck breast pieces are also available sometimes and can be roasted or broiled slightly rare. Quail were once considered a game bird but because they are now only available farmed they are considered poultry. Try them for their subtle taste and delicate texture.

All sorts of game birds are now farmed and, although they may not have been hung enough to develop a really game-like flavor, it is exciting to be able to buy them so easily. Squab always taste delicious but are best stewed as they can be tough if roasted. Similarly, pheasants, which can also be dry, are excellent in a stew, their flavor enhanced by other ingredients. Partridges have a delicate taste and texture and can be beautifully juicy when not overcooked; but of all game birds plump grouse are my favorite birds to eat, as they have a distinctive flavor and a lot of succulence. All game birds take very well to slightly sweet, fruity accompaniments and also, which fewer people realize, to a number of aromatic spices.

Clockwise from top: A thick honey and apricot sauce with fresh mint tops duck pieces in Dark Glossy Fruited Duck (page 192); Chicken in Almond and Coconut Milk (page 190) served with saffron-flavored rice; Roasted Chicken with Cilantro and Lime (page 191) are roasted with flavored cream cheese under the skins and bacon strips over the breasts, then served with a sauce made from pan juices; Steamed Chicken in Yellow Pepper and Dill Sauce (page 190); Duck Filets in Pastry with Leek Sauce (page 193) with potatoes; Cornish Hens with Mystery Sauce (page 193) accompanied by steamed baby carrots.

PREPARATION

When choosing a whole fresh bird, look for one with a compact and rounded shape, plump breasts, dry and unmarked skin and pliable legs. Chickens, turkeys, ducks and geese should smell fresh, which means very little smell at all; if they have been stored too long an off odor is easily distinguishable, even through plastic. Always remove tight plastic wrapping when you get home and leave the bird in the refrigerator on a large plate for no longer than its sell-by date, covered only loosely with waxed paper so plenty of air can circulate around it. If the bird comes with its giblets be sure to save them for the stockpot (page 29); they can be frozen until you are ready to use them.

Poultry pieces do not need cleaning before cooking but whole birds should be well rinsed. Whether you truss the bird or not is a matter of personal preference but I like the neater shape it guarantees. Although there are traditional ways of cooking certain birds, almost all poultry and game is more versatile than you would think. It can be roasted, pot-roasted, boiled, steamed, stewed, barbecued, grilled, broiled or fried.

Duck is best either roasted or grilled as this achieves a delicious crispy skin, but it is also good cut into pieces and stewed, with some starchy ingredient such as dried beans to absorb its delicious fat.

I think roast goose is a fine sight for a special occasion, especially if it is served with a moist and aromatic fruity stuffing. Turkey is also traditionally roasted but it can be dull and dry. You can add far more character to turkey by stewing parts or boned breasts or using diced meat in stir-fries. Game birds are usually roasted but are also good stewed, especially pheasant and squab.

CLEANING AND TRUSSING CHICKEN

Most prepared roasting birds are sold with the legs held together by a fastener. Whether or not you stuff the bird (page 176), replace the fastener with string. Trussing helps keep the bird in a good compact shape for even cooking, easier carving and to retain the juices for more tender flesh. A simple method is to pull up the legs and tie together. Make sure the neck skin is pulled under the bird and wings tucked underneath.

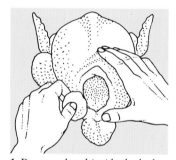

1 *Put your hand inside the body cavity and pull away the pad of fat just inside. Wash the bird inside and out under running water and dry with paper towels.*

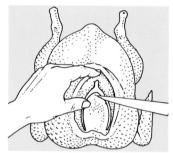

2 *Working at the neck end, pull back the neck flap. Cut out the wishbone, if desired, for easy carving. Pack stuffing, if used, in neck end and pull down the skin.*

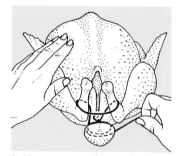

3 *Using a piece of string 5 times the bird's length anchor one end around the tail and loop the long end around one leg and then the other and back around the tail to draw the legs and tail together.*

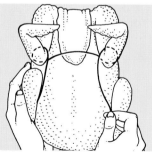

4 *Take the string to the back, passing between the thigh and body, then turn the bird over. Loop around one wing and across to the second wing, securing the neck flap. Loop again and pull up the wings to the body. Pass string back to tail and tie.*

Chicken pieces are so versatile and can be combined with endless ingredients. Here Aromatic Chicken with Pilaf (page 191) combines apple, onion, chicory and bulgar to make a puree.

CUTTING UP CHICKEN

Cutting up a bird yourself is quite straightforward if you have a good sharp knife. A pair of poultry shears is useful but not essential. Be sure to allow plenty of time when you try this the first time.

One of the advantages of cutting up a whole bird yourself is that you get a selection of pieces, such as the breasts and thighs. The other advantage is that you do not lose the 'oysters', two tender pieces of meat along the backbone. These small pieces of dark meat are traditionally known as the 'chef's treat'.

This method of cutting makes 8 pieces.

HANDLING POULTRY AND GAME BIRDS

• I cannot over-emphasize the importance of safe handling of poultry, particularly chickens and turkeys. All foods contain bacteria, some of which can cause food poisoning if allowed to grow at room temperature and not destroyed by thorough cooking.

• Buy birds that are well wrapped. Check the sell-by date and avoid any with torn packaging.

• Get the birds home as soon as possible, then store in the refrigerator or freezer until required. Cook fresh birds within 3 days.

• Frozen birds must be completely thawed before cooking. Follow instructions on the packaging. You can check the thawing by putting your hand inside the cavity. If some ice is still present, it needs further thawing. Cook as soon as the bird has thawed.

• It is best to thaw birds as slowly as possible to produce the most tender flesh, so thaw them in the refrigerator on a plate with a rim. This prevents the juices from dripping onto other food. Place on a shelf below cooked meats.

• Do not put frozen birds in hot water to thaw.

• Do not refreeze thawed poultry, even after it has been cooked.

• Always wash hands and utensils after handling raw poultry. Scrub chopping boards well in hot soapy water – don't just wipe them with a damp cloth. This cuts down on the chance of cross-contamination.

• Do not allow raw and cooked meats to come into contact with each other.

• Cook all poultry thoroughly. Potential problem bacteria such as salmonella thrive and grow in warm temperatures. If food is only half cooked, this is an ideal breeding ground for germs. Salmonella bacteria grow slowly in temperatures less than 50°F, (10°C) but cannot survive in temperatures above 160°F (70°C) for 2 minutes. These temperatures are reached when food is properly cooked. At this temperature, poultry juices will run clear. Any hint of pinkness indicates further cooking is needed.

• When boiling a mixture with raw poultry meat in it, bring the mixture to a boil as quickly as possible and boil for 30 seconds to kill the bacteria.

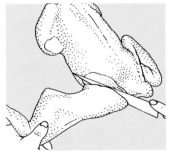

1 *With the bird breast side down locate the 2 oysters either side of the backbone. Loosen them with a sharp knife, putting the tip of the blade underneath and cutting them free from the skeleton without completely cutting the oysters off.*

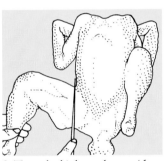

2 *Turn the bird over breast side up. To remove the legs cut through the skin between the legs and breast, pulling the legs away and cutting through each joint to the backbone and including the oyster. The oysters should come away with the thighs.*

3 *To cut up the leg use your finger to locate the joint between the drumstick and thigh on one side, then cut straight through the joint with a sharp knife; repeat with the other leg. Cut off the lower legs and discard or save for use in the stockpot (page 29).*

CUTTING UP DUCK

The technique for cutting up a duck is different from that for a chicken because ducks have different shapes and so much less meat in relation to bone.

It is also easy to remove breast filets. Remove the backbone, then cut off the leg and thigh portions. Cut along the breastbone, and use the knife's tip to cut away the meat.

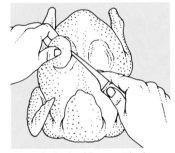

4 *Turn the bird around with the neck end facing you, then cut through the wing joints, cutting off some of the breast flesh with each piece for more generous portions. Cut off the wing tips and discard or save for use in the stockpot with the lower carcass.*

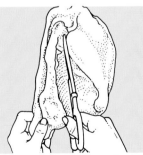

5 *Using poultry shears, if available, split the carcass, cutting away the backbone from the breast, then reserve the lower carcass and save for use in the stockpot.*

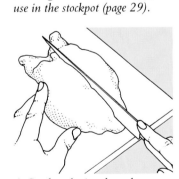

6 *Cut lengthwise along the breastbone with a knife, then remove the bone, if desired, producing 2 portions. Add the bones to the stockpot.*

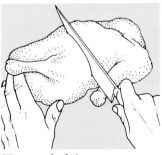

To cut a duck into quarters *cut through and discard the backbone which can be used for making stock (page 29). Then turn the duck over so it is breast side up. Split the duck in half through the breast, then cut each half again crosswise making 4 quarters, allowing bigger portions at the wing ends.*

BONING AND STUFFING

I love stuffed dishes, whether they are vegetables, fish or meat, so I am always inspired by a boneless bird. Years ago I used to buy whole boned chickens so I could stuff them with good things, tie them up into neat parcels and then roast them. Nowadays, although it is far easier to find boned pieces of chicken, it is impossible to find boned whole birds. A stuffed boned chicken, either to roast and eat hot or to poach, and eat cold, can be such a delicious pleasure to create that it is worth learning to bone poultry yourself for special occasions.

Open- and tunnel-boning are the two classic professional techniques for boning birds before stuffing. Open-boning, where the bird is cut open and the bones removed from the inside is the easiest technique to learn.

Tunnel-boning, which leaves the skin and flesh whole, is best for larger birds such as duck but it takes more practice.

Using different colored ingredients for stuffing a whole bird and arranging them in a definite pattern produces impressive-looking slices that can be beautifully arranged on a serving plate. The flavors of the stuffing also enhance the meat and help avoid blandness. Include ingredients with striking colors such as red, green or yellow peppers, black and green olives, spinach leaves, pistachio nuts, dried fruit and so on. In a traditional French galantine you might add ground meat. Stuffings are not always a solid mixture of ingredients; in chicken Kiev, for example, a boned chicken breast is stuffed with flavored butter, then breaded before cooking.

OPEN-BONING AND STUFFING CHICKEN

A boned bird has endless possibilities for stuffing and serving, and, hot or cold, a stuffed boned bird is easy to cook through evenly.

Boning a whole chicken may seem tricky at first, but with practice it will soon become easier. Three things help – a good, short-handled, sharp, thin-bladed boning knife, a pair of poultry shears and some knowledge of the bird's anatomy so you can figure out where the bones lie. Do not cut the skin while you are working as the stuffing may burst through during cooking.

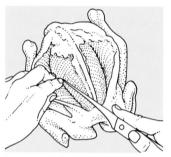

1 *Unwrap the bird and lay it breast side down. Cut a line along the backbone, beginning at the neck end. Working the blade under the skin, shave the flesh away from the backbone in a back and forth motion. Pull the flesh away with one hand while you cut with the other.*

2 *Work your way down around the leg and wing joints, carefully scraping and shaving as you go. Cut through the joints with poultry shears to free them so you can get to the rest of the flesh. Sometimes you can ease the flesh from the bones simply with your fingers.*

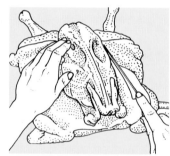

3 *With the bird still breast side down work your way along the rib cage, shaving and scraping close against the bones. Take care not to cut the skin over the breastbone where the flesh is very thin. The carcass should now lift out in one piece and can be used in the stockpot (page 29).*

4 *Cut off the lower legs and discard or save for use in the stockpot. Working from the inside remove the leg bones on either side by scraping away the flesh first from the thigh bone, then from the drumstick. Sever the white ligaments, pull the bones free and remove.*

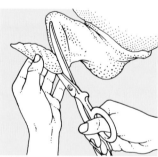

5 *Cut off the wing tips. To remove the wing bones hold each wing and carefully scrape away the flesh. Twist the bones free and remove. Cut off the tail and discard. Lay the bird flat, skin side down, and turn the leg and wing flesh into the center to make a neat shape.*

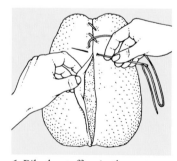

6 *Pile the stuffing in the center and wrap the sides around it, taking care not to overlap the skin too much. Secure with kitchen string, using a trussing needle. Weigh the stuffed bird and roast as normal (page 178) but for 25 minutes per 1lb (500g) plus 25 minutes extra.*

BONING A CHICKEN LEG

An easily boned chicken leg (the drumstick and thigh together) can be stuffed and baked or coated in crumbs and deep fried.

Scrape the flesh away from the top of the thigh, working your way down the bone. Do not cut the skin. Pull the flesh down and outwards as you scrape. Cut through the joint and discard the thigh bone. Stuff the thigh cavity only, leaving the drumstick bone in and stitch the top closed.

TUNNEL-BONING DUCK

A duck has a much higher bone to meat ratio, so it is worth boning and stuffing one, if only because it makes it easier to carve. Boning and stuffing are also a good way to stretch a duck to feed a larger number of people.

Normally only the breastbone and backbone are carved out in this style of boning. The legs and wings are left to add shape to the boned and stuffed bird.

A good boning knife and poultry shears are essential. Take care not to cut the skin, so the juices and stuffing do not escape during cooking, resulting in a dry bird.

A tunnel-boned duck stuffed with a mixture of yellow peppers, red onions, chopped walnuts, raw spinach and stewed apricots, and then roasted makes an impressive easy-to-carve party dish.

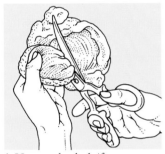

1 *Untruss the duck if necessary and cut off the wing tips and lower legs. Rinse the duck inside and out with cold running water and pat dry with paper towels. Stand the duck upright on its neck end. Cut off the tail and discard.*

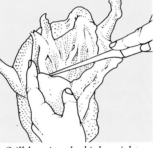

2 *Still keeping the bird upright, carefully scrape the knife against the bone structure, and start to cut the flesh away from the bones, pulling back the freed flesh with one hand as you cut with the other.*

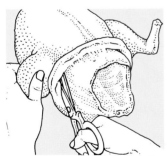

3 *When you get to the legs and wings, cut through the joints from the inside with poultry shears. Leave the legs and wings alone as they are not boned in this method, unlike open-boning. This makes the stuffed bird look more natural.*

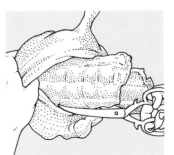

4 *Use poultry shears to cut the rib cage from the main whole carcass, then pull out the skeleton and discard or use in the stockpot (page 29). Trim and stuff the bird. Using a trussing needle and string stitch up the neck end for a neat roasting shape.*

STUFFING AND SERVING BONED POULTRY

• One of the simplest and most successful poultry stuffings is a mixture of fresh herbs, such as tarragon, dill or cilantro with finely chopped ginger, garlic, finely grated lemon rind and a little soft butter or olive oil. Use it to stuff boned thighs, breasts and whole birds.
• Flatten boneless legs, thighs and breasts for rolling or folding around a stuffing by putting them under wet parchment paper and pounding with the side of a meat mallet, heavy flat knife or rolling pin. This way you can put a chunkier stuffing of chopped ingredients in the center and bring the meat around it to enclose like a package.
• Ingredients particularly good for stuffing mixtures are pieces of grilled and skinned peppers (page 55), sautéed onions, chopped mushrooms (especially portabella or shiitake), pine nuts, pistachio nuts and walnuts, cooked wild rice, grated carrot, grated cheese, grated citrus rind, chopped tomatoes, chopped dried apricots, peaches or prunes and chopped spinach.
• A little root vegetable puree (page 53), such as parsnip or celeriac, is a good binder for the more chunky ingredients,

such as vegetables and nuts, in stuffing.
• Another excellent stuffing is cream cheese, particularly the kind with garlic and herbs, or blue cheese – use this instead of the traditional butter in a chicken Kiev.
• There are all sorts of flavor enhancers you can stir into stuffing mixtures including tomato puree, sun-dried tomato paste, olive paste, finely chopped anchovies, roasted pepper puree, caponata or pesto.
• Boned thighs and breasts can be stuffed and wrapped in puff pastry, then decorated with scraps of pastry and glazed with egg yolk. Bake in a preheated oven, 425°F, 220°C for the first 20 minutes, then at 325°F, 160°C for another 20 minutes. Decorated with scraps of pastry and glazed with egg yolk, these exciting little packages are perfect for dinner parties as they can be prepared well ahead, and kept in the refrigerator before cooking. They will even keep warm for a short while in a low oven before serving.
• Use thinly sliced strips of bacon to wrap around stuffed and rolled boned pieces of poultry for extra flavor.

ROASTING

The smell of a roasting bird never fails to excite the taste-buds. Roasting is one of the simplest ways of cooking, and carefully done it can produce exquisite results. Even though a roast chicken is nowadays perhaps the meal we are more used to than anything else, a glistening, golden bird still has an aura of feasting about it.

When done thoughtfully, roasting is probably in the end the most satisfying way of cooking chicken, turkey, Cornish hens, duck, goose and most game birds. Chicken, turkey and Cornish hens should be cooked until all the flesh has turned from pink to white, but it is equally important that they should not dry out, losing both

tenderness and flavor. For smaller birds a medium or high heat is best and there are various ways to make sure that moisture is not lost, particularly from the breast. With most birds olive oil or butter, spread either on top of or pushed under the skin, or a few strips of bacon over the breasts, will do, but some larger birds need basting during roasting. Duck and goose have so much fat that they do not need any extra to keep them moist.

Game should be cooked at a higher heat and must never be overcooked so that it remains juicy and slightly pink inside, particularly as with small birds it is only the breast that is fleshy enough to eat.

ROASTING TURKEY OR CHICKEN

Basting and careful timing are essential if turkey legs are not to dry out before the breast meat is cooked. With the larger birds, it is sometimes recommended to cut off the legs and roast them separately. Using a baster during roasting also helps keep the meat tender and juicy. If you put the bird on a rack in the pan the juices are easier to get to.

I recommend that birds should only be stuffed in the neck end; roast any leftover stuffing in an ovenproof dish.

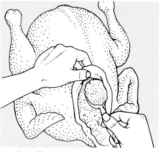

1 *If stuffing, spoon the stuffing into the neck end and truss (page 174). Add an onion, lemon halves or herb sprigs to the body cavity for flavor. Weigh and calculate cooking time (opposite).*

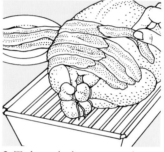

2 *To keep the breast moist during cooking, cover it with strips of bacon or lift the breast skin and, using your fingers, spread the flesh with butter or cream cheese (opposite).*

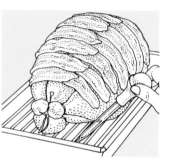

3 *Brush the legs with oil or rub with butter. Using a baster or spoon, baste the bird in its own juices 2 or 3 times during roasting. Any bacon needs to be removed for the last 20 minutes of roasting to brown the breast to an attractive golden color.*

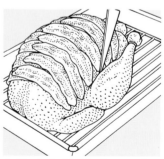

4 *Check the bird for doneness by piercing between the thigh and breast. Clear juices should run out. If there is even a hint of pink, return the bird to the oven for further cooking.*

Roast Pheasants Indian Style (page 192) served with okra and a curried mushroom sauce. This preparation is good with chickens as well.

ROASTING DUCK OR GOOSE

Because these birds are so fatty they do not need extra fat to keep them moist but they do need basting during cooking. For a rich, dark glaze and crisp skin on roasted duck or goose I often rub the skin with honey or sugar as well as salt about 30 minutes before the end of cooking.

For a flavorful gravy to serve with roast duck, I nearly always put 2 orange halves in the body cavity. This way the mingled juices can be poured out at the end of cooking to be added to the gravy.

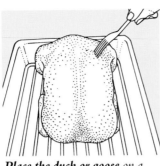

Place the duck or goose *on a rack in the roasting pan and pierce the skin all over with a fork. This allows the fat to run out during roasting and helps the skin become crisp and golden. Save the fat for roasting potatoes (page 57).*

ROASTING CHART

All timings are guidelines only. Check for doneness by piercing the bird between the thigh and breast. For just cooked birds, the juices should run clear. (Or, use a meat thermometer which should reach 160°F, 70°C.) If not return the bird to the oven. Juices from just pink birds such as ducks should have a slight pinky hue. Allow an extra 10 minutes cooking time for stuffed birds. After roasting, allow the bird to sit for 10–15 minutes to firm up for easier carving.

Bird	Temperature	Time
Chicken	375°F, 190°C	Allow 20 minutes per 1lb (500g) plus 20 minutes
Cornish hen	375°F, 190°C	45–75 minutes total cooking, depending on size
Duckling	400°F, 200°C	Allow 20 minutes per 1lb (500g) for 'rare' and 25 minutes for fully cooked
Goose	350°F, 180°C	Allow 20 minutes per 1lb (500g) plus 20 minutes
Pheasant	400°F, 200°C	50 minutes total cooking
Guinea fowl	400°F, 200°C	20 minutes per 1lb (500g) plus 25 minutes
Wild duck	400°F, 200°C	1–2 hours total cooking
Grouse	425°F, 220°C	35–40 minutes total cooking
Quail	425°F, 220°C	30 minutes total cooking
Partridge	425°F, 220°C	40 minutes total cooking
Turkey 8–10lb (3.6–4.5kg)	325°F, 160°C	3½–3¾ hours
11–12lb (5–5.4kg)		3¾–4 hours
12–14lb (5.4–6.3kg)		4–4¼ hours
14–16lb (6.3–7.2kg)		4¼–4½ hours
16–18lb (7.2–8.1kg)		4½–4¾ hours
8.1–9kg (18–20lb)		4¾–5 hours

FLAVORING AND SERVING ROAST BIRDS

• For flavoring butter to spread under the skin of a bird while roasting you can include fresh herbs, particularly tarragon, crushed or finely chopped garlic and fresh ginger, or ground aromatic Sichuan pepper and five-spice powder for a Chinese flavor. Ground Indian spices or curry paste with chopped fresh cilantro leaves add an Indian touch.

• For a more elaborate result also try pesto sauce, finely chopped anchovies with garlic, finely chopped arugula or watercress with cinnamon, finely grated lemon and orange rind, sun-dried tomato paste with fresh chopped basil and even slices of black truffle.

• A mixture of butter and an equal quantity of Brie or garlic and herb cream cheese is also very effective spread under a bird's skin.

• With small game birds I often put some garlic and herb cream cheese inside the body cavity – when emptied out at the end of roasting and mixed with the juices this makes the most delicious gravy, particularly with the addition of a little dry or medium sherry.

• Stuffings add both flavor and a different dimension to a roast bird. A stuffing should be simply a mixture of good flavors and textures. Eggs can be used to bind the mixture if it is dry but moist ingredients usually hold together well.

• For ducks and geese fruit and nut stuffings are ideal with combinations of apple, dried apricots, peaches or prunes, fresh plums, walnuts, pecans, hazelnuts, almonds and pistachio nuts.

• Pistachio nuts also go well in a well seasoned, ground poultry or pork stuffing mixture.

• Whole wheat breadcrumbs make a good stuffing mixed with lemon juice and rind and plenty of fresh herbs.

• Pommes soufflées (page 43), are similar to "game chips" which are traditional with game in England. If you want to avoid the smell and labor of deep-frying you can buy the best frozen French fries you can find, toss them in some game drippings and heat them on a baking sheet in the oven.

• Mashed potatoes also go well with the juices of roast birds – try infusing a few threads of saffron into hot milk or cream before mixing it into the cooked potatoes when you mash them (page 53).

KEEPING BIRDS MOIST

Buttering under the skin is an excellent way of stopping the breast meat from drying out and at the same time adding flavor. I also rub the skin with olive oil or butter and sprinkle it with sea salt to produce a crisp golden appearance when cooked. Another way of keeping the bird moist is to lay a large sheet of buttered foil over it, but not wrapped tightly, or you simply produce a steamed, rather than roasted, bird.

Another way I sometimes use for large birds is to drape the bird with cheesecloth dipped in plenty of melted butter which you remove for the last 30 minutes so the bird can brown well.

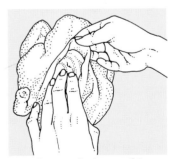

Gently ease the breast skin *from the meat, working between them with your fingertips and being careful not to tear the skin. Spread a generous amount of flavored butter at room temperature evenly over the meat and around the breast area of the bird. Finally, rub the skin with olive oil or a little more butter. The bird is now ready for roasting (see chart left).*

FRYING *and* STIR-FRYING

Ever since I treated myself to a heavy copper frying pan sautéing and stir-frying have become my favorite ways of cooking. As it has deep sides the pan is perfect for both sautéing and shallow frying or pan frying, which are the best ways of retaining the succulence of larger pieces of poultry with the bonus of an enticingly golden, crisp exterior. It is much easier to control the heat of the oil when frying by gas as the heat can be changed instantly if you see that it is becoming too hot or cool. With most electric units it is a question of moving the pan off the heat briefly while it cools a little. With all frying it is important to watch and adjust the temperature the whole time you are frying, and never to leave the stove.

For deep-frying the temperature of the cooking oil should be high and more exact – between 350°F and 385°F (180°C and 195°C). Butter is not suitable for high or deep-frying temperatures so use a vegetable oil. One of the things people have against deep-frying is the smell of the oil, so I like to use peanut oil which has practically no aroma. The pieces of poultry are usually dipped in a coating of egg and breadcrumbs and should not be too large or they will burn on the outside before cooking through. The temperature of the oil will fall when you add the pieces and from then on you must watch and regulate the heat so that a normal chicken piece will turn a rich golden brown in 7–10 minutes.

Duck and goose are so fatty that they should only be dry pan-fried, and you will have to pour off the fat which will emerge from them. Slivers of skinless duck or goose can be successfully sautéed.

FRYING CHICKEN

Fried chicken either with a crisp crumb or a light flour coating is a quite delicious way to cook young birds. Deep-frying is best for crumb coatings, shallow frying, also called pan frying, and sautéing are best for flour-coated birds. Unseasoned dried breadcrumbs give the most attractive color coating, but you can also use matzo meal or cornmeal. White breadcrumbs, which I prefer, give a golden coating.

It is important to fry at the correct temperature. If the oil is too hot, the skin and coating will start to burn while the center is still raw. If the oil is not hot enough, the coating will not crisp enough to form a barrier between the oil and the meat and the cooked chicken will be too greasy.

Cut a chicken into 8 pieces (page 175) and remove the skin to lower the overall fat content, if desired.

Tasty-looking shallow-fried chicken drumsticks with moist juicy meat inside a rich golden brown coating of paprika-seasoned flour. Using paprika or other spices adds extra flavor and color to the flour coating.

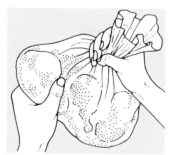

1 *To prepare chicken pieces for deep-frying toss the chicken first in seasoned flour in a plastic bag until well coated. Shake off the excess flour. Have a bowl of beaten egg and one of breadcrumbs ready.*

2 *Dip floured pieces first in egg, then in crumbs, spooning the crumbs over evenly. For a thicker crunchier crumb repeat the egg and crumbing. Chill on a plate for 1 hour. This helps the coating stick to the meat.*

3 *Half fill a deep-frying pan with oil. Heat the oil to 375°F (190°C) or until a cube of white bread browns in 30 seconds. Lower 3 or 4 pieces at a time into the basket, and cook for 7–10 minutes depending on size. Drain well on paper towels. Repeat with the remaining pieces, reheating the oil first.*

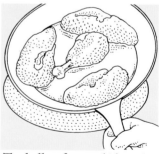

To shallow fry *toss chicken pieces in seasoned flour in a plastic bag. Shake off the excess flour. Heat 4–6 tablespoons vegetable oil in a heavy frying pan until nearly smoking, then add the pieces, shaking the pan to keep them from sticking. Cook over a medium heat for 12–15 minutes, turning once.*

STIR-FRYING

Stir-frying in a wok is a traditional Chinese way of cooking meats and vegetables, although a wok is not strictly necessary. Any large, deep, heavy frying pan will do.

Chicken, being lean and tender, is the ideal meat for stir-frying. Very thinly sliced duck breast is also successful, especially if you remove the fatty skin and cook the slivers of meat quickly so they remain pink and juicy.

Ingredients for stir-frying should be cut into thin, even-sized slices or strips, cubes or dice – some small vegetables such as snow pea pods can be added whole. Vegetables, such as zucchini, which only need brief cooking are excellent.

At the end of the cooking you can add some liquid and cornstarch to form a shiny thickened sauce, but I frequently find that the cooking juices with a little extra liquid are all that are necessary. Quantities for stir-frying need not be exact but for 4 people you will need about 1lb (500g) boneless chicken, depending on the quantity of other ingredients. Use about 2 tablespoons of oil for each 1lb (500g) ingredients.

Thinly sliced duck breast is an excellent choice for a stir-fry dish. Slices of shiitake mushrooms, yellow pepper, fresh gingerroot and garlic add delicate flavorings, and thinly sliced green onions are delicious stirred in at the last moment before serving.

1 *Slice skinless poultry breasts across in thin slices and marinate (page 182). Slice vegetables to roughly the same size, leaving small ones whole, and lay them out in the order of cooking. Prepare flavorings such as peeled and chopped garlic and ginger, chopped herbs or ground spices.*

2 *Heat the oil in a wok or large frying pan over a high heat. Stir in the drained marinated poultry slices (reserving the marinade) and cook for 3–4 minutes, stirring constantly. Then add the ginger and garlic, or spices, but no fresh green herbs yet. Stir constantly for 1 minute.*

3 *Stir in the prepared vegetables, starting with those that take longest to cook and adding the remainder at 30 second intervals. Cook, tossing and stirring the vegetables for a few minutes, until all the vegetables are tender but still crunchy. It helps to shake the wok occasionally.*

4 *Pour in the marinade and a little extra soy sauce, sherry, lemon juice or stock. If you like a shiny sauce mix 1 teaspoon cornstarch with 1–2 tablespoons of water until smooth, then stir in. Boil the sauce, stirring for 1 minute until thickened. Stir in chopped green onion or fresh herbs. Serve at once.*

MAKING THE MOST OF FRYING

• When making up an egg and bread crumb coating first season the bread crumbs, which can be either white or brown, white making the most golden crust. As well as sea salt and black pepper, dried herbs, particularly oregano, are a good addition. Ground spices such as coriander, cinnamon or whole cumin or caraway seeds are also excellent for adding extra flavor to the coating.

• Finely grated fresh Parmesan cheese and paprika, mixed with bread crumbs give the browned chicken a reddish tinge.

• Extra-crunchy ingredients to add to flour include finely chopped nuts, matzo meal, cornmeal, rice flour and, a favorite of mine, semolina.

• A little semolina added to a normal egg and bread crumb coating also adds crunchiness.

• Boned turkey and chicken breasts are ideal to cut into nugget-size pieces, then coat with batter and deep fry. They are also perfect to cut in thin slivers for stir-frying; in this case they need no coating, only seasoning, and if more flavor and tenderness are needed, marinate them beforehand (page 182).

• I often finely chop skinless chicken and turkey filets in the food processor, or by hand. The meat can then be formed into small balls and sautéed. Because chicken and turkey breast meat tends to be dry and bland, seasoning and extra moisture are important. Extra finely chopped fresh herbs, spinach, zucchini, tomato, finely grated lemon rind or grated cheese will all add moisture.

• A very successful way of using the above balls is to press a cube of cheese into the middle of each one. The cheese melts during cooking so that the ball reveals a delicious liquid center. Try blue cheese, mozzarella or goat cheese.

• With shallow frying or sautéing, the small amount of oil and butter you use really makes a difference in the flavor of the sauce so use extra virgin olive oil, creamy unsalted butter or, for a nutty flavor, walnut or hazelnut oil. With Chinese-style seasonings, try using a very little toasted sesame oil.

• Be sure to save the fat that accumulates in the frying pan after frying pieces of duck or goose to make the best roast potatoes (page 57).

GRILLING *and* BROILING

There are moments when one longs for the natural taste of food which grilling and broiling bring out. The only drawback to grilled poultry and game birds is that the pieces can dry out, and this is why marinating is particularly useful for ingredients you are going to grill or broil. Marinating keeps in and adds natural moisture and flavor, as well as being a tenderizer. A yogurt marinade alters the texture of the meat most noticeably as you will realize when eating Indian grilled and baked tandoori meats. As well as yogurt, marinades can be made from a mixture of oil and lemon juices, or wine.

Whole chicken breast filets are too bland and lean to grill without marinating – they can be extremely dry and dull. If you cut them up into pieces, marinate them well and skewer them flanked by vegetables for kebobs, however, they will have tenderness, moisture and flavor.

Pieces of chicken, duck and other game birds all grill well. Cornish hens are extremely tender so they just need seasoning but not marinating, and are best split before grilling to make them the right thickness to cook evenly all the way through.

The best tastes of all are those of food grilled over the embers of a wood fire, particularly if you use aromatic fruit woods like apple wood. Charcoal is also wonderful, with a smell which transports me instantly to the Mediterranean or Middle East. But the smell of marinated birds broiling under an ordinary gas or electric broiler can be almost as evocative, if lacking the romance of an outside meal.

MARINATING POULTRY

There are several simple ways to marinate poultry. A liquid marinade is oil with another liquid such as lemon juice, wine, fruit juice or various alcohols plus seasoning. Or, a moist marinade can be simply a seasoned yogurt mixture.

Flavors can also be added to the meat with a dry marinade; simply rub spices and herbs directly into the skin and leave overnight. Keep marinating pieces in a covered, non-metallic dish in the refrigerator and spoon with the marinade from time to time. Leave at least 1 hour.

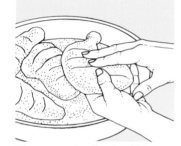

Yogurt marinades should be rubbed into the meat. Deep slashes help the marinade penetrate and tenderize the meat. Place the meat in a shallow, non-metallic dish, spoon over any remaining marinade, cover and place in the refrigerator.

BROILING POULTRY BREASTS

When broiling you must watch carefully and adjust the heat if the outside of the breasts are browning too quickly, giving no time for the centers to cook properly. Broiled duck breast filets are a great favorite in my house. They are simple and quick to do, and when thinly sliced lengthwise into pink juicy strips, look and taste sophisticated.

For either duck or squab breasts I usually make a slightly sweet marinade which could be a mixture of olive oil, orange juice, a little sherry or balsamic vinegar, with finely chopped garlic and fresh herbs such as tarragon, dill or oregano. Season the marinade with plenty of black pepper and sea salt and place the breasts flesh side down in a dish in which they fit closely so that the marinade is all around them. Spoon the marinade over the breasts from time to time.

Before broiling rub the skin with either honey or sugar and salt so that the skin blackens and crisps under the hot grill and forms a dark border to the pink flesh when the breasts are sliced. A certain amount of charring adds a smokiness I like.

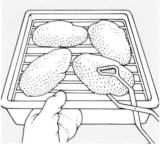

Place marinated duck breasts under a hot broiler for 3–5 minutes until the skin is dark brown, then turn over and repeat on the other side. The meat inside will be pink and juicy.

To broil chickens evenly, cut along the backbone and flatten.

KEBOBS

Kebobs made with various pieces of boneless turkey or chicken, interspersed with colorful vegetables, look pretty and are simple and fun to put together. Marinate skinless pieces of meat for extra tenderness and flavor.

Grilled kebobs are usually served with a sauce, which could be an Indonesian satay sauce made with spiced peanut butter, or one like Japanese yakitori, based on soy sauce. Or make yogurt-based sauces with an Indian touch by stirring in a little curry paste and chopped fresh cilantro.

Marinated pieces of skinless chicken are threaded onto skewers with strips of yellow and red peppers, button mushrooms, slices of zucchini and fresh herbs to make colorful tasty kebobs.

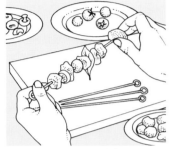

Colorful kebobs Fill skewers with marinated 2in (5cm) cubes of boneless meat, alternating with vegetables all roughly the same size. Brush with oil and cook under a hot broiler or on a grill, turning once or twice, basting with boiled marinade.

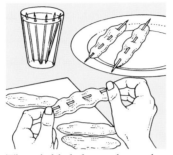

Threaded kebobs are skewered accordion-style onto wooden skewers, which should be soaked in water beforehand to prevent them from burning. Cut skinless and boneless pieces of poultry into long strips about ½in (1cm) wide and marinate before skewering.

BARBECUING TIPS

• One of the things it is easy to forget when there is suddenly a fine day and you are filled with enthusiasm about having a barbecue is to start in good time. Charcoal or wood must be left until the flames have subsided to produce just smoldering, white-looking charcoal or glowing embers before starting to cook. This process will take at least 30 minutes.

• Precook whole birds or 2 large halves to save time barbecuing. Finishing over the charcoal or wood adds the authentic smoky taste but the meat may not be quite so aromatic or succulent.

• To cook a whole bird or large poultry pieces entirely on the barbecue you can make a loose hood of foil (these days many barbecues have their own lid) which keeps in the heat so that cooking is more even and makes the poultry even more intensely smoky in flavor.

• When cooking over wood remember that fruit woods will add their aroma to the meat, as will pieces of woody herbs such as rosemary or bay added to the embers or to charcoal. Juniper wood produces the most wonderful aroma.

• Let marinades add variety to barbecued food. Oil-based marinades can be olive, sesame or other vegetable and nut oils, mixed with lemon juice, wine, sherry or other alcohols, aromatic vinegars and soy sauce or various fruit juices.

• Add chopped garlic and fresh ginger, spices of all kinds, herbs and pastes such as tomato, and aromatic peppers such as green peppercorns and Sichuan pepper to a liquid marinade.

• Yogurt, seasoned with herbs, spices or Indian pastes is a very effective marinade as it tenderizes the toughest meat if left for several hours.

• Sesame seeds mixed with a marinade add crunchiness and extra flavor.

FLATTENING

This is a most attractive and tasty way of grilling or broiling small birds such as Cornish hens and quail. The birds are opened out flat, then prevented from curling back to their original shape during cooking by being held in position with two long criss-crossed skewers.

In Britain and Ireland this process is called "spatchcocking" because of an Irish expression for preparing an impromptu meal for unexpected guests. A chicken was 'dispatched', or killed, before being quickly split, flattened and then fried.

Cook the birds simply basted with oil and seasoning or marinated with spices and herbs which will give an attractive speckled appearance to the cooked birds. Grill them for 5–10 minutes on each side according to size, basting during cooking. Sprinkle with fresh lemon juice to serve, if you like.

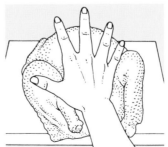

1 Using a large very sharp knife or poultry shears, cut through the backbone and open out the bird, flattening it firmly with the palm of your hand.

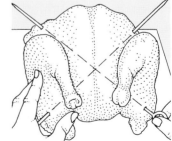

2 Stick metal skewers or long wooden satay sticks diagonally through the bird to hold it flat. Quail can be skewered side by side, 2 birds on 1 skewer.

STEWING *and* POT-ROASTING

Stewing and pot-roasting are long, gentle methods of cooking in a covered pot, which need minimum attention but can produce the most delectable results. With slow cooking the meat gradually becomes meltingly tender and absorbs the essence of ingredients and flavorings with which it is cooked. These methods are ideal for older poultry and game birds which might otherwise be rather tough and dry. Squab, pheasant and mallard are ideal candidates, as well as mature chicken.

Stews are usually made from parts or smaller boneless pieces of meat and cooked in a covered Dutch oven. The liquid in which stews cook is plentiful and often thickened, and vegetables are usually added during cooking. Stews can also have unthickened juices, and can be cooked on top of the stove. Pot-roasting and braising are very similar as the ingredients are cooked with little or no liquid and vegetables are usually added so the meat juices flavor the vegetables and vice versa. Pot-roasting is for whole birds, whereas both whole and cut up birds can be braised.

Preliminary frying of the meat adds both color and flavor but is by no means obligatory if you have little time. After the frying, liquid is added in which the ingredients cook; this can include wine, good stock, the marinade mixture if the meat has been marinated, fruit juices or even cream.

The most important thing about slow cooking is that it really is slow; the liquid should be barely trembling. Too high a temperature toughens the meat, and the flavors of meat, vegetables and seasonings merge better without the turbulence of boiling. Vegetables should be added at different times, depending on how long they take to cook. Add green vegetables, such as broccoli or snow peas, at the end of cooking so they remain bright green.

Casseroled Quail in a Pear Tree (page 192): quail cooked slowly with pears and tomatoes. Quail are ideal birds for stewing as it prevents their delicate flesh from drying out.

STEWING CORNISH HENS

I often stew or braise Cornish hens, and you can adapt this method for squab or other game birds with vegetables of your choice. First quarter lengthwise 2 fennel bulbs, finely chop 3 cloves garlic and a 2in (5cm) piece fresh ginger and skin and chop 1lb (500g) tomatoes (page 48). Have ready 4 Cornish hens, 3 strips orange rind, 1 teaspoon ground mace, 1 tablespoon all-purpose flour, ½ cup (125ml) stock and the juice of 1 orange. Serves 4.

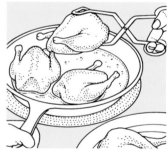

1 Heat a small amount of olive oil and butter in a heavy frying pan over a high heat. Brown 4 whole or halved Cornish hens all over, then remove from the pan and set aside.

2 Fry the fennel until golden, then add the garlic and ginger for 1 minute. Transfer to a Dutch oven with the tomatoes, orange rind and mace. Stir in the flour, add the stock and orange juice and season. Then return to the heat.

3 Bring to a boil, stirring until the sauce has thickened. Add the Cornish hens on top of the vegetables, cover and cook in a preheated oven, 300°F, 150°C for 2½–3 hours until the birds are very tender when tested with the tip of a knife.

POT-ROASTING PHEASANT

This is an excellent method for cooking game birds, such as pheasants, which can be tough and dry. If you cook a few vegetables in the dish, too, they will also add flavor. The liquid of a pot roast, gently reduced by long simmering, turns into an intense sauce. Before cooking, slice 2 onions and have ready 2 teaspoons sugar, 1 teaspoon crushed juniper berries, 2 teaspoons ground coriander and 1lb (500g) well-scrubbed whole small carrots. One pheasant serves 2–3.

Or, use your favorite vegetables to flavor other birds. Parsnips and turnips with a little added honey are successful, as are skinned and chopped tomatoes.

Cornish hens are delicious cooked by a slow method such as pot-roasting. Slices of pumpkin and small onions are cooked with the birds to give added flavors.

1 *Heat 2 tablespoons olive oil and 1oz (25g) butter in a Dutch oven over a fairly high heat. Fry the pheasant on all sides until browned. Remove the pheasant using wooden spoons so the skin isn't pierced; set aside.*

2 *Add the sliced onions and stir until browned. Stir in the sugar, juniper berries, ground coriander and carrots. Season with salt and pepper. Return the browned pheasant to the Dutch oven on top of the vegetables.*

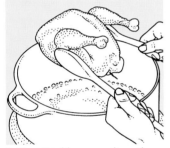

3 *Add about ⅓ cup (75ml) dry vermouth or white wine, cover and cook in a preheated oven, 325°F, 160°C for 2–3 hours until tender. Transfer to a warm serving dish.*

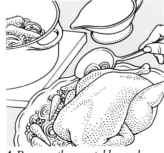

4 *Remove the vegetables and arrange around the pheasant. To make a sauce add ⅔ cup (150ml) heavy cream to the juices and bring to a boil for about 2 minutes, stirring.*

FLAVORING STEWS AND POT ROASTS

• Fresh herbs should always be added to stews at the very end of cooking. If a bouquet garni was added at the beginning of cooking discard it and replace with fresh herbs for serving.

• Sweetness brings out savory flavors and sweet vegetables such as carrots, parsnips and sweet potatoes can be very effective cooked with game birds.

• Fruit such as pears, apples and plums are excellent with pheasants, but need only be added halfway through the cooking or they become too mushy.

• Dried fruits, particularly apricots and prunes, are excellent in a game stew.

• Cinnamon has a special affinity with chicken.

• Game is good cooked with a few whole cloves and some caraway seeds. Coriander seems to go well with almost everything, and you can experiment with many other spices, including Chinese five-spice powder.

• Soy sauce, as well as wines, spirits, liqueurs, citrus and other fruit juices, tomato juice and puree and good stocks can all be used for the liquid in stews and pot roasts.

• Cream stirred into a stew at the end, or used to make a sauce for pot-roasted birds, always adds a luscious sophistication to a dish. Sour cream or plain yogurt can also be used. Do not boil the juices after adding yogurt or they will curdle.

• Apart from soft, sweet onions, some of the other vegetables I particularly like in stews and pot roasts which take well to slow cooking are leeks, bulb fennel, eggplant, parsnips and, of course, carrots and tomatoes.

• Zucchini can be cooked slowly, too, but I prefer them added towards the end of the cooking so they are still slightly crunchy and brightly colored in comparison to all the other soft, mellow-colored ingredients.

• Cremini mushrooms, which have more body than the ordinary button variety, are the best to use for long cooking. For a special treat, try fresh shiitake mushrooms or soaked dried mushrooms for their intense flavors.

POACHING *and* STEAMING

Poaching and steaming are simple, healthy and efficient ways of cooking which retain moisture, tenderness and flavor in a bird. Both these methods have the advantage of using no added fat. Poaching is particularly good for stewing hens and older game birds which could be tough.

Poaching is often confused with boiling but 'poaching' is a far better term because the important thing to remember is that although the liquid surrounding the bird is brought up to the boil initially, it should thereafter barely simmer, retaining only a gentle shuddering instead of bubbling. This is because strong boiling toughens birds and makes them stringy; it is the gentleness of simmering which results in the tender fine texture characteristic of poached poultry. Game birds, which tend to be dry, are also very good poached, especially with whole spices and fruit juices in the liquid.

For poaching, it is important that a bird is completely immersed in the liquid but since the flavors will dilute too much in a large quantity of water use a Dutch oven in which the bird, and vegetables if using, fit tightly. Apart from being eaten as a main course with its vegetables, the meat from a poached bird is excellent in pot pies or for sandwiches, salads, or any dish which requires cold poultry or game. After removing the bird the flavorful liquid can be eaten as a delicate broth on its own or reduced and thickened and used to make a sauce or soup.

Steaming is a slower cooking process than poaching and is excellent for boned chicken or turkey breasts and other pieces of boneless poultry. Steaming can be done on any rack or tray suspended over boiling water as long as it is tightly covered. If you do not have a steamer it is possible to improvise by using two heatproof plates large enough to fit over the top of a saucepan. Place thin slices of poultry on the surface of one plate over a pan of simmering water. Top with an upside-down plate and leave for about 5 minutes until the meat is cooked through.

POACHING A WHOLE CHICKEN

As well as whole birds, poultry pieces can also be poached successfully to keep the flesh moist and tender. **The Chicken Breast Rolls with Wine and Parsley Sauce recipe (page 190) uses chicken breast filets which are wrapped up like a jelly roll round a flavorful filling and then poached.**

Poach the bird with a selection of coarsely chopped vegetables and other flavorings such as fresh herbs and spices for 20–25 minutes per 1lb (500g), according to the age and size of the bird. Time from when the water comes to a boil. Good vegetables for adding flavor to the poaching water are chopped onions, carrots, leeks or celery.

Test the bird for 'doneness' as you would do for roasting (page 178), and if the juices run clear the bird is cooked through. If you intend dicing the meat you can actually cut into the leg to check whether it is cooked or not.

If you are eating the bird cold, for a moister texture, allow the cooked bird to cool in the liquid. This is not, however, recommended in warm weather when the bird should be cooled out of the stock as quickly as possible, then stored well covered in the refrigerator for up to 3 days.

1 *Truss the bird (page 174) with kitchen string before poaching, if you like, so it retains its shape after cooking. Place the bird in the smallest saucepan it will fit and fill with water. Add the coarsely chopped vegetables of your choice and any other flavorings.*

2 *Season with fresh herbs and spices, of your choice, then bring to a boil. Skim any foam that rises to the top, then partially cover, lower the heat and simmer gently until cooked and the juices run clear when tested with the tip of a knife.*

STEAMING

Steaming is an ideal method for cooking tender pieces of poultry breast, especially if they have been marinated beforehand in Chinese- or Japanese-style sauces.

You can use a traditional metal steamer that fits on top of a saucepan, or a modern electric one, but perhaps the most attractive way to steam is using an oriental bamboo steamer that fits into a wok.

The best cuts of poultry for steaming are breasts, or small whole birds such as quail or Cornish hens. Old birds can be tenderized by first steaming them whole, and patting them dry before rubbing with aromatic flavorings and roasting.

Steaming oriental-style, using an attractive bamboo steaming basket and flavorings such as whole star anise, finely sliced green onions and fresh cilantro leaves. Far from being a bland method of cooking pieces of poultry steaming can impart some exciting flavors to the lean flesh as well as keeping it moist.

1 *Marinate chicken breasts for steaming oriental-style in light soy sauce, dry sherry and a few drops of sesame oil for 10 minutes. Slash the breasts each side for even heat penetration. Place in the top of a steamer.*

2 *Half fill the bottom of the steamer with water and bring to a boil over a high heat. Add a selection of fresh herbs or other flavorings to the water. This will give extra flavor to the steamed poultry.*

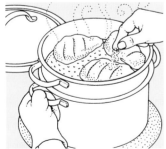

3 *Place the top half of the steamer over the water, making sure no water comes through the holes. Sprinkle sliced green onions, shredded ginger or spices over the poultry. Cover and steam about 10 minutes until the juices run clear when tested with a knife.*

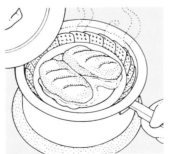

Adapt a collapsible metal steamer so you can steam marinated food without losing all the delicious juices into the boiling water below. Remove the central handle from the steamer and place the poultry on a small heatproof plate in the bottom.

POACHING AND STEAMING TIPS

• To preserve a chicken's white flesh rub it all over with lemon juice before poaching in water with lemon juice or white wine vinegar added to it.
• Additions to poaching water can be whole spices of all kinds, bay leaves, rosemary, tarragon, thyme or other strong herbs, coarsely chopped garlic, lemon and orange rind, whole peppercorns including green and Sichuan, tamarind pods, saffron and, for extra bite, 1 or 2 dried red chilies.
• I like to poach chicken pieces in aromatic tea such as Earl Grey which produces a delicate and interesting flavor, as well as a darkly stained exterior.
• Liquid additions to poaching or steaming water can be wine, sherry, Pernod for its aniseed flavor, and fruit juice.
• There are ingredients you can add to the cooking liquid which will color the eventual sauce when poaching. Tomatoes will add a light orangy red color, but you can also add 2–3 teaspoons paprika and some tomato puree to strengthen this. Saffron gives a yellow color, at a cost, but if the sauce is to be spicy you can add turmeric instead.
• If you grow marigolds in your garden the flowers will add a yellow color but no discernible taste.
• To make the liquid green you can either use spinach leaves or wrap compressed spinach leaves up in cheesecloth like a large bouquet garni so that the green juices come out during the cooking. The spinach should not be in the water for more than 1 hour or it will lose its bright green color.
• If there is not much cooking liquid left after the bird has been removed you can reduce it after straining it through a fine sieve and to make an excellent sauce without extra thickening, simply stir in heavy cream and boil for a minute or two. As a last touch, add chopped fresh green herbs.
• In addition to marinating pieces of poultry before steaming, you can also flavor the simmering water underneath with slivers of onions, fresh gingerroot, carrots or celery. This water can then be used to make sauces, as with poaching liquid (opposite), but it will probably not have such a full flavor. Or place poultry pieces on a bed of tasty lovage or mint leaves to impart more flavor.

CARVING *and* CUTTING

One of my earliest memories is of my father sharpening the carving knife with a steel. Being a jazz enthusiast, and an old-fashioned English eccentric, the sharpening process was always done to a jazz rhythm and, in fact, the sliding and clicking noises of steel against steel fitted it perfectly and produced a marvelously sharp knife as well.

An important step towards successful carving is to rest the bird in a warm place for 10–15 minutes after taking it out of the oven – this 'sets' the flesh and makes it easier to slice neatly. Remember to include this resting time when you calculate what time to start cooking the bird for a particular meal (page 179). Also, always remember the supreme importance of the knife's sharpness for successful carving; a blunt carving knife can induce fury and result in a wrecked bird. Slices should be as thin as you can manage and arranged on the plate rather than just thrown haphazardly onto it. Leg and wing pieces should be cut off as neatly as possible.

There are some people who never really take to carving and others who pride themselves on it. If you are the cook there are so many other things such as the vegetables or the gravy to attend to at this stage in the meal that it is worth asking if any of your guests, or a member of the family, would like to carve.

CARVING ROAST TURKEY OR CHICKEN

There is actually nothing difficult or mysterious about carving but a really sharp knife, ideally sharpened by a steel, is a must (page 16). Remember to cut across the grain of meat. This requires a little simple knowledge of anatomy and which way the meat fibers run. Cutting across the grain of meat shortens muscle fibers and means more tender meat. It is also worth remembering that white meat comes from the breast and dark meat from the rest of the body and the legs. Ideally you should serve a selection of both to your guests.

Don't be tempted to carve too far ahead or you may lose valuable meat juice. It is better to serve good juicy slices freshly cut than to try and save a few minutes.

Turkey and chicken are carved in the same way, while ducks and geese require a slightly different technique because of their different body shapes (opposite).

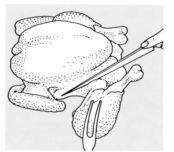

1 *Before starting to carve, remove all the trussing strings if the bird was trussed. Work on one side of the bird at a time. Cut through the thigh and breast skin, then pry the thigh away from the body. Locate the socket joint and pull the leg away from the body, cutting through the joint. There is no need to cut through the actual bone.*

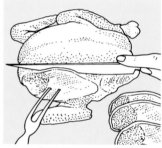

2 *Cut down across the breast in ¼in (5mm) slices, including stuffing if possible, otherwise spoon out the stuffing. Cut enough for 1 portion, then cut some leg meat. If you are carving a large turkey, you can save time by slicing the breast in advance and putting it back on the carcass before bringing the bird to the table.*

If carving a cold turkey for a large number it is worth thinking about attractive presentation. Arrange the carved slices in piles of white meat, dark meat and stuffing on a large plate with a garnish. Here, a few fresh cranberries, pieces of fresh fig and some cilantro leaves make a simple finishing touch.

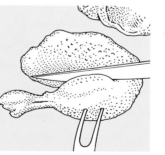

3 *Next, separate the thigh from the drumstick, slicing down between the joint. If the bird is small, however, you can leave the leg whole. For a better presentation cut or pull off the knuckle at the end of the drumstick and discard.*

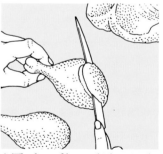

4 *The legs of larger chickens and turkeys should be carved into smaller pieces. For leg meat, hold the drumstick away from you and cut off slices. Cut the thigh across into several pieces. Discard the wing tip and only serve the wing if you are running out of other meat.*

CARVING DUCK OR GOOSE

Small ducks can be simply cut into quarters for serving but I prefer the long, narrow slices of breast meat achieved by normal carving. Larger ducks and geese are carved as below. Remember that because of the high bone content on these birds there is much less meat on them than on other poultry.

To carve a stuffed boned duck (page 177) remove the trussing strings and cut crosswise into neat, thin slices. If you make the stuffing with colorful ingredients this looks attractive presented on a pretty plate on a buffet table.

A roast goose is an old-fashioned tradition to serve on festive occasions.

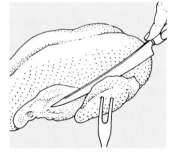

1 *A long thin-bladed knife is useful for carving a duck or goose. Pull the wings and legs away from the body and cut firmly through the joints. Put the legs aside for carving later. Wings on ducks have little meat and are not usually served.*

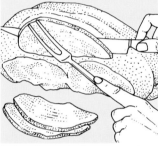

2 *Neatly cut the breast meat into long thin slices, working the full length of the carcass from the sides up toward the breastbone. Remove the slices carefully holding them between the carving knife and fork.*

3 *Large duck and goose legs can be carved into further pieces as for larger chickens or turkeys (opposite). Cut the leg into 2 pieces, thigh and drumstick, by slicing down between the joint. Cut slices off the drumstick and cut the thigh into several pieces.*

SMALL BIRDS

Pheasants can be carved in the same way as small chicken. For small guinea fowls, partridges and wild duck half a bird is usually just the right amount for each serving. Cut it before you bring it to the table. Small Cornish hens and quail are served whole. Allow 1 hen or 2 or 3 quail per person, depending on how large appetites are. Even young game birds can be tougher than farmed poultry and will need to be cut on plates after serving with sharp or serrated steak knives.

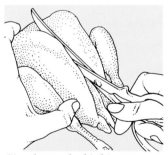

Simply cut the bird *in two through the breastbone and backbone with sharp poultry shears, then to serve place cut side down on individual plates. If you don't have poultry shears, use a sharp chef's knife.*

PRESENTING CARVED POULTRY AND GAME BIRDS

• Some Cornish hens are a bit too big to serve 1 per person, so instead of serving them on individual plates I usually halve the cooked birds and arrange them on a large serving plate with sprigs of fresh herbs or a cream sauce poured over them.
• Squab look wonderful all together on a serving plate with a glaze of seasoned honey warmed with a little balsamic vinegar spooned over them. This glaze can also be used with grouse on individual plates.
• A platter of cold carved meat is greatly enhanced by greenery. Lay the pieces on a bed of pretty greens such as the oak leaf or curly lettuces, feathery frisée, or simply watercress. If you grow it in your garden lovage leaves make a good border.
• You can also sprinkle fresh herbs such as dill, fennel or chopped parsley over the platter.
• I often make a mixture of lemon juice or good, fruity wine or sherry vinegar with extra virgin olive oil and plenty of chopped herbs, seasoned with sea salt and black pepper, and spoon it over the arranged meat – this both adds flavor to the meat and prevents it from drying out.

• Another way of presenting cold chicken or turkey is to arrange a wide border of thinly sliced breast edged with greens around the plate and then mix the small pieces of meat with either plain yogurt or mayonnaise and plenty of chopped fresh herbs and seasoning, and spoon it into the middle of the plate.
• A quick way of making Indian-style cold chicken or turkey, which is particularly useful for a party, is to stir curry paste into yogurt then mix with the carved meat and plenty of chopped fresh cilantro leaves.

CHICKEN IN ALMOND AND COCONUT MILK *(172)*

The character of this dish is Indian but you would be most unlikely to find almonds in the dishes of southern India or coconut milk in those of the north. My recipe combines both. It is quick to make, and convenient too, as it can be made ahead and reheated when required. Serve with saffron-flavored rice or Basmati Rice with Crisped Grains (page 114). *SERVES 6*

1 cup (75g) finely shredded
  unsweetened coconut
2 cups (450ml) boiling water
1 tablespoon sunflower oil
1oz (25g) butter
2 onions, finely chopped
1 teaspoon ground cardamom
1 teaspoon ground coriander
1 teaspoon ground cumin
1in (2.5cm) piece fresh gingerroot, peeled
  and finely chopped
1 large clove garlic, finely chopped
½ cup (75g) ground almonds
3–5 pinches chili powder
Salt
6 boned and skinned chicken thighs
Handful of fresh cilantro leaves, coarsely
  chopped

Put the shredded coconut in a bowl, pour over the boiling water and leave for at least 30 minutes.

Heat the oil and butter in a Dutch oven over a fairly high heat. Add the chopped onions and fry, stirring occasionally, until browned. Add the ground spices and the chopped ginger and garlic. Stir occasionally, then add the ground almonds and stir over the heat for another minute until thickened and brown. Remove the casserole from the heat.

Strain the water from the soaking coconut into the Dutch oven through a sieve. Using your hand squeeze the coconut in the sieve over and over again until all the liquid has been squeezed out of it. Discard the leftover coconut. Stir the coconut liquid into the casserole and season to taste with chili powder and salt.

Add the skinned pieces of chicken. Bring the mixture to a boil, cover and leave to simmer gently over a very low heat for about 1 hour. Remove from the heat and stir in the chopped cilantro leaves just before serving.

STEAMED CHICKEN IN YELLOW PEPPER AND DILL SAUCE *(172)*

I devised this recipe for a visiting friend on a low-fat diet. The pepper and dill sauce tastes almost creamy so it has none of the austerity of a dieter's dish. *SERVES 4*

2 yellow peppers, seeded and coarsely
  chopped (page 49)
3–4 large cloves garlic, halved
⅔ cup (150ml) water
Salt
4 chicken breast filets, skinned and cut
  crosswise into thin slices
Generous handful of fresh dill, chopped
3 tablespoons plain yogurt
3–4 pinches cayenne pepper
Fresh dill to garnish

Put the chopped peppers and garlic in a saucepan with the water and sprinkle in a little salt. Bring to a boil, cover and simmer gently for about 20 minutes until the peppers are very soft. Remove from the heat. Put the pepper, garlic and water in a food processor and process to a smooth puree. You can then strain through a fine sieve if you want an extra-smooth puree, but I don't think this is necessary.

Place a fairly shallow serving dish into a low oven to warm. Put the slices of chicken breast in a steamer and steam over boiling water for about 5 minutes until the slices are white all the way through. Arrange the chicken pieces in the warm serving dish, cover loosely with foil and keep warm in the oven.

Spoon the pepper puree into a saucepan and heat gently, stirring. Stir in the chopped dill and yogurt, then remove the sauce from the heat without allowing it to boil. Season to taste with cayenne pepper and salt. Pour the sauce over the chicken and garnish with more fresh dill. Serve at once.

CHICKEN BREAST ROLLS WITH WINE AND PARSLEY SAUCE *(186)*

Here chicken breast filets are wrapped round a thin layer of lemon rind, cottage cheese and capers in this delicious and easily made dish. The chicken rolls are then gently poached in the oven and served with a delicate, translucent sauce made with the cooking juices. Serve with hot new potatoes or buttered noodles and a green vegetable such as French beans. *SERVES 4*

Finely grated rind of 2 lemons
3 teaspoons capers, finely chopped
1 tablespoon cottage cheese
1 teaspoon sugar
Sea salt and black pepper
4 large chicken breast filets, skinned
4 tablespoons lemon juice, strained
⅔ cup (150ml) white wine
2 teaspoons cornstarch mixed with a small
  amount of water
1 teaspoon clover honey
Large handful of parsley, finely chopped

Put the grated lemon rind, chopped capers, cottage cheese and sugar in a small bowl and mix together thoroughly. Season well with crushed sea salt and black pepper.

Cut the chicken breast filets in half crosswise and lay spaced apart on a large sheet of wet parchment paper or foil on a firm work surface. Put another sheet on top and beat the filets evenly with a rolling pin or heavy flat implement until the pieces of breast are spread out and fairly thin.

Spread the lemon rind, cottage cheese and caper mixture thinly on each piece of chicken, then roll up fairly loosely like a jelly roll.

Lay the rolls, cut side down, in a fairly shallow ovenproof dish in which they fit closely in a single layer. (By putting the chicken rolls close together you prevent them from unrolling during cooking.) Pour the lemon juice and wine over the rolls.

Cover the dish with foil and leave to marinate for at least 30 minutes before cooking. If you have time to marinate the chicken for several hours, put the dish in the refrigerator but bring it out to return to room temperature 30 minutes before cooking.

Cook the chicken rolls, still covered

with foil, in the center of a preheated oven, 375°F, 190°C for 35–40 minutes until white and just lightly cooked through. Test with the tip of a knife; there shouldn't be any pink juices. Carefully pour all the juices off into a saucepan and leave the dish of chicken rolls in a warm place while you make the sauce.

Stir the cornstarch and water mixture into the juices. Bring to a boil, stirring as the sauce bubbles and thickens for at least 5 minutes. Stir in the honey and season to taste with salt and black pepper. Finally stir in the chopped parsley and remove from the heat. Pour any juice that has come from the chicken rolls while you made the sauce into the finished sauce and stir in before spooning over the rolls and serving.

AROMATIC CHICKEN WITH PILAF (174)

In this aromatic dish pieces of chicken are cooked on top of the puree of apples, onion, garlic and chicory mixed with bulgar, also called cracked wheat. The mixture produces a wonderful combination of contrasting flavours and textures, and the pilaf is made even tastier by the juices of the chicken which run into it as it cooks. Serve with a crisp green vegetable such as broccoli, and with sautéed potatoes or buttered noodles.   *SERVES 6*

½ cup (75g) bulgar
2 tablespoons olive oil
1 large onion, sliced
5–6 whole allspice berries
3 large cloves garlic, coarsely chopped
1in (2.5cm) piece fresh gingerroot, peeled
*   and coarsely chopped*
4 large apples, unpeeled, cored and fairly
*   thinly sliced*
4 heads Belgian endive, sliced
Salt and black pepper
6 chicken pieces, such as breasts,
*   drumsticks or thighs*
Extra virgin olive oil
3 tablespoons plain yogurt
1 clove garlic, finely chopped
3 tablespoons pine nuts or
*   split almonds*

Put the bulgar in a bowl, cover with plenty of cold water and leave to soak for at least 10 minutes.

Meanwhile, put the olive oil in a large, deep frying pan over a medium heat. Add the sliced onion and stir for 1–2 minutes, then add the allspice berries, garlic and ginger, apples and endive. Cook, stirring frequently, for 10–20 minutes or until the apples and onions are soft but not browned. Sprinkle with a little black pepper and salt.

Spoon the mixture into a food processor, picking out the whole allspice as you do so. Process until smooth, then check the seasoning again – the puree should be well seasoned at this stage as it is going to be mixed with the mild bulgar.

Drain the bulgar, squeezing out the excess water with your hand, then stir it into the puree. Spoon the mixture into a large, wide ovenproof Dutch oven and spread level.

Rub each of the chicken pieces with a little extra virgin olive oil and sprinkle with salt and black pepper.

Arrange the chicken pieces on top of the puree and bulgar, then cover the Dutch oven and cook in the center of a preheated oven, 375°F, 190°C for 1 hour. Remove the Dutch oven from the oven and increase the temperature to 475°F, 240°C.

Put the yogurt in a bowl and mix in the garlic. Using a pastry brush apply this mixture thickly over the chicken pieces. Scatter the pine nuts or split almonds on top all over.

Return the uncovered Dutch oven back to the oven at the very top for 10–20 minutes until the pieces are tinged with brown. Remove from the oven and serve right from the Dutch oven or on individual plates.

ROASTED CHICKEN WITH CILANTRO AND LIME (172)

One small chicken per person is generous but half of one, is, I think, definitely skimping. A whole bird on your plate also looks more impressive so serve this for a small dinner. Flavorful cheese under the skin and bacon on the breast keep the birds tender.   *SERVES 4*

3oz (75g) cream cheese
1 tablespoon lemon juice
Large bunch of fresh cilantro leaves
2in (5cm) piece fresh gingerroot, peeled
*   and very finely chopped*
Finely grated rind and juice of 2 limes
4 1lb (500g) chickens
12–16 strips bacon
1¼ cups (300ml) heavy cream
Salt and black pepper

Put the cream cheese into a bowl with the lemon juice and work with a wooden spoon to soften and mix. Reserve about 2 tablespoons of the smallest cilantro leaves and chop the remaining leaves coarsely. Stir the chopped cilantro, ginger and grated lime rind into the cheese mixture.

Lift up the skin of the chickens from the neck end and carefully insert your fingers to separate the skin from the flesh. Cut a small slit in the skin of the inside leg of each bird and stick a finger in to loosen the skin from the thighs, too. Using your fingertips place the cheese paste under the skin of the birds and press from the top to distribute the paste all over the breasts and the thighs. Place the strips of bacon over the breasts and thighs of the chickens, cutting the bacon to fit. Put the chickens in a roasting pan and cook in a preheated oven, 375°F, 190°C for 40–45 minutes. Transfer the birds to a warmed serving platter or individual plates.

Add the lime juice to the cooking juices in the roasting pan, then place it over a fairly high heat. Bring the juices to a boil and stir for 1 minute. Stir in the cream and boil again, still stirring, for 2–3 minutes until the sauce has thickened quite a bit. Remove from the heat and add the reserved cilantro leaves with salt and black pepper to taste.

Pour the sauce into a sauceboat to serve with the chickens or, if they are already on individual plates, spoon the sauce onto each plate.

DARK GLOSSY FRUITED DUCK (172)

This is a dish evocative of Morocco where meats, spices and fruits are often mixed together – with delicious results. It is very simple to prepare and so it is perfect for a dinner party. Serve with saffron-flavored rice or Basmati Rice with Crisped Grains (page 114) and a green salad.   SERVES 4

4 quarters of duck or 1 large duck, jointed (page 175)
Sunflower oil
3oz (75g) dried apricots
2 large cloves garlic, finely chopped
3 teaspoons paprika
2 teaspoons ground cinnamon
¾ teaspoon cayenne pepper
⅔ cup (150ml) apple juice
2 tablespoons honey mixed with ⅔ cup (150ml) warm water
4 tablespoons lemon juice
⅓ cup (50g) whole natural almonds
Salt
Good handful of fresh mint leaves, chopped

Pierce the skin of the duck quarters all over with a fork. Heat a little oil in a large frying pan and fry the duck quarters over a fairly high heat on both sides until they are just brown. Transfer the duck to a large saucepan and add the apricots, garlic, spices, cayenne pepper, apple juice, honey and water mixture, lemon juice and almonds. Bring the liquid to a boil, then cover and simmer gently for about 45 minutes or until the duck is tender and just cooked through, but still slightly pink.

Using a slotted spoon, remove the duck, apricots and almonds and arrange on a serving dish with the almonds mostly on top. Keep the dish warm in a very low oven.

Boil the remaining saucepan juices rapidly until they are reduced, thickened and glossy. Add salt and more cayenne pepper to taste. Just before serving, reheat the sauce, stir in the chopped mint leaves and spoon the sauce over the duck quarters.

STEWED QUAIL IN A PEAR TREE (184)

In the autumn when my garden is full of rather hard pears I find this simple stew a marvelous way to make use of them. They seem made for the delicate flavor of quail, which have more flesh on them than you would think. Don't be alarmed by the quantity of garlic – cooked long and gently it becomes sweet and mild.   SERVES 4

1 tablespoon olive oil
1oz (25g) butter
8 quail
1 small red pepper, seeded and finely sliced (page 49)
1 large bulb fennel, trimmed and thinly sliced (page 46)
1 teaspoon fennel seeds
6–8 cloves garlic
4 firm pears, peeled, quartered and cored
Salt and black pepper
14½oz (411g) can chopped tomatoes

Put the olive oil and butter in a large Dutch oven and heat to a fairly high heat. Add the quail, in batches if necessary, and turn until lightly browned all over. Remove the birds to a plate and keep on one side. Reduce the heat to medium, then add the sliced pepper and fennel to the Dutch oven and cook, stirring often, until softened. Add the fennel seeds and the whole cloves of garlic. Cook for another minute or two, then remove from the heat.

Arrange the pear pieces among the vegetable mixture and season with salt and black pepper. Place the quail on top, in 2 layers if necessary, and spoon the chopped tomatoes evenly over each quail. Season again with a little salt and black pepper. Cover the Dutch oven and cook just above the center of a preheated oven, 375°F, 190°C for 1–1¼ hours. Transfer to a serving dish or serve straight from the Dutch oven.

ROAST PHEASANTS INDIAN STYLE (178)

If you roast pheasants without seasoning them they can be dry and bland, and so one of the best ways to treat them is to use a spicy marinade. Serve with saffron-flavored rice and a green salad.   SERVES 6

FOR THE PHEASANTS AND MARINADE
2 oven-ready pheasants
2 large cloves garlic, very finely chopped
3 tablespoons peanut oil
2 tablespoons tomato puree
1 tablespoon wine vinegar
2 teaspoons ground cumin
3 teaspoons ground coriander
1 teaspoon ground cardamom
½ teaspoon each ground cloves and cayenne pepper
4 tablespoons lemon juice
Juice of 1 orange
FOR THE SAUCE
2oz (50g) butter
2 teaspoons each ground cumin, ground cardamom and ground coriander
8oz (250g) mushrooms, thinly sliced
4 tomatoes, skinned and finely chopped
2 large cloves garlic
2in (5cm) piece fresh gingerroot, peeled and finely chopped
1 heaping tablespoon tomato puree
1¼ cups (300ml) hot water
⅓ cup (75ml) coconut milk
Cayenne pepper
Salt
Handful of fresh cilantro leaves, coarsely chopped

Using a small sharp knife, cut 3 slits in the skin on each side of the pheasants' breasts and 1 slit in each thigh. Put the chopped garlic in a bowl with the peanut oil, tomato puree, vinegar, ground spices and cayenne pepper. Mix thoroughly, then rub the mixture over the birds pushing it into the slits and under the breast skin, too. Put the seasoned birds in a roasting pan, cover the pan tightly with foil and place in the refrigerator for several hours or overnight to marinate.

Add the lemon and orange juices to the roasting pan, cover with foil again and roast in the center of a preheated oven, 325°F, 160°C for 1½ hours, basting occasionally with the juices. Remove the foil and continue roasting, uncovered, for another 30 minutes until the birds are browned.

Meanwhile, melt the butter in a large saucepan over a medium heat. Add the ground spices and stir, then add the sliced mushrooms, chopped tomatoes, garlic and ginger and stir again until the mushrooms and tomatoes have softened. Mix the tomato puree with the hot water and add to the mushroom and tomato mixture.

Cover the saucepan and simmer very gently for 20–30 minutes, then add the coconut milk and cook until the sauce reduces and thickens. Season to taste with cayenne pepper and salt and remove from the heat.

Transfer the cooked pheasants to a carving board. Pour the juices from the roasting pan into the saucepan of sauce, stir and reheat. Check for seasoning and add the chopped cilantro leaves. Pour the sauce into a pitcher and serve with the carved pheasants.

DUCK FILETS IN PASTRY WITH LEEK SAUCE (172)

The first *magrets de canard* (duck breast filets) I ever ate were in a little restaurant in Paris; they were grilled pale pink, succulent and tender and it seemed to me to be the greatest luxury to be eating just the breast of the duck without struggling to get the meat off the bones of a leg. This recipe is another way of using breast filets. If you like, you can make the rolls without using the fatty duck skin, although it does add extra flavor.   *SERVES 4*

4 duck breast filets
Good handful of fresh mint leaves,
 chopped
5–6 stalks fresh tarragon leaves, chopped
2in (5cm) piece fresh gingerroot, peeled
 and very finely chopped
1 tablespoon marmalade
Salt and black pepper
17.3oz (490g) package puff pastry,
 thawed if frozen
2–3 long leeks, trimmed and thinly sliced
 (include the green parts)
Juice of 1 orange, strained
4 tablespoons lemon juice, strained
4 teaspoons sugar
1 cup (250ml) heavy cream
1 egg yolk, beaten

Pull the skin off the duck filets and if using, pierce each one all over deeply

with a fork. Keep on one side. On a large, flat surface lay out 2 large sheets of wet parchment paper. Put 2 filets on each piece of paper spaced well apart. Wet 2 more large sheets of paper and lay them on top. Pound very hard with a rolling pin or heavy flat implement until the filets have spread out and are as flat as you can get them. Repeat this procedure with the fatty duck skin, beating it out to roughly the same size as the filets.

Put the herbs, ginger and marmalade in a bowl and mix together thoroughly. Season with salt and black pepper. Spread the mixture onto each breast fillet then, roll up fairly loosely like a jelly roll. Wrap a piece of skin around each roll.

Cut the pastry into 4 equal-sized pieces and roll out thinly until big enough to wrap up the rolled duck breasts. Wrap each duck roll in pastry making a neat package, cutting off the excess uneven pieces and moistening the edges of the pastry to seal.

Roll out the trimmings and cut out a leaf or two to decorate each package if you like (page 245). Pierce a small hole in the top for the steam to escape. Put the packages in the refrigerator until 30 minutes before you plan to eat.

Meanwhile, prepare the sauce. Put the leeks in a saucepan with the orange and lemon juices and the sugar. Cover and boil over a low heat for 15–20 minutes until the leeks are soft. Put the leeks and juices in a food processor and process until very smooth. Add the cream and process again. Then season with salt and black pepper. Transfer into a saucepan and keep on one side.

Brush the packages all over with egg yolk and bake in the center of a preheated oven, 425°F, 220°C for 20–25 minutes until a rich golden brown all over. Reheat the sauce shortly before the duck packages are ready. Boil it for 2–3 minutes and pour into a warmed serving pitcher.

CORNISH HENS WITH MYSTERY SAUCE (172)

Cornish hens really are a treat but are mild in flavor and benefit from an interesting sauce. Both sweet and salty, the dark sauce in this recipe is a mystery because no one can ever guess what it is made from. Serve the grouse with new potatoes and either snow peas or broccoli.   *SERVES 4*

1 small–medium parsnip, peeled and cut
 into small pieces
4–5 large cloves garlic, coarsely chopped
8oz (250g) mushrooms, coarsely chopped
 (include the stalks)
1¼ cups (300ml) fresh orange juice
4 tablespoons soy sauce
Black pepper
4 small Cornish hens
Salt
2oz (50g) unsalted butter
1 heaping tablespoon fresh tarragon leaves

Put the parsnip, garlic and mushrooms in a saucepan with the orange juice, soy sauce and a sprinkling of black pepper. Bring to a boil over a high heat, then cover and simmer gently for about 45 minutes until soft, saucey and dark in color. Then process the mixture to a puree in a food processor. You should have a thick sauce. Taste for seasoning and leave on one side until the Cornish hens have finished roasting.

Meanwhile, wipe the birds inside and out, sprinkle with salt and pepper and put a generous chunk of butter inside each bird. Rub the remaining butter on the bottom of a roasting pan and add the birds breast side up. Cook in the center of a preheated oven, 350°F, 180°C for 45 to 60 minutes, basting occasionally. Cornish hens should be fully cooked and are done if the juices run clear when the bird is pierced between the leg and the breast. Remove the birds from the roasting pan (making sure that the juices from inside the bodies empty into the pan) and put them on warmed individual serving plates while you finish the sauce.

Pour the sauce into the roasting pan with the buttery juices, put it over a medium heat and bring the sauce to a boil, stirring constantly. Then stir in the tarragon leaves, boil for a moment more and either pour the sauce into a sauceboat to serve with the Cornish hens or spoon it directly next to the hens on the individual plates.

SAUCES and DRESSINGS

Sauces are the most important, yet, perhaps the most daunting area of cooking. The day I made my first flour-based white sauce, however, I suddenly realized the creative possibilities that cooking held, and how exciting it could be. For this reason, I would always advise new cooks to learn to make this most reliable of sauces as soon as possible. Flour-based sauces have sometimes been out of favor but they should not be scorned; they are the perfect base for variation, and can be adapted to suit all kinds of dishes; once mastered they also give you confidence to attempt the more tricky, emulsified sauces. Good sauces can transform and enhance your cooking, can raise humble or leftover ingredients to sublime heights, and can widen your repertoire immeasurably. Confidence is the vital first step to making them.

I think people are often alarmed by the long list of impressive sounding names for sauces, implying endless time-consuming and complex methods. If you understand that all sauces stem from a very few basic methods, and that different names often mean only a change of ingredient rather than technique, this should encourage you to become a saucemaker.

Since the textures and flavors of sauces are so crucial to the wonderful final results, they do need constant attention. Depending on the type of sauce the consistency can range from satin-smooth to frothy, and from transparently thin to creamily thick, but the texture must always be as much of a pleasurable characteristic of the sauce as the flavor. Taste your sauce constantly as you make it, and feel it against your tongue – there are many adjustments you can make along the way if it doesn't seem right; lumps can be destroyed by pressing the sauce through a fine sieve, a sauce which is too thick can be thinned by beating in cream, milk or stock or a very thin sauce can be reduced by boiling to a thicker consistency.

The point of a sauce is to enhance and complement the flavors of the ingredients it is served with, sometimes very subtly and sometimes by being in complete contrast. The seasoning of the sauce itself needs to be both careful and thoughtful; you must bear in mind the sauce's final destination – sauces should always have an additional last minute seasoning, and therefore it is best to add seasoning at several points during cooking. Season only lightly at first in the case of sauces where the basic mixture is reduced at the end to thicken the texture and intensify the taste.

Although a sauce should have a much more concentrated flavor than say a soup or the juices of a stew, it should contain no individual seasoning or ingredient which dominates enough to obliterate the taste of the food it is eaten with. Remember, too, that all flavors become more assertive as they cool, so care must be taken when making a cooked sauce which is then to be served cold. The taste of a sauce, of course, also depends on the basic ingredients, which need to be top quality and really fresh because although a good sauce can transform dull ingredients, nothing can redeem a bad sauce. The techniques of even the trickiest sauce-making can be learned, practiced and perfected, but in the end it is the tiny and personal adjustments to its seasoning by the cook which can make the entire meal memorable for long afterwards.

Clockwise from the top left: Plum and Shallot Sauce with Fresh Mint (page 212), flavored with freshly squeezed orange juice, to serve with pork, duck, ham or game; Chunky Horseradish Sauce (page 212) is made with prepared horseradish, chopped onion, sour cream and seasonings; Red Velvet Sauce (page 213) combines tomatoes, red peppers and green peppercorns to complement vegetables, meat, poultry and pasta; Kumquat Sauce with Dill (page 212) includes apple juice and raspberry vinegar ; Indian Spiced Mushroom Sauce (page 212) made from mushrooms, spices and cream; Ragù (page 213) is a classic Italian meat sauce for serving with pasta. Center: Coconut Sauce (page 213) uses coconut milk to make an accompaniment for exotic fruits.

BASIC WHITE SAUCES

White sauces provide a neutral base which can be varied for many purposes. The two classic white sauces are both flour-based; basic white sauce made with milk, and velouté sauce made with stock. These sauces are made from a roux – equal amounts of butter (or oil) and flour, cooked together. It is important for the roux to be cooked for a few minutes before the liquid is added, so the final sauce does not taste of raw flour. You can avoid a lumpy sauce by sprinkling in the flour to make a smooth and soft roux that is easy to beat the liquid into. It is safest to add cold milk to the hot roux for white sauces. Although cold milk takes longer to come to a boil, hot milk can be beaten in quickly with a wire whisk. It also helps to stir the sauce constantly as you add the liquid. If the sauce does go lumpy, you can try beating out the lumps with a whisk or process it in the food processor until smooth.

Make these sauces ahead, then reheat for serving. To prevent a skin from forming, melt a little butter on the surface, then whisk it in while reheating. Store, covered, for 2–3 days in the refrigerator.

BASIC WHITE SAUCE

The quantities of flour and fat used to make this versatile sauce are varied to produce different consistencies for different uses. For 1¼ cups (300ml) thin pouring sauce use ½oz (15g) each butter and all-purpose flour; for a medium sauce for coating use ¾oz (20g) each butter and plain flour; and for a thick binding sauce for making soufflés, 1oz (25g) each butter and flour.

1 *Melt the butter in a heavy saucepan. Whisk in the flour until the roux is blended and sandy colored. Cook for 2 minutes, whisking constantly. Remove the pan from the heat.*

2 *Gradually whisk in 1¼ cups (300ml) milk. Return to the heat and whisk until the sauce thickens and boils, then simmer for 2–3 minutes, whisking occasionally. Season to taste.*

For a quick version, *use the classic quantities (above) and put the fat, flour, milk and seasoning into the pan at once. Bring to a boil, stirring constantly with a wooden spoon, until thickened. Simmer for 2 minutes, season well, then use as required.*

To make a parsley sauce *make a medium coating white sauce (above) and stir in a finely chopped large bunch of parsley. Simmer gently for 1–2 minutes, then season to taste. Serve with boiled meats, steamed chicken breasts, fish cooked in any way or with vegetables.*

BÉCHAMEL SAUCE

This classic French sauce is identical to a basic white sauce, except it is made with milk infused with herbs and spices for more flavor. It is also made in varying consistencies like the basic white sauce (left). Use anywhere white sauce is called for. Once made it is important to simmer the sauce until reduced and fully thickened, stirring frequently. Makes about 1¼ cups (300ml).

Many ingredients, including pre-cooked ones, can be stirred into a béchamel sauce at the end of cooking. The cheese sauce (below) is good with fish, eggs and vegetables.

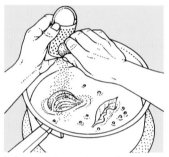

1 *Place 1¼ cups (300ml) milk in a heavy-based saucepan with ½ onion, 8–10 black peppercorns, 1 bay leaf and a pinch of freshly grated nutmeg. Bring the milk to a boil, then remove the saucepan from the heat, cover and set aside for 10–12 minutes for the flavors to infuse into the milk.*

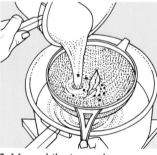

2 *Meanwhile, in another saucepan, prepare the roux (left), then remove from the heat. Strain the milk into the roux, whisking immediately, and discard the flavorings. Return the saucepan to the heat and bring to a boil, whisking constantly until the sauce thickens, then simmer gently for 2–3 minutes, still whisking. Season to taste with salt and pepper.*

To make a cheese sauce, *make a thin béchamel sauce; remove the saucepan from the heat. Stir in 1¼ cups (125g) grated Parmesan or Cheddar cheese and 1 teaspoon Dijon mustard, stirring until the cheese melts; do not return to the heat again or the cheese may become stringy. For extra flavoring, stir in either grated nutmeg or a sprinkling of caraway or cumin seeds.*

VELOUTÉ SAUCE

A good, flavorful stock is the most important ingredient in a velouté sauce. This stock need not be specially made; usually it is the cooking liquid of the ingredient the sauce is to be served with, such as poached fish, chicken or veal. Skimming during cooking gives this sauce its distinctive velvety appearance, hence its name which is derived from the French word for 'velvet'.

The mushroom and cream variation (below) is often used to make a chicken stew and the shellfish variation (below) uses leftover shells to enhance the flavor of the shellfish poaching liquid. It is an ideal sauce to serve with poached crab, lobster or shrimp.

To make 1¼ cups (300ml), bring 1¾ cups (400ml) fish, chicken or veal stock (pages 28–31) or shellfish cooking liquid to a boil, skimming the surface. Meanwhile, prepare a roux (opposite) with ¾oz (20g) each butter and flour and cook for 2 minutes until grainy and golden colored. Remove from the heat and cool slightly.

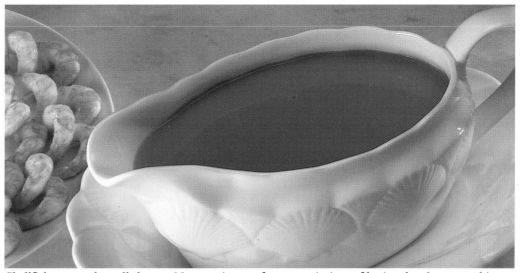

Shellfish sauce, also called sauce Nantua, is one of many variations of basic velouté sauce and is flavored by using the reserved shells and poaching liquid from the shellfish.

1 *Gradually whisk about three-quarters of the boiling stock or cooking liquid into the slightly cooled roux. Return the pan to the heat and bring the mixture to a boil, whisking constantly, until the sauce thickens.*

2 *Lower the heat and simmer the sauce gently for at least 15 minutes to concentrate the flavor, stirring from time to time. Skim occasionally with a large slotted spoon until the surface of the sauce is clear.*

3 *Use the sauce as it is, or pass it through a fine sieve into a clean saucepan. Whisk in 1–2 tablespoons heavy cream or cold butter and season to taste. Thin down with the remaining hot stock, if necessary.*

FLAVORING WHITE SAUCES

• Transform a quickly made white sauce by adding spices with the butter at the beginning and a little lemon juice or wine vinegar at the end.

• Add cream and fresh tarragon to a white sauce to serve with grilled chicken. Or, if you roast the chicken, stir the pan juices into the tarragon sauce just before serving.

• Season a white sauce to coat cauliflower, broccoli or baby carrots with freshly grated nutmeg, and add whole caraway or dill seeds.

• For a delicious and quick accompaniment to hot, fresh beets add sour cream and chopped fresh parsley to a white sauce at the end.

• To make a white garlic sauce, add 1–2 cloves crushed garlic to the butter before adding the flour for the roux, and stir it for 2–3 minutes over a low heat.

• I stir curry paste into white sauce with a little lemon juice to make an instant dish of curry when I'm in a hurry. Just pour the sauce over pieces of cold chicken or turkey in a saucepan and heat them together before turning into a serving dish – chopped fresh cilantro stirred in just before serving makes the dish even better.

• Many additions to a velouté sauce are the same as for a white sauce, but added ingredients taste more intense in a velouté sauce. Shellfish butter, pounded crab or chopped lobster, shrimp or smoked fish stirred in at the last minute, are wonderful.

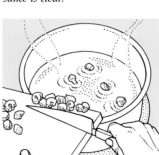

To make mushroom *and cream sauce (or sauce suprême) use chicken stock (page 29) to make the velouté sauce (above), adding 4oz (125g) chopped mushrooms after the boiling stock is incorporated into the roux. Complete steps 1 and 2, then strain the sauce through a sieve, as in step 3, and whisk in ¼ cup (50ml) heavy cream. Season with salt, pepper and a squeeze of lemon juice.*

To make shellfish-flavored *sauce (or sauce Nantua) to serve with poached shellfish save the shells and liquid from poaching the shellfish. Make the roux and add 1¾ cups (400ml) boiling poaching liquid, as in step 1 (above). Add the reserved shells and simmer for 15 minutes. Strain the sauce into a clean saucepan. Return to the heat and for an extra rich sauce whisk in 1–2 tablespoons cold butter.*

BROWN SAUCES *and* THICKENERS

Brown flour-based sauces are made in the same way as white velouté sauces (page 197), but they depend on a well-browned roux and brown stock (page 28) for their color, as well as for their very rich flavor. They most often accompany roast or sautéed meat and game.

The most classic brown sauce is espagnole sauce, so called because it was originally made with a fine, cured ham from Spain. Traditionally, this was a complicated sauce,

often taking days to prepare. It is still time-consuming to make but is an essential part of many of the traditional rich sauces we associate with fine French cooking.

Nowadays, however, most people only have time to make simple brown sauces with a basic browned roux and brown stock. Probably our most popular 'brown sauce' is basic brown gravy, made from the drippings and juices of roasted meat, game or poultry and thickened with flour.

BASIC BROWN SAUCE

A good stock is essential for a brown sauce. Bring 3¾ cups (900ml) beef or veal stock (page 28) to a boil and simmer until slightly reduced to concentrate the flavor. This recipe makes about 2 ½ cups(600ml). Freeze any extra you don't want.

 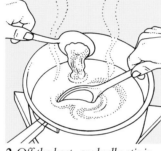

1 *Melt 1oz (25g) butter in a heavy saucepan and stir in 1oz (25g) all-purpose flour. Cook the roux for 3–4 minutes over a medium heat until it is well-browned, stirring constantly so as not to burn the roux.*

2 *Off the heat, gradually stir in the slightly reduced hot stock and 1½ tablespoons tomato puree. Return the pan to the heat and bring to a boil, then simmer for 20–30 minutes, uncovered, skimming occasionally. Season.*

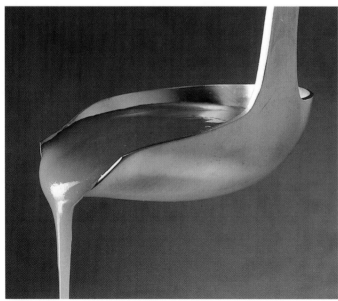

A basic brown sauce gets its deep color and full flavor from a brown roux and reduced brown stock.

CLASSIC ESPAGNOLE SAUCE

To make about 5 cups (1.2 liters) espagnole sauce, use approximately 10 cups (2.4 liters) rich brown meat stock which should have a full flavor and color, as well as plenty of gelatin from the bones (page 28). Espagnole sauce is rarely served on its own, because it takes several hours to make, but instead, is used as a base for other sauces. (See hunter's sauce in box opposite.)

Because it does take so long to make, it is worth making a large quantity and freezing some for later use. Freeze in 1¼ cups (300ml) blocks and reheat from frozen, slowly stirring occasionally, then boiling for 2 minutes.

1 *Bring 10 cups (2.4 liters) beef or veal stock (page 28) to a boil. Simmer and skim the stock until it reduces to about half its original volume. In a second saucepan, heat 6 tablespoons (75ml) vegetable oil. Add 4oz (125g) diced smoked bacon and cook for 2 minutes. Add 2 diced onions and 2 diced carrots to the saucepan and cook gently until the vegetables begin to soften.*

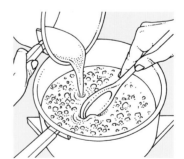 

2 *Sprinkle over a generous ⅓ cup (50g) flour and stir until well blended. Cook for 4–5 minutes, stirring frequently, until the roux becomes a rich brown color, taking care not to let it burn. Remove the pan from the heat. Stir three-quarters of the hot stock into the roux and softened vegetables. Return to the heat and bring to a boil, stirring constantly, until thickened.*

3 *Add 1 large bouquet garni (page 10), 2 halved small tomatoes, 2 tablespoons tomato puree, and simmer for 2–3 hours, uncovered, skimming often. Reheat the remaining stock and add little by little to the saucepan as the sauce thickens and reduces. Strain the sauce, if you like, before using. Stir in 1–1½oz (25–40g) diced chilled butter and season if necessary.*

QUICK SAUCE THICKENERS

Sometimes a sauce needs thickening at the last minute and there are several traditional methods that do not require great skill. A beurre manié, simply equal amounts of flour and butter kneaded to a paste, added just before the end of cooking, thickens and enriches. As the butter melts it distributes the flour throughout the liquid. Other thickeners are cornstarch, arrowroot or potato starch. These thicken with very little cooking as they work more quickly than wheat flour. Egg yolks and cream are used to thicken and enrich velouté sauces.

To make a beurre manié, knead together about ³⁄₄oz (20g) each all-purpose flour and butter with a fork. Bring 1¼ cups (300ml) sauce to a boil, then drop in small chunks of beurre manié, stirring until the sauce thickens. Beurre manié can be stored in the refrigerator for several weeks; use as necessary.

A simple way to thicken sauces is by stirring in equal amounts of butter and flour, called a beurre manié.

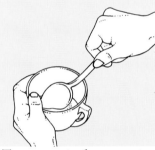

To use cornstarch, arrowroot or potato starch to thicken 1¼ cups (300ml) sauce, bring the sauce to the boil. Mix 2 teaspoons thickener with 1½ tablespoons cold water or stock, then whisk into the hot sauce, whisking until slightly thickened.

To thicken and enrich 1¼ cups (300ml) hot velouté sauce, mix 1 egg yolk and 1–2 tablespoons heavy cream in a cup, then stir in a little hot sauce. Whisk this mixture into the sauce over a low heat, whisking constantly until thickened. Do not boil.

TRADITIONAL GRAVY

Although I prefer an unthickened gravy many people consider a traditionally thickened brown sauce an essential part of Sunday dinner. When you make a roast either use my quick gravy (page 157) or this more traditional method. Be sure the flour cooks until brown so it doesn't taste uncooked when the gravy is served.

After roasting, pour off all but 2 tablespoons fat from the roasting pan and place the pan over a medium heat.

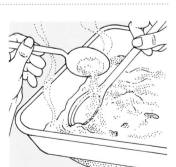

Sprinkle in 2 tablespoons flour. Stir for 4 minutes until rich brown. Add 2 cups (450ml) hot stock or vegetable water, stirring up all the bits off the pan, and cook until thickened. Season.

FLAVORING BROWN SAUCES

• Sauté thin slices of sharp red plums or firm, fresh apricots to add to a basic brown sauce to serve with duck, pork or game. Or simmer coarsely grated orange rind in the sauce when you are making it.
• For a piquant brown sauce, sauté 1 small finely chopped onion in butter when you make the roux until very soft, adding 2–4 pinches of cayenne pepper and 2 teaspoons paprika half way through the sautéing, then stir in ¼ cup (50ml) red wine vinegar at the same time as adding the stock.
• A spicy brown sauce is excellent with game birds, chicken or turkey – add curry paste, 1 finely chopped onion and 2 crushed garlic cloves to the roux and cook slowly for at least 5 minutes before pouring in the hot brown stock. Just before serving, stir in a handful of coarsely chopped fresh cilantro leaves. Or, use individual ground Indian spices such as cardamom and coriander for a spicy sauce.
• Finely chopped fresh ginger is a good addition with garlic to a roux. Flavor and enrich a spicy brown sauce at the end of cooking with about ¼ cup (60ml) coconut milk.
• To make hunter's sauce or sauce chasseur soften 2–3 chopped shallots and 4oz (125g) chopped mushrooms in ½ oz (15g) butter. Add a generous ¾ cup (200ml) dry white wine and reduce by half. Add 1 cup (250ml) basic brown or espagnole sauce and 2 tablespoons tomato puree and simmer for 15 minutes. Stir in 2 tablespoons diced cold butter and 1 tablespoon chopped parsley. Serve with grilled or roasted meat or game.
• I also love the flavor of coarsely chopped capers added to a brown sauce at the end.
• Meat glazes, which are simply meat, poultry and game stock boiled until reduced to a thick, syrupy consistency, with an extremely concentrated flavor, add great finesse when stirred into a brown sauce after cooking. For extra richness, finish by whisking in ½–1oz (15–25g) diced cold butter.
• The appearance of a brown sauce is often improved, and a refreshing element given, if you stir a handful of chopped fresh herbs such as dill, tarragon, basil, chives or flat-leaf parsley into the sauce just before serving. Chopped sorrel loses its bright color and seems to dissolve into the sauce when it is boiled for a minute or two, but it adds a delicious sharpness.

HOT EMULSIFIED SAUCES

Hollandaise, béarnaise and butter sauces are my favorite sauces; they are all hot emulsified sauces made by whisking two or more ingredients into an emulsion. All these sauces are light, yet rich and have many variations, such as orange-flavored hollandaise. These sauces have a reputation of being difficult because the egg yolks can easily curdle and ruin the sauce. This can be overcome by using a food processor, although the technique of making them by hand can easily be mastered with a little practice.

When making these sauces by hand you must take time to heat the yolks and butter sufficiently. Heat slowly over a low heat in a heavy saucepan because too high a heat will cause them to curdle. The safest way to make them by hand is to use a heatproof bowl set over a pan of simmering water (below) or use a double boiler (page 18).

Each egg yolk will absorb about 2oz (50g) of butter. Using clarified butter (page 96) also helps prevent curdling but for less experienced cooks it is probably easier to use softened butter rather than melted butter. Use unsalted butter if possible. Start by adding the butter in small spoonfuls, then when the sauce thickens it can be added in larger amounts until the sauce is smooth and creamy.

CLASSIC HOLLANDAISE SAUCE

If the sauce separates or curdles, remove from the heat and immediately whisk in an ice cube. This lowers the temperature and usually saves the sauce. If not, start again with 2 fresh yolks, slowly whisking in the curdled sauce until a new emulsion forms.

You should make hollandaise sauce just before serving, but it will keep for about 30 minutes in a bowl set over simmering water if you stir often. Serve with poached eggs, fish and vegetables. Makes about 1¼ cups (300ml).

1 *Separate 3 egg yolks and whisk them with 1 teaspoon sugar, 1 tablespoon water, 1 tablespoon white wine vinegar and 1 tablespoon lemon juice in a heatproof bowl set over a saucepan of simmering water until well mixed and foamy.*

2 *Over a very low heat, continue whisking the egg yolk mixture until the whisk leaves a trail on the surface. This should take about 3 minutes. Be careful the bottom of the bowl doesn't actually touch the water or the yolks may scramble.*

3 *Remove from the heat and whisk in 6oz (175g) softened butter, cut into pieces. Add piece by piece at first, then several at a time until the hollandaise sauce is thick but still light enough to pour. Season to taste with salt, pepper and more lemon juice.*

BÉARNAISE SAUCE

Béarnaise sauce uses the same technique as hollandaise, but it is slightly thicker and has a much more concentrated and pronounced flavor because the flavorings are reduced. Serve with grilled or roasted lamb, beef and full-flavored fish like salmon or monkfish.

For 1¼ cups (300ml), boil 3 tablespoons each white wine vinegar and dry white wine, 10 crushed peppercorns, 2–3 chopped shallots and 1 tablespoon chopped fresh tarragon until reduced to 1–2 tablespoons. Strain, cool slightly and place in a heatproof bowl set over a pan of simmering water.

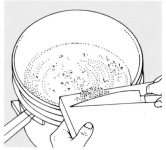

Whisk 2 egg yolks *into the reduction until foamy. Continue whisking over a low heat for about 3 minutes until the whisk leaves a trail on the surface. Remove from the heat and whisk in 4oz (125g) softened butter, a small piece at a time, until the sauce is thick. Stir in 1 tablespoon chopped fresh tarragon.*

FLAVORING HOT EMULSIFIED SAUCES

• For an orange-flavored hollandaise sauce, which goes well with broccoli, asparagus or cauliflower, whisk a little finely grated orange rind into the egg yolks, followed by the lemon juice, wine vinegar and 3–4 tablespoons fresh orange juice. Omit the water. Add a little more butter if necessary to thicken the sauce as desired.

• Reduce a scant ⅔ cup (150ml) fish stock made with white wine (page 31) to 2 tablespoons and use instead of lemon juice in a hollandaise sauce to serve with simply cooked fish.

• Flavor hollandaise sauce by stirring in chopped fresh herbs just before serving – try dill, tarragon and basil.

• For a good sauce to serve with egg dishes, grilled fish or new potatoes, stir 2–3 tablespoons of smooth pureed cooked fresh or smoked fish or grilled, skinned and pureed red or yellow peppers into a hollandaise sauce.

• If you are not a purist, there is no reason why you should not try many of the variations mentioned above for béarnaise sauce as well.

• For a tomato-flavored béarnaise, I like adding tomato puree (made from fresh, butter-sautéed tomatoes, if possible) and strips of fresh basil leaves to the finished sauce, leaving out the tarragon in the classic recipe – this goes beautifully with grilled chicken.

QUICK METHODS

WHITE BUTTER SAUCE

The food processor and microwave oven can both be used to make foolproof hollandaise and béarnaise sauces in minutes. Because eggs are not as well cooked as in the classic methods (opposite) the use of pasteurized egg products is recommended. And, since the butter is melted, the sauce is less creamy. However, I don't think there is anything wrong with using these modern methods, especially as it encourages people to make sauces they might otherwise be apprehensive about.

This version of hollandaise sauce, like the classic, becomes ethereal if you fold in stiffly beaten powdered egg whites equivalent to 2 to 3 whites just before serving. This lightens the sauce and increases the volume. Béarnaise sauce can also be made by these quick methods, using the quantities opposite.

I love this simple butter sauce, often known by its French name of *beurre blanc*; it makes an elegant accompaniment to fish, vegetables and egg dishes. Because this sauce does not contain any egg yolks it is more likely to separate than the other hot emulsified sauces, and it really should be made just before serving. It only takes a few minutes to make.

When adding the butter in step 2 be sure to whisk vigorously so it emulsifies before melting and becoming oily. If the sauce does separate, it cannot be rescued unlike the sauces that contain egg yolks, so you will have to start again. It is important to use unsalted butter. Makes about 1¼ cups (300ml).

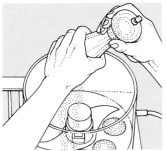

1 *For food processor hollandaise, use the same ingredients as for classic hollandaise (opposite). Melt the butter in a pan, taking care not to let it burn by stirring as it melts and then leave it on one side. Put the pasteurized egg product, salt and pepper in the processor and blend for 15 seconds until creamy and lightened.*

2 *In another pan, heat the sugar, water, vinegar and lemon juice. With the machine still running, add the warm sugar, water, vinegar and lemon juice and process in. Add the melted butter in a slow steady stream until the mixture emulsifies and forms a smooth creamy sauce. Adjust the seasoning if necessary.*

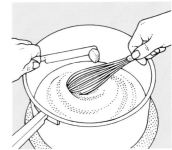

1 *Boil 2–3 finely chopped shallots with 3 tablespoons each white wine and white wine vinegar in a heavy saucepan until reduced to 1–2 tablespoons and thick and syrupy. Add 1 tablespoon heavy cream and boil again until reduced to 1–2 tablespoons. (This step can be done ahead.) Adding the cream helps to stabilize the sauce before the butter is whisked in.*

2 *Over a low heat, whisk in 10oz (300g) diced chilled butter, little by little until incorporated. Increase the heat and bring just to a boil, whisking constantly and vigorously to stabilize the emulsion. You can either strain out the shallots or leave the sauce as it is. Season with salt and pepper to taste, using white pepper to avoid any black specks, and serve at once.*

For microwave hollandaise, *cut 4oz (125g) cold butter into large pieces and soften on Defrost (30%) for 1½ minutes. Remove from the microwave. In another bowl, beat pasteurized egg product equivalent to 2 egg yolks with 1 tablespoon lemon juice, 1 teaspoon French mustard, and salt and black pepper. Heat on Full (100%) for 40 seconds. Remove the bowl and stir well, then beat in the softened butter in pieces until creamy and thickened.*

Rich hollandaise sauce is a traditional accompaniment for delicately poached salmon with fresh dill.

COLD EMULSIFIED SAUCES

Mayonnaise is the most popular and well known cold emulsified sauce. It should be thick and creamy and the key to making it both safely and successfully is to heat the egg yolks, vinegar, water, sugar, mustard, salt and pepper to boiling before beating in the oil. Have the oil at room temperature as mayonnaise can easily curdle if the oil is too cold or if it is added too quickly.

Making mayonnaise by hand is easily mastered, but with a food processor it is magically quick. I think making the sauce by hand is very satisfying and enables the cook to feel the texture thicken, but using a food processor means that a homemade sauce with a flavor so different from commercial variations can be produced in minutes.

The flavors of mayonnaise, as well as other salad dressings, derive mainly from the oil used – so use good-quality oil and experiment with the wide variety of oils now available. In France, mayonnaise and salad dressings are often made entirely with olive oil but this is sometimes too overpowering for a delicate fish or vegetable dish. A good idea is to use half vegetable oil, such as sunflower, and half olive or other flavored oil. You can also vary the taste by using different-flavored vinegars, such as a herb or a wine vinegar. If you are making a tomato mayonnaise by adding tomato puree, use the slightly sweet balsamic vinegar.

CLASSIC MAYONNAISE

Make mayonnaise with a whisk, or, for the faint-hearted, a hand-held electric mixer to beat in the oil. Adding a small amount of Dijon mustard to the yolks, along with the lemon juice and seasoning, helps the sauce to emulsify as well as flavoring it. The proportion of oil to egg yolk can be varied, depending on the consistency desired, but in general, 1 egg yolk 'holds' about ⅔ cup (150ml)) oil; if too much oil is added or if you add it too quickly, the sauce separates.

If the sauce does separate or curdle, there are several ways to save it. Begin with a clean saucepan and another beaten egg yolk and a pinch of salt and slowly whisk the curdled mixture into the new egg yolk over low heat until it emulsifies again. You can also whisk the curdled mixture into a little mustard, lemon juice or vinegar, but be careful of these strong flavors.

Store in the refrigerator for 2–3 days, but bring it to room temperature before stirring or it could curdle. Mayonnaise is the ideal sauce to serve with cold fish, poultry, vegetables, eggs and salads. There are many popular variations too, such as aïoli, a garlic-flavored mayonnaise. Makes 1¼ cups (300ml).

FOOD PROCESSOR MAYONNAISE

Using a food processor saves time and there is little risk of curdling, but it does make a lighter texture and color. This recipe could be prepared in a blender as well.

Use the quantities as for Classic Mayonnaise (left), using 1 whole egg, beaten well, instead of the 2 egg yolks to help lighten it.

In a small saucepan, stir together the beaten egg, vinegar, water, sugar, mustard, salt and pepper. Cook over very low heat, stirring constantly until the mixture just comes to a boil. Remove from the heat and let stand 4 minutes. Pour the mixture into the bowl of the food processor and, with the processor running, very slowly add the oil. Once you have added about 1¼ cups (300ml) oil, stop the machine and check the texture. If the mayonnaise is too thin, continue adding oil, and if too thick add 1 or 2 tablespoons lemon juice, light cream or plain yogurt. Makes 1¼ cups (300ml).

AÏOLI

Aïoli is a thick glossy garlic mayonnaise that is used to accompany the classic French Provençal dish called aïoli, a large dish of poached salt cod, boiled meats and vegetables. Aïoli is also delicious served with fish soups, cold poached fish and shellfish, salads, hard-cooked eggs or cold meats and spread on slices of toasted French bread.

If you are in a hurry you can add 3-5 cloves crushed garlic to commercial mayonnaise or some already prepared Classic Mayonnaise (see left) or use a pasteurized egg product and skip the cooking step. However, it really doesn't take much time to prepare aïoli from scratch when you use the food processor or blender method (above).

For a mellow garlic flavor, add the garlic to the egg mixture before cooking. For a more robust garlic flavor, add the garlic to the cooked egg mixture in the processor just before you start processing in the oil. It is important to use a fruity extra virgin olive oil to achieve the full flavor characteristic of this sauce. Don't be tempted to cut the olive oil with a less flavorful oil as you might when making Classic Mayonnaise. Makes about 1¼ cups (300ml) aïoli.

1 *In a small saucepan, whisk 2 egg yolks with 1½ tablespoons lemon juice or white wine vinegar, 2-3 teaspoons Dijon mustard, 1 teaspoon sugar and a little salt and white pepper until the mixture is well blended and lightened. Heat just to a boil over very low heat. Pour into a small bowl placed on a tea towel and whisk to cool slightly.*

2 *Gradually add up to 1¼ cups (300ml) oil, drop by drop, whisking constantly. It is easy to add the oil drop by drop if you just let it drip off a spoon. Do not add the oil too quickly or the mixture may curdle. When the sauce begins to thicken, pour the oil in a very slow stream until the mayonnaise reaches the desired consistency. Season to taste.*

TARTAR SAUCE

Homemade tartar sauce is well worth making as it bears no resemblance to the bottled variety, and is delicious with all sorts of things, especially cold or hot fish, poultry, vegetable and egg dishes. It is made by emulsifying mashed hard-cooked egg yolks with oil, then adding capers, gherkins and the chopped hard-boiled egg whites.

For a quick version of tartar sauce add gherkins, capers and finely chopped herbs to classic mayonnaise (opposite).

Tartar sauce will keep covered for 2–3 days in the refrigerator. Makes about 1¼ cups (300ml).

Mash 3 hard-cooked egg yolks with 1 tablespoon Dijon mustard, salt and pepper. Gradually beat in 1¼ cups (300ml) sunflower oil, as if making mayonnaise, until the sauce is thickened. Stir in 1–2 tablespoons lemon juice, 2 tablespoons each chopped gherkins, capers, tarragon and the chopped egg whites.

Golden homemade mayonnaise, with a tarragon-flavored variation and rouille (see box below), a piquant chili-flavored mayonnaise, served with fish soups in France.

COATING WITH MAYONNAISE

Although mayonnaise is often used to bind fish, poultry, vegetable, pasta and egg dishes and salads, it can also be thinned to coat cold foods. Adding a little lemon juice, wine vinegar, warm water, plain yogurt, whipped cream or milk thins mayonnaise to a coating consistency for dressing salads made with raw or lightly cooked vegetables and other ingredients.

If the mayonnaise needs to be thin, but still keep its shape for coating fish or poultry pieces, gelatin can be added. Use ½ package gelatin softened in 3–4 tablespoons water, wine or stock. Heat to dissolve completely and allow to cool to room temperature, then whisk into 1¼ cups (300ml) mayonnaise. If you like, decorate the coated fish or poultry with fresh herb sprigs and chill to set before serving.

NO-EGG 'MAYONNAISE'

A mayonnaise-like sauce, excellent with cold or grilled fish and meat, can be made by adding oil to a base of a light vegetable puree instead of the egg yolks used in mayonnaise. This sauce can also be made with a base of smooth fish puree or caviar to make a delicious accompaniment to egg dishes and chunky salads, including potato salad.

I like using sweet peppers for this kind of sauce, or pureed eggplant as in eggplant pâté (page 97). Purees made from root vegetables also work well. The amount of oil you need depends on what base you use for the sauce, as these obviously vary in density and texture. For strong-flavored purees, I use olive oil, and for more subtle ones, sunflower, grape seed or a mixture of oils. Makes about 2 to 2½ cups (450–600ml).

FLAVORING MAYONNAISE

• My favorite additions to mayonnaise are finely chopped anchovies and crushed garlic; sun-dried tomato paste mixed with tomato puree and strips of fresh basil; chopped capers; fresh dill and whole grain mustard; coarsely crushed green or pink peppercorns; garlic which has been roasted in its skin until soft, then skinned and crushed to a puree; the juice of fresh ginger squeezed through a crusher and chopped fresh cilantro; and many chopped fresh, tender herbs such as tarragon, dill, chervil, savory and lovage.

• I particularly like green mayonnaise, made by mixing in chopped, blanched and well drained spinach (adding sorrel leaves, too, if you have them) or blanched and chopped watercress to the mayonnaise. If using a food processor, add the blanched leaves to make the sauce a uniform green.

• The delicious red chili sauce, rouille, which is spooned in small quantities into hot soups and stews, can be made by first pounding a fresh red chili and several cloves of garlic in a mortar and then continuing as for classic mayonnaise (opposite), but using extra virgin olive oil and adding tomato puree instead of vinegar or mustard.

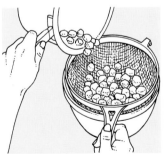

1 *To make a pepper-flavored no-egg 'mayonnaise', seed and coarsely chop 12oz (375g) yellow peppers (page 49). Place in a saucepan with just enough water to cover. Bring to a boil, then simmer for about 10 minutes until the peppers are very soft. Drain, discarding the water, and set aside until the peppers are cool or rinse in cold water to cool.*

2 *Put the peppers in a food processor with 1 tablespoon white wine vinegar, 2 teaspoons sugar and 1–2 teaspoons Dijon mustard and process all together to a puree. With the machine running all the time, add 7–9 tablespoons sunflower or grape seed oil, drop by drop, until fairly thick. Season and chill until ready to serve.*

SALAD DRESSINGS

It is well worth making your own salad dressings, especially since it is now so easy to make such exciting salads. Many lettuces that were once only available in Europe are now sold here, adding to the appeal of salads.

Classic vinaigrette contains mostly oil, so choose the oil you use carefully. Many interesting types of high-quality oils are available, so the combination of flavors is almost endless, but the choice usually depends on the salad to be dressed. Olive oil, for example, is a natural partner for a tomato and mozzarella cheese salad, and a nut-flavored oil goes well with salads containing nuts, mushrooms or bitter leaves, while a plain sunflower oil is many people's choice for a simple tossed green salad.

A good basic formula for an oil-and-vinegar dressing is about 3–5 parts oil to 1 part vinegar or lemon juice, depending, of course, on how sharp you like your dressing and the flavor of the ingredients. If dressing a leafy green salad, be sure the greens are clean and dry so the dressing coats the greens and clings to them.

For convenience, dressings can always be made ahead in a large quantity, but they do taste best when freshly made. The quick way to make most dressings is to put all the ingredients in a screw-top jar and shake. Although it's best to toss a salad at the last minute to avoid wilted soggy greens, an alternative for a simple dressing is to toss the greens with oil alone a short time ahead. Then when you are ready to serve the salad, toss the oiled leaves with a little flavored vinegar or lemon juice and season well.

VINAIGRETTE DRESSING

A few plain lettuce leaves can be turned into a gastronomic delight with a good vinaigrette dressing. Opinions vary as to how sharp it should taste, but I prefer a little more oil than the classic proportions of 1 part vinegar to 3 parts of oil, and I like to use extra virgin olive oil as its fruity flavor can be really appreciated. All sorts of different oils and vinegars can be used for a variety of results, and lemon juice can be used instead of vinegar. Dark, matured balsamic vinegar, which is sweet and rich-tasting, makes a very special vinaigrette, as does delicious sherry vinegar which is also slightly sweet and not strong.

For a smoothly emulsified vinaigrette, it is best to add dry mustard, but I often use Dijon mustard and personally like mild whole grain mustards best of all. It is not necessary to use mustard at all if you don't like it. Traditionally, vinaigrette is made by whisking the oil gradually into the vinegar and mustard mixture, but I find vigorous shaking of all the ingredients in a screw-top jar successful, and far easier. Makes about 1¼ cups (300ml).

1 *Put 2 tablespoons wine vinegar, 1 teaspoon sugar and 2 teaspoons dry or Dijon mustard into a screw-top jar. Replace the lid securely and give the jar a really good shake. If making dressing to store for any length of time, choose a jar with a plastic-coated inner lid so the vinegar doesn't affect it.*

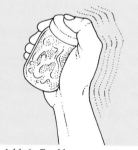

2 *Add 6–7 tablespoons extra virgin olive oil to the jar, replace the lid securely again and shake vigorously until the dressing has lightly emulsified. Season to taste. Store, covered, in the refrigerator. Before using, bring the jar to room temperature for at least 30 minutes before the dressing is needed and shake again.*

VINAIGRETTE VARIATIONS

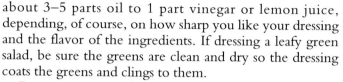

There are endless variations of vinaigrette dressing (see box opposite), but here are 3 of the most usual ones. You can, of course, add other flavorings as well to any of these suggestions.

The taste of garlic in a salad dressing should not be overpowering, but in moderation I think crushed garlic is a wonderful addition for many salads.

I almost always use a little mustard in any vinaigrette and very often chopped fresh herbs, too. Whole grain mustard is my favorite and I often add a little soy sauce with the vinegar to add extra flavor.

Usually 1 small *crushed garlic clove is enough to add a garlicky flavor to the vinaigrette unless you want a much stronger taste. Shake the dressing before using. If you don't want to bite on tiny bits of raw garlic, you can leave the dressing standing with the garlic for a bit, then strain the vinaigrette through a sieve when ready to use.*

Add 2 tablespoons *chopped, fresh herbs such as dill, fennel, chervil, savory, mint, tarragon and lovage for a stronger flavor, and shake in the dressing. This herb variation is useful with meat, poultry and fish salads.*

For a honey and mustard *variation, add 2–3 teaspoons whole grain or Dijon mustard or 1 teaspoon dry mustard and 1 teaspoon honey to the vinegar and mix together before adding the oil.*

YOGURT DRESSING

Plain yogurt is an extremely useful ingredient for salad dressings. It can simply be used on its own, seasoned to taste and freshly chopped herbs such as mint added, or you can mix it into a vinaigrette base with very little olive oil or into mayonnaise or sour cream. For a mousseline-style dressing, add some whipped heavy cream.

Use either fat-free plain yogurt, or low-fat yogurt for a richer, thicker dressing. Or, try mascarpone. Makes about 1¼ cups (300ml).

A classic vinaigrette is the ideal dressing for a simple salad of sliced tomatoes with sliced black olives and finely shredded leaves of fresh basil.

Strain the juice of 2 small lemons into a bowl and mix in 1¼ cups (300ml) plain yogurt with a wooden spoon. Season with salt and freshly ground black pepper and add finely chopped fresh mint or other herbs. A mint-flavored yogurt dressing is a good alternative to traditional mint sauce or jelly with roast lamb. It is also ideal for dressing potato salads.

CHEESE DRESSINGS

Because cheese dressings are fairly strong in flavor and heavy in consistency use them to coat crisp greens and vegetables. Use iceberg, romaine, spinach and radicchio leaves with cucumber, radishes, fennel and other crisp vegetables. Soft leafy greens and delicate flavors are just overpowered by these cheese dressings.

The most popular cheese dressings are made with a blue cheese, preferably French Roquefort or Italian Gorgonzola for a more exciting taste, but for economy use blue.

To make a blue cheese dressing, make 1¼ cups (300ml) vinaigrette (opposite). Mash or crumble 2oz (50g) Roquefort, Gorgonzola or other blue cheese in a small bowl, then whisk in the vinaigrette dressing. This is especially good with spinach salad and for shredded red cabbage.

To make a cream cheese dressing, beat 3oz (75g) softened cream cheese until creamy. Add 2 finely chopped green onions and 2 tablespoons chopped parsley, then beat in 1 cup (250ml) vinaigrette dressing (opposite). Serve with sliced hard-boiled eggs and tuna fish.

EASY WAYS TO ADD FLAVORS TO SALADS

• Different oils, vinegars and mustards make it possible to achieve a great variety of flavors from a vinaigrette; for cooked vegetables and substantial mixed salads with crunchy ingredients, I like the rich, fruity taste of extra virgin olive oil, but for more delicate, leafy salads, it can be made less assertive by diluting it with grape seed or sunflower oil or using light olive oil.
• Walnut and hazelnut oils are strongly flavored and should be mixed with a blander oil; they

are delicious for leafy salads, especially those containing feta or goat cheese and bitter leaves such as chicory and frisée combined with nuts.
• Wine vinegar can be either white or the richer red, which I prefer for most dressings, but fruit vinegars such as raspberry, which smell almost scented, can be effective in delicate, subtle or slightly sweet salads.
• Sweetness is an important ingredient in a salad dressing to bring out all the flavors; I usually

use a little honey (opposite) or light brown sugar instead of the more classic granulated sugar.
• Try adding aromatic crushed green or pink peppercorns, or even a little chopped fresh red chili, for a bold flavored piquant dressing.
• For an oriental vinaigrette to serve with Chinese greens and bean sprout salads, use sherry vinegar and add crushed garlic and fresh ginger with soy sauce and a mixture of sunflower with a little toasted sesame oil.

• Apart from yogurt dressings, seasoned sour cream is very useful for dressing potato and other cooked vegetable salads. Add all sorts of ingredients, including chopped fresh herbs, whole grain mustard, crushed green peppercorns, grated horseradish, chopped anchovies, onions and gherkins or capers, and curry pastes with chopped fresh cilantro leaves. These dressings also make effective coatings for cold chicken and fish, instead of mayonnaise.

FRUIT *and* VEGETABLE SAUCES

Savory fruit and vegetable sauces are based on the cooked reduced puree of the fruit or vegetable, and are usually used in small quantities as a condiment rather than as a covering sauce. A fresh tomato sauce, for example, can accompany soufflés, gratins, fried fish or vegetable cakes as well as many pasta dishes to complement the dish's flavor.

Tomatoes are so versatile they are used as the base for many of these sauces. A cooked tomato sauce is classic and can be made all year round. Pasta sauces, barbecue sauce, ketchup, chili sauce, relishes and salsas are also based on tomatoes or tomato sauce. Almost any cooked vegetable, however, can be softened with butter or oil, plain yogurt, or cream and used as a sauce or as a base for another sauce, soup or soufflé. Herbs are also used as a base for many savory sauces, such as basil for pesto sauce, a traditional Italian accompaniment to pasta, and mint sauce, always a favorite for serving with roast lamb.

Fruit purees are also used as the base for creating sauces which are classic with certain dishes; apple sauce with pork, cranberry sauce with chicken, turkey and ham, Cumberland sauce with roast game and pâtés and plum sauce with duck, ham or pork.

Fruits or vegetables for these savory sauces do not have to be pureed however – I often prefer, particularly with fruit sauces, to leave pieces of fruit soft and mushy to give texture to the sauce and I like to stir in chopped fresh green herbs at the end which add a fresh taste to the sauce and enhance its appearance.

FRESH TOMATO SAUCE

This is one of the most useful and also one of the best tasting sauces of all. This recipe is a simple version I have devised, and I think it is hard to beat. It can either be used on its own or as a base for other sauces. A good tomato sauce goes with every kind of ingredient from meat, fish and vegetables to pasta. When you don't have time to make this sauce, use the quick tomato sauce (page 89) that uses canned tomatoes.

The best fresh tomatoes for cooking are the plum variety, if you can get them, and I only use the ones that are really ripe and deep red; when plum tomatoes are in season, make a large quantity of sauce and freeze it in separate containers. Mix in 1–2oz (25–50g) butter at the end for a richer sauce. And, if the tomatoes you are using are not really ripe and full of flavor, stir in 1 tablespoon tomato puree.

It doesn't make much difference to the color of the finished sauce if you substitute white wine for red. Finely shredded fresh basil is a wonderful addition stirred in just before serving. Makes about 5 cups (1.2 liters).

1 *Melt 2oz (50g) butter with 4 tablespoons olive oil in a large saucepan. Add 3–4 large chopped garlic cloves, 2lb (1kg) skinned and chopped tomatoes (page 48), ⅔ cup (150ml) red wine, 2 teaspoons sugar and a little salt.*

2 *Bring to a boil, then simmer over a low heat, stirring often, for 20–30 minutes until the tomatoes are completely soft and the sauce thickens as desired. Season to taste with crushed sea salt and plenty of freshly ground black pepper.*

TOMATO SALSA

This south of the border import has rapidly become one of the most popular sauces in the supermarket today. Even more delicious than the dozens of prepared choices on the shelf, this fresh homemade tomato salsa couldn't be easier to make. In addition to its traditional role as a dip for tortilla chips, this peppy sauce can add excitement to grilled meats, fish or vegetables or salad dressings.

For 6 servings, peel and quarter 5 medium-size fresh ripe Italian or plum tomatoes. Shake out and discard the seeds; coarsely chop the remaining tomatoes to make 2½ cups. In a non-metal bowl, combine the tomato with 1 4½ oz (140g) can chopped green chilis, drained, 2 tablespoons lime juice, ½ teaspoon sugar, ¼ teaspoon salt and 4-6 dashes hot red pepper sauce. Cover the salsa and refrigerate for 1-2 hours. When ready to serve, stir in 2 tablespoons chopped fresh cilantro or flat-leaf parsley leaves. Surround with tortilla chips to serve traditionally, or use as a sauce with cooked foods.

CUMBERLAND SAUCE

Cumberland Sauce is basically a redcurrant jelly sauce flavored with citrus rind and port. Traditionally served at room temperature with roast venison, this sauce is equally delicious with hot or cold lamb, ham, beef, tongue, and especially pâtés and terrines.

To make about 1¼ cups (300ml) sauce, you will need 1 cup (250g) good-quality redcurrant jelly and about ¼ cup (50ml) ruby port. Remove the rinds of 1 orange or ½ orange and ½ lemon and cut into fine julienne strips. Bring the rind and ⅔ cup (150ml) water to a boil for 2-3 minutes. Drain and rinse under cold water. Melt the redcurrant jelly in a small saucepan; squeeze the juice from the fruit and add to the pan. Stir in ¼ teaspoon each ground cinnamon or ginger and dry mustard, 1 finely chopped shallot and the port; simmer for 3-4 minutes until the jelly is melted and shallot softened. Strain; stir in the peel and cool until thickened and syrupy. For a clear sauce, simmer with the rind and then strain.

MINT SAUCE

I never really liked mint sauce as a child, but I think it must have been because I had only tasted a bottled variety made with strong malt vinegar and too much sugar. Home-made mint sauce, using really fresh mint and good wine vinegar is quite a different thing. I also like using sherry vinegar for its rounded flavor or cider for its mildness. For variation add 1 teaspoon ground cumin, which has a great affinity both with lamb and mint. Serves 4–6.

Put a handful of finely chopped fresh mint and 1 teaspoon sugar in a bowl. Stir in 2 tablespoons boiling water. Add 2 tablespoons white wine vinegar and leave for at least 1 hour.

TART FRUIT SAUCES

All sorts of fruits can be used to make enhancing sauces to serve with pork, ham, duck, goose and game, and cranberry sauce is traditionally served with turkey.

Either simply stew the fruit with a little sugar until soft and thick, or sharpen it with vinegar or lemon juice as a little acidity cuts the fattier meat. I prefer apple sauce to be cooked until mushy, but not smoothly pureed. If you like, stir in 1 heaping tablespoon plain yogurt before the sauce cools. Serves 4–6.

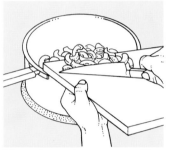

To make apple sauce, put 1lb (500g) peeled and sliced cooking apples in a saucepan with 2 tablespoons sugar and 2 tablespoons lemon juice. Cook, stirring, until soft. Remove from the heat and leave to cool.

IDEAS FOR FRUIT AND VEGETABLE SAUCES

• Make vegetable puree sauces from red or yellow peppers, spinach, watercress, parsnips, carrots, leeks, zucchini, fennel or eggplant. Cook the vegetables by boiling, grilling or sautéing in butter, then puree and thin with cream, yogurt or stock if necessary.
• For the smoothest possible vegetable sauce, pass the puree through a fine sieve after blending in a food processor.
• Fresh plums, blackcurrants, apricots, gooseberries, whole kumquats or chopped tangerines and, of course, cranberries, can all be stewed with a small amount of sugar, and a little water or orange juice to make thick, shiny sauces delicious served cold or hot with pork, ham, duck and game. Sharpen them with lemon juice or wine, cider or raspberry vinegar.
• To make an oriental-style dipping sauce, boil together 2 tablespoons lemon juice, ½ cup (125ml) soy sauce, 1 tablespoon cider vinegar, 2 tablespoons sugar, a grated 1in (2.5cm) piece fresh ginger and 2 cloves finely chopped garlic for 1–2 minutes. Cool, strain and stir in 2–3 tablespoons sliced green onions. Serve with shrimp tempura (page 129).

Pesto, a traditional Italian sauce for pasta, is made with fresh basil, olive oil and toasted pine nuts.

PESTO SAUCE

In Liguria, Italy, where this basil sauce for pasta originated, there are vast fields of basil plants stretching as far as the eye can see. The smell as the basil is picked in the warm sun is exquisite. You can recapture this fantastic smell if you make pesto at home, particularly if you pound the leaves and other ingredients in a mortar and pestle, which is the best way of making it if you have time. For speed, however, process all the ingredients in a food processor, adding the cheese last. Keep in well-sealed jars in the refrigerator or freeze. If you haven't enough basil use some parsley. Makes about 1¼ cups (300ml).

 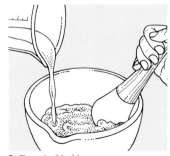

1 Toast 1oz (25g) pine nuts in a high oven or toss in a dry frying pan for 1–2 minutes. Put about 1 cup (50g) coarsely sliced fresh basil leaves, 2 coarsely chopped garlic cloves, the toasted pine nuts and a good pinch of salt in a mortar. Press and grind with the pestle until the mixture becomes a paste.

2 Beat in ⅔–¾ cup (150–175ml) olive oil, starting with a drop at a time and gradually increasing to a steady stream, as if making mayonnaise (page 202). Stir in 4 tablespoons freshly grated Parmesan and 2 tablespoons grated pecorino cheese, or use all Parmesan cheese if you can't obtain pecorino.

SWEET SAUCES *and* SYRUPS

Sweet fruit sauces are usually based on fruit purees, or jams and jellies, and can be cooked or uncooked. In general, they are thinner than the tart fruit sauces (page 207) as they are intended to be served with or to glaze cakes, pies or tarts. Fruit-based purees can be sweetened and are sometimes thinned and flavored with a liqueur or lemon juice. Both these ingredients help to bring out the flavor of the fruit and prevent discoloration.

I think the most popular sauce for puddings is chocolate – it is usually used with ice cream and other frozen desserts, but is also delicious with poached fruit, especially pears. Vanilla, coffee and brandy, along with orange, almond, cherry and other flavored liqueurs can be stirred in for extra flavor or to complement a particular pudding. Cinnamon also has a special affinity for chocolate.

Another type of sweet sauce is based on sugar syrups. To make these syrups, sugar and water are cooked together to a certain density which is calculated by the proportion of water to sugar or measured on a special thermometer (page 23). A sugar syrup can be flavored with vanilla, cinnamon, ginger, mint and many liqueurs to serve with a wide array of desserts.

UNCOOKED FRUIT PUREES

A fruit sauce for pouring, also called a coulis, can be made in minutes in a food processor. Soft fruit and fruit pulps are the easiest as they need little preparation and tend to have the brightest colors. Raspberries, strawberries, blackberries, blackcurrants, blueberries, kiwi and mango all make vividly colored purees which look spectacular on a plate with other sliced fruit arranged on top. The amount made depends on how juicy the fruit is.

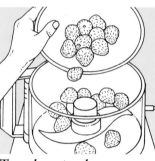

To make a strawberry *puree, process hulled berries in a food processor or blender with a little fresh orange juice and water until smooth. Strain and sweeten the sauce if you want.*

RASPBERRY SAUCE

The most famous fruit sauce is Melba sauce, a raspberry sauce prepared especially for the opera singer Nellie Melba by Escoffier while he was working at the Savoy Hotel in London in 1892. It was intended to coat a poached peach served on vanilla ice cream, which is still a wonderful combination of flavors known as Peach Melba.

When fresh raspberries are not in season, use frozen ones. Makes about 1¼ cups (300ml).

Purée 2 cups (300g) raspberries *with a little lemon juice, water and sifted confectioners' sugar. Strain through a fine nylon sieve. Stir in 2 tablespoons framboise (raspberry liqueur), if desired.*

SUGAR SYRUPS

A simple solution of sugar dissolved in water is very useful for a number of sweet recipes, from soaking fruit, sponges, cakes, savarins and baba au rhum, to making sorbets and sauces. The technique is easy but needs a little care.

It is vital that all grains of sugar are dissolved in the water before boiling, otherwise the solution may crystallize around the remaining grains. To prevent this, use a heavy saucepan, preferably copper or aluminum for even heat distribution, and brush down the sides of the pan while the sugar grains dissolve, using a pastry brush dipped in cold water.

Syrups are measured in terms of densities according to their final use. The rapid boiling in step 2 evaporates the water thereby concentrating the density. A low-density or light syrup of 1lb (500g) sugar to 5 cups (1 liter) water is used for fruit salads, poaching fruits, soaking sponge cake, baba au rhum and savarins; a medium-density syrup of 1lb (500g) sugar to 2½ cups (500ml) water is used for candying fruits; a high-density or heavy syrup of 1lb (500g) sugar to a scant 2 cups (450ml) water is used for making sorbets and ice creams.

If you wish to keep sugar syrup for a couple of weeks in the refrigerator, add 1 teaspoon of liquid glucose, available at candy supply stores, after it has cooled. This keeps it from crystallizing.

1 *Put the sugar and cold water into a large heavy saucepan and heat slowly to dissolve the grains, stirring occasionally with a wooden spoon. As the sugar dissolves, brush down the sides of the pan using a pastry brush dipped in cold water to remove any grains of sugar. It is very important not to allow the water to boil until every grain of sugar has dissolved.*

2 *Increase the heat and bring to a rolling boil, without stirring at all. Boil for about 2 minutes or until the syrup is clear. Remove the pan from the heat and leave to cool. For an orange- or lemon-flavored syrup add orange or lemon juice at this stage. When the syrup is cold use as required or store in the refrigerator in a screw-top jar, adding 1 teaspoon liquid glucose if necessary.*

SWEET WHITE SAUCE

Here is a simple dessert sauce to which you can add all sorts of flavorings – grated lemon, lime or orange rinds, brandy, sweet sherry, almond extract, vanilla extract and so on.

For an economical chocolate version, mix 1 tablespoon cocoa powder with the cornstarch before cooking and add some unsweetened chocolate, broken in small pieces.

You can make this useful sauce in advance, then just gently reheat it when ready to serve. Makes about 1¼ cups (300ml).

Mix 1 tablespoon *cornstarch with a little milk from 1¼ cups (300ml). Bring the remaining milk to a boil with 1 tablespoon vanilla sugar (page 235). Pour the hot milk onto the cornstarch mixture, beating well, then cook, stirring, until thickened.*

Thick and glossy Hot Spiced Chocolate Sauce (page 213) complements the fresh taste of a pear lightly poached in syrup.

HOT CHOCOLATE FUDGE SAUCE

Very simple to make, this chocolate fudge sauce is decadent and perfect to serve over homemade ice cream. Try it with coffee, chocolate, strawberry or traditional vanilla ice cream (page 235). It is particularly good poured over bananas or sliced fresh pears, topped with chopped, toasted nuts. It keeps well in the refrigerator for about a week and still stays quite runny, although it thickens a bit. Before serving, reheat gently in a saucepan without boiling. Makes about 2 cups (450ml) to serve 4–6.

1 *Melt 2oz (50g) butter in a small saucepan with 2oz (50g) unsweetened chocolate, broken in pieces. Stir until smooth, then beat in 2 tablespoons cocoa powder. Beat in 4oz (125g) light brown sugar or dark brown sugar for a stronger, more fudgy taste.*

2 *Slowly add 7fl oz (200ml) evaporated milk, 1 teaspoon vanilla extract and a pinch of salt. Boil for 1 minute, then set aside to cool slightly. Serve while still warm over scoops of ice cream, fresh fruit, such as strawberries, or a slice of cheesecake.*

HARD SAUCE

When I was a child, hard sauce was the only thing which would make me eat steamed Christmas pudding. I still adore this rich mixture of sugary, brandy-flavored butter which melts on the steaming pudding. For a very smooth sauce, all confectioners' sugar can be used, but I think a combination of sugars is best to give the texture a slight crunchiness. Cover and store in the refrigerator for up to 1 week but remove about 1 hour before serving. Makes about 1¾ cups (400g).

FLAVORING SWEET SAUCES

• Butterscotch is one of my favorite sweet sauces to pour over ice cream, or over soft fruit. I make it with 3oz (75g) unsalted butter, 3/4 cup (150g) light brown sugar and 2 tablespoons light honey such as orange blossom or clover. Melt the ingredients together in a saucepan and then boil for 1 minute; for a finishing touch stir in a little lemon juice or heavy cream at the end.
• Chopped toasted hazelnuts can be stirred into butterscotch, hot fudge or chocolate sauces just before serving.

• For a fresh orange sauce, sweeten 1¼ cups (300ml) freshly squeezed orange juice and the juice of 1 lemon with a little honey or sugar in a saucepan. Stir in 1 teaspoon cornstarch or arrowroot mixed with 1 tablespoon water. Bring to a boil and stir constantly for 2 minutes until the sauce has thickened. This is a good sauce for gingerbread served with or without cream as well.
• I often dress fruit salads, particularly those containing strawberries, or it could be simply a bowl of strawberries,

with a fresh orange syrup: dissolve ¾ cup (175g) sugar in the strained juice of 3 oranges and 1 lemon, then bring to a boil and cook rapidly for 3 minutes. Leave to cool before pouring over the fruit.
• Yogurt, mascarpone and crème fraîche are a boon for making quick sweet sauces. For mocha sauce, stir in strong black coffee and grated chocolate. Other good additions are chopped, toasted nuts, fresh fruit purees and caramel or a little concentrated orange juice and finely grated rind.

Put 8oz (250g) soft *diced unsalted butter into a bowl and beat in 1 cup (75g) confectioners' sugar and ¼ cup (50g) light brown sugar. Little by little, beat in 4–6 tablespoons brandy according to taste. Use rum instead of brandy if you prefer.*

CUSTARD *and* CREAM SAUCES

Sweet egg custard is a wonderful sauce as well as being the base for many other puddings, ice creams and mousses. Although you can flavor it with endless variations such as lemon or orange rind, coffee, chocolate and a variety of liqueurs, the flavor of real vanilla from an infused vanilla bean is hard to match. Pastry cream, also called *crème patissière*, a rich filling for fruit tarts, cakes, napoleon, éclairs and profiteroles, is simply thickened custard.

A sweet sabayon, or the Italian version, zabaglione, is a rich mousseline sauce, so special it can even be served as a

pudding on its own. Really an emulsified sauce of beaten egg yolks, sugar and a liqueur, usually Marsala, it is cooked carefully over a low heat, like hollandaise sauce. It can also be poured over fruit and then glazed under a grill at the last minute.

Sweetened and flavored whipped cream, also called *crème Chantilly*, has many uses. As a sauce it can be spooned over desserts and served with fresh fruit but it can also be used for a pastry filling like pastry cream. Flavor it the same way as custard and pastry cream (see box opposite).

REAL VANILLA CUSTARD

This really is a special treat. It is so good that the French serve it with many of their pastries as *crème anglaise*. In traditional custard recipes, the milk and eggs are stirred for ages in a bowl set over a saucepan of simmering water, but I find if you just scald the milk and pour it from a height onto the eggs, then stir it over the lowest heat possible you can speed up the process without running the risk of curdling.

To obtain the flavoring of true vanilla, split a vanilla bean lengthwise and remove the seeds with a pointed knife. (The seeds intensify the vanilla taste.) Place the bean and seeds in a saucepan and add 1¼ cups (300ml) each milk and light cream. Bring just to a boil and remove from the heat. Set aside, covered, for 15–20 minutes to infuse the flavor. This is delicious hot or cold served with cakes, pies, fruit salads and tarts (page 220). Makes about 2½ cups (600ml).

1 *Beat 4 egg yolks (or 1 whole egg and 2 yolks) together in a bowl. If planning to serve the custard thickened and cold, beat in 2 teaspoons cornstarch.*

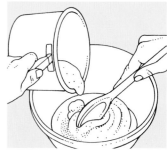

2 *Reheat the vanilla-flavored cream and milk just until tiny bubbles appear around the sides of the saucepan but do not boil. Remove at once and pour gradually onto the eggs from a height, beating hard until all the milk and cream are added. Strain the mixture through a fine sieve back into the saucepan.*

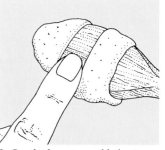

3 *On the lowest possible heat, stir constantly until the custard thickens to the consistency of light cream: if you draw your finger across the back of a custard-coated spoon it should leave a clear line. Pour the custard immediately into a pitcher to cool and serve warm or cover with a piece of plastic wrap so a skin doesn't form. This will keep for up to 2 days in the refrigerator.*

Real vanilla-flavored custard sauce elevates a homemade apple pie to an upscale dessert.

PASTRY CREAM

More hardy than whipped cream or *crème Chantilly*, (below) pastry cream has numerous uses as a filling for éclairs or profiteroles (page 255) and fruit tart bases.

Although quite simple to make, pastry cream does need swift stirring to prevent any lumps from forming. If it does get lumpy beat it well when cold or process it in a food processor. You can flavor it in the same way as custard (see box right). Pastry cream will keep for up to 2 days covered in the refrigerator. Beat well before using. Makes about 1¼ cups (300ml).

1 Blend together 3 egg yolks, ¼ cup (50g) sugar, ½ teaspoon vanilla extract and 3 tablespoons each cornstarch and all-purpose flour in a heavy saucepan over a low heat. Gradually mix in 2 cups (450ml) milk, stirring constantly as you pour.

2 Slowly bring to a boil, stirring constantly until thickened. It will look alarmingly lumpy at first but keep stirring and the sauce will become smooth. Cook for 1 minute.

3 Remove the saucepan from the heat. Leave to cool, stirring occasionally to prevent a skin from forming. For additional flavor, beat in 2 tablespoons brandy, rum or sherry.

FLAVORING CUSTARD AND CREAM SAUCES

• You can flavor a custard sauce with flavorings other than vanilla; infuse grated orange, lime or lemon rind in the milk and cream instead of the vanilla bean for citrus custards; stir in 2–3 teaspoons instant coffee to the hot milk and cream as well as the vanilla bean for a coffee sauce; grate 3oz (75g) unsweetened chocolate into the hot vanilla-flavored milk and cream and stir until melted for a chocolate sauce.

• For honey custard sauce, sweeten the milk and cream with 2 tablespoons well-flavored honey instead of sugar and stir until melted.

• Liqueurs, such as rum, brandy, kirsch or an orange liqueur, can be stirred into the custard at the end of cooking.

• A little ground cardamom enhances an orange custard, and ground nutmeg or cinnamon are good with a plain vanilla custard.

• Other ingredients can also be added to the custard such as chopped toasted nuts, crushed macaroons or finely chopped prunes, raisins, dried apricots or crystallized ginger.

• To make a light mousseline custard sauce, whisk reconstituted powdered egg whites equivalent to 2 egg whites with a pinch of salt until they hold soft peaks and then fold them gently but thoroughly into the sauce just before serving.

• If, like me, you love lemon and orange curd, you can make a delicious citrus sauce by following the recipe for custard sauce but omitting the vanilla and using fresh, strained orange and lemon juice for the liquid instead of milk and cream – this sauce is wonderful for a variety of desserts including gingerbread (page 269), upside-down cakes (page 218) or hot sponges (page 266).

CRÈME CHANTILLY

This is simply sweetened and flavored whipped cream. Sometimes, 1–2 tablespoons brandy or a fruit liqueur are folded in. Whip heavy cream with vanilla sugar (page 235), using 2 tablespoons sugar for each 1¼ cups (300ml) cream, or to taste. Use like pastry cream (above), spoon over desserts or serve with fresh fruit. Coarsely grated chocolate is good folded into crème Chantilly and looks pretty too.

SABAYON SAUCE

In France, this light and frothy mousseline sauce is known as sabayon and is spooned over fruity desserts. When freshly made and warm it is delicious served with a simple sponge cake. In Italy, when flavored with sweet rich Marsala and extra sugar it becomes the classic dessert zabaglione.

For a sauce, allow 1 tablespoon sugar to each egg yolk. For zabaglione, allow 2 tablespoons sugar and 1 tablespoon of Marsala per yolk. The method of making them is almost the same. Makes about 1¼ cups (300ml).

1 To make sabayon sauce, put 4 egg yolks and 4 tablespoons sugar in a heatproof bowl and beat until frothy, ideally using an electric mixer. If making zabaglione whisk in the Marsala at this stage. Scrape down the sides of the bowl with a rubber spatula.

2 Set the bowl over a saucepan of gently simmering water and continue beating the mixture until thick. Make sure the bottom of the bowl does not touch the water, or the eggs could scramble. It helps to lift the bowl occasionally to check the water underneath.

3 The sauce is thick enough when the beaters leave a ribbon trail on the surface when lifted. For sabayon sauce, stir in 2 tablespoons sherry or sweet white wine and cool, beating occasionally. Zabaglione is usually served hot straight from the pan in tall, elegant glasses.

PLUM AND SHALLOT SAUCE WITH FRESH MINT *(194)*

Plums, with their natural sharpness, are ideal to serve with pork, duck, ham or game. Like apricots, they are a fruit which often has more flavor when cooked, and they go well with the slight sweetness of shallots. Serve hot or cold.   *SERVES 4–6*

6oz (175g) shallots, peeled but left whole
1lb (500g) red plums, pitted and sliced
1¼ cups (300ml) freshly squeezed orange juice
¼ cup (50g) sugar
1 tablespoon sherry vinegar
Salt and black pepper
Handful of fresh mint, finely chopped

Put the shallots and plums into a saucepan with the orange juice and sugar. Bring to a boil, then cover and simmer very gently for about 30 minutes until the shallots are completely soft and the plums are saucy. The juiciness of plums varies, so if you feel the sauce should be thicker, uncover the pan and boil to reduce the juices slightly, then stir in the vinegar and season to taste with salt and black pepper. Just before serving, stir in the chopped mint.

CRANBERRY SAUCE

A traditional accompaniment to your Thanksgiving turkey, cranberry sauce is good with other roasted and grilled meats as well.   *SERVES 6*

1 12oz (350g) package cranberries
1½ cups (300g) sugar
1 cup (250ml) water or orange juice

Sort the cranberries and discard soft ones. Combine cranberries, the sugar and water in a medium-size saucepan. Heat to a boil over low heat and cook, stirring, until thickened. Chill until firm.

CHUNKY HORSERADISH SAUCE *(194)*

Fresh horseradish root is available in most supermarkets and adds a unique flavor and heat to sauces in which there is some acidity. The easieast possible horseradish sauce is made by combining prepared horseradish with sour cream. The recipe that follows requires only slightly more effort and is the perfect partner to hot or cold roast beef and grilled fish or shrimp.   *SERVES 4–6*

1 cup (250ml) sour cream
1 medium-size sweet onion, coarsely chopped
⅓ cup (75g) freshly grated horseradish root or prepared horseradish
¼ teaspoon salt
¼ teaspoon sugar

In a non-metal bowl, combine the sour cream, chopped onion, horseradish root, salt and sugar. Spoon into a serving dish; cover and refrigerate until ready to serve. If covered tightly, this will keep 3-4 days in the refrigerator.

To vary this sauce, add crunch and a pretty pink color by folding 1 small raw beet, peeled and finely grated, into the prepared mixture just before serving.

KUMQUAT SAUCE WITH DILL *(194)*

I once visited kumquat orchards in Israel and the little trees massed with their brilliant orange fruit were a charming sight, like a miniature world. Kumquats have a pleasantly sharp and piquant flavor and the edible skin is quite thin. This is the perfect sauce for serving with roast or grilled duck.   *SERVES 4*

8oz (250g) fresh kumquats, cut in half lengthwise and seeds removed
1¼ cups (300ml) unsweetened apple juice
1 heaping tablespoon sugar
2 teaspoons raspberry vinegar
2 teaspoons cornstarch or arrowroot
About 1 tablespoon chopped fresh dill
Salt
2–4 pinches cayenne pepper

Put the kumquats into a saucepan with the apple juice, and bring to a boil, then simmer gently for about 20 minutes until they are very soft. Stir in the sugar, then

remove from the heat and stir in the raspberry vinegar.

Put 1 tablespoon of water in a cup, add the cornstarch or arrowroot and mix until smooth, then stir the mixture into the softened kumquats and return to the heat. Bring to a boil, stirring, then simmer gently, still stirring, for about 2 minutes until the sauce is thickened and translucent. Stir in the chopped dill and remove the saucepan from the heat. Season to taste with salt and cayenne pepper and serve the sauce warm.

INDIAN SPICED MUSHROOM SAUCE *(194)*

Cultivated mushrooms are greatly improved by spices, and this creamy sauce transforms roast and grilled chicken or lamb. It is quite piquant despite the cream. Serve the sauce with pasta dishes. Or, you can make a delicious egg curry by slicing hard-cooked eggs and mixing them in with the sauce. The meatier cremini mushrooms are ideal for this sauce if available.   *SERVES 6*

2oz (50g) butter
1 tablespoon peanut or sunflower oil
2 teaspoons ground coriander
1 teaspoon ground cumin
1 teaspoon ground cinnamon
2in (5cm) piece fresh gingerroot, peeled and finely chopped
3 large cloves garlic, finely chopped
6oz (175g) mushrooms, finely chopped including stalks
2 tablespoons tomato puree
½ cup (125ml) water
4 tablespoons lemon juice, strained
1¼ cups (300ml) heavy cream
Salt
2–4 pinches cayenne pepper
Handful of fresh cilantro or mint leaves, coarsely chopped

Melt the butter and oil in a heavy saucepan over a medium heat, then add the ground coriander, cumin and cinnamon and the chopped ginger and garlic. Stir the spices for a minute or so and then add the chopped mushrooms. Stir until the mushrooms begin to soften, and then add the tomato puree, the water and the strained lemon juice.

Mix the contents of the saucepan thoroughly and bring to a boil, then lower the heat and simmer very gently in the open pan, stirring occasionally, for 15–20 minutes. Bring to a boil again (if the mushroom mixture is very liquid boil for a few more minutes to reduce it slightly) and add the heavy cream.

Stir and boil the mixture for about 2 minutes, then remove the saucepan from the heat. Add salt and cayenne pepper to taste and stir the coarsely chopped cilantro or mint leaves into the sauce just before serving.

If you want to make the sauce well in advance, which you can, add the fresh herbs after you have reheated it gently.

RED VELVET SAUCE (194)

Peppers are a marvelous ingredient for sauces and you can vary the color of the sauce according to the pepper used. But I use red peppers again and again for their vibrant scarlet which you can make even more dramatic with a sprinkling of coarsely chopped flat-leaf parsley when the sauce is on the plate. This is a lovely, light sauce and is excellent with meat, poultry, vegetables and pasta dishes. I particularly like it with grilled lamb or chicken. *SERVES 4*

2 tablespoons olive oil
1 tablespoon lemon juice
4 tablespoons water
1 tablespoon tomato puree
1 large red pepper, halved, seeded and
  finely sliced (page 49)
1 large onion, coarsely sliced
3–4 cloves garlic, coarsely sliced
Salt
2 teaspoons bottled green peppercorns,
  drained and crushed
1–3 pinches cayenne pepper

Put the olive oil, lemon juice, water and tomato puree into a heavy saucepan and add the sliced pepper, onion and garlic and a little salt. Cover the pan and bring to a boil, then lower the heat and simmer gently for 15–20 minutes, stirring occasionally, until all the ingredients are completely soft.

Pour the contents of the saucepan into a food processor and process to a smooth puree, then spoon the sauce back into the saucepan. Add the crushed green peppercorns and bring the sauce just up to a boil again. Remove from the heat, add salt and cayenne pepper to taste and serve hot in a sauceboat or bowl.

RAGÙ (194)

Ragù, or Bolognese sauce, is a meat sauce to serve with all sorts of pasta including lasagna (page 84). If it is cooked long and very gently, it becomes rich, almost creamy, and aromatic with the addition of herbs and grated nutmeg. Make the sauce in advance and keep it in the refrigerator for up to 4 days, or freeze it, and then reheat from frozen while you cook the pasta. To make it really creamy, you can stir in a little heavy cream before serving. *SERVES 4*

2oz (50g) butter
2 tablespoons olive oil
1 onion, finely chopped
1 stick celery, finely chopped
1 carrot, finely chopped
12oz (375g) extra lean ground beef
3 large cloves garlic, finely chopped
1 cup (250ml) dry red wine
⅔ cup (150ml) milk
14½oz (411g) can chopped tomatoes
1 rounded tablespoon tomato puree,
  dissolved in ⅓ cup (75ml) water
1 teaspoon dried oregano
2 bay leaves
¼ whole nutmeg, grated
Salt and black pepper
Handful of fresh parsley, finely chopped

Melt the butter with the olive oil in a wide, heavy saucepan over a medium heat. Add the chopped onion, celery and carrot and stir until the vegetables are beginning to brown, then add the ground beef and the finely chopped garlic and stir briefly just until the meat has completely broken up and lost all of its redness.

Pour in the wine, increase the heat and boil, stirring frequently, for a few minutes until the wine has evaporated. Then add the milk and boil, stirring all the time, until that has evaporated, too.

Stir in the chopped tomatoes, tomato puree mixture, oregano, bay leaves, and nutmeg. Season carefully with salt and black pepper.

Stir the mixture and bring to a boil, then cover the saucepan and leave to barely simmer over the lowest possible heat for at least 2 hours, stirring occasionally and adding a little water if the mixture looks dry at all. Finally, remove from the heat and adjust the seasoning to taste. Before mixing with the pasta, stir the chopped parsley into the sauce.

COCONUT SAUCE (194)

Making coconut milk from fresh coconut is a laborious business, but using a can of prepared coconut milk makes it very easy. This creamy sauce is a wonderful accompaniment for fruit salads made out of mainly exotic fruits, such as mangoes, lychees, passion fruit or star fruit. *SERVES 6*

14oz (400ml) can coconut milk
½ teaspoon salt
2 tablespoons sugar
1¼ cups (300ml) heavy cream

Put the coconut milk into a saucepan and heat just to simmer over a low heat. Add the salt and sugar and stir until all the sugar has dissolved. Allow to simmer for about 10 minutes to reduce. Remove from the heat and stir in the cream, then pour into a bowl and refrigerate to chill before serving.

HOT SPICED CHOCOLATE SAUCE (209)

I love watching a hot chocolate sauce solidifying as it runs down ice cream. The sauce must be pure chocolate, and a little added sour cream and cinnamon brings out the best in it. Be careful when you melt the chocolate that the hot water beneath it never boils. If the chocolate does get too hot and it 'seizes' and thickens, briskly stir in a little warm water. *SERVES 4–6*

6oz (175g) unsweetened chocolate,
  broken into pieces
2 teaspoons vanilla extract
⅓ cup (75ml) sour cream
1 teaspoon ground cinnamon

Put the chocolate into a heatproof bowl set over simmering water or in the top of a double boiler. Add the vanilla extract, sour cream and cinnamon and stir until melted and smooth.

DESSERTS

I have to admit that this is the chapter closest to my heart. I have always loved desserts – I love making desserts, I love eating desserts, I even love just looking at desserts. I do have a sweet tooth, but I don't enjoy things which taste only of sweetness – there must either be an exceptional texture, or an element of sharpness, usually provided by the addition of lemon juice, to temper the sweetness.

My friends say they can always recognize my desserts by their sweet but sharp character, for example the Hot Lemon and Passion Fruit Soufflé in the Recipe Collection on page 238. I also love chocolate; dark, moist chocolate pudding cakes, served either with crème fraîche or an intense fruit coulis, are a great favorite. I often bring lemon in with chocolate, too; a sharp lemon tart glazed with melted chocolate is wonderful. With fruit I also enjoy the sharp intensity of flavor which you can find in passion fruit and blackcurrants, but delicate combinations, such as lightly cooked fresh apricots with the flowers from two or three elderflower heads are absolutely magical, too.

Cream, I feel, has to be used judiciously; too much cream without a strong taste to cut it, can make a dessert too rich, which I hate. I often mix a little plain yogurt into whipped cream to temper the richness or I use crème fraîche or mascarpone, which is delicious and tangier than cream. For those wishing to cut down on fat, the virtually fat-free sour cream is useful in desserts as an alternative to cream, because it actually tastes more creamy than even whole milk plain yogurt.

Making desserts is one of those areas of cooking which can often give you the feeling that you have raised a magic wand at some stage in the preparation. Results can be ethereal as with the lightest soufflés or melt-in-your-mouth mousses; they can also be warm and reassuring, like apple pie or an old-fashioned bread pudding fragrant with cinnamon and vanilla. They can be light and dreamy like an angel food cake filled with cream and summer fruit; rich and luxurious as in the darkest chocolate mousse or real vanilla ice cream; frosty and cooling as in delicately perfumed sorbets, and fruit ice creams; or tangy and refreshing as in fruit compotes. The last course sets the seal on the meal and must never be a disappointment.

As a dessert should echo the season, the weather and the mood of the occasion, it must also complement the main course to the advantage of both. A heavy meat course such as a hearty roast is best followed by something juicy and fruity like stewed fruit or a refreshing sorbet. A rich fish like salmon is also better followed by a really good salad of summer berries, whereas spicy foods, however rich, somehow make the taste buds appreciate creamy, milky puddings.

A dessert can be a truly artistic creation, and those inclined can spend a lot of time and thought on the final appearance. It is also important to realize, however, that just a swift sprinkling of nuts, grated chocolate, sugar crystals or flower petals, or a dusting of sifted confectioners' sugar or cocoa powder, can transform an ordinary looking dish into something really special. I certainly prefer simple decorations to swirls of piped cream.

Clockwise from top: Quince Pudding Brûlée (page 240) with sweetened cream cheese and quinces under a caramelized top; luscious fresh raspberries encased in a mascarpone and chocolate mixture in Chocolate Ripple Heart with Raspberries (page 241); ever-popular Summer Pudding (page 238) with a hint of orange; Passion Fruit and Orange Puddings (page 239) with a creamy sauce; Banana and Pecan Pie with Cranberry and Orange Coulis (page 241) uses puff pastry for the top and bottom crusts; Queen of Puddings with Fresh Poached Apricots (page 239); and an individual Crème Brûlée (page 240).

MILK *and* EGG DESSERTS

People used to talk of puddings in a slightly disparaging way as reminiscent either of school or poorer times. But when they started appearing in upscale restaurants everyone rediscovered that they can also be delicious. Rice (either wild, aromatic or arborio, and brown as well as white), semolina, tapioca and cornstarch are all being used for puddings today.

The best rice pudding I have ever had was made by my grandmother (who must have been one of the first health-food enthusiasts); she used brown rice and brown sugar and gentle, slow cooking to produce a nutty, creamy, caramel-flavored pudding with a wonderful, shiny brown skin. But other ways of cooking and flavoring puddings can have their charms, too. An excellent and often somewhat lighter rice pudding can be made by cooking the rice on top of the stove, stirring it often. This pudding will not form a skin like baked rice pudding and is excellent eaten cold. You can add cream and flavoring such as cinnamon to taste while you are cooking the rice, and you may stop cooking it the moment the rice is the exact texture you want. You can also stir in plain yogurt or whipped cream after it has chilled.

Baked egg custards should be rich and yolky (add an extra egg yolk or two) with an irresistible light smoothness. They can be baked in a dish or in molds with a sauce which tops them when they are turned out, as in crème caramel. Egg custard is also responsible for the creamy layers in bread and butter pudding.

TRADITIONAL BAKED RICE PUDDING

This classic old-fashioned pudding should be rich and creamy – never a solid white lump of rice.

I always use light brown sugar for flavor, and finely grated lemon rind to make it even better.

Because the character of the pudding is to be creamy there is no point in using skim or low-fat milk – use full-fat milk.

To make enough for 4 people you will need ⅓ cup (63g) short grain white rice and 2½ cups (600ml) milk.

1 *Rinse the rice and put it in a buttered 3¾ cup (900ml) ovenproof dish. Stir in 2 tablespoons light brown sugar, the finely grated rind of 1 small lemon, a pinch of salt and then 2½ cups (600ml) milk.*

2 *Dot the top of the pudding all over with little pieces of butter and freshly grated nutmeg and bake, uncovered, in a preheated oven, 300°F, 150°C for 1–1½ hours, stirring once after the first 30 minutes.*

Creamy baked rice pudding.

BREAD AND BUTTER PUDDING

The best bread and butter puddings have a golden crusty top, rich creamy egg custard, plump fruit and not too much bread.

To serve 4 you will need 4–6 slices well-buttered bread with crusts removed, cut into triangles, about ⅓ cup (50g) raisins and 2 tablespoons candied peel.

To make the custard whisk together 2 eggs plus an extra egg yolk with ¼ cup (50g) sugar, then whisk in 1¼ cups (300ml) milk and ⅔ cup (150ml) heavy cream and set aside.

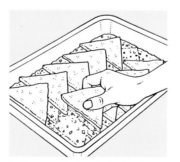

1 *Arrange the bread, buttered sides up, in layers in a 5 cup (1.2 liter) buttered ovenproof dish, sprinkling raisins and candied peel between the layers. End with a layer of bread. Or, dot with marmalade instead of fruit.*

2 *Strain the custard mixture on top of the bread and leave to soak for 30–45 minutes. Bake, uncovered, in a water bath (right) in the center of a preheated oven, 300°F, 150°C for 1–1¼ hours until the pudding is golden and slightly risen.*

USING A WATER BATH
A water bath, or bain marie, is a roasting pan of hot water for cooking food slowly at a low temperature. The hot water prevents the food from overheating and curdling. Steam rising from the water keeps the food moist and prevents it from drying out. For baking egg custards and egg thickened puddings put the pan of water in the oven when you preheat it, so the water heats up before you set the dish in it. The water should come halfway up the sides of the dish.

BAKED EGG CUSTARD

It is easy to forget the pure and simple goodness of this dish. Crème caramel (below) is a variation with a caramel sauce topping.

If possible use a vanilla bean in the custard, as the flavor of real vanilla makes all the difference, but, if necessary, substitute 2 teaspoons vanilla extract. You can make a baked egg custard simply with 3 or 4 eggs but I prefer a richer version made using 3 whole eggs plus 2 extra yolks with 2½ cups (600ml) milk. These quantities serve 6.

IDEAS FOR MILK AND EGG DESSERTS

• Ground nutmeg, cinnamon and mace are spices which enhance puddings, and a crushed cardamom pod or two boiled with the milk to flavor it is wonderful.
• For something deliciously exotic use coconut milk in place of the milk you use to make a pudding and flavor it with cardamom.
• Brown rice can also be used for puddings and produces a nice, nutty flavor and texture but cook the pudding slower and for longer with about a quarter more milk than normal to prevent it becoming too solid.
• I once made a wonderful bread and butter pudding using slices of Italian panettone, a light, dry yeasted cake with fruit and peel.
• Saffron, infused in the milk for rice pudding first, is a luxurious addition which will give a pudding a rich yellow color and distinctive taste.
• Crème caramel can be varied by substituting orange juice for the water.
• A little ground vanilla bean adds extra vanilla flavor to milk or cream.
• Prepare individual baked egg custards or crème caramels by dividing the mixture among 4–6 ramekin dishes. Cook in a water bath for 30–40 minutes.

1 *Put the milk in a saucepan with ⅓ cup (75g) sugar, a split vanilla bean and a sliver of lemon rind. Bring just to a boil, then cover, remove from the heat and set aside for 10 minutes for the flavors to infuse.*

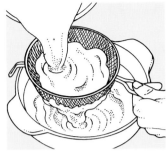

2 *Whisk the whole eggs and egg yolks together to mix, then pour into the warm milk, whisking all the time. Strain the custard mixture through a sieve into a buttered 4 cup (1 liter) ovenproof dish.*

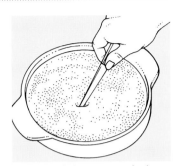

3 *Put the dish in a water bath (opposite) in the center of a preheated oven, 325°F, 160°C and bake for about 1 hour or until firm and a knife tip inserted in the center of the custard comes out clean.*

CRÈME CARAMEL

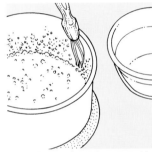

1 *Stir ¾ cup (150g) sugar with ⅔ cup (150ml) water in a small saucepan over a low heat until dissolved. Brush any sugar crystals from the side of the pan with a wet pastry brush.*

2 *Bring to a boil, without stirring, and boil until golden. Tip the pan to make an even color, then pour the caramel into a 4 cup (1 liter) soufflé dish and tilt to coat the base.*

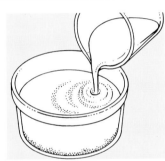

3 *Prepare the baked egg custard mixture (above). Strain the mixture into the soufflé dish and bake in a water bath as above. Set aside to cool, then invert the custard onto a serving dish.*

Coconut Cream Custard (page 241) makes an excellent dessert to follow a spicy meal, and can be accompanied by fresh exotic fruits such as star fruit, mango and kumquat, as here.

OTHER DESSERTS

There are a number of old-fashioned desserts that used to be just memories until they were rediscovered to satisfy the craving for heart-warming home-made desserts experienced by a generation of young adults who were denied them while growing up. Today it would be hard to find the dessert menu of an upscale restaurant that doesn't list a cobbler, crisp or pudding of some sort.

Warm, sweet and aromatic these dessert traditions deliver a reward far greater than the effort necessary to create them. Simple ingredients are put to the best use - fresh fruit in season and frozen or canned fruit out of season produce a spectacular Blueberry Cobbler or Cherry Crisp, while just ingredients from the cupboard create the Brownie Pudding.

BLUEBERRY COBBLER

The filling for this fruit cobbler can be varied by using any ripe fruit or a mixture of fruit. As some fruits are tarter than others, if using a fruit other than blueberries, the filling should be tasted for sweetness before the topping is added. This recipe will serve 6 people.

Combine ¼ cup (50g) light brown sugar and 2 tablespoons cornstarch in a 2 quart (1.89 liter) saucepan. Gradually stir in ½ cup (118ml) cold water and 1 tablespoon lemon juice. Bring to a boil over medium heat, stirring constantly until thickened. Fold in 4 cups (600g) blueberries, pitted cherries, or other fresh fruit cut to berry size. Pour fruit filling into a 6 cup (about 1½ liter) round baking dish or soufflé dish.

To make cobbler topping, combine 1 cup (125g) all-purpose flour, 1 tablespoon sugar, 1½ teaspoons baking powder and ¼ teaspoon salt in a bowl. Cut in 2oz (50g) butter with a pastry blender or 2 knives until the mixture resembles coarse crumbs. Make a well in the center and add ¼ cup (60ml) milk and 1 egg, mixing with a fork to form a soft but not sticky dough. Drop the dough by large spoonfuls to cover the entire surface of the filling.

Place the baking dish on a rimmed baking pan and bake in a preheated 350°F, 180°C oven for 25 to 30 minutes. Cool 10 minutes, then serve from the dish.

CHERRY CRISP

For a Cherry Crisp that will serve 6 people, prepare the filling from the Blueberry Cobbler recipe above using 4 cups (600g) pitted fresh, frozen, or drained, canned sour cherries and ½ cup (100g) granulated sugar for the ¼ cup (50g) light brown sugar. Pour filling into a 6 cup (about 1½ liter) baking dish.

To make the crisp topping, combine ½ cup (63g) all-purpose flour, ¼ cup (50g) light brown sugar, ½ teaspoon cinnamon and ¼ teaspoon salt in a bowl. Stir in 2oz (50g) melted butter until the mixture resembles coarse crumbs. Then, fold in 1 cup (72g) old-fashioned rolled oats and ½ cup (50g) coarsely chopped walnuts or pecans. Sprinkle the crumb mixture evenly over the surface of the cherry filling.

Place the baking dish on a rimmed baking pan and bake in a preheated 350°F, 180°C oven for 25 to 30 minutes. Cool 10 minutes, then serve from the dish.

BROWNIE PUDDING

Also known as Chocolate Pudding Cake, this saucy dessert can be assembled quickly and served just a few minutes after it has been removed from the oven. The wonderful aroma of a Brownie Pudding baking in the oven fills your kitchen and is a great way to greet guests arriving for dinner or a family coming home on a cold winter evening.

To make enough Brownie Pudding to serve 6 people, combine 1 cup (125g) all-purpose flour, ½ cup (100g) granulated sugar, 3 tablespoons unsweetened cocoa powder, 2 teaspoons baking powder and ¼ teaspoon salt in a medium-size bowl. Stir in ⅓ cup (85ml) milk, 3 tablespoons vegetable oil, 1 teaspoon vanilla and ½ cup (50g) coarsely chopped walnuts or pecans to make a stiff batter. Spoon the mixture into a greased 8in (20cm) square baking pan or dish.

Combine ½ cup (100g) light brown sugar and ¼ cup (30g) cocoa in a small bowl; sprinkle over the brownie mixture in the baking pan. Pour 1½ cups (360ml) hot water over all and bake in a preheated 350°F, 180°C oven for 40-45 minutes or until the top surface looks dry with some thickened pudding bubbling at the edges. Cool 5-10 minutes, then serve from the pan. Scoops of vanilla ice cream or sweetened whipped cream make a delicious topping.

IDEAS FOR OTHER DESSERTS

• To make a pineapple upside-down cake, generously butter a deep 9in (23cm) cake pan. Arrange 5 or 6 fresh or canned pineapple rings in the bottom with a dried apricot in the center of each. Sprinkle ½ cup (100g) light brown sugar over the fruit and top with the batter for the One-bowl Layer Cake (page 265). Bake in a preheated 350°F, 180°C oven for 30-35 minutes. Then test for doneness (page 263). Immediately loosen the cake and invert onto a heatproof serving plate. Remove pan immediately.

• To vary upside-down cakes, top with apples in the fall, cranberries for the holidays, rhubarb for springtime, and peaches for mid-summer.

• Small individual cobblers, crisps, pudding cakes and other desserts can be made by dividing the recipe into buttered, deep ramekins or custard cups. Place the filled cups on a baking sheet before baking about half the time necessary for it to bake all in one dish.

• Add dried fruit to the fresh fruit in a cobbler or crisp filling to make combinations such as apple-apricot, or cranberry-raisin.

• Slightly softened vanilla ice cream into which some cinnamon or nutmeg has been stirred makes a flavorful sauce for these desserts. Or, beat sweetened heavy cream just until very soft peaks form and stir in some brandy or liqueur.

APPLE ROLL-UPS

A cider and brown sugar glaze tops these fruit-filled biscuit rolls. This recipe makes 9 servings.

Combine ¼ cup (60ml) apple cider, ¾ cup (150g) light brown sugar and 1 tablespoon lemon juice in a 9in (23cm) square baking pan.

Combine 2 cups (250g) all-purpose flour, 3 tablespoons granulated sugar, 3 teaspoons baking powder and ¼ teaspoon salt in a bowl. Cut in 4oz (100g) butter with a pastry blender or 2 knives until the mixture resembles coarse crumbs.

1 *Stir a generous ¼ cup (60ml) milk and 1 egg into the flour mixture, stirring with a fork to form a soft, but not sticky dough. Turn out onto a floured surface and knead lightly to form a ball, then roll out to a rectangle about ½ in (1cm) thick.*

2 *With a spatula, spread the rolled-out biscuit dough with ½ cup (150g) apricot preserves and sprinkle with 2 large tart apples which have been cored, peeled and coarsely shredded. Roll up the biscuit dough like a jelly roll to enclose filling*

3 *Cut the filled biscuit roll crosswise into 9 slices. Place the slices with a cut side down into the cider and brown sugar mixture in the baking pan. Bake the roll-ups in a preheated 400°F, 200°C oven for about 20 minutes or until the biscuit dough is brown and the syrup mixture bubbles.*

4 *Remove baking pan from the oven. Immediately loosen the roll-ups from the edges of the pan and invert them onto a heatproof serving plate. Drizzle any cider syrup remaining in the pan evenly over the top of the roll-ups. Set aside to cool 10 minutes, then serve with vanilla ice cream.*

CHRISTMAS PLUM PUDDING

In Colonial times, steamed puddings were some of the nation's most popular desserts all year round. Many homes did not have an oven and steaming or boiling was the easiest way of producing a cake-like dessert in an open hearth. As reliable ovens became a part of every home, baked desserts, which could be made in a much shorter time, took over the dessert table. It is only at the holiday season that we look back to our family traditions and take the time to make such seasonal sweets as steamed plum pudding. In truth, it really isn't much trouble. Once steaming, the pudding can sit on a back burner and mind itself, except for the occasional additions of water, while the cook goes on with other holiday preparations. And, the spicy aroma it produces in the kitchen reminds your family that this seasonal treat is soon to be theirs.

I have evolved this recipe over the years to achieve what I feel is the perfect pudding – dark and rich but light in texture. For the perfect spherical shape I have experimented with cooking the pudding in a floured cloth and wrapping it in foil, but my large, round aluminum rice steamer lined with foil is ideal. Round steamed-pudding molds are also available. Of course, it could be made in any shaped mold. The quantities here will also fill two 5 cup (1.2 liter) pudding molds. Christmas pudding can, of course, be made with butter, but as it is such a strong flavored mixture, I don't think there is much point. I prefer to use suet or you could use vegetable shortening. You can completely make the pudding up to a week ahead; then wrap and refrigerate it until you are ready to reheat it. On Christmas Day, all you have to do is steam the pudding for an hour to warm it and keep it moist before serving. This recipe makes about 12 servings.

The traditional accompaniment to this steamed Christmas Plum Pudding is Hard Sauce (page 209). More like a frosting than a sauce, this easy-to-prepare mixture of sugar, butter and brandy can be made a week ahead, spooned into a decorative serving bowl, covered and refrigerated until about an hour before it is to be served. Then set it out at room temperature to warm up to a spoonable consistency.

½ cup (75g) candied cherries, coarsely chopped
1 cup (175g) pitted prunes, coarsely chopped
1 cup (175g) candied peel
1¼ cups (175g) seedless raisins
1¼ cups (175g) golden raisins
1¼ cups (175g) currants
¾ cup (75g) pecan or walnut pieces, coarsely or finely chopped
5 cups (250g) fresh bread crumbs
8oz (250g) shredded suet
6 eggs, beaten
⅔ cup (150ml) stout
3–4 tablespoons brandy, rum or whiskey

1 *Put the dried fruit, nuts, bread crumbs and suet in a large bowl and mix with a wooden spoon. Stir in the eggs, stout and enough brandy to make a mixture which just drops from the spoon. Refrigerate for a few hours.*

2 *Line both halves of a rice steamer with buttered foil, letting it overlap the edges. Fill both halves, then clamp shut and press the foil edges together. Or, butter, fill and cover a pudding mold. Put the pudding on a rack in a large saucepan and add hot water to come 2in (5cm) up the mold.*

3 *Cover and steam for about 6 hours, adding more boiling water as necessary. Remove pudding from the pan and allow to cool. When cold uncover the pudding, then rewrap it in a layer of fresh parchment paper, followed by one of foil. Refrigerate until you are ready to prepare for serving (left).*

TARTS *and* PIES

A pie or tart always seems like a treat to me, whether it be an old-fashioned double-crust pie filled with fruit such as apples, peaches, or cherries, or an elegant open tart with the most delicate wafer of pastry as a base. Pies and tarts provide endless opportunity for experiment and new ideas. They can suit all seasons, all occasions and hold a wide variety of enticing ingredients.

There is nothing better than a fresh fruit pie in season. You can tell it is springtime when rhubarb pies appear on the table. Berry, cherry and peach pies herald the arrival of summertime, while apple, plum and pear pies mean autumn has arrived. And, the holiday season is surely here when cranberry mixtures start to appear.

Double-crust or deep-dish pies offer an opportunity to decorate the top crust artistically. Pieces of left over pastry can be cut into decorations such as simple leaf or flower shapes (page 245). I often cut out letters to spell out a message identifying the contents of the pie or even the occasion for which it has been made. The pastry recipe on page 248 produces a generous crust so there will be plenty to use for decorating.

The traditional dessert pies that follow include a selection of holiday favorites. But don't just make them once a year; they will make an impression at any occasion. The crust recipes, savory pies and a few more sweet options may be found in the Pastry chapter.

OPEN TART

Open tarts or pies look attractive because the filling is visible. To prepare an open apple pie, prepare the pastry on page 246 and prepare the apples as for Double-crust Apple Pie (opposite), omitting the ginger. Bake as Double-crust Apple Pie but with a round of foil covering the fruit for the first 25 minutes.

An Italian Cheese Tart (right) is a traditional open tart made with sweet pastry. The cheese filling is flavored with lemon and almond. To serve 6 use a 9in (23cm) tart pan with removable bottom.

1 *Make conventional pastry (page 246) adding 3 tablespoons sugar and 1 tablespoon lemon rind to the flour mixture. Roll out three-quarters of the pastry and line tart pan. Trim edge, reserving the trimmings. Pierce bottom all over with a fork.*

2 *In a bowl mix together 15oz (475g) ricotta cheese, ⅓ cup (75g) sugar, 2 eggs, 2 tablespoons each flour and lemon juice, 1 tablespoon lemon rind, and 1 teaspoon almond extract. Spoon the mixture into the prepared pastry shell.*

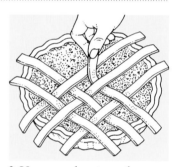

3 *Use reserved pastry and trimmings to make ½in (1cm) wide strips. Arrange in a lattice pattern over the tart. Trim off the edges and press to seal. Glaze pastry with milk. Bake in a preheated oven, 400°F 200°C for 25–30 minutes.*

DEEP-DISH FRUIT PIE

A deep-dish pie should be made with slightly thicker pastry than that for an open tart. For covering a 1½ quart (1.4 liter) oval dish, you will need pastry made with 2½ cups (300g) flour, 7oz (200g) butter, 1 teaspoon salt and 2-3 tablespoons well-chilled water (page 246). Using a pie bird prevents the pastry from falling in on the fruit filling.

Spoon about 2lb (1kg) stewed fruit without too much juice or 2–2½lb (1–1.2kg) fruit filling, sugar and any flavoring, such as spices, around the pie bird.

1 *Roll out about one eighth of the pastry into a strip as wide as the rim and long enough to go around the edge of the dish. Carefully lay the strip in position all along the rim of the dish, pressing the edges with your fingers to seal them together.*

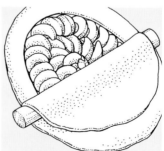

2 *Roll out the remaining pastry to cover the dish. Brush the pastry strip with water, then lay the large piece of pastry on top, using a rolling pin so it doesn't stretch. Cut a small hole for the pie bird. Press the edges to seal. Chill for 20 minutes.*

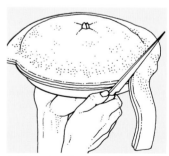

3 *Trim the edges, then glaze with milk or egg yolk beaten with a little water. Bake at 400°F, 200°C for 20–30 minutes until the pastry is golden. If the filling is not precooked, continue baking at 325°F, 160°C for another 20 minutes.*

PECAN PIE

Prepare conventional pastry (page 246). Roll out to an 11in (28cm) round and use to line a 9in (23cm) pie plate. Fold under edge of pastry at rim and crimp. Line with parchment paper and beans and bake blind for 7 minutes (page 245).

In a bowl, beat together 4 eggs, 1 cup (328g) light corn syrup, ⅓ cup (75g) granulated sugar, ⅓ cup (75g) light brown sugar, 2 tablespoons each flour and melted butter and 1 teaspoon vanilla extract. Fold in 2 cups (200g) coarsely chopped pecans. Spoon into the prepared pastry shell.

Bake in a preheated oven, 350°F, 180°C for 50 minutes or until the center appears set if the pie plate is gently tapped. Remove to a wire rack and cool completely. Store in the refrigerator until ready to serve. Top each serving with a spoonful of sweetened whipped cream.

PUMPKIN PIE

Prepare conventional pastry (page 246). Roll out to an 11in (28cm) round and use to line a 9in (23cm) pie plate. Fold under edges of pastry at rim and crimp. Line with parchment paper and beans and bake blind for 7 minutes (page 245).

In a bowl, beat together a 15oz (425g) can pumpkin, 4 eggs, ⅔ cup (150g) light brown sugar, 2 tablespoons melted butter, 2 teaspoons vanilla extract, 2 teaspoons ground cinnamon, 1 teaspoon ground ginger and ½ teaspoon ground nutmeg. Fold in ¾ cup (180ml) light cream. Spoon into the prepared pastry shell.

Bake in a preheated oven, 350°F, 180°C for 50 minutes or until the center appears set if the pie plate is gently tapped. Remove to a wire rack and cool completely. Store in the refrigerator until ready to serve. Top each serving with a spoonful of sweetened whipped cream.

DOUBLE-CRUST APPLE PIE

To make the double-crust apple pie shown on page 210, you will need 1½ times the recipe for pastry on page 246. Divide the pastry into 2 balls. Roll out one ball to make an 11in (28cm) round of pastry and use it to line the bottom, side and rim of a 9in (23cm) pie plate. Combine 3lb (1½ kg) tart cooking apples, peeled, cored and thinly sliced, with 2 tablespoons lemon juice. Arrange in the lined pie plate alternating with a mixture of ½ cup (100g) granulated sugar, 2 tablespoons all-purpose flour, and 1 teaspoon ground ginger and ending with apples.

Brush the pastry on the rim of the plate with water. Roll out the remaining ball of dough to a 10in (25cm) round and place over the apples; poke a hole in the center. Trim and pinch together pastry at edge. Roll out pastry trimmings and cut out as many leaves as possible. Moisten backs of leaves and arrange around hole in center of pie. Sprinkle top of pie with granulated sugar and bake in a preheated 400°F, 200°C oven for 30 to 35 minutes or until juices bubble at center hole. Serve hot or cold with light, heavy or sweetened whipped cream or vanilla ice cream.

FLAVORING TARTS AND PIES

• I use all-purpose or eating rather than cooking apples for both apple pies and tarts, as they hold their shape better and have a fuller flavor. For an open tart fry peeled apple slices in butter until soft, adding sugar and spices if desired and a little lemon juice which will form a caramel-flavored sauce around the apples.

• Remember that plums and berries produce quite a lot of juice during cooking so it is a good idea to precook them with sugar but no extra liquid; if necessary, you can evaporate some of the juice by boiling until it is syrupy and strongly flavored.

• Spices often enhance a fruit pie. Apples and pears take well to cinnamon, cloves or nutmeg.

• In the summer, chopped fresh mint goes well with all berry or cherry pie fillings.

• To vary the flavor of a pie or tart add a little brown sugar or honey to the fruit mixture or replace some of the flour in the crust with ground nuts, such as ground almonds.

• Upside-down tarts are similar to upside-down cakes, but use pie crust (page 246) or puff pastry or cookie crust (page 249) instead of a cake mixture. They look so beautiful with glossy fruit on a crisp caramelized base. Brush the pastry with water and sugar just before baking. It is important to remember that after baking the pastry you should reduce the oven temperature to 325°F, 160°C for the last 30 minutes or so to insure that the fruit is mellow-tasting and soft enough.

• For upside-down apple or pear tarts I don't peel the thin slices of fruit – the colored border of skin both looks and tastes better.

This Caramelized Orange Tart (page 238) is cooked upside down so that the pastry is extra crisp and the thin seedless orange slices, honey, butter and cinnamon combine to make a wonderful caramel filling.

FRESH *and* DRIED FRUIT SALADS

Fruit is beautiful to look at, wonderful to taste, simple to serve and good for you. With modern methods of cold storage and swift refrigeration, fruit from all over the world is now available at any time of year. But despite the choice all year round, seasonal fruit still holds a special charm and attraction.

When choosing fruit, inspect it very carefully. Colors should be bright, even sparkling; the skins taut but the fruit slightly soft to the touch, and a light aromatic smell should be noticeable. Hard fruit which has to ripen further at home should be arranged at room temperature on a dry surface and not touching each other.

Ever since I first tasted 'apricot leather' – a sheet of compressed dried apricot puree – in the Middle East as a young child, dried fruit has been one of my passions. It is altogether different from fresh fruit. Stewed with a little water, brown sugar and lemon juice, dried fruits such as prunes or apricots make a lovely simple dessert with whipped cream or custard, or they can be made into full-flavored fruit compotes, ice creams, purees and sauces as well as fillings for tarts and pies. They are also good in many spiced savory dishes.

Fruit salads can be made with either fresh or dried fruits or a mixture of both. Always think of a combination of color and texture as well as taste when composing a fruit salad. I like to make an orange-and-lemon-flavored fruit juice syrup for fruit salad instead of just sprinkling the fruit with sugar. Berries and cherries are nearly always a marvelous ingredient but I think that apples are far better kept to eat whole or to cook in other desserts.

PREPARING FRESH FRUIT

Many fruits need no more preparation than just rinsing in cold water, though apples and pears may need a good scrub. Berries deteriorate very quickly after contact with water, so they should not be rinsed until ready to use.

Many fruits such as apples, pears, quinces and peaches swiftly discolor when cut and exposed to the air but you can prevent this by rubbing the cut surfaces with lemon juice or by putting the pieces into a bowl of water with lemon juice added to it, or in a light sugar syrup (page 208).

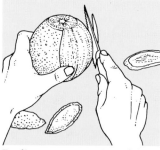

Peeling an orange *One of the simplest ways is to cut off the very top and bottom of the fruit, then cut off the skin and pith carefully in vertical strips, using a small serrated knife. Trim off any of the remaining bitter white pith and discard.*

Sectioning an orange *Slice down between the membrane and flesh on either side of a segment with a sharp knife, working over a plate or bowl to catch the juices. Repeat on the other side and pull away the section. Continue with the remaining sections.*

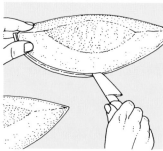

Preparing a large melon *Cut the melon in half lengthwise and scrape out the seeds. Cut each half into wedge-shaped slices. Loosen the flesh from the skin with a knife, then cut the flesh into pieces. Or use a melon baller to scoop out the flesh into balls.*

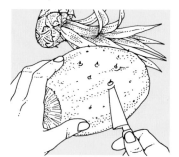

Peeling a pineapple *Cut off the crown and base, then hold the pineapple firmly upright on a chopping board and cut off the peel in vertical strips. Remove the remaining eyes with the tip of a sharp knife. Cut across into slices or chunks, cutting out the center core.*

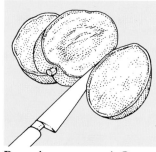

Preparing a mango: 1 *Cut through the mango horizontally as close as possible to the seed on each side. Peel the center section containing the seed and cut the flesh away from around the seed as neatly as possible. Cut the flesh into pieces or cubes as required.*

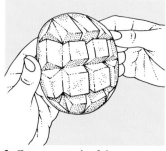

2 *Cut across each of the remaining side sections of the mango in a checkered pattern, cutting down as far as the peel but without piercing it. Then push up the skin from the center so that the cubes of flesh are exposed. Cut them away from the peel with a sharp knife.*

Pitting fruit *Using a small sharp knife cut along the groove in the fruit through the flesh to the seed, then use both hands and give a sharp twist to each half of the fruit to loosen the seed. If the flesh still clings to the seed use a teaspoon to pry out the seed and discard.*

FRESH FRUIT SALAD

Some of the fruit salads I had as a child put me off for many years. Over-sweet and with dull combinations of fruit, including the inevitable canned cherries, they gave no hint of how inspired a fruit salad can be. Think of the color of the fruit and how the flavors will complement each other. I usually use syrup made from strained fresh orange juice sharpened with strained lemon juice and mixed with a dash of liqueur (page 209). Allow about 1¼ cups (300ml) syrup for about 2lb (1kg) fruit. Except when soaking fruits in wine or in liqueur beforehand, it is best to make up fruit salads only shortly before serving.

A colorful fresh fruit salad made with nectarines, raspberries and blueberries. A fresh orange juice syrup gives an extra gloss to the fruit and prevents discoloration.

1 *Rinse and dry any firm fruit not being peeled. Prepare the fruit, by hulling berries and slicing or cutting larger fruit into chunks. Apples and pears discolor very quickly so it is best to leave their preparation until last.*

2 *Gently mix the pieces of fruit together in a bowl and sprinkle with lemon juice or liqueur, and sugar to taste if not adding syrup later. Cover the bowl tightly with plastic wrap without touching any fruit and chill in the refrigerator.*

3 *Prepare the fresh orange juice syrup mixture (page 209) and chill well. Shortly before serving, pour the chilled syrup over the fruit and gently toss to coat all the pieces of fruit thoroughly. Serve in a pretty glass bowl to show off all the fresh fruit colors.*

DRIED FRUIT COMPOTE

A dried fruit compote makes a sophisticated dessert out of stewed fruit. Presoak the fruit if necessary so that it softens. Place fruit and liquid together in a saucepan and cook gently on top of the stove for about 20–30 minutes until soft and plump. Strain off the juices and reduce them in a small saucepan. Put the fruit in a bowl, pour over the reduced glaze and mix, then chill before serving.

USING FRESH AND DRIED FRUIT SALADS

• Fresh fruit can make the easiest but often the most welcome end to a meal. If you are serving a selection of whole fruit it simply has to be well rinsed and arranged attractively in a bowl or on a serving platter.
• Classic fruit combinations include peaches or nectarines with red raspberries, melon and strawberries with orange juice or orange segments, and apricots with raspberries.
• Prunes and apricots make a good combination for a dried fruit salad.

• Mixtures of berries can be excellent simply sprinkled with lemon juice and sugar and chilled briefly before serving.
• When in season the juice of blood oranges makes a beautiful fruit-juice syrup (page 209) to use for fresh fruit salads.
• Wine or fruit liqueurs are often used to steep fruit in, so that the fruit absorbs the flavor before the fruit salad is assembled. The steeping liquid can be reduced and made into a thin syrup.
• Whipped cream mixed with plain yogurt, or fat-free sour

cream is an excellent low-fat alternative to plain whipped cream to serve with fruit salads.
• A smooth fruit puree or coulis (page 208) of raspberries, blackbrries or other berries can be lovely for serving with fruit salads, too.
• For a mango salad sprinkle the slices or cubes of fruit with lemon juice, and then make a coconut dressing by reducing coconut milk with a pinch of salt and sugar to taste. Chill before using.
• A mixed citrus salad is nice

with slivers of caramelized rind and a clear honey dressing.
• My favorite fruit salad is a generous mixture of fresh raspberries, strawberries and any other available berries which I combine with blackberries which have been simmered in a saucepan with sugar to bring out their juices and then cooled.
• Garnishes for fruit salads can include slivers of nuts, strips of fresh mint leaves, grated fresh coconut and raisins or chopped dates soaked in wine or liqueur.

OTHER FRUIT DESSERTS

Stewed and poached fruit can be cooked either on top of the stove or in a covered dish in the oven. Stewed fruit, cooked over a higher heat and stirred while cooking, becomes soft and mushy. Poached fruit is lowered into a flavored sugar syrup and cooked gently until just soft enough to pierce through easily with a knife while still holding a perfect shape. Fruit can also be sautéed in butter and eaten warm: the sugary juices become caramelized and the flavor of the fruit is enriched by the butter.

Fruit fool, an easy-to-make English dessert, is made by adding cooled pureed stewed fruit to whipped cream. Low-fat alternatives to whipped cream include plain or vanilla-flavored yogurt or fat-free sour cream. Egg custard can be used, too. Fruit puree is also good gelled and as a sauce to spoon onto a dessert plate around baked desserts.

Finally don't forget fresh fruit molds and terrines. Cool and refreshing, they make a simple but impressive end to a meal when made in a decorative shape.

STEWING FRUIT

Stewing is a simple technique of softening fruit so it can be made into a smooth puree, used as a pie filling or simply eaten as fruit soup with a topping of yogurt. Stewed fruit purees are so versatile that they can be served on their own or slightly sweetened to make a 'natural' sauce for other fruit, or combined with whipped cream to make a fruit fool.

Only very hard fruits such as under-ripe pears, apples or plums need much liquid for stewing. Most ripe fruits contain enough juice to cook in the syrup formed by added sugar dissolved in their own juices. A little lemon juice added with the sugar sharpens the taste, and you can use honey instead of sugar.

Apricots are the best dried fruits to stew: soak and simmer gently in just enough orange and lemon juices sweetened with brown or white sugar to half cover the apricots.

Put fresh fruit to be stewed into a saucepan with sugar and little or no liquid. Stir over the heat until the sugar has dissolved, then cover and simmer until the fruit is soft.

POACHING FRUIT

Poached fruit is cooked very gently in a light syrup (page 208) so it still holds its shape. It can be eaten hot or cold, with or without its syrup and makes a simple but elegant dessert. Firm fruit such as pears, apples and plums hold their shape best when poached, but with juicy fruits you can use a heavier sugar syrup which delays the point when they begin to collapse. Lemon juice added after cooking counteracts the sweetness.

1 *Place a single layer of sliced or whole peeled fruit carefully in a wide saucepan of hot syrup. Make sure that the fruit is fully covered by the syrup.*

2 *Cover and poach very gently until the fruit is just soft when pierced with a small knife. Remove from the heat, cover and leave for several minutes.*

MAKING A FRUIT PUREE

For the smoothest puree, *process the stewed fruit in a food processor, then push through a fine sieve using the back of a spoon. Or you can simply use either the sieve or processor alone for a slightly less smooth result.*

For a fruit fool, *whip heavy cream until it forms soft peaks and is about the same consistency as the puree, then gently fold the same amount of stewed or pureed fruit into the cream. Chill well before serving.*

MAKING EXTRA-SPECIAL FRUIT DESSERTS

• Fools are nicest when they have a little texture, so I tend to use very soft stewed fruit for fools without pureeing it. Smooth purees are better for sorbets and ice creams, or for a fruit coulis (page 208) to accompany fresh fruit.

• If making a fool from strong-colored fruits such as blackberries you can achieve a marbled effect by mixing in the whipped cream with a minimum of strokes.

• Green grapes or apricots stewed with elderflowers take on a scented muscatel flavor and make irresistible compotes. If you have some muscat wine, such as Beaumes-de-Venise, add a little to the fruit syrup before serving it with whipped cream.

• Decorate fruit desserts with strips of fresh mint leaves, feathery fennel and dill leaves, curls of plain chocolate or toasted, flaked or chopped nuts.

• Flavor syrups for poaching fruit with fruit juice or wine and whole spices such as mace, cinnamon, black peppercorns and cloves if appropriate.

• A simple compote of poached fruit can seem more sophisticated if it contains an interesting liqueur. Experiment with what you have at home. Stir it at the end of the cooking time for the strongest flavor.

• As well as using fruit juices, you can also make gelled fruit desserts with sweetened wine or lemon juice or with the cooled juices of stewed fruits.

• Fresh pineapple and kiwi fruit contain an enzyme which destroys the setting power of gelatin. If you want to use fresh pineapple juice in gelatin you must boil it for 3 minutes.

MAKING GELLED FRUIT DESSERTS

Gelled fruit desserts can be made with unflavored gelatin or flavored gelatin dessert mixes. Unflavored gelatin comes in envelopes of about 2¼ teaspoons. This will normally set 2 cups (424ml) liquid (which serves 4), except in very hot weather when you will need a little extra gelatin. You should also use a little more gelatin for a firmer set when you have a tall or complicated mold. Vegetarians can set gelled molds with agar-agar. following package instructions.

1 *Put 1 cup (240ml) fresh fruit juice in a saucepan with ¼ cup (50g) sugar. Stir 1 envelope gelatin into the liquid. Heat gently, stirring until sugar and gelatin have dissolved.Do not allow to boil.*

2 *Pour the warm liquid into a bowl containing another 1 cup (240ml) cold fruit juice and stir thoroughly to mix before pouring into a gelatin mold. Cool completely, then chill in the refrigerator for 6–8 hours until the mold is firmly set.*

3 *To turn out, gently loosen the edges by pulling them back with your fingers. Dip the mold into a bowl of hot water for just 1–2 seconds. Place a wet serving plate on top, then holding firmly with both hands, invert the mold and give a strong shake.*

MAKING A FRUIT TERRINE

Gleaming fruit terrines are easy to make, especially when the fruit is added randomly. To make one with set layers of fruit you must allow the gelatin to set between each layer. You can use slightly sweet white wine instead of fruit juice.

To serve 6–8 use 2½ cups (600ml) fruit juice such as freshly squeezed orange juice sweetened with 2 tablespoons honey and a selection of prepared fruits such as strawberries, the segments of 6 oranges and about 1lb (500g) fresh raspberries.

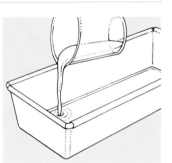

1 *Make up 2½ cups (600ml) fruit juice gelatin with 1¼ envelopes unflavored gelatin (above), and pour a small amount into a 9in (23cm) loaf pan or a ring mold to coat the bottom. Chill for about 15 minutes until set. Do not chill the remaining gelatin.*

2 *Add the prepared fruit in random layers, pressing down well as you go, then slowly pour in the remaining gelatin in a slow trickle until the pan is full. As you pour tap the pan on the bottom so the gelatin works its way down around the fruit.*

3 *Chill until well set. Unmold by loosening the edges, pulling them back with your fingers. Dip the pan in a bowl of hot water for 1–2 seconds only, then invert on a wet serving plate and give a strong shake. Reposition the mold if necessary. Slice to serve.*

This glistening fresh fruit terrine uses slices of orange, seedless grapes and raspberries to make a decorative dessert. The gelatin was made from white wine, colored with raspberry cordial. Like all fruit terrines, it can be served with cream or a fruit puree.

MERINGUES

The sculptural, overblown and fragile appearance of meringues never fails to thrill and they are an easy way to impress. Simple, old-fashioned meringues baked slowly at a very low heat until the edges turn slightly brown always bring me nostalgic memories of childhood.

Meringue can be used to great effect as the frosting on Baked Alaska, for pie or tart shells, to top lemon meringue pie and other tarts, or to transform a plain dish of stewed fruits (page 224). Tortes can be made using meringue layers instead of sponge cake or pastry. A meringue topping is cooked at a higher temperature and more quickly than individual-shaped meringues so it has been heated through but not dried inside. Meringues can be made with egg whites or pasteurized meringue powder. If using egg whites it is important to heat them thoroughly.

Like other apparently tricky culinary techniques, making meringues successfully is really quite straightforward. There are three basic methods, Swiss meringue being the easiest, but Italian meringue is the most stable and useful. I use Italian meringue to make ice cream (page 234).

SWISS MERINGUE

Swiss meringue is used for making simple shells or for topping a pie. A wire whisk and copper bowl will produce the most voluminous egg whites of the lightest and finest texture (page 77), however an electric beater works quite well. Be careful not to overbeat the egg whites or the meringue might 'weep' during baking. Any trace of yolk in the egg whites will prevent the whites from forming stiff peaks.

Two egg whites will make enough meringue for 12–16 shells or enough to top an 8in (20cm) pie.

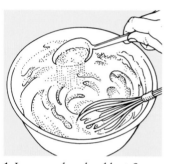

1 *In a very clean bowl beat 2 egg whites until they hold their shape and form soft peaks. Beat in 2 tablespoons superfine or vanilla sugar (page 235), beating until the meringue is smooth and glossy. With a large metal spoon gently fold in ⅓ cup (75g) more sugar.*

2 *To top a pie, spread the mixture over a hot, baked tart, being careful to leave no gaps. Use a spatula to make decorative peaks. Bake in a preheated oven, 350°F, 180°C for 15–20 minutes or until lightly tinged. Serve immediately or at room temperature.*

COOKED MERINGUE

Also known as *meringue cuite* this type is used for making petits fours, layers and meringue baskets, as well as for topping pies. Although difficult to work, its main advantage is that it keeps in the refrigerator, covered, for 1–2 days before using.

Put 2 egg whites and 1 cup (125g) confectioners' sugar in a heatproof bowl set over a pan of simmering water and beat until the mixture forms a very stiff meringue. Remove from the heat and continue beating the meringue for a further 10–15 minutes until cool. This amount makes enough to cover one large pie.

A sumptuous Raspberry and Chocolate Meringue Cake (page 240). Light meringue rounds flecked with toasted hazelnuts are sandwiched with raspberries, cream and a rich chocolate filling. Cocoa powder and superfine sugar are sifted on top as a final decoration.

ITALIAN MERINGUE

Similar to white Fluffy frosting, Italian meringue is most often used for topping puddings and for piping. Boiling sugar syrup is poured on to whisked egg whites, which, as a result, are partially cooked, making the mixture more stable and versatile than Swiss meringue.

This meringue holds its foam for a few hours before use or baking, which is why it is excellent for piping into shapes or making into baskets or discs. Italian meringue also forms the basis of some of the lightest and most successful ice creams (page 234).

To make the sugar syrup (page 208), use 1½ cups (250g) granulated sugar and 1 cup (125ml) water.

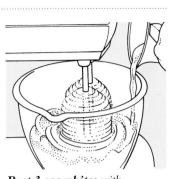

Beat 3 egg whites with ½ teaspoon salt in a clean bowl until stiff and glossy. (For ease, use an electric mixer but not a food processor.) Pour the boiling sugar syrup into the egg whites in a thin, steady stream, beating constantly until the mixture is smooth, very stiff and glossy. Allow the meringue to cool before using. This amount is enough to make two 9in (23cm) layers or baskets.

Piping decorative meringue fingers and stars. Use plain or fluted tips and allow a little space between the shapes for expansion.

SHAPING AND FLAVORING MERINGUES

• Use Swiss meringue for making individual shapes, and Italian or cooked meringue for making pavlovas, baskets or layers for meringue cakes.
• Homemade meringues sandwiched with whipped cream make a delicious tea-time treat.
• You can vary meringues and meringue toppings for pies, tarts and stewed fruit by adding toasted flaked or chopped nuts, grated fresh coconut, citrus fruit rind or grated chocolate.
• Coarsely grated chocolate or chopped pieces can either be incorporated in the meringue mixture or sprinkled on top – the chocolate melts lusciously into the meringue as it cooks.
• Add cocoa powder to a meringue mixture and then grate chocolate on top for all-chocolate meringues.
• Extra superfine sugar sprinkled over a meringue topping will make it brown attractively and glisten. Raw sugar or coffee sugar crystals are especially effective as they remain crunchy.
• As a topping for a large mince pie or an apple tart add ground mixed spice or cinnamon to the meringue mixture. You can

also fold in a handful of currants and candied peel.
• When filling a meringue shell do so only very shortly before you want to eat, and if possible spoon a layer of whipped cream, cream cheese or pastry cream onto the meringue before adding the fruit to prevent the juices from soaking into the meringue and softening it.
• To make one of my favorite desserts, *oeufs à la neige* or floating islands, poach ovals of meringue in simmering water, then chill and serve on a sea of custard made with the egg yolks (page 210).
• A meringue mixture incorporating ground nuts makes the lightest torte layers to frost together with vanilla or lemon custard made from the yolks (page 210).
• Two circles of meringue sandwiched with fresh ripe fruit and whipped cream or lemon curd (page 302) makes a spectacular summer dessert.
• Meringue can also be used to add a contrast of texture to smooth dishes. Fold some crumbled meringue into smooth ice cream before freezing.

SHAPING AND BAKING MERINGUE

Before shaping meringues prepare a baking sheet with greased parchment or aluminum foil.

To bake meringue shapes preheat oven to the lowest setting, 225°F, 110°C for 2½–3 hours until the meringue dries out and peels off the parchment easily. If the meringue sticks to the parchment after baking it hasn't been baked enough. Cool on a wire rack to crisp.

To make shells gently mold the mixture by shaping between 2 spoons and place on a prepared baking sheet.

To make a pavlova or basket shape, pile a mound of Italian or cooked meringue on a prepared baking sheet. Use the back of a large spoon to form a rim around the edge of the basket.

To make a meringue layer draw a circle on parchment on a baking sheet. Use a pastry bag fitted with a plain tip and pipe in coils in a continuous circle, beginning in the center.

SWEET SOUFFLÉS *and* MOUSSES

The experience of chilled cream poured over a light, steaming hot sweet soufflé is heavenly. You can make a hot soufflé with fruit puree, melted chocolate or lemon, orange or other strong-tasting fruit juices blended with flour and milk to make a sauce base just as you do when making a savory soufflé (page 76).

Because of the large quantity of bland egg whites in hot sweet soufflés, and egg whites and cream in chilled soufflés and mousses, use flavorings strong enough not to get lost. Pureed and stewed apricots, for example, are excellent base flavorings. Lightly cooked fresh blueberries add their unique character to a soufflé, and orange is one of my favorite flavors.

Chilled soufflés are, in fact, not really soufflés but actually mousses with plenty of beaten pasteurized egg whites incorporated into them then set with gelatin. They are called soufflés because of their high soufflé-like appearance, the result of the mousse mixture being spooned into a soufflé dish with a foil or parchment collar rising above the rim. When the collar is removed after chilling the dessert has the appearance of a dramatically risen soufflé.

Chilled mousses can be flavored with fruit, fruit juices, liqueurs or chocolate. They are richer than chilled soufflés because they contain more eggs and have a more velvety texture. They are not necessarily set with gelatin, unlike chilled soufflés.

HOT SWEET SOUFFLÉ

Hot Lemon and Passion Fruit Soufflé (page 238) here made as individual soufflés. The dark golden tops, dramatically speckled with the passion fruit seeds, are lightly dusted with confectioners' sugar just before serving.

A hot sweet soufflé is made on the same principle as a savory soufflé (page 76), with a sweetened white sauce base to which you add the egg yolks and your chosen flavoring. The desired consistency is like a thick custard but not so thick that all the air will be knocked out of the egg whites when they are folded in. If you are using a fruit puree or fairly juicy fruit as flavoring, you will need to add less milk when making the sauce base than if you are making a savory soufflé. The base of a hot sweet soufflé can be prepared well ahead, leaving only the beating and folding in of the egg whites to do just before baking the soufflé.

This Grand Marnier soufflé is a classic dessert. To serve 3–4 make a white sauce from 2oz (50g) butter, ⅓ cup (40g) all-purpose flour, 2 teaspoons grated orange rind and ¾ cup plus 2 tablespoons (200ml) milk (page 196). Add 1 tablespoon sugar. You also need 4 separated eggs and 1 egg white.

Stir 3–4 tablespoons Grand Marnier into the sauce, then beat in the egg yolks thoroughly. Beat the egg whites until they stand in soft peaks and fold into the soufflé mixture. Spoon into a buttered 6 cup (1.5 liter) soufflé dish that has been coated with sugar or ground almonds. Bake in a preheated oven, 375°F, 190°C for about 25 minutes until well risen but still slightly wobbly. Dust the top of the soufflé with a little confectioners' sugar and serve at once.

IDEAS FOR SOUFFLÉS AND MOUSSES

• Pureed exotic fruits such as mangoes (with added lemon juice) and passion fruit also make a good base for soufflés and mousses (see Hot Lemon and Passion Fruit Soufflé page 238).
• Fresh summer berries such as raspberries and strawberries can be crushed or pureed and sieved with a little lemon juice to bring out their flavors. If you can find them, red currants make a nice addition to raspberries. Toss both fruits briefly with sugar over the heat in a saucepan until the sugar just dissolves and the juices start to run. Then puree and sieve the fruit to use as the base in mousses and soufflés.
• For chocolate mousses or chilled soufflés the chocolate tastes at its most dark and luxurious if it is melted with a little strong black coffee.
• Adding a liqueur, rum or brandy to a fruit puree makes the resulting soufflé or mousse taste more sophisticated. An apple puree made with lemon juice to keep the apples white, and flavored with Calvados is excellent in a cold soufflé. Or, use Curaçao for an orange soufflé decorated with caramelized orange rind, or instead of rum or brandy in a chocolate mousse.
• Decorate the chilled lemon soufflé (opposite) with chocolate curls (page 231), an edging of crystallized violets, or prettiest of all, edible flowers such as fresh wild violets or rose petals.
• The chilled lemon soufflé (opposite) can be set in a jagged-edge chocolate bowl (page 231) instead of using a soufflé dish.
• Caramelized nuts for decorating chilled soufflés and other puddings are easy to do; simply rinse the slivered, chopped or whole nuts to dampen, stir them in some superfine sugar to coat and toss in a very hot dry pan for 1–2 minutes until they caramelize. Turn them at once onto parchment and separate them as much as possible before the caramel hardens.

CHOCOLATE MOUSSE

Chocolate never goes out of fashion; a chocolate mousse is always popular, and rightly so. Serve it well chilled in pretty glasses or little pots.

Chocolate mousse is usually piped with whipped cream but I prefer a sharper mixture of whipped cream and yogurt, which I spoon smoothly over the top of each serving. For decoration add glazed orange rind or grated chocolate.

To make 4–6 mousses use 6oz (175g) unsweetened chocolate and 4 yolks or 2 whole beaten eggs.

1 *Break the chocolate into a heatproof bowl and add 2 tablespoons strong black coffee. Put the bowl over a saucepan of gently simmering water and stir with a wooden spoon until the chocolate is melted.*

2 *Add yolks and cook, stirring, until the mixture reaches 160°F, 90°C. Remove from heat; add 1 tablespoon soft butter and ½ tablespoon rum or brandy. Beat dehydrated whites equivalent to 4 whites until they make soft peaks.*

3 *Fold the egg whites quickly but thoroughly into the chocolate mixture with a large metal spoon. Spoon the mixture into ramekins or small glasses and chill for at least 4 hours or overnight before decorating.*

CHILLED LEMON SOUFFLÉ

This light and refreshing dessert looks very dramatic rising well up above the edge of the dish. This was the first dessert I ever made and I still think it is excellent and refreshing. If you like a particularly sharp lemon taste, dissolve the gelatin in extra lemon juice instead of water. To serve 4–6 use 4 egg yolks or 2 whole beaten eggs, dehydrated egg whites dissolved in water equivalent to 4 whites, ⅔ cup (125g) sugar, the finely grated rind and juice of 3 lemons and ⅔ cup (150ml) heavy cream. Use a lightly buttered 4 cup (946ml) soufflé dish.

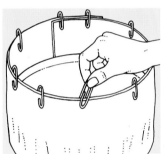

1 *Cut a strip of foil or waxed paper which when folded in half lengthwise is twice the depth of the dish and will fit around the sides with an overlap. Oil one side of the folded foil or paper, then mold it around the outside of the dish, cut edges up. Secure the paper with paper clips or tie with string.*

A rich chocolate mousse always makes an attractive dessert. Served here in individual glasses, the mousse is decorated with plain yogurt and curls of glazed orange rind.

2 *Put a heatproof bowl over a saucepan of simmering water. Add the egg yolks and sugar and mix well. Add the lemon rind and juice and beat thoroughly until thick and temperature reaches 160°F, 90°C.*

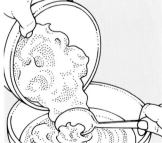

3 *Soften 1 package unflavored gelatin in 3 tablespoons of water then heat until gelatin dissolves. Fold into the egg yolk mixture. Chill until mixture starts to thicken. Whip cream to soft peaks, then fold into the mixture.*

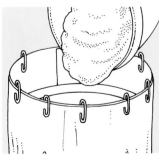

4 *Beat the egg white mixture until fairly stiff, then fold into the lemon and egg yolk mixture gently but evenly with a large metal spoon. Pour into the prepared soufflé dish and level the surface carefully with a spatula.*

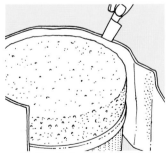

5 *Chill well for at least 4 hours. When set, remove the paper clips or string and run a spatula dipped in hot water between the 2 layers of paper or foil. Carefully peel away from the mixture. Decorate before serving.*

USING CHOCOLATE

Chocolate makes the most popular desserts of all. Hot, cold, or frozen, any chocolate dessert is always welcome – as long as you have not stinted on a generous concentration of chocolate. Good-quality semi-sweet dark chocolate should be used in all chocolate cookery. The most important thing is that it should contain a high proportion of cocoa solids – at least 50 per cent. Milk chocolate can only be used for coating or decoration as it will not add enough flavor in baking and is too sweet for most recipes.

Unsweetened cocoa powder is the solid brown part of the cocoa bean with the cocoa butter removed. The darkest, most chocolaty cakes of all can be made with plenty of unsweetened chocolate and a tablespoon or two of cocoa powder replacing some of the flour or ground nuts. In fact, chocolate can replace flour altogether – a hot chocolate soufflé is the only soufflé that doesn't need flour. For baking, cocoa powder added to chocolate intensifies both color and flavor but don't add it to melted chocolate to make a cake frosting as it makes the chocolate grainy.

White chocolate has the consistency but not the taste of chocolate as it is made only with cocoa butter, milk and sugar. It can be used to make a good chilled mousse, set with gelatin, which you can serve with a dark chocolate sauce – but it is not easy to melt (except in a microwave) and use for coating.

MELTING CHOCOLATE

Melting chocolate can be tricky, even for experienced cooks. As the cocoa butter content varies so much with different kinds of chocolate, it is extremely difficult to gauge just how long it will take to melt. If left a moment too long, or if the heat is too high, the mixture can easily turn into a hard, dry lump. Usually the damage will have been done and the smooth glossy consistency lost but you can try to restore the chocolate by adding butter, milk, cream or water and beating it again.

To melt chocolate break it into small pieces. Put the pieces in a completely dry heatproof bowl and set over a pan one-third filled with hot, but not boiling, water. Do not let the bowl touch the water, or the chocolate will become lumpy. Leave, uncovered, for 6–12 minutes, stirring until the chocolate is completely melted and smooth.

Melting chocolate should be done very slowly and with a watchful eye or it may scorch.

MAKING THE MOST OF CHOCOLATE

• There are a few ingredients which complement chocolate particularly well and seem to bring out its flavor even more; strong black coffee and cinnamon are two of them. Ground cardamom is also extremely effective. Vanilla is another compatible flavor but ideally it should be vanilla from a vanilla bean or use vanilla sugar (page 235).

• Gooey chocolate cakes (page 273) are marvelous with a fruit filling between the layers – raspberries are ideal. You can also make a fresh citrus curd (page 302) filling using orange or lemon juice.

• During the summer months complement a simple bowl of berries with a pitcher of chocolate sauce (make this by melting semi-sweet chocolate with a little water and then stirring in sour or light cream). Pour over the fruit, or onto each plate before you arrange a serving of fruit on top.

• Chocolate shreds or grated chocolate can be incorporated into ice creams with dramatic results. Make a lemon or vanilla bombe (page 237) and fill the hollow in the center with grated chocolate. Pack down and cover with extra ice cream and refreeze. When you spoon into the unmolded bombe the chocolate tumbles out.

• Chop chocolate into small pieces and add it to bread pudding, as well as to lemon or orange cake mixtures – it will melt into the cake in a delicious way as it cooks.

• Sprinkle grated pieces of chocolate onto cakes as soon as they come out of the oven so the chocolate melts in a haphazard pattern on top.

• A smooth chocolate glaze looks beautiful on a cake or poured over individual cakes. Before it has set you can decorate it further with chocolate curls (opposite).

• Melting 4oz (125g) chocolate with ½–1oz (15–25g) sweet butter makes a good coating consistency for covering cakes. For a less rich coating substitute 2 tablespoons of sour cream, light cream or plain yogurt for the butter.

• A good chocolate filling for a sponge cake can be made by melting chocolate and adding to butter whisked with a little icing sugar, then whisking in chopped toasted hazelnuts.

• Make a sauce of chocolate melted with water to serve with chilled lemon soufflé (page 229) instead of cream.

• If making an ice cream by the Italian meringue method (page 227), pour a thin stream of melted chocolate onto the mixture at different points before freezing to produce swirls of hard chocolate in the smooth ice cream.

• A thin layer of melted chocolate makes a delicious topping for a cheesecake.

CHOCOLATE DECORATIONS

Chocolate decorations are surprisingly easy to make and can transform almost any dessert or cake into a spectacular, professional-looking showpiece (see box opposite). A good-quality semi-sweet chocolate will produce excellent results.

Any leftover chocolate can be melted again and used in a sauce or cake filling or coating.

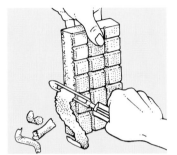

Making curls *Use a swivel-blade vegetable peeler to shave off curls from the side of a block of well-chilled chocolate.*

Grating chocolate *Gently rub a lightly chilled bar of chocolate along the coarse edge of a standard vegetable grater.*

Coating fruit *Leaving the stems on, wash and pat dry fruits such as strawberries, cherries and grapes. Dip each fruit halfway into a bowl of melted chocolate and leave to set on a tray lined with a sheet of parchment.*

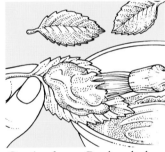

Coating leaves *Brush melted chocolate on the shiny upper side of a clean, non-toxic leaf. Leave to dry on parchment, then peel the chocolate off the leaf, starting at the stem end. Rose and mint leaves work best.*

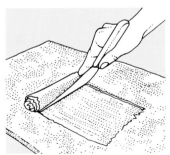

Making scrolls *Thinly spread melted chocolate as smoothly as possible on a clean flat surface and leave to set. Firmly push the edge of a pastry scraper away from you into the chocolate at a shallow angle and carefully scrape the chocolate so it comes off in long scrolls.*

Making shapes *Pour a ¼in (5mm) layer of melted chocolate on a baking sheet lined with parchment. Leave until set but still slightly soft. Carefully remove the chocolate and peel off the paper. Use cookie cutters or a sharp-pointed knife to cut out shapes.*

This jagged-edged chocolate bowl, filled with fresh strawberries, makes a simple but dramatic dessert.

MAKING A CHOCOLATE BOWL

This chocolate bowl began as an experiment but I now use it again and again as a container for fillings such as chilled soufflés, fruit mousses, fruit- or liqueur-flavored ice creams or whipped cream mixed with berries. I have even filled it with a fresh fruit gelatin (page 225) – but wait for the gelatin mixture to become cold before pouring it into the bowl.

Use either a bowl or a cake pan depending on the shape you want. To coat a fairly large deep bowl 200g (7oz) semi-sweet chocolate should be sufficient.

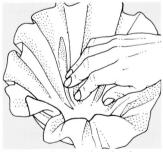

1 *Line a deep bowl with a large sheet of parchment, folding and pressing it down so it roughly fits the bowl. Bring the edges of the paper up above the bowl. Break the chocolate into a small bowl and add 1½ tablespoons water. Set over a pan of hot water until melted and stir in 1oz (25g) butter until smooth.*

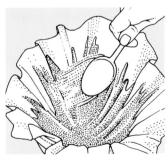

2 *Pour the chocolate into the lined bowl. Using the back of a spoon or spatula coat the bottom and sides thoroughly, drawing the chocolate around the top to give a jagged effect. Chill until firm. Holding the top of the paper lift out the chocolate bowl and gently peel the paper off the chocolate in strips.*

CHEESECAKES

I remember my mother telling me about the wonders of American cheesecake long before I ever tasted one. In those days the cheesecakes in England where I was living were the continental style, studded with raisins and cooked in an open pastry case. The dense, creamy richness of the baked American cheesecake on its crunchy cookie crust is something quite different. Very different again is the unbaked cheesecake set with gelatin. This kind of cheesecake is lighter than a baked cheesecake. It is served chilled and always on a cookie base and, in my opinion, should be flavored quite sharply with lemon, tasting best with a fruit topping.

What surprised me as a child was that cheesecakes do not really taste of cheese. Made with cream, curd, cottage or, indeed, any soft, bland white cheese which is then sweetened, mixed with eggs and often flavored with lemon, the taste of cheesecake is more like a rich, eggy cream with a hint of sharpness. Cheesecakes are also much more like a tart than a cake: they do not rise like cakes, they are far more creamy and dense and they nearly always have either a base or a crust.

At one time cheesecakes were all the rage. Everyone made them, sometimes not terribly well, and they were an inevitable dinner party and buffet dish. As with quiches this may have resulted in over exposure. Now that there is such an enormous variety of soft white cheeses available, many far lighter and less rich than full-fat cream cheese, it is worth remembering how wonderful cheesecakes can be. For me, the best of all remains the baked type, the American type I was told about, chilled and served without a topping but with a bowl of ripe fruit and perhaps a fruit coulis sauce (page 208).

CHEESECAKE CRUSTS

Make cheesecake crusts from either cookie crumbs or pastry. The most important thing to remember with either is that they must never be thick and soggy. I prefer the crunchiness of the cookie crust – it is also the easiest to make and can be varied according to the kind of cookies you use: vanilla wafers, chocolate wafers, graham crackers or gingersnaps and finely chopped walnuts are all good. Always use a loose-bottomed or springform pan (page 21).

For unbaked cheesecakes, bake cookie crusts blind (page 245) for 10 minutes at 350°F, 180°C, then cool on a wire rack before filling. Otherwise, chill the cookie crust until firm before filling and baking.

Pastry is the traditional crust for continental-style cheesecakes and can also be used with the baked kind of cheesecake. Use either sweet pastry (page 248) or sweet hot butter pastry (page 249) which is more cookie-like than many pastries. Chill the pastry before using.

To make a cookie crust combine 2 cups (175g) cookie crumbs in a plastic bag. Mix with ¼ cup (50g) brown sugar and 3oz (75g) melted butter. Press over the bottom, and up the side if you like, of a 9in (23cm) springform pan. Chill before filling.

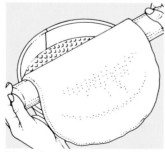

To make a pastry crust roll out the pastry and use to line the bottom and side of a buttered 9in (23cm) springform pan. Chill the pastry crust for at least 20 minutes before filling with the cheesecake mixture and baking.

FLAVORING CHEESECAKES

• Although a cheesecake should taste rich and creamy you can, if you want, keep the fat content down by using one of the low-fat cheeses, the ultimate being virtually fat-free yogurt cheese. On the whole the creamier the cheese the smoother the texture will be.

• If you use egg yolks only in a cheesecake the texture will be richer and more creamy than if you use the yolks and whites.

• You can flavor cheesecakes with chocolate by adding cocoa to the cheese mixture for a baked cheesecake or melted plain chocolate for an unbaked one. You can also ice the top with a layer of glossy melted chocolate mixed with a little sour cream.

• Incorporating a thick puree of fruit with the cheesecake mixture makes a fresh-flavored cheesecake.

• Plain cheesecakes are greatly improved if you use vanilla sugar (page 235).

• Use light brown sugar or honey to vary the taste of your cheesecakes.

• A wonderful cheesecake with the fragrance of muscatel can be made by folding about 2 tablespoons elderflowers into the mixture before baking. Top with green grapes in a glaze cooked with elderflowers.

• To give a chilled uncooked lemon cheesecake a more lemony flavor dissolve the gelatin in hot lemon juice instead of water. To top the cheesecake pour on a thin layer of strained lemon juice with added sugar and gelatin and leave to set.

• Ground spices such as cinnamon and nutmeg can be added to a cookie or pastry crust for extra flavor.

• One of my favorites for flavoring a cheesecake crust, whether cookie or pastry, is to add grated lemon or orange rind to the crust mixture.

• Toppings can vary from the slightest whisper of confectioners' sugar to an elaborate arrangement of glazed fruits. For glazing I use melted and strained apricot jam, red currant jelly or a seedless red raspberry preserve, according to the fruit I am using.

• Another way of topping cheesecakes is to arrange slices of uncooked fruit in a pattern on top of the mixture before chilling. You can also use apricots, raspberries or plums stewed to a thick jam-like consistency.

• Instead of fruit, top a cheesecake with caramelized nuts (page 228), turning them right from the pan onto the cheesecake so they stick together.

BAKED CHEESECAKE

There are two basic kinds of baked cheesecake: the continental style and, my favorite, the American baked type. To serve 6–8 use a 9in (23cm) springform cake pan with either a cookie or pastry crust which should be well chilled before filling.

You can use any kind of soft white cheese to make both kinds: the flavor will not be quite as rich and creamy with the low-fat cheeses but still very pleasant. Cottage cheese should be sieved before using. Quark, a low-fat skimmed mild soft cheese, also works well. Medium-fat ricotta cheese is another traditional cheesecake ingredient. If you want to make a continental-style cheesecake, use the same amounts of curd cheese, sugar and eggs as below but omit the cream and fold in a handful of golden raisins, then bake as below.

After baking, remove from the oven but leave the cake in the pan until cool, then using a knife to loosen the edges gently remove bottom and sides (page 21). Dust with confectioners' sugar just before serving. The higher you hold the sieve above the cheesecake the more delicate the layer of sugar.

UNBAKED CHEESECAKE

This cheesecake is quite different in character from either of the baked cheesecakes. It is set with gelatin and chilled so that it tastes more like a mousse. Use an 8in (20cm) springform pan with the bottom only lined with a cookie crust (opposite).

I think these cheesecakes are for summer eating and should be sharply flavored with lemon and topped with fresh fruit which can be glazed or sprinkled with superfine or confectioners' sugar at the last moment. You can use cottage cheese, farmer's cheese, yogurt or cream cheese.

1 *Beat together 12oz (375g) soft white cheese and ¾ cup plus 2 tablespoons (175g) sugar, then beat in the grated rind and juice of 1 lemon followed by 2 egg yolks. Fold in 1 package unflavored gelatin softened and dissolved in 4 tablespoons water or extra lemon juice.*

1 *In a large bowl beat together 8oz (250g) each of cream cheese and cottage cheese and 1¼ cups (250g) sugar; beat in ⅔ cup (150ml) heavy cream and 4 beaten egg yolks thoroughly, a little at a time.*

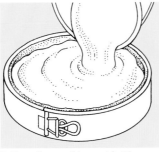
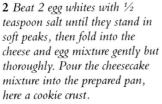

2 *Beat 2 egg whites with ½ teaspoon salt until they stand in soft peaks, then fold into the cheese and egg mixture gently but thoroughly. Pour the cheesecake mixture into the prepared pan, here a cookie crust.*

2 *In separate bowls beat ⅔ cup (150ml) heavy cream and powdered egg dissolved in water equal to 2 egg whites to soft peaks. Fold the cream into the cheese mixture; fold in the whites.*

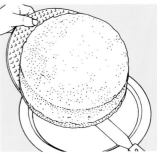

3 *Pour the mixture carefully into the prepared pan over the cookie crust and chill for several hours or overnight. Remove from the pan carefully and transfer to a serving plate. Decorate with fresh fruit.*

3 *Bake in a preheated oven, 325°F, 160°C for about 1 hour until just firm, the top is golden and a skewer or tip of a knife inserted in the center comes out clean. Turn off the heat and leave the cheesecake in the oven with the door slightly ajar for 30 minutes. Leave to cool completely on a wire rack, then carefully release the sides of the pan and transfer to a serving plate.*

A rich and creamy baked cheesecake with a crisp cookie crust.

SORBETS *and* ICE CREAMS

Homemade ice cream is well worth making – commercial ice creams can be excellent but they are never quite the same. In my experience ice creams and sorbets are also one of the most popular desserts of all, and they are not much trouble to make.

An ice cream maker, although creating the smoothest results, is not essential; the parfait-type ice creams (which is the method I use most) made with a base of Italian meringue (page 227) gives smooth results with no beating at all at mid-freezing point. Other ice creams and sorbets can be beaten very easily halfway through the freezing if you have a powerful electric beater or a food processor.

Sorbets and water ices are certainly the most refreshing of all desserts, which is why they are sometimes served in between courses at elaborate feasts. Sorbets consist of a sugar syrup and flavorings such as fruit juice or puree or a liqueur, sometimes with beaten pasteurized egg white or an Italian meringue added halfway through to make them lighter and smoother. Savory sorbets can also be served as a first course. A granita is a juice or alcohol-flavored sorbet mixture which is mashed with a fork when it is almost frozen to give it the consistency of crystallized snow.

With both ice cream- and sorbet-making remember a few key facts. Flavors are subdued by freezing so your original unfrozen mixture should be extra-strong tasting. Sugar and alcohol both inhibit the freezing process so mixtures with a lot of sugar and alcohol in them will be far softer. On the other hand, ice cream and sorbet mixtures with liquid ingredients such as watery fruit purees freeze harder and tend to crystallize.

BASIC FRUIT SORBET

Blackberries make a delicious fruit sorbet because of their strength of flavor. Use this method here for other flavored sorbets. Raspberries or strawberries won't need cooking, only mashing.

To make a blackberry sorbet for 6, you will need 1¼ cups (250g) sugar, 1¼ cups (300ml) water, sieved puree made from 1lb (500g) blackberries and dehydrated egg whites dissolved in water equal to 2 egg whites. Heat the fruit with just a little sugar until the juices run, then puree.

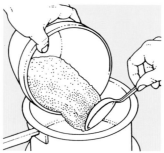

1 *Dissolve the sugar in the water in a small saucepan over a low heat, then increase the heat and boil rapidly for 3–4 minutes without stirring. Stir the fruit puree into the sugar syrup and then set aside to cool.*

2 *Spoon the cold syrup and fruit puree mixture into a shallow freezerproof container and freeze for 1–2 hours until the sorbet mixture is mushy. Then beat the egg white mixture until it stands in soft peaks.*

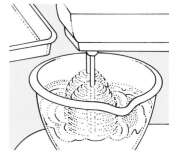

3 *Turn the frozen mixture into a bowl and beat until softened, then fold in the egg white mixture. Return to the container and freeze. Transfer to the refrigerator for about 15 minutes before serving to soften the sorbet*

MAKING GRANITA

A granita or water ice is an Italian invention and makes a refreshing finish to a rich meal. Granitas are simple to make as they are only made from sugar, water and a flavoring. To serve 6 you will need 1¼ cups (250g) sugar, 2½ cups (600ml) water and 2½ cups (600ml) freshly squeezed fruit juice.

To make, dissolve the sugar in the water over a low heat and then increase the heat and boil briskly for 5 minutes without stirring. Remove from the heat and set aside to cool.

Stir in the fruit juice, then transfer to a shallow freezerproof container and freeze until almost frozen. Stir through lightly with a fork and return to the freezer. When firm, granular and not too solid, spoon into tall glasses and serve.

Fruit sorbets make a refreshing dessert and because of their softness are usually served in individual glasses. From the top: mango, lemon and orange sorbets.

MY FAVORITE ICE CREAM

This Italian meringue method makes a light and smooth parfait-type ice cream which needs no beating halfway through the freezing. Unless you have used a large quantity of fruit puree (thus adding a lot more water) the ice cream will be soft enough to spoon straight from the freezer. If the ice cream seems too hard to scoop, transfer it to the refrigerator for 15–30 minutes before serving.

To serve 6–8, you will need 2 egg whites, a pinch of salt, ¾ cup plus 2 tablespoons (175g) sugar, 6 tablespoons water and 1¼ cups (300ml) heavy cream and flavoring such as 4–6oz (125–175g) melted chocolate, 3–4 tablespoons well-sweetened thick fruit puree to taste or 2–5 tablespoons liqueur, again to taste. The exact amount depends on how liquid the flavoring is. For a toffee-like flavor use light brown sugar instead.

Chocolate Peppermint Ice Cream (page 239) is flavored with peppermint extract and pieces of chocolate peppermint candy.

1 *Make an Italian meringue with the egg whites, salt, sugar and water (page 227). Continue beating for about 2 minutes until the mixture is cool and thick. Fold the flavoring of your choice into the mixture.*

2 *Whip the cream until it is thick but not too stiff, then quickly fold it into the egg white mixture. Spoon the mixture into a freezerproof serving mold or bowl and freeze for several hours or overnight before turning out.*

IDEAS FOR ICE CREAMS AND SORBETS

• Ice creams and sorbets can be flavored with almost anything you can think of – just try to imagine your favorite flavors and combinations and then make them into something frozen.

• Try a tomato sorbet with strips of fresh basil leaves for an excellent first course or palate-refresher in the middle of a multi-course meal.

• Canteloupe, charentais or other aromatic melons with added sharpness of lemon can be used for both ice creams and sorbets.

• When adding ground spices to ice creams toast them first in a hot, dry pan for a minute to bring out their full aromas.

• If made with a really aromatic home-produced honey, a honey ice cream can be perfect, especially served with an apple tart. Or, you can make apple and Calvados sorbet, or a simple Calvados ice cream to accompany a hot apple pie.

• Sauces are nearly always a welcome accompaniment to ice cream. They can be hot or cold: chocolate (see Hot Spiced Chocolate Sauce page 213), caramel, butterscotch or smooth fruit purees for vanilla and other creamy ice creams.

• Thin cookies are nice as an accompaniment. Freezer cookies (page 277) are particularly useful – keep a roll of cookie dough in the freezer and then slice it very thinly and bake to make delicate fresh cookies whenever you need them at short notice.

• To make vanilla sugar simply keep vanilla beans in a sealed jar of sugar. The sugar will absorb the flavor of the beans, and you can use it instead of plain sugar.

TRADITIONAL VANILLA ICE CREAM

A true, smooth, old-fashioned vanilla ice cream is made with a rich egg yolk custard and a real vanilla bean for genuine flavor.

Long, thin, brown vanilla beans give the richest vanilla flavor, and the tiny dark seeds add slight speckles and more flavor to the creamy ice cream.

To serve 6, you will need 1¼ cups (300ml) light cream, 1 vanilla bean, 4 egg yolks, ½ cup plus 2 tablespoons (125g) vanilla sugar (below) and 1¼ cups (300ml) heavy cream.

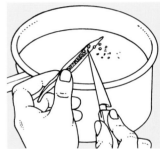

1 *Put the light cream in a saucepan. Split the vanilla bean lengthwise and add the seeds and bean to the pan. Bring the cream just up to a boil. Remove from the heat, cover and infuse for 30 minutes. Remove the bean.*

2 *Beat the egg yolks and sugar until pale and creamy. Reheat the vanilla-flavored cream until nearly boiling, then pour gradually into the egg yolk mixture, beating or stirring all the time. Put the bowl over a saucepan of gently simmering water and stir with a wooden spoon until the custard begins to thicken. Cool, stirring often.*

3 *Beat the heavy cream until thick but not stiff and fold into the custard mixture. Pour into a freezerproof dish and freeze for 3–4 hours. Remove the mixture and beat, preferably in a food processor, and then return to the freezer. Repeat at least once more at hourly intervals. To serve, soften the ice cream in the refrigerator for 10 minutes.*

FROZEN DESSERTS

There is something about freezing desserts which makes them seem even more impressive, almost like something out of a fairy story. In fact, many chilled desserts can taste even better when frozen, and are particularly useful because, unlike sorbets and some ice cream recipes, they do not need beating halfway through the freezing and can usually be served straight from the freezer. All kinds of mousses and chilled soufflés fall into this category, as well as cakes layered with ice cream, meringue cakes and charlottes edged with lady fingers.

Layered ice cream bombes, ice cream or sorbet spooned into containers such as scooped-out oranges, tangerines, and the ever-impressive baked Alaska are all ways of turning an ice cream mixture into a more elaborate and magnificent end to a special meal.

You can even make a molded holiday dessert using an ice cream mixture combined with chestnut puree which has brandy- or rum-soaked fruit, nuts and spices incorporated into it. Make it in a pudding mold, then turn out and garnish festively.

Frozen soufflés can be made in the same way as chilled soufflés (page 229), using a foil or waxed paper collar which is then removed to reveal what looks like a dramatically risen dessert.

ICED CHOCOLATE MARQUISE

A chocolate marquise can either be chilled or frozen but I think it is best as an ice cream. As it is a dessert which can be made well ahead and is extremely impressive it is ideal for a special dinner party. The marquise is sliced across in thick slices to serve, and accompanied with cream or sour cream to spoon either over or underneath the slices. To turn out the marquise for serving rub the outside of the pan with a hot cloth, then slip a warm spatula carefully between the cookies and the pan. Invert onto a serving dish, giving a good shake.

The quantity here serves 6. Use about 25–30 lady fingers or finger cookies, ⅓ cup (75g) granulated sugar, 6 tablespoons brandy or rum, 2 tablespoons water, 4oz (125g) semi-sweet chocolate, 1 tablespoon half-and-half, 1 envelope unflavored gelatin, 3 egg yolks, dehydrated egg white dissolved in water to equal 2 egg whites, 2 tablespoons superfine sugar and ¾ cup (175ml) heavy cream plus extra chocolate for decoration.

Frozen chocolate marquise, a rich chocolate mixture encased in lady fingers which have been soaked in a liqueur syrup, is decorated with grated chocolate.

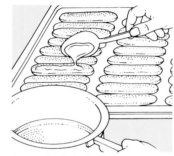

1 *Lay the lady fingers in a shallow dish. Dissolve the sugar in the brandy or rum and water over a low heat, then boil for a second or two before spooning over the lady fingers. Leave for 30 minutes or more until the syrup is absorbed, carefully turning over each lady finger once.*

2 *Line the bottom of a 9in (23cm) loaf pan with a piece of parchment cut to fit. Line the bottom and sides of the pan with the soaked lady fingers, cutting off neatly along the top of the pan with a sharp knife. Use the cut-off lady finger tops to fill in any gaps.*

3 *Melt the chocolate and half-and-half in a heatproof bowl set over a pan of gently simmering water. Soften the gelatin in about 3 tablespoons water, then stir it into the melted chocolate. Beat the egg yolks with the sugar until pale and thick, then beat into the chocolate and heat to 160°F, 90°C. Cool, stirring often.*

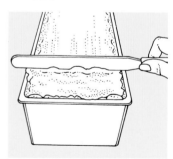

4 *Beat the cream until thick, and in a second bowl beat the egg white mixture until soft peaks form. Fold the cream into the chocolate mixture, followed by the egg whites. Spoon into the lady-finger-lined pan, smooth the top with a knife and freeze for several hours until firm. Unmold (above) onto a serving plate and top with grated chocolate, if desired.*

ICE CREAM BOMBE

Traditional bombes are made with contrasting layers of ice cream and sorbet. A thick fruit puree in the center can replace some of the sorbet to make a pretty variation. Ice cream should always be used on the outer layer as it freezes the firmest.

Metal molds with lids are best as they both freeze and unmold quickly. Most bombe molds are dome-shaped but they can also be square or even rectangular. Freezerproof gelatin molds and pudding molds can be used also.

To serve 4–6, you will need a 4 cup (1 liter) mold, ½ recipe strawberry sorbet (page 234), and ¾ to 1 cup (250g) blueberries stewed to a thick jam-like consistency (page 224).

To make the bombe ice cream mixture use 1 cup (200g) sugar, ½ cup (125ml) water, 4 egg yolks, finely grated rind and juice of 2 small oranges, 1¼ cups (300ml) heavy cream and 1 teaspoon vanilla extract. Dissolve the sugar in the water over a low heat, then increase the heat and boil rapidly for 1 minute. Remove from heat. Beat the egg yolks, then, still beating, pour on the hot syrup. Add the orange rind and juice. Continue beating the mixture until cool. Chill. Lightly whip the cream and fold it into the mixture. Fold in the vanilla extract and any other flavoring such as liqueur. Freeze until solid, beating 2 or 3 times at hourly intervals.

Ice cream bombes can be constructed in many different ways, using various flavors and textures to create a dramatic effect when the bombe is turned out. The bombe here has a pale outer layer of homemade orange-flavored ice cream with a second contrasting layer of strawberry sorbet and a center of fresh blueberries which have been lightly cooked so that they are thick and jam-like.

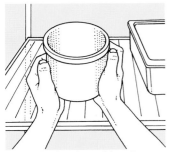

1 *Put the bombe mold in the freezer to chill for 2 hours. Soften the frozen bombe mixture for the outer layer until it spreads easily. Take care when you remove the chilled mold because it can 'burn' your fingers.*

2 *Using the back of a spoon line the mold with an even layer of bombe mixture 2.5cm (1in) thick. Cover the mold and return to the freezer for 2–3 hours until the layer of bombe mixture is firm again.*

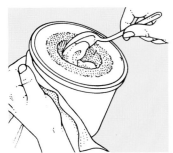

3 *Remove the mold from the freezer and quickly fill the center with the strawberry sorbet, leaving a hollow in the center. Freeze for 1 hour until firm. Fill the hollow with the thick blueberry puree, then cover and freeze for 8 hours.*

4 *To unmold, dip the bombe mold quickly in a bowl of hot water, then remove the top and invert onto a chilled serving plate, holding firmly with both hands. Soften the bombe for about 30 minutes in the refrigerator before serving.*

IDEAS FOR FROZEN PUDDINGS

• If you make a chocolate bombe you can have a center of ice cream flavored with peppermint so that the whole thing resembles a peppermint candy; thin peppermint candies can also be added to the bombe in layers.

• Successful bombe combinations include chocolate ice cream with lemon sorbet, apricot and lime ice creams, Calvados ice cream and apple sorbet, strawberry ice cream and orange sorbet and raspberry ice cream with blackberry sorbet.

• Fruit incorporated into bombes should be cooked with sugar until thick and jam-like, soaked in a liqueur, or, if fresh, mixed with a light sugar syrup (page 208) to keep it from solidifying to ice.

• If using dried fruit in a bombe soak it first in a little sherry, brandy or liqueur before using, unless it is already very soft.

• A wonderful dessert is a lemon sorbet frozen in a bombe mold, turned out onto a plate and frozen again before you pour a thick, hot chocolate sauce over it all just before putting it on the table.

• If using sponge cake for an ice cream cake you can soak it in a liqueur or a fruit syrup before assembling it. Ice cream cakes can also be layered with meringue layers instead of lady fingers.

• Meringue can also be used to add texture to smooth dishes. Bake a layer of crisp meringue, then crumble it and fold it into an ice cream mixture before freezing. Crushed cookies or macaroons can be used in the same way.

• A rich chocolate mousse made with gelatin is best of all when frozen and covered with strips of orange peel which have been boiled to soften and then boiled in an orange juice and sugar syrup (page 208) until it has reduced to coat the peel – this kind of candied peel is useful as a garnish or folded into all sorts of frozen desserts.

• When making Baked Alaska, use meringue powder and try folding chopped nuts into the meringue or a little coarsely grated chocolate which will begin to melt into the meringue during baking.

HOT LEMON AND PASSION FRUIT SOUFFLÉ *(228)*

Instead of a flour roux, this soufflé has a tangy lemon curd base. You can make the base in advance which will leave you only the whites to whisk and fold in shortly before you put the soufflé in the oven. Instead of one large soufflé, the mixture can also be divided between six ⅔ cup (150ml) ramekin dishes, in which case cook for 12–15 minutes only. This dessert is delicious served with a fruit puree of damsons, raspberries, blackberries or strawberries as a sauce.   *SERVES 6–8*

> *4 passion fruit*
> *⅔ cup (150ml) lemon juice*
> *5 large eggs, separated*
> *½ cup plus 2 tablespoons (125g) sugar*
> *Finely grated rind of 2 lemons*
> *½ teaspoon salt*
> *Confectioners' sugar for dusting*

Cut the passion fruit in half. Scoop out the flesh, juice and seeds from 2 passion fruit and put in a glass measuring cup with the lemon juice. Sieve the juice from the remaining passion fruit into the cup. Discard the seeds. Mix the contents of the cup thoroughly with a fork.

Put the egg yolks in the top of a double boiler or in a heatproof bowl which will fit over a saucepan of water. Stir in the sugar, then add the lemon and passion fruit mixture a little at a time.

Set the double boiler or bowl over gently simmering water and stir with a wooden spoon until the mixture is thick enough to lightly coat the back of the spoon. Remove the bowl from the heat, stir in the grated lemon rind and set aside until cold.

Meanwhile, butter a 4 cup (946ml) soufflé or other deep ovenproof dish. Put the egg whites in a large bowl with the salt and beat with an electric beater until soft peaks form. Using a large metal spoon, lightly fold the egg whites into the cooled lemon and passion fruit mixture until well incorporated.

Spoon the mixture into the buttered soufflé dish and bake just above the center of a preheated oven, 300°F, 150°C for 50–60 minutes until the top of the soufflé is dark golden brown. Lightly dust the top of the soufflé with sifted confectioners' sugar and serve at once while it is still puffed.

CARAMELIZED ORANGE TART *(221)*

I first made this upside-down tart using the typically Moroccan flavorings of honey and cinnamon after a holiday in southern Morocco, where the scent of orange blossom and the taste of fresh orange juice had dominated our days. Serve the tart warm with cream, crème fraîche or plain yogurt.   *SERVES 6–8*

> *FOR THE PASTRY*
> *1⅓ cups (175g) all-purpose flour*
> *⅓ cup (75g) sugar*
> *½ teaspoon salt*
> *3oz (75g) butter, just melted*
> *1 egg, beaten*
> *FOR THE FILLING*
> *1½oz (40g) butter*
> *4 generous tablespoons honey*
> *2 teaspoons ground cinnamon*
> *5–6 small seedless oranges*

To make the pastry, sift the flour, sugar and salt into a bowl. Stir in the melted butter using a wooden spoon, then thoroughly mix in the beaten egg until the dough is smooth. Press the dough into a ball, cover it with plastic wrap and leave to chill in the refrigerator for at least 1 hour.

To prepare the orange filling, melt the butter and honey gently in a saucepan, then stir in the cinnamon. Pour the mixture over the bottom of a 25cm (10in) flan dish (the fluted ones turn out nicely). Slice the unpeeled oranges across as thinly as possible. First lay a pattern of orange slices on the bottom of the dish on top of the butter and honey mixture, then add the remaining slices on top in overlapping circles.

Roll out the pastry on a floured surface to a little larger than the size of the flan dish. Roll the pastry back over the rolling pin and lift it onto the dish. (If the pastry breaks, just press it together again – it won't show.) Press the edges firmly down within the flan dish and pierce 2 or 3 holes in the pastry.

Bake the tart in the center of a preheated oven, 400°F, 200°C for 25 minutes, then reduce the oven temperature to 325°F, 160°C and bake for another 1¾–2 hours – the pastry will turn a rich dark brown. Remove the tart from the oven and set aside for 5–10 minutes to cool slightly before inverting onto a large serving plate.

SUMMER PUDDING *(214)*

Summer pudding is a simple but brilliant creation. Ideally you should turn out a dome entirely dark with absorbed juices but always keep some of the cooking juices in reserve to pour over the pudding after turning it out in case some of the bread still shows. All kinds of juicy summer fruit can be used but a good proportion of blueberries and raspberries is important. Serve with more berries and cream.   *SERVES 6*

> *⅔ cup (150ml) fresh orange juice*
> *4 tablespoons lemon juice*
> *¾ cup plus 2 tablespoons (175g) sugar*
> *1lb (500g) blueberries*
> *8oz (250g) red currants or strawberries*
> *1lb (500g) raspberries*
> *1 small loaf unsliced day-old white bread*
> *Extra fresh fruit to decorate*

Put the orange and lemon juices and the sugar in a saucepan and stir over a medium heat until the sugar has dissolved. Bring to a boil, then add the blueberries and red currants or strawberries. Cover and cook over a low heat for 8–10 minutes until the juices have run and the fruit is soft. Stir in the raspberries and remove from the heat.

Cut the loaf of bread into thin slices and a cut circle of bread to fit the bottom of a 5 cup (1.liter) pudding mold. Cut off and discard the crusts. Line the bottom and then the sides with overlapping slices of bread, leaving no gaps. Fill the mold with the fruit mixture, reserving any remaining juices and then top with more layers of bread. Put a saucer or small plate on top and weigh it down. Chill for several hours or overnight.

To serve, turn it out onto a serving plate, pour the reserved fruit juices over it and arrange some fresh fruit on top.

PASSION FRUIT AND ORANGE PUDDINGS *(214)*

These moist yet cakelike little almond molds are delectable. Remember that ripe passion fruit have very wrinkled skins. *SERVES 6*

FOR THE PUDDINGS

4oz (125g) butter, softened
¾ cup (150g) light brown sugar
Finely grated rind of 2 oranges
4 passion fruit
¾ cup (125g) ground almonds
3 large eggs, lightly beaten
Confectioners' sugar for dusting

FOR THE SAUCE

6 passion fruit
Juice of 2 oranges
2 tablespoons sugar
⅔ cup (150ml) heavy cream

To make the puddings, first butter 6 timbale molds or custard cups and put a round of parchment cut to fit in the bottom of each.

In a mixing bowl beat the butter and light brown sugar until soft and fluffy, then beat in the grated orange rind. Cut the 4 passion fruit in half and spoon the insides of 4 halves into the bowl with the beaten butter and sugar, then strain the juice from the remaining halves and add to the bowl; discard the seeds. Beat in to break the flesh up and disperse the seeds, then alternately beat in the ground almonds and the beaten eggs.

Spoon the pudding mixture into the individual molds and bake in the center of a preheated oven, 375°F, 190°C for 25–35 minutes until a small sharp knife inserted in the center of a pudding comes out clean. Leave the puddings in the molds for at least 10 minutes, then run a knife around the edges to loosen them and turn out onto a cooling rack, removing the discs of parchment. Leave until completely cool.

To make the sauce, cut the 6 passion fruit in half and spoon the insides out into a sieve set over a bowl. Rub with a wooden spoon until as much juice as possible has gone through the sieve. Discard the mass of seeds. Strain the orange juice through a fine sieve into the bowl and add the sugar, stirring thoroughly so that it dissolves. Finally stir in the heavy cream. Refrigerate the sauce until needed.

To serve, spoon the sauce equally onto 6 individual plates, place a pudding in the center of each and sprinkle confectioners' sugar on the puddings through a fine sieve – I like enough to make them completely white on top.

CHOCOLATE PEPPERMINT ICE CREAM *(235)*

If you have a weakness for chocolate peppermints, this is the ice cream for you. *SERVES 6–8*

3/4 cup plus 2 tablespoons (175g) sugar
½ teaspoon salt
2 large eggs, well beaten
1¼ cups (300ml) heavy cream
½ teaspoon peppermint extract
Dehydrated egg white dissolved in water to equal 4 whites
1 5oz (150g) box wafer-thin chocolate after-dinner mints, cut into small pieces
Mint leaves to decorate

Put the sugar, salt and eggs in a bowl and gradually beat in the cream until well mixed. Stir in the peppermint extract, set the bowl over a pan of simmering water, stirring with a wooden spoon for 10–15 minutes until the mixture has thickened slightly. Pour into a larger bowl and leave until cold.

Beat the egg white mixture until soft peaks form, then fold it gently but thoroughly into the cold custard. Stir in the pieces of chocolate after-dinner mints.

Pour the ice cream mixture into a freezerproof serving bowl and freeze for several hours. Thirty minutes before serving decorate with mint leaves; transfer to the refrigerator to soften slightly.

QUEEN OF PUDDINGS WITH FRESH POACHED APRICOTS *(214)*

Queen of puddings is an old-fashioned pudding that has been made since Colonial times. I like to use fresh apricots when they are available instead of the usual jam. Later in the summer blackberries are excellent, too. Serve this pudding either hot or well chilled and with cream if desired. *SERVES 6*

2 cups (75g) fresh white bread crumbs
1¼ cups (300ml) milk
1¼ cups (300ml) light cream
Finely grated rind of 1 lemon
2oz (50g) butter
3 large eggs, separated
¾ cup (150g) sugar
1lb (500g) fresh apricots, halved and pitted
6 tablespoons light brown sugar
4 tablespoons lemon juice
Pinch of salt

Butter a 6–8 cup (1.5–1.8 liter) ovenproof baking dish and sprinkle the fresh white breadcrumbs evenly in the bottom. Put the milk and cream in a saucepan with the lemon rind and butter and heat until just warm. In a mixing bowl beat the egg yolks lightly with ½ cup (100g) of the sugar, then gradually beat in the heated milk and cream. Pour this mixture into the baking dish over the breadcrumbs and bake in the center of a preheated oven, 350°F, 180°C for about 25 minutes or until just set when lightly touched in the center.

Meanwhile, put the apricot halves in a saucepan with the brown sugar and lemon juice and stir over a medium heat until the sugar has dissolved. Cover the pan and simmer gently for 10–15 minutes or until the fruit is soft. If the fruit has produced a lot of juice remove the lid and boil rapidly to reduce it to a thicker syrup. Remove from the heat and set aside.

When the custard and breadcrumb mixture is ready remove the dish from the oven and gently spoon the apricots evenly on top. Beat the egg whites with the salt until stiff, then fold in the remaining ¼ cup (50g) of sugar. Pile the meringue on top of the apricots and return to the oven for another 15 minutes until the meringue is golden brown and crisp on top.

QUINCE PUDDING BRÛLÉE (214)

This light and creamy pudding is perfect for a large Sunday dinner. If your quince feel very hard you can gently poach them for about 5 minutes before arranging them in layers in the dish.   *SERVES 8*

> 1½–2lb (750g–1kg) ripe quinces or hard
>   pears
> *Lemon juice or white wine vinegar*
> 6 tablespoons dark brown sugar
> 12oz (375g) cream cheese
> *Finely grated rind of 1 large lemon*
> 1¼ cups (250g) sugar
> 1¼ cups (300ml) heavy cream
> ⅔ cup (150ml) sour cream
> 6 large eggs, separated
> 1 teaspoon vanilla extract
> ½ teaspoon salt

Peel and core the quince and slice very thinly, dropping the slices immediately into a bowl of water to which you have added a little lemon juice or white wine vinegar. Drain the quince slices and arrange them in the bottom of a deep 10–12 cup (2.4–3 liter) flameproof dish. Sprinkle all over with the brown sugar.

Beat the cream cheese with the grated lemon rind and ¾ cup plus 2 tablespoons (175g) of the sugar until soft. Gradually beat in the cream, sour cream, egg yolks and vanilla extract. Beat the egg whites with the salt until soft peaks form, then fold into the creamy mixture. Pour on top of the fruit slices.

Bake in the center of a preheated oven, 350°F, 180°C for 35–40 minutes until the pudding is a rich golden brown on top. Remove from the oven and leave for about 5 minutes.

Meanwhile, preheat the broiler to a high heat. Sprinkle the remaining sugar evenly all over the top of the pudding and place it under the hot broiler until the sugar has melted and become caramelized, brown and glossy, watching all the time to catch it at the right moment. Serve either warm or chilled.

RASPBERRY AND CHOCOLATE MERINGUE CAKE (226)

This meringue cake is one of the most useful summer party desserts as it can be assembled up to 3 hours before you eat.   *SERVES 6–8*

FOR THE MERINGUE
> 4 large egg whites (size 1)
> *Pinch of salt*
> ¾ cup plus 2 tablespoons (175g)
>   superfine sugar
> 1 teaspoon vanilla extract
> 1 teaspoon white wine vinegar
> 3 tablespoons cornstarch
> ¼ cup (25g) toasted chopped hazelnuts
FOR THE FILLING
> 3oz (75g) semi-sweet chocolate, broken
>   into pieces
> 1 tablespoon water
> 4 large egg yolks
> 6 tablespoons milk
> 2 tablespoons granulated sugar
> 2½ cups (375g) raspberries
> ⅔ cup (150ml) heavy cream
> *Cocoa powder*
> *Extra superfine sugar*

Line the bottom of 2 ungreased 7in (18cm) cake pans with rounds of parchment cut to fit. Beat the egg whites with the salt until stiff, then beat in half the superfine sugar, a little at a time. Gently fold in the remaining superfine sugar, the vanilla extract, vinegar, cornstarch and chopped hazelnuts using a large metal spoon. Divide the mixture between the pans and bake just below the center of a preheated oven, 275°F, 140°C for about 1½ hours until firm to the touch in the center. Place a tea towel on a wire rack, turn out the meringues and remove the parchment.

While the meringues are baking make the filling. Put the chocolate in a small saucepan with the water and melt over a very gentle heat. Stir until smooth, then set aside. Put the egg yolks, milk and granulated sugar in the top of a double boiler or a heatproof bowl set over a pan of gently simmering water. Stir until the mixture has thickened. Stir in the chocolate and transfer to a bowl to cool.

When the filling and meringues are completely cold place one meringue on a serving plate and spread with the chocolate mixture. Put a layer of raspberries on the chocolate, reserving a few for the top of the cake. Beat the cream until stiff

and spread it over the raspberries, then place the second meringue on top. Chill until almost ready to serve. Sprinkle cocoa powder through a fine sieve all over the cake and gently arrange the reserved raspberries in a pattern on top. Sprinkle all over with a little superfine sugar, again through a sieve.

CRÈME BRÛLÉE (214)

Crème brûlée, or 'burnt cream', is decadent but irresistible: a smooth creamy custard topped with a delicious crisp caramel glaze. It is usually made in individual little pots or ramekin dishes.   *SERVES 6*

> 2½ cups (600ml) heavy cream
> 1 vanilla bean
> 5 egg yolks
> ½ cup plus 2 tablespoons (125g) sugar

Put the cream in a saucepan with the vanilla bean and heat gently until almost boiling. Remove from the heat, cover and leave to infuse for 10 minutes. Remove the vanilla bean.

Beat the egg yolks in a bowl with ¼ cup (50g) of the sugar until light in color. Gradually add the hot cream, beating all the time until evenly mixed, then pour the mixture slowly and equally into 6 ramekin dishes. Put the ramekins into a roasting pan and pour in enough hot water to come halfway up the sides of the dishes. Bake the custards in the center of a preheated oven, 300°F, 150°C for about 1 hour until just set – don't let the surface brown.

Meanwhile, preheat a very hot broiler. Sprinkle the remaining sugar evenly over the top of the custards then put them under the broiler for 2–3 minutes until an uneven caramel color. Cool and chill before serving.

BANANA AND PECAN PIE WITH CRANBERRY AND ORANGE COULIS (214)

This easily made winter dessert is one of those which receives enthusiastic praise from all who taste it. The chilled cranberry and orange coulis pairs perfectly with the warm richness of the pie. For convenience make the pie in advance, refrigerate it, then glaze and bake it shortly before your meal.   *SERVES 6–8*

FOR THE COULIS
1¼ cups (175g) fresh cranberries
1¼ cups (300ml) fresh orange juice
4 tablespoons lemon juice
½ cup (125g) plus 2 tablespoons
   granulated sugar
FOR THE PIE
½ 17.3oz (490g) package puff pastry,
   thawed if frozen
8oz (250g) cream cheese
6 tablespoons light brown sugar
1 large egg, beaten lightly
3–4 firm bananas (depending on size)
Finely grated rind and juice of 1 lemon
¾ cup (75g) shelled pecan halves
Milk and superfine sugar for glazing

Make the cranberry and orange coulis first. Put the cranberries in a saucepan with the orange and lemon juices and bring to a boil, then cover and simmer gently for 10–12 minutes until the cranberries pop and become saucy.

Add the granulated sugar and stir until dissolved. Process the mixture in a food processor until it is as smooth as possible – for perfect smoothness press the puree through a sieve. Turn the coulis into a serving bowl and chill.

Generously butter a 20–23cm (8–9in) flan dish. Cut the pastry in half and shape it into 2 rounds. On a lightly floured surface roll out 2 circles, one about the size of the flan dish and one slightly larger. Pierce the circles all over with a fork and line the dish with the larger circle.

Put the cream cheese and light brown sugar in a bowl and beat until fluffy. Thoroughly beat in the beaten egg. Mash the bananas with the lemon juice and stir immediately into the cream cheese mixture with the halved pecan nuts and the lemon rind.

Spoon the mixture into the lined flan dish and lay the other circle of pastry on top. Cut off the excess pastry neatly, moisten the edges lightly with water and press around the edges to seal. Roll out the pastry trimmings. Cut out some decorations, moisten them on one side and arrange on top of the pie. Brush the top of the pie with milk and sprinkle evenly all over with superfine sugar, then bake in the center of a preheated oven, 400°F, 200°C for 30–35 minutes until the pastry is a rich, crispy brown. Serve hot or warm with the chilled coulis as a sauce.

CHOCOLATE RIPPLE HEART WITH RASPBERRIES (214)

Use a fairly shallow heart-shaped cake pan or gelatin mold and this rather indulgent pudding of raspberries enclosed in a streaky mixture of mascarpone and dark chocolate will look especially effective. If you use a metal mold without a non-stick coating it is best to line it with plastic wrap before adding pudding mixture.   *SERVES 6*

5oz (150g) semi-sweet chocolate, broken
   into pieces
2 tablespoons water
1lb (500g) mascarpone
6–9 tablespoons confectioners' sugar, sifted
1 package unflavored gelatin
3 tablespoons water
3/4 cup (125g) raspberries
Cocoa powder for dusting

Lightly oil a 3¾ cup (900ml) heart-shaped cake pan or gelatin mold. Put the chocolate and the 2 tablespoons water in the top of a double boiler or in a heatproof bowl set over a pan of barely simmering water and melt. Stir until smooth. Set aside to cool only slightly.

Put the mascarpone in a bowl and beat in the sifted confectioners' sugar. Soften the gelatin in the water and heat, stirring, until completely dissolved, then beat swiftly into the mascarpone. Stir in the melted chocolate, leaving plenty of white streaks in the mixture.

Put the raspberries in the bottom of the mold and spoon the mascarpone and chocolate mixture on top, tapping the mold gently so the mixture settles around the raspberries. Refrigerate for at least 1 hour until set.

To turn out, loosen the edges of the mascarpone mixture with your fingers, then invert on a serving plate and dust the top with cocoa powder.

COCONUT CREAM CUSTARD (217)

This is a good dessert to follow a spicy meal and can be accompanied by fresh exotic fruits. I like to serve the custard soon after it has been baked although you can, of course, make it well in advance and refrigerate it.   *SERVES 6*

1¼ cups (300ml) heavy cream
14oz (400ml) coconut milk,
1 teaspoon salt
3 large eggs
2 egg yolks
½ cup (75g) sugar
⅓ cup (50g) unsalted cashew nuts,
   chopped

Put a roasting pan three-quarters full of water on the center shelf of the oven and preheat the oven to 325°F, 160°C. Put the cream and coconut milk in a saucepan and stir over a medium heat until the mixture starts to simmer. Stir in the salt and remove from the heat. Put the eggs, egg yolks and sugar in a bowl. Beat together thoroughly, then beat in the hot coconut milk mixture a little at a time.

Sprinkle the chopped cashew nuts in the bottom of a 5 cup (1.2 liter) soufflé or other similar ovenproof dish. Pour the cream and egg mixture into the dish and place it in the pan of water in the oven. Bake for 1–1¼ hours until the custard feels set to a very light touch in the center but still wobbles slightly if you move the dish. Remove from the oven and let cool.

PASTRY

Perfect homemade pastry is a dream – rich and buttery, but at the same time light, with a crumbly or flaky texture. Yet many competent and even inspired cooks never attempt to make pastry. It may well seem that only the greatest skill could produce such a variety of textures from the same few basic ingredients – pastries which vary enough to suit quite different purposes, but many pastries are really quite easily achieved.

I love experimenting with pastry to try and create a texture and taste I haven't achieved before. Yet I used to be one of those who felt they couldn't make pastry – that was until the day I was told to add more fat and less water when making a simple pie crust and to take as little time as possible cutting the fat into the flour. The result was wonderful, and from then on I found pastry-making a real pleasure; once you realize how easy it is to produce a light and flaky piecrust, your cooking repertoire can be enormously extended.

There are many types of pastry: conventional pastry or piecrust, short European-style pastry, cookie crust or mürbteig, puff pastry, choux or cream puff pastry, and phyllo or strudel pastry, all with possible varieations. Puff pastry is made in a way which layers the flour and fat, creating a light, crisp flaky dough – it is exquisite but it does take time and some practice to achieve perfect results. Phyllo or strudel pastry is a type of layered pastry, but it really does need practice and skill to make successfully, and it is far easier to buy the paper-thin sheets. Choux or cream puff pastry is made in an entirely different way: cooking the flour into a paste and beating in whole eggs to make it rise and expand when baked – it is the most unbelievable pastry of all, and yet one of the easiest and most infallible. There are also special mixtures that function as pastries for specific recipes, such as a biscuit topping for a meat pie, tamale or cornbread topping for a tamale pie.

Successful pastry depends on using good ingredients in the exact proportions, although as you become more experienced, you can alter these to a degree. Flour, fat and liquid, the most important ingredients in pastry, can vary in flavor and quality, and care should be taken to choose the best. A soft wheat cake flour is said to be the best for pastry as it develops less gluten, but I have also had excellent results using white bread flour. Whole wheat flour or ground nuts can be substituted for part of the flour in some pastry, depending on what fillings are to be used, but I have never yet tasted an all whole wheat flour pastry which was truly successful.

Sugar – granulated or confectioners' – is added to dessert pastry to give color and sweetness. Vanilla, lemon or orange rind, spices and herbs can also be used to flavor pastry. Pastry is such a useful ingredient that it is convenient to have it on hand. Ready-made fresh and frozen pastry is an acceptable alternative to homemade, particularly puff pastry, which is time-consuming to make, and certainly phyllo or strudel pastry.

Sweet and savory pastry dishes suitable for all occasions, clockwise from top left: Lime and Strawberry Tart (page 258) with a creamy, lime-flavored filling; Phyllo Pie with Caramelized Apples and Pine Nuts (page 258); an individual Sweet Onion, Garlic and Saffron Tart (page 259) served with a radish and mixed lettuce salad; Pizza Rustica (page 256) filled with different cheeses and vegetables and garnished with fresh herbs; and Steak and Kidney Pie (page 259) made with a caraway-flavored biscuit top and served here with brussels sprouts and carrots.

BASIC PASTRY TECHNIQUES

The most important thing to remember when making pastry is *to handle the dough as little as possible.* Work with chilled ingredients as quickly as you can. If overworked, the dough will shrink during baking and be tough after baking. Before refrigerating, flatten the dough to a round of even thickness and wrap carefully for even chilling without drying the edges. Chilling the dough before baking allows it to 'relax' and firms the fat to prevent shrinkage. If the chilled dough is a little too firm for rolling, let it soften briefly at room temperature first.

Dough can be stored at this stage for two to three days, or it can be rolled out and shaped, then refrigerated and stored. It can be also baked, cooled, wrapped and stored for two to three days in an airtight container. Or, if not using immediately, it is best to freeze the dough, already rolled out into its pan. Do not freeze for longer than three months. You can then bake the dough from frozen when you are ready to use it.

After rolling out, use the dough to line or cover shallow or deep pie plates, flan or tart pans or tartlet pans. Pie edges can be finished with a simple fork or finger-pinched edge or a fancy border made from the trimmings (opposite). Any pastry trimmings can be used to decorate pie tops or to make shapes for use as decorations (opposite). I enjoy cutting out appropriate shapes such as a chicken to go on a chicken pie, or a short simple message or name.

MIXING PASTRY DOUGH

Most pastry for pie crusts is made by blending together chilled butter, flour and water. Mix the dry ingredients in a large bowl. Quickly work in the butter with your fingertips, until the mixture resembles coarse crumbs. Or, use a pastry blender or 2 knives scissor-fashion (page 246) to cut in the butter lightly. Stir in chilled water (or beaten egg yolk for a richer pastry) with a fork until the dough begins to hold together, then quickly form the dough into a ball and flatten slightly into a round. Wrap well in plastic wrap and chill for at least 30 minutes.

To work in butter *or other chilled fat, pick up small amounts of diced butter and flour and quickly rub with your fingertips high above the bowl, letting the crumbs fall back into the bowl. Continue until all the fat is incorporated and the mixture resembles fine bread crumbs, then add the water and mix to a dough.*

ROLLING OUT PASTRY DOUGH

Before rolling out the chilled dough, allow it to soften until slightly pliable so the edges do not crack and break. Dust a dry work surface and rolling pin with flour. Use the pin to flatten the pastry round into the correct shape before you roll it out.

Roll out from the center *to the edges, giving a quarter turn each time to make a round. Push the sides in with your hands to help the dough to keep its shape.*

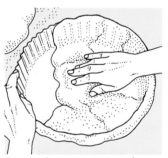

Very rich, sweet pastry *often sticks to the rolling pin. Instead, pat into position in the pan with your fingertips. The cracks won't show after baking.*

LINING PLATES, PANS OR DISHES

It is usually unnecessary to grease a tart pan, pie plate or dish, as the fat in the pastry prevents it from sticking. The thickness of pastry depends on the type of container used and on the filling. For most fillings, ⅛in (2.5mm) is adequate but thicker pastry may be required for heavy pies or deep fillings.

The example here shows how to line a fluted loose-bottomed flan pan but the technique is the same for a pie plate or dish.

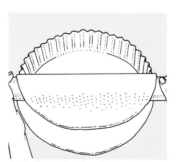

1 Roll out the dough into a round about 2in (5cm) larger than the pan. Roll half the dough back on the rolling pin and transfer to the center of the pan. Unroll, being careful not to stretch.

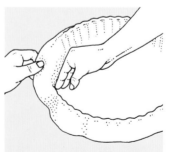

2 Gently lift the edges of the dough with one hand while pressing into the base and side of the pan. If using a dish, press the dough into the side so pastry does not shrink during baking.

3 Roll the rolling pin lightly over the top edge, cutting off any excess dough with a knife. If there is time chill in the refrigerator before baking either blind (opposite) or with a filling.

DECORATIVE PIE EDGES

A simple fluted or crimped edge, fancy border or decorated pie top adds interest to plain tart fillings or a large top crust of pastry.

After making your pie, reroll the trimmings and use a cookie cutter or knife to cut out enough leaves, hearts, or other shapes such as animals or people to decorate the pie, if you like. You can even cut out letters to spell names for special occasions.

To help the decorations stick, brush them with water before applying to the pie. Or, glaze the surface of the pie with a beaten egg and add the cut-outs, then glaze again before putting it into the oven to bake.

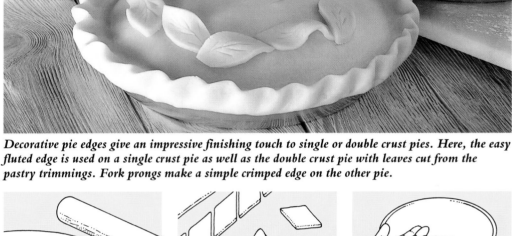

Decorative pie edges give an impressive finishing touch to single or double crust pies. Here, the easy fluted edge is used on a single crust pie as well as the double crust pie with leaves cut from the pastry trimmings. Fork prongs make a simple crimped edge on the other pie.

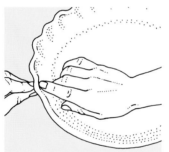

Make a fluted edge *by placing your index finger on the inside rim of the pastry and with the index finger and thumb of your other hand pinching against the first finger to make a flute.*

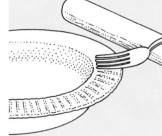

Make a simple crimped edge *by pressing fork prongs all round the edge of the pan. Or, press the tip of a pointed or round-bladed knife or spoon all around the pastry edge.*

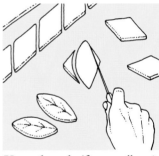

Use a sharp knife *or small aspic or cookie cutter to cut out leaves or other decorative shapes from the rerolled pastry trimmings. Use the back of a knife tip to mark the veins of leaves.*

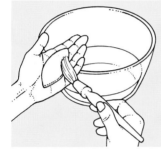

Brush the underside *of the decorative shapes with a little water, twist slightly, then position them on the top crust or edge of the pie. Glaze the pie before putting it in the oven to bake.*

GLAZES AND FINISHES

Glazing pastry dough adds shine and color to baked pastry, and a glaze can also be used to seal a pastry shell if a moist filling is being used. The most common glaze to use on savory pastry is a whole egg beaten with a pinch of salt and brushed on just before baking. Egg yolk beaten with 2 teaspoons water gives a slightly less shiny but even more golden color to the baked pastry. Milk or light cream can also be used for a lighter glaze.

Apply the glaze *before scoring or slashing the top crust so it does not soak into fillings or seal openings or edges. Egg glaze can also be used to secure pastry decorations in position.*

BAKING BLIND

To bake blind is to partially or completely bake a pastry shell without its filling: if the filling needs no cooking at all, bake the shell completely; if it needs only quick cooking, bake the shell partially. Prepare as right. Bake at 425°F, 220°C for 10 minutes, then lower to 375°F, 190°C and bake for 5 more minutes. The times will vary depending on pastry thickness. Remove the paper and beans. If baking the shell completely, bake for a further 8–10 minutes.

To bake blind *prick pastry bottom all over, line the unbaked pie shell with parchment paper 2in (5cm) larger than the pie. Fill with dried beans or rice, making sure they are placed right to the edge.*

BASIC CONVENTIONAL PASTRY

Conventional pastry is the easiest to make and most frequently used pastry. It is the basis of most fruit pies, tarts and even versatile savory flans, such as quiche Lorraine. The pastry dough can also easily be flavored, with herbs or spices for example, to complement the filling. The fat used can be butter, hard margarine, lard or vegetable oil depending on the baked flavor and texture you want. Increasing the amount of fat gives extra flavor and an even shorter pastry, though it will be more difficult to handle. If you have difficulty rolling out a rich pastry, press it into the container with your fingertips, pinching any cracks to seal so they will not show once baked.

The choices for filling piecrust are almost endless. Fruits and berries can fill open tarts or covered pies. Savory meat, fish, vegetable or cheese fillings can be bound in an egg-based custard and baked like a quiche, and piecrust pastry can be wrapped around a pâtés and other fillings for baking *en croûte*.

Piecrust made with 2 cups (250g) flour will make a 9in (23cm) open tart or pie or six 4in (10cm) tartlets. Pastry made with 2½ cups (300g) flour will make an 8in (20cm) double crust pie, or cover a 5 cup (1.2 liter) pie dish. Once a container is lined with the dough, chill it again for 30 minutes before baking. Conventional pastry shells can be baked blind (page 245) before filling if the filling is very runny or to be left uncooked.

CONVENTIONAL PASTRY OR PIECRUST

The basic piecrust recipe can be varied to suit the size of the plate or pan. The usual proportion is half the weight of fat to the weight of flour but if you like a richer and more crumbly pastry, use a little more fat and decrease the amount of liquid. A mixture of butter and vegetable fat makes a very light pastry.

Remember to handle the dough as little as possible, work with well-chilled ingredients and mix them quickly. The dough does not need to be perfectly blended because if it is overworked the baked pastry will be tough and shrink during baking. It is important not to use too much water as it, too, can toughen the pastry. Pastries with a lot of fat need hardly any water and will be rich, short and crumbly after baking.

To make pastry for a 9in (23cm) tart pan, you will need 2 cups (250g) all-purpose flour, ½ teaspoon salt, 4oz (125g) diced chilled butter and 2–3 tablespoons well-chilled water. For an open tart it is best to use a loose-bottomed flan pan for easy removal but a ceramic quiche dish with an unglazed bottom to help conduct the heat works just as well.

PIECRUST VARIATIONS
If you make piecrust with soft margarine or vegetable oil, the technique is different from the traditional method (above). Put the fat, chilled water and one-third of the flour in a bowl and cream together with a fork, then stir in the remaining flour and lightly knead to make a soft dough.

You can make piecrust in a food processor, rather than by hand, but take care that it isn't overworked – never let the dough form into a ball in the machine. Instead, I sometimes just combine the chilled butter and flour in the food processor until it resembles fine breadcrumbs, then transfer to a bowl and mix in the water by hand.

To make a rich, crisp cream cheese pastry, put 3oz (75g) butter and 3oz (75g) cream cheese with 2 cups (250g) flour and 2 tablespoons sugar in a food processor and blend until the dough just holds together. This dough will be difficult to roll out because it is so rich, so it will probably be easiest to pat it into the container or piece together as a top crust.

Using sour cream, rather than water in the basic pastry recipe (above) results in a tender pastry, ideal for wrapping pâtés *en croûte* (page 99) or making tartlet shells.

1 *Before you begin place a small bowl of water in the refrigerator to chill. Mix the flour and salt together in a large bowl. Add the well-chilled, diced butter and cut in with 2 knives used scissor-fashion until the mixture resembles fine breadcrumbs. Or, use your fingertips (page 244) or a pastry blender to work in the fat lightly.*

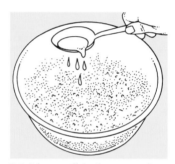

2 *Make a well in the center of the flour mixture and add 2 tablespoons well-chilled water, quickly and lightly mixing it in with a knife. The dough is moist enough if a little of the mixture squeezed between your fingertips sticks together; if it is too dry, add more well-chilled water little by little but be very careful not to add too much water which makes the pastry tough.*

3 *Press the crumbs together to form a more solid dough, picking up little flakes on the side of the bowl and gently kneading them together to form into a large ball. Only use 1 hand so you do not overwork the dough.*

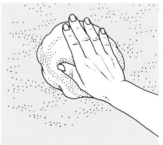

4 *Gently flatten the ball of dough on a lightly floured surface to a round so it chills evenly. Wrap well in plastic wrap and chill for at least 30 minutes before rolling out to the required shape. Allow to soften slightly before rolling.*

SAVORY FLAN TECHNIQUE

MAKING SAVORY TARTLETS

A savory flan, such as a quiche, made with conventional pastry is an ideal lunch dish or light supper when served with a crisp salad and some crusty French bread. Most flans use an egg custard as a base into which you set a selection of cooked and flaked fish, lightly sautéed or blanched vegetables, cheeses or any savory ingredient.

Prepare conventional pastry (opposite), using 2 cups (250g) all-purpose flour and 4oz (125g) butter. Roll out and line a 9in (23cm) flan dish or loose-bottomed tart pan and bake blind (page 245) for 15 minutes; remove the paper and dried beans. Prepare an egg custard by beating 4 eggs with 1¼ cups (300ml) milk and 1¼ cups (300ml) light cream. Serves 6.

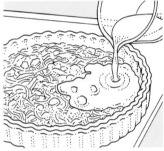

1 *Into the partially baked tart shell, scatter 4oz (125g) cooked diced ham and 4oz (125g) diced Brie or grated Cheddar cheese, or any other chosen filling. Place the flan dish on a baking sheet. Pour in the prepared egg custard.*

2 *Bake at 325°F, 160°C for about 45 minutes or until the mixture is set when tested with the tip of a knife. Serve the flan either straight from the oven, slightly cooled or at room temperature.*

FLAVORING CONVENTIONAL PASTRY

• One of the most usual variations is to make a delicious cheesy pastry by mixing finely grated strong-flavored cheese, such as aged Cheddar or Parmesan into the flour before incorporating the fat.
• A dark orange cheese will add a bright golden color to pastry, and another alternative is to crumble strong blue cheese like Gorgonzola or Roquefort into the flour before adding the fat.
• Herbed pastry is most successful with pungent dried herbs such as oregano, tarragon, thyme or dill. Very finely chopped fresh rosemary and tarragon and ground bay leaves also work well.
• You can make spiced pastries adding either one ground spice or a mixture of several. Turmeric gives a bright yellow color and a little curry powder imparts an instant Indian touch.
• Cumin, either whole or ground, combined with dried

mint, creates a Middle Eastern character and goes particularly well in a pastry crust for lamb dishes.
• Make a luxurious saffron pastry by heating a little milk with a good pinch of saffron strands and leaving to cool. Use this as the binding liquid instead of chilled water.
• Whole spices such as caraway, dill or fennel seeds are effective in a pastry to be used for cheese, vegetable or fish fillings, as is a mixture of finely grated lemon peel and a pinch of ground cardamom.
• Tomato puree can be added to both cheese and herb pastries, and will bind, so you need little, if any, water.
• For garlic pastry, add very finely chopped garlic and mix it evenly into the flour – chopped fresh ginger is good with garlic.
• Finely chopped fresh red chili adds an exciting bite to a spicy pie crust.

Individual savory tartlets can vary in size and shape, and are ideal for a first course or as bite-size canapés for a cocktail party. Bake the shells blind (page 245) before adding a sweet or savory filling. Cool on a wire rack.

The piecrust quantities (opposite) will make 18–20 small boat-shaped tartlets. If you bake the pastry shells in advance, you can store them in an airtight container for 2–3 days or you can freeze them.

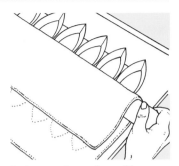

1 *Arrange the tartlet molds on a baking sheet in neat rows. Roll out the pastry to ⅛in (2.5mm) thick (page 244), then use the rolling pin to place it gently over the molds.*

2 *Use a small piece of surplus dough to gently press the rolled-out dough into each mould, pushing it well into the sides and base and taking care not to stretch the dough. Using a dough ball avoids making unecessary fingermarks in the dough.*

3 *Roll the rolling pin over the tops of the molds to cut off excess pastry. Pierce the bottom of each with a fork. Fill with parchment and beans and bake blind (page 245) for 8–10 minutes. Remove the paper and beans and bake for a further 6–8 minutes.*

Tartlet shells can be filled with many savory fillings to make interesting first courses or snacks. Here, the shells contain fried onion slices with finely chopped parsley, red pepper puree and plain yogurt combined with green onions and walnuts.

RICH PASTRIES

These rich pastries are crisper than plain piecrust, making ideal containers for free-standing tarts with creamy or fruit fillings. Even simple jam-filled tartlets become special when you make them with a rich pastry. The sweet hot butter crust pastry and chocolate crust pastry (both opposite) couldn't be easier to make, and the results are always wonderful.

You may find these rich pastries much more difficult to roll out than plain piecrust. I just use my fingertips to pat the dough into the pan or dish. When baked any small cracks will be gone, as if by magic.

If you are using a sweet rich pastry (below) for a fruit or custard tart, you can make the dough with ground nuts for a complementary flavor. Substitute up to half the amount of flour with ground blanched almonds, walnuts, pecans or hazelnuts and omit half the egg yolks. Because ground nuts do not contain the gluten found in wheat flour, this dough will be very difficult to handle. Don't even try to roll it out. Pat it out lightly instead with your fingertips. Sweet pastry can also be flavored with kirsch or other liqueurs, instead of the vanilla extract used in the recipe below.

SWEET PASTRY

This rich pastry, called *pâte sucrée* by the French, is crisp like a cookie because of the sugar and egg yolks it contains. Unlike ordinary piecrust, the key to success here is using butter that is soft at room temperature, not well chilled. To make a rich nut pastry to complement a fruit filling substitute ground nuts for half the flour in this recipe and only use 2 egg yolks. Try ground almonds, walnuts, pecans or hazelnuts.

To fill a 9in (23cm) tart pan, use 1⅔ cups (200g) all-purpose flour, ½ teaspoon salt (if using unsalted butter), 4oz (125g) diced, softened butter (preferably unsalted), ¼ cup (50g) sugar, 4 egg yolks and ½ teaspoon vanilla extract.

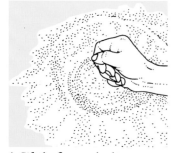

1 *Sift the flour and salt onto a work surface. Make a well in the center, circling from the middle outwards with your fist.*

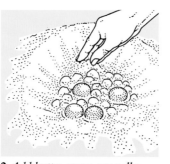

2 *Add butter, sugar, egg yolks and vanilla extract to the well. Use your fingertips in a quick 'pecking' motion to mix together.*

3 *As the mixture comes together use both hands to draw in the remaining flour and shape the dough into a ball.*

4 *Lightly knead the dough until smooth with the heel of your hand. Wrap the dough in plastic wrap and chill for at least 30 minutes before using.*

MAKING JAM TARTLETS

Little jam-filled tartlets make a rich dessert or snack. Use sweet pastry (left) and roll it out to about ⅛in (2.5mm) thick. These tartlets can't be patted into the pan because they are shaped with a cookie cutter, but if it is too difficult to handle, roll the dough between 2 sheets of waxed paper. Knead pastry trimmings together and reroll, cutting out more rounds until all the pastry has been used. Cut out little hearts or leaves to put on top of the jam, if you like.

Jam tartlets do not need blind baking because the jam reaches a high enough temperature to cook the pastry. Bake at 375°F, 190°C for about 10–12 minutes until the jam is bubbly and the pastry golden. Makes about 25 tartlets.

1 *After rolling out, dip a cutter in flour and cut as many rounds as you have muffin-pan cups, rerolling the dough as necessary.*

2 *Place pastry rounds into cups and press into the bottom and up the side of each. Chill for at least 30 minutes before baking.*

3 *Add about 1 heaping teaspoon jam to each cup, taking care not to overfill as the jam bubbles up during cooking, and bake (above).*

4 *Leave to cool for about 5 minutes. Then use a spatula to remove each tartlet, and place on a wire rack to cool further.*

SWEET HOT BUTTER CRUST PASTRY

This method is an unconventional but easy way to make pastry. I tried it out as an experiment years ago and have used it ever since. This pastry must be the easiest of all pastries to make, and produces a crisp, cookie-like crust, ideal to hold a filling. It can be baked blind without being weighted down and doesn't shrink during baking although it is best to chill the unbaked crust first. If desired, you can use strained orange or lemon juice instead of water, and include the finely grated rind, too, for extra flavor.

1 *To make enough sweet hot butter crust pastry to line a 23cm (9in) loose-bottomed flan pan, sift 1⅓ cups (175g) all-purpose flour, ½ teaspoon salt and 2 tablespoons confectioners' sugar into a mixing bowl and stir.*

2 *Gently melt 4oz (125g) butter and 1 tablespoon water in a saucepan, then gradually pour the warm liquid onto the flour mixture, mixing in with a wooden spoon until you have a soft dough.*

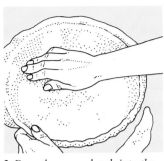

3 *Press the warm dough into the flan pan with your fingertips, lining the bottom and sides of the pan evenly. Press any cracks to seal together. Chill for at least 30 minutes before baking. If baking blind (page 245), pierce bottom lightly all over with a fork.*

FLAVORING SWEET PASTRY

- You might not think of adding herbs to flavor sweet pastry but I think very finely chopped rosemary or mint leaves added to the flour can be lovely.
- Finely grated lemon, lime or orange rind is delicious for mince pie pastry.
- A mixture of grated orange rind and ground cardamom, cinnamon or nutmeg is splendid for apple pie pastry.
- Make a honey-flavored pastry by sweetening the flour with honey instead of sugar; this works best if you melt 2 tablespoons honey with the butter as in the sweet hot butter crust pastry (above), omitting the water.
- Apart from the chocolate crust pastry method (right), flavor sweet pastry with chocolate by adding ¼ cup (25g) cocoa powder to the flour, or by stirring coarsely grated chocolate into the flour. This results in an interesting dappled effect. These chocolate pastries are good with finely grated orange rind, too.
- For a mocha flavor, use a very strong mixture of cold coffee as the binding liquid or, for a stronger taste, include some finely ground coffee in the flour.

CHOCOLATE CRUST PASTRY

This is another version of the sweet hot butter crust recipe (above) and is very simple to make. It produces a really dark and crisp chocolate crust, which is delicious baked blind and then filled with fresh blueberries, raspberries or other soft or exotic fruits which you can glaze or dust with confectioners' sugar or cover with flavored yogurt.

You can also use the baked crust as a container for ice cream, spooning in balls just before serving.

1 *To line a 9in (23cm) flan pan, sift 1 cup (125g) all-purpose flour, ½ cup (50g)) cocoa powder, ¾ cup plus 2 tablespoons (75g) confectioners' sugar and ½ teaspoon salt into a bowl; stir.*

2 *Melt 3oz (75g) butter and 1 tablespoon water in a saucepan, then gradually pour onto the flour and cocoa mixture, stirring with a wooden spoon. Knead briefly to form a dough.*

3 *Press the warm dough into a flan pan with your fingertips, lining the bottom and side evenly. Chill for at least 30 minutes before baking. If baking blind (page 245), lightly pierce the bottom all over with a fork. This pastry can be baked blind without being weighted down with dried beans.*

This luscious Blueberry Tart with a Chocolate Crust (page 258) is simple to make. The pastry is baked blind and filled with cream and fresh berries. Melted jelly is used for the glaze.

EASY PUFF PASTRY

Classic puff pastry is a light, flaky pastry which can be cut in a variety of shapes to make perfect containers for fillings of seafood, chicken, fish, ham or vegetables, or used to make sweet layered pastries. The flaky alternate layers of butter and dough rise as the oven heat melts the butter and turns the water to steam.

Although not as buttery as homemade puff pastry, which is very time-consuming to make, commercial puff pastry makes a perfectly acceptable and convenient alternative. However, the easy puff pastry given here provides almost as good results as the classic with much less work.

Whatever method of puff pastry you use, however, it needs baking at a high temperature. Unless the recipe or package instructs differently, bake the pastry at 425°F, 220°C for 8–10 minutes, to help the pastry to start to rise during baking, then lower the temperature to 375°F, 190°C for the remaining time. A dampened baking sheet which creates steam also helps the pastry to rise during baking and so does a roasting pan full of hot water on the shelf below.

MAKING EASY PUFF PASTRY

Easy puff pastry is quicker to make than traditional puff pastry. Begin by sifting 2 cups (250g) all-purpose flour into a bowl with 1 teaspoon salt. Add 2oz (50g) diced, chilled butter and rub or cut into the flour until the mixture resembles fine crumbs. Make a well in the center and pour in ⅔ cup (150ml) chilled water, mixing with a knife to form a soft, but not sticky dough. Form into a ball, wrap well in plastic wrap and chill for 15 minutes. On a lightly floured surface, roll out the dough to a neat rectangle about 6 x 18in (15 x 45cm). Keeping the edges straight as you work distributes the fat evenly.

1 *Cut 4oz (125g) more chilled butter into small pieces and dot evenly over the top two-thirds of the dough.*

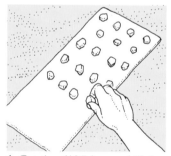

2 *Fold the unbuttered third of the dough, over half the buttered part of the rectangle. Fold the top third of the dough on top.*

3 *Make sure the butter is completely encased. Press the edges of the dough down with a rolling pin to seal in the air. Wrap the dough and chill for 20 minutes. Place the dough on a lightly floured surface.*

4 *Turn it so the seam sides are top and bottom. Keeping the edges straight, roll into a rectangle and fold into thirds (steps 2 and 3) twice more, always turning in the same direction. Wrap and chill for 20 minutes before using.*

MAKING PASTRY CASES

Easy puff pastry, as well as homemade or commercial puff pastry, can be formed into a variety of shapes, most of which are baked blind (page 245) so they remain crisp when a sweet or savory filling is added.

Vol-au-vents, deep pastry circles in a variety of sizes, are perhaps the best known pastry shells made from puff pastry. The quantity of easy puff pastry (left) will make about eight 4in (10cm) diamond-shaped cases.

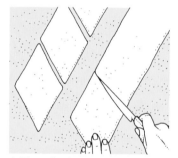

1 *To make diamond-shaped pastry cases, roll out pastry thinly to about ¼in (5mm) thick. Cut out 4in (10cm) wide strips, then cut into diamonds.*

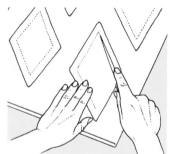

2 *Place the diamonds on 1–2 dampened baking sheets. Score a line 1in (2.5cm) inside each diamond, cutting halfway down; this will form the lid.*

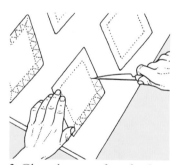

3 *Glaze the top surface of each diamond with an egg glaze (page 245) and cut to decorate the edges. This helps the pastry rise. Pierce the lids so they don't rise too much. Bake at 245°F, 200°C for 10 minutes until golden and well risen.*

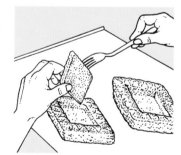

4 *After baking, the center of the diamond will have risen to form a lid. Carefully cut out the scored pastry lid and peel off any uncooked dough. Store in an airtight container and use within 24 hours. Fill with your chosen filling just before serving.*

Use commercial puff pastry and a filling of jam and apple slices for this quick Fruit Pastry.

USING PUFF PASTRY

• Add character to puff pastry by sifting dry flavorings such as ground spices, dried herbs or even ground toasted hazelnuts or almonds into the flour before adding the water.
• An extremely easy and featherlight cheese-flavored pastry which is as effective as puff pastry for cheese straws can be made by mixing together 1 cup (125g) all-purpose or whole wheat flour, 2 teaspoons baking powder, ½ teaspoon cayenne pepper and 6oz (175g) grated cheese. Work in 4oz (125g) diced well-chilled butter, then add 2 egg yolks and stir to make a dough. Press into a ball and chill. Roll out and cut into sticks. Bake toward the top of the oven at 425°F, 220°C for about 10 minutes.
• Commercial puff pastry is excellent for wrapping meat, fish or chicken to cook *en croûte*, as the flavors of the food seep into the pastry, yet it holds together as a crust far better than homemade pastry. Use an egg yolk glaze (page 245) for savory ingredients cooked *en croûte* in a puff pastry crust.
• Sweet puff and quick puff pastry pie tops and pastries can be given a caramel glaze by brushing lightly with a cold, heavy sugar syrup (page 208).

MAKING FRUIT PASTRY

Use one 17.3oz (490g) package of puff pastry and 1lb (500g) peeled eating apples to make this jam and apple dessert with a semi-open top. You can replace the jam with mincemeat (page 306) or sweetened and flavored cream or farmer's cheese. Instead of apples, you can also use pears or firm fresh apricots.

Thaw the puff pastry and roll out one package to a 8 x 15in (20 x 38cm) rectangle. Place on a greased baking sheet. Spread with jam to within 1in (2.5cm) from the edges. Top with thin peeled apple slices in neat rows, mounded up. Brush around the edges with water.

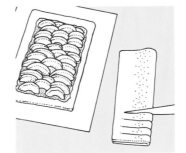

1 Roll out the second package of pastry to a 9 x 16in (23 x 40cm) rectangle. Lightly dust with flour and fold in half lengthwise. With a sharp knife, cut crosswise through the folded edge to within 1in (2.5cm) of the unfolded edge at ½in (1cm) intervals. Place the folded pastry over the filling with the fold in center; unfold, cutting off excess.

2 Seal the outside edges of the fruit-filled pastry by pressing down firmly with a bent index finger, then lift edges all around by cutting into the pastry edge with the back of a knife as you press. Glaze the pastry with an egg yolk glaze (page 245) and bake at 400°F, 200°C for 20–25 minutes until the pastry is puffed and golden.

SAUSAGE ROLLS

Good homemade sausage rolls are simple to make, especially if you use commercial puff pastry. The secret lies in using a good-quality ground meat or bulk sausage to which you can add your own flavorings, such as whole grain mustard, finely chopped fresh herbs, crushed garlic, chutney or even some crumbled blue cheese.

Allow 8oz (250g) of meat and ½ of a 17.3oz (490g) package puff pastry. Makes 2 large sausage rolls or 12 bite-size ones to serve with drinks.

1 Roll out the folded pastry on a lightly floured surface to a 12 x 6in (30 x 15cm) rectangle. Spread with your chosen flavoring. Or, add the flavoring by mixing it in with the meat.

2 Shape the meat, dusting lightly with flour, to the same length. Wrap it in the pastry, sealing the edge with beaten egg and placing cut-side down on a lightly greased baking sheet.

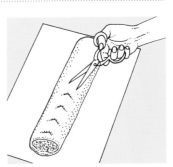

3 Snip the top with scissors 6–8 times, or cut into individual rolls. Glaze well with beaten egg (page 245) and bake at 400°F, 200°C for about 20 minutes until golden.

PHYLLO AND STRUDEL PASTRY

The word 'phyllo' in Greek means leaf, which is what the sheets of this extra-thin dough are like. Commercially made phyllo pastry is also suitable for making quick-and-easy strudel recipes. Phyllo and strudel pastry made from flour, water, salt and oil is stretched to develop the gluten in the flour until the dough is so thin that you can actually read through it! It can be made at home but it takes skill and practice to achieve perfection and hardly seems worth the time or trouble when fresh or frozen phyllo is so easily available. A package of fresh phyllo will last up to a month in the refrigerator and several months if frozen. Once you have defrosted phyllo dough, however, do not re-freeze it.

Phyllo pastry lends itself equally well to sweet or savory fillings, and always provides a delicate crisp result.

WORKING WITH PHYLLO

Phyllo is a versatile pastry which can be formed into many shapes or used to fill flan pans or other containers. It is very easy to use. The two important things to remember are to thaw frozen phyllo in the refrigerator to prevent any excess condensation from forming, which causes the sheets to stick together, and to keep any dough you are not using covered with a damp tea towel to prevent it from drying out. It is best to use clarified butter (page 96) for brushing the sheets, but olive oil or melted shortening can also be used. A light brushing is all that is needed. Use a sharp knife to cut the pastry neatly to avoid compressing the edges. Bake to a deep golden color to ensure it is cooked through. A brushing of oil or melted butter before and after baking helps moisten the pastry, but it often cracks anyway because the layers are so thin and crisp.

Versatile phyllo pastry is used for spinach and feta-filled phyllo packages and phyllo cups filled with ratatouille (page 59).

SHAPING PHYLLO PASTRY

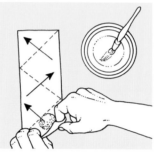 

To make phyllo packages: 1 *Cut 1 sheet phyllo pastry into 3 x 9in (7 x 23cm) strips. Brush 1 strip with melted butter and keep the remainder covered with a damp tea towel. Place 1 large teaspoon filling, such as chopped spinach and crumbled feta cheese in the bottom right-hand corner. Fold the bottom edge to meet the left side, forming a triangle and enclosing the filling.*

2 *Fold this triangle straight up, so the left sides are flush. Repeat these folds, working from left to right, until you reach the top. Tuck in any flap of leftover pastry. Brush with melted butter. Place on a lightly greased baking sheet and repeat with remaining strips to make more parcels. Bake at 375°F, 190°C for 12–15 minutes; brush again with melted butter.*

To make 4 phyllo cups: 1 *You need 4 buttered ramekins or shallow tartlet pans and 2 phyllo pastry sheets. Use 1 sheet at a time and cut each sheet in half; then each half into quarters. Working with 4 quarters at a time and keeping the remaining pastry covered, lightly butter the phyllo. Place 1 piece in a ramekin dish. Place another quarter crosswise over the first 1 and continue with 2 more quarters.*

2 *Gently crimp and make the corners stand up. Repeat with the remaining phyllo to make 3 more cups. Place the ramekins on a baking sheet and bake at 375°F, 190°C for 5 minutes until crisp. Remove the cups from the ramekins and fill with hot or cold savory ingredients, such as finely chopped ratatouille, soft white cheese mixed with herbs, spices or spinach, taramasalata or other fish pâtés.*

CLASSIC APPLE STRUDEL

This traditional dessert of light, flaky pastry layers enclosing spiced apple slices was originally Hungarian, but now it is usually associated with Austria. The strudel can be made ahead (it will keep in a freezer for a few weeks) but reheat before serving.

You can get a light, crisp, flaky result by using commercial phyllo pastry. Unwrap the dough and keep it covered completely with a damp tea towel.

For this classic apple strudel, peel, core and thinly slice 3 large cooking apples. In a large bowl, toss the apple slices with ⅓ cup (75g) sugar, ⅔ cup (75g) raisins, ¾ cup (75g) chopped walnuts, 1 teaspoon ground cinnamon, ½ teaspoon grated nutmeg and 1 tablespoon lemon juice. Set the filling aside while preparing the dough.

You will need 4 sheets phyllo pastry and about ¾ cup (75g) dry bread crumbs to assemble the strudel. Melt 4oz (125g) butter for brushing the pastry. Grease a large baking sheet with melted butter.

1 *Uncover the phyllo pastry and place 1 sheet on the greased baking sheet; keep the remaining pastry covered. Brush with melted butter and sprinkle with about one third of the bread crumbs.*

2 *Keeping the unused pastry covered, repeat the layering of phyllo sheets, brushing each one with melted butter and sprinkling with bread crumbs. Do not sprinkle crumbs on the top layer.*

3 *Drain the juices from the prepared apple filling. Spoon the filling along one side of the phyllo, placing it about 2in (5cm) in from the end to about 2in (5cm) from each of the long edges.*

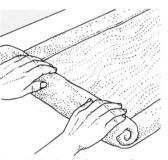

4 *Fold the long edges over the filling, then fold the end flap over to enclose the filling. Gently roll up the strudel like a jelly roll (see Chocolate Cream Roll, page 267), being careful to keep the long edges tucked in as you roll.*

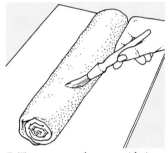

5 *Turn over so the seam side is underneath. Brush the strudel with melted butter. Bake at 375°F, 190°C for about 30 minutes until the pastry is golden and the apples are tender when pierced with a skewer.*

6 *Remove the strudel from the oven and brush with melted butter. To serve, cool slightly and transfer to a serving dish. Dust lightly with confectioners' sugar. The strudel can be served warm or at room temperature.*

FILLING PHYLLO PASTRY

• Use phyllo pastry for little stuffed appetizers. Prepare as for phyllo cups (opposite) but add a filling before baking, then pinch the tops together to make ruffled tops, like beggar's purses, and bake. The easiest fillings are farmer's, cream or crumbled feta cheeses, seasoned and mixed with chopped herbs, spices, chopped anchovies, chopped green onions, spinach, tuna, sliced mushrooms, sun-dried tomato paste, crumbled crisp bacon or diced ham, coarsely grated Parmesan, pesto sauce, curry paste or grated raw carrot.

• Precooked fillings for phyllo cups can be various kinds of cooked or smoked fish and seafood (crab is wonderful) mixed with herbs and seasonings, or ratatouille-type mixtures of cooked vegetables.

• Make large phyllo pies with layers of buttered fillo and a spicy ground meat mixture.

• Double crust phyllo pies can also be made enclosing fillings of precooked meat, game, poultry, fish, vegetables, cheese and eggs – a good way of using leftover Thanksgiving turkey.

• Make an impressive dome of rice encased entirely in crisp phyllo pastry: line a pudding mold with several layers of phyllo, well brushed with butter, and fill with a cold moist or buttery pilaf mixture with chicken, fish or other ingredients. Cover the top with the pastry and bake at 375°F, 190°C for 45 minutes, then turn out onto an ovenproof plate. Return to the oven for 10–15 minutes until golden.

A sweet use for phyllo pastry is apple strudel, made by wrapping spiced apple slices and raisins between delicate layers of pastry.

CHOUX PASTRY

This is truly a magical pastry, as a pasty thick sauce is transformed into incredibly light, crisp cream puffs. Even though the results give the opposite impression, choux paste (the name in French means cabbage because that's what the little puffs resemble) must be one of the easiest pastries to make as long as you follow a few simple rules.

It is also wonderfully versatile and after the first stovetop cooking stage will happily wait to be baked: the paste will keep for up to a day in the refrigerator. When ready to bake the paste needs no rolling – you simply pipe or spoon it onto a dampened baking sheet into all sorts of shapes from tiny little puffs to large gougère rings.

As canapés, bite-size cream puffs can be served hot and crisp with creamy and spicy chicken or fish fillings or cold with taramasalata or mayonnaise- or crème fraîche-based mixtures. Baby walnut-sized puffs can be flavored with curry spices and cheese, then deep-fried as beignets and served warm, dusted with grated Parmesan cheese.

The classic, elegant chocolate éclair, which must be nearly everyone's favorite treat, is surprisingly easy to make and can reappear in a different shape as the ever-popular dinner party dessert, profiteroles, or cream puffs, stuffed with custard or ice cream and served with either a hot or cold chocolate or butterscotch sauce.

MAKING CHOUX PASTRY

There are two stages of making choux pastry, the mixing of the paste in a saucepan followed by baking in a hot oven when the thick paste puffs up miraculously into whatever shape is required. Because of this double cooking, it is important that the eggs, which give choux paste its delicate lightness, are not added too soon or they will set and cook in the heat instead of expanding dramatically in the oven.

It is also important when melting the butter in the water (in step 2) not to let it come to a boil before it has completely melted. When the flour is added all at once it looks quite alarming, but, press on with the beating, and smoothness will soon be restored. For a crisper choux pastry, use bread flour although all-purpose flour can also be used. Do not, however, use self-rising flour.

Because choux pastry puffs up and out so much, leave lots of space for expansion when you pipe or spoon the paste on the baking sheet. As with puff pastry, a little moisture on the baking sheet and a roasting pan of water on a lower shelf of the oven provides steam which again helps with the rising during the second stage of cooking.

1 Sift ¾ cup (100g) bread flour with a pinch of salt into the center of a sheet of waxed paper and place by the stove so you will be able to pour the flour into the saucepan all at once. Put 3oz (75g) chopped butter into a medium-size saucepan with ¾ cup plus 2 tablespoons (200ml) cold water.

2 Melt the butter without stirring and bring slowly to a boil, still without stirring. When boiling immediately remove the pan from the heat and pour all the flour into the pan at once, slightly bending the waxed paper in the center to form a funnel. Beat the flour and butter immediately with a wooden spoon.

FLAVORING CHOUX PASTRY

- Fillings for small cream puff canapés can be either mayonnaise or cream cheese mixed with fresh herbs, finely chopped smoked salmon, crumbled Roquefort cheese, sun-dried tomato paste with fresh basil leaves, chopped tuna with fresh garlic, and many other seasonings. Taramasalata makes a delicious filling, a thick red pepper puree with chopped fresh herbs is an exciting surprise, and the famous Italian combination of spinach with ricotta cheese is always good.
- Profiteroles are best known with a chocolate sauce, but are also delicious with caramel and butterscotch sauces, or with fresh fruit purees, sweetened to taste which serve as a thick sauce (page 208).
- Profiteroles can be filled with whipped cream or a mixture of cream and plain yogurt or mascarpone – you can also streak the whipped cream with a little cooled, melted chocolate, or you can fill the profiteroles with ice cream and then top with hot chocolate fudge sauce (page 209).
- To make sweet fritters, deep-fry spoonfuls of choux paste, then sprinkle with vanilla sugar (page 235) and serve with cream or ice cream.

3 The mixture will look awful at first, but keep beating with the wooden spoon and it will soon form a smooth glossy paste that comes cleanly away from the side of the saucepan. Set aside to cool slightly, about 10–15 minutes. Meanwhile, beat 3 eggs together in a glass measuring cup with a fork.

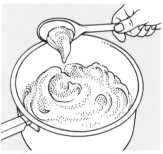

4 After the paste has cooled, gradually add the beaten eggs in stages, beating well after each addition with a wooden spoon until the egg is incorporated; you may not need all the egg. The mixture is ready to shape or pipe when it is of a manageable consistency and still firm enough to hold its shape.

USING CHOUX PASTE

How you shape choux paste before baking is what determines what it becomes. Spoon the paste into a pastry bag fitted with a small nozzle, about ½in (1cm) wide. The easiest way is to put the bag fitted with the tube into a glass measuring cup (page 24) and fold the top of the bag over the top of the cup. Spoon in the paste, then remove the bag and twist closed ready to pipe.

Choux pastry is nicest served crisp, so after baking it is best to pierce it to let out the steam or cut it open and scoop out any soft paste inside. Then return the pastry to the turned-off oven for a few minutes to dry out.

After baking, cream puffs can be filled with hot savory fillings, or left to cool and then filled with sweet fillings. Éclairs are traditionally filled with whipped cream or pastry cream (page 211) and then coated with a smooth chocolate sauce (page 230) or simply melted chocolate softened with a little butter or cream. In the summer include a few fresh raspberries mixed in with the whipped or pastry cream.

Profiteroles are usually filled with whipped cream or pastry cream and drizzled with chocolate sauce. Chopped, toasted hazelnuts are also excellent mixed in with the cream.

Chocolate-covered éclairs and profiteroles, decorated here with a fresh raspberry sauce (page 208) and fresh raspberries, are two popular uses for choux pastry.

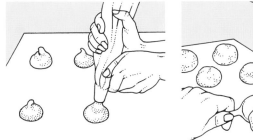  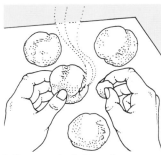 

1 *To make profiteroles or cream puffs, lightly grease 1 or 2 baking sheets and splash with water. Fill a pastry bag with the choux paste. Pipe 18–20 balls, about the size of a walnut, onto the baking sheets, spacing them well apart to allow for expansion.*

2 *If you do not have a pastry bag and tip, simply spoon large teaspoonfuls onto the prepared greased and wet baking sheets, spacing them well apart. Bake at 400°F, 200°C until the profiteroles are golden brown and crisp on the outside.*

3 *Remove the baking sheets from the oven and cut open the profiteroles carefully. Scrape out any uncooked paste and return the shells to the turned-off oven to dry out for about 5 minutes. Transfer to a wire rack and cool until ready to fill.*

To make éclairs, *pipe about 18 7cm (3in) lengths onto a lightly greased and wet baking sheet as for profiteroles, cutting the paste from the nozzle with a wet knife. Bake as for profiteroles, then transfer to a wire rack and cool before filling and coating.*

GOUGÈRE

Choux paste is not always sweet. It can also be flavored with strong grated cheese and baked and served with a delicious filling as in this classic French dish in which the paste rises up dramatically to produce a spectacular ring. The paste can either be spooned around a shallow ovenproof dish enclosing a filling, as here, or it can be spooned or piped into a large ring on a greased and wet baking sheet and baked. After baking split in half horizontally and spoon in your chosen filling.

Make up the choux paste (opposite), then stir in 3oz (75g) strong Cheddar or Gruyère cheese, cut into fine cubes or grated coarsely. Season well. Make a filling of either 8oz (250g) smoked flaked haddock or diced mushrooms mixed with 1¼ cups (300ml) white sauce (page 196), flavored with sautéed onions and carrots, 1 teaspoon of curry powder and finely chopped fresh parsley. You can also add leftover poultry, meat, finely chopped vegetables or crumbled, crispy fried bacon.

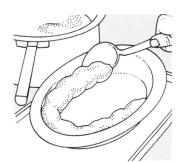 

1 *Grease a very shallow pie or other ovenproof dish, about 9in (23cm) long. Place the dish on a baking sheet and spoon the cheesy paste around the sides, mounding it up well.*

2 *Spoon the filling into the center, sprinkle with a little grated cheese, then bake at 400°F, 200°C for 35–40 minutes until the gougère is risen and golden brown. Serve at once.*

SAVORY PIES

Just as easy to prepare as their sweet look-alikes, savory pies make a hearty and comforting main dish that is assembled about an hour ahead and popped into the oven, allowing the cook time to concentrate on other things. For even greater convenience, most filling and topping choices can be prepared several hours ahead and refrigerated until ready to assemble

Savory pies offer great opportunity for creativity. While some combinations are traditional, chefs today lead the way in mixing and matching fillings and toppings to create a variety of combinations. Just add a pastry, puff-pastry, biscuit, cornbread or cobbler top to any meat, poultry or fish stew to make an elegant and traditional dish for brunch, lunch or dinner. (Make sure the stew is not too liquid so the sauce does not seep out under the pastry.) Or, combine an herbed custard, one or more kinds of cheese and roasted, grilled or fresh vegetables in a savory pastry crust to make an open tart or quiche. These delicious single-crust pies or tarts are excellent hors d'oeuvres, appetizers, first courses or vegetarian meals.

MAKING A PIZZA RUSTICA

There are dozens of fillings for this hearty Italian main dish pie traditionally made around Easter. Substitute strips of smoked mozzarella cheese for the meat for a lenten meal. Conventional pastry offers a quick alternative to the traditional yeast-raised crust. This recipe serves 6.

Lightly grease an 8in (20cm) deep round springform pan. For the filling combine 12oz (375g) chicken tenders, ¼ cup (60ml) dry white wine, 1 clove of garlic, finely chopped, ½ teaspoon fresh thyme leaves and a pinch salt in a small bowl. Set aside at room temperature while preparing the rest of the filling and the pastry (if longer than 30 minutes, refrigerate). Thoroughly rinse and drain 1lb (500g) baby spinach leaves. Steam or boil the spinach until soft. Drain very well. Combine 15oz (425g) ricotta cheese, 8oz (250g) shredded mozzarella, 1 cup (46g) fresh bread crumbs, 2 tablespoons finely chopped fresh basil leaves, 2 cloves garlic, finely chopped, and ¼ teaspoon salt. Beat in 1 egg. Separate 1 egg; beat the yolk and 1 tablespoon heavy cream to make a glaze; reserve the white for step 6. To make the crust, prepare a double recipe Conventional Pastry (page 246). Flatten the dough and score into quarters.

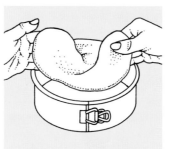

1 On a floured surface, roll out three-quarters of the dough to a 14in (36cm) round. Fold the rolled dough lightly in half and lower into the greased springform pan. Unfold the dough and press it down smoothly and evenly to line the bottom and side. Allow edges of dough to hang over rim of pan. Keep remaining dough covered.

2 Drain the marinade from the pieces of chicken into the cheese filling and stir to combine. Spoon half of the filling into the pastry-lined pan and arrange the chicken pieces in a layer over the top. Stir the cooked spinach into the remaining half of the filling and spoon over the chicken pieces, mounding the filling slightly and making six holes in it.

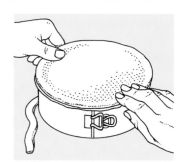

3 Roll out the remaining dough to a 9in (23cm) round for the top of the pizza. Moisten the overhanging edge of dough in the pan and place the pastry top over the filling. Press the edges of the dough together to seal. Trim the overhang of the dough so that it is even with the side of the pan and crimp the edge decoratively if desired.

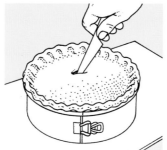

4 Set the pan on a baking sheet and glaze the top with the beaten yolk mixture (page 245). Make a small hole in the center of the top to allow steam to escape during baking and insert a piece of rolled foil into the hole. Reroll any pastry trimmings you may have left over and cut out leaves or flowers to decorate the pie top as desired.

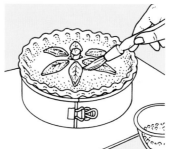

5 Attach the decorations by lightly pressing them into the glaze. Glaze the top again. If making the center flower (see page 242), set it into a well-greased ring of crumpled foil and bake it separately. In a measuring cup beat together ½ cup (120ml) heavy cream, the egg white, any remaining glaze and a pinch each of salt and pepper.

6 Insert a funnel into the rolled foil and slowly pour the cream mixture into the pizza. Bake in a preheated 350°F, 180°C oven for 65 to 75 minutes or until the center of the filling reaches 170°F, 75°C. After 35 minutes, check occasionally and cover the top of the pizza with foil when it appears to be getting too brown.

CHICKEN POT PIE

In some parts of the country a pot pie is a top-of-the-stove stew with squares of dough similar to noodle dough boiled in it. But in most areas, this traditional chicken mixture with a crisp brown oven-baked pastry or biscuit crust is what people think of as chicken pot pie.

Although you can start by boiling a stewing chicken to make the filling, these days chicken pot pie is most often made as a delicious way of using up the cooked chicken and broth left from a roast chicken dinner. If you don't have leftovers, refrigerated or thawed, frozen cooked chicken pieces and canned broth will do. This recipe serves 4.

Lightly grease a 1½ quart (1.4 liter) shallow casserole or baking dish. For the filling, melt 2 tablespoons butter in a 3 quart (2.84 liter) saucepan. Add 1 large onion, coarsely chopped, and ½ red bell pepper, chopped; cook, stirring, until vegetables have softened and slightly browned. Add 1½ cups (360ml) homemade or canned chicken broth, 1 large potato, peeled and cut into chunks, and 1 large carrot, peeled and sliced; bring the mixture to a boil. Cook 10 minutes.

Meanwhile, combine 1 cup (240ml) milk and ¼ cup (36g) flour until smooth. Gradually stir into broth mixture and bring to a boil over medium heat, stirring constantly until thickened. Fold in 2 cups (272g) cooked chicken pieces, 1 cup (142g) frozen green peas, 1 teaspoon fresh or ¼ teaspoon dried thyme leaves and salt and pepper to taste. Transfer to the greased casserole.

To make the crust, pepare a single recipe of Conventional Pastry (page 246). Shape into a flattened ball of dough and roll out to a round 1½in (4cm) larger than the top of the casserole. Place dough on casserole and allow the edges to overhang the side; fold the dough under and crimp the edge decoratively allowing it to rest on the edge of the casserole. Use any pastry trimmings to make decorations for the top of the pie if desired. Make a small hole in the center of the top to allow steam to escape during baking and score crust into quarters.

Set the casserole on a baking sheet and bake in a preheated 350°F, 180°C oven for 35 to 40 minutes or until the crust is golden brown and the filling bubbles. Remove casserole to a heatproof platter and serve the pot pie directly from the casserole.

TIPS FOR SAVORY PIES

• Both conventional pastry and biscuit dough can be flavored with herbs, spices, garlic and other flavorings to make exciting pie crusts.
• The addition of sesame or other seeds to a pastry or biscuit topping gives it more flavor and texture. You can also add flavor and tenderness to a crust by using cream or broth for the liquid in the recipe. For a special treat, add some shredded cheese to the flour mixture when making the pastry or biscuit crust for a savory pie.

• Try adding whole wheat, rye, or buckwheat flour to the all-purpose flour in a savory pie crust. The addition of oatmeal, cornmeal or chopped nuts gives a crunchy texture to the topping.
• Buttered sheets of phyllo dough with seasoned bread crumbs between the layers can give an exciting new look to your favorite meat, poultry or fish pie.
• For variety, use different fresh herbs, sesame oil, soy sauce or fresh ginger in your favorite savory pie fillings.

TAMALE PIE WITH CORN BREAD TOPPING

Tamale pie can be made with an unleavened crust of Masa Harina or a leavened cornbread topping. This version includes a corn bread recipe that could also be used on its own to bake a small loaf of corn bread or 6 corn muffins. The following recipe serves 6.

Lightly grease a 1½ quart (1.4 liter) shallow casserole or baking dish. For the filling, heat 1 tablespoon olive oil in a 3 quart (2.84 liter) saucepan. Add 1 large onion, coarsely chopped, and 1 green bell pepper, chopped, and 2 cloves garlic, finely chopped; cook, stirring, until vegetables have softened and slightly browned. Add a 14½ oz (411g) can stewed tomatoes, a 15oz (425g) can red kidney beans, drained, 2 tablespoons cornmeal, 2 teaspoons chili powder, 1½ teaspoons fresh or ½ teaspoon dried oregano leaves, and salt and pepper to taste. Bring to a boil over medium heat, stirring constantly until thickened. Fold in 1 cup (142g) frozen yellow corn and transfer to the greased casserole.

To make the topping, in a medium bowl, combine 1 cup (125g) yellow cornmeal, 2 tablespoons sugar and 2 teaspoons baking powder, 1 teaspoon fresh or ¼ teaspoon dried oregano leaves, and ¼ teaspoon salt. Stir in 1 egg and ⅓ cup (75ml) milk just until dry ingredients have been moistened. Spoon over chili mixture in casserole.

Set the casserole on a baking sheet and bake in a preheated 350°F, 180°C oven for 35 to 40 minutes or until the corn bread is golden brown and the filling bubbles. Remove the casserole to a heatproof platter and serve the tamale pie directly from the casserole.

LAMB AND VEGETABLE PIE

Garlic and rosemary enhance the flavor of this robust winter pie. For family occasions it is easier to prepare this aromatic mixture in one casserole, but for a company dinner, bake individual pies and elegantly decorate each crust. Just make an extra half recipe of pastry and assemble the pies in 6 or 8oz (177 or 237ml) baking dishes. This recipe serves 4.

Grease a 1½ quart (1.4 liter) shallow casserole or baking dish. For the filling, melt 1 tablespoon butter in a 3 quart (2.84 liter) saucepan. Add 1½lb (750g) cubed leg of lamb; sauté until browned on all sides. Add 1 large red onion, chopped, and 2 cloves of garlic, chopped; cook, stirring, until slightly browned. Add 1½ cups (360ml) water and 1 large potato, peeled and cut into chunks; bring mixture to a boil. Cook 30 minutes.

Meanwhile, combine 1 cup (240ml) dry red wine and ¼ cup (50g) flour. Gradually stir into boiling lamb mixture and return to a boil, stirring constantly until thickened. Stir in 1 teaspoon fresh or ¼ teaspoon dried rosemary leaves, and salt and pepper to taste. Transfer to casserole.

To make the crust, prepare a single recipe of Conventional Pastry (page 246) adding ½ teaspoon fresh or ⅛ teaspoon dried rosemary leaves to the flour. Roll out crust, place over filling, bake in a preheated 350°F, 180°C oven for 35 to 40 minutes or until the crust is golden brown and the filling bubbles. Remove casserole to a heatproof platter and serve the lamb and vegetable pie directly from the casserole.

PHYLLO PIE WITH CARAMELIZED APPLES AND PINE NUTS *(242)*

Serve this spiced tart with cream, yogurt or crème fraîche. *SERVES 6–8*

4oz (125g) butter
2lb (1kg) eating apples, peeled, cored, halved and thickly sliced
6–9 tablespoons pine nuts
3 teaspoons ground cinnamon
⅔ cup (125g) light brown sugar
Finely grated rind and juice of l lemon
12 oz (375g) phyllo pastry, thawed if frozen
Confectioners' sugar

Melt 2oz (50g) of the butter in a large frying pan over a medium heat. Fry the apples and toss them in the butter until soft. Add the pine nuts; stir for a minute. Stir in the cinnamon, and after 1 minute add the sugar and lemon rind and juice. Stir the boiling mixture until the juices have evaporated. Remove from the heat.

Melt the remaining butter and brush a large baking sheet, ideally a round pizza pan, with a little butter. Lay 2 sheets of phyllo pastry overlapping on the baking sheet. Brush thinly with butter, then lay on another 2 sheets of phyllo on top in the opposite direction. Continue for 3–4 more layers. Spoon the apple mixture on top in a circle. Fold the overlapping edges of the pastry over the mixture. Brush another 2 sheets with butter and lay them on top of the apples. Cover with another 2 buttered sheets in the opposite direction. Repeat with all the pastry, brushing the top sheets with butter. Press to seal in the apples and make a crinkly border, pinching with your fingers.

Bake at 400°F, 200°C for 35–45 minutes until the top is browned. Transfer to a serving dish. Just before serving dust with confectioners' sugar.

LIME AND STRAWBERRY TART *(242)*

With this pretty tart – in which a mouthwatering mixture of fresh lime slices and strawberries top a creamy filling encased in crisp sweet pastry – you will feel you have produced a dessert which might have come from a patisserie.   *SERVES 8*

FOR THE PASTRY
125g (4oz) unsalted butter
2 cups (250g) all-purpose flour
½ teaspoon salt
¼ cup (50g) sugar
2 large egg yolks
FOR THE FILLING
3 fresh limes, thinly sliced
1¼ cups (250g) granulated sugar
7–8oz (200–250g) medium or full fat cottage, farmer's or cream cheese
4 tablespoons light cream
⅓ cup (75g) superfine sugar
Grated rind and juice of 1 lemon
2 large eggs, beaten
1¼ cups (250g) fresh strawberries, hulled and halved

To make the pastry, melt the butter, then set aside. Sift the flour, salt and sugar into a bowl. Add the egg yolks and mix well, then pour in the melted butter and mix until the dough sticks together and forms a ball. Chill for at least 1 hour before shaping. If it is too firm for rolling, let it soften at room temperature first. Roll out to a circle and line a 9in (23cm) loose-bottomed metal flan pan, using your fingertips to pat it into position. Chill until ready to add the filling.

Meanwhile, put the lime slices in a small saucepan and just cover with water. Simmer, covered, for 20 minutes. Strain off ⅔ cup (150ml) water, and drain the slices. Put the measured water back into the pan with the granulated sugar. Dissolve the sugar, then simmer for 2 minutes until thickened. Add the limes and simmer, uncovered, for about 5 minutes. Set aside to cool.

Put the soft cheese into a bowl and mix in the cream and superfine sugar. Gradually stir in the lemon juice, then the beaten eggs. Mix thoroughly and lightly stir in the lemon rind. Pour into the chilled pastry shell.

Preheat a baking sheet in the oven at 350°F, 180°C. To bake place the tart pan on the hot baking sheet and bake for 25–35 minutes until the pastry edge is

well browned. Remove the tart from the oven and cool. Drain the lime slices from their syrup. Arrange the strawberries and lime slices on top of the tart, and then spoon the syrup over all. Remove the tart from the pan before serving. Serve immediately.

BLUEBERRY TART WITH A CHOCOLATE CRUST *(249)*

This miraculous little tart can be adapted to any season by using any berry which is available. Try it in particular with raspberries. *SERVES 6*

FOR THE CHOCOLATE CRUST
1 cup (125g) all-purpose flour
¼ cup (25g) cocoa powder
⅓ cup (50g) confectioners' sugar
½ teaspoon salt
3oz (75g) butter
FOR THE FILLING
1 cup (250ml) heavy cream
1 rounded tablespoon plain yogurt
1–1½ cups (250–375g) fresh blueberries
3 generous tablespoons raspberry jelly
1 tablespoon lemon juice

To make the crust, sift the flour, cocoa, confectioners' sugar and salt into a bowl and mix. Melt the butter and pour into the flour mixture a little at a time, stirring to make a dough. Press evenly over the bottom and about 1½in (4cm) up the sides of a buttered 6in (15cm) loose-bottomed cake pan, leaving an uneven edge. Chill for 20–30 minutes.

Put a large piece of parchment paper inside the pan, coming up well above the rim. Fill with dried beans and bake blind (page 245) in a preheated oven, 400°F, 200°C for 25 minutes. Remove the beans and parchment paper and put the crust back in the oven for another 5 minutes. Cool slightly then put the pan on a jam jar and carefully push down the cake pan sides (page 20). Use a thin spatula to transfer the crust onto a serving plate. Leave until cool.

Not more than ½ hour before serving, whip the cream until stiff, then fold in the yogurt. Spoon the mixture into the crust and level the surface. Arrange the blueberries on top. Melt the jelly with the lemon juice until smooth, then boil for 2–3 minutes. Remove from the heat, let the bubbles subside and then drizzle over the blueberries. Serve within the next 15 minutes.

SWEET ONION, GARLIC AND SAFFRON TART *(242)*

Of all savory tarts I think I like onion the best. In this recipe the sweet softness of boiled garlic and gently cooked onions are held in a rich eggy custard tinged with the subtle taste of saffron. Don't be alarmed by the quantity of garlic; when cooked in this way it is sweet and mild. To make six individual tarts instead of one larger tart, use 10cm (4in) tartlet pans. *SERVES 4–6*

FOR THE PASTRY
1⅓ cups (175g) all-purpose flour
1 teaspoon salt
½ teaspoon cayenne pepper
4oz (125g) butter
1 tablespoon water

FOR THE FILLING
1 cup (250ml) heavy cream
Approximately 10 saffron strands
8–10 cloves of garlic, unpeeled
1½lb (750g) onions, thinly sliced
2 tablespoons olive oil
1oz (25g) butter
1 generous teaspoon sugar
1 large egg
2 egg yolks
Salt and black pepper

To make the pastry, sift the flour, salt and cayenne pepper into a bowl. Melt the butter with the water, then pour into the flour gradually, mixing until you have a warm dough. Press the dough evenly over the base and sides of a 9in (23cm) fluted loose-bottomed flan pan. Chill for at least 30 minutes. Meanwhile, heat the cream and saffron until just boiling, then stir and set aside, stirring occasionally.

Place the garlic cloves in a small saucepan of water, bring to a boil, then simmer for 10–15 minutes until soft. Drain and set aside. Soften the onions in the olive oil and butter in a frying pan over a gentle heat, stirring, until soft but not browned. Transfer to a mixing bowl with any oil and butter from the pan. Squeeze the cloves of garlic out of their skins into the bowl, cut them in half lengthwise and add the sugar. Beat the cream, saffron, whole egg and 2 yolks. Add the onion and garlic mixture. Season with salt and pepper and stir.

Pierce the base of the pastry shell. Bake at 425°F, 220°C for 10 minutes, then turn the heat down to 350°F, 180°C. Spoon the onion mixture into the pastry shell, return to the oven and bake for 25–30 minutes, until the center of the filling feels only just set to a light touch. Serve warm.

STEAK AND KIDNEY PIE *(242)*

The savory filling for this hearty biscuit-topped meat pie may be cooked ahead, making it a good dish for busy days. *SERVES 6*

FOR THE FILLING
3 tablespoons all-purpose flour
½ teaspoon salt
¼ teaspoon black pepper
2lb (1kg) beef round steak, cut into 1in (2.5cm) pieces
3oz (75g) butter
1 very large onion, sliced
8oz (250g) mushrooms, halved
⅔ cup (150ml) dark beer
1 8oz (227g) can stewed tomatoes
1 bay leaf
¼ teaspoon ground allspice
6 lamb kidneys, skinned, quartered and cored or 3 calves' kidneys, chopped

FOR THE BISCUIT CRUST
1 cup (150g) all-purpose flour
1½ teaspoons baking powder
¼ teaspoon caraway seeds
¼ teaspoon salt
⅛ teaspoon ground nutmeg
2oz (50g) cold butter, sliced
1 large egg, beaten

To make the filling: In a plastic bag, combine the flour, salt and pepper. Add the steak pieces and shake to coat completely. Melt 2oz (50g) of the butter in a large Dutch oven, and fry the onion until golden. Transfer to a bowl. Cook the mushrooms in the Dutch oven for a few minutes, then transfer to the bowl. Melt the remaining butter in the pan and brown the beef all over. Return the onions and mushrooms to the Dutch oven. Stir in any remaining seasoned flour along with the beer, tomatoes, bay leaf and allspice.

Preheat oven to 350°F, 180°C. Cover the Dutch oven and heat on top of the stove until the meat mixture comes to a boil. Place in the oven and bake for about 1 hour. Add the kidneys and bake 20-30 minutes longer or until the meat is almost tender. Remove from the oven. Discard the bay leaf and set the meat mixture aside to cool 10-15 minutes so it is no longer steaming when you add the biscuit crust.

Meanwhile, make the biscuit crust. Combine the flour, baking powder, caraway seeds, salt and nutmeg in a bowl. Cut in the butter with a pastry blender or 2 knives. Stir in the beaten egg. If necessary, add a little water to make a manageable dough. Form into a ball. Roll out the dough on a heavily floured baking sheet to fit the top of the Dutch oven, or transfer the meat mixture to an oven-proof casserole and roll the dough to fit the top of the casserole. With a spatula, carefully slide the biscuit top from the baking sheet onto the meat mixture.

Return the pie to the oven and bake 20-25 minutes or until the biscuit is baked through and lightly browned. Serve from the Dutch oven or casserole.

If desired, the meat mixture may be cooled completely when it has been removed from the oven after cooking for about 1½ hours and is almost tender. Transfer it to a tightly covered container and refrigerate it until about 45 minutes before serving (no longer than 24 hours). Then prepare the biscuit crust, reheat the meat mixture, assemble the pie and bake as directed above.

CAKES and COOKIES

I don't think anyone who decides to make a cake does it as a chore – to me it seems almost like a holiday. Both cake- and cookie-making are not strictly necessary tasks and therefore should be pure pleasure; the pleasure of mixing the batter or dough, the pleasure of seeing how it becomes miraculously transformed in the oven, and finally, the intense pleasure, shared with family and friends, of eating what you have made. Many people feel they can't make cakes, either after suffering one disaster, or before having made a cake at all. But once anyone has made a successful cake and seen how it can be the center of attraction, they are usually hooked.

Like pastry- and bread-making, cakes never seem to turn out exactly the same way twice. All sorts of things – the kind of flour, the type of oven and the temperature of your kitchen – seem to make a difference, but this should be part of the excitement. The cake will be your creation and you must use your judgement. If you remember a few rules, many cakes are foolproof, and the simplest homemade cake is always tremendously appreciated for its unique character and the real flavor of natural ingredients.

The most important thing to remember about cake-making is not to open the oven door until the cake is at least three-quarters baked. If you do, cold air will rush in and the cake may sink if it has not had time to set through to the center.

Cakes vary tremendously in style according to the method used to make them. Layer cakes, the classic, which should be moist, springy and buttery, are made by creaming butter and sugar and beating in the eggs. On the whole, cakes containing a lot of butter are made by the creaming method, whereas with less rich mixtures, you can simply cut the butter into the flour. A sponge cake seemed particularly magical to me when I first made one; this is a fat-free cake in which the eggs and sugar are beaten until thick and creamy over hot water before folding in the flour. The mixture rises dramatically into the lightest cakes which are then put together with cream and jam or fresh fruit, and eaten as soon as possible – though this is never a problem.

Fruit cakes can be made both by the creaming method for rich and buttery mixtures, or by cutting the butter into the flour for plainer, lighter cakes. They can either be dotted sparsely with fruit as in a cherry sponge cake, or packed with different fruits as in traditional holiday fruit cakes. Some cakes can be so full of fruit that the result is simply fruit held together by a cake batter; this is expensive but very delicious. All kinds of dry fruit and nuts can be used: with fruit cakes it is always possible to be adventurous and vary combinations. Moist and sweet one-bowl cakes such as gingerbread are extremely easy to make as the butter is melted and simply stirred into the other ingredients.

Cakes do not necessarily need elaborate icing; a sprinkling of sieved confectioners' sugar or superfine sugar on top of the cake can look very attractive, while a thin coating of glacé icing covered with a few fresh edible flowers is often the prettiest decoration of all.

Homemade cookies are as popular as cakes and can be made much more immediately – literally minutes – before you want to eat them. They are also a good thing to give children to do on an uneventful afternoon and they can be stored in a tin or frozen.

A selection for dessert, afternoon tea or snack time, clockwise from top: crystallized edible blossoms elegantly decorate Frosted Sponge Cake with Lemon Curd and Blueberries (page 279); a coconut-flavored sweetened cream cheese filling frosts together the layers of Exotic Chocolate Cake (page 279); toasted hazelnuts add flavor and a crunchy texture to Chocolate and Hazelnut Thins (page 278); individual portions of old-fashioned, moist gingerbread (page 269) are topped with pieces of crystallized ginger; coated with confectioners' sugar, Snowballs (page 278) are round pecan biscuits with a rich taste like shortbread; fresh strawberries, shredded orange rind and a sprinkling of superfine sugar decorate the light-textured Orange Velvet Cake with Strawberries (page 278).

BASIC BAKING TECHNIQUES

To be praised as a good cake baker is perhaps one of the great culinary accolades, and to achieve this goal you are best armed with basic cake chemistry.

Heat has a specific effect on liquids, flours, eggs, fats and sugars, which also react with each other during baking. Too low a heat and the cake will not bake thoroughly in the center, producing a solid, sticky mass. Too high a temperature bakes the cake's outside quickly, causing a hard crisp exterior that forces any uncooked middle mixture to push up and erupt in a peaked and cracked appearance. Yet light, sponge cakes, for example, need quite a high heat to prevent them from becoming as flat as cookies.

Ideally, ingredients should be at room temperature, particularly eggs which curdle more easily when cold, and butter, which mixes so much more easily when soft. Cakes should be made with soft white wheat flour. Except for some fruit or vegetable cakes, I think whole wheat flours are too dense to be used on their own but can be mixed with white. Leavening agents are necessary for butter cakes, but fruit cakes and fat-free sponge cakes have air mechanically introduced through beating.

Superfine and brown sugars cream easily with butter, allowing lots of air to be beaten in. Granulated sugar will make an acceptable cake but gives speckled top crusts. Fats not only add flavor and color but also keeping qualities. Butter always gives the nicest flavor, but margarines make excellent cakes, too. This is why fat-free sponge cakes have to be eaten very fresh, and richer cakes actually improve with keeping. Rich cakes also cut far better if left for a day or two in an airtight tin first.

PREPARING PANS

One of the keys to successful baking lies in preparing the pans. Good quality non-stick pans need no preparation unless they are to be used for a rich fruit cake, which will need protection from the long baking with 1 or 2 sheets of parchment paper inside the pan, between the pan and cake mixture.

To make it really easy to turn out the cake, line the bottom of the pan with a round of paper. Non-stick baking parchment needs no greasing but waxed paper does; secure it to the pan with a little oil or butter.

Pans for sponge cakes *are best brushed with oil or melted shortening, then the bottom lined with a round of paper and greased again. Dust inside the pan with flour and tap upside down to remove any excess. Just brush pans for creamed cakes on the base and sides with oil or melted butter.*

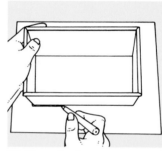

To line a loaf pan, *trace around the bottom on waxed paper, then cut out. Grease the pan, fit the paper in the bottom and grease again. Most loaf pans are lined on the bottom only. To line the sloping sides use a larger sheet of paper and cut into the corners as for a jelly roll pan (below).*

To line a deep square pan, *cut out a bottom as for a loaf pan (left), then 2 paper strips, each just a bit longer than 2 sides and 1in (2.5cm) taller. Grease the pan, fit in the bottom paper, then the long strips in 2 sections, pressing each well into the corners to crease. Lightly grease the paper.*

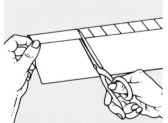

To line a deep round pan: 1 *Cut out a strip of paper just longer than the circumference of the pan and 2in (5cm) taller. Fold in about ¾in (1.5cm) along 1 edge of the strip, then snip along the edge to the fold lines at 1in (2.5cm) intervals.*

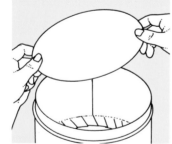

2 *Trace around the pan bottom on waxed paper and cut out a round. Grease the pan bottom and sides, fit in the long strip first, curving the snipped edge around on the bottom of the pan. Fit the round on top and lightly grease the paper. Do not flour.*

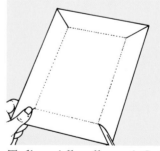

To line a jelly roll pan: 1 *Cut out a sheet of waxed paper large enough to cover the bottom of the pan comfortably and well up the sides. Trace the pan bottom, then fold along the lines to crease. Cut diagonally into the 4 corners to the traced line.*

2 *Lightly grease the bottom and sides of the jelly roll pan, fit in the prepared waxed paper, overlapping the corner diagonals for a snug fit. Secure these corner overlaps with metal paper clips, then lightly grease the surface of the paper.*

PREPARING BAKING SHEETS

Baking sheets for cookies
should ideally be rigid and
flat, and be rimless or with
just 1 rim, so you can transfer
the baked cookies easily onto
a wire rack to crisp as they
cool. If the baking sheets are
too thin and light the oven's
heat will cause them to
buckle. It is best to buy good-
quality baking sheets with a
dark surface, so they absorb
heat to produce crisp cookies
(page 20).

It is a good idea to have
several baking sheets, as
homemade cookies in
particular spread during
baking, taking up extra room.

Lightly grease most baking
sheets with a thin coating of
vegetable oil before adding the
dough to be baked. Doughs very
high in fat, such as shortbread,
however, are baked on ungreased
baking sheets. After baking, just
wipe the sheets with paper towels
to keep them well seasoned.

**To test fruit cakes such as Our Favorite Boiled Fruit and Nut
Cake (page 278) for doneness, insert a metal skewer in the center.
If no uncooked mixture adheres to it, the cake is baked.**

BAKING CAKES

A reliable oven is essential for successful cake and cookie
baking. Most are reliable, but no two ovens are quite the same,
so recipe times should be taken only as guidelines, and you
should test for doneness a few minutes before the time given in
any recipe. Because temperature is so vital in baking, an oven
thermometer is useful, and should be hung near the top part of
the oven, unless it is a convection oven. It is a good idea to read
through your user's manual before baking.

Try not to peek into the oven until the cake has had time to
set, especially for light cakes which might sink. And when you
do check, do so very quickly and shut the door again gently. In
general, position cakes on the shelf just above the center of the
oven and turn the cake if it is browning too quickly on one side.

After baking, test for doneness and then let cakes cool in their
pans and cookies cool on a baking sheet for a few minutes to
settle and firm up before transferring to a wire rack to cool
completely. Sponge cakes need 5–10 minutes cooling time
in the pans; fruit cakes 30–60 minutes; cookies 1–2 minutes.

Sponge cakes are baked if the
top springs back when lightly
pressed with a fingertip. Also, look
at the cake sides, and if they have
started to shrink away from the
side of the pan, the cake is baked.
If not baked, return to the oven
for a few minutes, then retest.

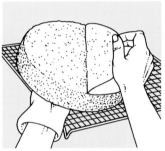

After a cake has rested in its pan
(left), invert it onto your hand
and peel off any lining paper
immediately so the bottom of the
cake does not become soggy. Turn
bottom down on a wire rack to
cool completely. Leave until cool
before icing or storing.

HINTS FOR SUCCESSFUL BAKING

• Always preheat ovens before
baking and ideally use an oven
thermometer to get an accurate
temperature reading.
• Take care to measure cake and
cookie ingredients accurately –
the correct proportions are
important for success.
• Use eggs at room temperature,
so they incorporate air more
easily. This results in lighter and
crisper textures.
• Always use butter for a rich
flavor but hard margarines or
vegetable shortening can be used
for simple everyday cakes as they

give better volume when beaten
or creamed.
• Hard fats cream better and
lighter if left out to soften at
room temperature for a few
hours before using. Otherwise
soften on Defrost (30%) in
a microwave for just a few
seconds before using.
• To hold mixing bowls steady
when beating place them on
a folded damp tea towel.
• When adding eggs to creamed
butter and sugar be careful that
it doesn't curdle, as this can
knock out air from the cake

mixture. If it does curdle, add
a tablespoon of flour to restore
the smoothness and beat again.
• Sift flour, spices and leavening
agents onto a sheet of waxed
paper when ingredients need to
be added all at once, or into
a bowl if added gradually.
• Always mix with wooden
spoons, and fold in ingredients
with large metal spoons so you
knock out as little air as possible.
• 'Dropping consistency' is
when the mixture drops easily
off a wooden spoon when given
a sharp shake. Stiff consistency

needs firmer shaking than
dropping consistency.
• Brush pans and lining paper
lightly but thoroughly with
either oil, melted butter or
melted vegetable shortening.
Wipe off excess oil with a
crumpled piece of paper towel.
• Don't wash cake pans and
baking sheets if possible. Often
they just need a wipe with paper
towels or a clean damp cloth.
This helps keep them seasoned,
so there is less chance of baked
cakes and cookies sticking
during cooking.

CREAMED *or* BUTTER CAKES

Creamed cakes have an unadulterated flavor of fresh, natural ingredients which is impossible to match in commercially made cakes. The best creamed cakes contain all butter because it results in wonderfully moist, rich and springy cakes which are deservedly popular; a freshly made layer cake is the best cake of all. A true butter flavor is supremely important and it is worth spending a little extra to get it. Sunflower-oil margarine can be used but follow the one-bowl method (opposite).

Butter cakes are extremely versatile and suit anything from a children's birthday cake to a fruit-topped upside-down cake (page 218) for a family meal.

The key to a good butter cake is lightness as well as rich flavor – every stage helps to achieve this. Begin by creaming the butter very thoroughly with the sugar using either an electric mixer or a wooden spoon. Superfine sugar is best to use because it dissolves most easily into the butter – the cake mixture will become light, fluffy and smooth.

The creamed mixture should be soft enough to just drop from the mixing spoon – if it seems too stiff, you can fold in a little liquid, which like all the ingredients, should be at room temperature. This can be milk, fruit juice or a strongly flavored liqueur such as rum or brandy but whichever you choose it should always be added gradually.

GOLDEN LAYER CAKE

The combination of fat, sugar, flour and eggs has served cooks well as the basis of simple cakes, buns and desserts. As you beat to cream the sugar and fat, air is incorporated in the mixture. Chefs sometimes do this initial creaming with a clean hand as hand warmth softens the fat and makes the sugar dissolve easier, but electric beaters or a wooden spoon will do as well. If you are using a wooden spoon, it helps to place the bowl on a folded tea towel or dish cloth to stop the bowl from sliding on the surface.

After the eggs are beaten in, flour sifted with a leavening agent is carefully folded in and the mixture moistened with a little liquid, usually water or milk. The mixture can then be baked as a single deep cake and sliced in half after baking or baked side by side in two cake pans.

This golden layer cake is simply filled with jam and sprinkled with superfine sugar but buttercream (page 274), whipped cream and soft cream cheese with crushed fruit are all memorable fillings. To make a chocolate butter cake, replace ¼ cup (32g) of the flour with cocoa powder. Makes one 18–20cm (7–8in) cake, enough to serve 4–6 people.

1 *Lightly grease two 7–8 (18–20cm) cake pans. Preheat the oven to 350°F, 180°C. Beat together 4 oz (125g) softened butter and ⅔ cup (125g) vanilla superfine sugar (page 235) until pale, light and fluffy. Continue beating for about 5 minutes until all the sugar has dissolved. It is easiest if you use an electric mixer.*

2 *When all the sugar has dissolved the mixture should no longer feel gritty. Lightly beat 2 eggs, and add half to the creamed butter and sugar. Beat thoroughly until well combined, then beat in the remaining egg, adding 1 tablespoon flour if the mixture looks as if it is beginning to curdle or separate.*

3 *Sift 1 cup (125g) self-rising cake flour over the creamed mixture. Fold the flour in with a large metal spoon, then fold in 2 tablespoons water or flavored liquid. Spoon into the prepared cake pans. Bake on the same shelf for 20–25 minutes, then test for doneness (page 263).*

4 *Cool for 5 minutes in the pans, then turn out and place bottom down on a wire rack. When cold, spread 1 cake with 2–3 tablespoons jam, then top with the other cake and dust the top with sifted superfine sugar. Or, use one of the filling suggestions (above).*

A homemade golden layer cake frosted together with raspberry jam makes a simple family dessert.

ONE-BOWL LAYER CAKE

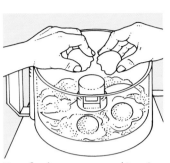

It is possible to make an excellent layer cake by beating all the ingredients together at once, but the fat must be quite soft for it to be successful. Very soft butter gives the best flavor or you can use soft tub margarine, but not a low-fat spread which contains too much water. Because air is not beaten in during the initial creaming, extra baking powder is needed and the baked texture is slightly more coarse.

This method is ideal for preparing in a food processor. Use this mixture as a quick layer cake or upside-down cake (page 218).

In a food processor combine 4oz (125g) softened butter and ⅔ cup (125g) sugar, 1 cup (125g) self-rising cake flour, 2 eggs and 1–2 tablespoons water. Process the mixture for 1 minute, then spoon into 2 greased 7–8in (18–20cm) cake pans. Bake as for Golden Layer Cake (opposite).

A selection of butterfly and plain cupcakes. Ice as you like, then decorate with sugared almonds and crystallized flowers.

FLAVORING CREAMED CAKES

• For a butter cake with a true, traditional vanilla flavor, split a vanilla bean and extract some of the seeds with the tip of a knife. Add these to the butter and sugar as you cream them together. You can also use vanilla sugar (page 235).
• Use half light or dark brown sugar instead of ordinary granulated sugar for a more distinctive flavor.
• I sometimes add taste and texture to butter cakes by stirring in whole caraway or cumin seeds, chopped toasted hazelnuts or chopped fresh rosemary or lavender leaves.
• If you are making small cakes, place a piece of chocolate in the middle of the mixture as a surprise center. A little jam or a piece of fresh fruit, such as apricot or plum, are also good.
• There are many ways to fill a layer cake apart from jam and whipped cream. My favorites are lemon-flavored buttercream (page 274), sweetened mascarpone with raspberries stirred in, farmers' or cream cheese sweetened with confectioners' sugar with a little lemon juice and finely grated rind, jam with fresh berries or cherries mixed into it, and fresh lemon or orange curd (page 302).
• Toppings for butter cakes can

be a smooth glazed top (page 274) which you can decorate with edible flowers, toasted nuts or sugar decorations – I always glaze with lemon juice instead of water as I prefer the sharp lemony taste.
• Caramelized nuts (page 228) are an ideal decoration for cakes.
• If you want to ice a cake's top and sides, buttercream icing (page 274) is the most suitable. This can be flavored with finely grated lemon or orange rinds, melted chocolate, coffee, liqueurs or other flavorings.
• Layer cakes can either be filled or covered completely with whipped cream, especially if they contain fresh fruit in the center. Softened cream cheese, sweetened and whipped with confectioners' sugar, is another good quick icing.
• The most lemony cake is made by piercing the hot cake with skewers and pouring a lemon-juice-flavored sugar syrup (page 208) all over which the cake absorbs as it cools.
• You can also make an alcoholic cake in the same way by pouring over it a rum- or brandy-flavored syrup.
• Make butter cakes in loaf pans. Add some fresh cranberries or blueberries, glacé cherries, or other dried fruits or nuts to the mixture for interest.

MAKING SMALL CAKES

Use the Golden Layer Cake recipe or the one-bowl variation for cupcakes and other individual cakes. These are just right for children's parties as you can make lots of delicious variations. Flavor them by adding 2 teaspoons finely grated orange or lemon rind, or 1 tablespoon orange flower water or rosewater to replace the water.

Cool the cakes in the papers. Top with buttercream (page 274), glacé icing (page 274) or sifted confectioners' sugar and decorate.

Put 18 cupcake papers into cupcake pans. Preheat the oven to 375°F, 190°C. Divide the batter between the papers, filling each three-quarters full. Bake for 15–17 minutes, then decorate as you like.

To make butterfly cakes, cut rounds from the tops of cupcakes. Spoon on 1 teaspoon buttercream and add a little jam. Cut the cake round in half and position as wings on top. Dust with confectioners' sugar.

For small coconut cakes, divide the batter between 8–10 timbale molds. Bake on a baking sheet for 18–20 minutes. Cool in the molds, then on wire racks. Brush with melted jam and roll in 1 cup (75g) toasted coconut.

SPONGE CAKES

Sponge cakes are the lightest cakes of all; certainly the fat-free sponge cake deserves its usual description of 'feather light'. This soft-textured, delicately flavored cake has no added leavening agent, relying simply on the volume achieved by beating eggs over a pan of hot water. Because of this, it is vitally important that the eggs are fresh so that they beat better, and that the flour is thoroughly sifted to make it as fine as possible so it can be folded very gently into the eggs without breaking down the air bubbles. Substitute 2 tablespoons of the flour for an equal amount of cornstarch to make it even finer.

Classic sponge cakes, although soft in texture, dry out quickly, so they should always be eaten on the day they are made, but this is not difficult as no other cakes disappear so fast! Other sponge cakes include Angel food cake which rises to great heights because it is made only with egg whites and the dry ingredients. Entirely fat-free, it is a favorite low-calorie dessert. Chiffon cakes are sponge cakes made with whole eggs, vegetable oil and baking powder. They are finer in texture and moister than the other sponge cakes and are often flavored with lemon or orange rind, chocolate, coffee, spices or ground nuts.

CLASSIC SPONGE CAKE

A light, golden sponge cake is one of the easiest cakes to make, especially if you use a hand-held electric mixer.

Usually only all-purpose flour is used for making this style of cake. If you use self-rising flour, the cake can rise too much and then collapse. For a more exotic flavor, fold in 1 tablespoon rosewater or orange flower water along with the flour.

Preheat the oven to 325°F, 160°C. Brush a deep 8in (20cm) cake pan with oil or melted butter, then flour the bottom and sides well, shaking out the excess flour (page 262).

1 *Beat 3 eggs with ⅔ cup (125g) vanilla superfine sugar (page 235) in a heatproof bowl over simmering water using an electric mixer or rotary beater, until the mixture is fluffy, pale and thick and leaves a trail when the beaters are lifted. The mixture must be very thick. Do not let the bottom of the bowl touch the water.*

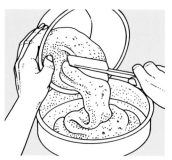

2 *Remove the bowl from the heat and beat the mixture for 2 minutes more. Very gently, using a large metal spoon, fold in 1 cup (125g) all-purpose flour. Pour the mixture into the prepared pan and bake for about 45 minutes until the top is golden and springs back when lightly pressed with a fingertip.*

3 *Cool the cake in the pan for 5 minutes, then turn out and place bottom down on a wire rack to cool completely. Cut in half horizontally with a long serrated knife, then frost together with jam and whipped cream or crushed fresh fruit. Dust the top with finely sifted confectioners' sugar, just before serving, if desired.*

The soft, delicate texture of a sponge cake shell makes it a perfect base for a shortcake. Add extra richness with a layer of pastry cream (page 211) or whipped cream under the fruit, if you like.

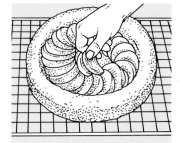

Use the sponge cake *mixture to make fruit shortcake. Grease and flour an 8in (20cm) indented cake pan. Make up a reduced quantity mixture of 2 eggs with ⅓ cup (75g) sugar and ⅔ cup (75g) all-purpose flour as in step 1. Bake for 25–30 minutes as in step 2, then cool as in step 3. Fill with fresh fruit and brush on a melted jelly glaze.*

MAKING JELLY ROLL

To make a jelly roll, simply use the basic sponge cake mixture (opposite) but make it with self-rising flour instead of plain to give a better volume. The thin flat cake is rolled and cooled around parchment paper so it keeps its characteristic shape. Preheat the oven to 425°F, 220°C. Line a 12 x 9in (30 x 23cm) jelly roll pan with greased parchment paper (page 262). Sift 1 cup (125g) self-rising flour into a bowl.

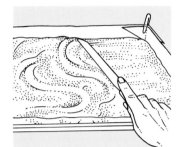

1 *Make the sponge cake mixture (opposite) as in steps 1 and 2. Pour into the prepared pan and spread level with a spatula. Bake for 8–10 minutes until just firm to the touch.*

2 *Sprinkle a large sheet of parchment paper with superfine sugar. Turn out the cake onto the sugary paper, peel off the lining paper and trim the edges. Roll up with the sugar paper inside. Cool.*

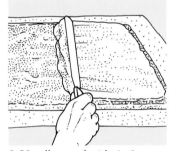

3 *Unroll; spread with 4–6 tablespoons red currant jelly or seedless red raspberry jam to 1in (2.5cm) from the edge.*

4 *Reroll the cake and discard the sugar paper. Dust with confectioners' sugar through a small, fine sieve, then serve.*

This Chocolate Cream Roll is easily made from the basic sponge cake recipe, substituting ¼ cup (25g) cocoa powder for an equal amount of flour. It is filled with whipped cream.

LADY FINGERS

These homemade lady fingers are very useful for making trifles or charlottes or to serve with sorbets and fruit compotes. To serve as cookies, frost two sponge fingers together with buttercream (page 274). A delicious way to serve lady fingers is to dip both ends in melted chocolate, then leave to set on waxed paper until firm.

The basic sponge cake mixture (opposite) makes 18–20 fingers. If you don't need them all at once, freeze in a plastic container so they don't get damaged, or store for several days in an airtight container. Preheat the oven to 400°F, 200°C. Lightly grease and flour 2 baking sheets (page 263).

FLAVORING SPONGE CAKES

• Sponge cakes have a delicate, delicious taste which should not be masked by strong flavoring. I like adding a little orange flower water, rosewater or violet flavoring to the cake mixture and then simply filling the baked cake with whipped cream and topping it with sieved confectioners' sugar. Crystallized rose or violet petals also make a pretty decoration.
• Finely grated lemon, orange or lime rinds are other flavorings for the sponge cake mixture, and with these a filling of fresh lemon or orange curd (page 302) with whipped

cream is delicious.
• A sponge cake is the perfect summer cake, as fresh berries are an ideal filling. Raspberries and cream is one of the best mixtures of all, while strawberries taste wonderful mixed with fresh orange curd, or whipped cream containing a little orange juice and finely grated orange rind.
• Peaches or nectarines, peeled, sliced and tossed with lemon juice to stop them discoloring, are excellent with red raspberries and whipped cream, or with whipped cream with yogurt folded into it.

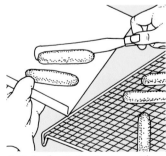

1 *Make up the basic sponge cake mixture. Fit a large pastry bag with a ¾in (1.5cm) tip; stand it in a measuring cup and fill with the mixture, refilling as necessary (page 24). Pipe 3in (7cm) lengths onto the prepared baking sheet, using a wet knife to cut off the mixture.*

2 *Bake for 5–7 minutes until golden, changing the 2 baking sheets to opposite racks halfway through baking. Cool for 2 minutes on the baking sheets, then transfer the lady fingers with a spatula onto a wire rack to cool completely. Store in an airtight container.*

DRIED FRUIT *and* SPICE CAKES

On a crisp autumn day, there are few things more satisfying than a spicy slice of cake filled with raisins and other dried fruit. Although there is nothing unappealing about spice cake in July, as the weather turns chilly we seem to crave the old-fashioned warmth and heartiness of molasses, dried fruit and spice. Originally popular because the richness of the spicy cake portion and the moistness of the fruit made these traditional cakes keep well into the winter and even improve with age, they have become an integral part of our culture.

We hear that, except for their once-a-year holiday fruit cake, people are using glacé fruit much less than they used to. In the place of the intensely sweetened peels, bakers are opting for the natural sweetness and appealing flavors of the increased variety of dried fruits now on the market. With choices such as dried sour cherries, blueberries, strawberries, mango, peaches, and pears as well as with the more familiar dates, figs, prunes, apricots and raisins, it is possible to create many different dried fruit cakes that will appeal to everyone.

For everyday eating, the easy-to-make Fruit and Nut Cake can be varied by changing the spices and the kinds of dried fruit or nuts included. The aromatic homemade Gingerbread will be perfect for your Halloween and Thanksgiving celebrations. And, the traditional fruit cake is rich with butter and eggs, crowded with fruit and nuts, slow baked, moistened with spirits, and ready for your holiday entertaining.

PREPARING DRIED FRUITS

These days dried fruits come ready to be used straight from the package. If you have a package that has been opened for a while and have to moisten the fruit, dry it thoroughly on paper towels and then toss in a little flour in a sieve. This distributes the fruit evenly and prevents it from sinking to the bottom while the cake is baking.

I like to use larger dried fruit, too, such as chopped prunes, dates and apricots in my fruit cakes. Because these are sticky it is a good idea to toss them in flour, as well.

Glacé fruits *need no special care before being added to the dry ingredients or batter of a cake. However, to prevent clumping it is a good idea to shake cherries in a little flour in a sieve to coat lightly before adding to the cake mixture with other ingredients.*

This spicy fruit and nut cake has a topping of chopped nuts for an extra special touch.

FRUIT AND NUT CAKE

This family-style cake is ideal for midweek eating. Unlike the traditional holiday fruit cake (opposite), this version is leavened with baking powder and uses a variety of dried rather than glacé fruit. I like to change the nature of its appearance by sprinkling the top with nuts or crushed cube sugar or even sparkling decorating sugar. The richness is provided by the butter.

Preheat the oven to 350°F, 180°C. Grease and line an 8in (20cm) deep square cake pan or two regular 8in (20cm) square cake pans.

1 *Sift 4 cups (500g) all-purpose flour, 2 teaspoons baking powder and 2 teaspoons pumpkin pie spice into a bowl. Work in 8oz (250g) butter until the mixture resembles fine bread crumbs. Stir in ⅔ cup (125g) each of brown sugar and granulated sugar.*

2 *Beat 2 eggs with 6 tablespoons milk and the finely grated rind of 1 lemon. Beat into the cake mixture with a wooden spoon, until a smooth dropping consistency is achieved. If the mixture is too dry add a little extra milk and beat in. Carefully fold in 1lb (500g) dried mixed fruit with a large metal spoon.*

3 *Spoon into the pan, leveling the top. Sprinkle with chopped nuts and bake for 45 minutes, then reduce the temperature to 325°F, 160°C and continue baking for about another hour. If using 2 pans, test for doneness after the first 45 minutes. Cool, then turn out right-side up onto a wire rack.*

RICH FRUIT CAKE

What Christmas celebration is complete without a dark rich moist fruit cake presented with great pride? It takes time to make and bake and is expensive, but it is always worth the effort. When cool, wrap it well in waxed paper and foil and store for up to 3 months.

Grease and line a 9in (23cm) deep round pan or springform pan (page 262) and preheat the oven to 275°F, 140°C.

12oz (375g) softened butter
1¾ cups (375g) dark brown sugar
6 eggs, beaten
4 cups (500g) all-purpose flour sifted with 1 teaspoon ground mixed spices
2 tablespoons dark molasses, warmed
5 tablespoons brown ale or milk
2½ cups (375g) currants
2½ cups (375g) golden raisins
1⅔ cups (250g) seedless raisins
1⅔ cups (250g) pitted prunes, chopped
4oz (125g) glacé cherries, quartered
4oz (125g) candied peel, chopped
1 cup (125g) blanched almonds or walnuts, chopped
Grated rind 1 lemon
3–5 tablespoons brandy or rum

FLAVORING AND DECORATING IDEAS

• Dried apricots have a lovely sharp flavor and are delicious combined in a fruit cake with coarsely chopped almonds and crystallized ginger.
• Extra large raisins with dates and walnuts is a delicious combination, and so are glacé cherries with seeded raisins, candied peel and unsalted pistachio nuts.
• Make a smaller fruit cake by halving the quantities of flour, eggs, butter and sugar in the rich fruit cake (left) and omitting the milk and molasses. Double the amount of dried fruit, using a selection of chopped glacé fruits and cherries, pineapple and pears. Bake in a greased 23cm (9in) ring mold at 325°F, 160°C for about 1½ hours, then test for doneness (page 263).
• Fruit juices can be used in cake mixtures, instead of the milk.
• When "mixed spices" are used in cake mixtures, I like to use freshly ground individual spices to make my mixtures – ground cloves, mace, nutmeg, cinnamon and cardamom are my favorites.
• Try the gingerbread recipe (below) using honey instead of molasses and adding a little finely chopped fresh lemon peel.
• Substituting ground almonds for some of the flour gives a fruit cake a lighter texture. It is very important to use really fresh nuts in cake mixtures as stale nuts ruin the whole cake.
• Marzipan (page 275) and royal icing (page 275) are traditional toppings for English fruit cakes but if you don't like marzipan just brush the cake with a layer of melted jam and let it set before icing.
• To present a very different and striking fruit cake at a festive occasion, glaze the surface with melted red currant jelly, then scatter with silver balls, and decorate with a pattern of angelica leaves and berries made with bits of glacé cherry.
• Plainer cakes can be sprinkled with slivered or chopped nuts towards the end of the cooking.

1 *Cream together the butter and sugar well until pale and fluffy. Gradually beat in the beaten eggs, adding 1 tablespoon of the flour if the mixture looks like curdling. Fold in the spicy flour with a large metal spoon, stirring gently in a figure eight.*

2 *Gently mix in the molasses and ale or milk, all the dried fruits, cherries, peel, nuts and lemon rind. The mixture should be stiff but not dry. Spoon into the prepared pan, and level the top making a slight hollow in the center so the cake rises level.*

3 *Bake in the center of the oven for 6–6½ hours. Test for doneness (page 263), then cool in the pan for 1 hour. Pierce the top and slowly pour on the brandy or rum. Turn out, peel off the paper and invert onto a wire rack to cool completely before wrapping.*

GINGERBREAD

As no air is beaten into this style of moist cake, its lightness comes from a leavening agent, in this case, baking soda (bicarbonate of soda). I like to make gingerbread extra spicy by adding chopped crystallized ginger but you can also add some raisins or walnuts for extra texture. Because of its moistness, gingerbread will keep well if wrapped and left for a few days in an airtight container.

Prepare a 10 x 7in (25 x 18cm) shallow rectangular pan (page 262) and preheat the oven to 350°F, 180°C.

1 *Sift 1 cup (125g) all-purpose flour with 2 teaspoons baking soda, 2 teaspoons ground ginger and 1 teaspoon mixed spices into a large mixing bowl. Stir in 3oz (75g) chopped crystallized or stem ginger. Stir in 1 cup (125g) whole wheat flour.*

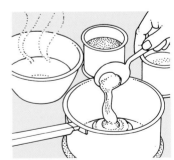

2 *Using a spoon dipped in hot water, measure out 4 tablespoons each of light corn syrup and molasses into a saucepan. Melt with 4oz (125g) butter over a low heat. Stir in 3 tablespoons brown sugar. Pour the mixture into the mixing bowl; beat well.*

3 *Mix in 1 beaten egg and ⅔ cup (150ml) milk. Pour into the pan and bake for about 45 minutes until a skewer comes out clean. Cool for 2–3 minutes, then turn out, peel off the paper and invert onto a wire rack. Cool completely and cut into squares.*

VEGETABLE, FRUIT *and* NUT CAKES

The idea of a cake made with vegetables may not seem irresistible, yet that is exactly what carrot cake can be. Flour or ground nuts are needed to hold the eggs, but grated carrots add a very desirable texture as well as moisture, sweetness and color. Grated zucchini and pumpkin also make delicious cakes – I particularly like pumpkin for its sweetness and brilliant color.

Flour is by no means obligatory in cakes, but it must be substituted by something which will support the eggs and butter. Ground nuts give the most richness and taste. You can use ready-ground almonds, but grinding nuts freshly in a food processor gives a better flavor and texture. You can also experiment with different nuts which are difficult to buy ready-ground, such as walnuts, pecans and hazelnuts – and I like grinding almonds which have not been blanched so that the ground nut cake is speckled with little bits of flavorful skin. The texture of the cake will vary depending on how finely you grind the nuts, so grind briefly if you want a really nutty, more crunchy cake. Fruits too, such as apples and pears, add moistness and body to cakes. If you use the sweet eating varieties the sugar can be reduced.

CARROT CAKE

To me this cake is impossible to resist. Moist and gooey, it can very well be eaten with nothing except a fine sprinkling of confectioners' sugar on top, or you can frost it together, top it or ice it completely with cream or farmers' cheese, softened and sweetened with confectioners' sugar. Grated parsnips are an excellent alternative to carrots, using ground mace and whole caraway seeds as the spices instead of cinnamon.

Carrot cake keeps well in an airtight tin, or wrapped in foil, and can be made the day before eating. The addition of chopped nuts is optional, but I think it makes all the difference to the taste as well as the texture.

Preheat the oven to 350°F, 180°C. Have ready a buttered 8in (20cm) deep round cake tin lined with a round of greased waxed paper or parchment (page 262). If the top of the cake begins to look a little too brown before it is completely baked, lay a piece of foil lightly over the surface and continue baking. Serves 6–8.

1 *Beat ¾ cup plus 2 tablespoons (175g) sugar with 2 rounded tablespoons honey and 1 cup (250ml) sunflower oil until well mixed. Beat in 3 large eggs, beating well after each addition until pale and frothy.*

2 *Stir in 1⅓ cups (175g) whole wheat flour, mixed with 1½ teaspoons baking powder, then stir in 2 teaspoons ground cinnamon, ½ teaspoon salt, 2½ cups (300g) grated carrots, and 1¼ cups (150g) chopped nuts.*

ADDING VARIETY TO VEGETABLE, FRUIT AND NUT CAKES

• Carrot cakes can be compact and chewy like the one above or light and fluffy. For a lighter cake, fold ¾–1 cup (75–125g) finely grated carrot into a basic sponge mixture (page 266) after you have added the flour and any spices.

• An unusual and glowing top for a carrot cake can be made by simmering coarsely grated carrots in a thick sugar and lemon juice syrup (page 208) and spreading the mixture on top of the cake when cold.

• Spices especially suitable to add to vegetable cake recipes are ground cinnamon, mace, nutmeg, cardamom, coriander, cloves and allspice.

• Finely grated orange or lemon rind is always a good, flavorful addition to vegetable cakes, too.

• Walnuts or pecans, ground in a food processor, have a rich oil which gives a very distinctive flavor to nut-based cakes. They are delicious in the ground nut cake (opposite) or used instead of flour in a chocolate cake recipe made with dark chocolate. Use ready-ground almonds for a milder, finer taste.

• Try adding candied peel and finely grated orange rind to a ground nut cake. Or, you can include a few golden raisins, chopped dried apricots, halved glacé cherries or uncooked fresh cranberries or blueberries.

• For an excellent orange cake, boil 1 unpeeled orange until soft, then cut in half and remove the seeds. Puree both the flesh and skin in the food processor, and mix this puree into the ground nut mixture (opposite) made with 6 tablespoons all-purpose flour as well as the 1 cup (75g) ground almonds.

• Add 2 tablespoons British bitter orange marmalade to the basic ground nut mixture (opposite) for another style of orange-flavored cake.

• For a delicious upside-down pear cake with a ground nut mixture, spoon a layer of honey onto the bottom of a generously buttered 7in (18cm) deep cake tin. Arrange thin pear slices in overlapping circles, sprinkle with lemon juice and then spoon in the ground nut cake mixture (opposite). Bake in a preheated 350°F, 180°C oven for 45–50 minutes. Let it rest in the pan for 10 minutes, then turn out upside down onto a serving plate. Serve the upside-down cake warm or at room temperature.

3 *Pour the mixture into the prepared cake pan and bake for 1½–1¾ hours until a thin skewer inserted in the center of the cake comes out clean. Leave to cool in the pan for about 10 minutes, then remove the cake from the pan and peel off the paper. Put the cake right-side up on a wire rack to cool completely. Dust the top with confectioners' sugar or raw sugar just before serving, if you like, or ice as suggested above.*

APPLE CAKE

In addition to our own favorites, there are countless apple cake recipes from all over the Western world, especially from other apple-growing areas like France, and New Zealand. The tang of the fruit balances well with a light toffee-like taste in this version. The fruit can be first peeled and chopped or cooked until fluffy and then mixed in.

This recipe has extra texture from the apple and crunchy streusel topping. It is moister than normal cakes and is nicest served warm with sour cream or crème fraîche. Try making it, too, with fresh, sweet pears or pitted and chopped fresh apricots or plums instead of apples. For extra flavoring add a little of your own mixed spices including cinnamon and nutmeg.

Preheat the oven to 325°F, 170°C. Grease and line the bottom of an 8in (20cm) springform pan with a round of waxed paper to fit (page 262). Lightly grease the paper.

1 *Beat 4oz (125g) softened butter with ¾ cup (150g) brown sugar until pale and fluffy, then beat in 2 eggs. Sift 2 cups (250g) all-purpose flour with 3 teaspoons baking powder and fold in with 2 tablespoons orange juice, 2 teaspoons grated orange rind and a few drops vanilla extract.*

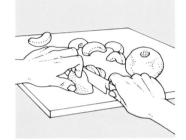

2 *Peel 1lb (500g) Golden Delicious or Granny Smith apples; core and chop into medium-size chunks. Stir them into the cake mixture. Turn into the pan and level the surface with a spatula. Tap the pan gently on the work surface so the mixture works its way down.*

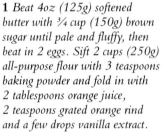

3 *Rub 1oz (25g) butter into ⅓ cup (50g) all-purpose flour until the mixture resembles crumbs. Mix in 2 tablespoons light brown sugar, 1 pinch ground cinnamon and 1 tablespoon chopped hazelnuts. Sprinkle over the cake. Bake for 1–1¼ hours or until a fine skewer inserted in the center comes out clean. Cool in the pan for 10 minutes; turn out and peel off the paper. Place right-side up on a wire rack to cool.*

GROUND NUT CAKE

Cakes made with ground nuts and no flour have a rich flavor and are very moist, but they also have a light and delicate texture. You can use ground nuts instead of some of the flour to improve the texture of fruit cakes, and chocolate cakes are excellent made with melted chocolate and ground nuts and no flour at all.

Vary the following simple recipe by using different kinds of ground nuts – hazelnuts are particularly good – and by adding chopped, toasted nuts, too, to the cake mixture. This cake has enough flavor and moisture to eat plain, but you can ice it, if you like or bake 2 cakes and frost them together with whipped cream, plain yogurt or fresh fruit. Serves 6.

Preheat the oven to 350°F, 180°C. Have ready a buttered and floured 7in (18cm) cake pan, the base lined with waxed paper or parchment (page 262).

1 *Beat 4oz (125g) softened butter and ⅔ cup (150g) sugar in a large mixing bowl until light and fluffy, then beat in the finely grated rind of 1 lemon and ½ teaspoon salt. Beat in 3 lightly beaten large eggs and add alternately with 1 cup (75g) ground almonds, beating well after each addition.*

2 *Pour the mixture into the prepared pan, smooth the top and sprinkle with raw sugar. Bake for 45–50 minutes or until a fine skewer inserted in the center of the cake comes out clean. Cool in the tin for 10 minutes before turning out, then peel off the paper and place right-side up on a wire rack to cool completely.*

A trio of cakes suitable for any occasion: apple cake served with sour cream, ground nut cake with a sparkling sugar topping and a carrot cake dusted with confectioners' sugar.

CHOCOLATE CAKES

If I had to choose one kind of cake above all others, it would certainly be a chocolate one, and there are clearly many others who share my passion. Because chocolate has real body, it is possible to make a chocolate cake with no support from flour at all – the cake will be soft, delicate and moist, ideal for a dessert. But there are many other kinds of chocolate cake, from the lightest sponge cake flavored with cocoa to the irresistible dense Sachertorte. Good-quality melted chocolate with a cocoa solids content of not less than 50 per cent, combined with a little powdered cocoa, makes the most chocolaty cakes of all. You can also add a little strong coffee to intensify the taste, and dark brown sugar instead of white.

Chocolate cakes suit all occasions; my family always chooses one for birthday celebrations, and chocolate cake for an everyday dessert cheers everyone up. They also make perfect desserts for entertaining, served with whipped cream or aside soft fresh fruit and fruit compotes. They are a delicious treat for mid-morning coffee – I must confess that I even like chocolate cake for breakfast!

SACHERTORTE

You can make this classic rich, chocolate cake from Vienna's Hotel Sacher easily at home. There are many different versions of the actual cake, but the crisp dark glossy icing with its sharp apricot layer underneath is always left relatively unadorned. I just decorate with chocolate leaves or you can add the name 'Sacher' drizzled in chocolate on top from a pastry bag. After icing, the cake can be stored for a day or two.

Preheat the oven to 325°F, 160°C. Grease and line a 9in (23cm) springform pan (page 262).

1 *Melt 5oz (150g) semi-sweet chocolate (page 230) and cool. Cream 4oz (125g) softened butter with ⅔ cup (125g) sugar, then beat in the chocolate and 4 egg yolks. Fold in ⅔ cup (75g) self-rising flour, sifted with 2 tablespoons cocoa powder, stirring in a figure eight motion.*

2 *Add 1 tablespoon rum, 1 teaspoon almond extract and 1 tablespoon water. Beat 4 egg whites until stiff, then carefully fold into the chocolate mixture. Turn into the pan and bake for about 50 minutes, or until the cake springs back when lightly pressed with a fingertip.*

3 *Cool in the pan for 10 minutes, then turn out and peel off the paper. Place the cake rightside up on a wire rack to cool completely. When the cake is cool, melt and sieve 3 tablespoons apricot jam and brush on the top and sides of the cake with a clean pastry brush.*

The ultimate in dark, rich chocolate cakes that few will be able to resist – chocolate fudge cake with walnuts, classic Sachertorte decorated with elegant chocolate leaves and gooey chocolate cake with whipped cream and chocolate curls.

4 *Meanwhile, dissolve ⅓ cup (75g) sugar in 5 tablespoons boiling water, then break in 4oz (125g) semisweet chocolate, stirring with a wooden spoon until the mixture is smooth. Boil for 1–2 minutes, then stir again and carefully pour over the cake top and sides, spreading with a spatula. Allow the chocolate icing to cool and set. Make chocolate leaves (page 231) and arrange them decoratively on top.*

GOOEY CHOCOLATE CAKE

Cake-eating is a most pleasurable indulgence, and the addictive qualities of chocolate make eating chocolate cake the most indulgent experience of all. The secret of a dark and gooey chocolate cake is that it should contain plenty of chocolate and little, if any, flour, but at the same time it should not be heavy. This is just such a cake.

Preheat the oven to 350°F, 180°C. Have ready two 8in (20cm) greased deep cake pans, each lined with a round of greased waxed paper or parchment (page 262).

After baking, leave the cakes in their pans to cool completely, then loosen the edges with a knife and turn out, removing the parchment. Frost the 2 cakes together with whipped cream or mascarpone and top with more cream or mascarpone and chocolate curls (page 231).

If you want to make this cake into a real orgy of chocolate, you can fill the middle with whipped cream, and then ice the whole cake with melted chocolate, into which you have stirred a little butter or cream. During the summer, fill the cake with fresh fruit such as raspberries, strawberries or peaches and whipped cream and cover with a simple sprinkling of confectioners' sugar.

IDEAS FOR CHOCOLATE CAKES

• Many flavorings go well with chocolate, but some have a special affinity; tangy orange or lemon, coffee and brandy, mint, cinnamon or cardamom.
• A dark chocolate cake filled and iced with a sharp lemon buttercream icing (page 274) is delicious. Or, ice the top with glacé icing (page 274) made with fresh lemon and fill the middle with lemon or orange curd (page 302).
• Marmalade can also be used as a filling.
• When you want to frost together a chocolate cake with cream, I think a slightly sharper taste is preferable to the richness of pure cream, so you can either fold yogurt into whipped cream or use crème fraîche as alternatives.
• A thick covering of coarsely flaked chocolate sprinkled with sieved confectioners' sugar looks very effective.
• To intensify the chocolate flavor of a chocolate sponge cake, add a little strong coffee to the mixture. If the cake has been made with melted chocolate, substitute ¼ cup (25g) cocoa for 3 tablespoons of the flour. You can also use dark brown sugar.

CHOCOLATE FUDGE CAKE

For this cake, a batter mixture, using oil, rather than solid fat, produces a light texture.

Make the chocolate icing while the cake is cooling. Sift 2⅓ cups (300g) confectioners' sugar and ¼ cup (25g) cocoa powder in a bowl. Melt 4oz (125g) butter with 4 tablespoons water, then beat into the confectioners' sugar until just runny. The icing does crack once set, if moved, so ice the cake on the serving plate with pieces of waxed paper under the cake.

Preheat the oven to 325°F, 160°C. Grease and line a 10in (25cm) square cake pan.

1 *Break up 8oz (250g) semisweet chocolate, put into a heatproof bowl set over a pan of barely simmering water and stir until the chocolate melts. Remove the bowl from the heat to cool.*

2 *Put the yolks of 5 large eggs into a large bowl, with ¾ cup plus 2 tablespoons (175g) dark brown sugar and beat thoroughly with a wooden spoon or electric mixer until smooth and thick.*

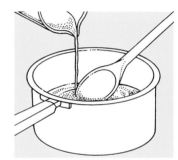

1 *Melt 4oz (125g) semisweet chocolate with ⅔ cup (125g) brown sugar in 1¼ cups (300ml) milk; stir in ⅔ cup (150ml) sunflower oil and 1 teaspoon vanilla extract. Sift 2¾ cups (350g) all-purpose flour, 2 tablespoons cocoa powder, 1 teaspoon baking soda and a pinch of salt into a large bowl.*

3 *Pour in the melted chocolate and beat thoroughly, then beat in 2 tablespoons hot water. Sift together 1 rounded tablespoon cocoa powder and 3 tablespoons all-purpose flour and stir into the chocolate mixture. In another bowl, beat the egg whites with ½ teaspoon salt until they stand in soft peaks but are not too stiff.*

4 *Fold the egg whites gently but thoroughly into the chocolate mixture. Pour the cake mixture into the prepared cake pans and bake for 15–20 minutes until the cakes spring back when lightly pressed with a fingertip. Cool completely in the tin, then loosen the edges with a spatula and turn out on to a serving plate.*

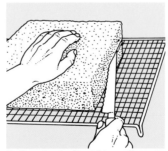

2 *Beat in the liquid ingredients, 1¼ cups (250g) sugar and 4 eggs. Pour into the pan and bake for 1 hour or until a skewer comes out clean. Cool for 5 minutes, then turn out and remove the paper. Put on a wire rack and slice in half. Cool completely.*

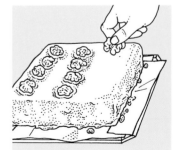

3 *Meanwhile, make the icing (above). Use some icing to frost the cake halves together, then pour the rest immediately over the top and down the sides. Decorate with 12 walnut halves and allow to set. Cut into 12 pieces to serve.*

SIMPLE CAKE DECORATION

Simple cake decorations are so much prettier than formal, elaborate icing which, although it can still transform a cake into an exciting and impressive centerpiece for a special occasion, doesn't exactly make a cake look edible. Simple decoration such as sifted confectioners' sugar on top is very effective, yet also reveals the mouthwatering aspects of the cake which make you want to eat it at once.

You don't need any skill to make attractive cake decorations, but it does require judgment. What must be learned is that, like painting a picture, there is a point at which it is time to stop. This is when the appearance is perfect and further decoration will begin to look like over-decoration. Since cake decorating is the same as any decorating, your color scheme is just as important. On the whole, one or two complementary colors are better than a random mixture. Certain combinations are especially effective: brilliant red, such as one perfect real red rose on dark brown chocolate, looks dramatic; silver looks lovely on white, and pale pink flowers with green leaves on the palest green icing look very summery.

BUTTERCREAM

This is a very versatile and easy icing which can be used as a filling, a coating and for simple piping. The only ingredients are softened unsalted butter and sifted confectioners' sugar, with added flavorings (such as vanilla, almond, peppermint, lemon juice and rind, or flower water) and colorings. You can mix the ingredients in a food processor.

Makes enough to fill and cover one 8–9in (20–23cm) round cake or top 18–24 cupcakes.

1 *Beat 125g (4oz) softened unsalted butter until light and fluffy. Sift 2 cups (250g) confectioners' sugar gradually on top, beating well with a wooden spoon. Scrape the sides of the bowl down with a rubber spatula.*

2 *Beat in a few drops of flavoring. Add coloring if desired, a drop at a time, from the tip of a toothpick. If the buttercream is too stiff, stir in 1 tablespoon milk, water or fruit juice to help to lighten it.*

3 *Spread the buttercream with a spatula first around the side of the cake, then on top. Run the tip of the knife back and forth over the top for a simple but effective pattern. Or bring the icing up over the cake in little swirls.*

GLACÉ ICING OR GLAZE

This is a very simple icing: just sifted confectioners' sugar and warm water. Because icing sugar is so sweet, glacé icing is often made with strained lemon juice, instead. The right consistency is reached when the icing flows thickly and finds its own level on a flat cake top.

Sift 1⅓ cups (175g) confectioners' sugar into a large bowl standing on a damp cloth. Using a wooden spoon, beat in 1 tablespoon warm water or strained lemon juice. Add more water or juice in dribbles until you have a syrupy consistency.

Makes enough to ice the top and side of an 8in (20cm) cake or 18 cupcakes.

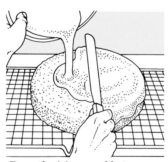

Pour the icing *steadily in an even stream onto the center of the cooled cake placed on a wire rack over a piece of waxed paper. Carefully spread the icing with a spatula, tapping the cake gently to discourage any air bubbles. Do not move the cake until the icing sets, which will be at least 4 hours, but attach any decorations to the icing while it is still fairly liquid.*

IDEAS FOR SIMPLE CAKE DECORATION

• I sometimes ice cakes with delicate icings on the serving plate rather than a wire rack. This prevents their appearance from spoiling when the cake is moved. Keep the plate's surface neat by placing pieces of waxed paper under the cake to be removed before serving (page 273).

• Decorations such as a pattern of fresh leaves, coarse coffee-flavored sugar crystals or silver balls can be positioned on top of a sponge, loaf or fruit cake which has been brushed with a thick glaze of melted jelly to give the cake a shiny glaze.

• Natural colored, halved angelica softened in warm water and then cut into holly leaves, makes a pretty Christmas pattern on top of a jelly-glazed fruit cake.

• Glacé icing before it sets is an ideal base on which to arrange fresh flowers and leaves, silver balls or slivers of orange peel.

• Sifted superfine sugar gives a frosty sparkle to the top of an uniced sponge cake.

• Chocolate curls (page 231) all over the top of a cake which has been iced with melted chocolate, look pretty dusted with lightly sifted confectioners' sugar – like a light snow fall.

• If you are decorating a cake with fresh, pesticide-free roses or other edible flowers, you will want to set aside some of the icing to do this as, for best appearance, fresh flowers should be placed on the cake within 1 hour of serving. You can dip the edges of the leaves into the icing and use them to decorate the cake – they look extremely effective.

USING MARZIPAN

A paste of ground almonds, sugar and egg white, marzipan is the traditional base for European cakes iced with royal icing (below). Ready-to-roll white marzipan is of excellent quality, and it can be lightly kneaded then rolled into shape. Brush the cake top with melted, sieved apricot jam to help the marzipan stick. Marzipan can also be an effective decoration on its own, with a pasteurized egg-white glaze and a sprinkling of sugar.

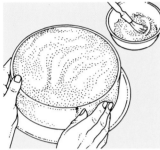

1 *For a 9in (23cm) round or 8in (20cm) square cake, brush the top and side with about 4 tablespoons sieved melted apricot jam. Knead 1lb (500g) white marzipan. Roll two-thirds to a strip to fit around the cake side, then press on and pinch together.*

2 *Roll out the remaining marzipan to fit the cake top, using the cake pan as a template. Lift on with the rolling pin and gently press into place. Press the edges to seal. Decorate with buttercream or completely frost over the marzipan.*

ROYAL ICING

This icing is used to make flowers and to frost and decorate gingerbread houses and holiday cookies. The icing holds peaks well and can be piped attractively, swirled decoratively or, if made runnier, dribbled from a spoon or piped from a small bag for writing or lacy patterns. Strained lemon juice adds flavor but will make the icing hard and brittle, so liquid glycerine is used as well. This makes enough to frost and decorate 1 gingerbread house or 48 medium-size holiday cookies.

For royal icing to be eaten, *beat together 1lb confectioners' sugar, 3 tablespoons meringue powder and ⅓ cup (75ml) water until very fluffy and stiff (about 5 minutes), and adding more water, a little at a time, if necessary to make the frosting manageable.*

For not-to-be-eaten *royal icing to be used on cookies for tree decoration or on a display cake or gingerbread house, beat together 1lb (500g) confectioners' sugar, 3 egg whites and ½ teaspoon cream of tartar in a large bowl with an electric mixer until glossy and fluffy. Add a few drops of water to adjust stiffness, if necessary.*

At all times, *keep top of bowl containing royal icing covered with a damp cloth towel to prevent icing from getting dry on the surface while you are working with it. Flavorings should be added with the water, but coloring may be added either during beating or as needed while working with the icing.*

EASY DECORATING IDEAS

The simplest decorating touch to a cake can often be the most effective. Easiest of all is a delicate dusting of sieved confectioners' sugar which totally transforms the appearance of a cake within seconds.

I like fresh flowers and pretty leaves as decoration best of all, and many flowers are edible, too. On cakes with buttercream or other icing, little silver balls dotted about on the icing look very pretty, as do crystallized violets, primroses or mimosa balls.

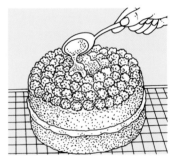

Arrange raspberries, *seedless grapes or halved strawberries all over the top of a cake. To glaze, melt 4 tablespoons red currant jelly with 1 tablespoon strained lemon juice, stirring until smooth, then spoon or drizzle over the fruit.*

Use strips of paper *to make a striped pattern. Lay the strips on the cake, criss-crossing if desired, sprinkle over confectioners' sugar through a fine sieve, then lift off the paper strips carefully one by one.*

Crystallize small flowers *and petals for decorating by brushing them with pasteurized egg white and dipping in superfine sugar. Lay them on a baking sheet in an airy spot for 1–2 hours until dry, crisp and frosty looking.*

COOKIES

Homemade cookies never stay around very long. They can be made very quickly on a last minute whim and are nearly always eaten just as quickly. Cookie-making is often something children can do, too. Cookie recipes are usually very easy and the results are delicious even when made by inexperienced cooks

In Britain cookies are called biscuits from the French *bis cuit*, meaning twice cooked, which was to preserve them. The word cookie comes from the Dutch *koekje*, meaning little cake. No matter what they are called, our cookie recipes have come from all over the world as immigrants came to settle this country. And somehow this convenient, hand-held, sweet, rich treat has captivated all generations.

Different types of ovens will have varying effects on just how the cookies bake, but as cookies arranged on a large baking sheet are unlikely to bake completely evenly in any oven, you should watch and turn the sheet around once, probably about three-quarters of the way through the estimated cooking time. Cookies can very suddenly become overcooked or burned, so keep an eye on them for the last few minutes of baking. It is always worth using real butter in cookie-making.

SHORTBREAD

Homemade shortbread is rich, buttery and has a good crunchy bite if the flour is combined with some semolina or rice flour. The dough is patted out into a neat round using a cake pan as a guide then baked slowly until very pale brown.

Preheat the oven to 325°F, 160°C. Cream 8oz (250g) softened butter with ⅔ cup (125g) superfine sugar. Sift 2 cups (250g) all-purpose flour, then mix with ¾ cup (125g) semolina or rice flour. Work lightly into the buttery mixture until the dough is soft but not sticky but take care not to overknead.

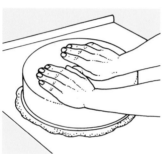

Cut the dough *in half and pat out each piece on a baking sheet into a neat 8in (20cm) round, using a cake pan as a guide. Pinch the edges, then mark into 8 wedges. Pierce with a fork. Bake for 30–40 minutes until golden. Cool for 5 minutes, then sprinkle with superfine sugar and cut into the wedges. Cool on a wire rack.*

IDEAS FOR COOKIES
• For children's parties, melting moments (above) can be rolled out and cut into different shapes with cookie cutters, such as stars and hearts.
• These cookies attract children more if you ice them with glacé icing (page 274); this can be colored either in 1 color or by mixing up 2 or 3 colors in separate bowls and making a pattern of colors on each cookie or making a selection of differently colored cookies. A plate of red iced hearts and white iced stars looks lovely.
• Also for children sprinkle colored sugar or sprinkles on top of iced cookies.
• Before putting a baking sheet of unbaked cookies into the oven, mark them with a fork or dot them all over with a skewer for a simple decoration.
• If you are making freezer cookies (opposite), you can make 1 ball of lemon- or vanilla-flavored dough and one of chocolate-flavored dough. Roll each into a thin circle, put the circles on top of each other and roll up like a jelly roll. Then wrap and freeze as instructed. When you slice and bake them, you will produce very decorative cookies with a dramatic swirl.
• Round cookies dipped in confectioners' sugar can be put back in the oven to glaze.

MELTING MOMENTS

You will be popular if you make some quick cookies when you have unexpected guests. These easy cookies really do seem to melt in your mouth. You can vary them by adding flavors to the flour such as finely grated lemon or orange rind, ¼ cup (25g) cocoa powder instead of 3 tablespoons of the flour and some chocolate chips too, chopped toasted nuts, vanilla extract, currants, finely chopped crystallized ginger and 1 teaspoon ground ginger.

These are best eaten the day they are made, but this isn't difficult! They are also a very good accompaniment to fresh fruit and compotes. Makes about 24 cookies.

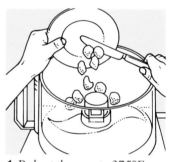

1 *Preheat the oven to 375°F, 190°C. Put 6oz (175g) softened diced butter into a food processor, then add 6½ tablespoons sifted confectioners' sugar, 2 cups (250g) sifted self-rising flour and ½ teaspoon salt. Add any extra flavoring if you want at this stage. Process the ingredients to a soft dough, taking care not to over process or the cookies will be tough.*

2 *Using floured hands, gather the dough into a ball, then roll out on a lightly floured surface until it is about ¼in (5mm) thick. Cut out rounds of dough with a floured cookie cutter or the rim of a glass, rerolling the dough as necessary, so that none is wasted.*

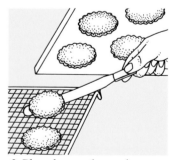

3 *Place the rounds on a large ungreased baking sheet and bake for 8–10 minutes until pale brown. Cool on the baking sheet for 1–2 minutes, then transfer carefully to a wire rack with a spatula to cool completely. Store the cookies in an airtight container.*

FREEZER COOKIES

Originally called icebox or refrigerator cookies, these are incredibly easy to make as well as being useful. Just form a rich dough into a roll and then wrap and keep in the freezer until ready to bake. That way, at any time and within minutes, you can produce thin, light, crisp cookies with a deliciously buttery flavor. These are perfect to serve with ice cream.

The richness of the dough makes the cookie roll easy to slice, and you can achieve far thinner cookies this way than by any other method I know. Slice as many cookies as you want from the frozen roll and then put the roll back in the freezer for another time.

Vary the cookies by adding flavorings to the flour before mixing with the butter and egg. Try finely grated lemon or orange rind, finely chopped nuts, cocoa powder (for chocolate cookies), finely chopped dried fruit or peel, shredded coconut, and ground or whole spices. Makes about 60 cookies.

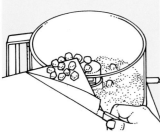

1 *Sift 1⅔ cups (200g) all-purpose flour with 2 teaspoons baking powder and a pinch of salt. Put 5 oz (150g) diced, cold butter into a food processor with 1 cup (200g) light brown sugar, 1 beaten egg, 1 teaspoon vanilla extract and the sifted ingredients. Process to a soft, smooth dough.*

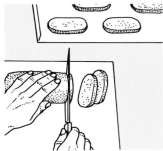

2 *Shape the dough into a 12–14in (30-35cm) roll; wrap and freeze for at least 30 minutes. Preheat the oven to 400°F, 200°C. Unwrap the dough and slice off as many cookies as you want with a serrated knife. Wrap the dough roll and put back in the freezer. Place the cookies ¾in (1.5cm) apart on a baking sheet and bake for 7–9 minutes, until golden.*

DROP COOKIES

Unlike most cookie mixtures this does not need rolling out; you simply drop the mixture off a teaspoon onto a greased baking sheet and flatten slightly before baking. It is a rich mixture, ensuring a crisp texture every time.

Flavor the basic dough with peanut butter or chocolate chips, currants, grated lemon or orange rind or chopped glacé cherries. Preheat the oven to 375°F, 190°C. Lightly grease 2 baking sheets. Makes 25–30 cookies.

1 *Cream 3oz (75g) softened butter or margarine with ⅓ cup (75g) sugar, then mix in 1 egg yolk and 1 cup (125g) flour, 1 teaspoon vanilla extract and 4 tablespoons milk or orange juice. Mix in chocolate chips or other flavoring (left).*

BROWNIES

Dark and chewy, these brownies keep well. Preheat the oven to 350°F, 180°C. Lightly grease a 7in (18cm) square cake pan. Put 4oz (100g) butter in a saucepan over low heat and stir until melted. Stir in 6 tablespoons cocoa powder, then add 2oz (50g) semisweet chocolate, broken into small pieces. Stir and remove from heat when melted. Put 2 eggs in a large bowl with ½ teaspoon salt and 1 cup plus 2 tablespoons (225g) light brown sugar and beat thoroughly until light and frothy. Then beat in the butter and chocolate mixture. Sift ½ cup (63g) self-rising flour onto the mixture and fold in lightly with a spoon. Stir in ⅔ cup (75g) chopped nuts if desired and pour into the pan. Bake in the center of the oven for 30 to 40 minutes – it should feel slightly under-baked. Cool in the pan then cut into squares and remove with a flexible spatula. Makes 12 brownies.

2 *Spoon 25-30 teaspoons, spaced apart, onto the baking sheets and bake for about 20 minutes, until the cookies are golden. Remove from the oven and transfer to a wire rack to cool. Store in an airtight container.*

From left to right: chocolate-flavored freezer cookies, plain buttery melting moments, chocolate chip cookies and rich, crunchy shortbread.

OUR FAVORITE BOILED FRUIT AND NUT CAKE *(263)*

This makes an extra rich, dark and moist fruit cake which lasts for months – except that it is always eaten up as soon as I make it! I make several of these cakes at the beginning of the holidays, as they are so useful for entertaining and busy-day desserts.   *SERVES 8–10*

> *Coarsely grated rind and juice of 2 large oranges*
> *Dark rum or water*
> *6oz (175g) butter*
> *¾ cup plus 2 tablespoons (175g) light brown sugar*
> *1¼ cups (175g) pitted prunes, chopped*
> *6 tablespoons crystallized ginger, chopped*
> *⅓ cup (50g) glacé cherries, chopped*
> *¾ cup (125g) golden raisins*
> *¾ cup (125g) currants*
> *¾ cup (75g) walnut pieces*
> *2 cups (250g) whole wheat flour, plus a little extra*
> *1 teaspoon baking soda*
> *½ teaspoon ground cloves (optional)*
> *2 large eggs, beaten lightly*

Place the orange juice in a measuring cup, bring up to 1¼ cups (300ml) with rum or water and put it in a saucepan with the butter and sugar. Melt the butter and sugar in the liquid over a low heat, then stir in the orange rind, prunes, ginger, cherries, golden raisins, currants and walnuts. Bring to a boil, cover, and simmer for 10–15 minutes, then remove from the heat and leave to cool.

Meanwhile, preheat the oven to 350°F, 180°C. Grease a 7in (18cm) round cake pan or a 6in (15cm) square one, and line the bottom with a round of parchment (page 262). Dust with flour.

When the fruit mixture is cool, stir together the flour, baking soda and ground cloves. Stir in the mixture from the saucepan, then stir the eggs thoroughly into the fruit and flour mixture. Pour the mixture into the pan and bake for about 1¼ hours or until the tip of a fine skewer inserted in the center comes out clean (page 263).

Leave in the pan for about 10 minutes, then loosen the sides with a knife. Turn out and peel off the paper, then place the cake right-side up on a wire rack to cool completely. If possible, store in an airtight container and leave for a couple of days before eating.

ORANGE VELVET CAKE WITH STRAWBERRIES *(260)*

Cakes made with oil rather than butter are quick to mix and have particularly smooth and light textures. This cake can be eaten either for dessert or as a snack.   *SERVES 8*

> *1¼ cups (150g) all-purpose flour*
> *3 tablespoons cornstarch*
> *2 teaspoons baking powder*
> *½ teaspoon salt*
> *1¼ cups (150g) confectioners' sugar*
> *6 tablespoons sunflower oil*
> *7 tablespoons freshly squeezed orange juice*
> *2 large eggs, separated*
> *Finely grated rind of 1 orange, plus rind shreds for decoration*
> *4 tablespoons mascarpone*
> *¼ cup (50g) superfine sugar*
> *1⅓–2⅓ cups (250–375g) small strawberries, halved and hulled*

Preheat the oven to 375°F, 190°C. Grease two 7–7½in (18–19cm) deep cake pans and line the bottom of each with a round of parchment (page 262). Sift the flour, cornstarch, baking powder, salt and confectioners' sugar into a large mixing bowl.

Put the oil into another bowl, strain in the orange juice and add the egg yolks. Beat the oil mixture together lightly, then add to the sifted dry ingredients and beat to a smooth batter. Stir in the grated orange rind. Beat the egg whites until they hold soft peaks and fold gently into the cake mixture.

Pour the mixture into the cake pans. Bake for 25–30 minutes until well raised and the cake surface springs back when lightly pressed with a fingertip. Leave the cakes in the pans for about 5 minutes, then loosen the sides and turn out. Peel off the paper and place right-side up on a wire rack to cool.

When cool and not too long before you want to eat, put 1 cake on a serving plate. Mix the mascarpone with the superfine sugar. Stir strawberries into the mascarpone, reserving some for decoration, and spread the mixture onto the cake on the plate. Top with the second cake. Decorate with reserved strawberries and orange rind, then sprinkle with superfine sugar through a sieve.

SNOWBALLS *(260)*

These delicious cookies are also called pecan balls and butter balls. They look more like snowballs with their sugar coating, but they taste like a nutty shortbread.   *MAKES 16–20*

> *4oz (125g) butter, softened*
> *¼ cup (50g) superfine sugar*
> *1 teaspoon vanilla extract*
> *1½ cups (150g) pecan halves, finely ground*
> *1⅔ cups (200g) all-purpose flour*
> *½ teaspoon salt*
> *Confectioners' sugar*

Preheat the oven to 275°F, 140°C. Grease a baking sheet. Beat the butter until very soft, then beat in the superfine sugar until fluffy. Beat in the vanilla extract. Stir in the pecans. Sift in the flour and salt and stir until mixed in.

Form the dough into balls the size of large marbles. Arrange on the baking sheet. Bake for 35–40 minutes. Remove from the oven and leave for 1–2 minutes. Sift confectioners' sugar into a bowl and dip each ball into it to coat with sugar – handle delicately as they are crumbly while still warm. Cool on a wire rack.

CHOCOLATE AND HAZELNUT THINS *(260)*

These quickly made cookies have the rich taste of brownies. They are good served with vanilla ice cream or a fruit compote – or simply eaten still warm as a snack.   *MAKES ABOUT 15*

> *4oz (125g) butter*
> *1oz (25g) semisweet chocolate, broken up*
> *1 teaspoon instant coffee*
> *⅓ cup (75g) dark brown sugar*
> *1 teaspoon vanilla extract*
> *1 egg, beaten lightly*
> *¼ cup (32g) all-purpose flour*
> *½ teaspoon salt*
> *⅓ cup (50g) skinned hazelnuts, toasted and chopped*

Preheat the oven to 375°F, 190°C. Butter a 10 x 12in (25 x 30cm) jelly roll pan. Melt the butter and chocolate together, over the lowest possible heat, stirring. Add the instant coffee and stir to dissolve. Remove from the heat and stir in the sugar and vanilla extract; then the egg. Sift in the flour and salt and mix until smooth.

Pour into the pan and spread evenly. Sprinkle the chopped hazelnuts over top. Bake for 12–15 minutes, turning the pan around half way through. The cookie mixture should firm up, but still seem soft – the cookies will crisp up on top and around the edges as they cool.

Cut at once into squares or rectangles. Cool in the pan for 1–2 minutes, then transfer to a wire rack to cool completely.

EXOTIC CHOCOLATE CAKE (260)

I have called this exotic because the cream cheese filling is mildly flavored with coconut milk – a classic flavoring for sweets in the Far East. The combination of chocolate, cream cheese and coconut milk is truly superlative. *SERVES 8*

FOR THE CAKE
  6oz (175g) semisweet chocolate, broken up
  5 large eggs, separated
  ¾ cup plus 2 tablespoons (175g) sugar
  2 rounded tablespoons cocoa powder
  2 rounded teaspoons ground cinnamon
  4 tablespoons water, warmed
  ½ teaspoon salt
  Confectioners' sugar
FOR THE FILLING
  2 tablespoons coconut milk
  ¼ teaspoon salt
  1 cup (125g) confectioners' sugar, sifted
  8oz (250g) cream cheese

Preheat the oven to 350°F, 180°C. Grease two 7½–8in (19–20cm) deep cake pans, and line the base with a round of parchment (page 262). Dust with flour. Melt the chocolate in a heatproof bowl set over a pan of simmering water, stirring occasionally. Remove the bowl from the heat.

Put the egg yolks into a large bowl, with the sugar and beat until pale and thick. Put the cocoa and cinnamon into a small bowl and gradually stir in the warm water until smooth. Stir into the melted chocolate, then beat the chocolate mixture into the egg yolks. Add the salt to the egg whites in another bowl and beat until they stand in soft peaks. Fold the egg whites into the chocolate mixture.

Pour the cake batter into the pans, and bake for 25–30 minutes until the cakes are firm to a light touch in the centers – the tops will probably be cracked, which is normal. Leave in the cake pans to cool – the cakes will sink slightly but this is also normal.

Meanwhile, make the filling. Beat the confectioners' sugar into the cream cheese. Beat in the coconut milk and set aside but do not refrigerate.

When the cakes have cooled, loosen the edges, turn out and remove the paper. Put one cake right-side up on a serving plate and spread the cream cheese mixture on top. Top with the other cake, cracked top up. Sift confectioners' sugar over the top and keep in a cool place, but not the refrigerator, until ready to serve. Do not leave out at room temperature longer than 2 hours. Refrigerate any leftovers.

FROSTED SPONGE CAKE WITH LEMON CURD AND BLUEBERRIES (260)

This beautiful white cake makes a wonderful celebration cake – to make it look really festive, top with crystallized flowers or edible fresh flowers such as violets. *SERVES 8*

FOR THE CAKE
  6 tablespoons self-rising cake flour
  2 tablespoons cornstarch
  ¾ cup (150g) vanilla superfine sugar (page 235), or plain superfine sugar
  4 large egg whites
  1 tablespoon cold water
  ½ teaspoon cream of tartar
  ¼ teaspoon salt
FOR THE LEMON CURD FILLING
  5 large egg yolks
  ⅓ cup (75g) sugar
  Finely grated rind of 2 lemons
  ½ cup (125ml) lemon juice
  1 cup (250g) fresh blueberries or other berries
FOR THE ICING
  Dehydrated egg white dissolved in water equal to 1 large egg white
  2½ teaspoons lemon juice
  2–2¼ cups (250–275g) confectioners' sugar, sifted

Preheat the oven to 275°F, 140°C. Line the bottom of 2 ungreased 7½–8in (19–20cm) deep cake pans with rounds of parchment (page 262).

Sift the flour and cornstarch together several times to make them extra fine. Sift the vanilla sugar and add 1 heaping tablespoon of it to the sifted flours. Put the egg whites into a large bowl with the water, cream of tartar and salt and beat with an electric mixer until they stand in soft peaks. With a large metal spoon, lightly fold in the remaining sugar, 1 tablespoon at a time. Fold in the sifted flours, a little at a time, sifting them directly onto the egg whites.

Pour the mixture into the pans and bake on the lowest shelf of the oven for about 1¼ hours until well risen and the cakes spring back when lightly pressed.

Meanwhile, prepare the lemon curd filling. Put the egg yolks into the top of a heatproof bowl set over a pan of simmering water. Stir in the sugar, lemon rind and lemon juice then cook over simmering water, stirring, until the mixture is thick enough to coat the back of a wooden spoon. Leave until cold.

Leave the baked cakes in their pans until cool, then loosen the sides with a spatula. Turn out and peel off the paper, then place right-side up on a wire rack to cool completely.

Put 1 cake on a large serving plate. Mix the blueberries into the cooled lemon curd mixture and then spread on the cake. Top with the other cake.

To make the icing, beat the egg white mixture until stiff, add 2 teaspoons lemon juice and beat in the confectioners' sugar, a little at a time. Beat in the remaining lemon juice; the icing should have a thick, spreading consistency. If it is not thick enough to hold peaks, beat in a little more sifted confectioners' sugar. Spread the icing all over the top and sides of the cake in small peaks. Decorate and leave in a dry, fairly cool place for several hours for the icing to set before cutting. Refrigerate any leftovers.

BREADS

Nothing whets the appetite as much as the smell of freshly baked bread filling the kitchen. There is something both soothing and rewarding about baking your own bread, and, once you have mastered the basic art and understood the principles of bread-making, you will realize how easy it is and will soon want to make it a regular part of your life, and even to try more ambitious recipes.

The great advantage of making bread at home is the opportunity to vary and mix flours and add all sorts of flavorings, seeds, grains and enrichments. In any case, even with an identical dough mixture, homemade bread is unlikely to turn out exactly the same two times in a row. The atmosphere in your kitchen, the weather and the oven, quite apart from the brand of flour, all make small differences. The brown bread which I make in the gas stove of our vacation cottage looks, feels and tastes quite different from the one I make at home – I always think it is better, but it may be that appetites are better and more appreciative as a result of outdoor life. The only disadvantage of homemade bread is that it does not contain preservatives, so that it doesn't last as long as commercial bread, but brown bread with added oil or fat lasts fairly well.

With your own bread, you can shape loaves as you like. If you want to make your oven more like a traditional bread oven for hand-shaped, free-form loaves, you can line an oven shelf with unglazed tiles before you turn on the heat – the extra heat from the tiles will make the dough increase in volume before a crust forms to stop it. Another easy way of making a lighter and crustier loaf (mainly with white breads or those with quite a large proportion of white flour) is to put a bowl of water on the bottom of the oven to increase the humidity, and you can also spray the bread a few times during baking with a fine spray of water.

No meal is really complete without some sort of bread to accompany it, and a few leftover ingredients can be made into an excellent meal by adding a fresh loaf of good bread. Bread is not only full of flavor, but of nutritional value too; it is rich in complex carbohydrates, vitamins, particularly the B group, iron, calcium and fiber. Breads made from whole wheat flour have more fiber than white breads.

When people think of bread, they think of a dough of flour and water, raised by yeast and then baked in an oven. Although this is true for the majority of breads, there is a surprising variety of breads, known as Quick Breads that use either a chemical leavening agent or no leavening agent at all. Tea breads, scones and soda breads, for example, use baking powder or bicarbonate of soda to make them rise, and breads such as flat chapatis and parathas from India are unleavened breads that rely solely on heat to produce steam inside them and make them puff up.

Most countries have evolved their own version of bread, based on local crops. From North America and Britain come breads using wheat; from Asia and Africa flat breads of barley, millet, corn and buckwheat; from Latin America tortillas made of corn and from Germany, Scandinavia, central Europe and Russia breads made of rye.

Bread comes in all different types, shapes and sizes; plain or rich, savory or sweet, or with added flavorings, breads range from the traditional loaf of sliced white bread to French brioches and croissants, Italian olive oil breads, German stollen and rye bread or Indian chapatis and parathas.

Clockwise from top right: Italian Hearth Bread with Black Olives and Rosemary (page 296) is quickly made with quick-rising dried yeast; Apricot and Currant Bread (page 296); Cheese and Tomato Swirl Loaf (page 297) combines the pronounced flavors of tomato puree and aged Cheddar cheese; Cheese and Green Onion Soda Breads (page 296) are topped with grated Cheddar cheese before baking ; traditional brioche (page 290) makes an elegant breakfast; Prune, Lemon and Honey Teabread (page 297) has a tangy lemon-juice syrup spooned over the hot loaf after baking; Seeded Brown Bread (page 297) combines sesame, pumpkin and caraway seeds as well as whole wheat and white flours.

BASIC BREAD TECHNIQUES

Most breads are made by adding yeast and liquid to flour to make a dough, which is then kneaded, left to rise, shaped, left to rise again and baked. Breads are easy to make but it is important to use the correct amounts of ingredients and you need time. Most yeasts do not like to be rushed!

Other important ingredients in bread-making are sugar, salt, fat and liquid. Sugar is the food yeast needs to make it grow. Fresh yeast can find enough natural sugar in the flour for fermentation but conventional dried yeast needs a little sugar added, when softening, to activate it. Salt is an essential ingredient as it not only improves the bread's flavor but also strengthens wheat's gluten and prevents the yeast from rising too quickly. Fat, in the form of butter, margarine, or oil, is not essential but it produces a moister bread which keeps longer. Too much sugar, salt and fat slows yeast down. Finally, the liquid used can be water or milk, or a mixture of both, and the amount used varies according to the flour's absorbency. The liquid should be added at the proper temperature for the kind of yeast being used. If it is too hot, the yeast will be killed.

USING YEAST

There are 3 types of yeast, and each is used in a different way. This chapter's recipes use only dried yeasts but here are the simple rules for using all yeasts. **Fresh yeast** is similar in color and texture to putty, and should be firm and easy to break. It is measured by weight and is usually blended with a warm liquid and then added to the flour, although it can also be worked directly into the flour. **Active dry yeast** is granular and comes in jars or packets. It must first be softened, and works better when a little sugar is added. Stir into warm water with a little sugar, then leave in a warm place for about 15 minutes until frothy. If the yeast does not froth, it is either too old to use or the water was too hot. **Quick-rising active dry yeast** is wonderfully simple and quick to use. It comes in fine granular form in packets or jars and is added directly to the flour, not mixed with liquid first. The majority of quick-rising yeasts need one short rising and one longer. Always check the package for directions; use a thermometer to check the water.

One ¼ oz (7g) packet of either active dry yeast or quick-rising active dry yeast has the rising power of a ⅗oz (17g) cake of fresh yeast.

BASIC BREAD

The ideal flour to use for yeast-risen breads is milled from hard wheat and is called bread flour. All wheat flour contains proteins which when moistened and beaten or kneaded develop into gluten. The gluten stretches like elastic and captures the carbon dioxide given off by the yeast, then hardens and forms the bread's structure. Several types of bread flour are available to bakers and in a few special baking supply stores. However, most of us have to make do with bread flour, all-purpose flour or whole wheat all-purpose flour. In health-food stores Graham flour, a coarser grind whole wheat flour, and flours made from other grains are available.

After mixing, the dough needs kneading to strengthen the gluten in flour. It is not difficult. Place the dough on a lightly floured surface. Fold it towards you, then push the dough down and away from you in a 'scrubbing' motion with the heel of your hand. Give a quarter turn and continue kneading for 10 minutes until the dough is smooth and elastic. The dough is ready when you press it and an impression remains.

To make 2 1lb (½kg) loaves, you will need 6 cups (750g) bread flour, 2 teaspoons salt, a pinch of sugar, ½oz (15g) butter, 1 packet quick-rising active dry yeast and about 2 cups (450ml) warm water.

1 Put the flour, salt and sugar in a large bowl and work in the butter. Add the yeast. Make a well in the center and pour in the warm water, mixing so all the flour is incorporated. Add a little extra water if necessary. Mix with a wooden spoon or your hands until the dough comes away from the side of the bowl. Place the dough on a lightly floured surface to knead.

2 Knead for 10 minutes until smooth and elastic, working in extra flour if necessary. Shape in a ball, put in a large bowl, oil the surface and cover the bowl with plastic wrap, trapping plenty of air. Leave to rise in a warm place for 20–30 minutes, until doubled. Knead again for 2–3 minutes to knock out all bubbles.

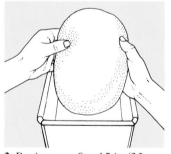

3 Pat into two 9 x 15 in (23 x 35cm) rectangles. Fold each up in thirds, smooth the top by rolling it on the work surface, then place in a lightly greased 9in (23cm) loaf pan, seam side down. Cover the pans and set aside to rise again in a warm place until the dough just rises to the top of the pan.

4 Bake at 400°F, 205°C for 20–30 minutes until well risen and brown. When baked, the loaves will sound hollow if you turn them out and tap the bottom. Cool on a wire rack. If not fully baked, return to the oven without putting them back in the pans. After a couple of minutes test again.

SODA BREAD

Soda bread is the quickest bread you can make and it is delicious as long as you eat it as fresh as possible, ideally the same day. It is made without yeast, relying instead on the chemical reaction of baking soda and cream of tartar with buttermilk to make the dough rise. To make 1 large loaf, you will need 4 cups (500g) all-purpose white or whole wheat flour or a mixture of the two, 2 teaspoons baking soda, 2 teaspoons cream of tartar, 1 teaspoon salt, 2oz (50g) butter, margarine or lard and about 1¼ cups (300ml) buttermilk.

A selection of whole wheat rolls, shaped as braids, knots and ovals, with an English-style cottage loaf (foreground) and braid, all made from the basic bread recipe.

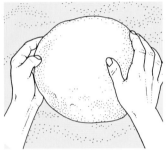

1 *Sift the dry ingredients together twice. Cut in the butter. Add the buttermilk slowly, mixing lightly to a soft but manageable dough. Without kneading shape into a 7in (18cm) round. Place on a greased and floured baking sheet.*

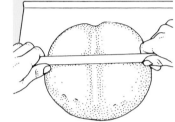

2 *Use the floured handle of a wooden spoon to press a deep cross on top. Immediately bake at 425°F, 220°C for about 30 minutes until the loaf sounds hollow when tested (opposite). Cool on a wire rack.*

SHAPING DOUGH

If baked on a baking sheet instead of in a pan bread dough can be made into many shapes, including rolls as well as loaves. Shape the dough before you leave it to rise a second time, unless you are using quick-rising yeast, in which case shape it after the first kneading.

Grease the baking sheet before adding the dough so the baked loaves do not stick. Test that they are baked by tapping on the bottoms (opposite) and then leave to cool on a wire rack.

***To make an oval loaf**, flatten the dough to a rectangle and roll up like a jelly roll (page 267), tucking the ends under. Place on a greased baking sheet. Cut 3 diagonal slashes across the top, then allow to rise.*

FINISHING TOUCHES FOR BREADS

• One of the nice things about making bread is that you can add different finishes giving it an exciting, or even a very personal, appearance. For example, cut deeply into the dough to make what will become dramatic patterns; diamonds, stripes or even a half sun image with its rays spreading out. Sprinkle some sesame or poppy seeds or cracked grains into the cuts.
• Seeds and grains of all kinds can be mixed into the flour of a whole wheat loaf, as well. I like to add green pumpkin seeds, sunflower seeds and whole grains of wheat; I soak them in water first to soften them slightly.
• Breads look beautifully shiny when they are glazed with either beaten egg, or egg beaten with milk or water at the second rising stage. You can also glaze a loaf just before you put it in the oven, but be very gentle when you brush on the glaze as a well-risen loaf can easily deflate.

• Give whole wheat bread a sheen too, by brushing with milk and water.
• Cracked wheat, sesame seeds and bran add texture and flavor to a loaf. Whole caraway seeds or cumin seeds give a definite taste which I like, especially with cheese.
• Bread need never be wasted – make fresh breadcrumbs in a food processor to use in stuffings, in cakes, or to coat foods before deep-frying. For toasted crumbs, toast thin slices of stale bread, put into a plastic bag and roll with a rolling pin, or process until fine in a food processor.
• Slices of stale white bread can be used for bread and butter pudding (page 216) and summer pudding (page 238), or cut into cubes and deep-fried to make croutons for soup (page 35).
• One of the most delicious breakfast uses for stale bread is to soak slices in beaten egg and milk, then fry in butter and sprinkle with cinnamon and soft brown sugar.

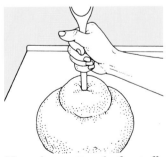

***To make a cottage loaf**, cut off one-third of the dough and shape both pieces into balls. Put the smaller ball on top of the larger one and place on a greased baking sheet. Push a floured wooden spoon handle through both balls.*

***To make a braid**, roll the dough into 3 pieces each 12in (30cm) long. Place side by side and braid from the center to each end. Pinch the ends together and fold underneath. Place on a greased baking sheet, then allow to rise.*

SAVORY BREADS

Savory breads are great fun to make, extremely delicious and provide an opportunity for creativity. They can be made either by using a flour rich in flavor or by adding savory ingredients to the dough. Rye flour is a popular flour to use for this purpose; examples include the traditional German and Dutch pumpernickels which are made entirely from rye flour. Because rye flour does not contain gluten, however, it makes a rather dense, heavy bread and is therefore best used with varying proportions of bread flour. Other flours to use in savory breads include barley flour which also has a low gluten content and produces a bread with an earthy flavor; cornmeal, with its lovely, distinctive, golden color, and malted wheat flour which has a sweet, nutty flavor and adds a certain moistness to the bread.

Many savory ingredients can be added to a bread dough, from the more familiar cheese, garlic, nuts, seeds and herbs to the less usual shredded zucchini, pureed pumpkin, sun-dried tomatoes, pine nuts, anchovies and pitted olives. Most savory breads should be baked a day before serving to allow their flavors to mature and make them easier for slicing. All are delicious served sliced and buttered, either on their own or as an accompaniment to soup, cheese, smoked fish or cold meats.

RYE BREAD

This recipe illustrates the use of rye flour which is stronger flavored than wheat flour. This version has a lighter texture than many other rye breads, for example pumpernickel, as it includes some gluten-rich bread flour. A variation can be made by adding seeds (below).

To make 2 round loaves, you will need 2 cups (250g) rye flour, 3 cups (375g) white bread flour, 1 teaspoon salt, 1 packet quick-rising active dry yeast, ⅔ cup (150ml) warm water, ⅔ cup (150ml) warm milk and 1 tablespoon molasses.

1 *Mix together the flours, salt and yeast in a large bowl. Mix together the water, milk and molasses. Add the liquid mixture to the flour and mix to a firm dough, adding extra flour if necessary. Knead the dough for about 10 minutes until it is smooth and elastic.*

2 *Shape the dough into a ball, oil the surface, put back in the bowl and cover with plastic wrap, trapping plenty of air. Leave to rise until double in size. Knead again for 2–3 minutes and shape into 2 smooth rounds. Place on a greased baking sheet, spaced well apart.*

3 *Cover and leave to rise again until double in size. Bake at 450°F, 230°C for 15 minutes. Brush the loaves with water, then reduce the oven temperature to 375°F, 190°C and bake for an additional 30–35 minutes or until they sound hollow when tapped. Cool on a wire rack.*

SEED BREAD

To vary the texture and flavor of rye bread, add whole seeds such as caraway, dill or cumin. Add 2–4 teaspoons of your chosen seeds to the flours in the basic recipe for rye bread (above).

Prepare as above but before the loaves rise the second time, lightly brush the surfaces with milk and then sprinkle with extra whole seeds, according to taste. Bake at 450°F, 230°C, for 15 minutes, then reduce the oven temperature to 375°F, 190°C, for a further 30–35 minutes. Cool on a wire rack.

IDEAS FOR SAVORY BREADS

• One of my favourite savory breads is cheese and onion bread; add grated cheese and finely chopped onion to the flour for bread dough before adding liquid. I use an aged Cheddar or Parmesan (fontina or provolone would be good as well) – and plenty of it, at least 6oz (175g) for 6 cups (750g) flour, with 1-2 onions – I like red ones for appearance. Frying the onion first to soften it and sweeten the taste is a good idea if there is time.
• Cheese bread is also excellent with added dried oregano or pieces of crisply fried bacon.
• Whole grain mustard adds a good flavor to cheese and to

many other savory breads.
• Chopped anchovies, grated Parmesan cheese and crushed garlic is another mouthwatering combination for flavoring savory bread.
• Many vegetables can be added to a basic bread dough; try adding grated carrots, parsnip, pumpkin, celeriac, turnip or rutabaga. They all go well with spices such as ground coriander or cardamom and grated nutmeg.
• Grated, cooked beets make an interesting scarlet loaf, that looks and tastes even better if you add some finely chopped, uncooked spinach to the dough.
• Finely chopped bulb fennel can be combined irresistibly

with plenty of grated Parmesan cheese, and a few fennel seeds.
• Mashed pumpkin and grated nutmeg, or ground cinnamon, is excellent to add to breads, or you can use a yellow pepper or tomato puree with some finely chopped tomatoes, olive oil and strips of basil.
• Olive oil improves most savory breads, and pesto sauce is an effective quick addition to dough when combined with extra olive oil. For extra flavor brush savory loaves with olive oil and salt before baking.
• Pitted, chopped olives and walnuts go well with olive oil in a dough. Try them in the stuffed olive oil bread (opposite).

VEGETABLE AND CHEESE BREAD

Ideal for a picnic or for serving when you don't want anything too sweet, this bread is made using baking powder instead of yeast. It is very easy to mix, requiring no kneading. It is particularly good sliced and spread with cream cheese.

Before mixing the ingredients, grease a large loaf pan with sunflower oil. Cut a piece of waxed paper to fit the bottom and lightly oil it. Begin by sifting together 1¼ cups (150g) whole wheat and 1¼ cups (150g) all-purpose white flours.

1 Mix in 2½ teaspoons baking powder, 1 teaspoon salt and 1 teaspoon each ground cumin and coriander to the sifted flours. Coarsely grate about 1 cup (125g) zucchini and 1 cup (125g) carrots into the bowl.

2 Mix in ¾ cup (75g) grated aged Cheddar cheese, 1 teaspoon fennel seeds, ⅔ cup (150ml) sunflower oil, 2 beaten eggs and about 4 tablespoons milk until just combined, then spoon into the prepared pan.

3 Bake at 350°F, 180°C for 40–45 minutes. After 25 minutes, sprinkle the top with some more grated cheese. Continue baking until a small skewer inserted in the center comes out clean. Cool on a wire rack.

STUFFED OLIVE OIL BREAD

The Italians make wonderful breads using olive oil for richness of flavor and texture, with delicious additions such as pitted, chopped olives or snipped sun-dried tomatoes, fresh or dried herbs, pieces of salami or cooked bacon, or grated cheese.

This stuffed olive oil bread is sensational served fresh from the oven, but it will keep for 1-2 days.

To make 2 loaves, mix together 6 cups (750g) bread flour, 1 teaspoon salt, 2 teaspoons dried oregano and 1 packet quick-rising active dry yeast in a large bowl.

A selection of savory breads: vegetable and cheese bread (left), rye bread (center) and stuffed olive bread with an Italian-style filling of pitted, chopped black olives and sun-dried tomatoes.

1 Make a well in the center of the flour mixture and pour in 5 tablespoons extra virgin olive oil and 2 cups (450ml) warm water. Mix into a firm dough, adding extra water if needed. Place on a lightly floured surface and knead for 5 minutes or until smooth.

2 Shape the dough into a ball. Pour 3 more tablespoons olive oil into the bowl, then return the dough, turning to coat it in the oil. Cover the bowl with plastic wrap, trapping in plenty of air. Set aside in a warm place to rise until double size.

3 Knead the dough for 2–3 minutes, then divide in half and knead again for 1 minute. Roll each half to a 12 x 8in (30 x 20cm) rectangle. Sprinkle with about 1½ cups (200g) of your chosen flavorings. Roll each piece up like a jelly roll (page 267).

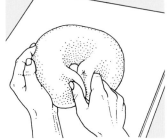

4 Place on greased baking sheets. Curl into rounds or leave in long rolls, sealing the edges with water. Cover and set aside to rise until double. Brush with more oil and bake at 400°F, 200°C for 35–40 minutes until golden. Cool the loaves on wire racks.

SWEET YEAST BREADS

The addition of sweet ingredients to bread is popular all over the world. Many of them are regional or festive specialities, and breads of this kind include stollen from Germany, fruit breads from Britain, pear bread from Switzerland and walnut bread from France.

Many are popular at a specific time of the year, such as Christmas or Easter, or make ideal breakfast treats. Fruity, spicy yeast breads make wonderful presents, too.

Some very rich, sweet doughs, such as for hot cross buns, start with a spongy flour and yeast mixture. This gives the yeast an extra boost so it develops a light texture even with all the rich ingredients. Dry ingredients can be mixed with the flour before the yeast is added but when a large quantity of dry, heavy ingredients are to be included, they should be kneaded into the dough after the first rising. Otherwise, they can hinder the rising of the yeast.

CURRANT LOAF

This is the basic recipe for an English currant loaf. You can vary the recipe by adding 2 teaspoons of ground mixed spices to the dry ingredients or use different dried fruits instead of the currants, such as chopped apricots, if you like.

To make 1 loaf, you will need 4 cups (500g) bread flour, ¼ cup (50g) sugar, 1 teaspoon salt, 25g (1oz) butter, ¾ cup (125g) currants, 1 packet quick-rising active dry yeast, 1¼ cups (300ml) warm milk and water mixed, and a little beaten egg and milk to glaze.

1 *Mix the flour, sugar and salt in a bowl and work in the butter. Add the currants, yeast and milk and mix to a soft dough. Knead until smooth, then put in a bowl, cover with plastic wrap, trapping in air, and leave until double size. Knead again briefly.*

2 *Shape to fit a large greased loaf pan (page 282). Brush with egg and milk beaten together. Cover and leave to rise until the dough nearly reaches the top of the pan. Bake at 425°F, 220°C for 30 minutes. Turn out and cool on a wire rack.*

FLAVORING IDEAS
• Chopped glacé apricots, peaches or mandarin oranges always add a touch of luxury to a currant loaf or stollen.
• Whole uncooked cranberries and coarsely grated orange rind, chopped soft, pitted prunes, candied citrus peel, grated lemon rind, chopped dried apricots and peaches, golden raisins, dark raisins soaked in brandy, coarsely chopped walnuts, pecans, hazelnuts or almonds, dates, angelica, crystallized pineapple and ginger and fresh blueberries are all good in sweet breads.
• Spices I like in sweet breads are ground coriander, cardamom (which is so wonderful with sweet things), allspice, cinnamon, cumin, cloves, ginger, nutmeg and saffron. Infuse the spices in a warm liquid before adding it to the flour.
• I like using honey instead of sugar for the sweetener in these doughs, and if I want a strong flavor and dark color, I use dark molasses.
• Grated orange rind enhances chocolate bread (opposite), and so does ground cinnamon, the spice which goes extraordinarily well with chocolate.
• Clear honey is an alternative glaze to milk and sugar or egg and milk. Use it to glaze hot bread or buns right after baking.
• A sprinkling of coarsely ground coffee or sugar crystals on top of a glazed loaf adds sparkle and crunch.
• Sesame seeds can be sprinkled on top of a glazed loaf before baking.

Slices of currant loaf and chocolate bread with hot cross buns and a German stollen loaf illustrate the varying styles of sweet yeast breads.

STOLLEN

This German bread is traditionally eaten at Christmas. There are many variations.

To make 1 loaf you will need 1½ teaspoons dried yeast and a pinch of granulated sugar, 6 tablespoons warm milk, 2 cups (250g) bread flour, ¼ teaspoon salt, 3oz (75g) butter, 2 tablespoons superfine sugar, 1 cup (150g) mixed dried fruit, ¼ cup (25g) quartered glacé cherries, ¼ cup (32g) chopped blanched almonds, ½ beaten egg and confectioners' sugar.

1 *Mix together the dry yeast, granulated sugar, milk and ½ cup (62g) flour. Leave in a warm place until frothy. Cut 2 oz (50g) butter into the remaining flour and the salt. Stir in the superfine sugar and all other ingredients.*

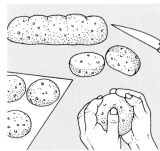

2 *Mix well and knead for 10 minutes. Cover and leave until double in size. Knead again 2–3 minutes, then roll into a 25 x 20cm (10 x 8in) oval. Spread with remaining butter. Make an indentation along the center.*

3 *Fold in half lengthwise. Put on a greased baking sheet, cover and leave to rise again until doubled in size. Bake at 400°F, 200°C for 30 minutes. Cool on a wire rack, then dust the stollen with confectioners' sugar.*

HOT CROSS BUNS

Traditionally in Britain, bread baked on Good Friday was marked with a cross, in honor of the crucifixion.

To make 12 of these delicious spiced buns you will need 1 tablespoon dry yeast and 1 teaspoon granulated sugar, a scant cup (225ml) warm milk, 4 cups (500g) bread flour, 1 teaspoon salt, 2oz (50g) butter, ¼ cup (50g) superfine sugar, 3 teaspoons ground mixed spices, ¾ cup (125g) currants, 1 lightly beaten egg and some corn syrup for glazing.

1 *Combine the yeast, granulated sugar, milk and 1 cup (125g) of the flour. Leave in a warm place until frothy. Sift remaining flour and salt and cut in butter. Stir in sugar, spice and currants. Add yeast liquid and egg and mix.*

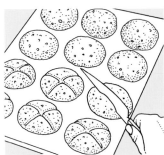

2 *Knead until smooth. Return to bowl, cover and leave until dough doubles in size. Knead for 2–3 minutes, then divide into 12 pieces and shape into balls. Put on a greased baking sheet, cover and leave until double in size.*

3 *Using the back of a knife, make 2 indentations on each bun to form a cross. Bake at 375°F, 190°C for 15–20 minutes until golden. Brush a little warmed corn syrup over each bun. Cool on a wire rack.*

CHOCOLATE BREAD

This is a wonderful breakfast bread. It is delicious spread thinly with butter and honey or homemade apricot or raspberry jam. The combination of melted chocolate and cocoa powder gives a lovely rich bread, which slices beautifully and toasts brilliantly. Try it spread with cream cheese.

Sift 5 cups (625g) bread flour, ½ cup (50g) cocoa powder, a pinch of salt and 3 tablespoons brown sugar into a large bowl then stir in 1 packet plus 1 extra teaspoon quick-rising active dry yeast. Melt 3oz (75g) semisweet chocolate in ¼ cup (50ml) milk, stir well and cool until warm.

Meanwhile, warm another 1 cup (250ml) milk, soften 5oz (150g) butter until just runny but not liquid, and beat 2 eggs together. Set all aside while the chocolate cools. Lightly grease two 9in (23cm) loaf pans.

Make a well in the center of the sifted flour mixture. Pour in the melted chocolate, the warm milk, softened butter and beaten eggs and mix together.

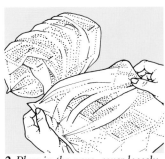

1 *Add extra milk in dribbles, if necessary, and knead until smooth and elastic. Set the bowl aside covered with plastic wrap to rise until the dough doubles in size. Knead again for 2–3 minutes and shape into 2 fat rectangles.*

2 *Place in the pans, cover loosely with plastic wrap and leave until the dough just reaches the tops of the pans. Uncover, then brush with beaten egg white. Bake at 400°F, 200°C for 30–35 minutes. Cool on a wire rack.*

CROISSANTS *and* DANISH PASTRIES

A yeast dough, spread with butter and repeatedly folded and rolled before being baked, produces a dough with flaky, puffy layers that can be used for a variety of delicious breads. The dough rises not only because of the yeast but also because of the moisture from the butter that turns to steam during baking and separates the layers into flakes.

Croissants conjure up breakfasts in France and are delicious served warm with steaming mugs of coffee or hot chocolate. Pull them apart to eat. They are usually made in the traditional crescent shape unless filled with chocolate

and shaped into a small roll. Croissants are luscious eaten on their own but may include sweet or savory fillings, such as chocolate or cheese. Sweet croissants are usually given a dusting of confectioners' sugar after baking.

There are many traditional shapes for Danish pastries, ranging from pinwheels to squares, and the filling for any shape can be savory or sweet. This can be as simple as a little grated cheese or ham or a handful of seeded raisins, or can be a more moist filling such as almond paste, apple puree or cream cheese.

CROISSANTS

Although croissants are time-consuming to make, the results are worth the effort. Do not substitute any fat for butter when making them.

French croissants are characteristically light and flaky because of the flour used to make them. When made with our flour, croissants have a more bread-like texture, but they are still buttery and good.

To make 12 croissants, you will need 1 tablespoon dry yeast and 1 teaspoon sugar, 1 cup (250ml) warm water, 4 cups (500g) bread flour, 1 teaspoon salt, 2 tablespoons vegetable shortening, 1 beaten egg, 8oz (250g) butter and a little extra beaten egg to glaze.

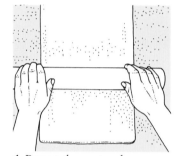

1 *Prepare the yeast and sugar with the warm water (page 282). Put the flour and salt in a bowl, and then cut in the shortening. Add the yeast liquid and beaten egg and mix to form a smooth dough. Knead until smooth. Roll out to a 20 x 8in (50 x 20cm) rectangle, keeping the edges straight. Soften the butter and divide into 3 equal portions.*

2 *Use 1 portion of butter to dot the top two-thirds of the dough, leaving a narrow border around the edges. Fold up the bottom third of the dough and fold down the top third of the dough. Seal the edges with a rolling pin, then give the dough a quarter turn. Press lightly at intervals, then roll the dough out to a rectangle again.*

3 *Repeat step 2 again with the next portion of butter. Roll out the dough as in step 2. Dot with the last portion of butter and fold the dough in thirds again. Cover with a tea towel and chill for 30 minutes. Then repeat the rolling and folding 3 more times without adding any more butter. Cover the folded dough and chill again for 30 minutes.*

FILLINGS AND FLAVORINGS

• Both Danish pastry and croissant dough can be spiced with a little ground cardamom, cinnamon or allspice, mixing it into the flour.
• All sorts of fillings can be made for Danish pastries. To make almond paste, the most traditional one, cream together ½oz (15g) butter and 3 tablespoons sugar. Stir in ⅓ cup (40g) ground almonds and just enough beaten egg to bind the mixture.
• To make cinnamon butter, another delicious filling, cream together 2oz (50g) butter, ¼ cup (50g) sugar and 1 teaspoon ground cinnamon. Or, try ground cardamom instead of

cinnamon. A little finely grated orange rind can also be added to the mixture for a refreshing filling.
• I love the more intense taste of dried apricots soaked and then stewed with lemon juice and sugar until soft and thick. Fresh apricots cooked in a pan with sugar and no liquid are also delicious, and in spring you can add a head or two of elderflowers to the fruit – you can also do this with berries, cooking them with sugar until they reach an almost jam-like consistency.
• Soft, fresh ricotta cheese, slightly sweetened and spiced is another good filling.

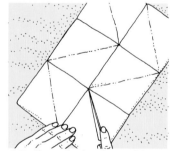

4 *Roll out the dough to a 20 x 12in (50 x 30cm) rectangle on a lightly floured surface, constantly patting in the edges to keep the shape. With a sharp knife, trim the edges neatly, then cut the dough in half lengthwise. Cut each strip of dough into 3 equal-sized squares and then cut each square in half diagonally to make 12 triangles.*

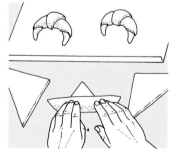

5 *Roll up each triangle, starting from the wide side and gently shape into a crescent. Any filling should be added before rolling each croissant. Put on ungreased baking sheets, cover and leave to rise for about 30 minutes until double in size. Brush with beaten egg. Bake at 425°F, 220°C for about 15 minutes. Cool on a wire rack.*

DANISH PASTRIES

Danish pastries are made in various traditional shapes. To make about 25 pastries, you will need 1 tablespoon dry yeast and a pinch of sugar, ⅔ cup (150ml) warm milk, 4 cups (500g) all-purpose flour, 1 teaspoon salt, 2 tablespoons vegetable shortening, 2 tablespoons sugar, 2 beaten eggs plus 1 for glazing, 10oz (300g) softened butter, a selection of fillings (see box opposite), glacé icing (page 274), and flaked almonds.

Butter-rich French-style croissants (above) and a selection of freshly baked Danish pastries, shaped as pinwheels, spirals and squares, contain a variety of flavorful fillings (see box opposite) and are decorated with glacé icing and almonds.

1 *Prepare the yeast and sugar with the warm milk (page 282). Put the flour and salt in a bowl and cut in the shortening. Stir in the sugar. Add the yeast liquid and 2 beaten eggs, mix to a smooth dough and knead.*

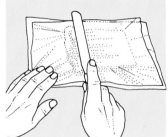

2 *Put the dough in a bowl, cover and chill for 10 minutes. Shape the butter between 2 sheets of waxed paper into a 7 x 5in (18 x 12cm) rectangle. Roll out the dough to a 16 x 8in (40 x 20cm) rectangle.*

FINISHING DANISH PASTRIES

3 *Put the butter in the center of the dough and fold the sides on top. Seal the edges. Give the dough a half turn, then roll into a 16 x 8in (40 x 20cm) rectangle. Fold the bottom third up and the top third down.*

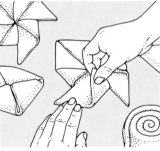

4 *Cover the dough and leave for 10 minutes. Turn and repeat rolling, folding and resting twice more. Cover and leave for 30 minutes. Roll out to ¼in (5mm) thick, make a variety of shapes (right) and add the fillings.*

Almond paste is a traditional filling for Danish pastries but many other fillings can be used (see box opposite). I often make a hazelnut filling, exactly like the almond paste but made with ground hazelnuts instead of almonds. Fresh lemon curd (page 302) is another delicious filling.

Make the dough (steps 1–4) and shape into either squares, spirals or pinwheels. After shaping and filling bake and decorate as in steps 5–6 (left).

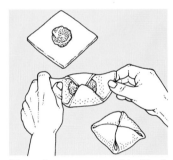

To make squares, *cut 3in (7cm) squares. Add the filling to each square and fold in the corners towards the center, securing the tips with beaten egg.*

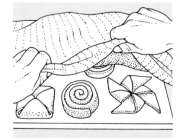

5 *Put shaped pastries on baking sheets, cover and leave for about 30 minutes. Brush with beaten egg. Bake at 425°F, 220°C for 15 minutes.*

6 *Place on a rack and pipe with glacé icing and sprinkle some with flaked almonds while slightly warm. Add extra decoration if desired. Cool.*

To make spirals, *cut a 10 x 4in (25 x 10cm) rectangle. Spread with filling and roll up like a jelly roll (page 267). Cut into 1in (2.5cm) slices and bake cut sides down on the baking sheets.*

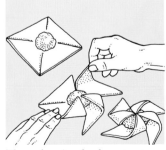

To make pinwheels, *cut out 3in (7cm) squares. Cut from each corner to within ½in (1cm) of the center. Add the filling to the center and fold in the points to the center, securing with beaten egg.*

BRIOCHES *and* SAVARINS

Butter and eggs can be added to a yeast dough to enrich it and produce a bread that is similar in many ways to a cake. The butter makes the dough soft while the eggs make it lighter and more moist, so that the finished bread almost melts in your mouth.

A brioche dough is the richest of all breads and can vary in shape and size from a small ball to a large crown shape. It can be served on its own or the dough can be filled with a sweet or savory filling such as sausage. Other breads made from a brioche dough include a kugelhopf, which is a bread from Alsace in eastern France, layered with a sweet fruit and nut mixture or a savory filling such as cream cheese and ham.

A savarin is also made from a brioche dough but has more liquid added to the dry ingredients. It is baked in a ring and then has syrup poured over it to give it a spongy texture. I sometimes replace the sugar syrup with melted honey simply mixed with lemon juice and jam or even whiskey. Individual savarins are known as babas, and are an excellent dessert to serve for a buffet.

TRADITIONAL BRIOCHE

In France, brioche (page 280) is traditionally served warm for breakfast, with conserves and a large cup of milky coffee. Brioche also makes delicious light toast and is wonderful spread with sweet butter and apricot jam. It should be baked in a brioche mold, which is a fluted pan with steeply sloping sides (page 20). The mold allows the dough to form a brioche's characteristic shape.

You will need 1½ teaspoons dry yeast and a pinch of granulated sugar, 2 tablespoons warm milk, 2 cups (250g) bread flour, 1 tablespoon superfine sugar, a pinch of salt, 2 beaten eggs, 3oz (75g) softened butter and a little extra beaten egg to glaze. This recipe makes one large traditionally shaped brioche or 12 individual brioches, although the dough can also be baked in a loaf pan (see box opposite).

For a saffron-flavored brioche, infuse a few strands of saffron with the milk, bringing both to a boil and then set aside until it is just warm and can be combined with the yeast and sugar.

Another flavorful variation is to add a selection of dried fruit such as snipped dried apricots, peaches or prunes to the brioche dough at the same time as you beat in the eggs and incorporate the butter in step 1.

1 *Prepare the yeast and granulated sugar with the warm milk (page 282). Put the flour, superfine sugar and salt in a bowl and add the yeast liquid. Gradually beat in the eggs. Using your hands, incorporate the softened butter. Knead to a soft dough, adding extra flour only if really necessary. Knead for 5 minutes until smooth.*

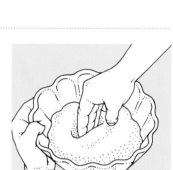

2 *Return the dough to the bowl, cover with plastic wrap and leave to rise until the dough doubles in size. Knead again for 2–3 minutes. Cut off three-quarters of the dough and shape into a ball. Place in a greased 5 cup (1.2 liter) brioche mold. Using three fingers, press a hole in the center of the dough down to the bottom of the mold.*

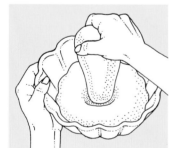

3 *Shape the remaining piece of dough into a cone. If necessary, slightly enlarge the hole in the main piece of dough with your fingers so that the pointed end of the cone will fit in neatly. Lower in the dough cone with the pointed end downwards. Gently pat the top of the dough cone to form the traditional well-rounded head on top of the brioche.*

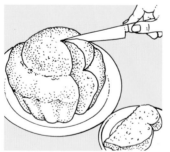

4 *Cover the mold with plastic wrap and leave to rise until the dough reaches the top of the mold. Lightly brush with beaten egg, avoiding the seam around the knob. Bake at 425°F, 220°C for 15–20 minutes, until golden. Turn out and serve warm, or cool completely on a wire rack. To serve, cut the brioche into vertical wedges.*

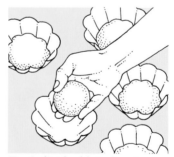

For individual brioches: 1 *complete step 1 (above). Put the kneaded dough back in the bowl, cover with plastic wrap and leave to rise until the dough doubles in size. Knead again for 2–3 minutes and divide into 12 pieces. Shape three-quarters of each piece into a small ball and put into 3in (7cm) diameter greased mini brioche molds.*

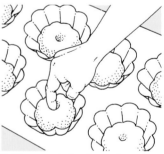

2 *Use your index finger to make a hole in the center of each brioche. Shape the remaining pieces of dough into small knobs and place in the holes. Press down lightly. Complete step 4 but bake the individual brioches for only 10 minutes. Turn out the brioches and serve warm, or leave to cool completely on a wire rack.*

SAVARIN

This rum-flavored yeast cake is served as a cold dessert with fresh fruit in the center. The mixture will also make 16 individual rum babas.

You will need 1 tablespoon dry yeast and 1 teaspoon sugar, 6 tablespoons warm milk, 2 cups (250g) bread flour, ½ teaspoon salt, 2 tablespoons superfine sugar, 4 beaten eggs, 4oz (125g) softened butter, ½ cup (125g) granulated sugar, 2 tablespoons each lemon juice and rum and 4 tablespoons apricot preserves.

Freshly baked rum babas and a large savarin filled with a selection of seasonal fruit. As the fruits vary with the time of year, the glaze can be flavored with different liqueurs and juices that are appropriate to the season. Serve with whipped cream if you like.

1 *Blend together the dried yeast, sugar, warm milk and ½ cup (50g) flour in a large mixing bowl and leave in a warm place for 15 minutes until frothy. Stir in the remaining flour, salt, superfine sugar, beaten eggs and butter. Beat well with a wooden spoon for 3–4 minutes until the mixture is well combined.*

2 *Pour into a greased 6 cup (1.5 liter) ring mold. Place a piece of plastic wrap over the mold, and leave to rise in a warm place until the dough has risen two-thirds up the sides of the mold. Bake at 400°F, 200°C for 30 minutes until the savarin is golden.*

3 *Cool for 5 minutes, then turn out of the mold to loosen. Return to the mold in order to add the syrup. Put the granulated sugar, 1¼ cups (300ml) water and lemon juice in a pan, dissolve and boil until reduced by half. Remove from the heat and stir in the rum. Pour the syrup over the savarin; set aside to soak in.*

4 *Unmold the savarin and leave it to cool completely on a wire rack. Meanwhile, gently melt the apricot preserves over a low heat in a small saucepan. Transfer the cooled savarin to a serving plate and brush with the melted preserves to glaze. Fill the center with a selection of fresh fruit and serve with whipped cream.*

IDEAS FOR BRIOCHES AND SAVARINS

• Brioche dough can be baked in a loaf pan as well as in the traditional-shaped mold. This makes it possible to cut the baked brioche into slices which can be used to make excellent sandwiches; as it is a rich and also slightly sweet bread, fillings such as duck, pork, ham and pâté are successful. Season slivers of duck or pork with a little soy sauce and chopped green onions.
• Brioche suits fillings of triple crème cheese or fresh goat cheese mixed with fresh herbs, chopped walnuts, smoked fish or fresh shrimp.
• Use brioche dough, with an added 3 tablespoons flour to

make a stiffer dough, to wrap savory fillings, such as a pâté or spicy ground beef mixture shaped into a loaf or sausage, any all-meat sausages or a piece of skinless, filleted salmon – all of which should be lightly precooked. Roll out the dough and enclose the filling, sealing the seams with cold water. Mark the top into a diamond pattern with a knife and brush with beaten egg. Bake at 425°F, 220°C for 15–20 minutes until golden brown.
• I like to vary the syrup for savarins and rum babas by substituting the juice of ½ a large orange or 1 small orange

for the lemon juice. You can also add kirsch instead of rum.
• The fresh fruits for the center of savarins and babas can either have syrup spooned over them, or marinate with a mixture of kirsch and superfine sugar for at least 1 hour before being spooned into the savarin.
• Instead of fruit, savarins can be filled with a thick vanilla custard (page 210) as well as with crème fraîche, sweetened ricotta cheese or simply with whipped cream.
• Glaze a savarin with melted apricot jam and make a pattern of glacé cherries, angelica and blanched almonds on top of the ring, glazing them as well.

For rum babas, make the mixture as in step 1, and adding ¾ cup (125g) currants. Pour into 3½in (8cm) greased rum baba molds and place on a baking sheet. Cover with plastic wrap, and let rise in a warm place. Bake at 400°F, 200°C for 15–20 minutes. Complete Savarin steps 3 and 4.

EXOTIC BREADS

Exotic breads include flat unleavened doughs, made without any yeast or other leavening agent. The techniques here cover chapatis which are unleavened whole wheat breads and parathas which are made from a similar dough but are layered with ghee (Indian clarified butter) or melted butter to produce a much richer, flakier bread. They are also shallow-fried instead of baked on a dry griddle.

Pita bread, although containing yeast, is often thought of as a flat bread. The puffed-up 'pocket' produced in baking makes it an ideal container for all kinds of wonderful fillings. I sometimes add extra flavor to pita bread by incorporating finely chopped fresh herbs or chopped black olives into the dough while I am kneading it. It is the oven's intense heat that makes these soft, thinly rolled-out doughs rise. During baking, moisture in the dough is converted to steam and this creates a pocket which makes the bread puff up. Yeast relies on a flour with a high gluten content, so unleavened breads can be made with flours with little or no gluten, such as cornmeal, barley, oatmeal, rye and buckwheat flours.

All these exotic breads are quick to make and really delicious but should be eaten as soon as possible after being made as they do not have the keeping qualities of most yeast-leavened breads.

PITA BREAD

Pita breads are the ideal bread for light meals and snacks as you can open them up and fill them with almost anything. Unlike most bread doughs which are allowed to rise before shaping, pita breads are shaped and left to rise. When baked, they rise further to produce a bread with a pocket.

To make 12, you will need ½ teaspoon sugar, 2 teaspoons salt, 6–7 cups (750–875g) bread flour, 1 packet quick-rising active dry yeast and 2 cups (475ml) warm water. If you want a nuttier tasting bread use one third whole wheat flour to two-thirds bread flour.

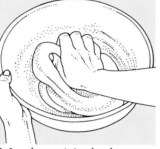

1 In a large mixing bowl, combine the sugar, salt, 6 cups (750g) of the flour and the yeast. Using a wooden spoon, stir in the water and mix to a smooth dough. Using your hands, slowly work in the remaining flour as necessary, kneading the dough along the sides of the bowl, until the dough is smooth and no longer sticky.

2 Knead for at least 5 minutes on a lightly floured surface until the dough is smooth and elastic. Divide the dough into 12 equal pieces. Shape each into a smooth ball, then cover with a damp tea towel. Working with 1 ball at a time, roll out each one to an oval about 9in (23cm) long. Flip the ovals over and lightly roll out any creases on the second side.

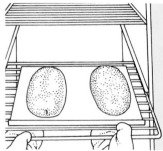

3 As each pita is rolled put it on a lightly floured surface and cover with the damp tea towel. Leave to rise in a warm place for 30–45 minutes. Place 2 pitas at a time on a preheated ungreased baking sheet and bake at 475°F, 240°C on the bottom shelf for about 3½ minutes until the pitas are puffed and browned on the bottom.

FILLING AND FLAVORING EXOTIC BREADS

• My favorite fillings for pita bread are well-spiced and garlicked ground lamb fried over a high heat and stirred until the meat is well separated and all the liquid has evaporated. Also try mixed salad with chopped fresh mint and goat cheese; cold chicken or lamb mixed with yogurt, ground cumin and chopped fresh mint; tuna mixed with a mild curry paste, yogurt and finely chopped green onions; sliced fennel or peppers, halved garlic cloves or eggplant fried in olive oil until soft, and spiced with ground coriander.
• Brush pita breads with olive oil

before baking and sprinkle with chopped blanched almonds, walnut halves or pistachios, or with tiny black or golden sesame seeds.
• For a good hot snack, make a depression in the pita dough, brush all over with olive oil mixed with 1 teaspoon paprika and break an egg over the depression. Sprinkle the egg and dough mixture with salt, pepper and dried oregano before putting into the oven to bake.
• In India, chapatis are normally used as the only implement for eating the meal and scooping up the juices, so they are almost

always a plain dough, though you may like to add some whole spices. Richer parathas, however, are eaten more as a bread on the side, and can contain delicious additions worked into the dough. Try fried onion or garlic slivers, chopped blanched almonds or pistachios, chopped cilantro and whole spices.
• Make a paratha into a snack meal in itself by adding not only onion, spices and cilantro, but also chopped hard-boiled egg and well-drained chopped, cooked spinach to the dough as well.

4 When baked, immediately wrap the pitas in a tea towel until cool enough to handle, then transfer to a wire rack. Bake the remaining pitas, two at a time. Serve warm or when cool, store in plastic bags, in the refrigerator for up to 1 week or in the freezer for up to 6 weeks.

CHAPATIS

PARATHAS

Chapatis are an unleavened bread and are the most common one served at an Indian meal. They are traditionally cooked on a *tava*, a flat Indian frying pan, but you can use a heavy frying pan or griddle. To make 8, you will need 2 cups (250g) whole wheat flour, 10–14 tablespoons water and a little ghee (Indian clarified butter) or melted clarified butter (page 96).

Like chapatis, parathas are an unleavened bread often served with an Indian meal. They are similar to chapatis but the difference is that once the basic dough is made, it is then rolled and layered with ghee or melted clarified butter (page 96) and then rolled out into a variety of shapes, including rounds, squares and triangles (the shape used here). Instead of ghee or clarified butter you can also use high-fat butter for cooking. Follow steps 1 and 2 of the chapati recipe (left), then continue as here. Makes 8 parathas.

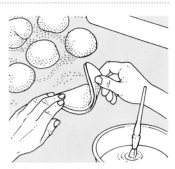

1 *On a floured surface, roll out 1 piece of dough to a circle about 4in (10cm) in diameter. Brush a little melted ghee or clarified butter on top. Fold the dough in half, brush more melted ghee or butter on top and fold in half again to form a triangle.*

1 *Put the flour in a bowl. Slowly mix in the water to form a soft dough. Knead for at least 5 minutes until smooth. Return to the bowl, cover with a damp cloth and leave for 30 minutes.*

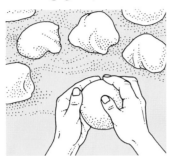

2 *Heat a dry, heavy frying pan or tava over a low heat until very hot. Meanwhile, divide the dough into 8 equal pieces and with floured hands, shape each one into a smooth ball.*

3 *Bake 1 chapati at a time. Put 1 ball on a lightly floured surface and coat in flour, then roll out to a circle about 12cm (5in) in diameter. Slap the chapati onto the hot pan.*

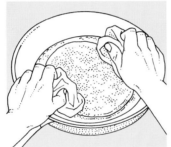

4 *Cook over a low heat and as soon as brown spots appear on the underneath, turn and cook the second side. Turn again and, using wads of paper towel, press on the edges so the chapati puffs up.*

2 *Roll out the triangle so that the sides measure about 6in (15cm). Cover with a damp tea towel while rolling out the remaining dough. Working with 1 triangle at a time, slap it on the hot frying pan or tava and, as soon as brown spots appear on the underneath, turn it over. Brush with melted ghee or butter and cook the second side.*

3 *Turn again and brush with more melted ghee or clarified butter. Using a spatula, press on the edges of the paratha and move it around the pan to make sure that it cooks evenly and is lightly browned. Remove from the pan and brush again with ghee or butter. Serve at once or keep warm in foil. Cook the remaining parathas in the same way.*

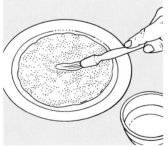

5 *Remove the chapatis from the frying pan or tava with a spatula and brush with melted ghee or butter. Serve the chapatis at once or wrap them in foil to keep warm while you cook the remaining chapati dough as in steps 3 and 4 above.*

Indian chapatis (left) and parathas served with traditional cucumber and yogurt raita and two spicy lentil dals. These breads are ideal to serve with curry, as well.

BISCUITS *and* TEA BREADS

Biscuits and tea breads are breads that are made without yeast. They are quick to make and are an irresistible alternative to plain bread. Tea breads are best when made the day before they are to be served so they can then be sliced without crumbling. Wrapped in foil, they can be kept for up to a week.

Biscuits, however, are best if eaten on the day they are made, as they go stale very quickly. The nicest thing of all is to eat them as soon as they come out of the oven and as they are so quickly made this is quite possible.

Both biscuits and tea breads are made with self-rising flour or all-purpose flour and a chemical leavening agent. Bicarbonate of soda is one of the most widely used of all non-yeast leavenings. When added to liquid and heated, it gives off carbon dioxide which expands and raises the dough. Cream of tartar is often used with bicarbonate of soda as together they react to produce carbon dioxide. Cream of tartar also helps to neutralize the soapy taste which bicarbonate of soda gives.

Baking powder, a ready-made mixture of bicarbonate of soda and cream of tartar, can also be used as a leavening agent for baking. It also contains a little starch, usually cornstarch, which helps keep it dry during storage.

If you like, you can sour milk for making a scone dough by stirring a little lemon juice into it. Use this to replace the milk, buttermilk or yogurt in the recipe below.

TRADITIONAL BISCUITS

This traditional recipe uses self-rising flour to make the biscuits rise but you can use other leavening agents; allow 2 teaspoons baking powder, or 2 teaspoons cream of tartar with 1 teaspoon baking soda to 2 cups (250g) flour. If not using self-rising flour, add ½ teaspoon salt to the flour mixture. Make the dough quickly and handle it as little as possible to keep the biscuits light.

To make 10–12 biscuits, you will need 2 cups (250g) self-rising flour, 3 tablespoons sugar, 1½oz (40g) butter or margarine, and ⅔ cup (150ml) buttermilk, milk or yogurt.

1 *Preheat the oven to 450°F, 230°C and put in a baking sheet. Sift the flour and sugar together into a bowl. Cut in the butter with a pastry blender until the mixture resembles coarse bread crumbs. Make a well in the center, pour in the buttermilk, milk or yogurt and mix lightly to make a soft dough.*

2 *Turn the dough onto a lightly floured surface and knead only very lightly just to smooth the underside. Turn the dough smooth side up and roll or pat it out to a thickness of about ¾in (1.5cm). Using a 2in (5cm) floured round biscuit cutter, cut out 10–12 biscuits.*

3 *Place the biscuits on the preheated baking sheet and dust the tops with a little extra flour. Bake immediately for 8–10 minutes until the biscuits are light brown and well risen. Cool slightly on a wire rack for 15 minutes. Serve the warm biscuits split, with butter and a good-flavored jam.*

For a traditional English teatime treat serve biscuits (scones) with thick raspberry jam and whipped cream.

To make fruit biscuits, stir ⅓ cup (50g) currants, raisins or golden raisins, and candied peel, if desired, into the flour and butter mixture in step 1 before adding the milk. Complete step 2 and bake as in step 3. These bicuits can be served plain or with jam and butter.

To make cheese biscuits, add about 1¾ cups (175–250g) finely grated aged Cheddar cheese and 1–2 teaspoons whole grain mustard to the mixture in step 1, but omit the sugar. Complete step 2 and bake as above with extra grated cheese sprinkled on top before baking.

RAISIN TEA BREAD

This recipe illustrates the use of self-rising flour as the only leavening in a bread. Like most tea breads, this bread is at its best if, after cooling, it is wrapped in foil and stored overnight before eating, allowing the flavor to mature. Serve the bread sliced and buttered.

To make 1 large loaf, you will need 3 cups (375g) self-rising flour, 2oz (50g) butter or margarine, ¾ cup (250g) golden raisins, currants or dark raisins, ¾ cup plus 2 tablespoons (200ml) milk, ¼ cup (50g) brown sugar and 2 lightly beaten eggs.

Buttered slices of raisin tea bread and a loaf of banana bread.

1 *Put the flour in a large bowl. Cut in the butter until the mixture resembles bread crumbs. Stir in the dried fruit. Warm together the milk and sugar, without boiling and stir into the dry ingredients with a wooden spoon. Add the beaten eggs and mix together well.*

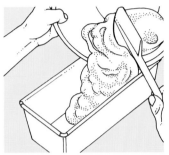

2 *Turn the mixture into a large loaf pan that has been greased and the bottom lined. Bake immediately at 350°F, 180°C for about 1 hour, until firm to the touch and a skewer inserted into the center comes out clean. Leave in the pan for 5 minutes, then turn out and cool on a wire rack.*

BANANA BREAD

This is a quick bread that is loved by children and adults alike. It is also an excellent way of using up over-ripe bananas.

If you like, you can add some finely grated lemon rind or 1 teaspoon mixed spices for extra flavoring.

To make 1 large loaf you will need 2 cups (500g) ripe bananas, 2 cups (250g) self-rising flour, 4oz (125g) butter, ½ cup (125g) sugar, 2 lightly beaten eggs and 2 tablespoons honey.

1 *Peel the bananas and mash them with a fork, adding some lemon rind, if desired. Put the flour in a bowl and cut in the butter until the mixture resembles bread crumbs.*

VARIATIONS ON TEA BREADS AND BISCUITS

• I think plain biscuits made with white flour, served with unsalted butter and homemade jam are best of all, but there are many variations . You can also make them with whole wheat flour or half whole wheat and half plain, which I prefer, and add some grated orange rind, 1 teaspoon ground mace and cinnamon, and ¼ teaspoon ground cloves.
• You can also leave out the sugar in a biscuit mixture so they are suitable to eat with savory accompaniments, such as soft cheeses or fish pâtés.
• Add chopped fresh herbs to a plain biscuit dough.
• Cheese biscuits are also delicious with chopped walnuts and chopped fresh sage or dried oregano added to the mixture.
• Add some crispy fried onion slivers or chopped green onions to a cheese biscuit mixture.
• To make scones, prepare any variation of the Traditional Biscuits opposite. Divide the dough in half and pat each half into a ¾ in (2cm) round. Cut the rounds into wedges and bake as for biscuits.
• All sorts of dried fruit can be used for tea breads, including dried apricots and peaches and chopped, pitted prunes.
• You can turn any tea bread into muffins. Just divide the batter into greased muffin pan cups and bake at 400°F, 200°C for about 20 minutes or until browned.
• Glaze tea breads by brushing with honey just as soon as they come out of the oven and sprinkle with toasted nuts or crushed sugar cubes.
• Grated lemon or orange rind or good candied peel usually enhances the flavor of a tea bread mixture, and many breads are nice in winter with spices such as ground mace, cinnamon, cloves or cardamom stirred in.

2 *With a wooden spoon, stir in the sugar, eggs, honey and mashed bananas, beating well. Turn the mixture into a large loaf pan that has been greased and the bottom lined.*

3 *Bake at 350°F, 180°C for about 1¼ hours, covering if necessary. Leave in the pan for 5 minutes, then turn out and cool on a wire rack. Serve sliced and buttered.*

ITALIAN HEARTH BREAD WITH BLACK OLIVES AND ROSEMARY *(280)*

Focaccia and *schiacciata* are both names for the flat, Italian hearth bread of which there are many varieties, but they all have one thing in common – the wonderful taste of fruity extra virgin olive oil and salt. It is best eaten warm. *MAKES 1 LARGE LOAF*

3 cups (375g) bread flour
1 packet quick-rising active dry yeast
4–5 teaspoons crushed sea salt
Leaves from 1 large sprig fresh rosemary, finely chopped
¾–1 cup (175–250ml) warm water
5–6 tablespoons extra virgin olive oil
¼–⅓ cup (40–50g) black olives, pitted and coarsely chopped

Lightly grease a large pizza pan or baking sheet. Put the flour in a large bowl with the yeast, 2 teaspoons crushed sea salt and all but 1 teaspoon of the rosemary leaves. Stir the dry ingredients with a wooden spoon, then pour in the water and 3 tablespoons olive oil, adding enough liquid to form a slightly sticky, soft dough. Turn the dough out and knead on a very lightly floured surface for 8–10 minutes until smooth and elastic.

Form the dough into a ball, and then press out with your hand into a free-form round, about 10–11in (25–28cm) in diameter and ½in (1cm) thick – the surface should be slightly undulating.

Carefully transfer the round of dough to the prepared pan or sheet. Using a wooden salad fork, pierce the surface deeply all over. Cover the pan loosely with plastic wrap. Set aside at room temperature for 1–2 hours until the dough has doubled in thickness and an impression remains when it is gently pressed.

Using a finger, press the pieces of olive slightly down into the dough at intervals, then drizzle the remaining 2–3 tablespoons olive oil over the bread, spreading it very lightly with your fingers to cover the surface completely, but leaving it to sit in pools in the indentations. Finally sprinkle with the reserved chopped rosemary and remaining crushed sea salt. Bake at 425°F, 220°C for about 20 minutes until golden brown.

CHEESE AND GREEN ONION SODA BREADS *(280)*

These are very quick to make and are delicious served as soon as they are baked for a light lunch or snack. Just slice them in half and fill with cream cheese and tomatoes or other fillings. *MAKES 6*

2 cups (250g) whole wheat flour
2 cups (250g) bread flour
2 teaspoons baking soda
2 teaspoons cream of tartar
1 teaspoon salt
½ teaspoon cayenne pepper
2½ cups (250g) aged Cheddar cheese, coarsely grated, plus a little extra for sprinkling over the tops
1 bunch green onions, trimmed and finely chopped
1 tablespoon whole grain mustard
1¼ cups (300ml) buttermilk or milk
A little olive oil

Mix the whole wheat flour, bread flour, baking soda, cream of tartar, salt and cayenne pepper together in a bowl. Stir in 2½ cups (250g) of the cheese and the finely chopped green onions. Mix the mustard with the buttermilk and add to the flour mixture, stirring until the dough leaves the side of the bowl.

Knead the dough briefly on a lightly floured surface. Form into a roll about 10cm (4in) in diameter and then cut into 6 pieces. Lay the rounds on a greased baking sheet, brush lightly with olive oil and sprinkle with the extra grated cheese. Bake at 400°F, 200°C for 20–25 minutes. Serve warm.

APRICOT AND CURRANT BREAD *(280)*

I find warm Apricot and Currant Bread to be one of the most irresistible brunch treats. Of course, any dried fruit could be substituted for these ones. *MAKES 1 LARGE LOAF*

4 cups (500g) bread flour
2 teaspoons salt
1 packet quick-rising active dry yeast
1¼ cups (300ml) warm water
1 tablespoon sunflower oil
3oz (75g) butter, cut into slices
½ cup (125g) light brown sugar
1½ teaspoons cinnamon
½ teaspoon ground nutmeg
1½ cups (175g) dried apricots, chopped
3oz (75g) currants

Grease a 10 x 8in (25 x 20cm) baking pan. Sift the flour and salt into a bowl and stir in the yeast. Add the water and oil, stirring with a wooden spoon to make a soft dough. Knead on a lightly floured surface for a few minutes until smooth. Put the dough in a lightly oiled bowl, cover with a tea towel and leave in a warm place until double in size.

Knead the dough on a lightly floured surface for about 5 minutes. Roll out into a rectangle about ¼in (5mm) thick. Dot half of the butter over the top two-thirds of the rectangle of dough, then sprinkle with 3 tablespoons brown sugar, ¾ teaspoon cinnamon, ¼ teaspoon nutmeg and half the chopped apricots and currants. Fold the uncovered bottom third of the rectangle up and the top third down, sealing the edges with a rolling pin. Roll out again to the same size rectangle and dot the top two-thirds of it with the remaining butter, 3 more tablespoons sugar, the remaining spices and the remaining apricots and currants. Fold and roll out the dough as before.

Put the pastry rectangle into the prepared baking pan, pressing it well to fill the corners and making a crisscross or diamond pattern with a sharp knife. Cover the baking pan loosely with plastic wrap and set aside in a warm place free from drafts until the dough has doubled in size.

Brush the bread lightly with oil and sprinkle the remaining sugar all over the top. Bake at 425°F, 220°C for about 30 minutes until a rich brown. If possible, eat while still warm.

CHEESE AND TOMATO SWIRL LOAF *(280)*

The smell of this bread cooking is wonderful and the first cut into it causes impressed amazement as a perfect swirl of red tomato bread is revealed within the cheese dough. Your secret is that, using quick-rising active dry yeast and with only one rising, it is extremely quick and easy to make.   *MAKES 1 LARGE LOAF*

6 cups (750g) bread flour
1 rounded tablespoon crushed sea salt
1 packet quick-rising active dry yeast
About 1 rounded tablespoon fresh chopped
   tarragon or 3 teaspoons dried oregano
1⅔ cups (375ml) warm water
2 rounded tablespoons tomato paste
2 teaspoons paprika
9 tablespoons olive oil, plus a little extra
1½ cups (150g) grated aged Cheddar
   cheese
¼ teaspoon cayenne pepper
2 large cloves garlic, crushed

Put the flour into a large bowl with the sea salt and yeast and mix together. Measure out 2½ cups (300g) of this mixture and place into another large bowl. Stir in the chopped tarragon or dried oregano. Pour ⅔ cup (150ml) of warm water into a measuring cup and stir in the tomato paste, paprika and 4 tablespoons olive oil. Using a wooden spoon, stir this mixture into the bowl containing the flour with herbs until it sticks together. Knead the dough on an unfloured surface for 2–3 minutes into a smooth ball.

Using either a wooden spoon or your hands mix all but 1 tablespoon of the grated cheese into the remaining flour, adding the cayenne pepper and the crushed garlic. Stir in the remaining warm water with 5 tablespoons olive oil. Knead the dough on a lightly floured surface for 2–3 minutes into a ball of fairly soft but just manageable dough.

Roll out the cheese dough on an unfloured surface into a large round about ¼in (5mm) thick. Roll out the tomato dough slightly thinner into a round almost as big. Lay the tomato dough on top of the cheese dough and roll up both doughs together like a jelly roll (page 267). Turn under at the ends.

Place the roll of dough on a large greased baking sheet, brush with olive oil and cut slanting slashes across the roll at 1–1½in (2.5–4cm) intervals. Sprinkle all over with the reserved grated cheese. Cover the baking sheet loosely with plastic wrap and set aside at room temperature in a place free from drafts for 1½–2 hours, or until the dough has doubled in size.

Bake the loaf for 20 minutes at 450°F, 230°C then reduce to 400°F, 200°C for another 20–25 minutes. Cool the loaf on a rack and eat while warm, or slice and toast.

SEEDED BROWN BREAD *(280)*

If you are busy during the day, make up this dough in the morning, leave it all day in the refrigerator to rise, then put the risen dough into the oven when you get home. Or you can mix the dough before you go to bed and have freshly baked hot bread for breakfast.
     MAKES FOUR 9IN (23CM) LOAVES

Soft butter or margarine
8 cups (1kg) whole wheat flour
4 cups (500g) bread flour
2 packets quick-rising active dry yeast
2 tablespoons crushed sea salt
4 tablespoons bran, plus a little extra
⅓–½ cup (75–125g) sesame seeds
½ cup (75g) pumpkin or sunflower seeds
2 teaspoons caraway seeds
½ cup (125ml) sunflower oil
3¾–4⅓ cups (900ml–1 liter) warm
   water

Coat four 9in (23cm) loaf pans very generously with soft butter. Combine the flours and yeast in a very large bowl, then stir in the salt, 4 tablespoons bran and all the seeds, reserving some sesame and pumpkin seeds. Add the oil and water, stirring until the mixture sticks together. Knead on a lightly floured surface just for a few minutes until smooth. Cut it into 4 pieces, shape and put into the pans (page 282). Cut a pattern in deep gashes on the tops and sprinkle the reserved seeds into the gashes, scattering the extra bran all over. Cover the pans loosely with plastic wrap and set aside in a warm place, free from drafts, until the dough has doubled in size. Or, refrigerate for 6 to 8 hours for the same result.

Bake at 450°F, 230°C for 20 minutes, then turn down the temperature to 400°F, 200°C for a further 20 minutes. Turn out and cool.

PRUNE, LEMON AND HONEY TEA BREAD *(280)*

This tea bread is glazed with a tangy lemon syrup, which is absorbed by the loaf.   *MAKES 1 LOAF*

1½ cups (175g) all-purpose flour
1 teaspoon baking soda
½ teaspoon cream of tartar
1 teaspoon ground mace
½ teaspoon salt
Grated rind and juice of 2 small lemons
2oz (50g) butter
2 tablespoons honey
4 tablespoons milk
1 large egg, beaten
1¼ cups (175g) soft, pitted prunes,
   coarsely chopped
2 tablespoons sugar

Sift the flour, baking soda, cream of tartar, mace and salt into a bowl. Stir in the lemon rind. Put the butter and honey into a saucepan and melt, stirring over a low heat and removing immediately when they are liquid. Using a wooden spoon, stir the milk into the flour mixture, followed by the melted butter and honey, then the beaten egg. Mix thoroughly to make a smooth, soft dough. Fold in the chopped prunes. Spoon into a well-greased 9in (23cm) loaf pan.

Bake at 325°F, 160°C for 40–50 minutes until well risen and firm to touch. Remove from the oven and pierce holes with a thin skewer right through the loaf at regular intervals all over. Strain the lemon juice into a saucepan, add the sugar, dissolve in the juice over a gentle heat and then boil rapidly for 2 minutes. Spoon the lemon syrup gradually all over the loaf, letting it soak in through the holes. Set aside to cool in the pan. When almost cold, turn out, loosening the sides with a knife if necessary and cool completely on a wire rack.

PRESERVES

There is something very satisfying about seeing pantry shelves, or even a shelf in the kitchen cupboard, lined with homemade preserves. Making preserves used to be a traditional practice for keeping foods out of season but now, with the availability of fresh foods all year round and the use of freezers, preserving has become a way of turning fresh foods into a delicious and lasting product. Making preserves is an enjoyable pastime and the finished products are extremely good in a quite different way from the fresh ingredients. Although commercial jams, jellies and marmalades can be excellent they never achieve the unique character of something homemade which also make lovely, very personal presents either to give or to be given.

The best time to make a preserve is when you have an abundance of produce growing in your garden such as berries or apples, or have been able to go fruit or berry picking.

Foods that are left in their natural state very quickly deteriorate, but if they are treated to extremes of temperature or to high concentrations of sugar, salt, vinegar or alcohol, their natural decaying process can be arrested. This is what preserving is all about – to take fresh foods in good condition and to keep them at this stage for a long period of time.

The original methods of preserving used were drying, smoking and salting which made use of the natural facilities available – sun, wind, smoke and salt. Using simple methods it is still possible to dry some foods at home, such as fruits, vegetables and herbs, but it is mostly done commercially. Nowadays large-scale smoking is rarely done at home, because few homes have a smoke house any more. Small domestic home smokers are available but they are designed to give the food flavor and it is then eaten immediately rather than preserved. Excellent home drying equipment has made it possible for people to once again dry fruits, vegetables, and even meat mixtures such as jerky. Fruit purees can be dried to make fruit leather and thinly sliced fruit can be dried to top desserts as in upscale restaurants.

Freezing is the most modern method of preserving and certainly the easiest, though it rarely improves the texture or flavor in the way that some preserving methods do. It needs no extra salt and often very little extra sugar, so is healthier than other methods of preserving. Its success as a method of home preservation depends on a low temperature destroying some microorganisms, in the form of bacteria, yeasts and molds, and making others dormant.

Other methods of preserving include the use of sugar. A high concentration of sugar prevents the growth of microorganisms and, combined with a high temperature, it preserves the fruits in jams, jellies, marmalades, curds and conserves. It is, therefore, important to follow a recipe accurately and never, for example, skimp on the amount of sugar to be used, as this is the main preservative.

Preserving with high concentrations of vinegar and alcohol are also more modern methods of preserving. Like sugar, a high concentration of these prevents the growth of microorganisms. Vinegar is used to preserve chutneys, relishes and pickles, and various kinds of alcohol are used to preserve fruits.

Preserves may look beautiful lined up on the pantry shelf and the intention may be to keep them for long periods – nevertheless, like all good food, the time comes when they must be eaten and enjoyed, so don't forget that that is what they are there for!

Preserves made throughout the year capture seasonal flavors. Back row, left to right: Fresh Raspberry Jam (page 309) is made with small amounts of orange and lemon juices to accentuate the raspberry flavor; Lemons Preserved in Salt (page 309) are made using a traditional Moroccan method and are ideal for adding extra flavor to meat stews: Orange, Lime and Sweet Pepper Chutney (page 308), flavored with turmeric and cardamom pods. Front row, left to right: Flower and Hazelnut Honey (page 308) is an easy way to transform ordinary honey into something extra special; (above) Mixed Pickled Mushrooms (page 309) can be made with any mushrooms in season; (below) Spiced Apricot and Tomato Relish (page 309), with ginger, cinnamon and cardamom, is ideal to serve with curries; (right) more jars of Mixed Pickled Mushrooms and Spiced Apricot and Tomato Relish.

JAMS *and* JELLIES

Jams and jellies are basically the same type of preserve, as both are made from cooked fruit to which sugar is added. It is the high concentration of sugar, combined with a high temperature, that enables the fruit to be preserved. The sugar also affects the fruits' setting quality, and the exact amount that is needed depends on the pectin strength of the fruit. These preserves will only set if there are sufficient quantities of sugar, acid and pectin present.

Fruits high in pectin include cooking apples, crab apples, red and black currants, gooseberries, quinces and Seville oranges. Fruits containing a moderate amount of pectin include cranberries, eating apples, blackberries, apricots and raspberries. Fruits low in pectin include bananas, cherries, elderberries, figs, melons, nectarines, peaches, pineapple, rhubarb, and strawberries. For low-pectin fruits any of the commercial pectin products give good results. Berries such as raspberries have a wonderfully fresh flavor if only boiled for a few minutes – using commercial pectin it is now possible to make successful jams this way which actually set.

There are two kinds of commercial pectin on the market, liquid pectin and powdered pectin. It is best to use the recipes that come with the product as the proportions vary for the different fruits and the different types of pectin.

CHOOSING FRUIT

The fruits used for jams and jellies should be firm and just ripe. Prepare according to the recipe, discarding any damaged parts. The fruit is then simmered to extract the pectin and acid it contains.

Only fruits with a high pectin content are suitable for jellies unless you use commercial pectin.

Any skin, core or seeds will be extracted when the pulp is strained, though damaged parts should be removed before using.

ABOUT PECTIN

Some fruits contain a lot of pectin and acid, while others do not. Preserves made with fruits low in pectin must have pectin added to enable them to set. Lemon juice is usually used to provide the acid along with commercially prepared liquid pectin or powdered pectin. Sometimes an acid only is added, such as citric or tartaric acid. These do not contain pectin but help to extract what natural pectin there is present in the fruit. Lemon juice improves the flavor of many fruits in any case.

TESTING FOR A SET

You can tell when a jam has been cooked enough by testing for a set. Remove the pan from the heat while you test as if the jam overcooks it will not set. If the test shows the jam mixture is still too liquid continue boiling and retesting every few minutes.

For a sheeting test, dip a metal spoon into the pan and lift out a little jam. Cool slightly, then let the jam drop back into the pan. If the jam does not run off the spoon but slides off in a sheet, setting point has been reached.

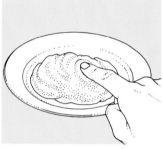

For a saucer test, put a little jam on a saucer into the freezer for a minute or so until just cooled. Push a finger gently through the jam. Setting point has been reached if the surface of the jam wrinkles.

JARRING AND STORING

Once a setting point has been reached, it is time to put the jam or jelly into jars. Stop boiling and let the fruit mixture stand for 15 minutes (this will stop fruit from rising to the top of the jars when you fill them), then remove any foam with a large slotted spoon. Stir to distribute the fruit.

Meanwhile, wash the jars well in hot water and rinse, then dry in a cool oven at 275°F, 140°C. It is easiest to handle the hot jars if you place them in the oven on a baking sheet. Use the jars while still hot so they will not crack from the jam, and fill them to within ⅛in (3mm) of the top. Wipe the rims and cover the still hot jam with a canning lid. Fasten tightly with a screw band and invert the jars for 5 minutes so the hot jam will sterilize the lid. Set the jars right-side up and let them cool completely.

Jams and jellies may also be processed in a boiling water bath. Place the jars in a canner and cover with boiling water. Boil for 10 minutes; remove from the canner and tighten the bands immediately.

After processing, wipe the jars clean, label and store in a cool, dry, dark place. Most jams can be kept for up to a year.

*Use a **wide-mouthed** metal funnel with a short neck, and a ladle with a lip and a long handle to fill jam and jelly jars. These help protect your hands from the hot mixture, as well as making filling a neater operation. Take care not to overfill the jars, lifting the funnel to check underneath as you pour.*

FREEZER JAMS

One of the most rewarding ways to preserve jams these days is to freeze them. The instructions for making freezer jams come with all commercial pectins and, because the cooking time is short, the resulting jams retain much of the flavor of the fresh fruit. Strawberry, raspberry, blueberry and peach jams are especially delicious when made by this method. After brief cooking, the finished jams are packed into jars and frozen, thereby eliminating any loss from poor sealing. When you are ready to use the jams, thaw and store in the refrigerator.

MAKING JELLY

Fruit for jelly is gently cooked to a pulp with any flavorings, and then left to drain through a jelly bag until all the juices have dripped out. If you haven't got a jelly bag (page 24), you can improvise by using a large double thickness of unbleached muslin. Whichever you use, scald the bag or muslin by pouring boiling water through it. Measure out the amount of extracted juice and return it to the cleaned preserving pan with the sugar, the quantity depending on the pectin content of the fruit. Pectin-rich extract needs 1lb (500g) sugar for each 2½ cups (600ml), while extract from fruit with a medium pectin content will set with 12oz (375g) sugar for each 2½ cups (600ml).

To make apple jelly, a fruit with a naturally high pectin content, you will need 3lb (1.5kg) cooking apples, 2½ cups (600ml) water and sugar (see method).

1 *Remove and discard any damaged fruit. Put the sliced apples and measured water in a preserving pan and simmer gently on a low heat, to extract as much juice as possible, for 30–45 minutes until the fruit is tender and thoroughly broken up. Stir occasionally with a large wooden spoon to prevent the fruit from sticking to the bottom of the pan.*

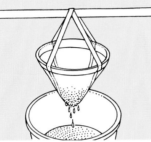

2 *Meanwhile prepare your jelly bag and bowl. If you don't have a special stand suspend the scalded bag from a broom handle placed between 2 chairs. Place a large bowl underneath the bag to catch the juice. Pour the cooked pulp into the bag and leave for at least 12 hours, until the dripping has stopped. Do not squeeze the bag at all or the jelly will cloud.*

3 *Discard the jelly bag pulp; measure extracted juice and return it to the pan. Add 1lb (500g) sugar to each 2½ cups (600ml) juice. Heat gently to dissolve the sugar, then bring to the boiling point as quickly as possible and boil rapidly for about 10 minutes or until the setting point is reached (opposite). Remove from the heat, skim, then fill into jars and cover (opposite).*

MAKING JAM

When initially cooking the fruit for a jam it is important to simmer it gently until it is very tender before adding the sugar, as cooking afterwards will not soften the fruit. Those with tough skins, such as plums, will take about 30 minutes, while soft-skinned fruit, such as strawberries, will take about 20 minutes or less. It is this cooking that releases the pectin from the fruit.

To make about 10lb (5kg) plum jam you will need 6lb (3kg) plums, 3¾ cups (900ml) water, 6lb (3kg) sugar and a chunk of butter.

1 *Put the plums and water in a preserving pan and simmer gently, stirring occasionally, for about 30 minutes until the fruit is soft and the contents reduced. Remove the pan from the heat. Meanwhile warm the sugar slightly in a low oven so it dissolves more quickly.*

2 *Stir in the warmed sugar until dissolved, then add the butter to reduce foaming. Return the pan to the heat, bring the jam to the boiling point as quickly as possible and boil rapidly for about 10–15 minutes.*

3 *Remove from the heat and test for a set (opposite). Remove plum seeds and carefully skim off any foam. It is not necessary to skim while the jam is boiling as too much clear jam would be lost. Fill into jars and cover (opposite).*

Making your own jams and jellies lets you capture the fresh flavors of seasonal fruit. From left to right: Spiced Apple Jelly with Mint and Dill (page 308), ginger-flavored pear jam and plum jam.

OTHER SPREADS

Some other ways fruit may be preserved as a spread include spicy fruit butters, sweet and buttery fruit curds and tangy citrus maramalades. Ever since the first apple trees were brought to this country, the fruit has been sliced, boiled down in big kettles and spiced to make a thick spread for bread. Butters can also be made from pears and quince. The small batch apple butter (opposite) is easy to prepare yet traditionally delicious.

Curds are usually made from citrus fruits and sugar which are thickened with eggs and butter. They have a thick, soft consistency and can be spread on bread or toast and used like jam or as a filling for a sponge cake or small tarts or other pastries (below). Because the addition of eggs diminishes a curd's keeping qualities these are not a true preserve, and should, therefore, be made in small quantities, kept in the refrigerator and eaten quickly – which is

not difficult, as they are so delicious.

Marmalades are often served with toast for breakfast but are also good in cakes, sauces and glazes and for mixing with cooked apples and plums. Marmalades are a method of preserving similar to that used for jam but they are nearly always made from citrus fruits, including oranges, lemons, grapefruits and limes. In Europe, Seville or bitter oranges are used for marmalade because they give a strong flavor and clear appearance.

Marmalades need to be cooked for longer than jams in order to really soften the peel which is much tougher than that of most fruits used in jam, to extract the all-important pectin which is found in the pith, seeds and membrane of citrus fruits, and to evaporate the larger quantity of water than is needed. If this is not done adequately the marmalade will not set properly.

LEMON CURD

I adore lemon curd and other fruit curds, and they really have to be homemade to taste authentic. As well as lemon juice, you can make fruit curds also with freshly squeezed lime or orange juice. Lemon and other citrus-flavored curds are easy to make by the traditional method as here but they can be made in a microwave in less than half the time (page 311).

This is the classic fruit curd recipe that you can use to make curds on top of the stove. To make 1½lb (750g) lemon curd you will need the finely grated rind and juice of 4 lemons, 4 lightly beaten eggs, 4oz (125g) unsalted butter and 1¾ cups (375g) superfine sugar.

1 *Put all the ingredients in the top of a double boiler or in a heatproof bowl over a saucepan of simmering water, making sure the bottom of the bowl does not touch the water. Stir continuously with a wooden spoon until the butter has melted.*

2 *Cook very gently over a low heat, stirring frequently, for about 20 minutes until the sugar has dissolved and the mixture is creamy and thick enough to coat the back of a wooden spoon. The mixture should not be allowed to boil or it will curdle.*

Small jars of lemon and orange curds make lovely presents. Use curds to fill pastry shells and to frost together butter cookies.

3 *Immediately strain the cooked mixture through a fine sieve, to remove any lumps of egg white, into small, clean, dry jars (page 300). Carefully fill the jars right to the top as the curd will thicken and shrink slightly as it cools and sets.*

4 *Cover the jars while still hot with waxed paper and fabric rounds and secure with rubber bands or with canning lids and screw bands. Store in the refrigerator and eat within 1–2 weeks as curds are not true preserves and do not keep for long.*

ORANGE MARMALADE

There are many different ways of preparing marmalade.

This is the traditional recipe for Seville orange marmalade. Coarsely or finely chop the peel according to your preference. To make about 10lb (5kg) marmalade you will need 3lb (1.5kg) Seville or other oranges, 4 tablespoons lemon juice, 15 cups (3.6 liters) water and 6lb (3kg) granulated sugar.

1 *Wash the oranges well, then halve them and squeeze the juice and seeds into a sieve set over a small bowl. Tie the seeds and extra membrane in cheesecloth. Slice the orange peel thickly or thinly, as desired. Put the sliced peel, orange juice, lemon juice, water and cheesecloth bag in a preserving pan. Simmer gently for 1–3 hours.*

2 *When reduced by about a half and the peel has become really soft, discard the cheesecloth bag. Add the sugar, stirring until dissolved, then boil rapidly for about 15 minutes and test for a set (page 300). When the setting point is reached, skim and cool for 10–15 minutes, then stir to distribute the peel. Fill in jars and cover as for jams (page 300).*

Sweet and tangy orange marmalade, with its golden color, is always appreciated at breakfast time.

APPLE BUTTER

This traditional spread was originally cooked down in large kettles outdoors. While this recipe has been reduced to fit into a standard saucepan, the aroma that fills your home as the apple butter is cooking will entice you to make the resulting delicious spread often.

To make about 3 cups (700ml) apple butter, peel, core and slice 3lb (1.5kg) tart cooking apples. Combine the apples with 1¼ cups (300ml) apple cider and 2 tablespoons lemon juice in a large, heavy, non-aluminum saucepan or Dutch oven. Cover and cook over very low heat, stirring frequently, until the apples have completely turned into applesauce. This will take about 20 minutes.

Stir 1½ cups (300g) sugar, 1½ teaspoons ground cinnamon, ½ teaspoon ground ginger, ¼ teaspoon nutmeg, ¼ teaspoon salt and ⅛ teaspoon ground cloves into the apple mixture. Return the mixture to a boil and cook uncovered, stirring frequently, until the apple butter has reduced to a very thick spread, which will take at least 1-1½ hours. The wider the surface of the saucepan you use, the faster the apple butter will thicken.

Spoon the hot apple butter into sterilized 8oz (237ml) canning jars (page 300), cover with standard lids and rings and process in a boiling water bath for 10 minutes. Or spoon into sterilized decorative jars, cover tightly and store in the refrigerator until ready to serve.

EXCITING FLAVORS FOR PRESERVES

• As well as using juice you can make fruit curds with smooth fruit purees which are not too thick (page 224). Purees made from stewed dried or fresh apricots, peaches, quince or pears stewed with lemon juice, or a seedless puree of raspberries all work well – but the fruit should be sieved after pureeing to make it really smooth.

• Few marmalades can beat homemade orange marmalade, but there are all sorts of other citrus fruits and combinations of fruits which produce an interesting change. Oranges can be combined with fresh pineapple or with lemons and sliced quinces, peaches or apricots.

• Grapefruit can be combined with oranges and lemons as in the traditional three-fruit marmalade.

• Kumquats make a good marmalade, either on their own or with blood oranges, and orange, lemon and rhubarb is a very good combination.

• Added flavor and interest can be infused into a marmalade mixture by including certain spices or herbs enclosed in a muslin bag in addition to the one which holds the oranges' seeds and pulp. Slices of fresh ginger, 1 or 2 tablespoons whole cloves, star anise, coriander seeds, cardamom pods, sticks of cinnamon, rosemary, lavender, bay or mint leaves, are just some possibilities.

• The inclusion of dried aromatic edible flowers such as elderflowers raises any jam to a magical level. Amazingly, the musty-smelling elderflower imparts a scented flavor of muscatel grapes to the jam. This is especially good with fresh apricot jam.

• Various liqueurs can be added to jams at the last moment before they are put into jars to make them more sophisticated and fragrant; brandy is excellent added to plum jam, and kirsch is a natural partner for cherry jam.

• Vegetables can be used in jams, jellies and marmalades. Winter squash and pumpkin are traditional, tomato can be used on its own or combined with other fruits, and onion makes a wonderful jam to serve with pâtés and cold meats.

• My favorite jellies are made from quinces, or crab apples – with their fragrant flavors and amber colors.

CHUTNEYS *and* PICKLES

I only began to enjoy chutneys after my first visit to India – the dark brown sticky mush which was called chutney at school had never captivated my taste buds. Away from India, chutney is less dry and sweeter, often more like a sweet and sour jam. Chutneys are made from a mixture of vegetables or fruits, or a combination of both, which is cooked with vinegar, sugar and spices that act as the preservatives. The ingredients are finely chopped or sliced and then cooked slowly to produce a smooth texture, whereas the ingredients in relishes are cut larger, the cooking time is shorter, and therefore the finished texture is chunkier. Use uneven or misshapen ingredients because their appearance is not important in the finished preserve.

Pickles are made from raw or lightly cooked vegetables or fruits which are preserved in clear, spiced vinegar. Only use crisp fresh ingredients. Vegetables are usually brined or salted to remove excess water which would otherwise dilute the vinegar and make it too weak to act as a preservative. Make sure you use a good-quality bottled vinegar with an acetic acid content of at least five per cent. The color of vinegar is no indication of its strength; either white distilled or the golden cider vinegar gives a good flavor and is economical. Use white distilled vinegar in light-colored pickles for a better appearance, but I like the flavor of white wine and cider vinegar best of all. Do not use copper or brass pans for these preserves because the vinegar reacts adversely with them. It is important to use vinegar-proof tops such as plastic-coated ones. If metal caps are used take care not to let the vinegar come into contact with the metal. Glass preserving jars with clip tops are ideal.

FRESH GREEN APPLE CHUTNEY

Very dark, sweet, mushy chutneys are a great favorite with many people, but I personally prefer fresh chutneys with clear colors and separate flavors.

All sorts of ingredients which don't need cooking can be used for fresh chutneys, which are light and refreshing. Using a food processor this technique based on fresh green apple with mint and coriander only takes minutes to make, and will keep in a covered jar in the refrigerator for up to 1 week. Serve with cold or roast meat and poultry, spoon it into curries and casseroles, eat it with crusty bread and cheese or in sandwiches, or mix it with cottage cheese for a delicious baked potato filling.

Put 1 peeled, cored and chopped cooking apple, 4 tablespoons lemon juice, 1 seeded green chili cut in half (page 49), 1 generous handful fresh mint leaves, 2 tablespoons fresh cilantro leaves and 1 teaspoon sugar into a food processor and process to a coarse paste. Add salt and cayenne pepper to taste. The mixture should be moist – if it seems too wet add some more mint leaves and process again.

IDEAS FOR CHUTNEYS AND PICKLES
• For safer long-term storage chutney mixtures can be processed for 10 minutes in a boiling water bath.
• Good chutney combinations include dried apricots and whole shallots and orange juice, rhubarb with thinly sliced whole orange, blackberry and apple with elderberries, seedless grapes with apples and green peppers, apples and prunes, quince and pear with thinly sliced whole lemons, grapefruit with pumpkin and golden raisins, plums and apples with slices of fresh ginger, and tomato with apricots and pears.
• Small tomatoes, skinned and then put in a jar with strips of fresh basil leaves before being covered with sweetened wine vinegar and seasoned with salt and cayenne pepper, make an excellent pickle.
• Slightly bland exotic fruits such as kiwis, mangoes and papaya, pickle well and go well with game and pork.
• After packing ingredients into the jar with spiced vinegar, pour a layer of extra virgin olive oil on top to add flavor. Store in the refrigerator.

TOMATO CHUTNEY

It is very easy to vary a basic chutney recipe so you can use more unusual combinations of different fruits and vegetables, as well as the overabundance from your own garden.

To make about 2lb (1kg) tomato chutney you will need 2 tablespoons mustard seeds, 1 tablespoon whole allspice, 3lb (1.5kg) skinned and quartered tomatoes (page 48), 1lb (500g) finely chopped onions, 1 teaspoon cayenne pepper, 1¾ cups (250g) golden raisins, 1¼ cups (250g) granulated sugar, 2 teaspoons salt and 2 cups (450ml) vinegar.

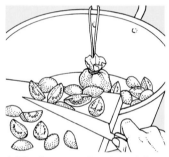

1 *Tie the mustard seeds and the allspice in a piece of cheesecloth. Gather up the corners and tie the bag securely with a piece of string, then tie to the handle of the preserving pan. Add the tomatoes, onions and cayenne pepper to the pan.*

2 *Simmer on a low heat for about 45 minutes, breaking down the tomatoes until they are reduced to a pulp. Add the remaining ingredients and continue simmering, stirring occasionally, for about 1½ hours, until the mixture is thick.*

3 *Remove the cheesecloth bag. Pour the hot chutney into clean, dry, preheated jars (page 300) and cover immediately with airtight, vinegar-proof tops. Store in a cool, dry, dark place for 2–3 months to allow the flavors to mature before use.*

SPICED VINEGAR

Spices are added to vinegar to give it a good flavor and they also help as a preservative. The vinegar can be used at once but if you keep it for several months the flavors will mature.

Preparing your own vinegar means you can add a wider variety of flavors. Whole spices are best for spicing vinegar as ground ones will make the vinegar cloudy. The spices can be varied according to choice but the following is a typical combination for 5 cups (1.2 liters) vinegar: 2in (3 x 5cm) cinnamon sticks, 2 rounded teaspoons whole cloves, 10 blades mace, 2 heaping teaspoons whole allspice and 2 heaping teaspoons black peppercorns.

Place the whole spices in a saucepan and add 5 cups (1.2 liters) white distilled or white wine vinegar. Bring just to a boil (do not allow to boil), then pour into a heatproof bowl and leave to cool and infuse for 2 hours. Store the vinegar with the spices in it in clean, dry bottles and seal well. Strain before use. If you keep it for about 2–3 months before use the flavors will intensify and improve.

Pickles and chutneys are surprisingly easy to make. Here are (clockwise from top right) pickled onions, tomato chutney, fresh green apple chutney and pickled red cabbage.

PICKLED ONIONS

This recipe illustrates wet brining, in which the onions are covered with a brine solution to remove their surplus water. Use ordinary table salt and spiced vinegar (above) which has more flavor than plain vinegar. Cauliflower florets can also be pickled in this way. Store for 3–4 months before using.

You will need 4lb (2kg) pickling onions, 1lb (500g) salt, 20 cups (4.8 liters) water and 5 cups (1.2 liters) cold spiced vinegar.

1 Put the unskinned onions in a large bowl. Dissolve 8oz (250g) salt in 10 cups (2.4 liters) water to make a brine and pour on top of the onions. Leave to soak for 12 hours or a little longer.

PICKLED RED CABBAGE

This classic recipe is an example of dry brining, where the vegetable is layered with salt. As well as red cabbage, it is also suitable for cucumber, tomatoes and squash. Slice cucumber and tomatoes and dice squash. Peel or not as you prefer. This is the only pickle that should not be allowed to mature, as it loses its crispness after 2–3 months. You will need 3lb (5kg) finely shredded firm red cabbage (page 45), 2 sliced large onions, 4 tablespoons table salt, 10 cups (2.4 liters) spiced vinegar (above) and 1 tablespoon brown sugar.

2 Drain the onions, then skin and cover with fresh brine, made with the remaining salt and water. Leave to soak for 24–36 hours, then drain and rinse.

3 Pack the onions into clean, dry wide-necked jars, to within 1in (2.5cm) of the top. Pour over the spiced vinegar and seal with vinegar-proof tops and process.

1 Layer the cabbage and onions in a large bowl, sprinkling each layer with salt, then cover with a clean tea towel and set aside for 24 hours. The next day, drain the cabbage and onions well, rinse off the surplus salt thoroughly and drain again.

2 Pack loosely into clean, dry wide-necked jars to within 1in (2.5cm) of the top. Heat the spiced vinegar gently, add the sugar and stir until dissolved. Pour over the cabbage and onions and cover with vinegar-proof tops. Store in the refrigerator.

GIFTS FROM YOUR KITCHEN

These special preserves include the less usual and more luxurious preserves. Some of them are an ideal method of preserving a small quantity of your favorite fruit or vegetable, while others are preserved in alcohol. All of them make very popular presents especially when you use attractive glass jars and labels.

Mincemeat, ever popular at Christmas, was originally a method of preserving meat without using the salting or smoking methods. Nowadays, however, it is a mixture of fruits, mostly dried, and spices, preserved in alcohol and sugar. Only the suet is a reminder of the past, although you can include a little lean ground beef, too, which adds flavor. I always make my own mincemeat but if you are short of time commercial mincemeat can be improved by stirring in fresh lemon juice, a little brandy, grated orange rind and peeled and chopped fresh cooking apples.

Fruits can be preserved in alcohol, in syrup alone and with spices in syrup and vinegar. The alcohol used in preserving fruits is usually brandy as it is the most compatible with the majority of fruits, including cherries, apricots, grapes, peaches, kumquats, pineapple and orange slices, but other spirits, such as kirsch, can be used. Kirsch goes well with cherries, pineapple and raspberries. Fruits in alcohol make delicious, quick and easy desserts and are also good mixed with fresh fruits. Fruits that are preserved with spices in syrup and vinegar can be served as accompaniments to meat and poultry.

It is possible to preserve some vegetables in oil including dried tomatoes, firm button mushrooms, olives, globe artichokes and grilled peppers but they should be stored in the refrigerator. Lemons can also be preserved this way and also by salting, which is a method that goes back to Roman times and is now much used in North African cooking (page 309).

MINCEMEAT

Make up large quantities of this brandy-flavored mincemeat, varying the ingredients to suit your family's favorite flavors. Give small jars as presents, or use to make individual mincemeat tarts with sweet pastry (page 248).

Although traditionally associated with the Christmas holidays, mincemeat can, of course, be used all year round, and it is always useful to have a jar in the cupboard. For mincemeat that will keep well, use a firm, hard variety of apple; a juicy apple may make the mixture too moist. Jar, process and store mincemeat in the same way as jam (page 300) but allow at least 2 weeks to mature before using. If it becomes dry, add a little extra of the original alcohol used.

To make 3lb (1.5kg) mincemeat, you will need ¾ cup (125g) raisins, ¾ cup (125g) golden raisins, ⅔ cup (75g) dried apricots, ⅔ cup (75g) glacé cherries, ¾ cup (75g) shelled pecans or walnut halves, 6–8oz (175–250g) cooking apples, the grated rind and juice of 2 lemons, 2oz (50g) cut mixed peel, ¾ cup (125g) currants, 4oz (125g) suet, ¾ cup (175g) plus 2 tablespoons light brown sugar, ½ teaspoon ground cloves, 1 teaspoon ground cinnamon and 6–10 tablespoons brandy.

1 *Finely chop the raisins, golden raisins, dried apricots, glacé cherries and nuts and put in a large bowl. Add the peeled, cored and chopped apple with the lemon rind and juice, mixed peel, currants, suet, sugar and spices. Stir in enough brandy to make a moist mixture.*

2 *Cover the bowl and refrigerate for 2 days. Then stir again, adding a little more brandy. Spoon into clean, dry jars, packing down well, cover, seal and process (page 300). Leave to mature for at least 2 weeks. If it becomes dry, add a little more brandy before using.*

BRANDIED CHERRIES

A wide variety of fruits can be preserved in alcohol but it is important that they are firm and fresh. The skins of pitted fruits must be pierced to allow the alcohol to permeate the flesh. Jar and cover the jars in the same way as pickles (page 305) and leave for at least 3 months before eating.

You will need 1lb (500g) cherries, 1¼ cups (250g) granulated sugar, 1¼ cups (300ml) water, 1 cinnamon stick and ⅔ cup (150ml) brandy, rum or kirsch.

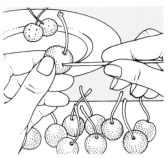

1 *Pierce the cherries all over with a clean toothpick or needle. Dissolve half the sugar in the water, then add the cherries and cinnamon stick and poach gently for 4–5 minutes.*

2 *Lift the cherries from the syrup and arrange in small, clean, dry preserving jars. Dissolve the remaining sugar in the reserved syrup, then bring to a boil for 5–6 minutes.*

3 *Cool the syrup, then measure and add an equal amount of brandy. Pour the brandy syrup over the cherries, seal with plastic-lined lids, process and leave to mature for 3 months.*

Colorful jars of pickled peppers are ideal to have on hand to serve with sliced meats and salami or cheese. When making cherries in brandy leave the stems on or take them off as you prefer.

PICKLED PEPPERS

Pickled vegetables can be used to liven up salads, in stews or as a pizza topping, and their vinegar can also be used in salad dressings. Peppers are always nicest grilled until blackened first and then skinned, as this gives them a wonderful mellow, smoky taste. To preserve peppers, you will need 4lb (2kg) red, green or yellow peppers – a mixture of all three looks very pretty. Sprigs of fresh herbs, peeled garlic cloves and spiced vinegar (page 305).

MORE IDEAS FOR KITCHEN GIFTS

• It is important to use standard canning jars and to process all preserves according to government standards if they are going to be held at room temperature.

• I like changing my mincemeat recipe a little each year and adding different ingredients like chopped pineapple, angelica, dried apricots, peaches and pears.

• All kinds of fruits can be gently poached in a sugar syrup (page 208) and then arranged in jars. You can make alternate layers of different fruits, half cover with a liqueur and then fill to the top with the poaching syrup (reduced to thicken). Jars should always be sterilized before using (page 300). Successful fruits to use are peeled peaches and apricots, quinces, pitted cherries, sliced mangoes, kiwi fruit and fresh figs – these last two need no cooking first.

• Halved clementines or pierced kumquats make an excellent accompaniment for roast game or pork: boil with spices in a mixture of water and wine vinegar until soft, then add sugar and after boiling again, pack the fruit into clean, dry jars. Reduce the syrup and pour over the fruit when cold.

• To store eggplant in oil, plunge thin slices into boiling white wine vinegar for 3–4 minutes, then drain and press thoroughly between paper towels to dry, pack in clean, dry jars, with paprika, black pepper, salt, crushed garlic and dried oregano between the layers. Cover completely with olive oil and store in the refrigerator.

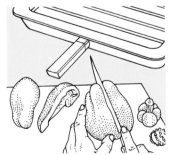

1 *Quarter the peppers lengthwise, then remove the stalks, cores and seeds. Arrange on a grill pan, skin-side up. Grill until completely black. Wrap in a tea towel and leave to cool for 10 minutes. Pull off the skins in strips (page 55), then cut the peppers into strips.*

2 *Pack the pepper strips into clean, dry jars, layering them with sprigs of fresh herbs and adding a peeled garlic clove to each layer. Pour over enough spiced vinegar to cover completely. Seal and process the jars. Store for about one month in a cool, dark place before using.*

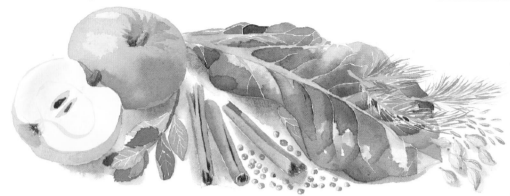

SPICED APPLE JELLY WITH MINT AND DILL (301)

Apple jelly is a delicious and pretty-looking accompaniment to roast lamb. I use spices which are often used with lamb in the Middle East and the green color is given by adding some spinach juice.   *MAKES ABOUT 4LB (2KG)*

3lb (1.5kg) green cooking apples, unpeeled, coarsely chopped
Good handful of fresh mint plus 2 tablespoons coarsely chopped mint
2 cinnamon sticks, broken
3¾ cups (900ml) water
4oz (125g) spinach, stems removed and coarsely chopped
1¼ cups (300ml) cider vinegar
3 teaspoons cumin seeds
3 teaspoons coriander seeds, crushed
6–8 cardamom pods, crushed
Granulated sugar
Generous bunch of fresh dill, divided into small sprigs

Put the apples in a preserving pan with the handful of fresh mint and broken cinnamon sticks. Add the water, bring to a boil and simmer gently for about 45 minutes, stirring now and then. Add the spinach about halfway through the cooking. When the apples are very soft and mushy, add the cider vinegar and boil for another 5 minutes.

Spoon the apple and spinach mixture into a scalded jelly bag (page 301) over a large bowl and leave to strain for at least 12 hours, without pressing, until the dripping has stopped. Tie up the cumin seeds, coriander seeds and cardamom pods in a cheesecloth bag, and wrap the 2 tablespoons of coarsely chopped mint in a second cheesecloth bag.

Measure the extracted juice from the apple and spinach mixture and put it in a preserving pan with 500g (1lb) of sugar for each 2½ cups (600ml) of juice.

Discard the pulp in the jelly bag. Put the pan over a medium heat and stir to dissolve the sugar, then add the spice and mint bags. Bring to a boil, boil rapidly for about 10 minutes, remove the pan from the heat and test for a set (page 300).

When the setting point has been reached, remove any foam with a large metal spoon. Add the dill sprigs to the jelly. Leave to cool for 8–10 minutes, then stir again and pour into clean, dry, hot jars (page 300), including some dill in each jar. Seal, process and store.

FLOWER AND HAZELNUT HONEY (298)

This is a wonderful way of making ordinary honey into something really special. Use either lavender or elderflowers from a health food store to infuse the honey with their magically scented flavor. Toasted hazelnuts give both taste and an exciting texture.   *MAKES 2LB(1KG)*

2lb (1kg) honey
2 tablespoons lavender or 3–4 clean-looking elderflower heads
½ cup (50g) toasted skinned hazelnuts, finely chopped

Spoon the honey into a saucepan. Add the lavender or pull the flowers from the elderflower heads and drop in. Heat gently, stirring, until just beginning to boil, then remove from the heat, cover and leave to infuse for at least 1 hour.

Reheat the honey until just boiling, then pour through a strainer into clean, dry, hot jars (page 300), stirring some chopped hazelnuts into each jar. When cool, cover tightly and store for at least 2 weeks before using. The hazelnuts will rise to the top of the jar while the honey is cooling so when it begins to set again, stir to redistribute them.

ORANGE, LIME AND SWEET PEPPER CHUTNEY (298)

This is a translucent, beautifully colored, mildly spiced chutney which goes especially well with duck, pork and venison. It is also excellent with cold turkey and ham. It is more like a thick fruit compote than a chutney though the onions and vinegar give it a definite savory taste.   *MAKES ABOUT 3LB (1.5KG)*

3 large oranges
5 limes
2 large onions, cut into ½in (1cm) pieces
9–10 large cloves garlic, halved
2 red chilies, seeded and finely chopped (page 49)
1 teaspoon turmeric
1¾ cups (375g) granulated sugar
1¼ cups (300ml) white wine vinegar
1¼ cups (300ml) fresh, unsweetened apple juice
1 teaspoon salt
10–12 cardamom pods, lightly crushed
6–8 whole cloves
1 large red pepper, cored, seeded and cut into ½in (1cm) pieces (page 49)
1 large yellow pepper, cored, seeded, and cut into ½in (1cm) pieces (page 49)

Scrub the oranges and limes with soapy water, rinse thoroughly in clean water and dry. Squeeze the juice out of the oranges into a heavy stainless steel or enameled saucepan, removing any seeds. Scrape the pith out of the orange shells with a teaspoon and discard, then cut the peel into small pieces. Cut the limes into eighths, discarding any pips.

Add the orange peel, lime segments, onions, garlic and chilies to the saucepan and stir in the turmeric, granulated sugar, white wine vinegar, apple juice and salt. Tie up the crushed cardamom pods and the cloves in a cheesecloth bag secured with a long piece of string and tie to the saucepan handle. Bring to a boil then simmer gently, uncovered, stirring occasionally, for 1 hour. Add the prepared peppers and continue to simmer gently for another 30–45 minutes, stirring more often with a large wooden spoon as the mixture thickens.

Remove the cheesecloth bag of spices and discard. Leave the chutney to cool in the saucepan. Then spoon into clean, dry jars (page 300), seal, process and keep in a cool place to mature for at least 2 weeks before using.

FRESH RASPBERRY JAM (298)

Some berry jams and ones made from non-pectin ingredients such as rose petals must be made with commercial pectin so the mixture sets with only the briefest of boiling and the fruits retain their juicy freshness.   *MAKES 3–4LB (1.5–2KG)*

2lb (1kg) dry, fresh raspberries
Juice of 1 orange, strained
4 tablespoons lemon juice, strained
Powdered or liquid pectin
4 ⅓ cups (875g) granulated sugar

Put the raspberries in a preserving pan with the strained orange and lemon juices. Add the pectin and sugar following the directions on the pectin product. When the setting point has been reached, pour into clean, dry, hot jars (page 300); seal and process.

LEMONS PRESERVED IN SALT (298)

After several vacations in Morocco, I have come to love these lemons which are used in many of their wonderful *tagines* (stews cooked in traditional earthenware pots). Slices of pickled lemons and their juice enhance chicken stew, and are good for a spicy lamb casserole which could also include dried fruits such as apricots or prunes. When matured, these lemons don't taste very salty, and the skin is soft and has lost all bitterness.   *MAKES ABOUT 1KG (2LB)*

About 1kg (2lb) fairly small lemons, plus
* about 6 lemons for extra juice*
About ½ cup (125g) sea salt

Scrub the lemons thoroughly with soapy water, then rinse well with cold running water and dry. Working over a bowl, cut the lemons lengthwise almost in quarters but stop before you cut right through at the stem end so the fruit still holds together. Remove any seeds.

Sprinkle a heaping teaspoon of salt into each lemon then pack very tightly into clean, dry, wide-necked jars (page 300), pressing down firmly with a spoon. Pour any juice which escaped while you were cutting the lemons into the jars. The juice should completely cover the lemons: squeeze out more from the extra lemons and use more lemons if necessary.

Put a weight such as a well-washed, suitably shaped stone or small saucer in the top of each jar so that no lemon rises above the juice, then cover the jars and leave at room temperature for 2–3 weeks. When the lemons are ready (the skins will be soft to cut) remove the weight. Once opened keep in the refrigerator and use as desired.

SPICED APRICOT AND TOMATO RELISH (298)

This relish is somewhat like a chutney but has a fresher, sweet-and-sour flavor.
    MAKES ABOUT 4–5LB (2–2.5KG)

500g (1lb) fresh apricots, halved, pitted
* and coarsely chopped (page 222)*
1½lb (750g) tomatoes, skinned and
* coarsely chopped (page 48)*
8oz (250g) shallots, quartered lengthwise
1in (2.5cm) piece fresh gingerroot, peeled
* and thinly sliced*
4–5 cardamom pods, crushed
1 cinnamon stick, in 1in (2.5cm) pieces
½ cup plus 2 tablespoons (125g) light
* brown sugar*
1 tablespoon honey
1¼ cups (150ml) cider vinegar
2 teaspoons green peppercorns

Put the prepared apricots, tomatoes, shallots, ginger, cardamom and cinnamon into a preserving pan, then stir in the brown sugar, honey, cider vinegar and green peppercorns. Bring to a boil and cook, uncovered, for about 20 minutes until the mixture is thick and soft. Spoon into clean, dry, hot jars (page 300), seal, cover and process. Store in a cool place for at least 3 weeks before opening.

MIXED PICKLED MUSHROOMS (298)

All over Eastern Europe and in Russia, pickled mushrooms are extremely popular, and rightly so. We had lunch once with an old lady in Prague who gave us four kinds of pickled mushrooms, some of which had an almost buttery consistency. Using a mixture of different mushrooms means there will be an interesting variation in textures and flavors. During a good autumn you could add some wild ones, too. Pickled mushrooms are delicious eaten on their own, with cheese or added to salads.
    MAKES ABOUT 3⅛ CUPS (750ML)

8oz (250g) cremini mushrooms
4oz (125g) shiitake mushrooms
4oz (125g) button mushrooms
4oz (125g) oyster mushrooms
3 tablespoons salt
1¼ cups (300ml) dry white wine
1¼ cups (300ml) white wine vinegar
2 teaspoons sugar
1 small red-skinned onion, thinly sliced t
2 large cloves garlic, quartered lengthwise
2 teaspoons pink or green peppercorns,
* crushed*
1 teaspoon coriander seeds
2 sprigs fresh tarragon, separated into
* leaves*
3–4 tablespoons extra virgin olive oil

If the mushrooms have any dirt on them, wipe with a damp cloth. Only cut off the bottom of the stalks, and cut any large mushrooms in half. Add the salt to a pan of water and bring to a boil, then add the mushrooms and boil for 4–5 minutes. Drain the mushrooms; set aside to cool.

Pour the dry white wine and white wine vinegar into a saucepan. Stir in the sugar then add the onion slices, garlic, crushed peppercorns, coriander seeds and tarragon leaves. Bring to a boil, cover and simmer for 5 minutes. Remove from the heat and leave to cool. Stir in the cooked mushrooms.

Pack the mushrooms and vinegar mixture with the spices, garlic and tarragon in clean, dry jars (page 300). Make sure the mushrooms are well covered by the liquid. Process, or spoon the olive oil over the tops. Cover tightly and store in the refrigerator. Leave to mature for at least 3 weeks before using. After opening, keep in the refrigerator.

FOOD SAFETY

Food safety has always been an important concern for the home cook. Over the years, dozens of rules have been passed from one generation to the next to serve as guidelines for preparing and serving food safely.

However, in the last decade, food safety concerns have arisen that were never a problem before. The mass production and marketing of food, increased import of both raw and prepared food products, trend towards greater home consumption of food fully prepared by the supermarkets, delis and restaurants, and the development of more resistant strains of bacteria, viruses, and molds has introduced new challenges in the prevention of foodborne illnesses.

New regulations covering the food production,

marketing and preparation industries continue to make the food supply safer but ultimately each cook is the last line of defense. Care in shopping, transporting, storing and preparing the food you serve can prevent most foodborne illnesses. And, "when in doubt, throw it out," is one age old bit of advice that is still valid.

Bacteria are by far the greatest cause of foodborne illness. Bacteria are everywhere but only some can cause illness and then only when allowed to multiply. The danger zone for food spoilage is from 140°F, 60°C to 40°F, 4°C. Foods should be cooked thoroughly and kept either above 140°F, 60°C or below 40°F, 4°C in order to ensure safety. The government recommends that no food be kept more than 2 hours at room temperature.

STEP-BY-STEP TO FOOD HANDLING SAFETY

At the market
• Always look for "sell by" dates on products and never purchase anything when the date is past.
• Choose pristine packages; never buy dented or bulging cans, packaged goods that are torn or opened, or frozen foods that are soft or covered with ice.
• Never buy products labeled "keep refrigerated" if displayed at room temperature. Do not buy eggs, cheese, luncheon meats or cooked meats or poultry displayed at room temperature.
• Shop last for all products that should be kept cold. Place meat, fish and poultry in separate plastic bags in the store, so they don't drip.
• If you can't get home from the store in 30 minutes, keep an ice chest in your car for perishables. In the summer, this is a good idea however quickly you can get perishables to a refrigerator.

At home
• Always keep a refrigerator thermometer on the top shelf of your refrigerator to see that the temperature is between 35°F, 2°C, and 40°F, 4°C.
• Periodically move it to the freezer to see that the freezer is at or below 0°F, -18°C.
• Wash refrigerator shelves frequently with hot soapy water.
• If items are going into the freezer, date and freeze them immediately.
• Keep meat, fish and poultry in separate plastic bags to prevent dripping. If drips occur, clean immediately,
• Use fish, poultry and ground meat within one to two days of purchase.
• Use luncheon meats and uncooked red meats within three days of purchase.
• Don't put anything in the refrigerator uncovered.

Before cooking
• Always thaw foods in the refrigerator or microwave; never at room temperature. Cook foods as soon as thawed.
• Wash your hands in hot, soapy water and cover any cuts or sores.
• Clean all surfaces and equipment that food will come in contact with.

While cooking
Keep all uncooked fish, poultry, meat and eggs as well as their drippings and discards such as shells and bones or fat away from foods that will not be cooked. It is really better to keep one board exclusively for fish, poultry, meat and mixtures that contain uncooked eggs.
• Always use a separate, clean cutting board for fruits and vegetables that will be served raw.
• Prepare all foods as close to serving time as possible.
• Cook meats and eggs thoroughly: Use an instant-read thermometer on all meats thicker than 1 ½in (3.5cm). On thinner cuts, the thermometer will not be accurate so make a small center cut and check visually.
• Ground beef, veal, and lamb must be cooked until no longer pink: at least 160°F,

71°C. Whole cuts must be cooked at least to medium-rare: 145°F, 63°C.
• Cook all pork at least to 160°F, 71°C.
• Poultry, including ground poultry, should be cooked to 180°F, 82°C. Turkey breast may be cooked to 170°F, 77°C.
• Poultry stuffing should be cooked to 165°F, 74°C.
• Eggs should be cooked until the yolks and whites are firm. Egg dishes should be cooked to 160°F, 71°C.
• Do not use oven temperatures lower than 325°F, 175°C when cooking fish, poultry, meat and eggs.
• Never baste cooked meats with marinades which have previously been in contact with raw meat.
• Always wash hands and all equipment used with uncooked fish, poultry, meat and eggs with hot water and anti-microbial soap as soon as possible.
• Clean cooking equipment thoroughly, including your microwave.

Serving
• Never return cooked meats to the same platter that raw meats were on.
• Keep hot food hot and cold food cold (see recommended safe temperatures above).
• Do not add fresh food to food that has been standing on a buffet. Use small serving dishes and replace food frequently.
• Do not allow cooked food to sit at room temperature longer than 2 hours.
• To serve leftovers, thoroughly reheat.
• Liquids should come to a full rolling boil.
• Solid foods should reach an internal temperature of 165°F, 74°C or be steaming hot in the center.

Storing
• Store leftovers immediately.
• Transfer large quantities of sauce, soup, or stew to shallow dishes or pans to cool as quickly as possible before you put them in containers and store them.

NUTRITION

Creative food preparation and nutrition must go hand-in-hand. A diet of the most deliciously creative prepared foods is not good for you unless it provides the nutrition you need. And, likewise, a perfectly nutritious diet is of no use if it is not delicious and satisfying enough that you will want to continue to eat it. Nutrition information varies from year to year and it is often hard to sort out the useful principles from the misinformation. As nutrition fads come and go, it is important to keep some basic principles in mind and to integrate nutritional foods into a long-term diet of delicious and exciting meals. Reputable nutrition advisors usually offer the following guidelines for healthy eating:

Eat a variety of foods, but in moderation.

Try to get your required nutrients from foods rather than nutritional supplements.

Find a diet that you enjoy, that allows you to maintain your desirable weight, and that includes a balance of carbohydrate, proteins, vitamin and mineral rich foods and, yes, a little fat.

THE BASICS

There are more than 40 different nutrients that are essential for good health. Making sure your diet includes all these is not as hard as it sounds. All foods contain a mixture of these essential nutrients and eating a varied diet makes it possible to get what you need from foods you like. It is not necessary to meet all these needs in one meal: look at your diet as a daily pattern of choices and make sure that you include some fruits, vegetables, grain products, dairy products and high-protein foods such as meat, poultry, fish, eggs and legumes in each day's meals.

Carbohydrates provide energy. Current government nutritional guidelines recommend a diet that emphasizes complex carbohydrates which metabolize slowly and provide energy over a long period of time. Foods high in complex carbohydrates include bread, rice, potatoes, pasta, corn, and other grains. Sugars are simple carbohydrates. They are a quick source of energy, but many have been so refined that they contain few other nutrients. Fruits are a good source of natural sugar that is associated with complex carbohydrates as well as other essential nutrients such as vitamins and minerals.

Proteins are body builders. You need an adequate supply of protein to build and repair body tissues. Proteins are made up of amino acids. Proteins from animal sources such as meat, fish, poultry, eggs and dairy products provide the combination of amino acids that you need, so they are called "complete proteins." Beans, grains and nuts provide protein but not in the exact combination that we need. They are called "incomplete proteins." Eating a variety of these foods, chosen in the right proportions, can provide all the necessary amino acids.

Fats can be found in both plant and animal food sources. Although some fats are liquid and some solid at room temperature, they all provide the same amount of energy per gram of fat. The relative merits of the various fats has been a hotly contested issue for some time but the important thing to remember is that fat provides long-term endurance, reserve energy, and is needed for many metabolic processes. Fat has an important role in the diet and natural fats such as butter and olive oil are delicious in many recipes.

Vitamins were isolated and defined early in the 19th century when it was discovered that some of the most puzzling diseases of the time were caused by a deficiency of these nutrients. There are thirteen compounds currently defined as vitamins: Vitmin A, Thiamin, Riboflavin, Niacin, Pyridoxine, Vitamin B12, Folic Acid, Pantothenic Acid, Biotin, Ascorbic Acid, and Vitamins D, E, and K. They perfom many necessary functions; all occur in a variety of foods.

Minerals also perform many necessary functions in the body and occur naturally in foods. Calcium, chlorine, magnesium, phosphorus, potassium, sodium, and sulfur are needed in the largest amounts, while others such as copper, fluorine, iodine, iron, zinc and up to 10 other inorganic elements are needed in trace amounts.

The government periodically issues charts showing their Recommended Daily Dietary Allowance for all these nutrients based on the most recent research. These charts as well as ones showing recommended weight in relation to height are revised about every 5 years and are available from the U.S. Government Printing Office.

DIET AND YOUR WEIGHT

There's no question about it: there is a mathematical correlation between your diet and your weight. Every gram of carbohydrate and protein that you eat is metabolized by your body to produce 4 calories of energy. If you exert enough energy to use up all the calories produced by the food you eat, none is stored; if you don't, you are likely to find it stored wherever your body is genetically predisposed to stockpile extra energy as fat.

This system used to insure survival when people were not certain when their next meal would be available. In fact, less than a century ago, Americans had to worry about diseases caused by insufficient food or lack of the right nutrients, but this is very rarely the case now. Our greatest problem today is overabundance. As the rate of obesity increases, even among young people, the risk of obesity-related illnesses such as high blood pressure, cardio-vascular disease, diabetes, and even some types of cancer has become a serious problem for our society.

WHAT TO DO

A healthy diet must be a way of life not a regime adopted occasionally just before bathing-suit season. It is healthy for your whole family to enjoy a lifetime of wonderfully prepared foods in small portions. It is not healthy to buy into the latest weight reduction fad. In fact, it could be positively dangerous.

TIME SAVERS

These days, everyone seems to be too busy to spend the time they used to spend in preparing family meals. In most families, both adults have a full time job as well as all the planning, managing, and at-home, hands-on care associated with taking care of a family. However, just as spare time drifted away, a household full of new kitchen appliances and equipment and a supermarket of new food products came into existence to help.

When asked about their most important concerns, homemakers almost always put preparing healthy and satisfying meals on the table for their families at the top of the list. Finding the time to do this well is difficult yet it is essential to the health and happiness of their families. When dinnertime arrives, most peope don't have any idea what they are going to have for dinner, but the busy cooks whose responsibility it is to have dinner ready know that whatever they choose to prepare, they can look to the latest time-saving conveniences to help.

MICROWAVE

There are very few homes without microwaves today. After several decades of trying to use this unique concept in cooking to replace conventional oven and top-of-the-stove cooking, cooks now have accepted the microwave as an essential accessory to conventional cooking appliances and let it do what it does best. While it is disparaged for its inability to bake and brown, there are many things for which it is the perfect choice. Here are some of them (in addition to reheating and popcorn making).
• One of the big advantages of microwaves is the way they cook vegetables: quickly, cleanly, and with the minimum of water and steam. They produce a good texture and maintain as many vitamins as possible; the vegetables will not boil dry and burn. You can cook them in the (microwave-safe) dish you are going to serve them in, saving time both in serving and clean up.
• Another area in which the microwave stars is in cooking fish. Fish is best cooked lightly and quickly and the microwave prevents overcooking. Cook on a microwave-safe platter; the juices it releases become its sauce.
• For a head start in cooking foods that will be finished on the grill, precook chicken, ribs or vegetables in the microwave. This insures that the inside is perfectly cooked without charring the outer surface.
• On evenings when you get home from work and dinner is still frozen solid, the microwave is the only way to thaw things safely in a hurry. Many things can even be thawed and cooked on the same plate in the microwave in a matter of minutes.

The microwave is the ideal choice for softening and melting. You can:
• Melt chocolalte in about 2 minutes on high power (100%) without it seizing and becoming stiff and lumpy.
• Dissolve gelatin on defrost (30%) for 2 to 3 minutes,
• Soften butter for baking on defrost (30%) for about a minute.
• Warm ice cream on defrost (30%) for 1 to 2 minutes to make it soft enough to scoop.

FREEZER

It is hard to believe that the home freezer has not been part of every kitchen forever. It has become such an essential part of our lives that we often install one in our offices and send our children off to college with a little one for their room. At home, the freezer not only stores commercially prepared foods, things bought in quantity, and leftovers, it also allows us to plan ahead and redistribute our time so that we can cook ahead for busy times. When cooking ahead to freeze for later use, always freeze things in small amounts. You can always add more than one container to a dish you are preparing, but it is very hard to divide a large container of frozen food. Here are some time savers that can be prepared ahead to make a last minute supper into a very special meal.
• There is nothing quite so good for sauces as homemade stock. Make it in bulk and freeze it in ice cube trays so it can be added to sauces and soups as needed. Once frozen, store in plastic freezer bags.
• An overabundance of fresh herbs from the market or your garden can be prepared and frozen to make herb ice cubes. Just chop the herbs and put 1 teaspoon in each space. Top with a little water and freeze. To use, put the cubes in sauces, or thaw and drain to sprinkle on meats and vegetables.
• At the height of the season, freeze edible flowers in ice cubes to serve in drinks at a later time.
• When you have extra bread, cut it into cubes or process it into fresh bread crumbs and freeze.
• Make a double recipe of pastry, then bake and freeze the extra shell, or freeze it unbaked for a pecan or pumpkin pie.
• When making tomato or pesto sauces, double the recipe and freeze the extra in ice cube trays to add flavor to sauces or soups.

FOOD PROCESSOR

One of the greatest time savers in the kitchen, the food processor has only been around for about 30 years. A welcome addition to the blender, which was good for liquids but inadequate for other chopping and blending, it has made it possible for us to prepare flavorful sauces, spreads, dips and doughs that would otherwise have been too time-consuming for most cooks to consider a part of their kitchen repertoire. The hand chopping of herbs, grinding of spices and seeds in a mortar and pestle, and the pureeing and shredding of vegetables had almost disappeared from our culture along with all the flavorful dishes made by those time-consuming methods when this one ingenious machine came along to make these steps easy. We have the food processor to thank for the return of fresh herbs and spices, pesto sauce, homemade sausage, colorful slaws, fresh fruit and vegetable purees and much more to the American kitchen. Processors are now available in various sizes, so you can find one the right size to fit on your kitchen counter all the time. It should be kept in a handy location. Here are some of the things it can do .
• Chop the overabundance of herbs that you are going to freeze (see Freezer, above).
• Prepare dips, condiments and sauces such as hummus, pesto, chutney and relish.
• Prepare bread and cookie doughs without having a cloud of flour settle over your counter tops.
• Finely chop cooked meats for salads and sandwich spreads.
• Grind uncooked meats for homemade sausages.
• Puree berries for dessert sauces and vegetables for purees and cream soups.

OTHER TIME SAVERS

Outdoor grill When the weather is good, cooking on an outdoor grill makes a weekday dinner into a special occasion. Although it doesn't take any less time to cook foods on the grill, it gets the heat and bustle of cooking out of the kitchen and other members of the family are much more likely to help with the cooking.

Bread machine With the help of a bread machine, you can bake a fresh loaf of homemade bread without coming near the kitchen. Today's versions of this popular appliance can be set on a timer to mix and bake your premeasured ingredients whenever you want. It can also be used to mix and raise dough mess-free for you to shape and bake in traditional ways.

Pressure cooker Now making a comeback, the pressure cooker is proving again it can help busy cooks make delicious pot roasts, stews, grains, beans, and soups in a fraction of the usual time. New security features make them easy and perfectly safe to use.

ENTERTAINING

There is nothing more satisfying than cooking for your family and friends. No matter the occasion, entertaining at home is a gift of time and creativity from you to the special people in your life. Even though everyone seems to be busier these days, more people are choosing to entertain at home than they did a decade ago because the relaxed atmosphere of home entertaining is a welcome relief from the pressure of the outside world.

With careful planning, you can make any party look effortless and enjoy the occasion as if you were one of the guests. It is never too early to start planning. Guest lists and menus for a formal event can be decided weeks, or even months, in advance as long as you build in some flexibility for last-minute changes. On the other hand, it is never too late to invite friends over for an impromptu get together inspired by a successful fishing trip, an afternoon of apple picking, or an abundant harvest from your garden. The following tips will help you get organized.

BE PREPARED

Entertaining is a way of life. Make your home party-ready by gradually collecting things that make entertaining easy. Keep notes on each occasion and decide how your work could have been made easier and if there are things you could have on hand that would help. Here are some ideas.
• Once you know how you like to entertain, you can save the price of rentals by stocking up on a plain pattern of the plates, glasses, and silverware you will need to serve the number of people you can entertain comfortably in your space.
• Serving pieces can be an eclectic mix and a collection of electric hot trays picked up at yard sales can be useful for buffets.
• Even for a stand up cocktail party, guests appreciate having some extra tray tables around to set plates and glasses on.
• Purchase enough matching white or ivory linens to cover the tables you are going to use and keep them just for entertaining. The decor of each party can be varied by adding colored napkins or scarves under the centerpieces.

PLAN AHEAD

Guest list, decor, and service style can be planned way in advance. Some considerations for each include:
• Sometimes the occasion dictates the guest list. If the group is small you might want to invite people who already know one another, but if inviting a crowd, it is fun to offer guests the opportunilty to meet new friends. Invitations can be written ahead and mailed at least 2 weeks before the party.
• Decor should be both attractive and unobtrusive. Make sure flower arrangements don't obstruct interaction between guests, and flower scents don't compete with the aromas of the food.
• Service style is determined by the number of people you have invited, the size and traffic flow of your space, and the amount of help you plan to have. Buffet service makes it easy to serve a large number of people with little help; for fewer people, a family-style sit-down meal can be managed with a little help; but a plated meal requires both kitchen and service help. The menu you plan will have to be determined by the service style you choose.

SELECTING THE MENU

Many things go into desiging the menu for a dinner party. If you have selected with care, the results will be impressive and the work will be manageable. Follow this game plan.
• Once you have determined how many people you are going to entertain and the style of service you are going to use, you can start the process by thinking of things that can be made successfully for that number of people and served comfortably in the way you have planned.
• The next important consideration is the availability of quality products in your area at the time of year you will need them. Finding the best possible raw materials is the cook's most important job. Select fresh local products wherever possible and get to know the best butcher and fish market in your area. If using seasonal products, have a second choice in mind just in case your first choice is not available or doesn't look good on the day that you shop.
• Plan some things that can be finished in the oven in the container in which they will be served.
• Select recipes that you are sure of. If you haven't tried a recipe, do so well before the party so you can change your mind if you are not satisfied with it.
• Keep in mind your guests' likes and dislikes; find out if anyone has any dietary restrictions. These days it is wise to plan to prepare a sparate vegetarian main course for those who do not want to eat meat, seafood or poultry. Be sure to make enough for the crowd as those who do eat meat will probably enjoy the vegetable dish as well.
• Keep a record of the menu and a list of the guests you have invited so you will not serve the same things if they come for dinner again.

MAKING IT WORK
A week or so before the party
• Make two shopping lists based on the recipes you have chosen - one for things that can be bought ahead and one for last minute things. Add beverages, paper and cleaning products to the buy ahead list.
• Check to see that you have all the equipment necessary to prepare the items you have chosen and the containers and silverware necessary to serve them.
• Start making ice or buy a few bags.

Several days ahead
• Iron tablecloths. You can even set the table and cover it with a clean sheet, if you want to save time on the day of the party
• Look over the recipes you have selected and pick out the steps that can be started ahead. Stock, pastry and cake layers can be prepared several days ahead and frozen.
• Confirm orders for food, flowers, etc.

The day before
• Most chopping and slicing can be done the day before. Vegetables can be trimmed a day ahead and peeled several hours ahead, if stored in the refrigerator. Be sure to cover strong smelling vegatables in the refrigerator so milder products don't pick up the odor.
• Complete all labor intensive steps.
• Purchase everything you need.

The day of the party
• Do all preparation early in the day.
• Have sink and dishwasher ready for easy cleanup.
• Delegate tasks to early guests who ask if they can help.
• Be confident. Enjoy the party.

The day after
• Thank everyone who helped.
• Return all borrowed items.
• Keep careful records of what you served and whether guests seemed to enjoy it or not.
• Keep a list of things that you would do differently and things that you would do the same next time.

GLOSSARY

Acidulated water Water that has been made acid by a dash of lemon juice or vinegar. It is used to immerse peeled or cut fruit and vegetables to prevent the discoloration which is caused by oxidation.

Agar-agar A vegetarian alternative to gelatin, made from seaweed.

Al dente Meaning, in Italian, 'to the tooth', this is used to describe the point when a food is cooked but still has just a touch of bite to it. Most often applied to pasta and vegetables.

Aspic A clear savory jelly made from clarified meat, fish or vegetable stock. It is used to glaze cold foods.

Bain-marie A water bath. Either a water-filled roasting pan (in the oven) or a double boiler with water in the bottom half (on top of the stove), for cooking gently at low temperatures or for keeping food warm.

Bard To cover meat, poultry or game with thin sheets of bacon fat or pork fat to prevent the flesh from drying out during roasting.

Baste To spoon fat, pan juices or a marinade over a food during cooking to prevent it from drying out.

Beurre manié Equal parts of butter and flour, kneaded together and used in small amounts to thicken and enrich soups and sauces.

Bind To add egg or other liquid to a mixture to hold the ingredients together.

Bisque A rich, creamy fish soup based on a thick puree.

Blanch To immerse briefly in boiling water.

Borsch A classic, brilliant red, Eastern European soup made with beets.

Bouquet garni A small bunch or cheesecloth bag of herbs, usually including fresh thyme, parsley and bay leaves, used to flavour soups, stews and sauces.

Brandade A Provençal dish of pureed salt cod, flavored with garlic.

Brown To sear the outside of meat and seal in its juices before stewing or braising.

Bruise To lightly crush an aromatic food such as garlic or ginger to release its flavor.

Bulgar Cracked wheat.

Caramelize To turn sugar into caramel by gentle heating so it dissolves and turns brown.

Clarify To remove impurities from stock. Also to remove the milk solids from butter by melting and straining.

Compote Fresh or dried fruit stewed in a sugar syrup.

Coulis A thin puree of fruit or vegetables, served as a sauce.

Court bouillon A poaching stock for delicate foods such as fish, shellfish and chicken. Usually made from vegetables and herbs with water and wine, wine vinegar or lemon juice.

Cream To beat butter and sugar together until the sugar has dissolved and the mixture is light and smooth.

Crystallize To preserve fruit by cooking in sugar syrup until translucent and sugar crystals

cover the surface. Also used to preserve pieces of fresh gingerroot.

Curdle Separation of a mixture into curds and liquids, due to overheating of egg and cream mixtures or beating together of cream or fat and sugar.

Cut in To mix butter and flour using a pastry blender or two knives until the mixture reaches a bread crumb consistency.

Cure To preserve meat or fish by drying, salting or smoking.

Deglaze To add liquid (usually wine) to a pan, scraping the cooking juices from the bottom, to form the basis for a sauce.

Degrease To remove the surface fat from a sauce, stock or soup.

Dhal The general Hindi term for lentils, peas and other legumes; also used for spicy Indian lentil purees.

Dice To cut food such as vegetables into ¼–½in (5mm–1cm) cubes.

Dropping consistency The point at which a mixture will drop off a spoon which is given a sharp tap.

Emulsify To bind together ingredients that would otherwise separate, such as oil or butter with water, vinegar or lemon juice, using an emulsifier like egg yolk.

En croûte Baked in a pastry crust.

Essence A concentrated aromatic liquid used to flavor foods.

Fillet To take flesh off the bones of fish.

Fold in To gently mix one ingredient with another beaten one using a cutting, lifting and turning-over movement of the spoon or spatula, so as not to knock out the air bubbles. It is best done with a large metal spoon, spatula or whisk.

Fumet A fish stock concentrated by reduction.

Galantine A dish of boned, stuffed and shaped white meat or poultry, cooked in aspic stock and glazed with aspic.

Garam masala An Indian mixture of roasted spices, such as coriander seed, cumin, cloves, cardamom and cinnamon.

Ghee Indian clarified butter.

Giblets The neck, liver, heart and gizzard (stomach) of a bird. They are useful to boil in stock for gravy, for example, but care must be taken to remove any bitter, yellowish coating on the gizzard.

Glaze To give a glossy coating to both savory and sweet foods. This can be done before cooking by brushing with milk or beaten egg, or after cooking by covering with aspic or sugar syrup, for example.

Gratin A golden breadcrumb or cheese crust on top of a dish browned in the oven or under a broiler.

Hull To remove the stalk and central core from berries such as strawberries.

Infuse To steep ingredients such as herbs, spices or tea leaves in a hot liquid so that the flavors seep out into the liquid.

Julienne Matchstick strips of vegetables, or citrus rind, often used as a garnish.

Knead To work dough with a pushing, pressing motion of the heel of the hands to strengthen the gluten in the flour.

Lard To thread thin strips of fat into lean meat before roasting, to moisten the meat while it cooks. Usually done with a larding needle.

Macerate To steep fruit in syrup, spirits or liqueurs to soften and absorb the flavor of the liquid.

Marinate To soak raw food in a liquid. This not only tenderizes and adds flavor, but also helps preserve the food. A marinade is usually a blend of wine, oil, vinegar, or citrus juice with herbs and spices.

Mirepoix A mixture of cut or finely diced vegetables.

Mousseline A puree of raw fish, poultry or pale meat into which unbeaten egg white, and often cream, are gradually beaten.

Oeufs mollets Medium-boiled eggs, with a just-firm white and semi-soft yolk.

Parboil To cook a food for a short time in liquid so that it is only partially cooked, to be finished by another method.

Pectin A natural gelling substance found in fruit and vegetables, needed in the setting of jams and jellies. Fruits high in pectin include cooking apples, quinces and some Seville oranges.

Phyllo Greek or Middle Eastern pastry made in paper thin sheets; also called strudel pastry.

Pith The bitter white part of the skin of a citrus fruit next to the zest.

Pot-roast To cook meat slowly in a tightly closed pan with some fat and a small amount of liquid.

Puree To mash, sieve or process food to a smooth consistency.

Reduce To concentrate a liquid by rapid boiling so that some of its water evaporates.

Refresh To immerse hot vegetables in cold water to stop the cooking process.

Roux Equal amounts of flour and butter (or oil), cooked together as the base for a sauce.

Sauté To cook in butter or fat until lightly browned.

Sear To brown the surface of meat very quickly over a high heat.

Shred To cut or tear into long fine strips.

Skim To remove any froth, foam or fat from the surface of a boiling liquid.

Steep To soak in liquid.

Stir-fry A traditional oriental cooking method in which equal-sized ingredients are cooked swiftly over a high heat.

Strain To remove any solids from a liquid by passing it through a sieve or cheesecloth.

Suet A thin layer of hard fat found around variety meats.

Tempura A Japanese dish of batter-coated, deep-fried fish, shellfish or vegetables.

Truss To tie poultry and game into a neat shape before cooking, for even cooking and to hold shape.

Yeast Fungus cells that multiply rapidly in suitable conditions to cause bread dough to rise. Yeast can be fresh or dried. Brewer's yeast is used in wine- and beer-making.

Zest The colored, oily outer part of the skin of citrus fruit. Used for flavoring or decoration.

INDEX

AUTHOR'S ACKNOWLEDGEMENTS

I am grateful to everyone who encouraged and helped me during the two years it took me to write the book: to my family, particularly my son Henry who has become my ally in the kitchen, to Gwen and Bert Grimmond whose help in the house and garden gave me time to work, to my friends John and Nicola Hilton, in whose house I cooked many of the recipes, and Christina Gascoigne, who listened patiently to my daily progress report. I am also grateful to Roz Denny, who independently checked everything in the book with her usual calm efficiency; to Sandy Carr, Fiona Holman and Beverly Le Blanc, my editors, who were unfailingly supportive however close the deadlines came, and to Susie Macdonald whose enthusiasm and swift typing of much of the manuscript was such a help. For this U.S. edition I am indebted to Joanne Lamb Hayes who has so meticulously prepared the book for American readers

Lastly I would like to thank my mother, who first introduced me to the pleasures of food.

CREDITS

The publishers would also like to thank the following individuals and institutions for the help, advice and information which they contributed towards the preparation of this book:

Judy Bastyra, Bodum, British Chicken Information Service, Elizabeth David Cookshop, Flour Advisory Bureau, Indigo, Leon Jaeggi & Sons Ltd, Norma MacMillan, Caroline Macy, Magimix UK Ltd, Stuart McClymont, David Mellor, Sea Fish Industry Authority, Petra Steenhamker, Susanna Tee, Villeroy and Boch Tableware Ltd, Josiah Wedgwood & Sons Ltd, Elizabeth Wolfe-Cohen.

Editorial Director Sandy Carr
Art Director Douglas Wilson
Editor Fiona Holman
U.S. Editor Joanne Lamb Hayes
Art Editors Sara Kidd, Michael Leaman
Deputy Editor Beverly Le Blanc
Deputy Art Editor Jane Haworth
Sub Editor Wendy Toole
Designer Sally Powell
Editorial Assistants Siobhan Bremner, Gemma Hancock
Photographers Clive Streeter, Struan Wallace,
Simon Wheeler (chapter openers)
Consultant Home Economist Roz Denny
Home Economists Mary Cadogan, Louise Pickford, Bridget Sargeson
Illustrations Diana Leadbetter (4-colour), Coral Mula (step-by-step)
Indexer Naomi Good
Stylists Rebecca Gillies, Jane Haworth